C. Brew G225
May 1995

*The Environmental
Imagination* 1995

The Environmental Imagination

Thoreau, Nature Writing, and the
Formation of American Culture

LAWRENCE BUELL

The Belknap Press of
Harvard University Press
Cambridge, Massachusetts
London, England
1995

To the memory of

Marjorie Henderson Buell

(1904–1993)

Contents

ABBREVIATIONS

J   *The Journal of Henry David Thoreau,* ed. Bradford Torrey and Francis H. Allen, 14 vols. (Boston: Houghton Mifflin, 1906)

LLR   Mary Austin, *The Land of Little Rain,* in *Stories from the Country of Lost Borders,* ed. Marjorie Pryse (New Brunswick: Rutgers University Press, 1987)

SCA   *Aldo Leopold, A Sand County Almanac* (New York: Oxford University Press, 1949)

PJ   *The Writings of Henry D. Thoreau: Journal,* ed. John C. Broderick (vols. 1–3) and Robert Sattelmeyer (vols. 4–). (Princeton: Princeton University Press, 1981–)

Wa   *The Writings of Henry D. Thoreau: Walden,* ed. J. Lyndon Shanley (Princeton: Princeton University Press, 1971)

*The Environmental
Imagination*

Introduction

⌁

A large intellectual gap exists between our sense of being actors in the world, of always being in place, and the "placelessness" that characterizes our attempts to theorize about human actions and events.

—J. Nicholas Entrikin, *The Betweenness of Place*

The only hope then lies not in identification with either pole of opposition, but in discovering . . . some larger grammar in which the words *culture* and *wilderness* may both be spoken.

—John Elder, *Imagining the Earth*

Environment is a structure which even biology as a positive science can never find and can never define but must presuppose and constantly employ.

—Martin Heidegger, *Being and Time*

THIS BOOK has refused to remain the modest undertaking I intended it to be. Planned as a history of Thoreauvian writing about the American natural environment, it has led me into broad study of environmental perception, the place of nature in the history of western thought, and the consequences for literary scholarship and indeed for humanistic thought in general of attempting to imagine a more "ecocentric" way of being.[1] I found that I could not discuss green writing without relating it to green thinking and green reading.

The result is an exploratory work with several foci rather than one. Its most frequent reference point remains Henry Thoreau: Thoreau the historical person; Thoreau's works, especially his central book, *Walden;*

his influence; and his stature as a representative of green American thinking. For no writer in the literary history of America's dominant subculture comes closer than he to standing for nature in both the scholarly and the popular mind. Yet Thoreau is really more my base of operations than my main subject. I am ultimately less interested in Thoreau per se than in the American environmental imagination generally, meaning especially literary nonfiction from St. John de Crèvecoeur and William Bartram to the present, but beyond this environmentally directed texts in other genres also. If, as environmental philosophers contend, western metaphysics and ethics need revision before we can address today's environmental problems, then environmental crisis involves a crisis of the imagination the amelioration of which depends on finding better ways of imaging nature and humanity's relation to it.² To that end, it behooves us to look searchingly at the most searching works of environmental reflection that the world's biggest technological power has produced; for in these we may expect to find disclosed (not always with full self-consciousness, of course) both the pathologies that bedevil society at large and some of the alternative paths that it might consider. That is this book's most ambitious goal. It is rendered even more formidable than it might otherwise be by the need simultaneously to refine and reevaluate some of the basic analytical premises used by "trained" readers of literature. I shall argue below that environmental interpretation requires us to rethink our assumptions about the nature of representation, reference, metaphor, characterization, personae, and canonicity. In one compartment of my mind, I like to think of this book as trying, with Thoreau as its chief touchstone, to re-theorize nonfiction as Gérard Genette reformulated narrative discourse using Marcel Proust as his central exhibit.³

I hope I do not need to spend many pages defending the reasonableness of the claim that "we must make the rescue of the environment the central organizing principle for civilization."⁴ Although many would not take then Senator Albert Gore's pronouncement literally (even committed environmentalists, I suspect, believe it in some moods more than others), no informed person would contest that it expresses an anxiety much stronger today than ever before in recorded history and likely to grow stronger. The rate at which public interest conservation groups formed in America between 1901 and 1960 sextupled between 1961 and 1980.⁵ "Not since the Industrial Revolution," observes environmental historian Donald Worster, "have the ambitions of modernization encountered such fierce and widespread resistance."[6] Since 1970 there has been unprecedented discussion, not just on a national but on a global scale, about the need to set limits to technoeconomic growth. If such a thing as global culture ever comes into being, environmentalism will surely be one of the catalysts.[7]

Although the creative and critical arts may seem remote from the arenas of scientific investigation and public policy, clearly they are exercising, however unconsciously, an influence upon the emerging culture of environmental concern, just as they have played a part in shaping as well as merely expressing every other aspect of human culture. One obvious sense in which this is true is that we live our lives by metaphors that have come to seem deceptively transparent through long usage.[8] Take for instance "progress," literally a procession or transit, which the democratic and industrial revolutions of the nineteenth century taught us to equate with "improvement," first with political liberalization and then with technological development. Whenever we use this word, unless we put it in quotation marks, we reinforce the assumption of a link between "technology" and the "good" and the assumption that continuous technological proliferation is inevitable and proper. To state this point is not to argue the reverse, merely to call attention to the power of language. How we image a thing, true or false, affects our conduct toward it, the conduct of nations as well as persons. Walden Woods in Concord, Massachusetts, has become a legal battleground because Thoreau's writings have led many to perceive it as sacred space that should be kept in its "natural" state. Novel-begotten stereotypes of Victorian England's industrial midlands are thought to have influenced internal migration to this day. Land reclamation and preservation throughout Denmark, starting in the mid-nineteenth century, was inspired by literary revivals of saga and folklore that infused erstwhile desolate heathlands with romantic meaning and potential.[9] These are but a few examples of how aesthetics can become a decisive force for or against environmental change.

But literary institutions, like all others, are cultural barometers as much as they are agents of change. The redefinition of "progress" was probably more an effect than a cause of technologism. Even countercultural institutions may act as safety valves that neutralize their oppositional force.[10] Take for example the problem of environmental doublethink. Awareness of the potential gravity of environmental degradation far surpasses the degree to which people effectively care about it. For decades it has been reckoned a major issue, but it has modified citizenly behavior only at the edges. Americans have become more energy-conscious but remain consumption-addicted. Nor is this paradoxical condition novel. For more than a century the United States has been at once a nature-loving and resource-consuming nation. This paradox, not unique to America but an exaggeration of a modern syndrome found worldwide, is sustained by acts of compartmentalization made habitual by the way our sensibilities are disciplined. The earth's most suburbanized citizens,[11] we like being surrounded by greenery but ignore our reliance on toxic substances that increase the comfort of our surroundings until waste disposal becomes a local issue—whereupon we are relieved when the incinerator gets built in the less affluent and politically weaker county fifty miles downwind. That our literature and journalism register this split consciousness is clear from a quick tour of the advertising pages of our leading conservationist magazines. Historically, artistic representations of the natural environment have served as agents both of provocation and of compartmentalization, calling us to think ecocentrically but often conspiring with the readerly temptation to cordon off scenery into pretty ghettoes. We honor their achievements best when we recognize them as prophetic but intermittent efforts to rise above the cultural limitations that threaten to becloud them. Their achievements are mirrors both of cultural promise and of cultural failure.

The failures are not, of course, simply a result of neglecting to translate perception into action; they are failures of perception as well—failures from which perhaps no human and certainly no westerner is exempt. Consider the case of Herman Melville. His sensitivity to physical environments was acute, even when one might least expect it, as in the heavily allegorical *Mardi* and the psychologically involuted *Pierre. Moby-Dick* comes closer than any other novel of its day to making a nonhuman creature a plausible major character and to developing the theme of human ferocity against animal nature. Yet Melville's interest in whales was subordinate to his interest in whaling, and his interest in the material reality of both was constrained by his preoccupation with their social and cosmic symbolism. Thus we should not be surprised by the contrast between the almost concurrent encounters of Melville and Charles Darwin with the Galapagos Islands. Darwin's visit in the 1830s as naturalist of the HMS *Beagle* was an astonishingly rich imaginative event. His discovery of large numbers of unique but related species on the different individual islands marked the beginning of his discovery of the theory of natural selection.[12] Melville, visiting the islands during his wanderings in the South Pacific a few years later, was equally impressed by them, but as an area of starkness and desolation that he turned to symbolic use in *The Encantadas,* a series of ironically titled sketches about the islands, and in his late poem *Clarel,* which likens the deserts of Palestine to the Galapagos. Melville's environmental imagination was too homocentric to allow him to respond as Darwin did. Even Darwin did not fully come to terms with what he had seen until years later.

"No intellectual vice," warns E. O. Wilson, "is more crippling than defiantly self-indulgent anthropocentrism."[13] Melville scarcely deserves such chastisement, but it is harder to exonerate the voluminous body of criticism on the subject of art's representation of nature. Wonderfully astute in some ways, in others this criticism is myopic. Like all specialized discourses, it has been driven by disciplinary imperatives that create a skewed elegance of result. For instance, to posit a disjunction between text and world is both an indispensable starting point for mature literary understanding and a move that tends to efface the world.[14] Other disjunctions follow from this one, like that between text and author and the collapse of the distinction between fiction and nonfiction. The problems are aggravated by the cloistral, urbanized quality of the environment in which this criticism tends to be practiced. When an author undertakes to imagine someone else's imagination of a tree while sitting, Bartleby-like, in a cubicle with no view, small wonder if the tree seems to be nothing more than a textual function and one comes to doubt that the author could have fancied otherwise.

A more affirmative way of stating all this is that an inquiry into the environmental imagination forces us to question the premises of literary theory while using its resources to expose the limitation of literature's representations. This bind is especially pertinent to the case of the American natural environment, which during the last five centuries has been constructed thrice over in a tangled ideological palimpsest. First it was constructed in the image of old world desire, then reconstructed in the image of American cultural nationalism, then reconstructed again in a latter-day scholarly discourse of American exceptionalism. Thus the territorial facticity of America has always been both blatant and opaque.

But I am getting ahead of myself, referring loosely to the "environmental imagination" without indicating the properties I have in mind and implying that it has yielded a unified body of thought and writing, as manifestly it has not. In the three following sections I try, respectively, to define my field of inquiry in general terms; to anticipate its conceptual limits; and to elaborate my reasons for focusing on Thoreau as writer and as cultural phenomenon.

What Is an Environmental Text?

This book ranges freely through the canons of western literature and occasionally even beyond, into the literature of Asia, Africa, and the Caribbean. But I shall concentrate especially on the literary history of the United States, in ways that will often seem odd from an orthodox standpoint. In my version of the history of the western hemisphere, the ecological colonization of the Americas by disease and invasive plant forms is as crucial as the subjugation of their indigenous peoples by political and military means.[15] William Bartram's botanical conquest of Florida is as notable an event of the American Revolutionary era as Patriot resistance to Britain. Although I broadly agree (while differing on specifics) with the many other Americanists who have seen pastoral ideology as central to American cultural self-understanding, I argue that American cultural distinctiveness in this respect must be understood in light of parallels to the conditions of other former colonies remote from Europe, whence Anglophone pastoral emanated. The key figure of the so-called American literary renaissance of the mid-nineteenth century is not Ralph Waldo Emerson, in this book's scheme of things, but Thoreau. The writings of Susan Fenimore Cooper are as significant as those of her more famous father. Darwin's *Origin of Species* was as catalytic an event for American thought as John Brown's raid on Harpers Ferry the same year (1859). Among the achievements of late nineteenth-century realism, the environmental nonfiction of Celia Thaxter, Mary Austin, and John Burroughs counts for as much as the novels of William Dean Howells and Mark Twain. Among intellectual developments during the Depression and World War II, Aldo Leopold's formation of a biocentric environmental ethics was as important as any. In the Cold War era, ecocide was always a more serious threat than nuclear destruction. In literary history since World War II, the resurgence of environmental writing is as important as the rise of magical realist fiction.

The combination of broad sweep and cranky hyperfocus of which I have just forewarned is, I think, in keeping with the nature of environmental representation, which is at least faintly present in most texts but salient in few. This we immediately see from a rough checklist of some of the ingredients that might be said to comprise an environmentally oriented work.

1. *The nonhuman environment is present not merely as a framing device but as a presence that begins to suggest that human history is implicated in natural history.* To take a couple of borderline cases, the American sequence of Charles Dickens' *Martin Chuzzlewit* barely qualifies, since the American West is little more than a backdrop for Martin's picaresque misadventures; but E. M. Forster's *Passage to India* clearly would, for it reflects at every level a version of the theory of determinism by climate posited by discredited police commissioner MacBryde: Forster seems seriously to consider that difference in latitude shapes emotions, behavior, art. But both novels seem peripheral cases compared with almost any novel by Thomas Hardy—or with the travel books Dickens and Forster quarried from the biographical experiences that underlay their two novels: Dickens's *American Notes* and Forster's *The Hill of Devi.*

2. *The human interest is not understood to be the only legitimate interest.* By this criterion, the boy's empathy for the bird's loss of its mate in Walt Whitman's "Out of the Cradle Endlessly Rocking" stands out by contrast to the comparative self-absorption of Percy Bysshe Shelley's persona in "To a Skylark" and John Keats's in "Ode to a Nightingale." "Cradle" is more concerned with the composition of a specific place, and Whitman's symbolic bird is endowed with a habitat, a history, a story of its own.

3. *Human accountability to the environment is part of the text's ethical orientation.* By this standard, William Wordsworth's "Nutting" comes closer to being an environmental text than his "Tintern Abbey," insofar as the function of landscape in the latter is chiefly to activate the speaker's subjective feelings of rejuvenation and anxiety, whereas the former remi-

niscence prompts him to retell a self-incriminating tale of his youthful violation of the hazel grove.

4. *Some sense of the environment as a process rather than as a constant or a given is at least implicit in the text.* By this criterion, James Fenimore Cooper's *Pioneers* is a more faithful environmental text than the four ensuing Leatherstocking Tales because it never loses sight of the history of the community's development from wilderness to town, while his daughter Susan's *Rural Hours,* a literary daybook of Cooperstown natural and social history, is a more faithful environmental text than any of her father's romances.

I deliberately keep this list short, wanting chiefly to give a flavor of how potentially inclusive *and* exclusive the category of "environmental" is, in my apprehension of it. By these criteria, few works fail to qualify at least marginally, but few qualify unequivocally and consistently. Most of the clearest cases are so-called nonfictional works, hence my special concentration on them here.

It is a provocative fact of literary scholarship that this concentration is unorthodox. That in itself is a reason for pursuing it here. American nature poetry and fiction about the wilderness experience have been studied much more intensively than environmental nonfiction.[16] Apart from *Walden* and a few other works by Thoreau, for practical purposes nonfictional writing about nature scarcely exists from the standpoint of American literary studies, even though by any measure it has flourished for more than a century and has burgeoned vigorously in the nuclear age. The *Companion to "A Sand County Almanac,"* published several years ago to honor the major literary work of 1949 by ecologist Aldo Leopold, calls the book a "classic," a classic of literary craftsmanship as well as an intellectual milestone in fathering contemporary environmental ethics.[17] Yet *Sand County* is not widely thought to be a classic of American literary history; it is a classic merely of the enclave canon of "nature writing" (so called with enthusiasm by partisans, but with condescension by most professional students of literature), whose canon remains today even more of an enclave than, for example, the canons of American ethnic literatures. Those are increasingly represented in our omnibus anthologies of American literature. Environmental nonfiction, however, gets studied chiefly in expository writing programs and in "special topics" courses offered as the humanities' tithe to environmental studies programs or to indulge a colleague's idiosyncrasies, rather than as bona fide additions to the literature curriculum. This market is supplied by a half-dozen or so anthologies whose increasingly high quality testifies to a thriving cottage industry, as does the publication of a Modern Language Association (MLA) guide for teachers of environmental literature.[18] Scholarship has begun to pick up,[19] and it may be expected to benefit from the broader theoretical and critical movement, still in its fledgling stages, that is starting to become known as "ecocriticism."[20] But such work is still far from becoming the fashion. Joseph Wood Krutch's salty pronouncement of the mid-1950s still rings true: "There are many courses in 'The Nature Poets' in American colleges. But nature is usually left out of them."[21]

Possibly students of American environmental writing ought to count their blessings. Lynn L. Merrill, in *The Romance of Victorian Natural History*, laments the uphill battle she faces for critical recognition of her genre in the absence of a British counterpart to *Walden*, which according to a 1991 MLA survey American professors consider the single most important work to teach in nineteenth-century literature courses (45 percent, ahead of 34 percent for *The Scarlet Letter* and *Moby-Dick*'s 29 percent). Merrill may have a point, although John Hildebidle argues precisely the opposite in his book on Thoreau as natural historian.[22] British counterparts like Isaac Walton's *Compleat Angler* and Gilbert White's *Natural History of Selbourne* are at best "minor classics." Even Darwin's *Origin of Species* does not have the "great book" status within British *literary* history that *Walden* enjoys in American literary history, despite several first-rate studies of Darwin's literary influence.[23] Yet *Walden*'s canonization does not betoken the broader legitimation Merrill implies. Unlike Emerson and Nathaniel Hawthorne and Whitman and Emily Dickinson, Thoreau is not deemed to have engendered any canonical progeny, at least within the field of literature (although Thoreauvians regularly enlist such heroes of moral reform as Lev Tolstoy, Mahatma Gandhi, and Martin Luther King, Jr., as fellow Thoreauvians); nor does the canonization of *Walden* of itself imply respect for the book as an environmental text.

American literary history thus presents the spectacle of having identified representation of the natural environment as a major theme while marginalizing the literature devoted most specifically to it and reading the canonical books in ways that minimize their interest in representing the environment as such. To put this abstract point in an immediate context: the grove of second-growth white pines that sway at this moment of writing, with their blue-yellow-green five-needle clusters above spiky circles of atrophied lower limbs, along a brown needle-strewn ridge of shale forty feet from my computer screen—this grove can be found in the pages of American literature also, but it is not the woods imagined by American criticism. The forest of American scholarship is the far more blurry and highly symbolic delta landscape of William Faulkner's "The Bear," built from chant-like reiterated and generalized images: a forest where treeness matters but the identities and the material properties of the trees are inconsequential. Faulkner encourages us to admire Ike McCaslin's growing prowess as a woodsman but to feel no obligation to emulate it.

Three decades have passed since the publication in 1962 of Rachel Carson's *Silent Spring* and the passage of the Wilderness Act, which marked the full-fledged emergence of environmentalism as a topic of public concern in America. During this time the environment has not only become a multifarious worldwide policy issue but also engendered within the academy new subfields in disciplines as varied as anthropology, philosophy, and law. Literary studies have lagged behind. Indeed, environmental representation seems to be of less interest to the average literary specialist than it was when systematic scholarly study of American literature began in the 1920s. To investigate literature's capacity for articulating the nonhuman environment is not one of the things that modern professional readers of literature have been trained to do or for the most part wish to do. Our training conditions us, on the contrary, to stress the distinction between text and referent. I do this myself; in fact, I feel a professional responsibility to do so at the outset of my course "American Literature and the American Environment." Taking a short nocturnal meditation by Wendell Berry, I peel off its layers of mediation and show, in turn, how it is structured by the American machine-in-the-garden convention (car headlights interrupt, then are absorbed in the silence), by the neoclassical prospect poem (as a hilltop meditation), and by the Ovidian metamorphosis plot (the speaker's foot roots in the ground at the end).[24]

The discovery of these frameworks excites my students; it furnishes them with sophisticated hermeneutical equipment that they soon wield deftly. But they also, and with reason, feel somewhat cheated. Must literature always lead us away from the physical world, never back to it?

Operating from the premise of intractable textuality, we find it hard to resist the resistance to nature that is second nature to us in our capacity as critical readers, whatever our behavior in everyday life. I think of myself as a pretty fair natural historian, yet I was bemused and chagrined at coming across this aperçu about William Cullen Bryant's poetry in a monograph from the dawn of American literary professionalization, Norman Foerster's *Nature in American Literature:* "Of the forty-five species [of flowers in his poems] it is rather odd that none, save the violet, reappears more than once or twice; when he wanted a flower, he generally picked a new one."[25] I was chagrined by the thought that I never would have discovered this tidbit for myself, bemused by the critic's assumption that readers would consider data on Bryant's botanical reach to be indispensable information. That kind of passion went out with new critical formalism in the 1940s and seems almost antediluvian today. As ecocritic Jonathan Bate remarks concerning British romantic studies, "some of the most eminent literary critics of our time have believed that Wordsworth was *not* a nature poet, or that there is no such thing as nature, or that if there is such a thing and Wordsworth was interested in it then that interest was very suspect on political grounds."[26]

Bate speaks especially of scholarship during the 1970s and 1980s, but the situation is long-standing. The best book ever written about the place of nature in American literary thought, Leo Marx's *The Machine in the Garden* (1964), advises us that what Thoreau says "about the location of meaning and value" is "that it does not reside in the natural facts or in social institutions or in anything 'out there,' but in consciousness," in the "mythopoeic power of the human mind."[27] In short, Thoreau was not really *that* interested in nature as such; nature was a screen for something else.

In defense of this view, one might argue that imagining figures like Wordsworth and Thoreau mainly as writers about nature imposes a test on them they cannot pass. Even readers sympathetic to literary naturism have made this argument.[28] At the end of a book devoted to Wordsworth's view of nature, Norman Lacey makes the now familiar point that Wordsworth was an observer of rather than a participant in the rustic ethos he celebrated: "He was not in a natural relation to physical nature nor to his own nature, nor to that Nature which he extolled in the dalesman . . . He stood in a no-man's-land between town and country."[29] The same could be said of all other Anglo-American writers who have taken nature as a subject. Always in their capacity as writers their relation to nature is, in Friedrich von Schiller's terms, "sentimental" rather than "naive," as Schiller took the ancient Greeks to be. They have sought from a position of acculturated distance to return to or realize their object.[30] The only problem with Schiller's theory is that the Greeks were sentimentalists too.

Discussions of environmental literature written from the perspective of intellectual or social history tend to underestimate this "sentimentalism." Take Max Oelschlaeger's account, in his history of the idea of wilderness, of Thoreau's excited reaction to the primordialness of Mount Katahdin. In a much-discussed passage in *The Maine Woods,* Thoreau declares,

> This was that Earth of which we have heard, made out of Chaos and Old Night. Here was no man's garden, but the unhandselled globe. It was not lawn, nor pasture, nor mead, nor woodland, nor lea, nor arable, nor waste-land. It was the fresh and natural surface of the planet Earth, as it was made forever and ever . . . It was Matter, vast, terrific . . . a place for heathenism and superstitious rites,—to be inhabited by men nearer of kin to the rocks and wild animals than we.[31]

For Oelschlaeger, "Ktaadn rekindles for Thoreau a primal or Paleolithic coming-to-consciousness of humankind's naked rootedness in and absolute dependence upon nature." Oelschlaeger sees the event as an experience that helped liberate Thoreau from Emerson's bookish homocentrism.[32] To this one might reply that Thoreau's rhetoric hardly shows naked rootedness and dependence on nature; that its consciousness is anything but Paleolithic; that it is in fact a studious exercise in romantic literary sublimity, in keeping with the many other stylizations throughout "Ktaadn" that mark it as a piece designed for periodical publication in the company of other romantic travel narratives, a favorite kind of nineteenth-century magazine fare, consumed with relish in many a Victorian parlor.[33]

Yet even literary Thoreauvians would hardly deny that the passage refers back to an experience of confrontation with an actual landscape that struck Thoreau as more primal than anything he had met before, and that the evocation of that landscape and what sort of relation human beings might sustain to it are crucial preoccupations for Thoreau here. Oelschlaeger's neoprimitivist reading may overstate the case, but his assumption that the passage processes the experience of contact with a particular place in the New England outback is just as valid as the assumption that it is culturally mediated. Indeed, these hypotheses imply each other. The one must acknowledge that reported contacts with particular settings are intertextually, intersocially constructed; the other must acknowledge that the nonbuilt environment is one of the variables that influence culture, text, and personality.

All environmental texts raise similar issues. Should we suppose that Bryant culled his literary flowers from woodsy rambles or from a chapbook of emblems? Should this or that literary expression of gratitude at one's return to nature be taken as responding to nature, or as disguising a human interest (the squire's evasion of the landless laborers evicted to make room for his park), or simply as affirming the tradition of nature affirmations? The answer to such questions is always "both." This ambidextrous response avoids opposite reductionisms: reductionism at the level of formal representation, such as to compel us to believe either that the text replicates the object-world or that it creates an entirely distinct linguistic world; and reductionism at the ideational level, such as to require us to believe that the environment ought to be considered either the major subject of concern or merely a mystification of some other interest.[34]

So far I have spoken chiefly to the former issue, of formal representation. But the second is equally important in adjudicating what literary texts are about. The most seminal theorists of the country-city polarity in English and American literary culture, Raymond Williams and Leo Marx, differ sharply in their personal responses both to country landscapes and to literary texts but agree in interpreting the polarity as having more to do with the clash of economic, political, and class interests than with landscapes as such. "Anti-urbanism," as Marx puts it, "is better understood as an expression of something else: a far more inclusive, if indirect and often equivocal, attitude toward the transformation of society and of culture of which the emerging industrial city is but one

manifestation."[35] What is troublesome about this statement is the implication that the biota itself is not likely to be anyone's primary concern.
The dramatic upgrading in recent years of the environment as a public
issue, such that feature articles even in middlebrow newsmagazines have
for the last decade been regularly devoted to it, shows the hastiness of
diagnosing environmental representation even in precontemporary times
as a screen for another agenda. The more the environment looms as a
self-evidently fundamental problem, the more problematic it seems to
minimize its importance for our precursors. If our present concern may
tempt us to overstate their concern, our past unconcern may have tempted
us to ignore theirs.

   This is not to say that environmental questions, whether in literature
or daily life, can be discussed in abstraction from other issues. Indeed, as
public anxiety about the environment seems ever more self-evidently
legitimate, it becomes all the more important to remain aware of the
other agendas that may accompany it. In the present case, it is well to
recognize from the outset that the retrieval of the natural environment
for purposes of literary representation is a project to which some cultures
have historically subscribed more enthusiastically than others, and that
in American literary history the dominant contribution has been made
by members of the dominant Euro-American subculture.[36] This opens up
a whole new set of considerations.

Environmental Response and Cultural Difference

So far I have chiefly emphasized how modern conventions of reading
block out the environmental dimension of literary texts. Yet from another
standpoint nature's prominence in the literature of the United States
might be seen as only too conspicuous: as the inertial effect of the time
lag between material conditions and cultural adjustment. The first writings about America were works of geographical description. Much colonial and early national literature was taken up with exploring, mapping,
and celebrating the land. The American literary renaissance of the antebellum period, influenced by romantic naturism, nurtured the image of
a wild, unsettled continent as an article of cultural nationalism well into
the age of industrial revolution. American literature to this day continues
to be more rustically oriented than the living habits of most Americans,

scarcely 3 percent of whom live on farms anymore. American criticism ✓ has repeatedly stressed the historic importance of pastoral, frontier, and wilderness themes to the American imagination.

The strange impression this nature-oriented version of the American literary-cultural heritage can create often emerges in the modern class-room. This any teacher knows who has tried to explain to a dyed-in-the-wool (sub)urban sophomore why Emerson was justified in thinking that country living stimulates the mind better than city life. The student has come face-to-face with what might be called the America-as-nature re-duction. By highlighting representations of rusticity and wilderness the American literary canon from Emerson through Faulkner perpetuates a historic tendency within American culture for intellectuals to imagine the ✓ heart of America as more rural than their own positions at the time of imagining.[37]

Obscure disaffected undergraduates are not the only ones who feel the artificiality of American naturism. Eminent critics have voiced similar complaints, such as Irving Howe's strictures on "the unconsidered respect good Americans feel obliged to show for 'nature.'"[38] Howe's nominal adversary is the general public, but what provokes his criticism is more fundamentally his coolness toward the whole Emerson-Thoreau line in American literary thought, which Howe considered "deficient in those historical entanglements that seemed essential to literature because ines-capable in life."[39] For a politically astute Jewish intellectual from New York, the heritage of American naturism seemed to impose a self-con-scious choice: assimilate or resist. Howe resisted. Alfred Kazin, also of urban background like the majority of leading American Jewish intellec-tuals, chose to assimilate, celebrating the naturist tradition in *A Writer's America* despite its dissimilarity to the experience of his formative years.[40] Both cases, Howe's and Kazin's, remind us that literary naturism is for many an acquired taste.

The Jewish American literary renaissance of the mid-twentieth cen-tury, of which they were leaders and exemplars, was the first of a series of intellectual movements of American minority cultures that will likely ✓ stand as one of the century's two most important developments in American letters besides the modernist revolution and the professionali-zation of American literary criticism and theory. The other development is the conception of writing and reading as gendered pursuits. The ethnic and feminist renaissances have made American writing and public intellectual life more faithful mirrors of the diversity of American society as a whole and offer a presumptive rebuttal to any one America-as-X approach. Within a mere two decades, it has become emphatically clear that orthodox versions of American literary naturism, like the myth of ✓ the American Adam, have been based on texts by Anglo-American males; that American men have historically written somewhat differently about nature than have American women; that their representations of nature contain misogynist and racist elements (such as the disparagement of settlement culture as feminine, the euphemization of slavery in nostalgic plantation and frontiersman tales, the manipulation of romantic scenery in the service of a gospel of expansionism); and that the closeness of felt interdependence between literary expression and the natural environment varies according to the cultures of race and gender as well as that of region.[41] Although we grossly oversimplify by equating the American environmental imagination with its hegemonic elements, no one can understand its workings without taking account of them. No inquiry can call itself informed which does not recognize that the idealization of nature in American literary mythography has historically been more a masculine pursuit than a female-sponsored endeavor, and that attitudes toward exurban space differ considerably among American cultural groups, the tendency to idealize it having run far stronger, by and large, in white and Native American writing than in Jewish American, Asian American, African American, and even American Latina/Latino writing.

This is not to say that no readers other than Anglo-American males can practice, enjoy, or find empowerment within "patriarchal" forms of writing like the wilderness romance, which imagines heroes like Cooper's Natty Bumppo and Faulkner's Ike McCaslin lighting out for a male domain free of genteel and feminized entanglements of civil society. In the course of her landmark critique of critical overgeneralization about these "melodramas of beset manhood," Nina Baym notes the readiness of her female students to identify with the male protagonist's will to freedom.[42] Indeed, this response is written into fiction by precontempo-✓ rary women, one "archetypal" pattern of which, as Annis Pratt and others have observed, is girlish indulgence of freedom within a natural setting as a resistance to the impending conformity of adult ladyhood. (Louisa May Alcott's *Moods,* George Eliot's *Mill on the Floss,* and Elizabeth Barrett

Browning's poetic narrative *Aurora Leigh* are cases in point.)[43] Although women's frontier fiction "does not present us with any female Natty Bumppos," as one feminist scholar wryly remarks, women writers might be said to have developed their own version of adapted wilderness romance as a primary plot model.[44] At the culmination of Marilynne Robinson's *Housekeeping,* for example, the adolescent narrator-protagonist Ruth and her aunt-mentor, fitly named Sylvie, burn down their house and desert small-town Montana for a vagrant life. Yet this denouement also goes to show that "natural appeal" cannot be cleanly separated from culturally sanctioned expression.[45] This is true not only of the appeal of wilderness romance for the male critics whom Baym criticized, not only of its influence on contemporary writers like Robinson, but also for the genre at its very point of canonical origin: the Leatherstocking novels of James Fenimore Cooper. For Cooper arrived at his plot by viewing the condition of the American frontier through the lens of the historical romance as developed by Walter Scott. Scott's opposition of England/bourgeois/modern/city versus Scots Highland/archaic/feudal/nature supplied Cooper with his basic narrative grammar.[46]

The case of the perplexed undergraduate, then, is a representative case, inasmuch as American tastes for writing and reading about the natural environment never were wholly "natural" to start with but always in some measure were culturally produced.

But this is still too simple a statement of the matter. When a historically "Anglo-American" or "male" formation like wilderness romance is read with pleasure or adapted with relish by a non-Anglo or non-male, the implication is not necessarily that the reader or writer has had to self-efface or migrate across a cultural gap in order to read so; for the cultures of ethnicity and gender themselves migrate. African American aesthetics afford some striking examples of this transition. In the one full-length treatment of the subject, Melvin Dixon argues persuasively for disassociating African American literary culture from Anglo-American romanticization of nature and wilderness. In Dixon's appraisal of African American history, the countryside is what you escape from, an area of chance violence and enslavement.[47] His argument is supported by the limited amount of research on the tepid African American interest to date in environmentalist causes and on ethnic differences in landscape preferences.[48] The variability of this situation becomes apparent, however, when we put it in broader geographical and historical perspective. Dixon's analysis would hold for South Africa, where even more than in the United States black intellectual life has concentrated in the cities while the English and the Afrikaners have been the pastoral idealizers—and chief landowners. Elsewhere in sub-Saharan African and Afro-Caribbean culture, however, particularly in Francophone regions, writers have often celebrated precolonial states of comparatively bucolic society, as I will discuss in more detail in Chapter 2. Their imagery, furthermore, has made sense to at least some politically conscious African Americans, such as those who imported it into 1960s cityscapes to imagine a Harlem "blunthead old sweet-daddy," "leaning on a post like some gaudy warrior / spear planted, patient eyes searching the veldt" or a rioter aroused by "the beat / of a war drum / dancing from a distant / land" "to hurl a brick through" a white storekeeper's window.[49]

But one does not need to invoke pan-Africa in order to detect a strain of African American pastoralism running parallel to and crisscrossing Euro-American regionalism, exemplified in its early modern phases by Jean Toomer's *Cane*, Sterling Brown's dialect poems in *Southern Road*, and Zora Neale Hurston's fiction and folklore. The displacement of Richard Wright's *Native Son* by Hurston's *Their Eyes Were Watching God* as the most often cited precontemporary African American novel suggests the greater readiness of African American intellectuals, having won a certain state of national acceptance, more assertively to reimagine the rural phase preceding urbanization as culturally formative.[50] In texts like Gloria Naylor's *Mama Day*, Toni Morrison's *Song of Solomon,* and Alice Walker's "Everyday Use," the rural South is counterpointed with the urban North so as to take on somewhat the same iconic-ironic resonance that the traditional New England or pseudo–New England village has done for many Euro-American writers of the Northeast and Midwest. Although African American scholarship may never rediscover a neglected counterpart to Henry Thoreau, its geographical space has come to seem less city-oriented than it had seemed a generation ago notwithstanding the demographic facts.

These glimpses of Jewish American and African American letters are meant to offset each other by suggesting that a hegemonic practice of environmental representation can present itself to another subculture either as a roadblock (Howe facing the implacable Concordians) or as an opportunity (regionalist conventions in the hands of Charles Chesnutt, Jean Toomer, Hurston, and Brown, revived a half-century later). The key difference between these cases is that the African American writers have felt able to draw on a cultural memory of a rural phase that intersected— both in its lyricism and in its ironies—with the likes of Mark Twain, Robert Frost, and Sherwood Anderson. That is another ground for hoping that a study focused on texts from the traditionally dominant American cultural group may illuminate more than just the dominant group. Indeed, even some "alien" elements in Euro-American literary naturism need not be thought of as hurdles or suppressants to those approaching the discourse from other cultural backgrounds, any more than representative democracy should feel alien to someone who has not grown up with it, but sometimes may be a way of giving voice to what otherwise might have gone unvoiced. A case in point is the lyric of nature meditation as practiced by some contemporary Native American poets.

Lyric subjectivity might seem, on the face of it, to be a form of expression hostile to the elements of Native American "difference" most often criticized as lacking in Euro-American culture: the sense of the individual as inseparable from tribe and bonded to place in a relationship in which nature is not "other" but part of a continuum with the human. In the Anglo-American postromantic nature lyric, on the contrary, one expects to find an individualized voice contemplating a scene from a certain emotional distance that it wishes to bridge. Yet the work of a leading Native American poet like Simon Ortiz does not consistently reflect such a "Native American difference." It is upheld in "The Creation, according to Coyote," a retelling of a story the poet's uncle told him. But "Bend in the River," a wistful panoramic view of a riverscape, is indistinguishable from the work of many Anglo nature poets, apart from a passing reference to a flicker's wing "tied to prayer sticks"—a detail easily imitated. Other poems mix modes; in "Spreading Wings on Wind," a view of the homeland during a plane flight, Ortiz speaks at one point in a troubled "modern" lyric voice ("I must remember / that I am only one part / among many parts / not a singular eagle / or one mountain"), at another point in a traditional medicine man's voice ("Breathe like this on the feather / and cornfood like this, this way").[51] It seems to me that Ortiz moves easily between "Native" and "Anglo" modes; that it would be foolish to think of him either as having been colonized by the master's program at the University of Iowa or as using western lyric conventions of persona and aesthetic distance to deconstruct them. Rather, like most Native American poets he practices a hybridized art, not just to represent a hybridized experience (the plane flight over native soil), but for the flexibility it permits (his lyric reminiscences of his father as person and as model in "A Story of How a Wall Stands" and "My Father's Song"). In fact, Ortiz has warned against the danger of "writing only what is expected of you because you are an Indian. I don't think that's a healthy sign of a growing person or a growing people."[52] In this he seems typical rather than unique among Native American writers.

One of the most conspicuous signs of convergence between "native" and "mainstream" in Native American fiction and poetry today is the motif of the (re)turn from the city to the rural place of cultural origin and spiritual centeredness. We see a version of it in N. Scott Momaday's *House Made of Dawn* (1968), the novel that ushered in the contemporary Native American literary renaissance. Ortiz makes use of it in "Spreading Wings on Wind," "Returned from California," and other poems. So do Michael Dorris's *Yellow Raft and Blue Water*, Louise Erdrich's *Love Medicine*, Leslie Marmon Silko's *Ceremony* and *Almanac of the Dead*—the list is long and likely to continue, if only because the motif is basic to the polycultural experience of educated Native Americans today. (Indeed, cultural hybridization seems to be in the process of becoming the American norm.)[53] But as with the case of African American literature's affinities with Euro-American regionalism, the (re)turn scenario in American Indian writing also resonates with "mainstream" writing: with Thoreau's *Walden,* with Willa Cather's *My Antonia,* with Wendell Berry's *Clearing* (a linked series of poems rededicating himself to his Kentucky boyhood agrarianism). Such cross-cultural affinities indicate, as I shall later try to show with respect to Silko, a commitment to imagining a less technologized, less "artificial" life that extends across lines of gender and ethnicity.

Yet by far the single most significant aspect of cultural difference with which we shall have to reckon pertains neither to ethnicity nor to gender but to anthropocentrism, that is to the parallax engendered by human-centered vision, particularly in the modern age of print culture and advanced technology. All living writers and readers, regardless of gender and ethnicity, are more or less constrained by it: by the ethnocentricity of the human estate. "Nature itself is an oppressed and silent class, in need of spokespersons." The nonhuman remains "banished from the Critique," under "the double domination of society and science."[54] In the west, only quite recently has rampant human exploitation of the nonhuman become a major public issue, and then only for reasons of species self-interest (keeping *our* environment safe), even though it had been the subject of systematic comment since turn-of-the-nineteenth-century humanitarian protest against mistreatment of domestic animals, not to mention more long-standing laws in certain regions that regulated the killing of game. Indigenous cultures have maintained a less dualistic spirit of partnership with the nonhuman, but not such as would keep them, for example, from hunting a species to extinction if it served their interest to do so.[55] As revisionary scholarship on race and gender has shown, nature has historically been not only directly exploited but also the sign under which women and nonwhites have been grouped in the process of themselves being exploited even while being relished as exotic, spontaneous, and so forth.[56] Even liberal critics of such exploitation, like Joseph Conrad in *Heart of Darkness,* have often abetted the "otherization" of the "native" or the "woman" by simplifying and exoticizing the one or the other as creatures of nature, whether baleful (like the "savage" throng that greets Marlow at Kurtz's inner station) or benign (like the "wild, wild eyes" of the "dear, dear sister" which the speaker of Wordsworth's "Tintern Abbey" affectionately but relentlessly appropriates in the interest of his self-centered meditation).

In short, nature has been doubly otherized in modern thought. The natural environment as empirical reality has been made to subserve human interests, and one of these interests has been to make it serve as a symbolic reinforcement of the subservience of disempowered groups: nonwhites, women, and children.

It is no easy matter to extricate oneself from these biases, to arrive at a more ecocentric state of thinking than western culture now sustains, without falling into other biases like environmental racism. Three avenues may be tried. First, to anatomize the pathology: to define its forms and dimensions. Second, to take stock of the resources within our traditions of thought that might help address it. Third, to consider alternative models, be they antique, exotic, or utopian. In this book, at different points, I try all three paths, but especially the second, building around queries like these. To what extent is the ambiguous legacy of western pastoralism adaptable to an enviromentalist end (Chapters 1–2)? How can the categories of literary theory be reenvisioned so as to bring the environmental dimension of literary texts into better focus (Chapters 3, 5–6, 12)? What happens when we try to reread Euro-American literature with biota rather than homo sapiens as our central concern? What then become the major discourses, and what fundamental informing—and reforming—perceptions do they bring to light (Chapters 4–9)? How does a green reading of literary accomplishment illuminate the history of public taste and help to shape its underlying values (Chapters 10–12)?

A more radical critic would want to caution to a greater extent than I do against relying for intellectual support on the likes of Thoreau and other disaffected westerners, and would tend to favor more than I do the prospect of a complete, ground-up reconstruction of western values in terms of some other paradigm—perhaps Taoism, or some Native American culture, or other aboriginal worldview. I agree that exogamous models need to be looked at, and I devote a limited amount of time to them here, within the limits of my competence to do so. But it seems to me less likely that at this point in history they will become paradigmatic than that they will assume a more subordinate place as ingredients of a new eclecticism toward which western thinking may evolve. If, as John Locke once wrote, in the beginning all the world is America, as the twentieth century nears its close the world has become sufficiently westernized to ensure for Euro-American culture, for better or for worse, a disproportionately large share in determining world environmental attitudes during the next century.[57] If nothing more, it is prudent to imagine how the voices of environmentalist dissent within western culture might help reinvision it and how they themselves must be critically reinvisioned in order to enlist them to this end. From that double-sided perspective, I end this chapter with some reflections on the uses I intend to make of Thoreau.

Thoreau as Reference Point

Henry David Thoreau, particularly the Thoreau of *Walden,* is this book's most conspicuous human protagonist. My final three chapters focus on his posthumous career as a cultural icon, and most of the others contain extended discussion of his work, especially his masterpiece. I have made

Walden a key point of reference for several reasons. One, frankly, is autobiographical. *Walden* was the book that first drew me, as a college student, to think seriously about what I did not yet know was called the American Renaissance, which later became my field of professional specialization. Since then I have taught *Walden* dozens of times and publish- ✓ ed several essays about it. Yet no other book I have lived with for so long a period has so resisted my power to explain what it is about it that matters to me. Densely written, with a refractory mixture of forthrightness and riddlesome reserve, *Walden* demands the kind of sustained, minute, but open-ended meditation that the narrator of Robert Pirsig's *Zen and the Art of Motorcycle Maintenance* wanted to give it by taking it apart passage by passage in discussion with his son Chris, or that Stanley Cavell actually did give it in his great essay *The Senses of Walden*, treating *Walden* as an offbeat form of philosophical reflection. This book follows their examples in its own peculiar way, by returning to *Walden*, in almost every chapter, for extended discussion from many different angles.

More important than these essentially private reasons for my choice of focus, however, is the extraordinary suggestiveness of Thoreau's Walden project (both the event and the book) as a record and model of a western sensibility working with and through the constraints of Eurocentric, androcentric, homocentric culture to arrive at an environmentally ✓ responsive vision. Thoreau's career can be understood as a process of self-education in environmental reading, articulation, and bonding. The composition of *Walden*, extending over nearly a decade (1845–1854), spans the critical stage. To read the published text in light of antecedent drafts and journal material is to see Thoreau undergoing a partly planned, partly fortuitous, always somewhat conflicted odyssey of reorientation such as I myself have begun to undergo in recent years, such as it seems American culture has been undergoing, such as I am asking the reader to undergo by reconsidering the place of the environment in our conventions of reading and writing. Because *Walden*,—that is, the whole project from Thoreau's first journalizing to the published text—seems to be so representative in the senses just named, I shall concentrate more on that phase of Thoreau's career than on his later *Journal* and essays, which show greater mastery of environmental fact, texture, and nuance. *Walden* interests me, then, not only because it is a comparatively more finished piece of writing but because it also isn't: because of the richness to the point of confusion of its various aims, the multiplicity and conflictedness of which Chapter 4 holds up as a microcosm of our broader inquiry. As I see it, the later Thoreau had a more coherent sense of intellectual and literary purpose, though he died before he could achieve a synthesis elegant enough to please him, whereas in *Walden* he achieved a richly tangled expression of the conflicting priorities that he would later manage more consciously to sort through.

Of course the Walden project might never have come to my attention had it not already been canonized before I was assigned to read the book in school. And of course my emphasis on Thoreau here self-evidently will seem more legitimated by his perceived status as a "major" writer than by my personal interest in him or my personal belief in his cultural representativeness. So Thoreau's canonicity itself must also be an important part of my analysis here.

My reasons for taking a special interest in Thoreau's iconic status go beyond issues of environmental consciousness. He was one of the first writers to be added to the American literary pantheon after it was erected in the late nineteenth century; and for this and other reasons noted below the history of his reputation makes an unusually interesting window onto American literary history. He is one of the few American writers to have become canonized as both a popular hero and a hero of high culture, and this fact in turn raises a number of pointed questions about what literary canonization means and ought to mean. Most especially I shall focus on the history of the "green Thoreau," on Thoreau's posthumous transformation into an environmental saint, as a barometer of the pulsations, limitations, and promise of green thinking in America.

In my treatment of these subjects, my primary aim is neither to defend the received canon as such nor to engage in canon bashing, although I do some of both, but to understand better what is involved in imagining a particular author or text—or genre—as canonical. My basic working assumption about canonicity is that canons are indispensable for formulating discourse about text-centered fields, provided that they are considered as provisional and subject to negotiation and change. I see it as desirable both that we have common reference points and that the reference points can be changed.[58]

Canonical writers may serve either as agents of critical anesthesia or as agents of provocation. The basic paradox of Thoreau's canonicity—

himself canonized, but not his nearest progeny—makes him an instructive example of this duality.

Thoreau's canonicity has, in a way, exercised a restricting influence, reinforcing for example the notion of androcentric pastoral escape as the great tradition within American literary naturism. To align the "plot" of *Walden* in terms of this motif with those of the Leatherstocking Tales, *Moby-Dick,* and *Huckleberry Finn* is child's play for seasoned Americanists. To see the restrictiveness of this procedure, one needs simply point, as Annette Kolodny and others have done, to what happens when we try to configure American literary naturism from a very different but at least as representative (albeit less prestigious) subject position—say, that of Mary Rowlandson's *Narrative,* or the affectionate and satirical narratives of Eliza Farnham and Caroline Kirkland about frontier life in Illinois and Michigan.[59] At once the cult of wilderness becomes demystified and an alternative, gynocentric paradigm suggests itself: domestic, garden-oriented, critical of the slovenliness and the aggressivity of a wilderness existence as portrayed in the literature of frontier heroism. These texts are hardly anomalous, either: Rowlandson originated an enormously popular genre, Kirkland and Farnham exemplify an extensive vein of middle-class women's frontier narrative whose importance has so far been recognized more in Canada than in the United States.[60] Their "female" configuration has been at least as salient in the history of American literature as the "male" configuration of wilderness romance.

But if women over time availed themselves of male wilderness romance, it is also true that men have availed themselves of the comparatively nonegoistic, context-responsive, and ethically sensitive mode of environmental writing that has been linked to the social history of American women. To focus discussion on Thoreau in the context of environmental nonfiction generally helps reveal this complexity. Although Thoreau has been pressed into the service of an exclusionary myth, he has himself been victimized by its foreshortenings. His characteristic genres—the journal, the travel narrative, the natural history essay, the local sketch, none of which have gained the critical prestige of wilderness romance or the romantic nature lyric—link him almost as closely to nineteenth-century women's writing as to men's. It was not coincidental that Kirkland happened to be the editor of the journal which published Thoreau's "Ktaadn," a magazine invested heavily in drawings, essays, poetry, and fiction dealing with the environment—albeit a more prettified environment than we find in the essay's most famous passages, as the illustrations accompanying the article version of 1848 show.[61] Thoreau's increasing commitment to minute realization of vignettes of local landscape and culture, during the 1850s, brought him into intersection with a thriving local sketchbook tradition that quite early in the antebellum period was taken over by women writers influenced by Washington Irving and Mary Russell Mitford and eventually culminated in late-century regional realism.[62]

There is a striking consonance between the more landscape-oriented works in this archive, like Susan Cooper's *Rural Hours* and Celia Thaxter's *Among the Isles of Shoals* (both ecocultural sketches of comparatively isolated places), and certain works of Thoreau not ordinarily considered central, like *Cape Cod,* as well as between the former works and the seldom discussed sections of *Walden,* like the sequence from "Former Inhabitants" through "Winter Animals." It is interesting to recall that Thoreau's most intimate collaborator in natural history pursuits was his sister Sophia, and that the most characteristic reason for discounting the importance of his essays and journals in that vein—namely, that they engage in minute description without adequate conceptual framing—has also been critics' commonest recourse for disparaging one of the supposedly distinctive talents of women writers. This is not to deny the masculinism of a writer who could be bluntly misogynistic and whose praise of the "wild" has inspired writers far more masculinist than he, such as Edward Abbey. My point is simply that the androcentric Thoreau, the Thoreau of the "imperial self," is exaggerated by accounts of literary history based on the standard canonical alignments. To imagine Thoreau not as the one American practitioner of the nature essay amid a group of male writers of wilderness romance and nature poetry, but rather as part of an extensive, variegated literature of environmental prose is to point toward a more complexly gendered Thoreau[63] and to contribute toward the rehabilitation of a literature whose extent and dimensions are still not fully appreciated even by specialists. Even today we are unnecessarily burdened, as Vera Norwood has demonstrated, by the misapprehension that women have avoided the field of environmental writing.[64] True, none is yet canonical, although the revival of interest in Mary Austin's work seems to be on its way to restoring her to the plane of eminence she enjoyed during her lifetime, as the peer of Willa Cather, whose rehabilitation one supposes came more quickly in part because fiction was clearly her preferred genre.[65] But the historical record shows that women literary naturists were a strong presence almost from the dawn of American literary emergence. To read Thoreau in light of this expanded conception of the environmental intertext is at once to redefine his cultural significance and to help revise our understanding of what counts as the American environmental imagination.

Historical and
Theoretical Contexts

CHAPTER ONE

Pastoral Ideology

The line between a mythic drama that helps to redeem people in
the here and now, and one that simply lends to an opiated
passiveness, is necessarily thin.

—Genaro M. Padilla, "Myth and Comparative Cultural Nationalism"

those who want to reform society according to nature are neither
right nor left

—Anna Bramwell, *Ecology in the Twentieth Century*

Persuade a careless, indolent man to take an interest in his garden,
and his reformation has begun.

—Susan Fenimore Cooper, *Rural Hours*

I START WITH THE SUBJECT of pastoral, for "pastoral" has become almost synonymous with the idea of (re)turn to a less urbanized,
more "natural" state of existence.[1] Indeed this entire book, in focusing
on art's capacity to image and to remythify the natural environment, is
itself a kind of pastoral project.

Historically, pastoral has sometimes activated green consciousness,
sometimes euphemized land appropriation. It may direct us toward the
realm of physical nature, or it may abstract us from it. These I take to be
the basic issues of ideology and representation posed by pastoral tradition, and the purpose of the next two chapters is to deal with each in
turn, with special reference to American literary history.

Pastoral's internal contradictions, inherent from antiquity, have intensified since classicism began to break down in the post-Renaissance. In

Greco-Roman literature, pastoral both satirized and replicated the hyper-civilization of urban life by portraying supposititious shepherds and other rustics in such stylized attitudes as playful exuberance and amatory despair. In English literary history, pastoral was further developed by Edmund Spenser, John Milton, and others as a highly learned, allusive discourse, as befit the element of playful artifice already present in Theocritus. Almost concurrently, however, pastoral conventions started to modify and multiply, so that in modern times it has become possible for one of its shrewdest interpreters to define, for example, gentry-class mimesis of urban working-class life as a version of pastoral.[2]

The modern transmutation that concerns me most is the enlistment of pastoral in the service of local, regional, and national particularism. Starting in the seventeenth century, pastoralism began to become substantialized in locodescriptive poetry (the country house poem, for instance) and, more grandly, in the representation of Europe's colonies as pastoral abodes, first by promoters and explorers, later by the settlers themselves as an article of cultural nationalism. The tendency to identify nation with countryside promoted by the English squirearchy became, in time, accentuated in England's colonies.[3] This identification had an ambiguous impact on pastoral representation, opening up the possibility of a more densely imaged, environmentally responsive art yet also the possibility of reducing the land to a highly selective ideological construct. The challenge this legacy poses for the ecocritical interpreter is to appreciate how compromised the pastoralizing vision thereby can become without losing sight of its constructive power. To face this challenge is imperative if only because pastoralism is a species of cultural equipment that western thought has for more than two millennia been unable to do without. Insofar as some form of pastoralism is part of the conceptual apparatus of all persons with western educations interested in leading more nature-sensitive lives, it is to be expected that pastoralism will be part of the unavoidable ground-condition of most of those who read this book. Even if, as is clear, pastoralism interposes some major stumbling blocks in the way of developing a mature environmental aesthetics, it cannot but play a major role in that endeavor.

After a short review of pastoral commentary, I shall reflect at greater length on the tendency among many writers and critics to want to represent the essential America as exurban, green, pastoral, even wild.

This green script I call pastoral ideology for short.[4] Partly because it has been treated with much astringency of late, I shall stress its constructive potential rather than its role as a blocking agent or inducer of false consciousness. But the positive case cannot be made except in awareness of the vulnerabilities.

A Short Retrospect of American Pastoral Scholarship

Nature has long been reckoned a crucial ingredient of the American national ego. Ever since an American literary canon began to crystallize, American literature has been considered preoccupied with country and wilderness as setting, theme, and value in contradistinction to society and the urban, notwithstanding the sociological facts of urbanization and industrialization. The critical urge to explain this preoccupation in terms of a general theory of American culture is almost as long-standing. It effectively starts with the first thesis book about American literature to endure, D. H. Lawrence's *Studies in Classic American Literature* (1923).[5]

Lawrence advanced a psychohistorical explanation of the American (male) writer as an escapee from civilization (that is, Europe). Though Lawrence himself often relished such literary results as James Fenimore Cooper's nature descriptions and the thrill of the chase in *Moby-Dick,* his critical judgment was that nature-quest narratives reflected an immature stage of psychocultural development, in which struggles between libidinal and repressive forces were acted out in processes that the authors them-selves only half grasped. In Leslie Fiedler's work on American fiction, this line of analysis was fleshed out and transposed. Fleshed out, in that Fiedler exposed more intricately than Lawrence how wilderness in Ameri-can writing serves as a liminal site for male self-fulfillment in recoil from adult responsibility associated with female-dominated culture in the set-tlements. Transposed, in that Fiedler's contrast between these two do-mains clearly makes the former seem even more resonant and inviting than it did for Lawrence. Fiedler thus became the key architect, albeit not the originator, of the hypothesis that the "mainstream" tradition in American narrative is romance rather than novel.[6]

Meanwhile, American Studies scholarship had been exploring in a sociohistorical rather than psychohistorical fashion the impact of Jeffer-sonianism on American literature. The landmark works were Henry Nash

✓ Smith's *Virgin Land* (1950) and especially Leo Marx's *Machine in the Garden* (1964). Marx showed how the European settler's dream of America as arcadia achieved its early national culmination in the agrarian vision of Jefferson's *Notes on the State of Virginia* (Query XIX), ironically on the eve of industrial revolution, and how major American writers from the transcendentalists through F. Scott Fitzgerald dramatized as a tragic losing struggle the conflict between that ideal and the emergent technocracy sponsored by middle America.[7]

The result of these and other achievements of the 1950s and 1960s was to reaffirm the concept of nature as one of the preeminently formative influences in traditional if not in contemporary American writing, an influence seen on balance as a positive cultural value notwithstanding the pathological aspects diagnosed by Lawrence and Fiedler. Those writers judged to have written most powerfully about the pastoral experience assumed, indeed, the status of social prophets: critics of corruption in the name of a purer American vision of a society founded on the order of nature.

This reading of American pastoralism as a social conscience was quickly challenged, however, when starting in the 1970s the same body of writing was reread as a form of hegemony rather than as a serious attempt at social redirection. Feminist scholars were the first to expose its exclu-
✓ sionary aspects. Nina Baym and Annette Kolodny showed that to identify the wilderness romance from Cooper to Melville to Twain as the core of the American novelistic tradition marginalizes women's fiction and women's history. Kolodny argued that women writers who fictionalized the frontier dreamed their own version of the male arcadian dream ("the mid-nineteenth-century American Adam and Eve, turning wilderness or prairie into a communal garden of domesticity"), and that the actual hardships women faced drove many of them to see frontier experience more as captivity than as adventure narrative. They aspired not to be freed from civic restraint but to see nature civilized.[8] In that respect, their values more closely resembled those of the "simple," mainstream pastoral that Marx contrasted with the "complex," troubled critique of technology he ascribed to major writers like Thoreau and Melville.

Meanwhile, the supposed oppositionalism of the "complex" pastoralists was itself questioned. Kenneth Lynn and Bernard Rosenthal argued that they too should be seen more as mainstream than as dissident voices.[9] New historicist scholarship of the 1980s extended this line of argument by radicalizing Smith's analysis of expansionism in a critique that indicted romantic naturism as an instrument of imperial conquest. Myra Jehlen, in *American Incarnation* (1986), directly linked Emerson's vision of the promise of the individual's mystical relation to nature to the middle-class myth of social contract as a compact of freeholders in a land of plenty.[10] Literary and artistic representations of natural sublimity came to be seen as an arm of American manifest destiny, creating for the Euro-American male "a veritable world elsewhere where he could rewrite and reread national policies of commercialism and expansionism in quite ideal terms."[11] In the early 1990s this revisionary equation (idealizing nature equals exploitation) spilled over from academic discourse into the public arena with the controversial National Gallery exhibit "The West as America," which shocked conservative viewers by adopting as its major premise the view that nineteenth-century American romantic representation of the West was built on an ideology of conquest.[12]

Hence the theory that American idealization of nature and wilderness has acted as a kind of moral tonic or social conscience has come to seem increasingly suspect—not that the various challenges to it form a united front. Neither the feminist critique of androcentric wilderness narrative nor the critique of pastoral as the idyllic face of settler-culture expansionism is internally monolithic, and they differ between and among themselves on such points as how far to press the distinction between major male writers generally. But the various revisionisms do add up to a diagnosis that the pastoralism of the American authors traditionally regarded as major ought to be looked at as conservatively hegemonic rather than as dissenting from an urbanizing social mainstream; and this assessment in itself is highly significant in at least two ways that transcend the specific point at issue. First, it bespeaks a shift from the hermeneutics of empathy that by and large marks pre-1970 new critical and myth-symbol American scholarship to a hermeneutics of skepticism that appraises texts more in terms of what they exclude or suppress. Second, and related, the newer scholarship stresses even more than the older scholarship did nature's function as an ideological theater for acting out desires that have very little to do with bonding to nature as such and that subtly or not so subtly valorize its unrepresented opposite (complex society): as the true direction of the pastoral impulse (Lynn, Rosenthal), as the provider of necessary legal protection and communal support (Kolodny), as the institutional grid in terms of which the "natural" is seen (Jehlen).

I would raise two questions about the directional movements I have just sketched. First, I would question the increasing marginalization of the literal environment in the explanation of what is most decisive and important among the agendas of American naturism. The conception of represented nature as an ideological screen becomes unfruitful if it is used to portray the green world as nothing more than projective fantasy or social allegory, as if *Walden* were to be read in the same way as François-René Chateaubriand's *Atala* or George Orwell's *Animal Farm*. It then becomes impossible to differentiate between a descriptive poem by Robert Frost or Mary Oliver (not to mention a descriptive narration by William Bartram) and an eclogue by Virgil or Spenser. An instructive case from British literary studies is the tendency in romanticist criticism following Geoffrey Hartman to type Wordsworthian nature as a *via naturaliter negativa*, a symbolic, opposing "other" that it was the poet's business to sublate. This is a brilliantly penetrating yet also dehydrated analysis, reminiscent of formalist readings of *Walden* that consider it merely a symbolic poem. These are characteristic results of a metropolitan-based enterprise of academic criticism for which it easily becomes second nature to read literature about nature for its structural or ideological properties rather than for its experiential or referential aspects. (More on this in the next two chapters.)[13] For now, I want to focus on my second concern, having to do with the ideological character of American nature representation per se. It strikes me both that the current revisionism has not gone far enough in stressing the "imperial" cast of American pastoral ideology, and that it has gone farther than it should, by making insufficient allowance for American naturism's ideological multivalence.[14]

Pastoral's Multiple Frames

What is most troubling about the social vision of classic American pastoral can be quickly illustrated by the conclusion of Thoreau's "Slavery in Massachusetts" (1854), a lecture delivered at the height of the controversy surrounding the case of the last escaped slave to be returned to slavery from that state. The final section constitutes what genre critic Andrew Ettin would call a pastoral inset within an otherwise political discourse.[15] "Slavery in Massachusetts" is indeed one of Thoreau's most incendiary performances, and its last section is one of its most provocative parts. However, that provocation arises not from any overt political radicalism but rather from the essay's abrupt-seeming swerve *from* radicalism. The late events in Boston, declares Thoreau, seem to have permanently shaken our peaceful lives.

> Who can be serene in a country where both the rulers and the ruled are without principle? The remembrance of my country spoils my walk. My thoughts are murder to the State, and involuntarily go plotting against her.

"But," he adds, recovering himself,

> it chanced the other day that I scented a white water-lily, and a season I had waited for had arrived. It is the emblem of purity . . . extracted from the slime and muck of earth. I think I have plucked the first one that has opened for a mile. What confirmation of our hopes is in the fragrance of this flower! I shall not so soon despair of the world for it, notwithstanding slavery, and the cowardice and want of principle of Northern men.[16]

After working through this metaphor for another twenty lines or so, Thoreau ends his lecture on the same sardonic but hopeful note.

Thoreau's denouement poses the same rhetorical question Shakespeare posed in his great sixty-fifth sonnet:

> Since brass, nor stone, nor earth, nor boundless sea
> But sad mortality o'er-sways their power
> How with this rage shall beauty hold a plea
> Whose action is no stronger than a flower?

The inset's scenario replicates this sonnet's answer: beauty is threatened by a harsh reality that somehow beauty may miraculously contain at last. Yet beauty's victory may be pyrrhic, in Thoreau if not in Shakespeare. In an Elizabethan sonnet, graceful idealization is expected. We build in sonnets pretty rooms, as Donne wryly wrote in "The Canonization." But in a political jeremiad, the retort pastoral is more suspect. "The remembrance of my country spoils my walk"—what sort of plea is that? Right-eous indignation seems to dissolve into a sulk.

There's no possibility that pitting the lily against the law was an isolated infelicitous mistake. Thoreau had done the same thing before, at the end of "Resistance to Civil Government," which stresses that his first action upon release from jail, after completing his interrupted in-town errand, was to join "a huckleberry party, who were impatient to put themselves under my conduct."[17] And only a month after delivering "Slavery in Massachusetts," Thoreau issued still another work where the same gesture occurs twice again, *Walden:* he concludes his critique of institutionalized reform at the end of the "Economy" chapter by displac-ing it with an image of freedom within nature; and he later retells the story of his imprisonment and release in miniature. What's disturbing about these incidents is the insouciance with which the persona turns away from social confrontation for the sake of immersion in a simplified green world. That was one of the points about Thoreau that most irritated the Brahmin establishment and bothered even his mentor Emerson. The now infamous passage in Emerson's funeral address, chiding Thoreau for being content to "be captain of a huckleberry-party" "when he might have been engineering for all America," might have been prompted by that passage from "Resistance to Civil Government."[18] In the 1960s parlor game (still common) of praising Thoreau at Emerson's expense, this passage is one of the texts cited against the guru. Yet one can understand why Emerson should have been moved to say it.

Indeed, not just quasi-pastoralists like Emerson but full-fledged ones as well have been hard put to deal with the Peter Pan–like side of themselves even at the very point of its indulgence. A telling moment of this sort occurs in the diary of one of Thoreau's most important succes-sors in the next generation of literary naturalists, John Burroughs. In a passage that makes an arresting complement to Thoreau's, Burroughs reports a springtime visit with a friend to the woods outside the city of Washington.

> It was a superb day without a cloud, with a soft wind—one of those strong, positive days—a he-day—impregnating the earth with the generative principle of sunshine. Just as we were about to enter one of those deep wooded nooks on Piney Branch, eager and expectant,

we saw two soldiers just ahead of us. I felt vexed and as if they had no business there. Had I possessed the authority, I should have ordered them back, for I could not get over the feeling that they would drive away something I was after, some influence, some wood spirit or kindly genie that needed to be approached as gently and devoutly as possible . . . though habitually I respect and love these Bluecoats above all men. So we were obliged to lie down on the leaves and wait till the pollution of their presence had passed off, and the privacy of the woods restored—the coy nymphs all back again.[19]

Unfortunately, Burroughs's troubles are compounded when he finds that the soldiers are out there for target practice.

Here, then, is a concrete example of one's walk being spoiled by the state. In relaying it, Burroughs discloses more than Thoreau. Being a dutiful Treasury Department bureaucrat and a pro- rather than antigovernment man, Burroughs is acutely, embarrassedly aware of his duplicity: of how his pursuit of nature's charms pulls against his role as good citizen. So he openly confesses to self-indulgent retreat from the arena as Thoreau does not. On a less conscious plane, the passage bears all the telltale marks of the discourse of nature-as-elite-androcentric-preserve: the generative metaphor so redolent of Burroughs's friend Whitman (the "he-day" "impregnating the earth"), the Fiedleresque ritual of male bonding in the woods, the obvious class difference between the meditative and military recreations of white collar and bluecoat. All of these signs can easily be read back into Thoreau the Harvard-educated and genteelly subsidized misogynist nature lover.

But can American pastoral be so easily pigeonholed? Let us look again at those two passages from Thoreau and Burroughs. There is another important difference between them other than the one just noted. The Burroughs passage does indeed present a scene of interrupted innocence thereby exposed as willful: the speaker shakes the dust of civilization from his feet, but then civilization breaks back in, revealing his capacity for doublethink. The Thoreau passage speaks directly from the start to the difficulty of shaking civilization off—the state invades even so private a sector as the state of nature. However much the lily is an agent of escape on the narrative level, rhetorically it's a bomb thrown at the state. In fact, given the lily's figural status as an indictment of the slime of the mundane, only in a partial sense does it usher us away from the original context and into a natural scene at all, although there is no reason to doubt that Thoreau met with it on an actual walk and that he wishes to describe some of the particulars of that encounter. Whereas the plot seems to support the notion of nature as a refuge from complexity, on the rhetorical level the flower is not so much a mystification as a self-conscious device for exposing public consensus as repressive and arbitrary.

Perhaps I have tried too hard to exonerate Thoreau here, but at least I should have shown that the job of setting a pastoral moment in an appropriate ideological frame is trickier than it might seem, indeed that the same decoding process may not suffice for reading lyrical celebrations of nature's beauty even in cases as ostensibly similar as these two. Two more examples will help to develop this point, the first from a latter-day Thoreauvian, the second from Thoreau himself.

Aldo Leopold's *Sand County Almanac* (1949) clusters a series of essays in an arresting three-part structure: first, a seasonally arranged series of prose poems and anecdotes set at Leopold's Wisconsin weekend retreat; second, topical essays inspired by different places elsewhere around the country; and third, a series of longer, more issue-oriented essays like "The Biotic Community" and "The Land Ethic" that press points of ecological doctrine. The aim is to create a symbiosis of art and polemic, such that environmental representation and lyricism exist for their own sakes yet also, ex post facto, as a means to make the reader more receptive to environmental advocacy. This approach turns what at first might seem mere pictorialism into something increasingly less innocuous. This is the obverse of Thoreau's approach in *Walden,* which opens with the doctrine of economy and later moves closer to description and narration. Leopold's tactic is to lull the reader into an idyllic mood, then broach the more controversial critique and solution needed to preserve the experience of beauty and intimacy with nature that has previously been dramatized. Beauty becomes a form of action, as Shakespeare's sonnet hopes it might.

Leopold's reversal of Thoreauvian procedure illuminates both writers in the way it intertwines art with activism. Leopold, like Ansel Adams and Eliot Porter in the field of photography, shows as his book moves through its various sections how the ostensibly self-contained and idealized artifact can serve the role of agent of change through strategic reframing: in their case, as Sierra Club books, calendars, promotional pieces, and the like; in Leopold's case, as the experiential dimension of an emerging rhetorical appeal.

We find a version of this also in an especially provocative passage in Thoreau's "Where I Lived and What I Lived For," in which with charming mock-innocence the speaker ruminates on the farm he almost bought instead of building his cabin.

> The real attractions of the Hollowell farm, to me, were; its complete retirement, being about two miles from the village, half a mile from the nearest neighbor, and separated from the highway by a broad field; its bounding on the river, which the owner said protected it by its fogs from frosts in the spring, though that was nothing to me; the gray color and ruinous state of the house and barn, and the dilapidated fences, which put such an interval between me and the last occupant; the hollow and lichen-covered apple trees, gnawed by rabbits, showing what kind of neighbors I should have; but above all, the recollection I had of it from my earliest voyages up the river, when the house was concealed behind a dense grove of red maples, through which I heard the house-dog bark.   (*Wa* 83)

This passage aims both to mesmerize with nostalgic charm and to unsettle readerly allegiances. It is lyricized to the point of narcissism (with the retreat to childhood fantasy at the end), but lyrical regression is not so much indulged in as transformed into sly satire. I chose this farm, the passage says, deliberately for the "wrong" reasons. I liked how inconvenient it was from the market center. I liked its dilapidation. Its one practical advantage (protection from fogs) didn't matter. My notion of use value is the opposite of yours, which is based on exchange—so there. Pastoral hedonism becomes indictment of the average farmer's plodding matter-of-factness. Altogether, Thoreau's strategy resembles what the domestic fiction of his day did when it challenged readers to take seriously the Victorian idealization of women's moral sensibility. Without exactly repudiating the status quo, agrarian rather than patriarchal in this case, Thoreau prods readers to consider how wide is the gap between scrabbling actuality and Jeffersonian ideal, according to which the ethos of farming empowers, not frustrates, the pursuit of culture.[20]

Here and elsewhere in pastoral, beauty never functions *only* as critique. At some level there is always the chance that the text will tempt the reader to see all sugar and no pill and that even hard thrusts will get deflected into quaint excursions. American texts are particularly susceptible to this because of the ease with which dissent can get co-opted as an aspect of consensus. As David Shi shows in his history of the dream of the simple life in America—a book bearing directly on pastoral art although not about aesthetics—the dream of a disencumbered, stripped-down life has the potential to become a socially disruptive force but also, given its historic sponsorship by hegemonic groups (like the Puritan fathers and the Founders), to become an ultrarespectable plank in American civil religion, as much of a placebo as *e pluribus unum*.[21]

Conversely, however, the dream of the simple life and the pastoral aesthetic can assume a more contentious form in proportion to the degree the establishment seems arrayed against them. A powerful motif in African American writing, emanating from slave narrative, is the denial to blacks of the bounty masters enjoy at their own expense. Frederick Douglass's *Narrative* crystallizes this beautifully in the image of the master tarring his garden fence so that any fruit-snatching slave will be found out and whipped. Richard Wright's "Big Boy Leaves Home" reinvents the classic American male-bonding-in-nature story in protest against the exclusion of blacks from the American arcadia. Ignoring a local farmer's proscription against blacks in his swimming hole, Big Boy and his friends enjoy a moment of innocence and release—interrupted by a spiral of violence: murder, lynching, and Big Boy's flight from the South.[22] In both cases white injustice is dramatized by the scene of exclusion from pastoral gratification. As a Sterling Brown poem pithily describes it,

> Some planters goes broke,
> An' some gits well,
> But dey sits on deir bottoms
> Feelin' swell;
> An' us in the crab grass
> Catchin' hell.[23]

Like many Euro-American pastoralists (although not Thoreau and Burroughs), Douglass, Wright, and Brown all composed their pastoral satires from urban bases of operation. Unlike their mainstream counterparts, they of course wrote under some fairly significant externally imposed constraints about subject matter. Aesthetic choice was focused if not dictated for Douglass and, to a lesser extent, for the other two by the traditional image of the "black" as a laborer in the agricultural south. Authors of antebellum slave narratives, like Douglass until he had extricated himself from white abolitionist sponsorship, could not stray much beyond that plantation-based image.[24] Later in the nineteenth century, one of the few ways open to the African American creative writer in search of a mainstream audience was to play the Uncle Remus card and write local color fiction and dialect poetry. Wright and Brown, two generations later, can be seen as exemplifying different ways of undermining the mainstream stereotype of blacks as Cudjoes—dark descendants of the yokels of neoclassical pastoral satire. But black American writers actually manipulated the stereotype from the start, as is clear for example from Charles Chesnutt's "The Goophered Grapevine" (1887), narrated by a northern white man of means who desires to take up viticulture in the more benign climate of North Carolina. He tells a charming tale of meeting at the farm he proposed to buy an Uncle Julius, who solemnly warns him that the previous owner had the vineyard hexed by a local conjure woman. The narrator buys the farm anyway and assuages Uncle Julius, whose defensive act he sees right through, with the post of coachman. Of course there are three conjurers, not just two: not just Aunt Peggy and Uncle Julius, but also Chesnutt passing as a purveyor of standard magazine fare before the average reader of his story in the *Atlantic Monthly*.[25] Chesnutt uses his pastoral scenario to set forth three examples of wily assertion including his own. It is a risky game; here as elsewhere pastoral ideology is double-edged; Chesnutt's strategy (as professional author) puts him in the role of hired contractor (like Aunt Peggy) and in a position to be neutralized (like Uncle Julius) by entering into authorship on those terms. But that this exceptional reflexivity, on top of everything else, is itself part of Chesnutt's game, folded into the tale's subtext, completes the pastoral thrust. This tale, and it is only one of many possible examples, shows that African Americans are not the uncouth rustics that the tale has to pretend they are because turn-of-the-century white culture does not want to hear about blacks on any other terms. The tale demonstrates that African Americans can gain control of the pastoral apparatus, whether "we" realize it or not. Indeed, Frederick Douglass had already shown this when he rewrote his childhood in *My*

Bondage and My Freedom in such a way as to emphasize his love of countryside to a much greater degree than his format permitted him to do in his earlier *Narrative,* and thereby to dramatize further the sense of the slave's exclusion from his rightful estate.[26]

Pastoral oppositionalism can also be seen in writers closer to the mainstream. Rachel Carson's *Silent Spring* (1962), which helped inspire contemporary radical environmentalism largely on account of its power as creative writing (see Chapter 9), starts out with an elegiac Thornton Wilderesque fantasy of the death of a typical Our Town. This pastoral inset trades strongly on the old dream of the simple life but is hardly a simple nostalgia piece, since it was intended and was perceived to be a direct challenge to the chemical industry. To read it as regressive fantasy is to read it the same way the pesticide industry's defenders wanted us to read it. A similar claim can be made on behalf of Wendell Berry's revival of Jeffersonian agrarianism as a weapon against agribusiness and what Berry sees as the myopic cosmopolitanism of the average American today. Clearly that agrarian vision has a different political valence for Berry than for Thomas Jefferson. For Jefferson it would have expressed something like the status quo. For Berry it is deliberately anticonsensual, an insurgency of the disempowered.[27]

This scattergram of examples should suffice to demonstrate that American pastoral representation cannot be pinned to a single ideological position. Even at its seemingly most culpable—the moment of willful retreat from social and political responsibility—it may be more strategized than mystified. As a final case study, I turn to pastoral prose by women writers, given that the literary pursuit of nature has so often been reckoned a male domain by traditional and revisionist critics alike.

Women on Nature

The feminist critique of wilderness romance should not block us from seeing how pastoral modes have functioned as a means of empowerment for women writers. While researching environmental writing and commentary from Thoreau's day to ours, I was surprised to find a significant degree of interdependence between the "major" male figures and the work and commentary of women writers less well known. Roughly half the nature essays contributed to the *Atlantic Monthly* during the late nineteenth century, the point when the nature essay became a recognized genre, were by female authors.[28] Among early appraisals of Thoreau, I found, unexpectedly—given the predominant notion of Thoreau as appealing more to men than to women—that commentaries by women were more likely to be favorable than those by men. The first posthumous fictional recreation of Thoreau was by a woman, Louisa May Alcott (*Moods* [1864]). The first book, to my knowledge, published by an outsider to the transcendentalist circle that celebrates nature as a refuge from hypercivilization with explicit invocation of Thoreau as model and precursor was written by a woman: Elizabeth Wright's *Lichen Tufts, from the Alleghanies* (1860). The first Thoreau Society was founded by a group of young women (1891); the first doctoral dissertation on Thoreau (1899) was written by a woman, as was one of the best early biographical studies of Thoreau.[29] John Burroughs and John Muir, the most prominent male literary naturists in the generation following Thoreau, present even more conspicuous cases of female affiliations. Both had mothers who played a major part in nurturing their love of nature; both as adults were sustained by the encouragement of women who shared that interest; a woman was one of the candidates for the post of Muir's literary executor (but was edged out by editorial patriarchy), and a woman actually did take charge of Burroughs's literary affairs (at his own request). Burroughs in particular was convinced that his most sympathetic readers were women; and his literary executrix, Clara Barrus, in her biography stresses that appeal, explaining that turn-of-the-century women looked on nature excursions as a means of liberation from the parlor.[30]

Patriarchy, in turn, considered nature observation, particularly botany, a quite safe pursuit for Victorian women. An anonymous writer for the *Maine Monthly Magazine* in 1837 spoke the consensus in affirming that "botany may be safely commended to the attention of young ladies without incurring the censure of any party." For the "practical pursuit of botany" was "peculiarly feminine. The dust and effluvia of the laboratory will never commend it to delicate nerves, while many of its tasks are scarcely within the limits of female strength."[31] American women, for their part, were quick to seize on this space for entrepreneurship as early as the mid-eighteenth century, when Jane Colden became the "first lady Linnaean."[32] That women would have been attracted almost as readily as men to natural history is in keeping with the prototypes for nineteenth-century representation of men's and women's experience vis-à-vis nature. These prototypes are not so discrepant as they are often made to seem by stark juxtapositions of wilderness romance and domestic fiction. Writers of both sexes commonly picture the early childhood stage of both sexes as a state of natural piety. The first books of Elizabeth Barrett Browning's poetic bildungsroman *Aurora Leigh* resemble those of Wordsworth's *Prelude* in this respect. The child-seer of Wordsworth's "Immortality Ode," that nineteenth-century literary fountainhead of Anglo-American natural piety, is virtually sexless or androgynous; and in American writing influenced by its vision the child is more often female than male.[33] In adolescence, female protagonists become socialized away from nature, while the male continues to enjoy freer mobility and the option of questing and of conquest within nature, which is frequently and revealingly symbolized as female. Starting well before Thoreau, male narratives of self-reliant cabin-dwelling isolatoes are common, whereas the commonest counterpart in women's narrative is the story of the "female hermit" who has not risen above society but fallen below it as a result of a disastrous love affair, usually extralegal, which has left her with a child, who usually dies. For women like Joanna, the hermitess of Shell-heap Island in Sarah Orne Jewett's *Country of the Pointed Firs,* nature is where you go if you have no place to go. Yet the personal bond to nature can also retain a more positive value for the mature woman protagonist who, as Annis Pratt and Barbara White put it, may "look back to moments of naturalistic epiphany as touchstones in a quest for her lost selfhood."[34] This is precisely how Thoreau pictures himself when confessing that one of his earliest childhood memories was of being taken to Walden Pond, so that by his return to live there "I have at length helped to clothe that fabulous landscape of my infant dreams" (*Wa* 156). A similar reenactment process is evident in the work of the early female Thoreauvian mentioned above.

Having being cosmopolitanized after an Alleghany girlhood and a purgatorial stint of pioneering in Illinois, Elizabeth Wright returns with a group of friends for a holiday in the woods of northwestern Pennsylvania. Self-conscious though she is about the element of playacting ("like overgrown children"), she considers herself a good woodswoman and longs "for the cool pure liberty of their hidden depths." To her companions, overbaggaged with "civilized rubbish," Wright quotes Thoreau on simplification, from which ensues a pungent commentary on how nature gives the lie to civilized distinctions and in particular to the niceties of conduct that hem tenderfoot women in. ("I wondered then, more than ever, where people ever get the absurd notion of talking about 'refined' and 'vulgar,' or 'masculine' and 'feminine' employments. It sounds as ridiculous as the French way of calling knives masculine and forks feminine. My knives are no more masculine than my forks. Elvira's shooting was as feminine as her curls, and the Professor's cooking as manly as his beard.") [35] Wright's keyed-up jauntiness reassures the more conventional reader that despite appearances of revolutionary fervor, her work will be a mere carnivalesque inversion of the proprieties. But it *is* an inversion: a sustained exercise in pushing limits whereby nature authorizes mid-Victorian woman to level the social distinctions that gall her.

Along the way, Wright also sets herself against stereotypical female appropriations of nature, such as the "satiny, perfumed" nature rhetoric in gift books or the "twaddle" of botany textbooks written for young women. [36] In the work of the less outspoken of the period's female naturists, such distinctions are more subtle, though not invisible. A case in point would be the nineteenth-century American literary season book that comes closest to rivaling Thoreau, Susan Cooper's unjustly neglected *Rural Hours* (1850, revised 1887): a calendar of natural and cultural history observations that reveals a Dorothy Wordsworth–like keenness of environmental perception. As Vera Norwood has shown, it is instructive to think of this text as a center of meditation on classic American nature writing in place of, say, the forest romances of her father, James Fenimore. [37]

At first sight, Susan Cooper seems sedately entrenched within the sphere of decorous floral observation. Unlike her litigious father, she does not confront head-on the burning contemporary sociopolitical issues any more than Dorothy Wordsworth does, and in this and several other respects *Rural Hours* exhibits the characteristic stylistic differences we have been taught to find in precontemporary women's narratives as opposed to men's: the figure of the experiencer is played down relative to the object described; the setting is more local, within the circuit of the writer's own daily excursions; and the mimetic level is less romanticized. The author's quiet eye, however, sees a number of things the eye of a James Fenimore Cooper novel tends to miss. In place of his romantic savagism, which sees Indians as a doomed archaic race because the twain can never meet, *Rural Hours* envisions a possible integration whereby "men of Indian blood may be numbered among the wise and the good, laboring in behalf of our common country." Whereas her father has Natty Bumppo elegize over the "wasty ways" of the settlers in *The Pioneers* and *The Prairie,* she makes specific recommendations about the conservation of trees before Thoreau did. Though hardly prepared to go so far as he in praising the wild above the good, Cooper shows a projective empathy for nature's rhythms as a corrective to the human-built: it is more than fortuitous that the book's structure implicitly asserts the need for the human order to accommodate itself to the natural as well as vice versa.[38]

As these examples suggest, Cooper's instinct, unlike Wright's, is to valorize the natural by incorporating it into a vision of society brought closer to nature, not to set society and individual free expression at odds. The latter is present only latently in *Rural Hours,* as for instance in Cooper's most detailed set piece of wildlife description, on hummingbirds, concerning which these two interesting points emerge: that their dainty diminutiveness is deceptive (hummingbirds are actually bold and confident), and that a major threat to their existence is their tendency to fly indoors and get trapped there. "We have repeatedly known them found dead in rooms little used," Cooper writes.[39] Clearly *Rural Hours* is not "The Yellow Wallpaper," but the prevailing sedateness of the female sketchbook norm warrants our being brought up by the muffled vehemence of such passages. Consequently, we should also see such a passage as embedding a more substantial challenge to status quo perceptions both about hummingbirds and the power or vulnerability of tiny creatures generally than we would ascribe to a passage of the same decibel level in Thoreau. To take another example, Thoreau risked nothing when he (guardedly) praised Walt Whitman, flanked as he was by sympathetic transcendental brethren; but for a female *Atlantic* contributor to begin a mid-1880s nature essay on grass with an epigraph from Whitman, not long after *Leaves of Grass* had been banned in Boston, was an act of risk taking, chaste though the ensuing discourse was by comparison.[40]

This undertone surfaces in Mary Austin's turn-of-the-century books and stories about the California desert, starting with *Land of Little Rain* (1903). Unlike Thoreau, Austin rarely parades the "I," and in keeping with a strong tradition in women's rural writing she ends *Little Rain* with a vision of community—an idyllic Mexican American village—that contrasts greatly with Thoreau's ironic "return" to Concord at the end of *Walden.* But the main narrative, typically for Austin, displays an assertive, somewhat prickly, sardonic persona. She disorients, for instance, by refusing to map her territory with English place-names. This reticence becomes part of a strategy, despite disclaimers of ignorance, for unfolding her environmental knowledge (including knowledge of non-Anglo cultures, Indian and Hispanic) and thereby pulling the whole territory away from prior Anglo claims to it—both legal and interpretative—into a domain of which she alone is the interpreter. She reinforces her control through peremptory declaratives: "This is the nature of that country," "Mesa trails were meant to be traveled on horseback," and so on (*LLR* 9, 83). In the process, Austin is careful to discredit masculine romance about the west à la Bret Harte, sketching *her* version of a remote frontier town in an anthropological realist retort to "The Luck of Roaring Camp." Ultimately the Austin persona beats Harte's in realism, in toughness, *and* in bonding to the environment.

To align Wright, Cooper, and Austin with Thoreau is to form a picture of "men's" and "women's" representations of nature and wildness blending into each other to the point that distinctions start to seem porous. *Walden* executes the antisocial, individualistic flight from the settlements featured in masculine wilderness romance, but the break is not total, the woods are not too dark and deep, the experience becomes domesticated as the lifestyle is expatiated and the protagonist's lococentrism stressed, and the persona remains always in dialogue with and to that extent always a member of the community whose norms he rejects. *Little Rain* tells no such story of the writer's repudiation of community and indeed barely allows the persona to exist as an independent character; but the persona speaks from the position of being *in* the wilderness and disengaged from the complacencies of settlement culture. Altogether, it seems that premodern women's pastoral was, like its Thoreauvian counterpart, capable of questioning the normative values that seemingly regulated it, and of exploring the claims of self-realization against those of social constraint.

Pastoral's Future

We have seen that the ideological valence of pastoral writing cannot be determined without putting the text in a contextual frame. As Houston Baker has said of how similar motifs are handled in white and black American writing, ostensibly similar terms can bear quite different iconic sequences depending on context.[41] The "retreat" to nature *can* be a form of willed amnesia, as in the Burroughs passage; but it means something different when held up self-consciously, as by Thoreau, to appeal to an alternative set of values over and against the dominant one. It means something still different when that alternative framework is employed by one like Elizabeth Wright, for whom that framework is not as predictable and acceptable a vocabulary as it was for a male writer of the same era. And it means something different when the alternative vocabulary is itself less conventionalized than it is for either Thoreau or Wright, both of whom are, after all, appealing to notions of the romantic and the picturesque that had strong imaginative currency for middlebrow readers of the age when found in their "proper" setting: namely, Wordsworthian poetry or, for that matter, Shakespearean sonnet. In effect, at the end of "Slavery in Massachusetts" Thoreau produces the "unacceptable" by imposing a stereotypical image from another context. From this use of nature should be distinguished Wendell Berry's appeal to an agrarian ideal of a nuts-and-bolts literalism that was normative in nineteenth-century thought but that today is far more alien to the average book reader than Thoreau's idiom. And from Berry's appeal might be distinguished still more revolutionary pastoralisms that never did have mainstream status to begin with, like the lesbian-ecofeminist vision of Susan Griffin's *Woman and Nature: The Roaring inside Her* (1978).

But the "ideological grammar" of American pastoral[42] cannot stop at trying to make distinctions among different categories of work. It must also recognize the crosscurrents that keep any example from being pure: on the one hand, the centripetal pull of consensualism that threatens to draw the radical text over into the sleepy safe domain of nature's nationism, the ho-hum pieties of American civil religion; and, on the other, the centrifugal impulse always incipient, though usually contained within modest limits, for pastoral to form itself in opposition to social institutions of whatever sort. This duality was built into Euro-American pastoral thinking from the start, for it was conceived as both a dream hostile to the standing order of civilization (decadent Europe, later hypercivilizing America) and at the same time a model for the civilization in the process of being built. So American pastoral has simultaneously been counterinstitutional and institutionally sponsored. This is a troublesome dichotomy. It is hard to keep one's eye on a target moving in two directions at once. But if, as Fitzgerald said, the test of a first-rate intelligence is the ability to hold contradictory ideas in the mind and still maintain the ability to function, serious readers ought to be equal to the task.

But how pressing an issue will pastoral continue to be? Given our present degree of industrialization, isn't it likely to become increasingly obsolete? Surely not. Environmental holocaust now seems not only a potential by-product of nuclear attack but also an imminent peril in its own right. Owing to this and other social disaffections, as Leo Marx and others have pointed out, we have since the 1960s been faced with the novel phenomenon of a "life-leaning ideology not based on a progressive world view," which challenges us to reexamine our most obstinate myth of historical development. The "wholly new conception of the precari- ✓ ousness of our relations with nature," Marx predicts—and I agree—"is bound to bring forth new versions of pastoral."[43] Hitherto, contemporary intellectuals have been accustomed to thinking of rusticity rather as they think of God: surely both are myths that effectively died out in the nineteenth century. Urbanization, even more tenaciously than seculariza- tion, is one of those larger myths in whose existence intellectuals continue to believe even after they disavow the doctrine of history's linear move- ment. The "age of ecology," as Donald Worster has termed the present era,[44] may not lead to more than a marginal change in social attitudes toward or public policy concerning further technological buildup; but even if it doesn't, indeed perhaps especially if it doesn't, pastoralism is sure to remain a luminous ideal and to retain the capacity to assume oppositional forms for some time to come. One conspicuous mark of its relevance is the contemporary tradition of environmental apocalypse literature: Carson's *Silent Spring,* Ernest Callenbach's *Ecotopia,* John Brun- ner's *The Sheep Look Up,* Jonathan Schell's *The Fate of the Earth.* The ephemeral quality of much of this writing does not rule out the possibility of a long-range impact.

Pastoral's likely future as an ideological force makes it all the more important to grasp its double-edged character. We would be quixotic to expect to sift "progressive" pastoral from "regressive" using some political program as a litmus test, even when it seems this could be done. For pastoral as ideological *form* tends to remain more or less constant even as ideological content changes. Set, for example, two Vietnam-era calen- dars of environmental observation and musing next to each other: Jean Hersey's *The Shape of a Year* (1967) and Josephine Johnson's *The Inland Island* (1969). The first is wholly accommodationist (pretty much oblivi- ous to politics, "hoping that just once somebody would write about what is *right with us* instead of what is wrong"). The second expresses strong dissent by thrusting vignettes of the "cancer in the body of the world" into the imagery of idyllic calm.[45] Yet these antithetical moves are, at a higher level of abstraction, identical in respect to holding up physical nature as a touchstone of value for the edification of one's culture. The striking contrast between the politics of Hersey and of Johnson is the exception rather than the norm. More often than not, accommodationism and reformism are interfused. The move to Walden is both a frontal assault on mainstream values like the protestant work ethic and a ritual reenactment of the pioneer experience, New England–style, with which the average American do-it-yourselfer can identify. It is a mistake to resolve either image into the other. These two faces are the Tityrus and Meliboeus of modern pastoral: the happy co-opted shepherd and the dispossessed, alienated shepherd of Virgil's first eclogue, where the convention of pastoral debate was first self-consciously ideologized. Which dimension gets stressed depends not only on who's writing but also on who's reading. In modern times, pastoral's forms and contradictions have intensified. In the next chapter I will discuss more fully what I take to be the single most fundamental reason for this: the enlistment of pastoral as a vehicle of national self-definition, specifically as a way of envisaging Europe's "new" worlds. We have yet to take full account of the complexity and irony of this process. Amidst the self-interestedness of the various proprietary projects, however, we can also see pastoral ideology functioning as a bridge, crude but serviceable, from anthropocentric to more specifically ecocentric concerns. For the pastoralization of new worlds, in spite of some of its original motives, also created a space for the eventual advancement of nature's claims on human society. Though at first new world nature looked to many like vacancy, emptiness waiting to be filled, this same vision—*mutatis mutandis*—became in time the basis for rallying support for an endangered plenitude. "Howling wilderness" has its reverse: "This living flowing land / is all there is, forever."[46] The myth of actual regions, even continents, as properly "unspoiled" has helped stimulate and bolster the authority of the ecological conscience as environmental deterioration has become too blatant to ignore. As this ecocentric repossession of pastoral has gathered force, its center of energy has begun to shift from representation of nature as a theater for human events to representation in the sense of advocacy of nature as a presence for its own sake.

CHAPTER TWO

New World Dreams and Environmental Actualities

⊖

When we come to natural gifts apart from book-learning [the Romans] are above comparison with the Greeks or any other people . . . In learning Greece surpassed us and in all branches of literature.

—Cicero, *Tusculan Disputations,* 1.ii

I get to know more about the concrete, social life of America from the desert than I ever would from . . . intellectual gatherings.

—Jean Baudrillard, *America*

The American writer inhabits a country at once the dream of Europe and a fact of history; he lives on the last horizon of an endlessly retreating vision of innocence.

—Leslie Fiedler, *Love and Death in the American Novel*

AMERICAN LITERARY NATURISM was a variant of a motif to be found worldwide among literary cultures in European languages generated by former colonies. Many, if not most, post-European literatures[1] harbor traditions of envisioning their cultures as nonmetropolitan spaces set apart from the imperium for better or for worse. That provincial self-conception has given rise to latter-day versions of the insecurity Cicero long ago evinced when formulating Rome's relation to *its* fountainhead, Greece, and to varieties of cultural nationalism that try to turn the European perception of the (post)colonial periphery into a cultural asset. From this have arisen myths of the frontier, of the bush, of Africanity.

Here we find the source of much of the ideological mobility of American pastoral. For in the service of cultural self-definition, pastoral has been used by European immigrants to underwrite a program of conquest and by indigenes to decry such conquest. It has been used by corrective forces within settler culture, in the way Emerson and Thoreau criticized the hypercivilized effeteness of Boston, and self-critically by postcolonial writers as V. S. Naipaul who accept metropolitan values. Sometimes it is hard to discern, as we have seen, whether a given text is being accommodationist or oppositional—whether a romantic landscape painting by Thomas Cole participates in the rhetoric of American expansionism or whether it should be seen as a protoenvironmentalist indictment of expansionism.[2] In this chapter I develop the case for new world pastoral's adaptability for ecocentric purposes in light of these complications and in turn its capacity to serve as something more than ideological theater: its capacity, in particular, to register actual physical environments as against idealized abstractions of those. Traditional pastoral, although vaguely localized, was so inclined toward the latter as to tempt one to conclude that "it thematizes the act of fictionalizing."[3] The Renaissance invention of Europe's new worlds under the sign of pastoral,[4] however, set all the following in motion: it held out the prospect that the never-never lands of pastoral might truly be located in actual somewheres; it helped energize quests, both selfish and unselfish, to map and understand those territories; and it thereby helped ensure a future interplay between projective fantasy and responsiveness to actual environments in which pastoral thinking both energized environmental perception and organized that energy into schemas. New world pastoral thus offered both to filter the vision of those enchanted by it and to stimulate them to question metropolitan culture itself (even while participating in it).

Two considerations make new world pastoral especially significant to our study. First, it promotes the idea of vast territories of the actual globe subsisting under the sign of nature. During the era of colonization this idea remains a rudimentary albeit luminous one, unaccompanied by any conservationist impulse—indeed quite the reverse. Still, it lays the groundwork for developing the myth of the land as properly unspoiled, a myth that can give shape and impetus to more recent environmental restoration projects.[5] Second, new world pastoral anticipates the modern would-be environmentalist's dilemma of having to come to terms with actual natural environments while participating in the institutions of a technologized culture that insulates one from the natural environment and splits one's allegiances. Modern environmentalists wishing to speak for the green world are contemporary new world pastoralists. Their challenge is also one of decolonization, insofar as they must fall back on conceptual instruments derived from metropolitan educations that have inevitably somewhat alienated them from the green world, whether they are genealogically settlers or indigenes. In order to inhabit their environment responsibly, in order even to see it, they have to perceive it as something other than just a green world, a dream, a concept. The green world myth is a start. It is the best they can perhaps do at a certain stage. It marks the beginning of the possibility of a mature conception of a heterotopic alternative to the poisoned environments that we increasingly find ourselves inhabiting.[6] But it can become productive only as people learn to use it in earth's interest as well as in humanity's, and this new responsibility cannot be assumed until one begins to look past the mythical vision as well as through it.

Settlers' Pastoral

When Wendell Berry calls on us to "think little," to look to the frugal Amish as a model, to mourn "our loss of contact with the earth," to believe in "the old idea" of Jeffersonian agrarianism, he intends to evoke thoughts not just of today but of the whole heritage of virtuous ruralism from which Americans have supposedly lapsed.[7] Nor is the agrarian jeremiad itself a genre original with him. It is already half-developed in America's first major work of literary agrarianism, Crèvecoeur's *Letters of an American Farmer* (1782), which begins with images of Farmer James's happy, thriving estate—the proper way of the new world, clearly—and ends with somber autobiographical reminiscence of the loyalist untimely ripped from that estate when revolution struck. Crèvecoeur's visions of agrarian prosperity in the middle colonies are not a homegrown American documentary so much as a European visitor's or immigrant's dream of what might be enacted, ventriloquized first through the letters of a model farmer writing to an English gentleman who had visited him, then in Crèvecoeur's more cosmopolitan authorial voice.[8] We witness American culture and writing at the moment of being dreamed by the European mind. The Jeffersonian legacy to which Berry today appeals was, in the first instance, a construct imagined by Europeans, although Jefferson gave it a republican turn.

Under new world conditions, some imported enterprises prove more adaptable than others. Silk production failed in the American South, while apple culture throve in the North. So with literary forms. American writers from Cooper to Henry James complained that the American social fabric was too flimsy for a novelistic mode of representation (meaning the novel of manners); but pastoral proved highly adaptable. Eighteenth-century intellectuals like Jefferson and Timothy Dwight readily formulated America's identity and promise in terms of a ruralist myth of provincial (later republican) virtue resting on its agrarian order, as opposed to an increasingly overpopulated, citified, industrializing Europe. In the antebellum period, the link between American cultural identity and exurban and preindustrial spaces became one of the enabling myths of American literary nationalism. The American environment became one of its most distinctive cultural resources.

European romanticism's canonization of nature afforded anxious post-colonials a means of converting a seemingly irreparable disadvantage (cultural underdevelopment) into an asset. "Americans sought something uniquely 'American,' yet valuable enough to transform embarrassed provincials into proud and confident citizens . . . In at least one respect Americans sensed that their country was different: wilderness had no counterpart in the Old World."[9] Monuments of high culture and storied association America may have lacked, but "here was a realm in which Americans could compete." When it came to landscape grandeur "we clearly had the Europeans beaten."[10]

By no means did all antebellum American writers feel such investment in cultural nationalism and such zest for wilderness. Literary nationalism was most vigorously promoted by a vocal minority: that fraction of Anglo-American male writers who held that American writing ought to differ sharply from European. Even this group was not nationalist all the time; Emerson's nationalism in "The American Scholar," for example, was hesitant and lukewarm compared to Whitman's preface to the 1855 edition of *Leaves of Grass*.[11] The same can be said of "wilderness" as an ideal. Slave narratives and domestic fiction, for example, were not written to promote a gospel of nature or wilderness. Yet such work also by and large reinforced the image of America as more countrified than the facts of contemporary economic transformation would suggest. Slave narrative did so by duress; it had no choice but to focus on plantation life.[12] Sentimental fiction often did so more affirmatively, generating images of rural domesticity (Sarah Hale's New Hampshire Thanksgiving in *Northwood*,

Harriet Beecher Stowe's Quaker Settlement in *Uncle Tom's Cabin,* Susan Warner's extended portraits of country living in *Wide, Wide World*) that provided more nuanced versions of the iconic scenes packaged for middle-class purchasers in the popular prints of Currier and Ives. By mid-century, women writers had become leaders in the genre of the village sketch, originally pioneered by Timothy Dwight and Washington Irving, ushering in what later became known as local colorism. In this tradition, until the twentieth century, for women as for men, virtue tends to correlate with rurality even when rurality includes poverty, gloom, and intolerance.

The persistent tendency for exurban environments to become the purview of the American writer to a greater extent than social data would predict was not unique to America. It also appears in nineteenth-century British literature: in Wordsworthian poetry, in the regional gothic of the Brontës, in Hardy's Wessex. Had the Alps not been lyricized by Goethe, Byron, Wordsworth, and the Shelleys, Thoreau might have been less drawn to Saddleback and Katahdin as literary subjects. The seeds for Thoreau's interests were actually planted in the neoclassical era, which one is tempted to contrast too starkly with romanticism as urban in spirit. Well before American pastoralists began to effect the historic innovation of translating what had traditionally been a sophisticated intellectual game into an ideological program for an actual society, certain British writers were inventing newly concretized versions of pastoral, such as the country house poem, to explicate and underwrite the ethos of emerging squirearchy. American writers borrowed freely from them.

But what I want chiefly to stress here is the family resemblance among settler cultures. A glance at traditional landscape poetry by Anglophone settler cultures in Canada, Australia, South Africa, and the United States tells the story.[13]

> By the smoky amber light
> Through the forest arches streaming,
> Where Nature on her throne sits dreaming,
> And the sun is scarcely gleaming
> Through the cloudlets, snowy white,
> Winter's lovely herald greets us
> Ere the ice-crowned tyrant meets us.
> (Susanna Moodie, Canadian,
> "Indian Summer")

Over plains and over woods
What a mighty stillness broods!
  . . . . .
Only there's a drowsy humming
From yon warm lagoon slow coming:
'Tis the dragon-hornet—see!
All bedaubed resplendently,
Yellow on a tawny ground—
Each rich spot nor square nor round,
Rudely heart-shaped, as it were
The blurred and hasty impress there
Of a vermeil-crusted seal
Dusted o'er with golden meal.
> (Charles Harpur, Australian,
> "A Midsummer Noon in the Australian
> Forest")

I am the shadow, the swift dream,
The stark loneliness of the tall tree,
The slow solitudes that stream
Star-deep through eternity.

I am the pain, the aching heart
That all must know who would be free:
The empty cup that the bleached lips part,
. . . And the pledge of immortality.
> (Brian Waldron Rose, South African,
> "The Veld")

A waif from Carroll's wildest hills,
    Unstoried and unknown;
The ursine legend of its name
    Prowls on its banks alone,
Yet flowers as fair its slopes adorn
    As ever Yarrow knew,

Or, under rainy Irish skies,
    By Spenser's Mulla grew;

And through the gaps of leaning trees
    Its mountain cradle shows:
The gold against the amethyst,
    The green against the rose.

    (John Greenleaf Whittier, American,
    "Sunset on the Bearcamp")

All four poets survey a vast, unpeopled, and (for that reason?) vaguely somber landscape, whose emptiness they fill with imagery in order to make it seem compelling and distinctive. Moodie unfolds one of the glories of upper North America, also celebrated by Yankee bards: the idyllic albeit ominous Indian summer, whose spectacular colors, which Moodie proceeds to describe, were unknown in Britain's less extreme climate. Her contemporary Harpur compensates for the eerie stillness of the Australian subtropics with a bright piece of natural history curiosa that remains true to the tonality of that landscape even as it takes on the protective coloration of first Wordsworth (the brooding mighty stillness echoing the "Westminster Bridge" sonnet) and then Emerson (compare both the meter and the imagery of this verse to "The Humble-Bee"). Rose (a mid-twentieth-century poet but a throwback to romanticism in style) gives to the landscape feature nineteenth-century South African poets had settled on as their country's most distinctive topographical mark[14] a metaphysical resonance as well as a provocatively ambiguous social valence. (In precisely whose interest are we to imagine the veld as offering freedom? Despite his apparent gesture back toward the *vortrekkers,* Rose obviously does not want to pin the association down.) Finally, the American romantic Whittier makes ingenuously plain the sense of embattlement lurking in the subtext of each poem—the awareness of the obscurity and poverty of local materials from a cosmopolitan point of view and the determination to do something about this. My river may be "unstoried and unknown," but the panorama is striking, not to be surpassed by Wordsworth's Yarrow and Spenser's Mulla.

Such poetry reflects the internalization by settler culture of the European equation of old world is to new world as town is to country. "Implicit in ——— is a natural mystery more powerful than the civilisation around its fringes . . . The mysterious untamed country is both literally and metaphorically at the centre of ———." This passage occurs in an essay from 1986 entitled "Landscape and the Australian Imagination," but the same has often been said about Canada and the United States.[15]

The equation of new world with nature, Leo Marx has shown in the case of British America, could yield antithetical schemas: arcadian utopia or dystopian desert.[16] This dyadic scheme has sometimes been used to sort out the different provincial enclaves. Marx links the tradition of dystopian stereotyping with Puritan New Englanders' evocation of the howling wilderness, the image of arcadia with the more temperate region of the more latitudinarian Virginia planters.[17] Some Canadian critics have pressed a distinction between Canada and the United States along the same lines, following Northrop Frye's dictum that Canadian poetry manifests "a tone of deep terror in regard to nature." As his student Margaret Atwood has put it, "Canadian writers as a whole do not trust Nature, they are always suspecting some dirty trick"—which Atwood takes satisfaction in regarding as a more mature, modern view than the Wordsworthian tradition of nature's benignity, which she sees as shaping American poetry to a larger degree.[18] Such dichotomies, however, do not take one very far: as Alan Heimert and Andrew Delbanco have shown, not all the Pilgrims who landed in 1620 saw Massachusetts in the lurid way William Bradford's history remembered it (Marx's dystopian locus classicus); and the case for persistent arcadianism in the Canadian lyric, whatever the environmental data, seems to be at least as strong as the case for a poetry of distrust or terror.[19] Altogether, both arcadian and dystopian imagery might best be reckoned a stockpile of prefabricated imagery subject to deployment, deformation, and commingling according to need.

A particularly fascinating manipulation of this sort occurred during the course of Australian colonial history: the arcadianization of the continent once Britain determined that Australia was more urgently required for purposes of emigration than for chastisement. "Barren shores and savage climes," Coral Lansbury observes, "had been eminently suitable for criminals, but now England had to divest itself of the needy, and a country fit for convicts was hardly to be recommended to the deserving poor." This English promotional line eventually resulted in what Lansbury terms, with slight but pardonable overstatement, "the complete transference of the Arcadian myth to Australia," where it "could maintain a vigorous literary existence related not to existing conditions but to a tradition inherited from England." She refers here especially to the romanticization of the bush in turn-of-the-century cultural nationalist poetry:

> You are the brooding comrade of our way,
> Whispering rumour of a new Unknown
>   . . . . .
> And freshening with unpolluted light
> The squalid city's day and pallid night.

This despite an exceptionally harsh interior environment and at a time when already three-quarters of the Australian population were living in cities and towns.[20] Lansbury suggests that any provincial outback, no matter how repellent, can be pastoralized if the social pressures and the individual poetic will are great enough. "Such was the Antipodean consummation of the old Renaissance paradise image," as another Australian critic dryly remarks of this same poem.[21] J. M. Coetzee and Stephen Gray have demonstrated the comparable struggle of precontemporary white South African writers to adjust the categories of the picturesque and the sublime so as to make some semblance of aesthetic concord out of a legacy of conquest and a resistant landscape.[22]

The family resemblances among settler-culture representations of new world environments as realms of the natural show the limits of an exceptionalist reading of American landscape representation. They demonstrate that American naturism is not wholly unique but rather one avatar of a pluriform new world naturism. The explicitly nationalist element in such landscapes—the rhetoric of "exceptionalism" itself—is one of the points at which environmental texts may be tied most closely to a politics of validation in terms of old world classifications (such as the ancient association of new world with the natural and the romanticist valorization of landscape). The same can be said, with concessions for their attempts to honor what genteel forms of naturism would edit out, of new world cultural nationalist reactions against traditional "pastoral" in the name of a wilder, autochthonous environment that European standards of beauty supposedly could not encompass: an aesthetic based on, for example, the American prairie, mountain, or desert; the Canadian north; the Australian bush. These variant cults of wilderness may assume an antipastoral, anti-European guise, but only to repeat in a grander way the gesture of putting the nation under the sign of the natural: America as crag, Canada as iceberg, Australia as outback.

Indigenes' Pastoral

The greatest occupational hazard of the pastoral imagination is its temptation to clear the scene of complicating features, especially human complications that might inhibit the aesthetic pleasure of privileged solitary communion with nature. Raymond Williams and his successors have shown how even "close observers" of the English countryside have overlooked or prettified the working classes. "The labourer," he writes, tends to be "merged with his landscape, a figure within the general figure of nature," viewed from a distance by the sympathetic but condescending observer.[23] In the final chapter of *The Country and the City*, Williams brilliantly develops the analogy of country and colony, noting how, as previously at home, "The lands of the Empire were an idyllic retreat, an escape from debt or shame, or an opportunity for making a fortune . . . New rural societies entered the English imagination, under the shadow of political and economic control: the plantation worlds of Kipling and Maugham and early Orwell; the trading worlds of Conrad and Joyce Cary."[24] That is the mentality which created the image of the Australian arcadia as Lansbury describes it. In this way, pastoral has underwritten myths of conquest abroad as well as of squierarchy at home.[25]

That settler pastoral cannot be so categorically arraigned is equally clear, however. Post-Revolutionary America's first enduring work of wilderness nonfiction shows this: *Travels in Florida*, by Philadelphia naturalist William Bartram. Bartram writes in a genre that has, with reason, been attacked for its complicity in and furtherance of colonizing projects. Linnaeus and his army of field-workers reducing the natural world to order is the deceptively apolitical face of Europe's imperial push. "Here is to be found," warns Mary Louise Pratt, "a utopian image of a European bourgeois subject simultaneously innocent and imperial, asserting a harmless hegemonic vision."[26] To some degree, Pratt's account of natural history as anticonquest (that is, conquest in the guise of passive observation, even to the point of "a certain impotence or androgyny" in the persona's self-presentation) certainly applies to Bartram's botanical conquest of Florida, as I seriocomically called it in the Introduction. Yet Bartram's

Travels cannot be conflated with *The Field-Book of a Jungle-Wallah*,[27] or even with Darwin's *Journal of Researches*, which reveals sympathy for graceful Polynesians, disdain for the more primitive Fuegians, and satisfaction that Van Diemen's land "enjoys the great advantage of being free from a native population." Bartram's idiosyncratic spirituality leads him to the brink of cultural relativism and biotic egalitarianism. He is as interested in and almost as nonjudgmental toward the Creeks and Seminoles as he is toward the white planters who also host him. Although one can link Bartram to more programmatic modern anthropological "constructions of the primitive," the link is closer between him and contemporary advocacy groups like Cultural Survival. As with Thoreau and Muir after him, Bartram's excitement by the sense that the country in which he finds himself really seems like a pastoral eden (despite the mosquitoes and the alligators) converts his intellectual ambitiousness into a defense of the region's integrity, not an apologia for conquest.[28]

In light of a work like Bartram's, we should not be surprised to find indigenes making pastoral serve their own counterhegemonic ends. Just as settler culture has tried to convert its perceived rusticity into cultural capital, so indigenes have used pastoral as a weapon against cultural dominance. Native American literature offers some outstanding examples of this technique. Leslie Marmon Silko's *Ceremony*, for example, traces the psychic reintegration of a war-damaged Indian GI through a process of native healing in a plot that appropriates many of the conventions of American wilderness romance in the interest of a neotraditionalist critique of mainstream civilization. The urban-military-industrial realm of white witchery is opposed to the remoter districts of the reservation where Tayo's healing largely takes place; secular science, modern psychiatry, and rational empiricism are opposed to traditional storytelling, myth-based ceremonial healing, and spiritual intuition; official cartographic coordinates and boundary lines are opposed to sacred space. The plot loosely follows a familiar Joseph Campbellish monomyth employed also by mainstream wilderness romance: separation from (reservation) settlement for a period of liminality and testing, mostly in comparatively wild settings, followed by the return to the settlement to assume a position of mature leadership. These patterns, along with some special complications to be discussed in Chapter 9, make the text rather compatible with the preestablished tastes of educated Euro-American readers, who Silko presumably expects to compose the largest faction of her audience. Especially striking in this regard is the motif of the wise, mixed-blood mentor, Betonie, who expounds an updated version of traditional native wisdom, whom Anglo-American readers familiar with wilderness romance are likely to think they recognize as an avatar of the role Faulkner's Sam Fathers plays in relation to Ike McCaslin or the one Cooper's Natty Bumppo plays in relation to Duncas Uncas Middleton and others of Cooper's Scottian wavering heroes. Not so much despite as because of the element of cultural advocacy in *Ceremony*, the basic grammar of mainstream wilderness romance does service in creating Silko's "Native American" countervision to Anglo-American technoculture.[29]

In modern times the most influential form of indigenous pastoral nationalism has been Negritude, defined by Léopold Senghor, its first theorist, as "the sum total of the values of the civilization of the African world," and more specifically "the communal warmth, the image-symbol and the cosmic rhythm which instead of dividing and sterilizing, unified and made fertile."[30] Negritude can be thought of as a pastoral mode because it evokes a traditional, holistic, nonmetropolitan, nature-attuned myth of Africanity in reaction to and critique of a more urbanized, "artificial" European order—and evokes it, furthermore, from the standpoint of one who has experienced exile and wishes to return. Like pastoral, Negritude was born before it was named. The Harlem Renaissance anticipated and influenced it;[31] even before that, the first black African novel in English, Sol Plaatje's *Mhudi* (completed in 1920, published in 1930, and issued in unabridged form in 1975), manifests it.[32]

The movement that called itself Negritude was fomented in the 1930s by Francophone intellectuals from the African diaspora centered in Paris, chief among them Senghor from Senegal and Aimé Césaire from Martinique. Negritude for them, like cultural nationalist pastoral for early settler culture, meant the inversion of the primary basis of their marginalization—blackness—into a source of pride and cultural self-definition. This inversion required a considerable amount of editing. In Césaire's great poem *Cahier d'un retour au pays natal* (1939), the work that made the term "Negritude" canonical, a stylized version of the Martinican homeland is created in the image of the returned exile's desire: stylized first as a stinkhole to the fastidious alienated returnee, then wrenchingly transformed into the place of salvation as the speaker accepts "ma race qu'aucune ablution d'hysope et de lys mêlés ne pourrait purifier / ma race rongée de macules / ma race raisin mûr pour pieds ivres."[33] At first, the speaker seems constrained to see his home the first way; then he wills himself into the latter perspective. By contrast, Camara Laye's memoir-novel *L'enfant noir* (1954), not a programmatic work but also an autobiographical speaker's attempt to define himself in terms of his Africanity after being Europeanized, achieves this goal more by documentary selection than by engineering appropriate symbolic images. Ostensibly, it is a success story of the author's rise from humble origins to an academic triumph that won him a scholarship to France. But the speaker represents himself more as a villager at heart than as a seeker after a position in the colonial elite; Guinea's capital of Conarky always seems less real than his home; by far the longest episode is the retelling of his circumcision ritual. We "know" that his father is part of the rising commercial-industrial order, running a successful shop near the local railway station. But the signs of economic transformation are played down. Altogether, *L'enfant noir* reminds an American romanticist of Thoreau's attempts to naturalize the railroad and to suppress the fact that he went to Walden, in the first instance, as much to write as to observe nature.

As *L'enfant noir* shows, Negritude, like settler pastoral, threatens to become self-limited as a means of representation by reason of having to accept the binary vocabulary that has been used to create margins or outposts in the first place. The narrator of *L'enfant noir*, presenting himself *as* dark child, does not account for himself any more fully than Thoreau does: he can write like a literary man but cannot define himself as such. He must portray himself as a simple creature who wound up leaving his beloved village through a combination of mere conscientiousness and lucky sponsorship. Indeed, he even denies himself the consolation of *sounding* sophisticated—unlike Thoreau, unlike his Nigerian near-contemporary Wole Soyinka, whose *Aké* recreates his childhood innocence with such tonal intricacy and multicultural allusiveness as to shame Anglo-American readers into realizing that Soyinka's Nigerian village origins might have been a likelier starting point for cosmopolitanism than their own. But clearly Camara Laye was no bumpkin. A work like *L'enfant noir* could not have been produced without a bicontinental awareness of Eurocentric expectations.[34] If Negritude and other forms of pastoral have a constitutional weakness, it is less on the side of naïveté than on the side of sophistication.

Within the African diaspora, no writer shows a keener awareness of this than St. Lucian expatriate Derek Walcott, who has indeed taken this insight as one of his major subjects, in such works as "The Star-Apple Kingdom," a Jamaica-centered poem that meditates on West Indian history and politics. The poem opens with a richly sardonic glimpse of the "shards of an ancient pastoral" that dot the island—remnants of colonial days "when the landscape copied such subjects as / 'Herefords at Sunset in the Valley of the Wye.'" Prime Minister Manley (the younger, never actually named) is ironically pictured as looking out nabob-style from "the Great House windows" at the rising slums and rabble below that he is powerless to control. The night comes on like "that black power / that has the assassin dreaming of snow, that poleaxes the tyrant to a sleeping child." In the long central part of the poem that follows, the figure of a black woman arises in his dream, claiming, "I'm the Revolution. / I am the darker, the older America." She is at once a kind of archetypal night goddess, the voice of the land imagined in terms of Afrocentric myth, and an epitome of revolutionary insurgency. This sequence climaxes when the dreamer cries out, seemingly in response to the "silent scream" that has been welling up in the breasts of all the inhabitants, both human and beast. This catharsis brings the dawn, and in an ending either hopeful or ironic, the mysterious woman in black is juxtaposed to the breakfasting prime minister, smiling (but not "decipherable" because of her wrinkles) "the same smile with which he now / cracked the day open and began his egg."[35]

Walcott leaves it studiously vague as to whether the imposing figure of the black woman represents anything more than a figment of the prime minister's imagination. Their final smiles make one doubt that the dream journey has affected him as much as the reader, make one wonder whether they are in cahoots somehow, like Cortez and La Malinche perhaps: whether the "threat" she represents is actually being manipulated by him as a form of self-purgative psychodrama that substitutes guilty excitement for practical action. These unresolvable questions, however, seem less vexatious when we perceive that the poem is structured in terms of the polarity between "ancient" pastoral—that is, pastoral of the Wordsworthian sort—and Negritudinist counterpastoral. The polarity immediately creates the dual suggestion that the mysterious black woman is both pastoralism's adversary *and* its duplicate: another utopian discourse that vies with the dream vision encoded into the older colonial landscape architecture, not to be dismissed but not to be considered demonstrably potent except as dream. It is potent especially in its capacity to haunt the

Eurocentric imagination with the specter of a rebellious counterpart to itself.

Senghor's own work bears out the logic of Walcott's ambiguous montage. Consider his vision of the eternal African female in "Nuit de Sine," an example of the prototype in terms of which Walcott created his more ambivalent and reflexive figure.[36]

> Femme, pose sur mon front tes mains balsamiques, tes mains
>   douces plus que fourrure.
> Là-haut les palmes balancées qui bruissent dans la haute
>   brise nocturne
> A peine. Pas même la chanson de nourrice.
> Qu'il nous berce, le silence rythmé.
> Ecoutons son chant, écoutons battre notre sang sombre,
>   ecoutons
> Battre le pouls profond de l'Afrique dans la brume des
>   villages perdus.

Sine was Senghor's home district, but the country of this poem is a country imagined in exile, a country that existed in mythic time ("forgotten villages") as much as historical time, indeed a country that referred as much to the European intertext as to African orature. For Senghor's favorite poem by his favorite poet, Baudelaire, a poem that he memorized and loved to recite, celebrates the poet's West Indian mistress with a similar yearning.[37]

> J'irai là bas où l'arbre et l'homme, pleins de sève,
> Se pâment longuement sous l'ardeur des climats;
> Fortes tresses, soyez la houle qui m'enlève!
> Tu contiens, mer d'ébène, un éblouissant rêve
> De voiles, de rameurs, de flammes et de mâts
>
> Un port retentissant où mon âme peut boire
> A grands flots le parfum, le son et la couleur;
> Où les vaisseaux, glissant dans l'or et dans la moire,
> Ouvrent leurs vastes bras pour embrasser la gloire
> D'un ciel pur où frémit l'éternelle chaleur.

Senghor deviates from Baudelaire in fundamental ways: he drops Baudelaire's master motif of his mistress's long hair, he locates the scene at the destination rather than the voyage thither, and he makes their mutual belonging to Africa rather than their relationship the subject of the poem. But the trope of the dark female other inspiring the vision of sensual bliss in a tropical paradise establishes so distinct a connection between the two passages that Senghor's adjustments seem almost as modest as Harpur's substitution of the dragon-hornet for the Emersonian humble-bee.

The Baudelairean model, then, became both a screen between the Gallicized poet and the culture of Sine and a powerful focusing lens that enabled Senghor to give a distinctive shape to the claims of his culture within the limits of the schema. This recalls the process of representation of physical environment in Anglophone settler culture. On the one hand, as one nineteenth-century Canadian critic noted, the post-European writer seemed condemned to the province of mimetic desire: "from the sheet of water a hand uprises as in the Morte d'Arthur, to grasp Excalibur, or as in Undine, to clutch the jewels . . . Again, no lover of Scott with a fair memory can sail among the craggy lakes of the Maritime Provinces without calling to mind numerous lines and verses of that poet, and without feeling inclined to half shut his eyes when he beholds a homespun petticoat in a dug-out, and to try and imagine that the rustic paddler is fair Ellen."[38] On the other hand, Scott's romantic highland imagery, Greco-Hebraic myths of arcadia, the modern vocabulary of the picturesque and the sublime, even traditional dystopian images of wilderness all supplied a conceptual apparatus in terms of which lands at first seemingly underdeveloped to Europeanized eyes might yield a fertile crop of aesthetic products, especially as nature became increasingly valorized with the rise of industrialization as the other in need of cherishing.

The Aesthetics of the Not-There

Post-European pastoral's enlistment in the service of these various projects of cultural self-definition confirms its ideological multivalence but intensifies the question of what new world pastoral has to do with actual environments. It seems to have more to do with reinvention of the non-European world as a mirror-opposite of certain European norms. Kwame Anthony Appiah tellingly remarks that

Postcoloniality is the condition of what we might ungenerously call a comprador intelligentsia: of a relatively small, Western-style, Western-trained, group of writers and thinkers who mediate the trade in cultural commodities of world capitalism at the periphery. In the West they are known through the Africa they offer; their compatriots know them both through the West they present to Africa and through an Africa they have invented for the world, for each other, and for Africa.[39]

This point surely applies to forms of cultural nationalism that define their region against Europe in terms of the pastoral difference.[40] The "comprador intelligentsia" phenomenon is precisely what makes possible interchanges like the cross-fertilization of American landscape painting by Claude Lorrain and Salvator Rosa or Francophone African poetry by Baudelaire and, ultimately, vice versa. Congolese masks inspire European abstract art; Senghor writes his "Masque négre," ostensibly about a sleeping African woman but dedicated to Picasso.[41] Nothing could be more logical.

One might therefore expect post-European pastoralists to have trouble getting beyond an intertextual level of engagement with the nature they so assiduously hold up as a mark of difference. So in fact it has been, although to a considerably lesser degree than in traditional pastoral from Theocritus to Pope. The seventeenth-century refocusing of pastoral to effect a textured rendering of a particular territory was a revolutionary development in principle, but in execution less so than it might seem.

The young Thoreau, albeit not the typical literary comprador, illustrates this point well. His home territory quickly became his literary subject, but to supercharge the Concord landscape with images from his reading was, as it were, second nature for him. This tendency is clear from the first essay he ever published ("I read in Audubon with a thrill of delight, when the snow covers the ground, of the magnolia and the Florida keys").[42] Pastoralizing the local by projecting upon it imagery imported from faraway continued to be a Thoreauvian hallmark. "For the first week" of his residence at Walden, the book tells us, "whenever I looked out on the pond it impressed me like a tarn high up on the side of a mountain . . . The very dew seemed to hang upon the trees later into the day than usual, as on the sides of mountains" (*Wa* 86). Thoreau's first recollected snapshot of pond gazing, which is also the reader's first glimpse of the pond, is thus a picture not of the thing itself but of the thing as it reminds him of a more romantically remote elsewhere. This Walden he will show us is no mere local niche. Rather, or in addition, it is a subalpine vista, or perhaps a rugged, leafy, tree-gnarled Adirondack landscape. The Walden journal, which begins as follows, makes his projection even clearer. "Yesterday I came here to live. My house makes me think of some mountain houses I have seen, which seemed to have a fresher auroral atmosphere about them as I fancy of the halls of Olympus." Thoreau goes on to recollect lodging the previous summer at a saw-miller's house in the Catskills, "which had this ambrosial character" (*PJ* 2: 155).[43]

Such rhetorical moves fill what otherwise might seem a prosaic landscape by turning winter into summer (the Audubon quote) or by giving arcadian resonance to an ordinary pondscape. In this way Thoreau is the descendant, if not the duplicate, of New England's early settlers. For them, old world frames of reference—the Exodus narrative, pastoral convention, a basketful of English place-names—became defenses against the heart of darkness. For Thoreau, these were the provincial's defense against dullness—and a means, he might hope, of getting a hearing, whether from foreigners or from his own similarly provincial compatriots.

To "fill" a landscape in this fashion also means emptying it, however: "Annihilating all that's made / To a green Thought in a green Shade," to quote Andrew Marvell's "The Garden." "I have my horizon bounded by woods all to myself"; "for the most part it is as solitary where I live as on the prairies"; "I had withdrawn . . . within the great ocean of solitude" (*Wa* 130, 144). Of course these stylizations are not the outright lies that anti-Thoreauvian debunkers have taken them to be. The evidence suggests that Thoreau's townspeople and contemporaries considered his move to Walden a significant distancing step; and even if they had not, Thoreau's claims make at least a degree of environmental sense. Even now, in the age of the solidly populated Northeastern corridor, one can live (for a price) within a half-mile of Walden Pond on a plot of no more then a couple of cozily landscaped acres at the end of a rustic cul-de-sac, backing up to a conservancy trail perhaps, and fancy that one is experiencing the "truth" of Thoreau's assertions, especially at night or in the winter. But even in the best of circumstances such an aesthetic experience requires editing out the noise of air traffic or of the cars on nearby Route 2, just as Thoreau largely edited out the pipe smoke and wagon traffic on the Wayland road (now Route 126).

A particularly striking case of emptying and filling in *Walden* occurs at the end of the "Sounds" chapter. The speaker empties the landscape by imagining himself alone with the owls and bullfrogs as night falls (125–126). He feels even too far away from human habitation to hear the roosters crow (127). But then, in a curious coda, he reflects on how delightful it would have been to have a cockerel nearby for a singing bird: "this foreign bird's note is celebrated by the poets of all countries along with the notes of their native songsters" (127). The desire to place oneself at a distance within new world nature gives way to what looks like a desire to domesticate the landscape with an exotic from India, with an exoticized replacement (the cockerel) displacing the ordinary domestic creature (the cock) that he has left behind in his retreat from town. The Walden naturescape begins to resemble Washington Irving's Alhambra. Thoreau's approach here is not fundamentally different from his more grandiose gesture of emptying and filling in "Ktaadn": on the one hand, he executes the America-as-nature reduction, clearing the rugged interior of all traces of human history; on the other hand, he imports the language of the sublime.[44]

The new world paradox of filling with pastoral accoutrements the ✓ landscape one has willed to be empty reaches a kind of extreme in latter-day Thoreauvian Edward Abbey. Abbey chose one of the loneliest environments possible as his literary province: the desert lands of southern Utah. Like John Muir and other western environmental writers, Abbey saw the element of self-deception in Thoreau's professed love of wildness and wanted both to chide and to fulfill Thoreau's self-styled narrative of return to the primal by bonding to a landscape far more primal than Thoreau ever knew: "a country with only the slightest traces of human history." Abbey's best-known book, *Desert Solitaire,* builds on a summer's experience spent as a park ranger in then remote Arches National Monument, interspersing vignettes of the park setting with essays about desert ecology and narratives of the author's increasingly daring adventures in primitivism (mountain climbing, rafting down the Colorado, going naked for a month in a branch of the Grand Canyon, and so on). Yet it soon becomes clear that this quest for the nitty-gritty will depend heavily on the imported imagery of the not-there.[45] Approaching his post-to-be for the first time at night, Abbey turns onto a dirt road, "into the howling wilderness" (of New England tradition). Summing up his reasons for going there, he describes his deepest purpose as "to confront, immediately and directly if it's possible, the bare bones of existence": Thoreau redivivus. Just as Milton could not attempt the unattempted without referring the attempt to the Aonian mount (even borrowing the trope of attempting itself), just as Thoreau turned to the classics as a way of returning to nature—so Abbey returns to the now classic Thoreau as a way of expressing his own turn to a more primal nature. That he finds a snug prefabricated trailer waiting for him at the end of his drive is a symbolically fitting happenstance. But in Abbey the paradox is most striking given the extreme of primality to which he says he wishes to go. "I dream of a hard and brutal mysticism in which the naked self merges with a non-human world and yet somehow survives still intact, individual, separate."[46]

This is a dream that cannot be fulfilled, partly because the dreamer does not unequivocally want it to be fulfilled. If only for safety's sake, the modern desert venturer, like the European explorers and settlers, cannot do away with the customary repertoire of tropes. One of the best things about *Desert Solitaire* is the degree to which Abbey realizes his self-division. This especially comes out in "Down the River," the report of a rafting excursion, as the persona repeatedly catches himself mythifying—imagining, for example, that a certain canyon might be "at last the *locus Dei*"—a spot with "enough cathedrals and temples and altars here for a Hindu pantheon of divinities." The jauntiness of this phrase alerts us to the recoil that's about to follow: "If a man's imagination were not so weak, so easily tired, if his capacity for wonder not so limited, he would abandon forever such fantasies of the supernal. He would learn to perceive in water, leaves and silence more than sufficient of the absolute and marvelous, more than enough to console him for the loss of the ancient dreams." The beauty of a statement like this is that it means exactly what it means. It aspires to go beyond an aesthetic misprision of the nitty-gritty while recognizing how hard it is to part with the romantic furniture we say we want to jettison. Abbey thus anticipates even those moments in the text that fail to make the persona's ineradicable romanticism explicit. Take for instance a later passage celebrating the harsh material isness of the desert: "Whirlwinds dance across the salt flats, a pillar of dust by day;

the thornbush breaks into flame at night. What does it mean? It means nothing. It is as it is and has no need for meaning. The desert lies beneath and soars beyond any possible human qualification. Therefore, sublime."[47]—To which the querulous reader replies: "Aha, this is duplicity. You say 'it means nothing,' but you remythify this with your pseudobiblical imagery of the burning bush and the pillar of dust and your allusion to the sublime." But such a retort is too literal-minded; Abbey has anticipated it by recognizing in advance that we cannot help taking some baggage with us as a protection against the demythified reality we desire and as the lens through which we must see it.

Abbey's innovation as a modern Thoreauvian, then, does not lie only in the side of him that this discussion bypasses—his evocation of an environment so wild that it actually lived up to the wildness Thoreau could only impose on the Concord landscape. Even more significant, to my mind, is how Abbey brings to fuller consciousness, as an object of contemplation and a species of aesthetic play, the wish fulfillment inherent in the use of allusive rhetoric to empty and to fill new world environments. Thoreau does this himself, as we have just seen; but Abbey supplies a commentary on Thoreau's practice by making explicit the element of duplicity when, for example, he flaunts his own double life as one who relishes drinking in the bars of Moab and Hoboken as well as playing ascetic in the desert. Here Abbey taps into, develops, carnivalizes the villager side of Thoreau's identity, which is deliberately mentioned only in passing. ("I am naturally no hermit, but might possibly sit out the sturdiest frequenter of the bar-room, if my business called me thither" [*Wa* 140].)

Among contemporary environmental nonfiction writers, none has developed to a greater degree than Annie Dillard the aesthetics of the not-there as a principle of environmental representation. The skittery, self-reflexive, context-shifting style of the following passage from her *Pilgrim at Tinker Creek* shows this well. The passage comes as part of a meditation inspired by looking at a mountain while sipping coffee at a gas station on her way home.

> I like the slants of light; I'm a collector. That's a good one, I say, that bit of bank there, the snakeskin and the aquarium, that patch of light from the creek on bark. Sometimes I spread my fingers into a viewfinder; more often I peek through a tiny square or rectangle—a frame

of shadow—formed by the tips of index fingers and thumbs held directly before my eye. Speaking of the development of *papier collé* in late Cubism, Picasso said, "We tried to get rid of *trompe-l'oeil* to find a *trompe-l'esprit*." Trompe-l'esprit! I don't know why the world didn't latch on to the phrase. Our whole life is a stroll—or a forced march—through a gallery hung in trompes-l'esprit.[48]

The speaker's fascination with the process of seeing, not the objects seen, is the central subject here. In this passage, she is frankly a maker of views, creating her camera angles by hand and analogizing her procedures to cubist art. The intertextual salad is entirely consistent with the metaphor of landscape looking as gallery walking: the snippet from Picasso, the quotes from Emily Dickinson ("slant of light") and Thoreau ("life is a stroll"). Thoreau would not have written quite this way, but the man who saw elongated bodies swimming in Walden Pond as "fit studies for a Michael Angelo" (*Wa* 177) would have understood. Dillard's master's thesis, fittingly, was a formalist interpretation of the symbolism of the central chapter of Thoreau's masterpiece. Thoreau's continual shifts of visual, historical, and metaphorical perspectives make "The Ponds" a fit choice for Dillard's exegesis.[49]

Abbey's understanding of the splits and self-deceptions in the nature seeker's psyche and Dillard's awareness of the observer's desire to package the environment in a series of freeze-frames carry Thoreauvian thinking almost to the point reached by contemporary analysis of the geographical imagination of the colonial era. Here, for example, is Paul Carter's commentary on the description early explorer of Australia John Lort Stokes wrote of himself as "once more stepping out over a terra incognita; and though no alpine features greeted our eyes as they wandered over the vast level, all was clothed with the charm of novelty."

> The landscape that emerges from the explorer's pen is not a physical object: it is an object of desire, a figure of speech outlining the writer's exploratory impulse . . . What invests the view with significance is the explorer's desire to make it signify: it is not that the explorer comes to the landscape with rigid preconceptions, European standards he is determined to impose. Rather, it is the mere fact of his "advancing," the motive that moves him, that clothes all about him in a veil of mystery. The mystery is of his own making, a resistance

dialectically constructed in order to give his own passage historical meaning. "The charm of novelty" is the figure of speech by means of which the explorer translates the view into a text, by which he renders it of interest to the reader—a cultural object the reader will desire.[50]

Carter refuses, admirably, to reduce Stokes's rhetorical grid to an exemplum of imperial possession. Without disputing that Stokes supported the imperial project or that his writing might have been enlisted in its service, Carter sees that this passage's framework mainly expresses Stokes's desire to articulate his wonderment in a shareable form. What enables Carter to see what he sees about Stokes's environmental imagination is that, like Abbey, he understands how easily physical objects become projections of pastoral desire and that, like Dillard, he is sensitive to the status of textualized landscapes as necessarily formalized attempts at *trompes l'esprit.* So one might infer that the path of Thoreauvian writing from antecedent, less self-conscious efforts of the (post)colonial environmental imagination must lead at last to the redefinition of the whole new world landscape project in terms of epistemological malaise about its element of cultural projection rather than as a quest to come to terms with the environment itself. Something like this very criterion, in fact, is offered by Peter Fritzell, in one of the most sophisticated monographs on American nature writing to date, as the standard of excellence separating the major practitioners of the genre (among whom he includes Abbey and Dillard as well as Thoreau) from the also-rans.[51]

Does this mean, then, that new world pastoralism is fated to spiral from projection to projection, from Eurocentric intertext (Stokes) to postcolonial intertext (Thoreau) to its more self-conscious filiations (Abbey, Dillard), with contemporary criticism and theory ensuring that the circle is drawn tighter and more quickly? The yes and the no of this question were driven home to me when thumbing through the issue of *Audubon* magazine that arrived as I was first pondering this chapter. My eye was caught by a lavishly illustrated ten-page advertisement: "Preserving Paradise: Natural Attractions of the Caribbean," a promotion piece sponsored by the tourist agencies of fourteen Caribbean and Central American states, designed to appeal to the desire for unspoiled (but accessible) environments and the ancient Eurocentric dream of undevel-

oped lands as edens. As such it is an entirely typical manipulation of new
world pastoral imagery in which the interests of indigene and settler are
made to mirror each other. Predictably, not a single indigene is photo-
graphed; nor is a single native cultural institution mentioned in the text,
although it is claimed that this edenic, peopleless landscape expresses the
spirit of native institutions ("individual governments and public and private
sector organizations throughout the Caribbean basin"). The heartening
statistic touted by the advertisers—that "recent polls" show "90 percent
of American consumers" to be "concerned about the environmental
impact of the things they buy"—seems unlikely to translate from doctrine
into changed environmental perception or behavior. The ecotourists appealed to in this ad are invited to remain as blinded as possible by desert
island clichés.[52]

This is one side of the post-European pastoral not-there. There is
another. The article immediately following discusses the threat posed by
the development of hydropower projects in northern Quebec to the life
of the James Bay Cree, who "risk losing the garden that has sustained
them for millennia."[53] Vignettes of endangered wildlife are interwoven
with sympathetic representation of the Crees' victimization by environmental racism. The stereotypical association of the periphery of empire
with pristine beauty is linked to an actual indigenous tradition of superior
environmental ethics, offered as a moral mirror in which American
readers are asked to see themselves as irresponsible consumers and ex-
ploiters. "The Appeal of Grand Chief Matthew Coon-Come" reads like
Chief Seattle's oft-quoted (and oft-doctored) oration of the 1840s: "We
survived on the land, and we did not leave a trace of our having been
there . . . What we had and used came from the land and went back to
the land. The land is sacred. It is a land of remembrance." The statement
cannot be strictly true. (The Cree left *no* trace? Where did the elsewhere-
cited "archeological evidence" of their ancient residence come from?) But
this seems like nit-picking when weighed against the point that post-
European pastoralism in this case is apparently serving the Cree as an
incentive to decolonization and as a means of bringing crucial documentary information to light, thus provoking in at least some outsiders an
environmental awakening that has proven, or so the article argues, not
only emotionally potent but at least somewhat consequential politically.
The article does in itself not prove that the literary imagination can get

"beyond" intertextuality, but it shows that intertextuality can accomplish something more than the recycling of stereotypes.

Attending to the Environment in a Postcolonial Context

To give a detailed sense of all that that "something" might comprise will take the rest of this book. Certainly it must be a mode of vision that neither simply recirculates clichés (the ecotouristical advertisement) nor simply deploys them in the service of some particular human interest group (the article on the Cree) but rather opens itself up as well as it can to the perception of the environment as an actual independent party entitled to consideration for its own sake. To do this except under extreme duress, like the desire to survive in a snowstorm, is no easy matter, because humanity *qua* geographer is *Homo faber,* the environment's constructor, and the sense of place is necessarily always a social product and not simply what is "there."[54] Nevertheless, although this condition imposes an asymptotic limit on anyone's environmental responsiveness, we would be obtuse in lumping all environmental representations together as fabricated impositions. Our earlier glimpse of William Bartram's *Travels* in relation to the imperial subtext of naturalist travelogue began to suggest how post-European pastoral perception can, both despite and because of itself, involve a reciprocal process of being defamiliarized and instructed by the environmental encounters even when one continues to rely on ancient torpoi for conceptual vocabulary. Two further vignettes will help to clarify. Both depict representatives of settler cultures struggling with the temptation to project images on the expanses of the American West.

One is by the first Anglo-American poet of the environment to produce a body of enduring work: William Cullen Bryant—now deemed a minor figure but likely to retain a modest niche. One of his anthologized efforts is a longish blank verse meditation on "the Prairies," the "gardens of the Desert," "the unshorn fields, boundless and beautiful, / For which the speech of England has no name." Ruminating on them, Bryant imagines their immense vista, their past inhabitance by the now vanished (*sic*) Indian, and their future settlement, as a New England village, by "that advancing multitude / Which soon shall fill these deserts." Whereupon "a fresher wind sweeps by, and breaks my dream, / And I am in the wilderness alone." This attempt to canonize a major district of the new world "for which the speech of England has no name" has inspired mixed reactions. According to Rob Wilson, "the poet confronts the natural sublime as a material malleable to the ideological dreams of power and self-making in Romantic America." For Barbara Packer, by contrast, to the extent that the poem displays a distinctive Americanness of perspective (and both critics agree that its aspiration to national distinctiveness is compromised by derivative language and imagery), that perspective consists in its vision of human littleness in the face of nature's grandeur.[55] There is evidence for both positions. Bryant's finale can be read either way: either as the experience of having one's agrarian daydream of village building swept away by the power of the wilderness, or as an act of poetic will, manipulating the wind Shelley-fashion to achieve sublime closure. To have it both ways at once is impossible. The ending is like Wittgenstein's rabbit-and-duck paradox: as you look at the cartoon outline of the head with bill(?) or ears(?), you can oscillate between the two gestalts but not conflate them. The dream of managing the environment opposes the dream of submission to it. One road leads to Gifford Pinchot, the other to John Muir. The first holds you in an appropriative relation to landscape, nature's controller. The second may lead you to try to respond to the landscape on its own terms, to try to get to know—and, if you are a writer, to articulate—its mysterious physiognomy in a more intimate, fine-grained way. Yet both states of the imagination follow logically from the experience—by no means uniquely American, as we have seen, but common to other settler cultures—of the "empty" landscape that seems thereby arrestingly different from any old world counterpart: the veldt, the outback, the prairie, the tundra.

Bryant's poem was one of the first of many attempts in verse and prose during the second quarter of the nineteenth century to celebrate the prairie as a region of the American imagination, a theme developed further by writers from James Fenimore Cooper and Washington Irving to Josiah Gregg and Francis Parkman. By the turn of the twentieth century, American authors had begun to open up another "desert" region, a region more literally so in the vernacular sense of the word: the arid lands of the Southwest. The harbinger was explorer John Wesley Powell, whose gripping *Exploration of the Colorado River and Its Canyons* concentrated on the rivercourses rather than the surrounding land; the first major popular success was Bret Harte; the first creative writer to make a sustained attempt to map the western desert as an ecocultural region was Mary Austin, in a series of nonfiction works and short stories beginning with *The Land of Little Rain* (1903).

Austin, author of our second vignette, continues to employ the vatic sublimities of earlier wilderness representation: the grand essentializing generalization; the conflation of indigenes with the environment ("the Shoshones live like their trees, with great spaces between" [*LLR* 57]); the empty landscape convention ("You will find [this region] forsaken of most things but beauty and madness and death and God" [103]). Indeed, throughout her career, Austin was only too ready to represent herself as the authoritative voice of the West and of Native American culture.[56] Yet fundamentally she conceives of the western environment and its pre–Gold Rush inhabitants in a more self-effacing manner. Ultimately, she wishes to define her role as that of the partly informed but partly baffled denizen of an environment that it takes several lifetimes to know. She knows enough to know that the sublime emptiness of the landscape is an artifact of the romantic westernizer's desire (16–17), even as she admits to feeling the pull of this desire, even as she exploits her tenderfoot reader's susceptibility to it. Austin repeatedly stresses the unobtrusive signs of life around her ("Go as far as you dare in the heart of a lonely land, you cannot go so far that life and death are not before you"); the arts of environmental accommodation required to survive in the desert, emotionally as well as physically; the models of adaptation offered by Shoshone, Paiute, and Chicano cultures; and the less satisfactory models, antimodels almost, offered by the lifestyle of the prospector and the frontier town.

Austin's three full-length individual portraits are especially revealing. The first is of a small-time prospector who spent twenty years hoping "to strike it rich and set himself up among the eminently bourgeois of London" (49). He does, then spends it all and returns to the West, having learned nothing. Here Austin gently satirizes the dogged repetition compulsions of gold grubbing, conflating the American and the British versions under the heading "the pocket hunter" (note that pockets are isolated deposits of rich ore). The second and third sketches are of Indian figures: a Shoshone medicine man held by the Paiutes "as a hostage for the long peace which the authority of the whites made interminable" (55); and an aging widowed Paiute woman of wondrous talent as a potter and basket maker, whom Austin admires for developing her trade to support herself and her child and for stoically accepting the blindness that eventually overtakes her. These two figures are models of admirable endurance, self-sufficiency, adaptation.

All three portraits involve self-projection. Austin herself was an initially unwilling emigrant (like the medicine man) from the Midwest, who created her own "wonders of technical precision" (the Paiute artist) (95), dreaming of financial success (the pocket hunter).[57] In this sense, the entire group is disguised lyric fantasy, on the same level as the empty landscape device. But to insist on this representation as the only truth in the portraits grossly flattens their extrospective character and blurs the distinctions among them. Austin endows her Indian figures with a more substantial self-sufficiency made possible by their powers of adaptation to the physical environment. In fact throughout her book she gives priority to the environment rather than these human-interest stories, which are austerely limited to interspersed vignettes. It is a mark of the maturity of her environmental vision, relative to Bryant's, that her protagonist is the land, more particularly the geography of its watercourses and the patterns of life created by water scarcity: the habits of life, the routes of travel, the visible marks on the landscape all being shown as shaped by the need of both animals and humans to adapt themselves to this basic necessity.

Austin's most fundamental adaptation of the empty landscape convention is to strip the landscape of the place-names and boundary markers assigned to it by the anxious settlers from the East, restoring the region's Indian name ("the country of the lost borders"). So much for imperial cartography. "Where it lies, how to come at it, you will not get from me," she says of the edenic Mexican village of the last sketch; "rather would I show you the heron's nest in the tulares" (143) This surely alludes to Sarah Orne Jewett's story "The White Heron," whose protagonist refuses to tell the eager collector where the heron can be found. For Austin, as for Jewett, the mark of insidership is the denizen's knowledge of the environmental particularity that is deliberately withheld from the uninitiated because the denizen's allegiance to maintaining the integrity of her environment has come to take precedence. This does not mean that either author has become wholly an insider to the life she describes. Austin's closing sketch of the "Little Town among the Grape-Vines" (a

Mexican American village) recalls Baudelaire in its discourse of the exotic other, its sentimental primitivism. It is a hermetic utopia, not a place localized. Nevertheless *Little Rain* has come a long way toward imagining a mode of living in terra incognita that respects the physical environment as the primary reality which must shape human thoughts and choices. The colonial legacy of the environment as the screen on which one projects romantic desire remains present, but diminishingly.

Even a writer who advanced from the Bryant stage of visionary enthusiasm to a more rigorous extrospection is not going to be able to see or articulate the natural environment on its own terms. The constraints of human perception, and of art, make zero-degree interference impossible. And yet not only can we dream of that impossible goal, as Dillard does when she imagines how it would be to see objects through the eyes of the blind who have just been restored to sight, we may also hope for concrete results. The contrast between Bryant and Austin shows this progression, not to mention the kind of evolution we shall witness when we look more closely at Thoreau's development within the space of less than a decade. Within the centuries-long series of recorded encounters between observer and landscape in American history are countless instances when the eye's "empire" is suspended and the eye is educated, the mind shaped, whether for the nonce or forever, by the land's template. "Rapt were my senses at this delectable view," Puritan poet Ann Bradstreet writes in "Contemplations." Her poem then converts this moment of contact into a pious exercise, but not before it has rendered the first autumn landscape described in the annals of American literature.[58] Bartram glimpses flocks of a previously undescribed bird, the anhinga, through an intertextual haze ("I think I have seen paintings of them on the Chinese screens and other India pictures"). He weaves them into a wishful fantasy of "little peaceable communities" "hanging over the still waters, with their wings and tails expended, I suppose to cool and air themselves, when at the same time they behold their images in the watery mirror"—but not before describing the birds with an attentive particularity that might not have been possible without the devotion to understanding bird behavior from the inside that produced this fancifulness.[59] For Bartram was, as Mary Austin described herself as a new arrival to the West, "spellbound in an effort not to miss any animal behavior, any bird-marking, any weather signal, any signature of tree or flower."[60]

It has been the distinctive mission of environmental nonfiction from Bartram to Thoreau to Austin and beyond to call this visible but over-looked American otherworld into being in such a way as to establish its integrity and standing apart from any irreducible lingering element of self-interest on the part of its discoverers.

The "transparent eyeball" state Austin defines can easily revert to the empire of the eye, with its alien agendas, personal or political. But the visionary state also and just as easily can lead one, as it did her, to look at the night sky and think: "Of no account you who lie out there watching, nor the lean coyote that stands off in the scrub from you and howls and howls" (*LLR* 17). Vision can correlate not with dominance but with receptivity, and knowledge with ecocentrism.

Contemporary literary theory, however, makes it hard to see this side of the story—and thus makes the prospect of environmental reorienta-tion, of awakening from the metropolitan dream, look more unlikely than it needs to be. Having complicated the theory of pastoral ideology, we must now confront squarely a more fundamental problem posed by literary theory: its skepticism about how texts can purport to represent environments in the first place when, after all, a text is obviously one thing and the world another.

CHAPTER THREE

Representing the Environment

⌁

The profound kinship of language with the world was thus dissolved . . . Things and words were to be separated from one another . . . Discourse was still to have the task of speaking that which is, but it was no longer to be anything more than what it said.

—Michel Foucault, *The Order of Things*

That everything we say is false because everything we say falls short of being everything that could be said is an adolescent sort of error.

—Hilary Putnam, *Realism with a Human Face*

I think of two landscapes—one outside the self, the other within. The external landscape is the one we see—not only the line and color of the land and its shading at different times of the day, but also its plants and animals in season, its weather, its geology, the record of its climate and evolution . . . One learns a landscape finally not by knowing the name or identity of everything in it, but by perceiving the relationships in it—like that between the sparrow and the twig . . .

The second landscape I think of is an interior one, a kind of projection within a person of a part of the exterior landscape . . . the speculations, intuitions, and formal ideas we refer to as "mind" are a set of relationships in the interior landscape with purpose and order . . . The interior landscape responds to the character and subtlety of an exterior landscape; the shape of the individual is affected by land as it is by genes.

—Barry Lopez, "Landscape and Narrative"

IDEOLOGY, the subject of Chapters 1–2, is after all only one of several filters through which literature sifts the environments it purports to represent. These filters begin with the human sensory apparatus itself, which responds much more sensitively for example at the level of sight than of smell and even at the visual level is highly selective: we perceive discrete objects better than objects in relation, and large objects much better than the average life-form (about the size of a small insect).[1] For these reasons our reconstructions of environment cannot be other than skewed and partial. Even if this were not so, even if human perception could perfectly register environmental stimuli, literature could not. Even when it professes the contrary, art removes itself from nature. Physical texts derive from dead plants. Even "imagistic" symbols like certain Chinese characters or visual configurations pronounced onomatopoeically are signs far more abstract than animal tracks on snow. Writing and reading are acts usually performed indoors, unachievable without long shifts of attention away from the natural environment. There is a crotchety justice to a late Victorian complaint about natural history essays: "Who would give a tinker's dam for a description of a sunset that *he* hadn't seen? Damn it, it's like kissing a pretty girl by proxy."[2]

Yet from another point of view the emphasis on disjunction between text and world seems overblown. To most lay readers, nothing seems more obvious than the proposition that literature of a descriptive cast, be it "fictional" or "nonfictional," portrays "reality," even if imperfectly. John Stuart Mill, who found solace in Wordsworth's compelling rendition of physical nature, would have been astonished by the stinginess of the modern argument that Wordsworth reckoned nature as at best a convenience and at worst an impediment to the imagination. Most amateur Thoreauvians would find equally strange the claim that in Thoreau's *Journal* "when the mind sees nature what it sees is its difference from nature," a million-word paper trail of unfulfilled desire.[3] In contemporary literary theory, however, the capacity of literary writers to render a faithful mimesis of the object world is reckoned indifferent at best, and their interest in doing so is thought to be a secondary concern.[4]

One basis for this divergence between commonsensical and specialized wisdom may be that the modern understanding of how environmental representation works has been derived from the study of the fictive genres rather than nonfiction. The consequence of this is suggested by the common omnibus term used for designating the sphere of the nonhuman environment in literary works: setting. It deprecates what it denotes, implying that the physical environment serves for artistic purposes merely as backdrop, ancillary to the main event. The most ambitious monograph on place in literature criticizes Thomas Hardy's evocation of Egdon heath (which "almost puts his work into the kind of place-saturated fiction which is expressly devoted to the assault upon a mountain") and commends by contrast the Parisian chapters of Henry James's *Ambassadors* as containing "the barest minimum of detail and the maximum of personal reflection on these details."[5] In "good" writing, then, it would seem that the biota has only a bit part. If we map literary history from this angle of vision, we reinforce the impression that attentive representation of environmental detail is of minor importance even in writing where the environment figures importantly as an issue. In American literature, the main canonical forms of environmental writing are the wilderness romance and the lyric meditation on the luminous natural image or scene. Cooper's *Deerslayer*, Faulkner's "Bear," Bryant's poem "To the Fringed Gentian," Whitman's "Out of the Cradle," Robert Frost's "Design"—of such is the core of these traditions comprised. It is easy to persuade oneself on the basis of the average critical discussion of these works that the literary naturescape exists for its formal or symbolic or ideological properties rather than as a place of literal reference or as an object of retrieval or contemplation for its own sake. It is unthinkable that Bryant could have sought to immerse himself in the natural history of the gentian, or Frost in observing spiders. And so professors of literature, whatever their behavior in ordinary life, easily become antienvironmentalists in their professional practice.

Yet the explanation cannot simply be that literature specialists mostly study novels and poems, for during the past two decades we have ranged freely across the human sciences, subjecting ethnography and phenomonology and even scientific monographs to literary analysis almost as readily as sonnets and short stories. Today, as Carolyn Porter has said, "we confront a virtually horizonless discursive field in which . . . the traditional boundaries between the literary and the extraliterary have faded."[6] No doubt we have derived our critical skepticism or disdain for the notion that literature does or can represent physical reality from the idea of writing as construct, whether this idea takes the form of the old-fashioned formalist theory of the literary work as artifact or the contemporary theory of writing as discourse. Thus, during the very half-century since Aldo Leopold, as environmental writing in America has unprecedentedly thriven, literary theory has been making the idea of a literature devoted to recuperating the factical environment seem quaintly untheoretical. All major strains of contemporary literary theory have marginalized literature's referential dimension by privileging structure, text(uality), ideology, or some other conceptual matrix that defines the space discourse occupies apart from factical "reality," as the epigraph from Foucault imagines having been done once and for all during the classical era. New critical formalism did so by insisting that the artifact was its own world, a heterocosm. Structualism and poststructualism broke down the barrier between literary and nonliterary, not however to rejoin literary discourse to the world but to conflate all verbal artifacts within a more spacious domain of textuality. Quarreling with this unworldliness, Marxist and Marxoid (for example, Foucaultian) models of analysis during the 1980s combined with poststructualism in Anglo-America to generate the so-called new historicism, which set text within context. But it did so in terms of the text's status as a species of cultural production or ideological work. In this type of formulation, literature's appropriation of the world in the service of some social allegiance or commitment seemed to render merely epiphenomenal the responsiveness of literature to the natural world either in its self-existence as an assemblage or plenum or in the form of a gestalt that can impress itself on the mind or text in the fundamental and binding way that the epigraph from Lopez envisages. It seems that literature is simply not thought to have the power to do this, that such power it might have is thought to have been overridden by the power of imagination, textuality, and culture over the malleable, plastic world that it bends to its will. Whitman, in "Song of Myself," may insist that "I lean and loafe at my ease observing a spear of summer grass," but there is no grass, no summer, no loafer (despite the title-page illustration done from a photograph of Whitman himself). No, there is only an image, a symbol, a projection, a persona, a vestige or democratic deformation of aristocratic pastoral (compare Thomas Gray's "disporting on the margent green"), a contortion of heptameter.

The historicist movement that succeeded poststructuralism as the dominant theoretical paradigm of literary studies during the 1980s attached greater importance than its formalist and structuralist predecessors to art's mimetic function and might thus seem to be more environment-responsive. Yet it turns out to interpose obstacles no less daunting to making the case for representation in the affirmative sense. The recent dismantling of nineteenth-century realism is instructive here.[7] Within a decade it has become almost hackneyed to point out that so-called realism, far from being a transparent rendering, is a highly stylized ideological or psychohistorical artifact that we have sloppily agreed to call realistic. The powerful rereading by art historian Michael Fried of the high point of realism in American painting, Thomas Eakins's *Gross Clinic,* is a striking example of the new orthodoxy in formation. Although Fried by no means denies the painting's graphic fidelity to documentary detail (the wincing observers, the blood on the scalpel, the almost violent dominance of the surgeon over the patient and the operating room), he argues that the painting is much more fundamentally shaped by intertextual and psycho-biographical forces. The referent, the text-clinic correspondence itself, seems almost epiphenomenal.[8]

Ironically, during the same period that "realism" has been deconstructed, historians and social scientists have often drawn on realistic fiction for evidentiary support. One cultural geographer, for example, praises John Steinbeck's *Grapes of Wrath* as providing "focus for instruction in migration, settlement forms, economic systems, cultural dualism, agricultural land use patterns, transportation technology and social change," as well as "a window on geographic phenomena broadly ranging from mental maps to economic infrastructures."[9]

And why not? I am not the first to wonder whether the discrediting of realism as an attempted transparency has gone too far. George Levine, for one, urges that "the dominant distaste for anything that smacks of the empirical" within the human sciences "needs to be overcome, just as the scientists' tendency to dismiss theory and antirealism must be." Levine contends that "the discriminations that have been obliterated between objectivity and subjectivity, scientific and literary discourse, history and fiction, are in effect, still operative" and that they "need to be recuperated, if modified."[10] His statement about differences in representational mode between disciplines I would apply to the literary field itself. There is a mimetic difference hard to specify but uncontroversial to posit between the Chicago of Theodore Dreiser's *Sister Carrie* and the places of Italo Calvino's *Invisible Cities,* a difference also between Calvino's cities and the cities of Marco Polo's original *Travels.* There is a difference between the relatively "uncomposed" western photographs of Timothy O'Sullivan and nineteenth-century landscape photographs of a more "luminist" persuasion like those by Thomas Moran.[11] In the theory—or countermyth—of representation that I develop in this chapter, these differences are not just symptoms of Dreiser's petit-bourgeois romance of commodities or Calvino's avant-gardist critique (or perhaps reflection) of the more abstract commodifications of contemporary globalized capitalism.[12] My account of the reality of these fictional realities does not deny that they can profitably be so read but focuses on the recuperation of natural objects and the relation between outer and inner landscapes as primary projects.

The Dream of Accuracy

Let us start by returning to the long-lost world of nineteenth-century realism, which actually has since been twice displaced. (Initially it was displaced by high modernism, which in turn supplied the intellectual foundations of the formalist phase of Anglo-American literary theory.) To that end, I invoke a quaint essay by the late nineteenth-century essayist, naturalist, and critic John Burroughs, "Nature and the Poets." Burroughs designed this essay as an addendum to an earlier piece in which he credited the true poet with greater insight into nature than naturalists have, because the poet "carries her open secrets in his heart." Without retracting this, Burroughs now seeks to expose poetry's lapses of accuracy, particularly those of "minor" poets, for Burroughs believes that "the greater the poet, the more correct and truthful will be his specifications." Thus Burroughs credits Emerson with knowing "the New England fields and woods, as few poets do," and Bryant slightly less so, while censuring an obscure poet from Kansas for imagining yews and nightingales there. As he conducts his tour of poetic landscapes, Burroughs piles up a sometimes incredibly picky catalog of ornithological and botanical lapses committed for the sake of melodic or imagistic euphony. Take for instance his strictures on Bryant's lines

> The mother bird hath broken for her brood
> Their prison shells, or shoved them from the nest,
> Plumed for their earliest flight.

"It is not a fact," complains Burroughs, "that the mother bird aids her offspring in escaping from the shell. The young of all birds are armed with a small temporary horn or protuberance upon the upper mandible, and they are so placed in the shell that this point is in immediate contact with its inner surface; as soon as they are fully developed and begin to struggle to free themselves, the horny growth 'pips' the shell . . . To help the young bird forth would insure its speedy death. It is not true, either, that the parent shoves its young from the nest when they are fully fledged, except possibly in the case of some of the swallows and of the eagle."[13]

This kind of commentary can cause a modern reader's eyes to glass over in a hurry and tempt one to explain the fussiness as an obtuse refusal to distinguish one discourse from another. Burroughs, to give him credit, remains fully aware that there *is* a difference, stressing at the end of his essay that the poet's proper role is not merely to chronicle nature but "to see it subjectively."[14] Mere objectivity, or scientific detachment, did not interest him; he wanted to make facticity regulate poetic license, not oppose it. His motto was "the beautiful, not *over* but *through* the true."[15] But from the standpoint of any prevailing aesthetic standard before or after, his was an extreme literalism. In later years, he pushed it even farther, instigating the "nature fakers" controversy, in which he and others decried the overuse of fantasy elements in contemporary animal stories.[16]

The fact that this teapot tempest started in America's then leading journal of literary opinion, the *Atlantic Monthly,* and effervesced to the point that even President Theodore Roosevelt became involved shows how much hotter an issue mimetic fidelity to the known facts of natural history was a century ago than now. In my Harvard University Library copy of Burroughs's "Nature and the Poets" is an ancient-looking graffito quibbling with the remark "the dandelion blooms occasionally through-out the whole summer"; the word "occasionally" is underlined and in the margin is written "very often."[17] That is how even some highbrow re-viewers challenged Burroughs's essay when it appeared in article form in the late 1870s: not by questioning whether it was ludicrously literal-minded but by finding fault with the accuracy of Burroughs's own observations.[18]

It is so easy to laugh at such punctiliousness today that it is all the more important as a test of our contrary assumptions to take Burroughs seriously as expounding an aspect of authorial proficiency and reading competence that in our time has been banished to the subconscious: not that it has disappeared altogether, but that, being disreputable, it lacks voice and remains in the same limbo position that Charles Taylor ascribes to the "ethics of inarticulacy" in moral thought.[19] We live in a time when it is more fashionable for art to replicate constructed objects (electric plugs, pop bottles, hot water bags) than sedate landscapes (or cityscapes) done to scale; but as we congratulate ourselves on outgrowing the mimetic illusion by making it the playful instrument of our will, the repressed overtakes us at every turn. Perhaps we encounter some untrained student or family member, a zestful amateur novel reader, who cannot avoid thinking that Melville was truly interested in whaling lore. Perhaps we recall our own excitement, before we became properly socialized, at Hardy bringing an English heath "to life," or Dickens the street scenes of London, or Richard Wright the world of a Chicago ghetto, or Edith Wharton the equally suffocating refinements of old-fashioned New York society. The willingness to admit that thick description of the external world can at least sometimes be a strong interest for writers and for readers, even when it also serves ulterior purposes, is particularly crucial in the case of the environmental text. Nonfictional nature representation, especially, hinges on its ability to convince us that it is more responsive to the physical world's nuances than most people are, selective though that response may still be. To give a sufficiently generous account ✓ of literature's environmental sensitivity, we need to find a way of conceiving the literal level that will neither peremptorily subordinate it nor gloss over its astigmatisms.[20]

Burroughs was not the first or most articulate spokesperson for the now disreputable aesthetic of classical realism. In the English-speaking world, its great fomenter was unquestionably John Ruskin, whose standards for the modern landscape painter were higher than Burroughs's standards for the nature poet. Aesthetic excellence, for Ruskin, was based on "*perfect* knowledge" of the properties of the object. Factual accuracy per se was not the artist's highest end for Ruskin, any more than for Burroughs, and on that account Ruskin followed the convention of his day by condescending to Dutch landscape painting. But he held "the representation of facts" to be "the foundation of all art," insisting that "nothing can atone for the want of truth, not the most brilliant imagination." Indeed, Ruskin, like Burroughs after him, went so far as to declare that "material truth is indeed a perfect test of the relative rank of painters, though it does not in itself constitute that rank."[21]

What most strikes me about Ruskin's stance in *Modern Painters* are not his categorical assertions, however, but his extraordinarily minute strictures on painterly rendering of all characteristic landscape items: how branches and twigs should ramify, how rocks should be differentiated, and so on. One unfortunate tree in a landscape by Nicolas Poussin elicits this verdict: "It has no bark, no roughness nor character of stem; its boughs do not grow out of each other, but are stuck into each other; they ramify without diminishing, diminish without ramifying, are terminated by no complicated sprays, have their leaves tied to their ends, like the heads of Dutch brooms; and finally, and chiefly, they are evidently not made of wood, but of some soft elastic substance, which the wind can stretch out as it pleases, for there is not a vestige of an angle in any one of them."[22] Here we see the same passion for ferreting out small errors that we saw in Burroughs, far more elegantly expressed, with a magisterial comprehensiveness that leaves one in awe of Ruskin's microscopic vision. The vehemence and subtlety with which he effected a quantum leap in the rigor of realist aesthetics carried, at least for some readers, the force of a revelation: he showed them that they had never looked at a tree before, in any true sense of looking. The experience of confronting Ruskin for the first time must have been comparable to the experience of first realizing that the generic use of the masculine pronoun might be ideologically loaded, or that *Heart of Darkness* perpetuates the imperial order as staunchly as it critiques it. Precisely such a reader was the young George Eliot, just then on the verge of beginning her career as the greatest of all Victorian realists. In a review of the third volume of *Modern Painters,* she praised Ruskin's "doctrine that all truth and beauty are to be attained by a humble and faithful study of nature, and not by substituting vague forms . . . in place of definite, substantial reality. The thorough acceptance of this doctrine," Eliot affirmed, "would remould our life; and he who teaches its application to any one department of human activity with such power as Mr. Ruskin's, is a prophet for his generation."[23]

Nonfictional Aesthetics: Dual Accountability

The pertinence of this mentality to the legitimation of environmental nonfiction is even more obvious than its pertinence to the realistic novel. By demanding that imaginary gardens have real toads in them, it makes discourse accountable to the object-world and thereby destabilizes the generic hierarchy of fictive over nonfictive, rendering the boundary porous to the point that artifacts appear arranged along a continuum of

facticity, the fictive judged in the first instance according to its fidelity to
the factual rather than vice versa. In this conceptual universe, the art of
discovery is valorized above the art of fabulation. Because it inevitably
goes too far, this aesthetic is vulnerable to the Wildean challenge (life
imitates art) that is the precursor of all modernist claims that discourse
overrides mimesis: the world is only a small part of me, as e.e. cummings
is said to have said. From *that* position, nonfiction becomes subsumed
by poesis, textuality, ideology, the unconscious. Clearly the claims of
realism merit reviving not in negation of these myths but in counterpoise,
so as to enable one to reimagine textual representations as having a dual
accountability to matter and to discursive mentation. I certainly would
not argue that classical realism is the only or even the best way of
restoring the object-world for art, for imagination, and for human life;
indeed, some of the most environmentally responsive writers have been
emphatic on the other side of the issue. Leslie Marmon Silko, for example,
insists that "a 'lifelike' rendering of an elk is too restrictive," offering no
more than the external particularity of a single creature.[24] The value of
classical realism as a test case is that it points up what contemporary
representation theory most vigorously suppresses.

   What I mean by "dual acountability" can be illustrated by a passage
from Barry Lopez's *Arctic Dreams: Imagination and Desire in a Northern
Landscape* (1986), which as the book's subtitle suggests is an environmental text distinguished for its exceptional sensitivity to the limits of
objective representation when the writer is placed in a totally unfamiliar
setting. Lopez ponders the question of how bears stalk seals:

   One of the most persistent of bear legends—that they cover their
   dark noses with a paw or a piece of snow when they are stalking a
   seal—may have originated with Eskimos, but the thought has the
   flavor of invention about it. At a distance of 1000 yards, the argument
   goes, you can barely distinguish a polar bear on the sea ice, but you
   can clearly see its black nose. How could a seal not notice it? It's
   possible that it does—and that is exactly what the bear intends. To a
   seal, a polar bear approaching in a straight line over flat ice, its
   lowered forequarters sliding along ahead of its hindquarters, would
   show very little body movement—the pushing motion of the rear legs
   does not break the outline of the hips. If the seal focuses on the dark

nose, the bear's shape falls into vague relief against the surrounding ice. And at that distance the nose looks like another seal resting on the ice. Because of an optical phenomenon, the size of the bear's nose does not begin to fill more of the seal's image of that part of the sea ice until the bear is almost on top of the seal. And at that point the bear rises and bounds toward it.

It is possible the bear goes down on its forequarters only to keep the horizon from showing up between its legs; but it is also possible it wants its dark nose down there on the ice where it looks like a seal.

"Without direct evidence," Lopez adds, "without setting up an experiment, one can only speculate." But even when that is done, "nothing—no laboratory result or field-camp speculation—can replace the rich, complex texture, the credibility, of something that takes place 'out there.'"[25]

The passage centers on two invented narratives, invented in the dual sense of fabricated and discovered: stories humanly made up but generated to explain an empirical fact, that the seal does not notice the bear. Lopez knows his theory is a fiction, and he defers to the authority of science; but the ultimate authority, to which both laboratory result and field-camp explanation must appeal, is what's "out there." The narrative of seal (mis)perception that Lopez makes up is a theory that might prove to be either fantasy or fact, in which respect it resembles, without equaling, a scientific hypothesis rigorously derived from laboratory data. Both must finally satisfy the mind *and* the ethological facts, which in both instances may refute them.

The notion of "dual accountability" is still vague. One can distinguish at least four levels of reference in literary discourse: to use Linda Hutcheon's taxonomy, the intratextual, the intertextual (the world of other texts), the autorepresentational (the text figured as a text), and the outer mimetic (the world outside the text).[26] All come into play here: the concern to establish narrative coherence, to signal participation of this story in a world of texts (the fable of the bear covering its nose), to acknowledge that the narrative may have created its own world, and to make the narrative faithful to the world. What differentiates Lopez's "nonfiction" from most "fiction" is not that he blocks out the first three (all of which point to relations within the domain of textuality), but that he gives more weight to the last, granting it a theoretical veto over the others.

This chapter's third epigraph, from an essay of the same period, amplifies Lopez's notion of how imagination mediates between landscape and desire. The contours of human subjectivity, as he sees it, are molded by the configurations of the landscapes with which a person has been deeply associated. Subjectivity is not a mere function of landscape; but it is regulated somewhat by landscape, and as far as Lopez is concerned landscape is the more interesting variable. In short, Lopez remains accountable to the facticity in terms of which he invites his arctic images to be judged.

Lopez's notion of "outer mimesis" in environmental nonfiction seemingly boils down to this. Literature functions as science's less systematic but more versatile complement. Both seek to make understandable a puzzling world. To a greater degree than science, literature releases imagination's free play, though the play is not entirely free, since the imagination is regulated by encounters with the environment both personal and mediated through the unofficial folk wisdom to which one has been exposed. Thus regulated, the mind is at leisure to ramble among intriguing hypotheses, and it is not only permitted but expected to present theory as narrative or descriptive exposition rather than as argument. A certain lyricism is thus also encouraged: the adventures and vacillations of the persona on the way to whatever conclusion or inconclusion is reached. So too is a degree of ethical reflection; the assertion that "nothing . . . can replace" is as much a moral as a factual statement. But in the long run the author is committed to offering a model or scheme of the world (the bear-seal narrative, in this case) that we are in invited to weigh according to our supposition or knowledge of its plausibility. Either intuition ("the thought has the flavor of invention about it") or field data can be invoked here. The narrative makes no pretense of total accuracy; it is a *theory* of natural history; but nature is the court of appeal. By Lopez's own account, we ought to value his bear-seal narrative less if it could be disproved, though we are also invited to value the free-swinging meditative process that leads up to it and accompanies it.

The foregoing stand as a short statement of the nonfictional aspiration. To get a firmer sense of the consequences of reading nonfictionally as opposed to fictionally, let us turn again to *Walden*. I want to juxtapose a passage from the Walden journal (16 July 1845) with the final version in the "Brute Neighbors" chapter of *Walden*. This is not Thoreau at his most exciting, but it would be hard to select a more useful juxtaposition for present purposes.

> Here is one has had her nest under my house, and came when I took my luncheon to pick the crumbs at my feet. It had never seen the race of man before, and so the sooner became familiar—It ran over my shoes and up my pantaloons inside clinging to my flesh with its sharp claws. It would run up the side of the room by short impulses like a squirrel—which resembles—coming between the house mouse and the former—Its belly is a little reddish and its ears a little longer. At length as I leaned my elbow on the bench it ran over my arm and round the paper which contained my dinner. And when I held it a piece of cheese it came and nibled between my fingers and then cleaned its face and paws like a fly. (*PJ* 2: 162)

> The mice which haunted my house were not the common ones, which are said to have been introduced into the country, but a wild native kind (*Mus leucopus*) not found in the village. I sent one to a distinguished naturalist, and it interested him much. When I was building, one of these had its nest underneath the house, and before I had laid the second floor, and swept out the shavings, would come out regularly at lunch time and pick up the crumbs at my feet. It probably had never seen a man before; and it soon became quite familiar, and would run over my shoes and up my clothes. It could readily ascend the sides of the room by short impulses, like a squirrel, which it resembled in its motions. At length, as I leaned with my elbow on the bench one day, it ran up my clothes, and along my sleeve, and round and round the paper which held my dinner, while I kept the latter close, and dodged and played at bo-peep with it; and when at last I held still a piece of cheese between my thumb and finger, it came and nibbled it, sitting in my hand, and afterward cleaned its face and paws, like a fly, and walked away. (*Wa* 225–226)

Through the several stages of composition, Thoreau developed both the "fictional" and the "nonfictional" elements. On the one hand, he stylized so as to stress the neighborliness of the little brute. For the first draft of *Walden,* Thoreau dropped "the race" of man and the reference to the mouse's "sharp claws"; he cut short the comparative mammalology; and he added the cute touches of playing bo-peep with the mouse and having it eat out of his hand.[27] In the fifth draft, he dropped the phrase "clinging to the flesh," so that in the published book the mouse simply scurries "up my clothes" without any sensation of discomfort.[28] These small changes ensured that the contact between mouse and man would seem more like an intimate, companionable interchange than the *Journal* version imagined it as being.

Yet even as Thoreau euphemized this passage he pushed it further toward documentary. Although he may not have intended "*Mus leucopus*" (a marginal note in his copy of the first edition) for the actual text of *Walden,* the first two sentences do explicitly frame the personal encounter as a natural history observation; with almost pedantic detail, he pins down the timing of it during the Walden experiment (when building, before laying the second story).[29] The vignette of Thoreau and the mouse is itself more personalized, but the passage as a whole does not focus so exclusively on an experience with one particular creature.

Read fictionally, the passage is conspicuous for its pastoral stylization, all the more so if we know its provenance. The infusion of natural history seems done in the interest of adding scientific authority to the author's conversion of wild creature into domestic creature. A nonfictional reading would hardly deny Thoreau's selective orchestration. But it would take fidelity to the evidence as a key ingredient in writing and editing; it would imagine the passage and its revisions as constructions from natural history and actual experience; and it would conclude that autobiography as such was less important than communicating, as Lopez puts it, a flavor of "the rich, complex texture, the credibility, of something that takes place 'out there.'" Does the consolidation of Thoreau's credentials as the Concord Pan really interest him so much here as the fact that a "wild" creature approached him so closely? Might the dramatization of intimacy have been warranted by the facts? Might not the *Journal*'s "nibled between my fingers" suggest that Thoreau did in fact hold it in hand? Might not Thoreau's passion for accuracy have been as important as his need to pastoralize?

A fictionalist reading tends to presuppose that the persona is the main subject, that selectivity is suppression, that represented detail is symbolic, that environmental knowledge (in either author or reader) counts for little. A nonfictionalist reading presupposes that the persona's most distinctive trait is environmental proficiency—not the professional scientist's command of data and theory but the working knowledge of someone more knowledgeable than we, who seeks to communicate what he or she knows in a shareable form. It presupposes that the persona's chief rhetorical resource is exposition, that the metaphorical and tonal and meditative complications enriching exposition cannot be distinguished as the sole or even chief ways in which the text becomes artful, that the text's outer mimetic function is as important as its intertextual dimension, and that its selectivity is an instrument for promoting knowledge rather than suppressing it. If the spirit of fiction is that a rose by any other name would smell as sweet, the spirit of nonfiction is that "without the name, any flower is more or less a stranger to you."[30] In other words, if environmental nonfiction shows itself ignorant of the known facts of nature, it does so at peril.

"What, a new nominalism? Must we study Roger Torrey Peterson's bird books in order to read literature?" I am tempted to reply: Yes, that would be a very good thing indeed, and not just for nonfiction but for fictive genres as well. In the case of Whitman's "Lilacs," for example, it is well to know why the hermit thrush (suggested by Burroughs) was Whitman's bird of choice, and to know enough about its habits to appreciate why it makes environmental sense for the thrush to be metaphorically but not metonymically connected with the lilacs. Environmental proficiency being a neglected art among the American bourgeoisie, I am all in favor of turning the resources of literature to its remediation whenever possible. But certainly neither I, nor Burroughs or Ruskin as we have seen, believe that the poet's or essayist's highest calling has ever been to teach ornithology. Rather, their view was that the potency of the environmental text consisted not just in the reader's transaction with it but also in reanimating and redirecting the reader's transactions with nature. This is a point on which Peterson's guides enlighten us, teaching us as they do a lesson in outer mimesis: the superiority, *for purposes of reference,* of the artist's drawing to the photograph and the unassisted eye. Peterson's schematic bird drawings, with their emphasis on a limited number of field marks, are highly abstract renderings that have proved, in the experience of veteran birders, to enable the student to identify the originals more effectively than would a denser mimetic image, such as a photograph in the Audubon Society field guide. The capacity of the stylized image to put the reader or viewer in touch with the environment is precisely what needs stressing as a counter to the assumptions that stylization must somehow work against outer mimesis or take precedence over it. We need to recognize stylization's capacity for what the poet-critic Francis Ponge calls *adéquation:* verbalizations that are not replicas but equivalents of the world of objects, such that writing in some measure bridges the abyss that inevitably yawns between language and the object-world.[31]

It should come as no surprise to find the aesthetics of dual account-ability applicable beyond the expository, in the realm of fictive poesis as well. Indeed, in poets like Whitman and Gerard Manley Hopkins, inward-ness produces outwardness, exuberance produces catalog.

> Glory be to God for dappled things,—
>   For skies of couple-colour as a brindled cow;
>   For rose-moles all in stipple upon trout that swim;
> Fresh-firecoal chestnut-falls; finches' wings;
>   Landscape plotted and pieced—fold, fallow, and plough;
>   And all trades, their gear, and tackle and trim.[32]

What makes Hopkins's exquisite responsiveness to environmental stimuli especially striking is the unlikeliness of it. He views landscape in a mood of prayerful exaltation that could easily have thrust him upward after glancing briefly outward. Indeed, properly speaking this is not a landscape at all. Hopkins creates a collage by darting in all directions at once in search of pied images. His fondness for collecting perceptual bits bespeaks a detachment of the aesthetic specialist from the ordinary landscapes and rhythms of country life. But how delicately responsive the poem is to the stimuli it registers! Who would have thought to see trout's "rose-moles all in stipple"? In this way, aestheticism produces environmental bonding. Literally, the poet sees a painted fish; effectively, the aestheticist distortion animates the trout and makes its body palpable. There can be no question that this is a live trout shimmering for an instant in Hopkins's imaginary pool. With another glance, Hopkins evokes the feel and look of chestnut-falls, with another the mottled look of the agricultural landscape. So the poem is after all not just a "space of accumulation" but a tiny energizer that disperses the reader's attention, in imitation of the poet's own, out to various points of environmental contact. Activating this process is an idiosyncratic blend of old-fashioned natural theology and new-fashioned delight in the materiality of natural *things.*[33]

The symbiosis of object-responsiveness and imaginative shaping that we have seen in the series of examples from Lopez to Hopkins, as well as in the theories of Burroughs and Ruskin, calls into question the charges of epistemological naïveté and ideological tyranny that have been leveled against "classic realism" by proponents of the theory of representation. "The strategies of the classic realist text," alleges Catherine Belsey, "divert the reader from what is contradictory within it to the renewed recognition (misrecognition) of what he or she already 'knows', knows because the myths and signifying systems of the classic realist text re-present experience in the ways in which it is conventionally articulated in our society."[34] Clearly this need not be so. Representational projects that aspire to render the object-world need not be monologic, may indeed be founded on self-division about the possibilities of such a project, may even make these self-divisions explicit to the reader, and are as likely to dislocate the reader as to placate her. Indeed it might be quite difficult to find among the realist classics a clear case of classic realism as Belsey defines it.

Environmental representation's power to invent, stylize, and dislocate while at the same time pursuing a decidedly referential project can be further illustrated by a botanical passage from Mary Austin's *Land of Little Rain*, which describes flowers blooming in the Sierras.

Austin

> They drift under the alternate flicker and gloom of the windy rooms of pines, in gray rock shelters, and by the ooze of blind springs, and their juxtapositions are the best imaginable. Lilies come up out of fern beds, columbine swings over meadowsweet, white rein-orchids quake in the leaning grass. Open swales, where in wet years may be running water, are plantations of false hellebore *(Veratrum californicum)*, tall, branched candelabra of greenish bloom above the sessile, sheathing, boat-shaped leaves, semi-translucent in the sun. A stately plant of the lily family, but why "false"? It is frankly offensive in its character, and its young juices deadly as any hellebore that ever grew.
>
> Like most mountain herbs it has an uncanny haste to bloom. One hears by night, when all the wood is still, the crepitatious rustle of the unfolding leaves and the pushing flower-stalk within, that has open blossoms before it has fairly uncramped from the sheath. (*LLR* 118)

Notice how quickly the passage comes to rest on the false hellebore plantations, which then blot out the rest of the landscape and become its sole denizens. Then the plantations become reduced to a single generic plant that dominates the whole foreground, and Austin proceeds to describe what could not possibly be perceived, even with the aid of mechanical gadgets: "the crepitatious rustle of the unfolding leaves and the pushing flower-stalk within." This language refers to actual processes, which at the visual level can be rendered by time-lapse photography, then in its pioneering stages of development.[35] But of course we cannot *hear* all this. Austin's stylization creates such a hyperfocus on the false hellebore plant as to suggest the effects of regional grotesque, like Wing Biddle-baum's monstrous-seeming hands in the opening story of Sherwood Anderson's *Winesburg, Ohio.* The plant, like the hands, expands to fill the universe of the text. This analogy could be pushed further, for the sudden, momentary glimpse of the grisly or the bizarre is an Austin trademark. Yet mimesis is not *forgone,* any more than it is in Anderson's representation of midwestern culture, or in the expressionist genre paintings of Thomas Hart Benton, who elongates hillocks, implements, and body parts. On the contrary, Austin might even be seen as Peterson's botanical counterpart: painting in words the equivalent of an illustration of *Veratrum californicum* for a turn-of-the-century flower book, the field marks impossibly but revealingly magnified. Similarly, Thoreau's mouse passage, with its combination of clinical documentary opening and personalized anecdote, recalls the interweave of data and autobiographical vignette to be found in his primary sourcebook for American mammalology, Audubon and Bachman's *Viviparous Quadrupeds of North America.*[36] The difference between these examples of artistry and the two handbooks lies not in the plenitude and fidelity with which objective detail is rendered but in the artist's desire to establish a counterpoint between the inner and outer landscapes. In these works the artist does much more than derealize the objective landscape through discursive imposition or preemption by intertext.

As the Austin passage partially illustrates, the act of imaging in words the actual but imperceptible demonstrates the importance of outer mimesis in environmental writing.

One has to visualize the life of these insects beneath the rushing-hard cold of Whitetail three: some kind of food was coming down that creek in large amounts, at a very rapid rate, and was being trapped

by these larvae. My mind goes back to the branches beneath Whitetail
three. There were not really that many, about one submerged limb
every ten yards, but there were many twigs and lesser branches along
the banks, dangling and submerged, also covered with caddis flies.
The animals had obviously taken up all the available space on those
twigs ranging from one the size of a pin to one the size of a railroad
tie supporting the bridge. The fact of these flies' dependence on twigs
for homesites was impressive only until one looked at the larvae with
a hand lens. Each larva lived in a house, constructed by itself. Each
larva's house was to the untrained eye so similar as to be identical to
every other larva's house, the detailed architecture and accoutrements
of each house built according to the same set of blueprints, and each
not only fastened to twigs but *made* of twigs. One sensed no colony
of caddis flies, as one senses a colony of cliff swallows, but rather
sensed a set of instructions within each fly larva that chose twigs to
build a house, arranged and glued those twigs in an identifiable
pattern, and finished the job by adding exactly two much longer
twigs, so that the final house resembled a tube with runners.[37]

In this passage from *Keith County Journal,* John Janovy, Jr., builds an
increasingly dense image of where and how the larvae of caddis flies build
their "houses" and what they look like. Janovy disclaims objectivity,
reminding us that his image is a constructed thing ("One has to visualize,"
"My mind goes back," "One sensed"), switching perspective back and
forth between the lab and the field. The little narrative in the last sentence,
so painstakingly detailed, is (he makes no bones about it) a complete
fabrication. Janovy could not possibly have seen the gene-driven nest-
building occur as he makes us see it—could not have seen it even under
a microscope, let alone with the naked eye. Yet the passage comports with
the entomological facts: the inner landscape is symbiotic with the outer.
His reflexiveness hardly amounts to a forfeiture of objectivity, much less
to proof that the passage has lost touch with its outer landscape. "Language need not know the world perfectly in order to communicate
perceptions adequately," as Annie Dillard writes in another connection,[38]
in the spirit of my epigraph from Hilary Putnam. Indeed, Janovy's "subjectiveness" itself, far from functioning simply as a compromising or
distorting agent, proves to be the means through which the larvae's

houses are realized as an actuality. Amateur nature lovers walking along the Whitetail in western Nebraska might not notice them; those that did might not recognize them; those that recognized them might not understand their construction. But those that do, like Janovy, in order to communicate what they know, would have to reinvent the scene with imagery they themselves could not possibly have seen, in order to make us see it. They would have to portray the scene, as here, with much more vividness and intensity and magnification than we would see it in the field, even with eyes awakened by this passage. The result is a more complicated version of Austin's magnified false hellebore plant. "Distortion" turns out in this case to thrust us closer than ever before to the object-world. "One has to visualize . . ." That is, one has to imagine. One has to invent, to extrapolate, to fabricate. Not in order to create an alternative reality but to see what without the aid of the imagination isn't likely to be seen at all.

of Blake

To reverse Emerson's conclusion to the "Idealism" section of *Nature,* perhaps the chief advantage of the dual accountability hypothesis in approaching the environmental nonfiction of Austin and Thoreau is that it is precisely the view least satisfactory to the mind.[39] It refuses to allow "mind" or "language" or "history" or "culture" to have its way over discourse unchecked. Whatever the conscious politics of the reader who espouses a philosophical antireferentialism in the domain of literary theory, that stance underrepresents the claims of the environment on humanity by banishing it from the realms of discourse except as something absent. It forbids discourse the project of evoking the natural world through verbal surrogates and thereby attempting to bond the reader to the world as well as to discourse: it forbids enabling the reader to see as a seal might see. From this standpoint, not mimesis but antireferentialism looks like the police. This holds not only for nonfiction but also for fictive genres, including poetry, which of all literary genres one might suppose to be nonreferential. Wendell Berry, for example, objects to defining poetry in terms of its specialization—that is, language; for "the subject of poetry is not words, it is the world, which poets have in common with other people." Berry's either/or rhetoric overstates the case, but the case is not trivial. "If a *culture* goes for too long," Berry writes elsewhere, "without producing poets and others who concern themselves with the problems and proprieties of humanity's practical connection to nature,

Berry

then the work of all poets may suffer, and so may nature."[40] This is a sobering thought, that the attenuation of mimesis might threaten nature itself. Yet, on reflection, we see that it is no less cogent than its opposite, that mimesis itself threatens nature by tempting us to accept cozening copies for the real thing.

Why Care?

It is not, after all, very hard to show that one of the projects of the environmental text is to render the object-world and that this project is sometimes best achieved through what would seem to be outright fiction or distortion. It is harder to give a searching explanation of why someone would want to do this. Berry's ring of self-evident finality warns us off, yet it is precisely here that we need to press him. Why, aside from commercial reasons, should an artist want to make minute extrospection a high priority? Why should writers like Janovy or Austin or Thoreau want to create landscapes in which obscure or overlooked objects become magnified or more densely rendered than they would be in the ordinary experience of them? Lopez's two-landscapes theory becomes mystical at this point. It is a description of a relational structure, not a theory of motive. I immerse myself in a landscape; it imprints itself on my mind; so my texts become a partial register of it. This is all very well; there is probably a lot of truth to it; but in the long run the theory of place osmosis is just as insufficient to explain the choice of a mimetic mode, and for much the same reason, as the theory of intertextuality is to explain the choice of a plot-oriented structure over an associative structure.

Doubtless no single explanation suffices. One is surely the sheer aesthetic and intellectual challenge of being held accountable to faithful rendering of the object-world. "Falsehood is so easy, truth so difficult," as George Eliot writes in the course of likening her painstakingly circumstantial account of rural vernacular culture in *Adam Bede* to Dutch realist painting. More relevant to environmental representation specifically, this sense of accountability may be intensified by a moral or even religious conviction as to the rightness of artistic conception being shaped by what the environment offers it: "no ideas but in things"; "first, there must be observance of the ruling organic law"; "God forbid that we should give out a dream of our own imagination for a pattern of the world." These three voices are, respectively, William Carlos Williams, John Ruskin, and Francis Bacon—all in their own ways great empiricists though of wildly different doctrinal persuasions.[41] That this ethos of deference to the object all too frequently yields to its opposite is clear enough—that Bacon can sponsor the manipulation of nature and that the Dutch realism he helped inspire can become an armature of the emerging commercial order.[42] But the more fundamental point is that the ethos—betrayed though it may eventually be—of basing art on disciplined extrospection is in the first instance an affirmation of environment over self, over appropriative homocentric desire. It affirms, as Gerard Manley Hopkins affirms in a burst of proto-Heideggerian exuberance, that

> Each mortal thing . . .
> Deals out that being indoors each one dwells;
> Selves—goes itself; *myself* it speaks and spells,
> Crying *Whát I dó is for me: for that I came.*[43]

As Norman Bryson has shown in the case of still life painting, the depiction of trivial objects can be a way of asserting art's primacy over matter (in the abstractions of Paul Cézanne or Juan Gris, for instance) or it can be a way of achieving (as in Juan Sánchez Cotán or Francisco de Zurbarán) a "renunciation of normal human priorities" and humbling the self by "forcing the eye to discover in the trivial base of life intensities and subtleties which are normally ascribed to things of great worth." "Opposing the anthropocentrism of the 'higher' genres, it assaults," at least in principle, "the centrality, value and prestige of the human subject."[44] The same, I think, could be said with even greater force about extrospective depiction of natural objects in the outdoors.

Discussing Austin, I likened her flower to the effect of regional grotesque, thinking at that point of the "hyperreality" that Bryson also notices in still life.[45] This notion of environmental art as a deliberate dislocation of ordinary perception deserves to be taken quite seriously. For the serious pursuit of natural history, from its premodern origins in the late Renaissance, has often been considered somewhat "grotesque." Field naturalists in the early republic were widely seen as eccentric misfits. William Bartram makes good-humored capital out of the trend, recounting for example the nickname the Indians gave him, "puc-puggy," the flower hunter (while also making it clear that they stood in awe of his botanical knowledge).[46] Cooper made the myopic pedantry of Obed Bat the butt of his humor in *The Prairie.* Thoreau repeatedly notes that his neighbors thought his preoccupation with nature absurd. Toward the end of the century, which was supposedly the heyday of amateur natural history, his English biographer Henry Salt made the same point about English attitudes in a book on Thoreau's English counterpart, Richard Jefferies : "the naturalist or nature student is everywhere looked upon by the generality of country-folk as a lunatic at large (except, of course, in those lucid intervals when he is engaged in 'killing something.')"[47] That the prejudice was not confined to the uneducated is clear from the opinion of young Charles Darwin's father that naturalism was a useless profession.

The passages quoted earlier suggest the basis for the prevalent sense of the naturalist as bizarrely out of step. They reveal "abnormal" ways of viewing objective reality. Normal people don't obsess on flowers the way Austin does or on insects the way Janovy does. Normal people don't train themselves to look the way Thoreau trained himself to look. The last entry in his immense *Journal* epitomizes the directional movement of his career in this regard. Thoreau contemplates the gravel of a railroad causeway. The individual pieces loom with a Brobdingnagian hugeness, the gravel "stratified like some slate rocks, on their edges, so that I can tell within a small fraction of a degree from what quarter the rain came . . . Behind each little pebble, as a protecting boulder . . . extends northwest a ridge of sand an inch or more, which it has protected from being washed away" (*J* 14: 346).

Thoreau and other literary naturalists are well aware they see things differently from the average person ("all this," Thoreau continues, "is perfectly distinct to an observant eye, and yet could pass unnoticed by most"); and at times this causes them to accentuate the whimsical and the grotesque. Thoreau does this with particular delicacy in his late essay "Wild Apples," a key naturist work in the Thoreau canon because the subject is so clearly also a self-image: a cherished Puritan legacy gone crabbed, cranky, and feral. In one sequence, the author describes his late fall foraging practices. "You would not suppose that there was any fruit left there," he chuckles, "but you must look according to system." "With experienced eyes," he draws forth the fruit from its secret "lurking-places," "perhaps with a leaf or two cemented to it (as Curzon an old manuscript from a monastery's mouldy cellar)," fills his pockets and ambles home, eating "one first from this side, and then from that, to keep my balance."[48] The essay is a display of field-naturalist apple lore and expertise wrapped in a charming portrait of a slightly dotty wild apple enthusiast that doubles as mock-confession and gentle mockery of the ignorant and perhaps uninterested reader's ability to read landscape.

The notion that intensely focused realistic mimesis of the natural world might be considered a form of grotesque has been pursued by Victorianists with respect to Pre-Raphaelite painting and the poetry of Alfred Tennyson, Robert Browning, and Hopkins. In the imagery used to depict the moated grange of Tennyson's "Mariana," Carol T. Christ notes that the very sharpness "conveys a sensitivity morbid in its emotional intensity": "The rusted nails fell from the knots / That held the pear to the gable-wall" and "Unlifted was the clinking latch." The precision, argues Christ, expresses the title figure's derangement. "Mariana's obses-sion with her desertion keeps her fixated in a static emotional attitude that makes the slightest movement or sound strike her with extreme sharpness . . . Objects appear to her with an acuteness that mesmerizes her"; "the slightness of these impressions conveys a blankness of a mind that under prolonged emotional strain seizes upon any object to find some release." This typifies Christ's analysis: the Victorians, as she says of the Pre-Raphaelites, "created a realism so exaggerated it became expres-sionistic."[49] Of Thoreau's apple manuscript somewhat the same could be said. But the magnification of the minute in Thoreauvian nonfiction is not the same as the hypersensitivity to objects in "Mariana." The situation can be clarified by John Everett Millais's notorious mid-Victorian paint-ing, *Christ in the House of His Parents* (1850), where a vernacular boy-Jesus who has hurt his hand is being comforted by working-class parents while standing in a carpenter's shop littered with shavings on the floor, tools and lumber cluttering up the background. The obvious agenda is to counteract religious sentimentalism by aggressively humanizing Christ. It is the visual equivalent of Whitman's "snag-toothed hostler with red hair redeeming sins past and to come."[50] But the painting, and the poem as well, must be read as revisionist allegories that deconstruct the allegorical mode by setting against it the world of vernacular fact where Jesus belongs. Otherwise, the hostler is gratuitous and the painting leaves the viewer unsatisfied by a "literalness that is . . . bothersome because it serves no expressive end."[51] Realistic mimesis is not the stalking horse for a revised theology; it *is* that theology.

What is true of Millais's carpenter shop is even truer of the natural environment of the environmental text. It requires us to remake our image of the world in terms of a criterion of value intentionally dislocating in its focus on the intractably and minutely factical. Janovy's passage on the caddis fly calls out as Whitman does elsewhere in the 1855 edition, insisting, "I swear I think now that every thing without exception has an eternal soul! / The trees have, rooted in the ground! the weeds of the sea have! the animals!"[52] Both affirm that the caddis fly is just as real as we are, has just as much right as you and I do to be taken as the center of the universe around which everything else shall revolve.

If this proposition seems hard to accept, consider another analogy. Think of environmental representation as akin to the novel of manners, where tea ceremonies, tiny conversational nuances, and minute gestures and variances of dress matter intensely.[53] The process of conforming to the codes begins when one accepts that the type of accent or dress one puts on really matters. At first we are not aware of the codes; then we perceive them as artifice; eventually we accept them as reality. So too with environmental literacy. We can think of it as a kind of culture, with local and historical variations, requiring efforts of study and adaptation.[54] What makes the analogy especially pertinent is that the niceties of manners fiction and environmental representation will probably seem to most readers of this book almost equally quaint. To require late twentieth-century urbanites to discriminate between edible and inedible plants in the forest or identify by feel different types of apples in a barrel (as John Burroughs claimed every New York farmboy could) seems about as finicky as to require them to be as conscious as Jane Austen and Henry James were of modes of proper chaperonage, polite replies to engraved invitations, and rituals for making social calls. Yet both are forms of competence in external affairs on which prestige and sometimes even survival have depended. People who continue to exhibit them after they no longer seem important we consider eccentric, with perhaps an admixture of respect for their knowledge of a lost art. The importance Lopez attaches to the reality of what's "out there" as a test of one's Arctic fictions reflects his awareness that in the cultures of the Arctic, both of aborigines and of scientific expeditioners, failures of accuracy may be life threatening.

In the late twentieth century, most westerners stand in much the same relation to the natural environment as a new immigrant to America without much prior knowledge of national custom. Regional terrain organizes itself for us in the guise of maps and highways; rarely do we bring its topography, system of watercourses, vegetation zones, and atmospheric patterns into focus as organizing forces when we drive rapidly through them on our daily commute. Insulated to such a degree from their direct influence, we do not feel them constituting us. Even if we have studied regional ecology, our daily routines may keep it from percolating through to the level of ordinary perception. The challenge, for those interested in assuming it, thus becomes to a considerable extent "reinhabitation": refamiliarizing ourselves with the physical environment that our preindustrial forebears perforce had to know better experientially, that their aboriginal forebears perforce knew better than they.[55] One way to answer this challenge is to sink one's roots more deeply in place. "It is only in the place that one belongs to, intimate and familiar, long watched over," affirms Wendell Berry for example, "that the hawk stoops into the clearing before one's eyes; the wood drake, aloof and serene in his glorious plumage, swims out of his hiding place."[56] This is the "bioregionalist" approach to self-education in environmental literacy.[57] Alternatively, Barry Lopez provides a complementary approach in his major books, *Wolves and Men* and *Arctic Dreams,* which draw heavily on sojourns among northern aboriginal peoples but are not localized anywhere and are inspired as much by intelligent eclectic reading in science, anthropology, and myth as by direct conversations with nature.

Nonfiction writers such as Thoreau, Austin, Berry, Dillard, and Janovy—and poets like Wordsworth, Frost, and Snyder—seem to have begun adulthood as youths with relatively modest degrees of eco-precociousness who became caught up in the quest for environmental literacy. In each case, one could deconstruct this interest, and the works that express it, by questioning whether environmental literacy was unequivocally of the first importance to them. For Janovy, it subserved his professorial ambitions as a parasitologist; for Dillard, it was artistic pigment, on much the same level as other forms of imagery; for Austin, it meant a one-way ticket out of a bad marriage and a dead town. By the same token, one could deconstruct our hypothetical immigrant's motives: very likely he or she was less interested in learning American manners per se than in using them as a means to another end. But certainly the pursuit of environmental or cultural literacy has been more valuable in the estimation of the people involved than to their debunkers.

The question then shifts from whether environmental facticity or environmental codes of manners matter in the formation of environmental writers' attitudes and works to whether today's readers should consider such matters important. The most obvious answer, although not the ultimate one, is that they make a difference in the way one reads. Even what seems a quite allegorical representation of nature may look quite different as one becomes more environmentally literate. As an example, take one of Henry Wadsworth Longfellow's few still-anthologized lyrics: his late poem "Aftermath."

> When the summer fields are mown,
> When the birds are fledged and flown,
>   And the dry leaves strew the path;
> With the falling of the snow,
> With the cawing of the crow,
> Once again the fields we mow
>   And gather in the aftermath.
>
> Not the sweet, new grass with flowers
> Is this harvesting of ours;
>   Not the upland clover bloom;
> But the rowen mixed with weeds,
> Tangled tufts from marsh and meads
> Where the poppy drops its seeds
>   In the silence and the gloom.[58]

These lines positively cry out to be read as an allegory of the scanty harvest of old age, as of course they are. In my teaching experience, few readers think of giving the poem anything but a symbolic reading. Few know that "aftermath" is an agricultural term for the second and inferior hay crop mown late in the season. That discovery changes one's reading of the poem: "we" can now mean working people as well as poets and other armchair harvesters; the poem's landscape now looks as much like the abstract of a literal farm as the concretization of a gestalt. We begin to credit Longfellow with having a certain taste for the poetry of earth as well as the poetry of moral abstraction. Perhaps he admired Keats for more reasons than one.

The initial failure of readerly vision doubtless reflects the attenuation of environmental knowledge ensuing from modern urbanization: the decline of poetry readers conversant enough with agricultural life to grasp the full meaning of "aftermath." Relative even to gentry-class premodernists like Longfellow, contemporary readers lead urbanized lives, whether in point of fact they reside as he did in Cambridge, Massachusetts, or in some leafy exurb. *This* concrete dissociation of sensibility, the loss of a culture of reciprocity with the natural environment, is more profound than the comparatively rarefied late Renaissance schism so termed by T. S. Eliot.[59] It conduces to the marginalization of the "descriptive" aspect of premodern poetry, to a preferred reading of images as a part of a symbolic construct or psychological landscape. Therefore, although the reader who does not know what "aftermath" literally means probably does not know what "rowen" looks like either, that ignorance is unlikely to cause anxiety (no student has ever asked me to explain); our reading priorities make inability to identify a particular kind of grass a unimportant. Yet "rowen" is the ancillary clue that will help remediate one's ignorance, for it is a synonym for the telltale aftermath—the second growth of grass.[60]

But a more cogent argument for environmental literacy than the historical one (based on its value in helping to decode writings of a bygone era) is simply that it is, if anything, getting more important as it seems to grow less. The impression that human affairs are not in fundamental ways subject to regulation by the environment is created by our ostensible success at regulating it. This blindness to the environment produces unintended destabilizing consequences like skin lesions from the ozone hole, owing partly to the products of cooling technologies that have insulated us from confronting the scandal of our environmental dependence. The situation is the obverse of Marxist reification theory. According to that theory, the bourgeoisie succumbs to a false impression of the givenness of the environment that has actually been created by the efforts of humankind. We have seen similar illusions at work in environmental aesthetics. What I have called the America-as-nature reduction in American literary studies disguises the roles of history and homocentrism in shaping what we fancy as the givenness of nature. But there is also a fallacy of derealization: the bourgeoisie's false assumption that environmental interventions in its planned existence are nothing more than fortuitous occasional events.[61] The notion of art (and other cultural practices) as discursive functions carried on within social "spaces" reinforces this mentality no less efficiently than air-conditioning. The facticity of the environmental other that faces the human practitioner collapses into the vision of a "dialectical relationship between the body and a space structured according to . . . mythico-ritual oppositions."[62] The contrary evidence is as simple as breathing subzero air, but in the discursive world such evidence can be repressed.

The desire to suppress the intimation of facticity surely runs deeper than mesmerization by literary theory, or even by the buffering accoutrements of commodity culture. Certainly a farming family living in a remote area before the dawn of modern medicine, transportation, and electricity would have been forced to conduct life with a much greater sense of environmental dependence than we have. But beneath this sociohistorical difference, respect for environmental facticity in any era might be felt to smack of acquiescence, fatalism, even death. Sooner or later, the implacable *thereness* of the external world is found to represent the adversary. No matter how resolutely cheerful or stoic one's temperament, in some moods or phases nature will metamorphose from possibility into fate, as for the aging Emerson.

It is striking in this regard that nowhere in modern aesthetic reflection has the animus against nature's givenness burst forth more spectacularly than in celebrations of the wonders of the most realistic of all media, cybernetically produced virtual reality (VR). Already it lies within technology's power to simulate an orchestra, a landscape, and any action or sensation in space with a finer and intenser degree of realization than the experience itself would bring. What thoughts does this prospect of hyperreality inspire? Not, of course, delight at having realized the world, but delight at mastery over it; for "In cyberspace, there is no need to move about in a body like the one you possess in physical reality. You may feel more comfortable, at first, with a body like your 'own' but as you conduct more of your life and affairs in cyberspace your conditioned notion of a unique and immutable body will give way to a far more liberated notion of 'body' as something quite disposable and, generally, limiting."[63] Undoubtedly one reason realist aesthetics has been criticized as an ideological apparatus is that in the much hotter medium of contemporary VR realistic mimesis does seem to have become a godlike instrument of totalitarian power. At last it seems almost in our power not only to image reality perfectly but to "participate" in that perfectly evoked reality without consequences, in experiences over which "we" if not the individual "I" maintain infallible control. Jean Baudrillard makes this linkage explicit in his dystopian account of what he takes to be the three "orders of simulacra": the realism of the classical era (which Baudrillard absurdly claims to have a "strict correlation" with the ascetic imperialism of the Jesuits), the epoch of mass production of the premodern industrial revolution, and the epoch of "digitality," of which the quintessential symbols are the computer and the genetic code. This succession, as Baudrillard defines it, is an arrogant displacement of reality ("the demiurgic ambition to exorcize the natural substance of a thing in order to substitute a synthetic one") that paradoxically has brought us, in the age of VR, "to the collapse of reality into hyperrealism, in the minute duplication of the real," since machines can now generate "a completely imaginary contact-world of sensorial mimetics and tactile mysticism"— "an entire ecology," he tellingly adds.[64]

As history, Baudrillard's essay is wildly sensationalized but thereby all the more revealing as myth: it lays bare the fear that underlies much 1980s historicist theory of representation as a part of the apparatus of modern capitalism, whose effective origins lie in Renaissance era imperialism and whose latter-day result is "the impossible totality of the contemporary world system," as Fredric Jameson writes in the course of a far more painstaking and nuanced analysis than Baudrillard's. Jameson's preferred symbol is not VR but the "hyperspace" of postmodern architecture like the Westin Bonaventure Hotel in Los Angeles, which unlike the products of Baudrillard's simulation machines is a massive eclectic assemblage that bears little relation to mimetic realism. But Jameson, too, diagnoses the postmodern dispensation in architecture as marking an intensified state of social control via environmental recreation to which the age of representational realism was the paleotechnic prelude. Jameson's architecture, like Baudillard's computers, stands "as something like an imperative to

grow new organs, to expand our sensorium and our body to some new
. . . perhaps ultimately impossible, dimensions."[65] And both are acutely
aware that this "imperative" does not begin with the individual consumer's desire (as the previous quotation from a VR entrepreneur disin-
genuously suggests), although it activates that desire. On the contrary, as
a *Business Week* feature on VR states with unintended grimness, "Cyberspace worlds that exist only in the electronic ether can be a powerful tool
in the hands of architects, engineers, and scientists" to "boost productivity, improve design, and provide more cost-effective training."[66]

Yet as one contemplates the resources of technologically assisted
representation in the era of postmodernity as Baudrillard and Jameson
describe it, one begins, on the contrary, to sense that one of literary
realism's advantages, which standard accounts of its ideological agenda
occlude, is precisely its comparative impotence: its inability to dominate
the physical world that its texts register, and with this an underlying
awareness of its own project as the inexhaustible challenge not of mastering
reality so much as trying quixotically to get nearer to it than the conventions of classical and romantic representation had permitted. Without
denying that aesthetic realism can validly be characterized from one
perspective as a waystation on the path toward total technological control
over reality, from another vantage point it signifies precisely the opposite:
a resistance to any such manipulation, "the nostalgia for a natural referent
of the sign," as Baudrillard slightingly calls what he takes to be western
culture's ineffective resistance to the succession of increasingly technologically sophisticated orders of simulacra.[67]

In short, paradoxical as it might seem, pondering the issue from an
ecocentric standpoint, one of the greatest advantages that linguistic attempts to represent reality, even those that are machine-generated, enjoy
over the simulacra of VR is precisely the comparative impotence that
requires writers to defer, as we have seen Ruskin and Burroughs defer, to
the authority of external nonhuman reality as a criterion of accuracy and
value.[68] Granted that this criterion can never be employed with the
objectivity writers claim; granted that their invocation of it presumes that
arbitration of what counts as adequate representation will be left to the
likes of them. From an ecocentric standpoint a criterion built on a
theoretical distinction between human constructedness and nonhuman
reality (Lopez's theory of the two landscapes) is far more productive than

a criterion based on the presupposition of the inevitable dominance of constructedness alone (Foucault's theory of discursive formations). This advantage the analogies of minute realism as grotesque and of ecocentrism as a code of manners underscore in different ways by calling attention to the status of nature-responsiveness as a kind of culture, or rather counterculture, that one must pursue in resistance to the intractable homocentrism in terms of which one's psychological and social worlds are always to some degree mapped. Lopez would doubtless want to argue that the humble aspiration of environmental mimesis, under these conditions, is far healthier for an individual, and for a society, than the arrogance of cyberspace.

CHAPTER FOUR

Walden's *Environmental Projects*

᪲

The question is not what you look at—but how you look &
whether you see.

—Henry David Thoreau, *Journal*

Man is altogether too much insisted on. The poet says the proper
study of mankind is man—I say study to forget all that—take
wider views of the universe.

—Thoreau, *Journal*

THOREAU IS THE PATRON SAINT of American environmental
writing. This eminence did not come easily to him. For more than a
generation after his death, he remained obscure; and in his relatively short
life he had to struggle to arrive at the deep understanding of nature for
which he is now remembered. Indeed, Thoreau spent his entire career
laboriously trying to sort out the competing claims of nature and culture.
It is especially in his partial odyssey from environmental naïveté to
comparative enlightenment that he looks most representative of his culture and mirrors most closely today's environmentalist ferment. Thoreau
started adult life from a less advantageous position than we sometimes
realize, as a village businessman's son of classical education rather than
having been versed in nature through intensive botanical study, agriculture, or more than a very ordinary sort of experiential contact with it.
Unlike William Bartram, he had no man of science for a father; unlike
Thomas Jefferson, he had no agrarian roots.[1] From early youth, he
enjoyed country rambles, but so did many of his contemporaries. His
first intellectual promptings to study and write about nature came from

books, school, and literary mentors like Ralph Waldo Emerson. Though he celebrated wildness, his was the wildness not of the moose but of the imported, cultivated escapee from the orchard that he celebrated in his late essay "Wild Apples."[2] His pursuit of nature thus became a fitful, irregular, experimental, although increasingly purposeful self-education in reading landscape and pondering what he found there: a process "of continuously mapping the world and locating the self" thereby.[3]

Thoreau's Development

In composing each of his four major books (the last two published posthumously), and throughout the history of his life as a thinking person, Thoreau pursued what might be called a strategy of substantialization. Each book centers on a relatively simple excursion or series of excursions: *A Week on the Concord and Merrimack Rivers,* on a two-week trip to the White Mountains of New Hampshire; *Walden,* on two years of bivouacking at the pond; *The Maine Woods,* on three journeys to Maine reported successively; and *Cape Cod,* on three trips to Cape Cod, conflated into a single narrative.[4] These he then expanded in the process of composition, as we see from their skeletal journal antecedents in the case of *The Maine Woods* and *Cape Cod,* and from the extensions of the original drafts of *Walden* and *A Week,* published by J. Lyndon Shanley and Linck Johnson, respectively.[5] In the case of *A Week,* Thoreau's first book, the amplifications mainly took the form of excursus meditations, some of them cannibalized chunks of earlier essays. What is distinctive about the three later books, by contrast, is the increase in representational density as the writing process advanced. In *Walden,* Thoreau increasingly elaborates the pondscape; he extends and subdivides a short piece on animals into two separate chapters; he fleshes out in great detail a terse seasonal progression from fall to spring.[6] *The Maine Woods* progresses through the three sections from magazine-piece romantic travel narrative ("Ktaadn") to much thicker botanical and anthropological description in "Chesuncook" and especially in "Allegash and the East Branch," which is longer than the first two sections combined, and in which the journal form takes precedence over the narrative line. Likewise, in *Cape Cod* the first four chapters, originally published in serial form, whisk us through the nearer regions of the cape, whereas the last six advance much more lingeringly from Wellfleet on.[7] The inner movements of the three later books, all of which took shape at intervals over long periods of time, reflect the shift in Thoreau's *Journal* during the 1850s as it became less a repository for thoughts, quotations, anecdotal vignettes, and drafts, and more a record of regular, meticulous daily extrospection. These shifts register Thoreau's development from the young transcendentalist literatus—with a strong bent for poetry and a still insufficiently appreciated stamina for ingesting *all* the elder English bards from John Gower to Michael Drayton to William Davenant—to the middle-aged ruralist for whom Virgil's *Georgics* were more compelling than his *Aeneid*, William Gilpin's literary prose about the picturesque qualities of the English landscape more readable than romantic poetry, and Darwin's *Journal of Researches* aboard *HMS Beagle* more significant than *Robinson Crusoe* or *Typee*.[8]

Thoreau is often thought of as Emerson's earthy opposite. But it would be truer to imagine him as moving gradually, partially, and self-conflictedly beyond the program Emerson outlined in *Nature*, which sacralized nature as humankind's mystic counterpart, arguing (in "Language") that physical nature could be decoded as a spiritually coherent system of signs. This theory of correspondence, derived chiefly from Emanuel Swedenborg, validated the authority of the inspired creative imagination as the means by which nature's meanings were to be read. The idea that natural phenomena had spiritual as well as material significance appealed strongly to Thoreau throughout his life, although he took a more empirical and "scientific" approach to nature after 1850; indeed, accompanying his growing commitment to exact observation and to keeping tabs on contemporary scientific thought was a lingering testiness at the myopia of its pedantry and formalism. (Ironically, Emerson himself was less critical of science and technology, although he was also far less knowledgeable.)[9] Hence Thoreau's famous explanation for his refusal to give a full answer to the Association for the Advancement of Science's query as to what kind of scientist he was: "I am a mystic, a transcendentalist, and a natural philosopher to boot" (*J* 5: 4). Yet Thoreau became increasingly interested in defining nature's structure, both spiritual and material, for its own sake, as against how nature might subserve humanity, which was Emerson's primary consideration.

It is important not to underrate Emerson's own environmentalist achievement. *Nature* took a great stride toward philosophic, or at least theologic, naturalism in holding up a nature more substantialized than the neoclassical cosmic abstraction called Nature as a mirror of moral health superior to human codes and doctrines. To object to miracles as not being one with "the blowing clover or the falling rain," as Emerson did in his Divinity School Address,[10] was a far more audaciously secularized advancement of physical nature's claims than to have indicted them for being "contrary to Nature." Emerson's religiophilosophical mode of reflecting on nature, however, may also have kept his talented disciple at a more ideational level of contemplation than he would have been drawn to if left to his own devices. (One of Harvard's natural historians is said to have remarked in exasperation to Bronson Alcott, "if Emerson had not spoiled him, Thoreau would have made a good entomologist.")[11]

Apart from the limits imposed by his Emersonian auspices and by classical education, in order to focus as intensively as he later did on natural history as a literary subject Thoreau had to overcome an intense preoccupation with himself, his moods, his identity, his vocation, his relation with other people. This narcissism he offset by defining as an essential part of his individuality the intensity of his interest in and caring for physical nature itself.

One of the reasons *Walden* is Thoreau's greatest book is that the transitional struggles of a lifetime are so fully reflected in it. I concentrate on it, therefore, not not only because *Walden* remains Thoreau's most enduring work but also because it embeds much of the history of his thinking about the natural environment as it unfolded from his apprentice years to his full maturity. For we should think of *Walden* both as product and as process, a work that took nearly a decade of accumulated experience and revision to complete: the decade that happened to be the most crucial period in Thoreau's inner life.

Let us start our examination with a section from the book's central chapter, "The Ponds." Here we see the romantic poet, as he reworked his material from the few simple descriptive paragraphs of his first draft (1846–1847), beginning also to become the natural historian and environmentalist.

In a previous chapter ("The Bean-Field"), Thoreau nostalgically remembers having been first taken to the pond at the age of four, "one of the oldest scenes stamped on my memory." In a pleasing self-indulgent fancy, the speaker goes on to muse that "even I have at length helped to clothe that fabulous landscape of my infant dreams"—referring ostensibly to his bean farming but presumably also to his book (*Wa* 155, 156). In "The Ponds," however, this reminiscence produces pain. "When I first paddled a boat on Walden, it was completely surrounded by thick and lofty pine and oak woods" (*Wa* 191). He lingers on this memory awhile. "But since I left those shores," he continues, "the woodchoppers have still further laid them waste, and now for many a year there will be no more rambling through the aisles of the woods, with occasional vistas through which you see the water. My Muse may be excused if she is silent henceforth. How can you expect the birds to sing when their groves are cut down?" (*Wa* 192). This is an arresting sequence for several reasons. First, obviously, because the outburst against woodchoppers abruptly halts the kind of nostalgic fantasy indulged just a little earlier. But it also piques our interest because of what it excludes. We are told that the choppers have *still further* laid waste the trees; yet no previous depredations have been mentioned. Perhaps the idyllic mood was so compelling that Thoreau could not bear to mention them, or (more likely, I suspect) Thoreau presumed that his nineteenth-century audience—which in the first instance he imagined as his inquisitive Concord neighbors—would take it for granted that the groves of youth had steadily been thinned. Such was indeed the case: the percentage of woodland in the town of Concord had steadily declined during Thoreau's lifetime, reaching an all-time low of little more than 10 percent almost at the moment Thoreau penned this sentence.[12]

Even more noteworthy, however, is the transience of the speaker's protest. It does proceed for another paragraph, chiefly devoted to complaints about the "devilish Iron Horse" that has "muddied the Boiling Spring with his foot." The speaker looks for a "champion" that will meet the engine "at the Deep Cut and thrust an avenging lance between the ribs of the bloated pest." But this pugnacity dissipates as the next paragraph assures us, "Nevertheless, of all the characters I have known, perhaps Walden wears best, and best preserves its purity." "Rather than directly engaging the realities it displaces," H. Daniel Peck observes, the Thoreauvian "Nevertheless" "deflects them, turns them aslant," smoothing "the temporarily ruffled surface of the pond."[13] A little later on, we are further reassured by the fancy that the railroad workers are somehow refreshed by Walden as the train whisks by: "the engineer does not forget at night, or his nature does not, that he has beheld this vision of serenity and purity once at least during the day" (*Wa* 192, 193). Thoreau has again transformed Walden back into a pristine sanctuary.[14]

This sequence dramatizes several important aspects of Thoreau's naturism. It shows that "thinking like a mountain" did not come any more naturally to him than it did to Aldo Leopold, in the famous essay of that title in which the father of modern environmental ethics confesses his slow awakening to awareness of the importance of predators to an ecosystem.[15] Thoreau seems first to have written *Walden* without mentioning the history of the abuses suffered by the Concord landscape,[16] though he was well aware of them. For example, the Concord and Fitchburg Railroad, laid along the west end of Walden Pond the year before Thoreau moved there, was a significant and highly visible cause of regional deforestation, for creating roadways and for fuel. Thoreau knew, furthermore, that forest conservation had already been advanced as a public concern. In the first section of the *Report on the Trees and Shrubs Growing Naturally in the Forests of Massachusetts* (1846), which Thoreau read soon after publication and consulted frequently thereafter, George B. Emerson had warned that "the axe has made, and is making, wanton and terrible havoc. The cunning foresight of the Yankee seems to desert him when he takes the axe in hand."[17] Yet even in the finished version of "The Ponds," produced amidst recurring *Journal* complaints about the philistine obtuseness of some of the clients for whom he worked as surveyor, Thoreau did not sound the preservationist note loudly. Why? Probably not because he feared readers would disapprove, but because the pastoralizing impulse to imagine Walden as an unspoiled place overrode his fears about its vulnerability to despoliation. One cannot argue simultaneously that sylvan utopia can be found within the town limits and that the locale is being devastated at an appalling rate; and the vision of a pristine nature close by appealed irresistibly to Thoreau for personal as well as rhetorical reasons. It was emotionally important to him to believe in Walden as a sanctuary, and it was all the easier for him to do so in the face of contrary evidence because of the myth of nature's inexhaustableness that mesmerized many of the astutest nineteenth-century minds. If Gerard Manley Hopkins, also a preservationist of sorts,[18] could declare near the end of the Victorian era that "nature is never spent" ("God's Grandeur"), how much easier for Thoreau, writing a generation earlier in a comparatively underdeveloped country, to relieve his chagrin at the local absence of the giant pines he saw being whisked by on railroad cars by thinking, "what a country we have got to back us up that way" (*J* 5: 299).

Even if Thoreau had stressed the issue of environmental degradation in *Walden,* he might not have opposed it primarily for nature's sake. In the passages we have reviewed, he laments the denuding of Walden mainly on grounds of personal taste, as a blow to "My Muse," as ruining the solace of the author's pondside rambles.

Yet the dominance of aesthetic considerations does not imply ethical anesthesia. As Leopold was later to observe in his essay "The Conservation Esthetic" (*SCA* 165–177), the cultivation of a noncomplacent bonding to nature at the aesthetic level is one of the paths to developing a mature environmental concern. So we should not minimize the potential impact of the challenge the speaker throws out at the chapter's end, when he declares of the ponds, "How much more beautiful than our lives, how much more transparent than our characters, are they! . . . Nature has no human inhabitant who appreciates her . . . She flourishes most alone, far from the towns where they reside. Talk of heaven! ye disgrace earth" (*Wa* 199–200). The language here teeters between the old-fashioned jeremiad's familiar call to moral purification and a more pointedly environmental protectionist eviction of fallen humanity from nature. Either way, Thoreau makes the spiritual renewal more closely dependent on nature appreciation than does Emerson, who would never have thought of calling Walden a "character." Finally, Thoreau's pleasing dramatization of the nurturing bond to nature, not only for the nostalgic speaker but even for the inattentive brakeman and engineer, is more likely to reinforce in attentive readers a sense of the rightness of an unsullied nature than to reinforce complacency in the railroad system as an unmixed good.[19]

Since Thoreau, when redrafting *Walden,* added much more to the second half of the book than to the first, it is not surprising that the sorts of alterations we have been considering reflect the changing ratio of homocentrism to ecocentrism as the book progresses. In "Economy," Walden figures chiefly as a good site for an enterprise. Nature is hardly yet present except as a theater for the speaker to exercise his cabin-craft in. Thoreau proceeds for fully one-ninth of the book before providing the merest glimpse of the pond. The section's message of simplification is certainly consistent with an "environmentalist" perspective, as it is for James Fenimore Cooper's Leatherstocking, but Thoreau does not as yet advocate it on this ground, as Natty Bumppo does from the very start of *The Pioneers* (1823). Not until "Higher Laws" does Thoreau restate his philosophy of abstemiousness as anything like an environmental ethic, questioning the killing and eating of animals and fish. This slow expansiveness of the sense of moral accountability toward nonhuman creatures is symptomatic. As *Walden* unfolds, the mock-serious discourse of enterprise, which implicitly casts the speaker as the self-creator of his environment, begins to give way to a more ruminative prose in which the speaker appears to be finding himself within his environment. The prose begins to turn significantly in this contemplative direction as it moves from the heroic classicism of "Reading," with its pedagogical didactics, to "Sounds," where the "language" of "all things and events" impresses itself on the speaker (111). The text seems at this point to discover, as Robert Pogue Harrison beautifully states, that "all that is to be learned about what is real and not real lies in the exteriority of our inner lives."[20] Thoreau's own language helps us put this directional movement of *Walden* in perspective. Earnest struggle partially gives way to receptivity, self-absorption to extrospection. Thoreau's favorite pronoun, "I," appears in the two opening chapters an average of 6.6 times per page; in the next six (through "The Village"), 5.5 times per page; in the next five ("The Ponds" through "House-Warming"—the last chapter in which the speaker modifies his environment, through plastering), 5.2; in the final five ("Former Inhabitants" through "Conclusion"), 3.6. Roughly inverse to these figures is his usage of the following cluster: "Walden," "pond(s)," and the various nominal and adjectival forms of "wild": once every 1.8 pages for the first two chapters, 1.1 times per page during the next six (through "Village"), 2.3 times per page during the rest of the book.[21]

These are crude indices. For a more complex understanding of Thoreau's revisionary processes, we must return to the microlevel and examine the use of a single telltale framing device. During the first pondside vignette in "Economy," the speaker devotes a sentence to remembering that "on the 1st of April it rained and melted the ice, and in the early part of the day, which was very foggy, I heard a stray goose groping about over the pond and cackling as if lost, or like the spirit of the fog" (*Wa* 42). An emblematic fowl, forsooth: suggesting both the spirit of nature and the uncertain spirit of the speaker, who has already chronicled his losses in symbolic form (hound, bay horse, turtle dove). The sentence uses the logic of correspondence delicately, evoking it but not depending on it for dogma—true to the uneasy tone of the image. In "Spring," to help draw the year into a symbolic circle Thoreau makes this image return: of "some solitary goose in the foggy mornings, seeking its companion, and still peopling the woods with the sound of a larger life than they could sustain" (*Wa* 313). This passage is actually the second of a two-part series of anecdotes, pursued through several paragraphs, the first of which begins: "I was startled by the *honking* of geese flying low over the woods, like weary travelers getting in late from southern lakes, and indulging at last in unrestrained complaint and mutual consolation. Standing at my door, I could hear the rush of their wings; when, driving toward my house, they suddenly spied my light, and with hushed clamor wheeled and settled in the pond. So I came in, and shut the door, and passed my first spring night in the woods" (*Wa* 312–313). Thoreau continues by describing the behavior of the "large and tumultuous" flock (he counts them: twenty-nine) as next morning they disport on the pond, then fly off toward Canada, "trusting to break their fast in muddier pools." Then, after brief mention of a duck flock, comes the solitary goose passage. This sequence is significant in several ways. First, it serves as a formal opening and closing device. Second, it confirms the move to a textured and extrospective rendering of the natural world, whose particularity is now so cogent that the exact number of the large flock must be reported. One wonders if Thoreau might have been trying to answer Emerson's challenge in "Literary Ethics" to "go into the forest" and describe the undescribed: "The honking of the wild geese flying by night; the thin note of the companionable titmouse, in the winter day; the fall of swarms of flies, in autumn, from combats high in the air . . . the turpentine exuding from the tree;—and indeed any vegetation, any animation, any and all, are alike unattempted."[22] Third, it suggests a recognition of the delicacy of the complementary project to which *Walden* is committed: to turn nature to human uses, as a barometer of and stimulus to the speaker's spiritual development. True, the geese are personified; they seem to participate in a logic of natural symbols: geese returning equals spring, which equals (we soon find, unsurprisingly) spiritual renewal. Yet their materiality is more immediately significant than their symbolism; when they arrive, the speaker goes indoors so as not to scare them. Though they seem to be projections of human desire ("peopling the woods with the sound of a larger life than they could sustain"), the difference between their realm and his is underscored. He provides no quick emblematic fix as he did in "Economy" ("like the spirit of the fog"). The correspondential framework remains implicit, but it is complicated by the facticity of the waterfowl and the speaker's respect for their interests. This respect is what begins to modulate Thoreau's romantic enthusiasm toward something like environmental awareness in the modern sense.

But the passage complicates the case I have been building for the correlation between *Walden*'s unfolding and the biographical unfolding of Thoreau's own environmental consciousness. For these developments are neither quite linear nor coextensive. It happens, for example, that the earliest surviving *Journal* entry that Thoreau used in Walden (from March of 1840, five years before the experience itself and still another comment on wild geese, by the way) was not inserted into the text until the *final* extant manuscript version (1853) (*PJ* 1: 119). Both of the geese anecdotes just discussed come from the time of the original Walden experience (*PJ* 2: 214, 192–193), and the language used in *Walden* closely matches the original *Journal* language. Nevertheless, although both anecdotes appear as early as the book's first draft (1846–1847), it was not until the latest extant manuscript versions that the material became fully elaborated. In version E (1852–1853), Thoreau first devised the sentence about shutting his door and passing his first spring night in the woods; and not until version F (1853) did he repeat the stray goose image in "Spring"—before that, it appeared only in "Economy"—in phrasing much less faithful to the *Journal* record than the late addition to "Spring."[23] In his revision, furthermore, Thoreau used the stray goose image at the head of a descriptive paragraph drawing on his increasingly extensive seasonal observations, begun in 1850, listing sundry other spring signs like pigeons, martins, frogs, tortoises. These details strengthen the naturalistic dimension of the image. So Thoreau revised to accentuate both schematic design (the circle of the year, the goose as a motif) and naturalistic detail more scrupulously respectful of nature's otherness and more "realistic" from the standpoint of the documentary record; and this revision entailed not simply drawing on the more mature findings of the post-Walden years, when Thoreau became increasingly the practicing naturalist, but also drawing on the writings of his "transcendentalist" period.

So Thoreau's biography, the composition sequence, and the "plot" of the published book do not correlate neatly. He began and ended his career fascinated by the vision of the natural realm as symbolically significant of the human estate. He could not get past the Emersonian axiom that "nature must be viewed humanly to be viewed at all" (*J* 4: 163). No matter how devoted a naturalist he became, he continued to need to organize his observations into aesthetic patterns. This need at times whetted his appetite for natural history (as when he hypothesized about the succession of forest trees, generalizing from some of his observations about the dispersion of seeds) and at other times reinforced him in the role of poet-mystic, seeking to find symbolic configurations within landscape, like the elaborate conceit about the moral significance of the intersection of lines of greatest length, breadth, and depth that he half-playfully, half-solemnly infers from his survey of Walden Pond.[24] In the revision of *Walden*, therefore, Thoreau sometimes moved backward from his later naturalist stage to his earlier (but still present) poet stage, as when he takes his initial (1846–1847) straightforward vignette of observing a striped snake arising from its torpid state and turns it into a symbol of regeneration in version C.[25] Generalizing in the aggregate, we can see in Thoreau's revisions an irregular movement toward discovery, retrieval, and respect for the realm of physical nature whose substantial reality must be honored in the face of any desire to appropriate it for didactic or aesthetic uses. Furthermore, Thoreau's aesthetic and mystical bents, as we shall soon see in more detail, in the long run furthered this process more than they impeded it.

To read *Walden* in sequence, bearing in mind the various stages of the manuscript, is to follow this movement through to a certain point in Thoreau's evolution, but not to the end. *Walden* does not contain Thoreau's most self-consciously environmentalist statements,[26] nor his most close-grained nature observations; and its most detailed passages of observation (the description of the ponds and the melting sandbank in "Spring," for instance) are allegorized more aggressively than is typical of Thoreau's later *Journal*. Partly on this account, Sharon Cameron asks us to think of *Walden* as a product got up for public consumption that seriously compromised, if it did not positively betray, Thoreau's deeper quest to fathom nature and his relation to it.[27] That to my mind is to carry a good point (about the *Journal*'s intellectual integrity and high seriousness) too far in the right direction and to understate the degree to which the same partial and ragged exploratory questing Cameron ascribes to the *Journal* can be observed at every level of Thoreau's achievement: his life; his journal; the genres in which he wrote for publication; the composition of *Walden,* *The Maine Woods,* and *Cape Cod;* and the sequential development of all his books. Respecting *Walden* particularly, I believe that its very "failures" enhance its representativeness both as a document of the environmental imagination and as a microcosm of Thoreau's achievement, for he was never able to get beyond an inchoate, fragmentary sketch of his grand effort to comprehend the Concord environment in its multidimensional totality.

Thoreau's biographers have carefully described his deepening commitment to the study of natural history during the 1840s and 1850s: his program of reading, his regime of fieldwork, his scientific knowledge. Textual scholarship has reconstructed to a reasonably complete degree the different stages of *Walden's* composition. I do not intend to repeat those findings here; rather I will draw selectively on them in the interest of an analytic account of Thoreau's developing environmental imagination that will double as a first attempt to map the typical emphases and lacunae of Thoreauvian writing generally.

Walden reflects Thoreau's commitment to not one but a cluster of distinct approaches to nature, none of which was wholly original or unique to him and thus all of which may be found widely pursued throughout American environmental prose, though reinforced by his example.[28] Some of these environmental projects were part of Thoreau's original intentions for the text, indeed of the experiment on which he based the text; some emerged later, between the two major bursts of compositional activity: 1846–1847 and 1852–1853. To understand fully what nature meant to Thoreau, we need to examine each of these projects with the understanding that we shall arrive at an overall picture that is somewhat blurry, shifting, and pluriform, not tidily coherent or reducible to one or two sweeping statements.

Thoreau's Projects

Thoreau began his literary career as a pastoralist of a more strictly traditional sort than many fellow writers of his day. One of his earliest dreams was the project of recovering for a time the feel of a pristine simplicity such as he associated with pre-Columbian America or—more typically—ancient Greece, in his schoolbook version of the Greeks as the symbol of the morning of the human race. (He reminded himself in 1840 that "the Greeks were boys in the sunshine . . .—the Romans were men in the field—the Persians women in the house—the Egyptians old men in the dark" [*PJ* 1: 154]). Walden, both the experience and the book, was a pastoral return in two symbolic senses as well as the literal: a psychocultural return, in the spirit of romantic sentimentalism defined by Schiller, to the Homeric world;[29] and a psychobiographical return, driven by Wordsworthian reminiscences of former times spent fully within nature, glimpses of which Thoreau allows us in the boyhood boating memories noted earlier. This nostalgia for youth later became intensified by nostalgia for life at Walden, kept alive by hundreds of additional visits, in body and in recollection, that Thoreau made to the site and memory of the experiment. So the parable from 1846–1847 of the author's long-lost hound, turtledove, and bay horse (*Wa* 17) came to apply as much to the Walden experience itself as to the past before the experience.[30] There is an exact—though buried—parallel between the vague sadness of that passage in "Economy" and the passage in "Conclusion" (added in 1853) that asserts, "I left the woods for as good a reason as I went there" (*Wa* 323), which in the 1852 *Journal* version reads "I left it as unaccountably as I went to it" (*J* 3: 216).

Pastoralism, as we have seen, may lead as easily to a factitious as to a factical ruralism, perhaps especially in postcolonials. Earlier I noted the irony that in the first *Journal* entries Walden Thoreau enthuses about his new environment by dwelling on the romantic elsewhere it reminds him of: "some mountain houses I have seen," which seemed bathed in "the very light & atmosphere in which the works of Grecian art were composed" (*PJ* 2: 155). Thoreau was well aware of the reductions of pastoral art ("the pasture as seen from the hall window" [*PJ* 1: 488]), but he was not above yielding to their blandishments, especially during that first excited summer.

One sign of Thoreau's yielding that also presaged (and, through his influence, helped to shape) the whole course of American literary naturism was the opening of a split between pastoral and agrarian sensibility in his work not present in early American literary naturism. Crèvecoeur and the Virginia planters domesticated the pastoral ideal in an agrarian context,[31] as did Jefferson's Yankee Federalist counterpart Timothy Dwight. Thoreau, however, generally satirized farming as part and parcel of the soul-withering false economy of the work ethic against which he set his own ethos of contemplative play, which approached crop growing in a willfully fanciful manner: "Shall I not rejoice also at the abundance of the weeds whose seeds are the granary of the birds?" (*Wa* 166). His favorite metaphor for necessary labor was the myth of Apollo tending the flocks of King Admetus (*Wa* 70; cf. *J* 4: 114)—a way of pastoralizing but spurning pasture duty at a single stroke. (It became one of his code phrases for days spent surveying [*J* 6: 185].) Thoreau's desire to imagine an actualization of the pastoral ideal more as leisure than as work drove him more often to picture the countryman as a Colin Clout than as a Lycidas. Nothing was easier for Milton than to imagine flock tending as a delightful pursuit precisely because, as Samuel Johnson remarked, he had no flocks to batten. Shepherding was a vicarious activity not expected of him in real life. Thoreau, by contrast, felt surrounded by townspeople who could not understand why he failed to tend his own flocks—that is, get ahead in some trade. To them, writing and botanizing seemed rarefied pursuits of no practical value. The prominence of stolid agriculturalists among the establishment in Thoreau's district provoked him into a mode of pastoralism condescending to actual farmers. This attitude eventually dominated the American literary naturist mainstream, with such partial exceptions as Robert Frost (in poems like "Tuft of Flowers" but less so in the satirical "Mending Wall" and not at all in the dreamy "After Apple-Picking") and with such few clear exceptions as Wendell Berry. In the tradition of Thoreau's unwillingness to write about social life at Walden, American literary naturists in general underrepresent community. The segmentation of "nature" from "civilization," "country" from "town," already endemic to pastoral becomes even more accentuated.[32]

Also conducive to schematic yet wholeheartedly ruralist vision was Thoreau's second project, the religiocentric inquest into the correspondence between the natural and the spiritual, derived from Emerson, on which I have already commented. Its logic helped undergird Thoreau's romantic Hellenism; it helped him see more than just fancifulness in the proposition that "morning brings back the heroic ages" (*Wa* 88); and that depth in turn opened up the possibility of converting "the faint hum of the mosquito, making its invisible and unimaginable tour" through the dawn into a symbolic "trumpet that recalled what I had read of most ancient history and heroic ages."[33] Thoreau's most extravagant exercise in the metaphysics of correspondence—the ethical significance of the pond's dimensions—was probably well worked out by the first draft of *Walden*.[34] In this series of examples—morning, mosquito, pond survey— we can see how a vision of correspondence has the potential to lead its devotee to a more textured perception of environmental detail, although this perception remains modulated by the deductive logic brought to it and was hardly an inevitable result. Swedenborg's writing is proof positive that an allegorical vision of nature does not necessarily induce naturism. But on a person attracted to nature to start with, it could have a catalytic effect. Without question, Thoreau's environmental perception remained energized throughout his life by a sense of natural piety, however secular his field notes became. In this sense, his mental makeup recalls the convergence of scientific curiosity and typological commitment in the thought of Jonathan Edwards.[35]

 A third Thoreauvian project involving a partially fortuitous conver- gence of piety and nature, but also at cross-purposes with the first two, was his pursuit of frugality. In principle, any habitat might do for this pursuit since its practical success depended on economic and moral self-regulation. In practice, Christian, classical, and romantic precedent all dictated a rural setting for such an experiment and a preindustrial mode of production. Hence Thoreau's sermon on economy and his droll critique in "The Bean-Field" of the contemporary movement to mecha- nize and intensify agriculture. Though he was more interested in the harvest of the spirit than in the hard-earned wisdom he mock-seriously imparted about how to grow beans, Walden—both the experience and the book—was also in one sense an agrarian experiment; and one may, without overstatement, describe Thoreau as "an articulate champion of the preservation of the values of subsistence farming."[36] For Thoreau's allegiances, when it came to choosing between options, were all against upscale commercialized farming and on the side of what is now called sustainable agriculture: a small-scale style of husbandry that produced for needs rather than gain and that observed the rhythms he found in the Roman agriculturalists whose works he read with increasing serious- ness in the latter stages of Walden's composition, for example Cato's *De Re Rustica* ("my 'Cultivator'" [Wa 84]).[37] Turning from that book to contemporary Concord, Thoreau was pleased to imagine that "the farmer's was pretty much the same routine then as now" and that "Cato but repeated the maxims of a remote antiquity" (*PJ* 4: 31). These lines exhibit Thoreau's wishful thinking, as he himself knew (see *J* 6: 108, for instance), but they illustrate his need to resupply a georgic dimension to his pastoral and ascetic commitments, notwithstanding the satirical barbs on farmers and farming he threw out in more poetical moods. Throughout his *Journal* Thoreau scattered unobtrusive references to the rhythms of the agricultural year—planting, manuring, haying—that reveal an attentiveness which contrasts with his slighting remarks about farmers, also liberally sprinkled throughout. These bucolic data are an important index of just how far Thoreau eventually moved from his earlier status as the pencil manufacturer's college-educated son.

This growth of interest in things agricultural, ironically, did not in itself set Thoreau apart from the Brahmin elite. On the contrary, it was faddish among affluent nineteenth-century Bostonians to take an active interest in farming methods. Thoreau hoeing his beans in ways contrary to ancient wisdom ("Beans so late!"[*Wa* 157]) was in some ways a writ-small version of contemporary merchant princes seeking to combine the roles of patriotic progressive agrarian and British country squire. But Thoreau's brand of reform opposed their attempt to play sponsor to new agricultural efficiencies in ways that only the wealthy could afford.[38]

A fourth project, Thoreau's interest in natural history, also came to maturity during the years of composing *Walden* rather than during the experiment itself. Over the last dozen years of his life, Thoreau made himself into an amateur field biologist of considerable skill: in botany especially, but also in zoology, ornithology, entomology, and ichthyology.[39] The most elaborate of his several aspirations in this line was the plan of devising a comprehensive account of the unfolding of the seasons as physical *and* mental events.[40] The first version of *Walden* does not deal with seasonal change as such until about the last tenth of the manuscript. Although Thoreau insisted in the first draft, "I am on the alert for the first signs of spring,"[41] he did not begin a detailed recording of seasonal flora and fauna until 1851, reaching a plateau of minute sophistication in 1852 ("my year of observation" [*J* 4: 174]), when he made an extraordinarily careful effort to chart seasonal changes through mid-May (*J* 4: 65). By the summer of 1851, he had begun thinking seriously of this log as a major literary venture: "A Book of the seasons—each page of which should be written in its own season & out of doors or in its own locality wherever it may be" (*PJ* 3: 253). About this same time, Thoreau became irrepressibly eager to identify first appearances of this flower or that bird, to discover foretastes or afterthoughts of one season in another, to identify microseasons—the season of leafing, the season of fogs, the season of fires—and indeed to think of each day as its own possible seasonal sign. The final version of *Walden* reflects Thoreau's growing phenological interest in the seasonal chronicle of its last major section ("House-Warming" through "Spring").

Thoreau's phenological investigations moved his thought toward the kind of inquiry Ernst Haeckel in 1866 first termed "ecology."[42] By late in his life, Thoreau's studies of plant succession and seed dispersal show the increasing scientific precision with which Thoreau pursued his holistic ecological vision.[43] What especially motivated him, however, was not the desire for empirical knowledge alone but also the desire for unifying patterns. The legacy of the Emersonian correspondence project continued to affect Thoreau's work even as he became increasingly committed to the scientific study of nature. At all stages of his life, Thoreau had an overriding penchant for conceiving of nature, as H. Daniel Peck puts it, in terms of "frameworks of cognition" that appealed to him for their aesthetic or ideational power as much as for their empirical and episte-mological solidity. Peck cites Thoreau's preference for essentializing sea-sonal data into phenomenological designs ("What 'makes' November is not its placement in the year's chronology, but its interrelated properties") and his interest in seeing the visual elements of the Concord environment as coherent arrangements, which Peck rightly says places Thoreau in the company of landscape theorists like Gilpin and Ruskin, despite his com-plaints about their bookishness.[44]

⑤ This interest in landscape aesthetics was a project in itself. Limited though Thoreau's formal knowledge of fine art was, throughout his adult life he liked to see land as landscape, as scene: to relish the elements of composition, self-containment, light, color, texture. It would be instruc-tive to tally up the number of hilltop meditations in Thoreau's *Journal*, many of which read like eighteenth-century locodescriptive prospect pieces. Thoreau was quite aware of the artificiality of the pleasure he experienced on such occasions, as when he remarks (in 1850) on the

I wonder if/when he read S. Cooper

"cheap but pleasant effect" of walking over the hills "ever and anon looking through a gap in the wood, as through the frame of a picture, to a more distant wood or hill side, painted with several more coats of air" (*PJ* 3: 105). Indeed, it became a kind of game with him to subject mundane objects to aesthetic transformation by using distance and perspective to defamiliarize and then order them. Filtering his perceptions through the slow dawn following a nighttime walk (one of dozens reported in the journal), Thoreau experiences "the sound of the [railroad] cars" as "that of a rushing wind" and hears "some far off factory bell" as a "matin bell, sweet & inspiring as if it summoned holy men & maids to worship" (*PJ* 4: 65). At first glance, these descriptions sound like classic machine-in-the-garden defensive reactions; but the entry registers no discomfort whatsoever about the baleful effects of industrialization, only a desire to make the ordinary seem poetic. Looked at in this way, Thoreau appears to be an epicure of natural processes who sees it as his business to tease out nature's theatricality and extravagance to the fullest possible extent.[45]

The five Thoreavian environmental projects I have somewhat artificially isolated so far each required Thoreau to approach nature through a certain kind of schematic, classifying lens, but they also had the effect of thrusting him toward a more particularized immersion. As he worked on and beyond *Walden,* what changed was not so much his commitment to ordering the environment as the precision of his apparatus for doing so, so as to make his schemas more environmentally sensitive. In the years between the first draft of *Walden* and the last, Thoreau greatly refined his perceptions, or at least his record, of environmental stimuli: his perception of the *variety* of apple blossom odors (*PJ* 3: 81), his sense of the texture of "the ripple marks on the sandy bottom of Flints Pond" (88), his sense of the likeness between "the quivering of pigeons' wings" and "the tough fibre of the air which they rend" (369).

A particularly striking case of this calibrated perception was Thoreau's sensitivity to microenvironments: niches within his township that assumed an integral character as he revisited and contemplated them.[46] "Certain localities only a few rods square in the fields & on the hills," he observed in 1851, "attract me—as if they had been the scene of pleasure in another state of existence" (*PJ* 3: 331). One such place was Saw Mill Brook, which he came to think of (in November 1851) as "peculiar among our brooks as a mountain brook . . . It was quite a discovery when I first came upon this brawling mountain stream in Concord woods" (*PJ* 4: 161, 162). He found another sanctuary in Miles' Swamp. "Here is a place, at last, which no woodchopper nor farmer frequents and to which no cows stray, perfectly wild, where the bittern and the hawk are undisturbed"(*J* 4: 281). In the summer of 1853, Thoreau undertook to name the various microenvironments of the "great wild tract" he had he decided to call the Easterbrooks Country north of Concord village and produced a roster of fifteen "places": the Boulder Field, the Yellow Birch Swamp, the Black Birch Hill, and so on (*J* 5: 239). The later versions of *Walden* reflect this microscopic discovery and invention process recorded in the journal. Here is an example of such transference (from the entry for 5 January 1850):

> Discovered a small grove of beeches to day—between Walden & Flints Ponds—standing by a little run which—at length makes its way through Jacob Baker's meadow and a deep broad ditch which he has dug—& emptied in to the River—A tree which has almost disappeared from Conc [*sic*] woods, though once plenty
>
> It is worth the while to go some mile only to see a single beech tree. So fine a bole it has so perfect in all its details
>
> —So fair & smoth its bark—as if painted with a brush—and fringed with lichens I could stand an hour and look at one.   (*PJ* 3: 43)

This entry inspired two passages in *Walden* that mention visits to particular groves or trees. The second and more famous one pictures the speaker "frequently" tramping "eight or ten miles through the deepest snow to keep an appointment with a beech-tree, or a yellow-birch, or an old acquaintance among the pines" (*Wa* 265). The first, part of the exordium to "Baker Farm," praises in a more documentary fashion the virtues of the beech, "which has so neat a bole and beautifully lichen-painted, perfect in all its details, of which, excepting scattered specimens, I know but one small grove of sizeable trees left in the township" (201). The playful extravagance of the one and the aesthetic fastidiousness of the other both arise out of the program of minute scrutiny to which Thoreau increasingly committed himself during these years. The culmination in *Walden* is the long sandbank passage in "Spring," wherein Thoreau detects "all the operations of Nature" at work (*Wa* 308) and constructs from this a playful-grandiose Goethian allegory of life as metamorphosis.[47] This passage, the height of Thoreauvian fancifulness in

Walden, contains some of the most rigorously empirical synthesizing observation culled from dozens of visits to the railroad embankment at the west end of the pond. In Thoreau's comparatively detranscendental-ized later work, the extravagance of his metaphysical leaps gets toned down, but the Blakean desire to transfuse minute particulars with cosmic significance stayed with him all his life.

I have not tried to make an *exhaustive* inventory of Thoreau's range of motives and analytical equipment in approaching nature. A complete survey could take an entire book—and has;[48] and even at that, there is bound to be endless dispute over the priority of one motive or another. Enough has been said to make a couple of complicated fundamental points very clear. First, multiple, shifting, and at times conflicting motives thrust Thoreau toward nature. The growing empiricism of his natural history project, for instance, was partially at odds with his "pastoral" and "correspondence" projects but also in some respects stimulated and even regulated by these more long-standing and more poetic interests. Second, the patchwork of convergent and dissonant motives just described, inter-acting with another dimension of his thought I shall get to in a moment, produced both a certain astigmatism and a wondrous acuity of environ-mental vision. One of *Walden*'s more frustrating charms is that it so easily loses the reader in the landscape of the text. Thoreau deliberately presents the Concord environment from the margin. He tells us more than we want to know about some of his favorite spots but leaves us with a fragmentary impression of the surroundings compared to what one would find in a more conventional report of traveling in Concord, such as Timothy Dwight's.[49] Though *Walden* supplies one or two sketchy panoramas of Thoreau's neighborhood, for the most part we cannot tell where anything is located in relation to anything else. Where is the bean field in relation to the pond? Where are the various ponds in relation to each other? Are the cellar holes of the "former inhabitants" scattered throughout the woods or clustered together? Where is Concord's single grove of "sizeable" beeches to be found? Just how sequestered from the public roads was Thoreau's cabin? All that the noninitiate can bring into focus if it occurs to him or her to think about such matters is that Thoreau lived a mile from any neighbor and a mile or so from town on the wooded shore of the pond. Small wonder it took the better part of a century to locate the site of his hut.[50]

Thoreau's eccentricity as a guide to his environment reflects partly his continuing commitment to a subjectified, aestheticized vision and partly his habit as a naturalist of organizing the environment in terms of its points of nonhuman interest instead of in terms of the directions and markers that most human beings depend on. This idiosyncrasy in turn points to the final environmental project I shall try to identify here, a project that might loosely be called political. I mean to suggest an interest in provoking social reflection and change rather than in the political process as such. This dimension of Thoreau's sensibility is notoriously hard to pin down, for Thoreau turned toward nature as both an accommodation of and a dissent from nineteenth-century norms. Insofar as *Walden* caters to armchair fantasies of returning to nature, it cannot be said to do anything more than pretend to challenge the status quo. But insofar as Thoreau must be read as seriously proposing the conversion of such fantasies into an actual lifestyle, *Walden* appears almost violently anticonventional. From one standpoint, Thoreau stands accused of retreating into privatism, into quietism, after an initial sermon that appears to attack the forces of capitalism and consumerism head-on. From another standpoint, however, that retreat is wholly consistent with his initial thrust: Thoreau seems to have assumed at some rather early point that readers (as opposed to the general public) will stay with him and complete the process of conversion to which they were already somewhat disposed by immersing themselves so completely in the life according to nature that they will refuse to reenter civilized life again on the same terms as before.[51] Thoreau's refusal to organize the Walden landscape tidily for his readers may be one sign of his intent to get us lost in it.[52]

Thoreau's politics of nature was further complicated by his deepening commitment to nature's interest over the human interest. His frequent insistence that he preferred the companionship of trees and animals was undoubtedly sincere, even if not the whole story. As he quickened his search for secluded pockets of wildness that he could savor as unappreciated, unfrequented jewels of the Concord region, it was a short step, in principle, to a self-conscious politics of environmentalism: a defense of nature against the human invader. But this step did not come as readily to Thoreau as a late twentieth-century reader, living in the post–Rachel Carson age of environmental apocalypse, might expect of so environmentally sensitive a person. As we have seen, Thoreau had preservationist leanings before he wrote *Walden;* but his most forthright statements came near the end of his life and were never published. Even at that, he was nowhere near writing the kind of extended treatise on environmental degradation that Vermont polymath George Perkins Marsh achieved with *Man and Nature* (1864), Anglo-America's first serious work of environmental history and the first major conservationist manifesto.[53] Thoreau would have seconded Marsh's indictment of society's degradation of nature, though he would have disputed Marsh's contention that the remedy for human engineering's errors was better human engineering. But the magnum opus Thoreau contemplated at the time Marsh was at work on his was an ecological *summa*, not a book of public policy. As we see from "The Succession of Forest Trees," the only piece published during Thoreau's lifetime, this work would have reproached the public more for failures of observation than for crimes against the land.[54] The circumstances of that lecture-essay's delivery dramatize Thoreau's political ambivalence: addressed nominally to farmers attending the annual county fair or "cattle show," it also announced to the broader scientific community the discovery of the principle of forest succession, which is Thoreau's main claim to fame as a pioneer of ecological science.[55] Thoreau speaks, as always, in a somewhat oppositional voice, as one who knows he's considered a crank and is proud of it, as one looking down on his audience from the height of superior wisdom about seed dispersion ("surely, men love darkness rather than light");[56] but the underlying aim of the address is less to disorder the status quo than to strengthen it, and by implication prove the author's value to society, by contributing useful new information to farmers and naturalists. Thoreau chides his audience on its ignorance of natural systems but does not advocate the radical reorganization of town property into parklands that he broaches in the peroration of the unpublished "Huckleberries," which calls for the sequestration of large riparian and woodland areas in every township.[57] These protoecological and protoenvironmentalist aspects of Thoreau's thought were symbiotic, but the first matured before the second, which was still in a relatively early state of formation by the time Thoreau died.[58]

That was predictable. Thoreau felt society's threat to him more keenly than he felt humankind's threat to nature, so it was not surprising that the process of first immersing himself in and then studying nature was more absorbing to him than the cause of defending the environment against its human attackers. Indeed, one could go still further and assert that Thoreau's ability to package nature usefully (as in "Forest Trees") or in an aesthetically pleasing way (as in "Autumnal Tints") served him as a more stable bridge between himself and elements of the larger society (local agriculturalists, urban and suburban readers) than he could sustain either in life or through his more explicitly political discourses. Even in the comparatively progressive Northeast, natural history topics were more widely palatable lyceum fare than abolitionist discourses.[59]

So Thoreau was not John Muir. Yet Thoreau leads to Muir; indeed, Thoreau became one of Muir's heroes. For both, a deeply personal love and reverence for the nonhuman led in time to a fiercely protective feeling for nature, which later generations have rightly seized on as a basis for a more enlightened environmental ethic and polity than the prevailing dispensation built on the view of American nature as an endlessly exploitable resource. For both Thoreau and Muir, aesthetics was continuous with environmentalism. Consider these quotations from the "Chesuncook" chapter of *The Maine Woods,* on which Thoreau was probably working at about the same time he put the finishing touches on *Walden.* First, from a central section:

> Is it the lumberman then who is the friend and lover of the pine— stands nearest to it and understands its nature best? . . . No! no! it is the poet; he it is who makes the truest use of the pine—who does not fondle it with an axe, nor tickle it with a saw.[60]

Then, from his final glimpse of the pine forests, the most forthright preservationist statement Thoreau ever published:

> Not only for strength, but for beauty, the poet must, from time to time, travel the logger's path and the Indian's trail, to drink at some new and more bracing fountain of the Muses, far in the recesses of the wilderness.
>
> The kings of England formerly had their forests "to hold the king's game," for sport or food, sometimes destroying villages to create or extend them; and I think that they were impelled by a true instinct. Why should not we, who have renounced the king's authority, have our national preserves, where no villages need be destroyed.[61]

From these passages it is easy to see why *The Maine Woods* was the book that first drew Muir to Thoreau and why Muir marked these passages in his own copy.[62] The progression is clear: from aesthetic pleasure and spiritual commitment to a politics of preservationism. This politics is also wary: Thoreau is careful to disassociate his "program" from the social evils of land sequestration under monarchy and to guard against the kind of abuse that we now call environmental racism.[63]

The Projects Reconciled

Appearances of self-contradiction notwithstanding, the development of Thoreau's thinking about nature seems pretty clearly to move along a path from homocentrism toward biocentrism. Nature was initially more a pastime for him, a place of recreational resort. Increasingly it became the environment in which he felt most comfortable. Then it became an occupation (or rather occupations, first literary and then botanical)[64] and finally a cause. Though at times his different levels of interest in nature came into conflict, the poetic with the scientific for instance, Thoreau rarely or never seems to have considered himself as conflicted about nature or his own relation to nature as he was about society and his relation to it. More specifically, Thoreau presents a clear case—as does John Muir—of pastoral aesthetics and romanticist natural piety interacting with empirical study and scientific interests (despite any tensions between them) to produce what we should now call an environmentalist commitment. For the purposes of this study it is especially important to appreciate how Thoreau's religioaestheticism contributed not merely a subjective impetus to this process of unfolding but also a more specific conceptual and stylistic apparatus for making this subjective bent shareable and contagious. We have seen that Thoreau came to practice a kind of "wilding therapy" as a method for keeping himself as defamiliarized as possible during what might otherwise have become boringly routine activities, imagining "the smallest brook with as much interest for the time being as if it were the Orinoco or Mississippi" (PJ 3: 140), walking at night in order to make him feel like the first or last man (PJ 4: 63 and following). Thoreau took common pastoral mystifications, like the transformation of remnant patches of well-trodden woodlots into green glades, and subjected them to such refinement and intensification as to reinforce within himself and transmit to his reader a will to transform the tame back into the wild and to preserve such wildness as presently exists.

As we ponder Thoreau's example on the eve of the sesquicentennial of his Walden experience, it is consoling to be able to say, as Auden did of Yeats, "You were silly like us." You were groping toward an ecological vision you never grasped; your environmentalism was fitful, your biocentrism half-baked. Fine. We mustn't succumb to mindless hero-worship. That would be unjust to the complexity that ought to increase one's interest in cultural heroes, not lessen it. But neither is it productive to "demystify" Thoreau and leave it at that. The onus of fitfulness and inconsistency lie more heavily on us. "After such knowledge, what forgiveness?" asks T. S. Eliot's Gerontion, who might have been talking about environmental knowledge.[65] We know much more than Thoreau did about how humans mispossess the environment but do less with what we know. If everyone lived like him, had the degree of environmental sensitivity at which he arrived, there would be no environmental problem. We should doubtless have other problems, but not that one. Even at this late date, most of us have immense difficulty holding consistently in mind how serious pollution, overpopulation, resource depletion, and species eradication have become, how rapidly these dangers increase, and how complicit we are in aggravating them. That Thoreau was already more aware of such problems than many of us speaks well for him, badly for us.

In this light, Thoreau's ragged progress through his various nature projects looks admirable, our quibbling shameful; and his lifework offers itself as a resource or laboratory in which we can study what is fruitful as well as risky about double-edged tools: tools like pastoral and correspondence and phenology and landscape aesthetics, which can in some contexts (even for Thoreau) become apparatus for exploiting nature, but in other contexts act as transforming agents to quicken or produce an environmentalist commitment.

Forms of Literary
Ecocentrism

CHAPTER FIVE

The Aesthetics of Relinquishment

> To cease from dominant-inspired relationships would be as violent a social and familial change as the attempt to refrain from sexual congress was at the turn of the first century A.D.; yet once a moral ideal has been proposed—and believed—it creates its own reality, its own validity.
>
> —Anna Bramwell, *Ecology in the Twentieth Century*

> The unit of survival is an organism-in-its-environment. If the environment fails to survive, so does the individual.
>
> —Freya Mathews, *The Ecological Self*

PART I BEGAN to give a sense of the capacity of environmental texts to model ecocentric thinking. We now need to identify more specific ways in which environmental texts act as carriers or agents of ecocentricity. That is the purpose of Part II: to discuss a series of imaginative structures in terms of which responsiveness to the natural environment has been cogently expressed in western and more especially in American writing. These chapters speak both to environmental literature's arrangement of the "human" and its arrangement of the "world." The first two chapters address the sense of personal presence in environmental texts, first as regards human subjects, then as regards the nonhuman. In a paradox that will seem comprehensible enough as I develop it, ecocentric literary vision may express itself both as a critique of the centrality and even the legitimacy of human assertion (Chapter 5) and as an ascription of something like human subjectiveness to the nonhuman world (Chapter 6). The next three chapters explicate some of the principal ways in which creative writers have perceived nature's structure and motion and reflect on why these particular figurations—season, place, catastrophe—have been so compelling.

This agenda is perforce selective. No fact about environmental writing is more fundamental than its pluriform nature. Many chapters could have been added: for example, a discussion of particular nonhuman subjects favored by creative writers—wolves, waterfalls, rivers, deserts, trees, mountains; an essay on travel narrative, on fictions of imaginary worlds, on hunting narratives, on the rhetoric of certain scientific writing, on the relation of text to visual illustration in environmental books, on prayers and hymns to the earth. Undoubtedly some of the most promising forms that ecocentricity can assume have not even occurred to me. The more these possibilities multiplied, however, the more clear it seemed that a comprehensive mapping, were that even feasible, would not be more helpful than some case studies dramatizing two fundamental points. First, most "modern" forms of environmental consciousness have ancient roots but, second, putting literature under the sign of the natural environment requires some major readjustments in the way serious late twentieth-century readers of literature are taught to read.

In this chapter I reflect on two forms of relinquishment that have fascinated American environmental writers. The more familiar is relinquishment of goods, of material trophies. Faulkner's Ike McCaslin lays down gun, compass, and watch in order to find Old Ben; later he tries to extricate himself from the curse his tribe has cast on the land by forgoing his inheritance. The more radical relinquishment is to give up individual autonomy itself, to forgo the illusion of mental and even bodily apartness from one's environment. This prospect can be pleasurable, like the burst of pantheistic exuberance of Emerson's "Bacchus" as the speaker imagines himself floating "at pleasure through all natures,"[1] but it can also be unsettling: the degree zero existence of Wallace Stevens's snow man; the orphean dismemberment into which the speaker of Whitman's "Song of Myself" feels betrayed by the sense of touch; or the uneasiness of Wendell Berry, as he begins to give himself over to farming, "afraid / one day my poems may pass / through my mind unwritten, / like the freshenings of a stream / in the hills."[2]

The first relinquishment supplies perhaps the commonest plot scenario in environmental writing. The second implies the dissolution of plot and calls into question the authority of the superintending consciousness. As such, it opens up the prospect of a thoroughgoing perceptual break-through, suggesting the possibility of a more ecocentric state of being than most of us have dreamed of. For "ecology does not know an encapsulated ego over against his or her environment," as ecophilosopher Holmes Rolston III has said.[3] But what sort of literature remains possible if we relinquish the myth of human apartness? It must be a literature that abandons, or at least questions, what would seem to be literature's most basic foci: character, persona, narrative consciousness. What literature can survive under these conditions?

Epics of Voluntary Simplicity

The best-known feature of *Walden* is that Thoreau built a cabin in the woods and dwelt there as an economic and spiritual experiment, which he presents as more deeply satisfying than the encumbered lives of his neighbors and readers. The summation and defense of this alternative life dominated the first draft of *Walden* and to a lesser extent the final text as well, "Economy" remaining by far the longest section. Reduced material wants, rustic habitation, self-sufficiency at every level, the cultivation of self-improvement through a disciplined life led largely in solitude—these were the ingredients. This formation has become a prototype, more so than Thoreau himself may have intended. As one disconcerted recent advocate remarks, "it is difficult to dispel the romantic image of Thoreau's cabin in the woods." Thus "the notion of voluntary simplicity" tends to conjure up "a hardy person or couple who have turned away from material progress, moved to a rural setting, and chosen a life of isolated and austere self-sufficiency," even though in principle simplicity of living might comport at least as well with certain forms of communitarianism and interdependence.[4]

Thoreau's story might not have been so memorable, however, had it been unprecedented rather than a re-created from an ancient dream that had in more modern times taken on new life as an ingredient of new world idealism. *Walden* was born into a literary culture better prepared to absorb an epic of simplification than Thoreau's skittishness about the marketplace's disinterest in his wares would suggest. When Thoreau whimsically compared himself, in "Economy," to the Indian basket maker unsuccessful at peddling his handiwork ("I too had woven a kind of basket of a delicate texture"), he doubtless wrote with his first book in mind (*Wa* 19). Whatever scars had been left by the utter commercial failure of *A Week on the Concord and Merrimack Rivers* (1849), certainly Thoreau was aware that his economy message was a more popular subject.[5] Respect for the simple life modeled on certain strains within Judeo-Christian and Greco-Roman thought, as well as the exigencies of frontier conditions, had been an integral part of Anglo-American civil religion from the start, existing in a kind of symbiotic antithesis with the ethic of consumerist capitalism for which American culture is much better known.[6] To be sure, Puritan and Quaker efforts to moderate entrepreneurial excess had not been very successful, nor did the founders' ethos of republican restraint prevent rampant greed during the middle period of national expansion. But the failures of simplicity ethics did not discredit the ethic; indeed, quite the contrary: the ethic took on a life of its own, serving "as the nation's conscience, reminding Americans of what the founders had hoped they would be and thereby providing a vivifying counterpoint to the excesses of materialist individualism."[7]

Such has been *Walden*'s role in sustaining this article of American civil religion. Thoreau was careful to root his critique of American culture within that culture, invoking for example not only Puritan antecedence (the austerity of Concord's first settlers) and "Spartan simplicity" (*Wa* 92), but also the Franklinian virtue of rigorous prudence in conducting business. He made his treatise on reform resonate in an offbeat way with contemporary genres like the young man's conduct book, the handbook on domestic economy, and the temperance tract.[8] To these he added models more exotic to his Protestant Yankee hearers, such as medieval and oriental asceticism, yet palatable enough as literary seasoning.

Under these circumstances it was to be expected that before Thoreau moved to Walden there should already have been three quasi-Thoreauvian experiments in voluntary simplicity from within the ranks of the transcendentalists alone. Nor is it surprising that one of *Walden*'s first enthusiastic readers, Daniel Ricketson, had serendipitously built a cabin retreat for himself on his New Bedford property. Thoreau and Ricketson were but two variants of a long-publicized type of American eccentric: the cranky hermit, who for a variety of possible reasons retreated to his (or her) secluded nook.[9] Not until modern times did Thoreau's bivouac emerge as the central precedent. The careers of the most Thoreauvian writers of the generation after Thoreau bear this out. In the early 1870s, John Muir probably built his shack over a Yosemite sawmill without thinking about Thoreau, even though he already had begun to read him. By the 1890s, John Burroughs was far more aware of Thoreau's shadow, often evincing a prickly, hypersensitive anxiety of influence; but Burroughs probably was not copying Thoreau when he built *his* cabin, Slabsides.[10]

In modern times, however, the commemoration of Muir and Burroughs as naturist prophets has been cross-pollinated by the myth of a Thoreauvian tradition, and Thoreau has come to exercise a more formative influence on the literature of voluntary simplicity. Take for example Henry Beston's *Outermost House* (1928) and Aldo Leopold's *Sand County Almanac* (1949), whose shacks on Cape Cod and in central Wisconsin themselves became sites of pilgrimage.[11] Both Leopold and Beston knew and quoted Thoreau; both declined to acknowledge any direct dependence on Walden (either the experiment or the book) as an incentive for their own experiments; yet both wrote about their experiences in such a way as to invite the comparison.

Beston: "I lived at the Fo'castle as undisturbed as Crusoe on his island" (71).
Thoreau: "For the most part it is as solitary where I live as on the prairies" (*Wa* 130).

Beston: "My fire was more than a source of heat—it was an elemental presence, a household god, and a friend" (6).
Thoreau: "My house was not empty though I was gone. It was as if I had left a cheerful housekeeper behind. It was I and Fire that lived there" (*Wa* 253).

Beston: "I woke last night just after two o'clock and found my larger room brimming with April moonlight" (111).
Thoreau: "I awoke to an answered question, to Nature and daylight" (*Wa* 282: also, like Beston's, the opening to a chapter).

Beston: "I began to reflect on Nature's eagerness to sow life everywhere" (128).
Thoreau: "I love to see that Nature is so rife with life" (*Wa* 318).

Perhaps, although I doubt it, the resemblances here signify nothing more than fortuitous convergences of similar kinds of experience and perception: the magnification of distance, the cherished intimacy of warmth, the light-flooded awakening, the awareness of plenitude. But even though they do not "prove" Thoreauvian influence as conclusively as, say, Anne LaBastille's naming one of her cabins Thoreau II, they make strikingly clear the minuteness of symmetry of which American epics of voluntary simplicity are capable—as well as the force of the underlying cultural formation.[12]

This is not to deny the diversity of such writing. A diagram of post-Thoreau simplicity literature might map the field along two coordinates: a mimetic continuum of dream to enactment and an ideological continuum of nominal to radical experiment. On the first continuum, at opposite ends would sit W. B. Yeats's escapist lyric "The Lake Isle of Innisfree" and the down-to-earth testimonials of Scott and Helen Nearing, *Living the Good Life* and *Continuing the Good Life*.[13] Inspired by listening to his father read *Walden,* Yeats fleetingly imagines a rustic retreat where he would plant "nine bean rows" and "live alone in the bee-loud glade." The Nearings patiently codify years of disciplined subsistence living on farms in Vermont and Maine, as they gradually build on the plan of half-day labor, half-day leisure, enlisting visitors in their regime. On the second continuum, a pair of representative opposites would be Roger Payne's depression-era manifesto *Why Work?* (1939), which advocates the lifestyle of the migratory hobo, relying on a curious yet coherent amalgam of Thoreauvian and Oxonian logic to argue for the feasibility and rightness of working only one day in seven; and journalist Charles B. Seib's *The Woods: One Man's Escape to Nature* (1971), which embalms the minutiae of Seib's weekend retreat place ("My son and daughter call it Walden South") and the cabin he built there ("finally, I had determined that my gabled roof would extend four feet beyond the front wall to provide shelter over part of the front deck"). These variants recall the slipperiness of *Walden* itself, which both describes a temporary withdrawal and gives prescriptions for permanent reformation, and which seems equally invested in the specificity of its own form of retreat and in allowing independent-minded readers like Payne to invent their own scenarios.[14]

The politics of these writers range from quasi-aristocratic (Yeats) to liberal bourgeois (Seib) to socialist (the Nearings) to anarchist (Payne).

This range fits the shiftiness of a precursor who was at once a bookish snob (see his defense of classicism in "Reading"), a vehement opposer of orthodoxy, and a self-styled pursuer of "enterprises" however odd, who won a degree of respect even from philistines for his pencil making and surveying skills. *Walden*'s ideological ambience can be pinned down more precisely, however, by comparing it to the Anglophone Protestant classic about homesteading that it most resembles: Defoe's *Robinson Crusoe*.[15] *Crusoe* was already a classic in Thoreau's day. Thoreau knew the Crusoe story well, both the original and several recent imitations, such as Mayne Reid's juvenile novel *The Desert Home* (1853) and Ephraim Squier's faintly *Typee*-like *Waikna; or, Adventures on the Mosquito Shore* (1855), about a beach- and junglecombing American artist-adventurer in Central America. In "Where I Lived," Thoreau alludes to Defoe via William Cowper's poem about Alexander Selkirk, fashioning a weak pun on his occupation from the famous line "I am monarch of all I *survey*" (*Wa* 82). But Thoreau's drift is antithetical to Defoe's. First, obviously, Crusoe is a case of *in*voluntary simplicity. He recreates civilization relentlessly, dragging up to his castle as much of the ship as he can and restlessly expanding his estate. Second, and no doubt related, Crusoe sets no value on leisure as such. He must forever work, if not at estate building then at Bible reading. His siestas are for self-protection only. Third, Crusoe hates solitude. Fourth, he reinstates without scruple the conventional structures of domination as Friday's master, the island's monarch, and the manipulator of fellow Europeans who land on the island. In this respect Crusoe is Prospero's legatee, another type of colonizer. He ransacks the environment to satisfy his needs as consumer and builder and alters it as quickly as possible from a state of nature to a state of gadgetry.

Thoreau was not wholly immune to the Crusoe syndrome. He condescends to ethnic others; he finds railroads and telegraphs more exciting than not; he imagines becoming the patriarch of a new Walden Woods settlement ("Former Inhabitants; and Winter Visitors"). Still, of the two, Thoreau is the sponsor of technological devolution and the attenuation of authority structures. Like their nightmarish complement, the gothic romance, *Crusoe* and *Walden* both cater to the great bourgeois (sub)urbanite anxiety: Can I survive when cast back on my own resources, without the usual social and material supports? But their prescriptions for survival greatly differ.

The significance of the Thoreauvian intervention can be appreciated by a glimpse at James Fenimore Cooper. Like Thoreau, Cooper often satirized the industrial and market revolutions and idealized antimaterialistic independent self-sufficiency. But he could not so readily imagine the larger course of American social history as other than a movement from frontier to increasing social complexity. This is clear from Cooper novels that run the gamut from first settlement to developed society, such as *The Pioneers* (a fictionalization of Cooperstown), *Wept of the Wish-ton-Wish* (seventeenth-century Connecticut), and *The Crater* (an imaginary Pacific island). Meanwhile, more conventional writers, like Mayne Reid, were reducing Cooper's romances of the forest to the simplistic formulas abetted not just by Defoe but by hundreds of colonial-era discovery and settlement narratives. In *The Desert Home*, the aptly named English family Robinson fights back from near extinction on the American prairie owing to poverty, Indians, beasts, thirst, and famine to create, in the end, a remarkable plantation in a remote oasis somewhere east of New Mexico and west of Missouri: a never-never land of plenty in which they have managed to tame antelopes, buffalo, bears, and even panthers. Happily, the Robinsons are discovered by another lost party, to whom they tell their amazing rags-to-riches story in a fashion that quaintly doubles as a melodramatic tale and a series of lessons in natural history, just before their return to St. Louis with a fortune's worth of beaver skins. Faithful Cudjo serves as their Friday. Reid affirms Crusoe's discovery that one can make "a fortune in the desert."[16] Cooper criticizes this mentality but builds his plots in recognition of the historical force of expansionism and the profit motive, like it or not; Thoreau opposes it more frontally by changing the plot.

If it is a plot. For the difference in ideological orientation between Defoe and Thoreau correlates with a difference in orientation toward narrative. Crusoe wills his story to complete itself; his triumph is in closure, the involuntary exile's safe return. Thoreau's closure is half-hearted: "I left the woods for as good a reason as I went there" (*Wa* 323)—a statement that Thoreauvians know to be even more equivocal in the original. ("I must say that I do not know what made me leave the pond—I left it as unaccountably as I went to it. To speak sincerely, I went there because I had got ready to go—I left it for the same reason" [*PJ* 4: 276].) Why Thoreau did not acknowledge his confusion more openly in *Walden* is unclear. Sheer defensiveness? Or perhaps he "knew" that books should have conclusions? In any case, *Walden* remains a book where the return is merely nominal. One could even go so far as to claim that the text reintegrates with society at the rhetorical level precisely through its message of divestment. Hence Wright Morris and others stress that whatever the technicalities of his return, Thoreau remains effectively in the woods at the end of *Walden*.[17] That he resists repatriation perhaps explains why Thoreau turns at the end of "Conclusion" to a new beginning: the beautiful bug emerging, the sun as morning star. Latter-day Thoreauvians like to repeat this gesture: Beston coming to rest with an image of "dawn seen over ocean from the beach," Joseph Wood Krutch ending the year *Finnegans Wake*–like with the sentence that started the book, Barry Lopez bowing to the spirit of the north at the end of the epilogue to *Arctic Dreams* as he did at the start of the preface, Annie Dillard revisiting the giant waterbug image with which she began *Pilgrim at Tinker Creek*.[18]

These circlings show the tendency of epics of voluntary simplicity to transform themselves into ritual. Here is still another point at which *Robinson Crusoe* illuminates Thoreauvianism. In both *Crusoe* and *Walden*, the action consists of microunits in which apparently trivial events loom extraordinarily large. The transportation of the Irish laborer's shanty to Thoreau's site is like the removal of the gods of Troy. The preparation of a simple loaf of bread for Robinson becomes a momentous labor: find the wheat, prepare the ground, sow it, grow it, build the oven, cook it. Thoreau magnifies the prospect of a mat on his floor as "the beginnings of evil" (*Wa* 67); Robinson reckons several pairs of shoes salvaged from the wreck as better than the eleven hundred pieces of gold (which he does not leave behind, however). The prized companionship of a parrot one has taught to talk, the owl hoot experienced as "such a sound as the frozen earth would yield if struck with a suitable plectrum, the very *lingua vernacula* of Walden Wood" (*Wa* 272). But there is also an immense difference between these sets of burgeoning minutiae: material goods regarded as traps rather than treasures, control over nature versus absorption into nature, ascesis as deprivation rather than as aesthetic.

Crusoe's enforced asceticism yields him a certain masochistic spiritual pleasure, effecting what he deems a conversion to pious sobriety. For Thoreau, ascesis leads to both spiritual and sensuous gratification. As Michael Warner remarks, Thoreau replaces the "ascetic self-relation of capitalism" with a "recuperative ascetics" in which chastity and polymorphous gratification are conjoined. ("The generative energy, which, when we are loose, dissipates and makes us unclean, when we are continent invigorates and inspires us" [*Wa* 219].)[19] To be sure, Thoreau makes this claim in "Higher Laws," during what appears to be an almost schizophrenic attempt to resolve the problem of "spiritual" versus "animal" natures with which he has wrestled throughout the chapter by abandoning nature for the safe refuge of mid-Victorian continence philosophy. "Nature is hard to be overcome," Thoreau insists, "but she must be overcome." Yet he turns out to mean not quite what we expect; indeed this passage may even be a deliberate tour de force to see whether he can snare (or lull) the dutiful reader into actually believing that he seriously means to disown the balance of *Walden*. For it immediately becomes clear that far from advocating *contemptu mundi*, Thoreau really desires the fullest possible engagement of the world, like that of "the Hindoo lawgiver" (Manu), for whom "nothing was too trivial," who "teaches how to eat, drink, cohabit, void excrement and urine, and the like, elevating what is mean, and does not falsely excuse himself by calling these things trifles" (*Wa* 221). It is difficult to apprehend Thoreau's point here because his own emulation of this desired state of recuperative ascetics appears, for the most part, not when he broaches the more sensational issues like sex and defecation but when he discusses "the trivial," "elevating what is mean." Thoreau's almost sybaritic relish in contemplating obscure environmental stimuli is the most typical instance. Voluntary simplicity of itself produces pleasure in the ordinary unobtrusive events that the life of simplification permits to become meaningful. The owl *might* have sounded merely "forlorn," but it is also "melodious." It is melodious because of the sensuous enrichment yielded by one of Thoreau's particular forms of discipline: concentration on the repetition of an event (so that the owl became "quite familiar to me at last, though I never saw the bird while it was making it"), analogical extension ("such a sound as the frozen earth would yield"), and synecdoche (the voice of Walden Woods) (*Wa* 271–272). The reader who has accepted the discipline of reading Thoreau will experience the ascetic aesthetic at another level, remembering the climactic passage on owls from the "Sounds" chapter, of which the passage just quoted is an incremental repetition.

What distinguishes *Walden* and other epics of voluntary simplicity from most traditional narrative plots, including that of *Robinson Crusoe*, is that the arrangement of its environmental furniture into linear corridors through which the protagonist strides becomes less important than what Thoreau suggestively calls deliberateness: the intensely pondered contemplation of characteristic images and events and gestures that take on a magical resonance beyond their normal importance now that the conditions of life have been simplified and the protagonist freed to appreciate how much more matters than what normally seems to matter. Here we see the effect of Thoreau's most cantankerous swerve from previous American models of voluntary simplicity—the Puritan, the Quaker, the republican patriot: his rejection of the work ethic as conventionally understood.[20] Of course, he could not abandon all discipline. He still enjoins a kind of vigilance over economic minutiae, espouses serious reading, and commends a moral rigor in "Higher Laws."[21] But Thoreau absolves himself from regular employment, takes pleasure in having farmed less rather than more his second year, recommends self-contained being over busy do-gooding. Roughly speaking, Thoreau turns pastoral into georgic: he elevates the Horatian and Virgilian love of rural retirement, a neoclassical motif of great resonance to the Anglo-American squierarchy, a motif on which Thoreau had written a college essay,[22] to the level of a lifework. Pastoral *otium* intensively cultivated rather than productive work as typically defined becomes the touchstone for a productive life. This nonlinear life is reflected in a nonlinear narrative, or rather a series of perceptions and events that do not constitute a narrative in any proper sense at all, but become contemplative occasions in whose delicacy of perceptual refinement the fruits of simplicity are savored.

Some readers will resist this side of Thoreau's genius. It is easier for the bourgeois reader (the typical Euro-American reader of Thoreau) to accept a myth of Thoreau as having written a purposeful saga of voluntary simplicity than a myth of Thoreau as experimenting with the rejection of work, purposiveness, linearity altogether. Thus we normalize the Walden sojourn by imagining it as an efficient way to get a lot of writing done, or normalize *Walden* by positing a firm aesthetic structure or ideational commitment. This tends to suppress both the worst and the best about Thoreau.

To take the "worst" first, the displacement of the work ethic by the gospel of *otium* is scandalous in the worst way: the internalizing of a mentality of civilized leisure—the highest form of life seen as refined recreation. English Thoreauvians like Edward Carpenter, Henry Salt, and Roger Payne immediately saw and valued this displacement, but it runs afoul of democratic ideology.[23] In Brahmin circles of Thoreau's day, this motive was better understood; and the disapproval of Thoreau stemmed as much from the judgment that he was unqualified to indulge it as from the disapproval of the motive itself. This can be illustrated by a tidbit from the annals of the Boston Society of Natural History, of which Thoreau was a corresponding member. Among this fraternity, the great necrological event of 1862 was not Thoreau's death but the passing of the society's first president, the well-endowed Benjamin Greene, trained in both law and medicine, who actually practiced neither but spent his life botanizing: a retiring man inarticulate in public situations, or so the memoir said. But Greene's "well known generosity in placing the results of his observations and his collections in the hands of those who could make the best use of them," not to mention his $9,000 bequest, made him a valuable citizen and entitled him to a full-dress biography, despite a far less productive life than Thoreau's.[24]

By freeing Thoreau from some of the curse of purposefulness, however, pastoral *otium* opened up for him the experience of place, of self as continuous with place. The long sequence of morning dooryard reveries at the beginning of "Sounds" marvellously captures this sense of place. Thoreau recalls learning (and tries to transmit) "what the Orientals mean by contemplation and the forsaking of works": "sheer idleness to my fellow-townsmen, no doubt; but if the birds and flowers had tried me by their standard, I should not have been found wanting" (*Wa* 111–112). The climax comes when, after reporting a not-too-arduous bit of house cleaning that involved taking his furniture outdoors, Thoreau affirms that "it was worth the while"

> to see the sun shine on these things, and hear the free wind blow on them; so much more interesting most familiar objects look out of doors than in the house. A bird sits on the next bough, life-everlasting grows under the table, and blackberry vines run round its legs; pine cones, chestnut burs, and strawberry leaves are strewn about. It looked as if this was the way these forms came to be transferred to our furniture, to tables, chairs, and bedsteads,—because they once stood in their midst. (*Wa* 113)

In this remarkable passage, Thoreau's colonization of his surroundings by his household effects gives way, when he relaxes and makes himself receptive, to the feeling of being constituted—lock, stock, and barrel—by the forms of nature. Ecocentrism replaces egocentrism.[25]

The feeling of luminous interchange with the external world as egocentrism gives way is hardly peculiar to Thoreauvian prose. We discern it also in imagist poetry (Williams finding that "so much depends" upon the juxtaposition of red wheelbarrow and white chickens), in phenomenology at its more lyric moments (Heidegger contemplating the thisness of the jug), and in haiku (Bashō experiencing a bunch of frozen sea slugs as an epiphany).[26] Thoreauvian writing aims especially to construct something like a complete world of such image-events, image-events moreover that we are given to understand the author experiences not just once but repeatedly, until their nuances become fully savored by slow internalization. The aforementioned reveries occurr "often," or at least "sometimes," after "my accustomed bath" (the Oriental contemplations), or "when my floor was dirty" (the furniture removal) (*Wa* 112). These events gain in resonance from the sense that they were ongoing, part of a praxis, not unique and nonrecurrent.

A common leitmotif in voluntary simplicity literature for registering the suspension of purposiveness and possessiveness is the pun on ownership. Thoreau derived this trope from Emerson's *Nature*, which assigns the poet a "property" in the "horizon," to which the individual farms he sees have no "title."[27] Similarly, in "Where I Lived," Thoreau observes that the poet often enjoys "the most valuable part of the farm," the landscape (*Wa* 82). Leopold takes up the game in "Great Possessions," the section of *Sand County Almanac* he considered his best—and the title he himself wanted for the book as a whole.[28] Leopold bemusedly imagines the birds on his property as demanding, nonpaying tenants. The underlying idea is that his great possessions reside in the birds, not in his "real" estate. Edward Abbey plays the role of Leopold's birds in *Desert Solitaire* when he usurps the government's control of Arches National Monument and removes all the surveyors' stakes—a slight oedipal dig at Thoreau's profession, perhaps. Annie Dillard buys a pet goldfish for her companion at Tinker Creek and names it Ellery Channing—thereby "becoming" Thoreau? Arnold Krupat's novella *Woodsmen; or, Thoreau and Indians* imagines a professorial would-be Thoreau who defends his tiny rural holding against a mafioso-type contractor only to cede it to a remnant Indian clan that claims prior ownership. All this troping on ownership simultaneously keeps alive the will to disengage from all material encumbrances and the inner awakening these writers see as the chief reward of that disengagement. Ownership becomes purified of possession and assumes its ideal form of acknowledgment, of avowal.

Self-Relinquishment

In avowing the relinquishment of goods, the literature of voluntary simplicity promises to restore the attenuated bond with nature. Ike meets the bear; Thoreau experiences the spring; Peter Matthiessen sees the snow leopard. The experiencer is refreshed and purified. But usually this process happens without the notion of the self being itself held up for examination. The potential problem inherent in this unself-consciousness becomes visible when the protagonist's small-mindedness obtrudes.

> In 1955, after adding a bedroom to the cabin, the blank wall with its single window annoyed me no end. Until I bought two Swedish junipers from a nursery to fill the vacant place. They have grown slowly and appear somewhat out of place among the oaks, pines and hollies. A small cedar that I transplanted nearby will soon catch the strangers.

This from one who "lived as simply as Henry Thoreau had at Walden Pond a century before."[29] His fussiness about tidying up his natural surroundings shows how much baggage he has carried into his pastoral retreat. Nor does this author even begin to imagine the kinds of complications that modern scholars have seen in the ideology of American individualism: that individual "separation" is part of a ritual of democratic consensus and that it is a specifically masculinist ritual.[30] Other challenges even more fundamental than these arise: such as the challenge from sociobiology, which would imagine selfness as genetically constrained by species being; the challenge from evolutionary biology, which would imagine *Homo sapiens* as a plastic category; and the challenge from ecology, which would question the very "notion of separate, skin-encapsulated beings."[31] Through these lenses a quite different version of the self is seen: Corpuscles float in a primal nutrient bath "of blood; intestines crawl about absorbing food in the manner of primitive worms; lungs absorb and excrete gases as do gills and leaves. No human organ would look out of place if planted in some Paleozoic sponge bed or coral reef.

Even our brain is an evolutionary onion, the core we share with fish and reptiles, the secondary layer we share with other mammals, and the outer layer we share with other primates."[32] This is David Rains Wallace, trying to reimagine the human body and mind in terms of the signs of evolutionary processes that link it to other organisms. We might consider even this surrealistic vision conservative insofar as it operates from the assumption that *Homo sapiens* refers to a unified assemblage of distinct parts. For as Neil Evernden points out, "it now appears that some of the organelles in our cells are quite as independent as the chloroplasts in plants."

> Mitochondria, the energy-providing structures within each cell, replicate independently of the cell and are composed of RNA which is dissimilar to that of the rest of the cell. Apparently the mitochondria move into the cells like colonists and continue their separate existence within. We cannot exist without them, and yet they may not strictly be "us." Does this mean that we must regard ourselves as colonies? . . . Where do we draw the line between one creature and another? Where does one stop and the other begin? Is there even a boundary between you and the non-living world, or will the atoms of this page be part of *you* tomorrow? In short, how can you make any sense of the concept of man as a discrete entity?[33]

His questions call for a vision of self-relinquishment far more sweeping than that afforded by the epic of voluntary simplicity— so sweeping that it is hard to imagine more than fitfully what a mental life rigorously conducted with that awareness as its guiding principle might be like. Among ontologists, none has been bolder or more inventive than Heidegger, and none more hospitable to a definition of the self in environmental terms. Heidegger defines human being precisely in terms of its "thereness," as *Dasein*. But when it comes to giving an account of human concern toward the environment in *Being and Time,* he seems to take it as self-evident that what ought to be stressed is the anthropocentric dimension of environment's use value, its "readiness-to-hand" rather than its "presence-to-hand," from which standpoint *Dasein's* concernfulness would stand exposed as a self-interested fiction.[34] Indeed, writers specializing in environmental representation who have taken it as their special mission to question anthropocentricity have been hard pressed to find counterfictions that would go as far as they are at the notional level prepared to go by way of relinquishing the privilege of selfhood.

> This is blasphemy, of course, to write about an animal like a toad in romantic and unscientific words, to give the wart factory a personality, a set of motives, a set of values and approaches to life that only few humans aspire to. The animals may be incredibly stupid, they may be locked in a most vicious struggle with one another for survival on the Arthur Bay beachhead, they may all be at this moment wishing they were not toads so they could be in town drinking beer with the college kids. Who knows what a toad thinks and feels?[35]

Here parasitologist John Janovy, Jr., recoils from his own professional callousness of killing toads en masse for research purposes but remains vexed by the impossibility of seeing from the toad's viewpoint. He immediately realizes how problematic is humankind's most instinctive way of reproaching itself for cruelty to animals, that is, to honor toads by ascribing personalities to them, and this realization frustrates him completely. How much harder, then, to hold firmly in the mind a vision of human beings in which the integrity of the individual mind seems anywhere near as porous and inconsequential as ecology says it is. Yet as ecophilosopher Freya Mathews has said, "if individuals are to retain any objective status within the domain of concrete reality, a new criterion of individuality will have to be found."[36]

The American literary imagination has made at least two significant attempts to develop such a criterion. The more long-standing and successful of these is, unsurprisingly, the more modest: an agrarian-tribal vision that imagines individual encounters with land contained by the imperatives of stewardship and community. American environmental writing has in this way tried to deal with the potential self-centeredness of voluntary simplicity thinking. Jeffersonian agrarianism supplies the mainstream paradigm, rural communitarianism the dissenting paradigm. The leading current exemplar, blending both elements, is Wendell Berry, author of several dozen books of poetry, nonfiction, and essays written since his return to the eastern Kentucky of his boyhood. Berry likes to think of himself as operating from the perspective of "each creature as living and moving always at the center—one of the infinite number of centers—of an arrangement of processes that reaches through the universe. The interlocking lives of the creatures, like a coat of chain mail, by which the creation saves itself from death."

This starting point leads Berry to a vision deeply hostile to the individual questing aspect of romantic naturism ("at times this wish to escape into nature is no such thing at all, but rather a poetic way of wishing to be a spirit"), a vision that imagines Gary Snyder and Alexander Pope as fundamentally akin, "though their ways of considering nature differ," in asking "the same practical questions about it: How do we fit in? What is the possibility of a human harmony *within* nature?" The answer for Berry lies in a sacramental, marriage-like commitment to sustainable agriculture in a place to which one bonds through long familiarity and "kindly use," and within which one is networked by participation in a community whose endurance absorbs the little life of the individual.[37] Berry gives splendid expression to this ideal toward the end of his elegy "At a Country Funeral."

> What we owe the future
> is not a new start, for we can only begin
> with what has happened. We owe the future
> the past, the long knowledge
> that is the potency of time to come.
> That makes of a man's grave a rich furrow.
> The community of knowing in common is the seed
> of our life in this place. There is not only
> no better possibility, there is no
> other, except for chaos and darkness,
> the terrible ground of the only possible
> new start. And so as the old die and the young
> depart, where shall a man go who keeps
> the memories of the dead, except home
> again, as one would go back after a burial,
> faithful to the fields, lest the dead die
> a second and more final death.[38]

Salvation lies not in personal knowledge but in the *community* of knowing, which itself is valuable not as (abstract) knowledge but only as enactment in the form of agrarian persistence: tending the dead man's furrow. This sacramental return to the land, sanctified by communally sustained memory, is the only form of self-fulfillment Berry will recognize as legitimate. The quest for self-realization as such he considers a "disease of the spirit." Indeed, he sees this "freedom" as a form of bondage: "Having a place, having a definition and limits, belonging to a kind unlike other kinds"—this, rather, is "the condition upon which we truly are set free." [39]

Berry's position is not so clear-cut as I have suggested. Interdependence also worries him, when it comes in the form of loss of economic self-sufficiency, such that a person never touches "anything that he has produced himself, in which he can take pride." Nor, this statement implies, would Berry presumably deny the individualist streak to the Jeffersonian agrarianism that he idealizes. Berry knows that Jefferson praised small-scale family farming for its promotion of an "independent, free-standing citizenry," knows that one of the grounds on which he distinguished between farmers and artisans was the reliance of the first on "their own soil and industry."[40] Crèvecoeur put the matter more baldly when he diagnosed the labor of the American cultivator as "founded on the basis of nature, *self-interest*; can it want a stronger allurement?"[41]

A century after Crèvecoeur, Willa Cather teased out the inner contradictions in agrarian thought in the form of Alexandra Bergson, the heroine of *O Pioneers*, in a way that anticipates Berry's thought. Alexandra is on the one hand a model of the nonexploitative, community-oriented agriculturist. She becomes head of the family in fulfillment of her dying father's wish; she farms successfully by conforming to the land's requirements, respecting the deep environmental knowledge of "crazy" Ivar, the mystical eccentric whom others shun; and the wealth she accumulates she seeks to give away. On the other hand, she also succeeds by speculating boldly, by making canny purchases and mortgages, by appropriating land-wise Ivar as a domestic oracle, by intimidating her unruly oafish brothers with the threat of the law. Her protocapitalist assertiveness cannot be separated from her "kindly use" of the land and her relinquishment of personal ambition.[42] This is not to say that Cather uses Alexandra to undercut the ideal that Berry's essays later promote; rather Alexandra's case shows, as Alexandra herself realizes, the inability even of a worthy ideal to work itself out without unintended consequences. On another level Cather and Berry are on the same footing of retrospect: both conjure up an infinitely receding epoch of simpler, more admirable rustic virtue exemplified by Alexandra's self-sacrificing devotion to her immigrant father's agrarian dream and by the "old idea" that "as many as possible should share in the ownership of the land and thus be bound to it by economic interest, by the investment of love and work, by family loyalty, by memory and tradition."[43] This retrospective idealization of the sublimation of self-interest by the bonds of loyalty, memory, and tradition reaches back at least as far as America's first agrarian classic, Crèvecour's *Letters*, and its imagination of model second-generation farmer James and model immigrant Andrew from the nostalgic vantage point of the Tory author's self-exile. Indeed, Raymond Williams has traced the Anglophone "escalator" of nostalgia for the vanishing "country way of life" back to Anglo-Saxon times.[44]

Berry frankly identifies his peaceable kingdom of the rural communitarian culture as an anthropocentric utopia. The farmer is the husbandman; the land is husbanded. His favorite analogy of man:woman = culture:nature is more problematic than he realizes, but he seeks to rehabilitate and purify it with an idealistic passion that can only be called patriarchal in the heroic sense.[45] Berry reckons the estate of humanity to be, in essence, as distinct from the estate of nature as male from female and considers any attempt to blur them as hubris. "The notion of romantic poets that they would like to turn and live with or as animals," insists Berry (alluding to section 32 of Whitman's "Song of Myself") "is a fantasy that has its counterpart in the notion of scientific and technological romantics that they will eventually turn and live with or as gods" (alluding here to Satan's temptation of Eve in *Paradise Lost*).[46] His vehemence, reminiscent of Blake's judgment on what he took to be Wordsworth's paganism, reflects the allure of that dream from early romantic times: the desire to reconceive, even remake, the human self in the image of nature.

A particularly striking enactment of this same heresy, the second experiment we shall consider here, is the attempt made by certain modern Anglo-American poets to imagine lyric personae as conduits or registers of environmental stimuli, thereby breaking from romantic subjectivism by taking one ingredient of romantic naturism to an extreme.[47] It is hard to imagine a literary project more committed to extricate art from homocentrism.

At the manifesto level, no postromantic assault on homocentrism has been more extreme than the "inhumanism" of Robinson Jeffers, which Berry would presumably consider horrifying. In Jeffers, agoraphobia reaches the point of cursing humanity itself for the sake of embracing the elemental forces, however bleak or violent. The melancholy, long, withdrawing roar that unnerved Matthew Arnold at Dover Beach was Jeffers's grim delight. His prescription for the hypercivilized is to put us in touch with hawks and eagles ("the destruction that brings an eagle from heaven is better than mercy") or, preferably, bedrock:

> Turn outward, love things, not men, turn right away from
> humanity,
> Let that doll lie. Consider if you like how the lilies grow,
> Lean on the silent rock until you feel its divinity
> Make your veins cold, look at the silent stars, let your eyes
> Climb the great ladder out of the pit of yourself and man.
> Things are so beautiful, your love will follow your eyes;
> Things are the God, you will love God, and not in vain,
> For what we love, we grow to it, we share its nature. At length
> You will look back along the stars' rays and see that even
> The poor doll humanity has a place under heaven.
> Its qualities repair their mosaic around you, the chips of strength
> And sickness; but now you are free, even to become human,
> But born of the rock and the air, not of a woman.[48]

The sheer force of this poetic statement, complicated by an unobtrusive deftness (the laconic deprecation of "if you like," the enigma of whether the tone of "your love will follow your eyes" is compassionate or disdainful, the rightness of the jerky off-rhyme of human and woman) helps explain why after years of self-prophesied neglect, Jeffers's poems are beginning to enjoy a certain vogue in today's age of unprecedented environmentalism. Jeffers's work has been celebrated as disclosing "an *ecological vision of divinity*" that proclaims the unity and holiness of the world of things.[49] In Jeffers, if anywhere, the Emersonian dream of nature as humankind's counterpart seems to have been purged of its theistic residue and to have assumed the status of an ecological ethic. Jeffers follows romantic lyric tradition in setting up the poem as a scene of instruction in which nature provides a moral mirror of the human condition, teaching humanity the way to be. But the mirror it holds up is not symbolically significant (like Emerson's rhodora, symbol of beauty, or Bryant's gentian, symbol of the opening to heaven at the moment of death) but simply its isness, its materiality. Jeffers restates the biblical precept that the test of adulthood is putting away childish things as a call to relinquish the plaything of humanism and become reborn as a child of rock and air. Things being God, self-realization lies in acceptance of the Stevens's snowmanlike or Yeats's-Ben-Bulbenlike reality of our thinghood.

Yet while Jeffers extirpates humanism at the level of the image, at the level of address he clings to authoritarian homiletics. Despite his doctrine, or rather in his anxiety to convey it, Jeffers does not allow his speaker to engage in the relinquishment of self that he preaches.

Jeffers's lingering Victorian moralism emerges more distinctly when we place "Signpost" alongside several other poems. William Carlos Williams's "Young Sycamore," for one:

> I must tell you
> this young tree
> whose round and firm trunk
> between the wet
>
> pavement and the gutter
> (where water
> is trickling) rises
> bodily
>
> into the air with
> one undulant
> thrust half its height—
> and then
>
> dividing and waning
> sending out
> young branches on
> all sides—

>hung with cocoons
>it thins
>till nothing is left of it
>but two
>
>eccentric knotted
>twigs
>bending forward
>hornlike at the top.[50]

Here the speaker is immediately possessed by the vision of the tree ("I must tell you"), the elaboration of which takes over the rest of the poem—as if the energy of the tree itself were dictating the poem's form. The poem's ordering is quite conventional—a blazon—but the effect of nature breaking through convention is created by the devices of inversion (blazoning from bottom to top), free verse, and the vertical graphics (short lines stretched down a whole page to create a saplinglike look). Greater suppleness of voice and prosody allows Williams to move further than Jeffers toward the goal of a poetics that would relinquish the superintending human consciousness. He almost seems to have realized his demand for an art that is "not 'realism' but reality itself."[51]

Yet Williams has not reached the asymptotic limit. He cannot give up prosodic formalism. He cannot give up the old tradition of the discrete orderly holistic image—as if the natural world were an infinite series of internally unified self-contained objects. Williams is partially amended in this respect by A. R. Ammons, whose poem "Center" is precisely about the nonexistence of centers:

>A bird fills up the
>streamside bush
>with wasteful song,
>capsizes waterfall,
>mill run, and
>superhighway
>to
>song's improvident

center
lost in the green
bush green
answering bush:
wind varies:
the noon sun casts
mesh refractions
on the stream's amber
bottom
and nothing at all gets,
nothing gets
caught at all.[52]

Ammons presents a more haphazard landscape than the surgically controlled domain of Williams's sycamore tree. Ammons initially makes it seem that the locus might have a center in the song of the nameless bird, which for awhile seems to sing beyond the genius of the waterfall and the highway: the idea of order in Ithaca, New York. But the rest is entropy: the answering birds (or rather the metonymic bushes) diffuse the sound; the sun diffuses its light; the poem's ending confesses that the poem's aesthetic net caught nothing. Relative to "Young Sycamore," not to mention Jeffers's "Signpost," the persona's relinquishment to nature's anarchic authority seems more complete.

Ah, but not so fast. The crafty Ammons *has* created a center after all. At the exact center of the poem is the bush, the word "bush," that is (line 11); surrounding it in triumphant symmetry, fore and aft, is the word "green," so that even though the act of attention to nature reported by the poem does not succeed in netting the macrocosm, the poem considered as a vertical verbal sequence is a manicured shrub after all: crescendo toward, diminuendo away from the bushy center. Then, too, one can hardly credit any of our three poets so far with relinquishing control of affect. They vary in their degree of emotional coloring, but all of them remain tightly monochromatic: Jeffers monotonously insistent, Williams breathily intent, Ammons coolly cognitive. To begin to get a sense of how it feels to feel oneself being permeated, overtaken by the earth, we have to turn to works like Theodore Roethke's horticultural reminiscences:

In my veins, in my bones I feel it,—
The small waters seeping upward,
The tight grains parting at last.
When sprouts break out,
Slippery as fish,
I quail, lean to beginnings, sheath-wet.[53]

These lines double as a mental transition back to boyhood and as the remembered experience of feeling one's own body, surrounded by plat upon plat of cuttings in father's fetid greenhouse, as if it too were a sprout about to pop. The tactile images, and the subdued turbulence and "grotesquification" of the *p* and *t* sounds, express the sense of being overtaken by the squamous biological world more urgently than the modulated muses of Jeffers, Williams, and Ammons.

Even Roethke does not approach the inchoate merge of humanity and nature attempted by Gary Snyder, in "Second Shaman Song" (from *Myths and Texts*):

Squat in swamp shadows.
    mosquitoes sting:
    high light in cedar above.
Crouched in a dry vain frame
    —thirst for cold snow
    —green slime of bone marrow
Seawater fills each eye

Quivering in nerve and muscle
Hung in the pelvic cradle
Bones propped against roots
A blind flicker of nerve

Still hand moves out alone
Flowering and leafing
    turning to quartz
Streaked rock   congestion of karma
The long body of the swamp.[54]

It was an inspired choice to follow traditional Chinese poetics by effacing the "I." This fits the ordeal of receptive endurance: the ordeal that the shaman must undergo before his ritual starts at the poem's end, where the speaker points to himself for the first and only time ("I dance" are the poem's two final words). He has allowed his body to become permeable to the point that his bones rub against the roots, and inside and outside can no longer be distinguished. (Is the "frame" a sacred cage or hut, or the frame of his own pelvis?) This erosion of boundaries is duplicated by the shifting of perspective (in the opening stanza, the speaker first seems to be squatting in the swamp, then engulfed by it, as if sunk in quicksand). As his hand "moves out" (as if of its own volition?), it takes on the look of first flowering plant and then quartz, rock. The metamorphosis is total: "The long body of the swamp." This is the rebirth Jeffers imagines but cannot image.

Perhaps Snyder cannot quite image it either. In a characteristic lapse or transcendence, depending on how you look at it, he introduces a piece of exotic pedantry, "congestion of karma," whose self-consciousness abruptly pulls us out of the muck. Still, this poem overall conveys as rigorous a relinquishment of homocentrism as one could expect a human lyric to achieve. And the same holds, albeit to a lesser degree, for the other poems just considered. The point of reading them all as partially successful but partially inhibited attempts is not to allow the critic to gloat over their failure to go all the way; for they emanate from sensibilities more heroic than those of most critics. The point is to underscore the heroic difficulty of achieving a thoroughgoing redefinition of the self in environmental terms.

It might seem that modernism had made such a redefinition easy. For the adjustments in persona, prosody, and image I have just been discussing have certainly to a large extent been enabled by such interdependent modernist cultural revolutions as the breakdown of trust in an autonomous self, the deterioration of faith in a symbolically significant universe, and a rejection of bound poetic forms. Under such circumstances, one might suppose that nothing would come easier to a late twentieth-century consciousness than imaging human selves as unstable constellations of matter occupying one among innumerable niches in an interactive biota. But such is not the case. It is hard not to care more about individuals than about people, hard not to care more about people than about the natural environment. Any attempt to compensate for these overbalances must struggle against large odds.

Environmental Nonfiction as a Fable of Relinquishment

The aesthetic of relinquishment in the long run fits environmental non-fiction better than lyric poetry and prose fiction. Insofar as such work takes as its starting point the decision to focus on the nonhuman, it tends to deny itself some of the most basic aesthetic pleasures of homocentrism: plot, characterization, lyric pathos, dialogue, intersocial events, and so on. Environmental nonfiction also often directly represents this displacement by making human figures hover at the edges of the text, sometimes hazing them as well as marginalizing them by showing them as doltish observers or ineffective predators. The most interesting cases are texts that do not maintain a single revision of the human-nonhuman ratio (which would allow the perceptual jolt to dwindle into normality) but instead keep it unstable, so that relinquishment remains more of an issue. Let us inspect three such cases, starting with a second look at *Walden*.

In treating *Walden* as a voluntary simplicity narrative, I failed to do justice to an important dimension of Thoreau's masterpiece not yet fully appreciated: the instability of the persona. Perhaps because Thoreau makes such a point at the start of the book that he intends to retain the "I," perhaps because we are trained to classify *Walden* as autobiography, perhaps for other reasons as well, readers seem inclined to suppose that Thoreau means for the persona-function itself to be thought of as remaining a constant element rather than a device subject to vacillation and change.[55] In fact, *Walden* shifts restlessly among a series of persona-functions: "I did," "I am doing," "I remember," "I believe," "There is," "There was"—each of which features the persona, or effaces it as the case may be, a little differently. Within these vacillations, the most conspicuous movement, briefly discussed in Chapter 4, is the book's partial shift away from egocentrism, as indexed by how often the "I" appears. I would argue that this alteration signifies a process of relinquishment and that the vacillations should be interpreted as a meditation on the question of the appropriateness of self-assertion in a mode of existence where individuality seems increasingly problematic.

Take a chapter that American literature specialists like to ignore: "Winter Animals."[56] It starts with the only piece of sustained action by the protagonist reported in the chapter: his itinerary as he treks to the neighboring town of Lincoln to lecture on winter evenings. This passage has a special interest as being the text's most explicit reference to an act of literary business directly related to the production of *Walden*—for presumably the lecture subject was the Walden experiment itself.[57] Yet the speaker stresses not that minor transaction but the intriguing dislocations of the nighttime winterscape, wherein the fishermen of Flint's Pond "loomed like fabulous creatures, and I did not know whether they were giants or pygmies"—"Esquimaux"—who sustain the illusion that this New England outback is as remote as "Baffin's Bay" (*Wa* 271). Self-focus gives way to extrospection, fellow humans become transformed into mythic near-animals as Thoreau imagines himself wandering "in a vast moose-yard well trodden, overhung by oak woods and solemn pines bent down with snow or bristling with icicles" (271). For the rest of the chapter, the speaker is largely passive ("I saw," "I heard," "I was waked"). A little beyond the halfway point, he yields even the authority of direct observation to the anecdotes of a salty old hunter, a more experienced woodsman than he. Then the chapter ends by sliding over to natural history cameos (squirrels, mice, hares, partridge), in which the speaker figure plays the bit part of attracting animals unintentionally by his store of provisions or scaring the game into visibility. Other than in the first paragraph, the speaker engages in no purposeful action; he mounts no sustained argument; he scarcely introspects; he increasingly allows his agenda and even himself to be defined by his environment. The chapter's emotional high point is the recollection—pulled in from another season, interestingly— of having "a sparrow alight upon my shoulder for a moment while I was hoeing in a village garden, and I felt that I was more distinguished by that circumstance than I should have been by any epaulet I could have worn" (276). Promotion to lieutenant hinges on the opposite of heroic striving: on an empathic effacement of human individuality into a state that other creatures might perceive as one of fellowship with them. The persona's decontrol of his impressions during the chapter imitates that effacement.

Sharon Cameron puts the matter well in reference to the later *Journal:* "The self is not to be empowered by nature. It is rather to be converted to nature."[58] Here as elsewhere, Cameron reads the *Journal* "against" *Walden,* which she regards as compromised by its status as a work for publication and thus the object of self-conscious ordering and closure. Yet the selfsame quest for conversion Cameron finds in the *Journal* also appears in *Walden* itself, in the form of the irregular and conflicted but distinct tendency of the speaking self to begin to yield his authority and his autonomy to the authority of the environment that he has come increasingly to know during the years of the experiment and of the book's writing. The relative "impurity" of this process, which Cameron might consider pusillanimous, actually enriches *Walden,* makes it a more capacious work of imagination, makes it also a more usable mirror and model of how to start moving from here to there.[59]

To the extent that the Thoreauvian self can be said to arrive "there" in *Walden,* the point of arrival is perhaps the famous sandbank passage in "Spring" (*Wa* 304–309), which minutely records the shifting formations of the mud flow and fantasizes exuberantly about what they symbolize. To be sure, Thoreau's imagery here has a certain self-conscious mannerism, as in the famous transparent eyeball passage in Emerson's *Nature,* wrought it would seem from a programmatic straining similar to the more elaborate conceits of metaphysical poetry, such as Andrew Marvell's "*Salmon-Fishers* moist" who "shod their *Heads* in their *Canoos*" like "*Antipodes* in shoes."[60] But whereas Emerson, or so I think, remains oblivious to the possibility that he sounds absurd, Thoreau is quite aware of looking at "a truly *grotesque* vegetation," as the mud lava reminds him "of coral, of leopards' paws or birds' feet, of brains or lungs or bowels, and excrements of all kinds" (305). What is important above all for my purposes, however, is Thoreau's vision of the coextensiveness of the human body with the inanimate earth. *Walden* breathes life into the biblical formula of humankind's earthy origins: "What is man but a mass of thawing clay" (307). Thoreau is in this respect on exactly the same wavelength as Wallace, who muses that "no human organ would look out of place if planted in some Paleozoic sponge bed."[61] Thoreau has gone as far as he can go in dispersing body into environment.

The metamorphosis is not, of course, as unconditional for Thoreau as it is for the post-Darwinian Wallace—yet that makes Thoreau all the more interesting. The environment he imagines has, despite the appearance of anarchic profusion, a tidiness to it: witness his triple correlations among leaf parts, human body parts, and the sounds of the nouns for these shapes (306). His manic exuberance has license to flourish only within an intellectual scheme; otherwise Pan-worship might turn to panic. This too is signaled by the use of "*grotesque.*" Thoreau italicizes it to show that he uses the word not just as an adjective of quality but also to refer to architectural art: an important doubleness, suggesting both the possibility of traumatic dislocation of the human estate and a metamorphic process safely under control. Cameron might call this compromise; I would call it the end point in Thoreau's epic of the autonomous self imagining with fascination yet hesitancy the possibility of relinquishing that autonomy to nature.

Aldo Leopold's *Sand County Almanac* presents a different but no less complicated drama of self-relinquishment. The starting points of these two works, both of which took nearly a decade to evolve, were somewhat similar. Thoreau, to hear him tell it anyhow, was asked some pointed questions about his life at Walden and decided to concoct a lecture or two on the subject treating his experience as an exemplum. Leopold was contacted by Harold Strauss of Alfred A. Knopf in 1941 with the proposition of writing a book for the layperson on "wild-life observation," "a personal book recounting adventures in the field."[62] But whereas for Thoreau, the focus on the protagonist's regime overshadowed the theme of yielding to the environment until he began to dedicate himself to natural history during the early 1850s, Leopold had to labor with the problem of inserting himself effectively into his presentation of environmental topics. This was not for lack of literary experience, for Leopold had been an amateur poet, essayist, and artist from his secondary school days and had begun giving popular ecological lectures, essays, and radio broadcasts well before Knopf contacted him. Yet both Knopf's editorial staff and Leopold's own associates had to prod this professor-forester into writing more of himself into his text. "Your lesson is much stronger," advised one of his former students, "if you try to show how your own attitude towards your environment has changed."[63] This advice referred specifically to Leopold's revised view of predator protection. In response, Leopold composed one of the book's best-known sections, "Thinking Like a Mountain," a meditation on the claims of deer and wolves that embeds a personal conversion narrative.

As published, *Sand County* has a three-part structure: first, a series of round-the-year essays set in "Sand" (actually Sauk) County, the site of the Leopold family's shack; second, a series of more discursive essays set in different parts of North America; and third, four more sustained and polemical essays in environmental ethics. Leopold arrived at this arrangement after deciding against a series of thirteen topical essays dominated, according to Dennis Ribbens, by "ecological preachment."[64] The first, most personal, "almanac" section of the book was not part of Leopold's original idea; he began working on it only after Knopf rejected the manuscript in 1944, urging him to stress the narrative element and confine himself to a single region of the country, and his former student Alfred Hochbaum advised Leopold to revise by building "the book wholly upon Shack backgrounds."[65]

Leopold's compromise, eventually published by Oxford rather than by Knopf, was to do it all: to personalize *and* focus his observations geographically (Part I), to range as widely as he wanted around North America (Part II), *and* to deliver his ecological manifesto (Part III). He retained his original didactic thrust, but in a somewhat subdued form. Even at that, Leopold did not quite get his way. Two weeks after Oxford accepted the manuscript, he died of a heart attack; a team of half a dozen friends and family, coordinated by his son Luna, then revised the work. Virtually no page was left unchanged; and though most of the alterations were small-scale, some were significant.[66] For example, Leopold intended to end the book with this sentence: "It is only the scholar who understands why the raw wilderness gives definition and meaning to the human enterprise" (*SCA* 200–201). But the revisers decided to reposition the first of the four final essays, "The Land Ethic," as the finale. Whereas Leopold saw "The Land Ethic" as the statement of principle from which the other essays on conservation, wildlife, and wilderness would follow, the revisers preferred the inductive approach of ending with the culminating ecological insight, the argument that all species are entitled to existence as a matter of biotic right.

We need a definitive edition of *Sand County Almanac* that distinguishes Leopold's own words from the published version. Yet the work of the revisers is not to be sniffed at. Most of their revisions were stylistic improvements. Posterity has confirmed their judgment of the importance of "The Land Ethic." Besides, it was Leopold himself who summoned them to their task, in a memo calling for help with revision prepared just a few days before his death. *Sand County Almanac,* then, presents an unusual, maybe unique, case of an individually generated work finished by committee, not over the author's dead body in the colloquial sense but according to his last wish. This wish was in keeping with Leopold's readiness to seek advice from all quarters from the project's very start. Probably no work of the American environmental imagination has eventuated from a more truly ecological process of creation than this.

But the irony of the ecological genesis of *Sand County* is that it took a community of opinion to get Leopold to develop in his text the figure of the individual, which left to his own individual devices he would have hesitated to do. Something in Leopold balked at personalizing his vision until his reticence was put under severe pressure by his various advisers. Knopf's market-oriented motive was different from Hochbaum's, but both stressed, in effect, that readers would be more interested in autobiographically tinted essays with a narrative line to them than in didactics or documentary. In essence, they counseled Leopold to produce something closer to autobiographical fiction than he originally preferred. Just why Leopold took so long to follow their advice may never be known. The distraction of other pursuits, the reluctance to compromise his arguments, the scholarly preference for objective presentation—these were some of the motives. It may also be that the prospect of a self-oriented presentation simply bothered him, both as an ecologist[67] and as a strong-minded and sometimes arrogant but increasingly philosophical and reflexive person, who, as his biographer reflects, "had disciplined himself into modesty."[68] As one ecofeminist critic observes, Leopold's concept of the land ethic seems to have been "conceived as a necessary restraint for a self that is driven by an inherently aggressive drive."[69]

So Leopold, under pressure to produce something autobiographical, devised two faces for his persona: the off-duty expert, in shirtsleeves as it were, who recedes into set-piece statements and natural history as he presents bits of forestry, birdlore, prairie vignettes, and the like; and the quizzical experiencer, who appears here and there throughout the text as a figure in the postures of desultory investigation, bemused meditation, and bafflement before the mysteries of nature. In the first sketch, "January Thaw," the speaker idly follows skunk tracks in the snow and wonders what drove the creature to leave its wintry nest. In the next, he delivers a charming, reverse-chronological fireside talk on the history of Wisconsin woods and wildlife for the past eighty years, as he relives the act of sawing through the rings of the oak tree that now fuels the fire. In the third, he ruminates on the return of the wild geese, wishing that "I were a muskrat, eye-deep in the marsh"—so as to understand their secrets better, perhaps (*SCA* 19). These are typical instances. The staging of each exhibit involves a set of strategic decisions as to how faintly or conspicuously to plant the persona and where, and how much to press or question or undercut his authority. Leopold distinctly prefers to have the persona hover on the edges.

The seeming parallel between *Walden* and *Sand County Almanac* regarding the pattern of irregular decline of emphasis on the speaker as the texts unfold is therefore somewhat specious. For Thoreau, the natural environment at first provided a theater for a self-reliance experiment and only belatedly became an interest in itself, as offering something beyond the discipline of voluntary simplicity to the self in search of self-purification. Leopold, by contrast, had no interest in conducting a self-reliance experiment. For him, the environment itself chiefly mattered. The difference in their attitudes was reflected in their actual nature experience, Leopold's at his shack and Thoreau's at Walden. The shack was a weekend place for the Leopold family to go to refresh and enjoy itself, but Leopold looked at it from the first as a serious long-term experiment in restoring an abused landscape. Planting several thousand trees annually is not the usual kind of family outing.

The subtle elegiac charm of *Sand County Almanac* arises from Leopold's awareness of the gap between the power/knowledge of experts on the one hand and the refractoriness on the other of both a nature resistant to human probes and a citizenry resistant to his doctrines. Perhaps it is in this last respect that Leopold's outlook is closest to Thoreau's. Dry irony for both serves as a rhetorical device used to pique an audience presumed to be somewhat obtuse or resistant and to insulate the author from attack.[70]

Although I have just said that the environment is what chiefly matters for Leopold, when we turn to Mary Austin's *Land of Little Rain,* we see that is not quite true. Like self-representation, representation of the environment in *Sand County Almanac* is finally a means for getting to the ecological ethics of the last section, which is set in no determinate region. Obviously Leopold's gospel can be fulfilled only when applied to particular locales; but as discourse *Sand County Almanac* is a homily wrapped in the guise of description, wrapped in the guise of autobiographical sketch. For Mary Austin, environmental representation is paramount, although she conveys an obliquely homiletic dimension (a plea for the West, and for Native American and Mexican American culture), as well as oblique autobiography.

Little Rain has two main subsections, each ending in a village sketch: of a frontier town called Jimville, an ecological disaster that somehow manages a hardscrabble existence, and a utopian oasis she calls El Pueblo de las Uvas. Other dominant motifs that help define the subsections include a natural history sequence (fauna in the first, flora in the second), a cameo sketch of an admirable Native American figure, a mapping of landscape in terms of trails, and images of Anglo-American enterprise (featuring prospecting in the first, ranching in the second). But these arrangements are not conspicuous; and Austin commits herself to boundary erasure at the outset by favoring the Indian name for the region ("The Country of Lost Borders") and warning the reader that she is an unmethodical cartographer. The most provocative example of evasiveness, however, is the chapter at the exact middle of the book, "My Neighbor's Field," in which Austin comes closest to localizing her cabin, her shack. She tells us enough to know that the field sits in some sort of community, next to her house. But we don't see the town (although Jimville, in the previous chapter, serves as an implicit surrogate); we don't see the house except in curt phrases like "under my window" (*LLR* 78); we don't even see the speaker as she looks out from her house. All we see is the field she looks at and envies her neighbor the possession of (calling him "Naboth," whom the biblical King Ahab slew for his vineyard). As he keeps it for a steer pasture and a real estate speculation, she notices with pleasure the "retaking of old grounds by the wild plants" (77).

Austin was a self-professed "fighting feminist,"[71] as she makes clear in the first village sketch, which she subtitles "A Bret Harte Town"—a swipe at the androcentric sentimentalism of Harte's Roaring Camp. Possibly she also sought to deconstruct Thoreau.[72] Be that as it may, the extravagance of her use of the empty center (not only no hometown, but no cabin, virtually no embodied speaker)—accentuated by placing the emptiness at the book's center—stretches to the point of parody some of Thoreau's own reticence and the trope of figurative possession in voluntary simplicity narratives. Austin's persona is so much more self-withholding than Thoreau's speaker that the pretense of land-envy in "My Neighbor's Field" reads like a caricature of romantic imperial selfhood.

Even if Austin did not intend such a caricature, her decision to empty the center of the text of town, habitat, and self comports with the diffusion of narrative angle throughout the work. Here and there she fleetingly gives her persona a shape and a history; more often she prefers the editorial "I" or "we" (which is sometimes literally plural). To a greater degree than Thoreau, Austin allows the book to be taken over by other peoples' stories and her speaker to imagine the desert as it might look through the eyes of birds and animals. In this diffusion of centers of consciousness, and her refusal to maintain an executive control over the perceptual center except at the level of the prescriptive aphorism, Austin adheres to what she sees as the ethic dictated by the place: "Not the law, but the land sets the limit" (9). This ethic exemplifies the double-edged quality of literary naturism as an ideological weapon. What kind of polity does "not the law, but the land" suggest? It *could* suggest a free-for-all frontier culture where the strongest gets the mostest. What better (and more commonly invoked) symbol of this culture than the image of a raw, empty landscape? Yet, of course, it is not the land's vulnerability but its resistance to capture that Austin wishes to stress. The maladaptiveness of outsiders to the region pleases her: that "of all its inhabitants it has the least concern for man" (45).

Here we see Austin fomenting the doctrine of the "hard and brutal mysticism" of the desert region that Edward Abbey later invokes to puncture armchair romanticism.[73] Here she differs markedly from the other literary pioneer of desert ecology, John Van Dyke, whose *The Desert* is a more traditional gallery of picturesque scenes. Austin, by contrast, reruns Thoreau's "The Ponds" like this:

> The lake is the eye of the mountain, jade green, placid, unwinking,
> also unfathomable. Whatever goes on under the high and stony brows
> is guessed at. It is always a favorite local tradition that one or another
> of the blind lakes is bottomless. Often they lie in such deep cairns of
> broken boulders that one never gets quite to them, or gets away
> unhurt. One such drops below the plunging slope that the Kearsarge
> trail winds over, perilously, nearing the pass. It lies still and wickedly
> green in its sharp-lipped cup, and the guides of that region love to
> tell of the packs and pack animals it has swallowed up. (*LLR* 114)

Austin's laconic voice registers the kind of environment "not bound to be kind to man,"[74] as Thoreau gingerly described the higher reaches of Mount Katahdin. It casts a cold eye not only on the charming myth of bottomlessness (which loses its Thoreaurian charm in this forbidding context) but also on the myth of its lethalness that the guides retail. The desertwise speaker relishes the tricksiness of this intractable region and the legends about it.

The combination of guarded impersonal voice and diffuse perceptual centers is an Austin hallmark. In imagining how she arrived at it, we need not merely or even mainly think of it as a revision of Thoreau. It puts Austin in the company of other premodern women environmental writers: like Thoreau's contemporary Susan Cooper, Sarah Orne Jewett, Willa Cather, and Celia Thaxter, whose major book, *Among the Isles of Shoals* (1873), was serialized in the *Atlantic Monthly* a generation before *Little Rain* (1903–1904). Thaxter in particular anticipated Austin by taking as her country of the imagination another remote, superficially forbidding region, a group of rocky islets off the New Hampshire coast. The desubjectification of the persona and the diffusion of perceptual center is common to their nonfiction, and the commonality makes historical sense. It reflects what premodern women were expected not to do (thrust themselves egotistically forward) and what they were supposed to do well (fine work with detail); but these conceptual constraints allow Austin, Thaxter, and others to bring into focus the necessity of approaching the environment on its own terms, not homocentrically.[75]

Such work exemplifies regional realism's ability to turn "improverishment" of place to imaginative gain. We are only now beginning again to appreciate how historically important this largely female-sponsored project was.[76] The effacement of ego that enabled women writers to avoid self-oriented narrative and write in a more "environmentally sensitive" manner resulted partially from cultural conventions they found irksome (Austin being a prime case in point), conventions that contemporary women writers like Annie Dillard and Anne LaBastille have felt free to flout in recomposing their own versions of quest narrative.[77] But however problematic the social causes that produced the result, the fact remains that Austin and Thaxter, and Susan Cooper before them, managed to cultivate a nonegoistic, ecocentric sensibility toward which Thoreau had to grope his way laboriously, as he slowly managed to get down on paper how much more being at Walden meant to him than an experiment in economic self-sufficiency, how much more was entailed in fathoming Walden than merely thinking about what it meant to him. If it is instructive to think of Thaxter and Austin as swerving away from Thoreau, it is no less so to imagine the evolution of Thoreau's style during the compo-sition of *Walden* as a process of learning to write more like them.

For none of them did relinquishment mean *eradication* of ego, how-ever. The aesthetics of relinquishment implied, rather, suspension of ego to the point of feeling the environment to be at least as worthy of attention as oneself and of experiencing oneself as situated among many interacting presences. "One's own landscape," as John Burroughs wrote, "comes in time to be a sort of outlying part of himself; he has sowed himself broadcast upon it, and it reflects his own moods and feelings; he is sensitive to the verge of the horizon: cut those trees, and he bleeds; mar those hills, and he suffers."[78] That seems to have been the sort of feeling that bonded Thoreau to his pondscape, Leopold to his sandy marshland, Austin to her neighbor's field, Thaxter to her rocks. So far is this emotion from ego *erasure* that one could accuse all these authors, including Burroughs, of using their seasoned understanding and their gifts of articulation as a way of securing snug little empires for themselves, hermetic spaces over which they can exert contemplative control, though the elements might defeat them in "real life." Yet much more conspicuous, finally, is their reluctance to assert such control, especially given the vastly increased risks they assume at being ruffled or wounded by perturbations in this greatly expanded space now continuous with, impinging upon, and interwoven with their own. Cut those trees, and I bleed. "If I take one step out of the center, I find myself a part of that circle—a circle made of chickens, chopped corn, mice, snakes, phoebes, me, and back to the chickens again, a tidy diagram that only hints at the complexity of the whole. For each of us is a part of other figures, too, the resulting interconnecting whole faceted, weblike, subtle, flexible, fragile."[79] This is Ozark beekeeper-writer Sue Hubbell, reflecting in a vein similar to Bur-roughs's sense of how farmers feel after long bonding to their niches. Hubbell's train of thought starts with the awareness of herself "setting the process in motion" by "putting a flock of chickens in prime mouse habitat," only to be overcome by the sense of being one among many actors in a much vaster and complexer habitat.

A passage like this, indeed like all the texts discussed here, shows the error of approaching environmental nonfictions as narratives of *either* disappearance *or* self-assertion of the personae. It is a constant temptation to read nonfiction as lyric, as the adventures of the "I." Up to a point that is warranted, and sometimes it may suffice. But we do not do full justice to environmental nonfiction if we read it as a *plot* of a disappearing "I." Peter Fritzell speaks directly to the issue in characterizing *Walden* as riddled by vacillation between "a highly personal point of view in which all or nearly all environmental factors are accounted for and given meaning by a person and, on the other hand, a kind of species-general point of view in which the person attains meaning only in public and impersonal environmental context."[80] Indeed, even this characterization is too rigid, as Fritzell goes on to note.

> To present an environmentalist's point of view in a personal voice. To immerse the person, the personal voice, in an environment. To deny the self and affirm the environment. To deny the environment and celebrate the self. To view the self as a product of its environment and the environment as a product of the self. To view the self as a metaphor for the environment and the environment as a metaphor of or for the self. Such is the habit and the strategy of the self-conscious ecologist, the man at Walden.[81]

This is an excellent description, true not only of Thoreau but of the polymorphousness of which the environmental sensibility has always been capable. Thoreau's prose is more atomized and jumpy than most, but the multiplicity of subject positions in relation to environment that Fritzell diagnoses here can be seen in other writers also.

In one respect, however, I would go a step further. The effect of environmental consciousness on the perceiving self, as I see it, is not primarily to fullfil it, to negate it, or even to complicate it, although all of these may seem to happen. Rather the effect is most fundamentally to raise the question of the validity of the self as the primary focalizing device for both writer and reader: to make one wonder, for instance, whether the self is as interesting an object of study as we supposed, whether the world would become more interesting if we could see it from the perspective of a wolf, a sparrow, a river, a stone. This approach to subjectivity makes apparent that the "I" has no greater claims to being the main subject than the chickens, the chopped corn, the mice, the snakes, and the phoebes—who are somehow also interwoven with me.[82] To get this point across, environmental writing has to be able to imagine nonhuman agents as bona fide partners. The checkered history of its attempt to do so is the subject of the next chapter.

CHAPTER SIX

Nature's Personhood

In those juvenile days, the bubbling brook, the trees, the flowers, the wild animals were to me persons, not things, & though not of a poetic nature, I sympathized with those *beings,* as I have never done since with the *general* society of men.

—George Perkins Marsh to Charles Eliot Norton

When the roar of the flood waters comes, water and rocks and trees are mutely indifferent, but when the mythmaker recounts the story of the flood, the tree is invested with the capacity of compassionate speech: "I too feel the waters rising, and see that you will drown; take hold of this branch." His fiction of object-responsiveness anticipates the actuality of object-responsibility, for though the tree does not speak, when it is itself remade into raft or boat (as when the indifferent rocks are rearranged into a dam), the world outside the body is made as compassionately effective as if every line and nuance of its materialized design were speaking those words. We come to expect this of the world.

—Elaine Scarry, *The Body in Pain*

IF THE PASSAGE from society to environment is dramatized by the plot of relinquishment, the bond between the human and nonhuman estates is expressed through the imagery of relationship. One of the dramatic developments in postromantic thinking about nature has been the decline and revival of the kinship between nonhuman and human. Its metaphysics withered in the last half of the nineteenth century; high modernism announced its death; modern ecologism has brought it back. In this chapter I shall try to make sense of that incongruous story, which is closely tied to the subject of the last, one motive for the personification of nature being to offset what might otherwise seem the bleakness of renouncing anthropocentrism.

Among the great Anglo-American modernists, none was more persistent than Wallace Stevens in exposing the self-delusion of imagining the object-world as our mystic counterpart or companion.

> Air is air,
> Its vacancy glitters round us everywhere.
> Its sounds are not angelic syllables
> But our unfashioned spirits realized
> More sharply in more furious selves.
> ("Evening without Angels")

> The spruces' outstretched hands;
> The twilight overfull
> Of wormy metaphors.
> ("Delightful Evening")

> Tonight there are only the winter stars.
> The sky is no longer a junk shop,
> Full of javelins and old fire-balls,
> Triangles and the names of girls.
> ("Dezembrum")

> The effete vocabulary of summer
> never says anything.
> ("The Green Plant")

> Trace the gold sun about the whitened sky
> Without evasion by the single metaphor.
> Look at it in its essential barrenness
> And say this, this is the centre that I seek.
> ("Credences of Summer")[1]

Yet such reiteration suggests how hard Stevens found it to exorcise his romantic propensities. He often seems to have wondered whether epistemological correctness was worth the sacrifice. For the countermovement is almost equally typical of him: the desire to remythologize, however playfully and conflictedly, as when he fantasizes in "Sunday Morning" about a future sun-worship replacing the Jesus cult.[2] Wryly inventing such fabulous scenarios and dismantling naive or shopworn fantasies were Stevens's ways of holding onto the dream in an age of atheism.

Such epistemological stuttering is one of the central problematics in environmental writing. It emerges most strikingly when a longing to revive the discredited construct overtakes the secularized imagination. Edward Abbey is Stevens's latter-day populist complement. Abbey grandly announces at the start of *Desert Solitaire* that "the personification of the natural is exactly the tendency I wish to suppress in myself, to eliminate for good." But he relapses at once, toying with the fancy that the two gopher snakes lurking somewhere near his trailer are "watching over me like totemic deities." This simile brings him up short.

> How can I descend to such anthropomorphism? Easily—but is it, in this case entirely false? Perhaps not. I am not attributing human motives to my snake and bird acquaintances. I recognize that when and where they serve purposes of mine they do so for beautifully selfish reasons of their own . . . I suggest, however, that it's a foolish, simple-minded rationalism which denies any form of emotion to all animals but man and his dog . . . It seems to me possible, even probable, that many of the nonhuman undomesticated animals experience emotions unknown to us.[3]

First he denounces personalization as imperial man's cardinal sin against empirical fact, then rejects rationalism and almost as vehemently affirms something perilously close to personification, as if the only way to dignify other creatures were to see them as more like ourselves. Some of the great convolutions of western intellectual history are writ small in these gyrations.

From Antiquity to Romanticism

In a celebrated essay, "The Historical Roots of Our Ecologic Crisis," Lynn White, Jr., blames Judeo-Christianity for technology's devastation of the environment, on the ground that it separated heaven from earth under the aegis of a monotheistic transcendent God and justified human lordship over the rest of creation. White proposes Saint Francis of Assisi (who preached to animals and birds and called the sun brother, the moon sister) as a countermodel for fellow Christians. White's argument has been justly questioned both at the level of cause and effect (was modern science not more invigorated by theism's decline than by its impact?) and at the level of its theological analysis (does the "dominion" granted humankind over the beasts of the field in Genesis mean domination or stewardship?).[4] Yet this much seems clear: Hebraic monotheism differed from polytheism in its emphasis on a single, transcendent God; and Christianity, although non-Gnostic versions of it rematerialized God by imagining Jesus as God in human form, further separated deity from earth by spiritualizing its utopian master image of a material promised land. The land of Canaan became an anagogic trope.[5] The New Testament represents Jesus as admiring the lilies of the field but reckoning them far less worthy in God's eyes than humankind.

Meanwhile, however, classicism had kept alive the imagination of an interanimate cosmos: of the land and the sea as gods and as comprising hosts of minor local deities; of humans as children of gods; of natural creatures as transformed humans (Daphne into laurel, Procne into swallow) or as transformable into human shape.[6] Even Lucretius, a scientific rationalist who advocated human control of the environment, enthusiastically reiterated, "How true remains, / How merited is that adopted name / Of earth—'The Mother!'"[7] What eventually became known as the "pathetic fallacy," the ascription of human feelings to nature, entered pastoral poetry with Theocritus.[8] The authority of classicism ensured that the Christian imagination would never go without models of nature and humankind as reciprocal forms of personhood. Thanks to Ovid, in Canto XIII of Dante's *Inferno*, trees bleed when their twigs are picked: they are transformed souls. Thanks to Theocritus and Virgil, not to mention various Renaissance precursors, the Puritan poet John Milton can enlist Neptune and the River Cam as witnesses at the inquest into the cause of Lycidas's death. Indeed, the personification of nature even has scriptural warrant. Psalm 148 calls on sun, moon, stars, waters, fire and hail, mountains, "beasts, and all cattle; creeping things, and flying fowl" to praise the name of the Lord.

Personification reached an apogee in late neoclassical literature. William Collins's "Ode to Evening," a typical period piece in this respect, invokes the hour as "chaste Eve," a thoroughly proper guide for this very proper Adam's recreations, as he casts his eye askance at the bright-haired sun sitting in his tent about to bed down, while the beetle "winds / His small but sullen horn," the evening star lights its lamp, and sundry nymphs and elves cavort.[9] In the next century, such stylizations came to seem intolerably artificial; yet this same climate in which literary fashion countenanced ornate personifications of any or all abstract qualities (pity, fear, hope, etc.) and elaborate anthropomorphism of minutiae like the sulky beetle signaled a breakthrough of great importance to the romantics: the dignification of the overlooked. By no coincidence, James Thomson's *The Seasons* (1726–1740), the first English poem to make natural processes its "protagonist," was also the first major fictive work to display the heightened sensitivity to the treatment and feelings of the brute creation that, as Keith Thomas observes, expressed itself "throughout the eighteenth century, and particularly from the 1740s onwards."[10] *The Seasons* contains appeals in favor of vegetarianism, against mistreatment of domestic animals, on behalf of wild creatures who suffer in winter. One longish passage denounces the honey harvesters' cruel and wasteful practice of smoking bees to death, as

> The happy People, in their waxen Cells,
> Sat tending public Cares, and planning Schemes
> Of Temperance, for Winter poor.
> ("Autumn," lines 1176–1178)

"O Man! tyrannic Lord!" Thomson moralizes,

> how long, how long,
> Shall prostrate Nature groan beneath your Rage,
> Awaiting Renovation? (lines 1189–1191)

To be sure, in ancient times bees had been thought a peculiarly enlightened species. They alone, observed Virgil in *The Georgics*, "hold the dwellings of their city jointly, and pass their life under the majesty of law."[11] In the Renaissance, it was thought that "they would not make honey if their owners were dirty, quarrelsome, or unchaste," and down through the nineteenth century the superstition lingered that they must be told of a death in the family or they might desert the homestead. In the rising climate of eighteenth-century speculation that animals might have souls, bees seemed likely candidates also.[12] Yet Thomson surpassed his precursors in his humanization of bees and other creatures entitled to the same charity as people. He reversed the Miltonic pastoral procedure of calling nature to account for the death of Lycidas. "Sympathy so intense, pity so genuine for the furred and feathered creatures of the countryside had never been expressed on such a scale."[13]

From Thomson it was a short step to Coleridge's salute "To a Young Ass" (1794): "Poor little foal of an oppressed race! / . . . I hail thee *Brother*—spite of the fool's scorn!"[14] The work, to be sure, was a minor one, of sentimentalist pastiche (compare Laurence Sterne's *Sentimental Journey:* "Nampont: The Dead Ass") and jejune revolutionary effluvium. Yet it was the mature Coleridge who went on to write the great English romantic poem about the consequences of mistreating the animal kingdom, "The Rime of the Ancient Mariner," whose protagonist sins by thoughtlessly killing the albatross and atones by expressing a spontaneous burst of affection for the slimy water snakes. Blake's "Auguries of Innocence" imagines a similar extension of moral accountability: "He who shall hurt the little Wren / Shall never be beloved by Men"; "Kill not the Moth nor Butterfly / For the Last Judgment draweth nigh." At times Blake goes so far as to imagine a complete interchangeability between animal and human:

> Am not I
> A fly like thee?
> Or art not thou
> A man like me?[15]

Small wonder that Josephine Miles, in her landmark study of anthropomorphic nature imagery in English poets from Collins to T. S. Eliot, found the highest incidence in Blake.[16]

Blake, with his distaste for scientism, would have been disgusted to learn that right behind him, in second place, was the botanical bard Erasmus Darwin, author of *Zoonomia* and *The Loves of the Plants,* pedantic poems that set Linnaeus to music. Yet the statistics make sense.

Blake and Darwin represent the two major, crisscrossing paths toward the blurring of the traditional hierarchicalizing boundaries separating the human estate from the rest of nature: the route of pietistic sentimentalism, which expanded the range of sensibility, democratized moral accountability, and used mistreatment of nature as an instance of the claims of the helpless against the powerful; and the route of natural history, which put nonhuman species and communities on the same footing as the human.[17] Not that natural history, any more than bourgeois sentimentalism, automatically led to biotic egalitarianism. Insofar as its primary business remained the objective description of natural phenomena and the formulation of these as system or law, it could do the very opposite: imagine beasts as Descartian machines and the natural historian's proper business as classification. The Linnaean naturalist, argues Foucault, "is the man concerned with the structure of the visible world and its denomination according to characters. Not with life."[18]

Yet in practice the discourse of natural history during the pre-Darwinian era reinforced the myth of kinship, reflecting an admixture of rhetorical strategy and authorial proclivity not easily disentangled. Gilbert White, for example, knew perfectly well that animal instinct was "blind to every circumstance that does not immediately respect self-preservation, or lead at once to the propagation or support of their species." Yet he also dilated on the "wonderful spirit of sociality in the brute creation," the "language" of birds, and striking instances of the mixture "of sagacity and instinct," such as an old tortoise who clearly recognized the "benefactress" who fed it—proof, declared White, that "the most abject reptile and torpid of beings distinguishes the hand that feeds it, and is touched with the feelings of gratitude!"[19] In Enlightenment America, the case was similar. In the magnum opus that set a new standard of elegance and precision in American ornithology, Alexander Wilson ascribed to the wood thrush "a shy, retired, unobtrusive disposition. With the modesty of true merit, he charms you with his song, but is content, and even solicitous, to be concealed." John J. Audubon, who superseded Wilson, moved a shade closer to objectivity but still felt impelled to remember "how fervently," after listening to the wood thrush sing at the end of a hard storm, "have I blessed the Being who formed the Wood Thrush, and placed it in those solitary forests, as if to console me amidst my privations, to cheer my depressed mind."[20] Audubon's "as if" was a simple trick to indulge the fantasy of kinship without lapsing into old-fashioned metaphysics. With the authority of such practices behind him, not to mention the age-old association of birds with poets, small wonder that Walt Whitman felt entitled to personify his "dear brother" hermit thrush in "When Lilacs Last in the Dooryard Bloom'd."[21]

Yet romanticism also put personification under new constraints. In neoclassical aesthetics, personification of general and abstract nouns seemed an apt expression of a stable universe; the rhetoricians of the later eighteenth century, however, defined prosopopoeia "so that it hinged on the verb rather than on the adjective or noun"; strength and sincerity of feeling became the test of merit.[22] Thus Wordsworth criticized William Cowper, in his poetic monologue expressing the loneliness of Alexander Selkirk (the original Robinson Crusoe) for picturing valleys and rocks that "ne'er sighed at the sound of a knell, / Or smiled when a sabbath appeared." For Wordsworth, Cowper's was a "language of passion wrested from its proper use." His more fastidious notion of the permissible limits is suggested by a passage from "The Ruined Cottage," later incorporated into *The Excursion,* in which an Old Man (later the Wanderer) commends "The Poets"—of old, presumably—who

> Lamenting the departed, call the groves,
> They call upon the hills and streams to mourn,
> And senseless rocks, nor idly; for they speak
> In these their invocations with a voice
> Obedient to the strong creative power
> Of human passion. Sympathies there are
> More tranquil, yet perhaps of kindred birth,
> That steal upon the meditative mind
> And grow with thought.

This passage says in effect that personification is a distortion of objective reality (the "senseless rocks") justified by lyric passion and that even as readers respond sympathetically they must not forget that it is in the first instance a willful abandonment of critical judgment, which perhaps—but only perhaps—has some basis in the nature of nature. One would like to think so but cannot be sure.[23] Thus Wordsworth vocalizes what neoclassical poets well knew, as their urbanity shows, but felt comfortable to

leave tacit: namely, that personification is a swerve from realism. Wordsworth's finickiness in raising poetic deception as an issue, and in chiding
Cowper for imagining rocks in civilized countries routinely sighing and
smiling, shows an increased commitment to literal fidelity as an issue of
aesthetic ethics. In the next generation, John Ruskin invoked a much
stricter criterion of representational realism, criticizing Wordsworthian
poetry on the same ground of excess passion. For Ruskin, the basis of
artistic excellence lay in the "unencumbered rendering, of the specific
characters of the given object, be it man, beast, or flower." "Material
truth" was "a perfect test of the relative rank of painters." Although
Ruskin allowed that personification of nature was often pleasing, indeed
sometimes mandatory, he categorically stigmatized it as "the pathetic
fallacy." [24]

Even in this altered climate, personification was not stamped out,
although it became more muted and oblique. Tennyson's "amorous odorous
wind" replaces Wordsworth's still Neoclassical line "The cataracts blow
their trumpets from the steep." We can trace this change, as Josephine
Miles does, in the form of an inside narrative of adjustments in aesthetic
perception resulting from greater attentiveness between the mid-1700s
and the mid-1800s to minuter phenomena and finer shades of feeling. [25]
The shift, however, clearly reflected as well the (somewhat reluctant and
self-divided) growth of the belief that natural processes should be explained in materialist terms and that nature's supposed sentience was
simple projection, not inherency. Such materialism made increasingly
fantastic neoclassical conventions underwritten by the hypothesis of a
great chain of being and romantic notions of the visionary imagination
underwritten by a myth of pantheism. Not until the mid-nineteenth
century would an author like Edgar Allan Poe have made a point of
diagnosing "the sentience of vegetable things" as a form of madness. [26]

Yet the rise of formal science did not so much discredit the notion of
"an occult relation between man and the vegetable," in Emerson's quaint
phrase, [27] as translate it. Indeed, the evolutionary hypothesis intensified
the claim of kinship by blurring the boundary between *Homo sapiens* and
other species. When Emerson issued the second edition of *Nature* (1849),
he expressed the ferment of evolutionary thought that Darwin was about
to formulate more rigorously, removing the 1836 epigraph granting nature
symbolic meaningfulness without sentience and replacing it with a poem

imagining the "worm" purposefully striving to become man. When Darwin explicated natural selection in *The Descent of Man* (1871), he granted that "the difference between the mind of the lowest man and that of the highest animal is immense" but argued that the differences were of degree, not kind: "the senses and intuitions, the various emotions and faculties, such as love, memory, attention, curiosity, imitation, reason, &c., of which man boasts, may be found in an incipient, or even sometimes in a well-developed condition, in the lower animals."[28]

Emerson's substitution shows the ease with which, in some minds, a spiritualized frame of vision could adapt itself to the new naturalistic teleology. Darwin's magisterial vacillation suggests the room for maneuvering within the Darwinian framework between strict and loose constructionist definitions of kinship. The resultant discords enliven late Victorian writing about nature, the point in history when the nature essay emerges as a recognized genre. The American scene can be approached by comparing the work of John Burroughs and John Muir, the genre's two most esteemed American practitioners at the turn of the twentieth century.

Personification in the Age of Victorian Realism

Burroughs was a nature-loving literatus self-taught in scientific theory; Muir studied botany and geology at the University of Wisconsin before he thought of becoming a writer. Ironically, it was Burroughs, after making his debut in the *Atlantic Monthly* as an Emersonian transcendentalist, who became the materialist conscience among literary naturists; while it was Muir, after receiving honorary doctorates from Harvard and Yale for (among other things) his knowledge of glaciers, who became the most vocal upholder of transcendentalist-style nature worship among his contemporaries.[29]

Burroughs's reputation was built on his skill as a chronicler of the eastern countryside, particularly the Catskill region where he was born and lived most of his life. Birds were his specialty. He set a high value on accurate observation ("The power to see straight is the rarest of gifts") and liked to think that here at least he had the advantage over Thoreau. ("Thoreau's thoughts are nearer to acts than mine. Yet I am more than his equal in powers of observation.") As Burroughs saw it, whereas the aims of Thoreau and Emerson were "mainly ethical," his own was to "paint the bird, or the trout, or the scene, for its own sake, truthfully anyhow, and picturesquely if I can." Whereas Emerson and Thoreau "drew readers to seek them personally," "my books do not bring readers to me, but send them to Nature." Burroughs's close ornithological descriptions (of habitat, song, nesting, fledging, feeding, and so on) justify this claim and explain why he preferred *The Maine Woods* and *Cape Cod* to *Walden*.[30]

At the same time, Burroughs thought of himself as a nature lover, not a scientist, and warned himself that "unless you can write about Nature with feeling, with real love, with more or less hearty affiliation and comradeship . . . it is no use." In his early work he unabashedly dramatized the sense of comradeship through personification: "It seems to me that I do not know a bird till I have heard its voice . . . The song of the bobolink to me expresses hilarity: the song sparrow's, faith; the bluebird's, love; the cat-bird's, pride; the white-eyed fly-catcher's, self-consciousness; that of the hermit thrush, spiritual serenity: while there is something military in the call of the robin." In later years, however, Burroughs became much harder on anthropomorphism in recoil against an upsurge of popular nature writers who, as he saw it, "grossly exaggerated and misrepresented the every-day wild life of our fields and woods." He had in mind the animal stories of such writers as Ernest Thompson Seton and William J. Long, who nettled Burroughs by overstating animal intelligence, representing instinctive behavior as conscious behavior (birds purposefully schooling their young), and crediting animals with impossible feats of ingenuity (devising splints to heal broken limbs).[31] Burroughs's irritation led him to define the nature of human-animal kinship more rigorously.

He concluded that "we are bound to misinterpret nature if we start with the assumption that her methods are at all like our methods." Burroughs denied that animals "are capable of any of our complex mental processes," except for "those that have been long associated with man, and they only in occasional gleams and hints." Animal artifacts like bird's nests suggest design, indeed seem like a perfect "type or epitome" of natural teleology, yet on closer inspection they appear "almost haphazard." Nature works "always in a blind, hesitating, experimental kind of fashion." Such psychic kinship as exists between human and animal lies rather at the level of the primary emotions—"fear, love, joy, anger, sympathy, jealousy."[32]

As this still generous list suggests, Burroughs by no means flatly debunked the idea of some sort of psychic continuum between human and nonhuman. While striving to minimize it, he kept glimpsing contrary evidence: signs of "disinterested" behavior in birds; signs of animal instinct governing human behavior; evidence supporting the Bergsonian theory that human and nonhuman realms both partake "of that universal intelligence, or mind-stuff, that is operative in all things";[33] similarities in courtship behavior between human and beast. But such evidence pointed in opposite directions. The older, consoling notion of kindred sensibility that in some moods this evidence seemed to support competed in Burroughs's mind with a newer materialist evolutionism: "the animal is father of the man"; the God of tradition is chimerical; "it is only by regarding man as a part of nature, as the outcome of the same vital forces underfoot and overhead that the plants and the animals are, that we can find God in the world."[34] Hence Burroughs's last major project: to try to reconcile modern science with the traditional demands of the spirit. He was too self-divided, and too honest in his self-division, to be able to achieve this reconciliation. "I am always inclined," he wrote late in life, "to defend physical science against the charge of materialism, and that it is the enemy of those who would live in the spirit; but when I do so I find I am unconsciously arguing with myself against the same half-defined imputation." Consequently, "it suits my reason better to say there is no solution than to accept a solution which itself needs solution."[35] But he did at least arrive at a mature, newly self-reflexive position respecting the myth of kinship, namely, to think of it as a need.

It was not a need of which he was proud. "Singular," he wryly remarked, "that we should have outgrown anthropomorphism so far as to deny personality to the separate forces of nature, but ascribe it to nature as a whole." He had in mind the myth of a purposeful universe: "what unthinking people call design in nature is simply the reflection of our inevitable anthropomorphism." He was quite willing to include himself among them:

Our religious natures are still Ptolemaic. The heavens still revolve around us. We do not with the eye of the flesh see ourselves . . . on a celestial body floating in space; we see ourselves as on an endless plain over and under which the heavenly bodies pass. It is only with the eye of the mind that we see things in their true relation and see that there is no up and no down, no under and no over, apart from the earth, and no God who rules.[36]

Intellectually, Burroughs accepted a "modernist" notion of the kinship between humanity and nature at the level of chemical and biological processes, but he could not imagine that anything less than a homocentric and spiritualized version of kinship, which he considered puerile, would satisfy the needs of the spirit.

When Burroughs first met Muir, both then in their fifties, the sedate Burroughs was put off by what he took to be Muir's pushy adolescent impetuousness, though they overcame their temperamental differences and made friends—albeit with an edge of competition.[37] Certainly a modern reader's first impression of Muir's writing is that it is much more youthful, more ingenuously romantic than Burroughs's subtle descriptive sketches or circumspect senescent ponderings. Muir never seriously considered that the "pathetic fallacy" might be fallacious. Among all the great American nature writers, he was the most striking case of spontaneous pantheism. Muir was not only a notional pantheist; he felt it experientially. He could look at a rock and see "a portion of Spirit cloth[ing] itself with a sheet of lichen tissue," and declare that it was no "more or less radically divine" than all other life-forms, which "high and low, and simply portions of God radiated from Him as a sun, and made terrestrial by the clothes they wear." He could look up at rugged peaks, see "mountains holy as Sinai," and exclaim,

> Wonderful how completely everything in wild nature fits into us, as if truly part and parent of us. The sun shines not on us but in us. The rivers flow not past, but through us, thrilling, tingling, vibrating every fiber and cell of the substance of our bodies, making them glide and sing. The trees wave and the flowers bloom in our bodies as well as our souls, and every bird song, wind song, and tremendous storm song of the rocks in the heart of the mountains is our song, our very own, and sings our love.[38]

Far from plunging Muir into agnostic doubt, science seemed "divine," an instrument for the geologist of the Yosemite hills to trace more profoundly "the working of the Divine Mind in their making." Muir not only seconded Wordsworth's dictum that "every flower enjoys the air it breathes" but also went so far as to claim the support of Darwin himself for the proposition that "plants have minds, are conscious of their existence, feel pain and have memories."[39] Reviving the quaint usage favored by the neoclassical poets, Muir spoke of "plant people," of beavers and wood rats as people, of gnats and mosquitoes as people. This was no metaphor. Muir, one comes to believe, really did see glaciers as messengers, feel the daisies "beam with trustfulness and sympathy," approach the sugar pine "as if in the presence of a superior being," and listen in Alaska to "the psalm-singing, lichen-painted trees."[40] For Muir, John Tallmadge rightly observes, "personification is the highest form of flattery," bespeaking reverence for nature and biotic egalitarianism.[41]

Muir's prolix enthusiasm and his inability to rise for very long above clichéd language make for more uneven prose than Burroughs produced, prose that at its worst exposes Muir as an out-of-date provincial trying to revive a secondhand transcendentalism to thrill the partakers of its genteel aftermath. But Muir's stylistic derivativeness belies the originality of his turn of mind. The young Muir was like thousands of intelligent, sensitive men and women of the nineteenth century who quarreled with, while also internalizing, the dogmatic protestantism of their childhood. But the form of his protest was unusual. It was to imagine God as having created the universe as a vast interwoven fraternity of absolutely equal members. "It never seems to occur to these far-seeing teachers," he wrote in a posthumously published journal of his late twenties, "that Nature's object in making animals and plants might possibly be first of all the happiness of each one of them, not the creation of all for the happiness of one. Why should man value himself as more than a small part of the one great unit of creation?" Even the smallest microorganisms, Muir added, "are born companions and our fellow mortals." Indeed, "why may not even a mineral arrangement of matter be endowed with sensation of a kind that we in our blind exclusive perfection can have no manner of communication with?"[42] The ecological thrust of Muir's later thought, as he became a more systematic scientist, derived from this vision of all the orders of creation as a community of equal companions.[43]

Throughout his work, Muir insisted to the point of obsessiveness on nature's companionableness, no matter how superficially forbidding. Camping at 11,000 feet on a climb up Mount Ritter, he had to admit that "in tone and aspect the scene was one of the most desolate I ever beheld. But," he continued, "the darkest scriptures of the mountains are illuminated with bright passages of love." To be sure, the night was "biting cold and I had no blankets"; he barely slept at all; but the sunrise totally eclipsed this discomfort: "How glorious a greeting the sun gives the mountains! To behold this alone is worth the pains of any excursion a thousand times over."[44] Such transformations of images of harshness into images of shelter and comfort are typical of Muir; they show how important to him it was, for whatever reason, to think of nature as his friend.

They also threaten to pull Muir back toward homocentrism: for in these passages he recreated nature in the image of his desire, and one of his chief desires was to use the great outdoors as a vast playground where he could have beautiful experiences and test his nerves and endurance. Indeed, at times Muir could be quite foolhardy and imperious, as when climbing an Alaskan mountain in a howling storm with a group of frightened Indians Muir blithely assured them, "I had wandered alone among mountains and storms, and good luck always followed me; that with me, therefore, they need fear nothing." In fact, he declared that "the storm would soon cease and the sun would shine to show us the way we should go, for God cares for us and guides us as long as we are trustful and brave, therefore all childish fear must be put away."[45] At moments like these, the nature-loving but Indian-disparaging Muir is not far from the machismo of a Theodore Roosevelt. But against this swagger must be set the more disinterested motive: Muir's desire to validate, by showing that he could experience even the most hostile environments as friendly, the vision of nature as a proper home for all its creatures. Muir's theology of an environment not created in humanity's special interest yet fundamentally compatible with all creatures' deepest interests made it unthinkable that there could be anything unnatural, much less wrong, about any degree of discomfort or suffering that might be inflicted on him during his ramblings. Continually to be able to turn fear into excitement, hunger and thirst into imaginative stimuli, was Muir's way of vindicating nature, even against the rebellion of his own body. Muir chided himself for feeling "weak and sickish" on one occasion when he had to do without bread, "as if one couldn't take a few days' saunter in the Godful woods without maintaining a base on a wheat-field and gristmill."[46] Not surprisingly, Muir praised the "Higher Laws" chapter of *Walden,* not despite but because of Thoreau's defenses of vegetarianism and chastity.[47] Thoreau's doctrine that "chastity is the flowering of man" (*Wa* 219–220) made perfect sense to a man like Muir, who felt a direct correlation in his own life between successful mortification of the flesh and peak experiences within nature.

The most popular work Muir ever wrote was, understandably, the kind of animal story Burroughs would never have written: about an unprepossessing, standoffish, intelligent little mongrel dog named Stickeen, which followed Muir on an Alaskan glacier excursion that got progressively more grim and dangerous. The climax comes when Muir negotiates a "sliver-bridge" over a crevasse that the dog fears to cross. Muir talks earnestly to the dog about how he must otherwise be left behind, how the wolves will get him. Finally the dog follows in Muir's footsteps, then cavorts joyfully, "screeching and screaming and shouting as if saying 'saved! saved! saved!'" Thereafter Stickeen and Muir are fast friends. The moral?—"there is no estimating the wit and wisdom concealed and latent in our lower fellow-mortals until made manifest by profound experiences."[48] Whereas Burroughs seldom lingers long on individual creatures, prefers to collage vignettes rather than focus on single species, and rarely allows affect to compromise observational precision and aesthetic detachment, Muir plays on the pathos of the animal-human bond for all it is worth—short of having Stickeen perform the physiologically impossible.

These contrasts suggest the diversification within nature writing during the late nineteenth century that led to Burroughs's attacks on what he took to be the fakery of certain upstarts in the field. The continued spread of humanitarian attitudes toward nature, especially domestic animals, and the technological and informational advances in visual and literary representation of natural history had produced a new genre in which creatures figured as protagonists in fictional narratives much more documentary and localized than the beast tales of traditional Aesopian allegory and folklore. At the romance extreme were programmatic works like Anna Sewall's *Black Beauty* (promoted on its appearance in 1890 as the *Uncle Tom's Cabin* of the horse).[49] At the documentary extreme were works in which human figures were secondary or nonexistent and the representation of animal life was accompanied by affirmations that it was drawn from life and true to natural detail. (Rudyard Kipling, Seton, and fellow Canadian writer Charles C. D. Roberts pioneered this genre.)[50] These writers sometimes set high standards of accuracy. (Henry Williamson claimed that he rewrote *Tarka the Otter* [1927] seventeen times in order to get the facts right.) Yet the practice of representing reality from the animal's perspective tended, as Roberts frankly said, to rest on the view that the intelligence gap "dividing the lowest of the human species from the highest of the animals has in these latter days been reduced to a very narrow psychological fissure." Such blurriness produced in practice the kind of hybrid that made Burroughs uncomfortable: "a psychological romance constructed on a framework of natural science,"[51] a rather precise description of the making of Muir's *Stickeen*. The original journal version of Muir's adventure made no reference to the dog that accompanied him—strong evidence that Muir wanted to create "an allegory on the worth of animals and their importance to mankind."[52]

With such motives operating even among empirically sophisticated literary naturalists, small wonder that even writers far more adamantly materialist in theory than Muir might still personify creaturely behavior. Ernest Ingersoll, a conscientious Darwinian whom Burroughs found unexceptionable, baptized a particular wasp he had observed "Madame Redbelt" and described the "little lady" as she built her nest singing "a low contented, humming song which told of hope and joy." ("And why not? She was constructing a home, a place for her babies . . .") Later chapters in this same book dealt with "Life Insurance for Wasps" and "A Kitten at School." Touches like these show the tendency of "realistic" animal stories to get "trapped by their own genre." To bond readers with their nonhuman protagonists, story writers anthropomorphized inordinately.[53]

The most interesting aspect of the genre, however, is not its susceptibility to deconstruction—any novice can point that out—but the pervasiveness of this doublethink and its persistence in the face of attempts by Burroughs and other apostles of rigor, including even President Roosevelt, to purge the field of exaggerators by scapegoating a few especially blatant "nature fakers." Presumably other motives were at play besides the drive for objective correctness.[54]

As far as Burroughs was concerned, one motive was doubtless the literary struggle of the fittest. Seton and Long represented a younger generation of suddenly succcessful market-oriented nature writers, threatening to dominate, with more compelling styles, a field in which Burroughs had until recently stood almost alone. As he aged, Burroughs had become increasingly anxious both about his waning zest for field studies and about the adequacy of his income. Under the circumstances, the urge to play the arbiter must have been irresistible. But the question remains of why the humanization of the animal world should have become so popular in the face of mounting "scientific" evidence to the contrary.

To begin with, readers traditionally imagined stories about animals as being stories about people. As Harriet Ritvo shows in her study of Victorian discourse on animals, Darwin tended to reinforce more than to interrupt this association.[55] A Darwinian "innovation" like the literary-naturalist convention of likening social to biological struggle was in this sense a new permutation of a much older structure of thinking. It is no coincidence that Jack London retold the plot of his social Darwinist animal story *The Call of the Wild* (1903), about a dog who ultimately became a wolf, in a novel about a tenderfoot seaman who musters enough brute will to defeat his wolfish captain (*The Sea-Wolf* [1904]). Both tales concern the recovery of "the dominant primordial beast" within oneself. Portions of the earlier story of the dog Buck read like analysis of class struggle in code, be the subject dog versus master or dog versus dog.[56] The animalistic combat motif is of course a staple leadoff device in naturalist fiction generally: the fight on the dunghill in Crane's *Maggie*, lobster versus squid in *The Financier*, Bigger versus the rat in *Native Son*, truck driver versus turtle in *Grapes of Wrath*. These prologues announce the social Darwinism of the human narrative to follow.[57]

Turn-of-the-century animal stories themselves rarely fall into the category of literary naturalism, however, even when showing predatory behavior, indeed quite the reverse. They attempt through a style of intimate documentary to counter the fear of nature's "primal brutality" by providing "evidence of dignity, beneficence, and morality in the natural world."[58] In Roberts's "Wild Motherhood," for instance, a wolf trying to feed his pregnant, three-legged dam attempts to rob a mother moose of a calf trapped in a pit; a woodsman, desperate to feed his sick wife and child, shoots both wolf and moose and is about to kill the calf as well ("no meat like moose-veal") when its "piteous bewilderment" by its dead mother's side makes him decide to take it home as a pet instead.[59] The plot turns the struggle for survival into domestic drama: wolf and man are alike as predators, but equally excusable on grounds of family emergency; moose and man are alike as caring parents, and the beast's tragedy, which the man has caused, smites the man's conscience and strengthens his resolve to be a good parent to mooseling as well as child. In short, beasts are both mirror and model. The naturalist novel dramatizes this duality for the sake of social Darwinist analysis; the animal story dramatizes it for humanitarian ends.

Roberts's story seems to bear out James Turner's view of why animal protectionism was a strong element of burgeoning middle-class humanitarian reform in nineteenth-century Anglo-America. Nostalgic about the dislocation from nature that industrialization wrought, anxious about the seemingly insoluble problems of the industrial system (both the bestialization of the lower classes and the threat of their unruliness), the reformers, argues Turner, turned to animal protection as a front on which humanitarianism could make progress without radical challenge to the social system. As part of this program, they projected their ethical standards onto the animal kingdom: "the animals served fallible people as mirrors, reflecting back their own better selves under the guise of the moral teaching of nature."[60] Through Turner's lens, we can read "Wild Motherhood" as a moral tale in which the stereotypical behavior of both wolf and woodsman is euphemized in order to regulate such behavior in society at large by exerting a domesticating influence on the reader.

To imagine animals as being imagined simply for purposes of societal reformation does not do full justice, however, to the extent to which turn-of-the-century personification sought to redefine the human estate by pressing nature's claims upon it. For instance, Sylvia, the heroine of Sarah Orne Jewett's "White Heron," is shown as protecting her alter ego, the heron, against the collector not because the heron is a symbolic extension of her but because she feels herself to be an extension of it. As her grandmother says, "the wild creatur's counts her one o' themselves."[61] Roberts's "Lord of the Air," about an eagle regaining its freedom after an Indian sells it to a rich American collector, does not appropriate the eagle as the symbol of the invaded Canadian wilderness but instead enforces the idea that humans ought not pillage nature and ought to respect a wild creature's wish to remain wild. When Muir imagines the forests of North America "rejoicing in wildness," then shuddering at "the bodeful sound" of axes ringing "out on the startled air," his personifications undermine human enterprise categorically. ("Any fool can destroy trees.")[62]

The controversies surrounding the pathetic fallacy and the humanization of animal behavior in the late nineteenth century reflect the ease with which literature could subserve contrasting social codes: a "masculinist" naturalist code (London) versus a "sentimentalist" naturist code (Roberts), a "sociological" code in terms of which nature mirrored the human scene versus an "ecological" code in the interest of which humanization dramatized nature's nature and nature's claims. Burroughs labored to disentangle these knots and arrive at objective truth. Muir, the less rigorous reasoner but the better judge of American audiences, sensed that the knots were better left untried. This was, in short, a complicated moment for literary history. Avant-garde western epistemology, long since secularized, had "discredited" the Emersonian notion of nature as humanity's spiritual counterpart; American protomodernist writers like Robinson and Frost were beginning to create lyrics about solipsistic projections of human vision onto nature, like "Luke Havergal" and "For Once, Then, Something"; and these poems were soon to be followed by Wallace Stevens's more sophisticated exercises in skepticism, with which this chapter began. If we take the Anglo-American lyric from Victorian to modern as our base of operations, we seem to find a story of increasing separation of mind from nature. Yet environmental prose, that neglected bastion of what we inadequately call the realist movement, was achieving an unprecedented degree of representational density, regulated by a positively Jamesean resourcefulness in the dispersal of narrative point of view among the orders of creation (reality seen through such reflectors as a bird, a wasp, a rabbit, a wolf, and so on). Transfusing these developments, in turn, was an incipient ecocentric ethics that would eventually challenge the utilitarian gospel of efficient exploitation of resources—the first organized conservationist ideology in America—as the paradigm for understanding humanity's proper relation to nature.[63]

This new naturism might seem to have stood opposed to modernist epistemology and poetics, the latter being an indoor, mental pursuit chiefly carried on around the major cities of Europe and the American East, rather than an outdoor activity associated with field observation and wilderness expertise. But the antithesis is oversimple. Within naturism, Burroughs played the modernist relative to Muir, with his pietistic organicism. Within high modernism, Stevens's lyrics mask a sense of loss similar to what Burroughs confesses—and an attentiveness to environmental detail almost as astute, notwithstanding Stevens's seeming disinterest in natural history as a body of knowledge. All parties remain interested in the possibilities of a properly modernized, properly demy-thologized myth of kinship though they disagree in their definition "properly."

In the twentieth century, "ecology" has supplied this myth. Here I refer not to the scientific subdiscipline called ecology, which rests on a set of specialist-sanctioned procedures for quantifying and predicting natural systems, but to the speculative edifices reared on its founding premise of interrelatedness: "There are no discrete entities." For the lay culture in which ecology is practiced, if not for practicing ecologists, ecology is "inescapably a relational discipline speaking a relational lan-guage," as Donald Worster avers.[64] Ecologists have witnessed the rise of various breakaway discourses within disciplines as diverse as biology, anthropology, and law that in different ways play nature's advocate by stressing the kinship between nonhumans and nonhumans.

The Persistence of the Pathetic Fallacy

A striking instance from the first of these fields has been the so-called Gaia hypothesis, fomented by British engineer James Lovelock, "the hy-pothesis that the entire range of living matter on Earth, from whales to viruses, and from oaks to algae, could be regarded as constituting a single living entity, capable of manipulating the Earth's atmosphere to suit its overall needs and endowed with faculties and powers far beyond those of its constituent parts."[65] Lovelock's user-friendly invocation of the Greek earth goddess was enthusiastically welcomed in New Age circles and treated with predictable skepticism by practicing scientists. Of late, Lovelock has begun to receive a more sympathetic hearing from the scientific community as a result of making such concessions as disclaiming the superorganism's intentionality. Lovelock has characterized Gaia merely as a "shorthand" for the theory that "the biosphere is a self-regulating entity with the capacity to keep our planet healthy by controlling the chemical and physical environment," specifically the regulation of the earth's at-mospheric content by the action of organic life. He is even said to have considered dropping the term as too metaphorical.[66] Yet clearly he wishes to claim that the earth is not merely a cybernetic *system* but also a unitary *organism* and to enforce the idea with the maximum impact. This he conveys through phrases like "the infant Gaia," "Gaia, the largest living creature on Earth," "Gaia was mortally stricken," "Gaia's intelligence network and intricate system of checks and balances," "Gaia herself," and "the intervention of Gaia."[67]

Personification of the planet helps Lovelock bond ecology to ethics. In a way reminiscent of Muir, Lovelock contends that humans "live within Gaia," that other species are "our partners in Gaia," that "all attempts to rationalize a subjugated biosphere with man in charge are as doomed to failure as the similar concept of benevolent colonialism." The co-optation of Lovelock's Gaia thesis by Euro-American counterculture seems to have taken him somewhat aback.[68] Yet Lovelock was probably not entirely unaware that his personification of earth was already current in occult and feminist circles.[69] Even if he had not been, he might have anticipated his Gaia's transformation into a cult hero by a culture prepared by Earth Day, *The Whole Earth Catalogue,* and best-sellers like *The Secret Life of Plants* (with chapters called "Plants and ESP," "Plants Can Read Your Mind," and "Force Fields, Humans and Plants"). Indeed, the increasing attention devoted in many arenas to the notion of a "living" planet shows not only the impossibility in modern culture of keeping the discourse of "serious science" distinct from the discourse of "popular superstition," but also the sense even among some scientists, despite fear and trembling, that a surgical separation is not desirable.[70]

Of course, from a cultural historian's perspective, the notion of myth-free scientific discourse is itself a myth. With this myth of surgical separation in mind Donna Haraway retells the history of primatology. Of the 1984 National Geographic film on Jane Goodall's work with chimpanzees in Africa, Haraway says, "Both the native scientific folk-epistemology about a finally validating 'empirical reality' and the popular ideology of scientific representation in the TV specials rely on the myth of the faithful copy, where interpretation or reinvention disappear, where history and its complexities can be finally repressed." The true history, as Haraway represents it, is a story of colonization—of primates, of African facto-tums, of women researchers pictured as stereotyped maternal nurturers of the primates amid solitary nature to propitiate the canons of voyeuristic sexism and savagism that obtain not just at the media level but within the discipline. Haraway directs her irony at institutions of research and their representation in the media rather than at the myth of kinship itself. This becomes clear when, halfway through *Primate Visions*, she interjects a sympathetic sketch of the different premises under which Japanese primatology operates, stressing among other points that the Japanese tradition "postulate[s] a 'unity' of human beings and animals" and that Japanese primatology is distinguished for its "comprehensive, detailed catalogue of the lives of *every* animal in a group." Haraway implies that the Japanese assumption of unity leads to more sensitive results than the western assumption of difference.[71]

So if Haraway punctures the romanticism of the scenes of kinship between Goodall and her chimps, and between Dian Fossey and her apes, she does so not on account of their falsity but on account of their betrayal of an ideal. Indeed, some of the research whose institutional ideology Haraway exposes has led to discoveries that give her comparatively uncritical portrait of Japanese research methods the ring of self-evident truth.[72] Thanks to primatologists' intensive work with chimps, we have a keener sense today than Darwin did of how "human" they can be. Intensive study of small-scale populations has led some ecological theorists to recognize the significance of individuality within animal populations.[73] Some zoologists have argued for the importance of studying the organism in terms of its subjective perceptual field.[74]

A third example of an attempt to press a discourse of "scientific" rationalism to a more generous acceptance of human likeness to nonhumans is the argument that natural "things" should, under the law, be considered jural persons. This position has a long prehistory, dating back to Jeremy Bentham's dictum of 1789: "the day *may* come when the rest of the animal creation may acquire those rights which never could have been withholden from them by the hand of tyranny."[75] Legislation against cruelty to animals, Bentham's immediate concern, was already underway; in America, federal protection of selected species began with the Lacey Act in 1900, first and still primarily adopted for utilitarian reasons but increasingly for aesthetic and moral reasons, until the Endangered Species Act of 1973 legalized the kind of comprehensive species and habitat protection that Aldo Leopold had in mind a quarter-century before, when he declared that all life-forms hold their existence as a matter of biotic right.[76] But the notion that a sequoia or a river or an ecosystem might be considered the legal equivalent of a person was most influentially set forth by Christopher Stone in his 1972 article (and later book) *Should Trees Have Standing?* Stone was moved to action by the case of *Sierra*

Club v. Morton, in which the club sought to prevent Disney Enterprises from building a resort in the Mineral King Valley in the Sierras of southern California. The Supreme Court ruled against the club on the ground that it would not suffer financial injury from the construction and thus had no standing. Stone's article received attention when it became the basis of Justice Douglas's dissenting opinion. Stone argued that the legal personification of a river was no more illogical than the status of a trust or a corporation; "the world of the lawyer is peopled with inanimate right-holders." Subsequent case law, Stone later acknowledged, rendered this innovation unnecessary by broadening the scope of what would count as injury sufficient to bring suit on behalf of the environment. But Stone continued to maintain the principle that "a society in which it is stated, however vaguely, that 'rivers have legal rights' would evolve a different legal system than one which did not employ that expression, even if the two of them had, at the start, the very same 'legal rules' in other respects."[77] The Endangered Species Act of 1973 institutionalized a less radical version of this thinking. For instance, in *Palila v. Hawaii Department of Land and Natural Resources,* the U.S. Court of Appeals, Ninth Circuit, found in favor of a native bird endangered by feral sheep and goats that had been allowed to roam on the slopes of the volcano Mauna Kea. "For the first time in American legal history," writes environmental historian Roderick Nash, "a nonhuman became a plaintiff in court." This was technically not so: the Sierra Club and others "brought this action in the name of the Palila," as the judge stated. But as regards as the effective consideration granted endangered species under the 1973 act, Nash might claim this technicality superfluous.[78]

The examples just surveyed demonstrate that the myth of human-nonhuman kinship has thrived, not withered, in the face of epistemological doubt about where humans stand in relation to the world. Clearly, the credibility of the notion of other beings as humanity's "fellow" creatures does not depend on a postulate of mystic correspondence between humanity and nature. Ecological and sociobiological models can nurture it equally well. Its persistence is not even dependent on being thought "true": indeed, the awareness of its fictiveness can, at least sometimes, actually add to its power. For with Stone the issue is not at all how to describe actuality but how to engineer a change in the legal and ethical status quo by a discursive innovation frankly announced as fictive. Haraway shows that kinship discourse expresses social conditions;

the reception of Lovelock's Gaia hypothesis shows that kinship discourse can make a social impact (in both professional circles and popular culture); but Stone explicitly argues what the others only imply: to change discourse is to change society. The success of the Sierra Club in *Palila* bears him out. The Sierra Club was itself the brainchild of John Muir, the great turn-of-the-century personifier.[79]

Granting species the right to exist has not, at least so far, meant forgoing the right to dominate them. As ethicist John Passmore observes, it is "not that animals have been given more power, more freedom, or anything else which might be accounted as a right" but that human power over them on certain specific fronts has been curtailed.[80] Indeed, the moral status of nonhuman creatures remains a vexed issue in environmental ethics. Even if animals are moral subjects, possessing ethical value, does it follow that they are moral agents? Should we include some unusually intelligent animals, like dolphins, and not others? Is it a "category mistake" to object to the difference between the great respect for the individual human agent in the tradition of liberal ethics and the lower valuation that the ecological community places on the worth of the individual organism?[81] To most who debate such questions, it still tends to seem self-evident that animals lack personality and agency in the sense that humans do and that respect for the individual makes more sense among people than among trees. But the more accustomed we get to thinking of trees as moral subjects, the more dubious these assumptions may come to seem and the more logical may seem those of Lovelock and Stone.

What literary inventions might be expected from an age of unprecedented, albeit somewhat ragged, sense of the interlinkage between humans and other creatures? In the balance of this chapter, I want to consider two different modalities.

The first and more conservative approach, which I shall treat more briefly, derives its energy and its discipline from observing the limits of a rigorously "realistic" sense of psychological probability while envisaging to the extent possible within those limits the interests and desires of nonhuman creatures as equal in affective force to the human desires. Two vignettes of fishing will suffice to illustrate.

> From force of habit, the eel thrust her snout inquisitively into the leaf
> litter under the log, adding to the terror of the frogs, but she did not

molest them as she would have done in the pond, for hunger was forgotten in the stronger instinct that made her a part of the moving stream. When Anguilla slipped into the central current of water that swept past the end of the log, the two young coons and their mother had walked out onto the trunk and four black-masked faces were peering into the water, preparing to fish the pool for frogs.[82]

> In the copper marsh
> I saw a stilted heron
> wade the tidal wash
>
> and I, who caught no fish,
> thought the place barren
> and that jade inlet harsh
>
> until the quick-billed splash
> of the long-necked heron
> fulfilled my hunter's wish.
>
> Then in the rising rush
> of those great wings far on
> I saw the herring flash
>
> and drop. And the dash
> of lesser wings through the barren
> marsh flew through my flesh.[83]

The first passage is from Rachel Carson's *Under the Sea-Wind* (1941), a portrayal of the bird and marine life that dwell in or migrate through the Chesapeake estuary and environs; the second is from an early collection (1957) by contemporary New England poet Philip Booth. *Under the Sea-Wind* updates the regional natural history tradition exemplified in its premodern phases by Gilbert White's *Natural History of Selborne* and Muir's *Mountains of California*. Booth updates romantic nature lyric, in which I-it poems about birds feature prominently: Keats's nightingale, Shelley's skylark, Bryant's waterfowl, Dickinson's robin. What especially differentiates the modern texts is their refusal to imagine nature existing for human benefit or yielding a moral for human consumption. The birds in Booth's marsh do not vibrate in response to the speaker, but vice versa. They do not symbolize his condition; he assimilates himself to theirs, becoming in imagination like the heron—or rather like the small fry who swing into action when the heron drops the fish. The speaker is pulled over the line from genteel Waltonish fisherman to avian hunter, and the poem's marshy-sounding off-rhymes playfully echo that immersion. So does the refusal to end the poem with a moralizing tag: the speaker is reduced to flesh.

Carson is comparatively indifferent to how a human observer might react on the spot to the events she describes. The *umwelt* of the eel interests her far more. Although she presses the point so gently that some will miss the sting, Carson takes humankind to be just another predator, more ominous but also more bumbling than the average. The fisherman remains Booth's center of consciousness even when humbled; Carson banishes her fishermen to the edges of her text—a common device of nature writing whose satirical implications are easily overlooked if we assume that focusing on the natural world by definition means evasion of social reality.[84] As for her portrayal of eel, frogs, and raccoons, Burroughs would have been delighted by the resoluteness with which she adheres to his view that wild creatures are instinctive rather than intelligent creatures driven mostly by appetite and fear. Carson was scrupulous about this. In her introduction she emphasizes the caution with which, for dramatic purposes, "I have deliberately used certain expressions which would be objected to in formal scientific writing." If she writes of "a fish 'fearing' his enemies," it is "not because I suppose a fish experiences fear in the same way that we do, but because I think he *behaves as though he were frightened*."[85] In the quoted passage, she carefully reminds us that the eel forages "from force of habit" yet remains in the current from "the stronger instinct." Even while respecting the distance between animal perception and ours, however, Carson incipiently humanizes her creatures by such devices as giving name and gender to her paradigmatic eel and a vocabulary that implies more purposiveness than she nominally ascribes ("inquisitively," "peering"). It is significant that her preface identifies the sea as the book's "central character." In these ways a bridge is built between her creatures' condition and ours. These touches express what seems to have been Carson's actual attitude toward her subject. Her editor and friend Paul Brooks recalls that Carson "felt a spiritual as well as physical closeness to the individual creatures about whom she wrote: a sense of identification that is an essential element of her style."[86]

Carson's approach to establishing kinship is, then, the obverse but not the opposite of Booth's. Both stresses the retention of the impression of kinship, but they approach this kinship from the opposite standpoints of their respective genres. Booth's lyric poem attempts to tailor the romantic projection of human self into bird in such a way as to meet modernist plausibility requirements. In Carson, kinship must be adumbrated within the bounds of documentary. So the two passages mark, as it were, subjective and objective coordinates of kinship thinking in a climate of modern sensitivity to the excesses of anthropomorphic projection and the ease with which the natural environment can become displaced by some human concern (like Burroughs's epistemological anxiety or Muir's quest for peak experiences). In both passages, the hierarchy of human and nonhuman communities becomes reversed relative to the nineteenth-century norm. For Darwin, "sympathy beyond the confines of man" was one of the prime marks of higher civilization, arising "from our sympathies becoming more tender and more widely diffused, until they are extended to all sentient beings."[87] He referred specifically to "humanity to the lower animals." This spirit of caring seems shared by Carson and Booth, without the sense of condescension. They write as outsiders imagining possible entrance to marshland communities seemingly more alive and genuine and interesting to them than themselves.

The other, very different tendency I want to discuss, at greater length, is the reinvention of mythic forms of representing nature's personhood. Here the agenda is not the humbling of the human observer but the reconstruction of human consciousness. For this discussion, we must return to the nineteenth century and Henry Thoreau.

Thoreau, Native American Spirituality, and Modern Neopaganism

When swapping anecdotes about teaching *Walden,* teachers like to tell about the student who misremembered Walden as the name of the hero. Usually the implication is that the student didn't read the book, but the error can be an honest memory lapse rather than a delinquency; for the author establishes an extraordinary personal tie with the pond. He writes of it as his "neighbor" (*Wa* 86), his "great bed-fellow" (272), his soul-mate in its isolation, himself feeling "no more lonely" than it: "What company has that lonely lake, I pray?" (137). Repeatedly he imagines Walden as a living thing. The pond is a hermit (194), a squaw (295), an eye, an iris (186, 176). It shuts its eyes when it freezes (282); it has a coat and skin (294); it licks its chaps (181); it whoops and farts (272). The speaker greets the pond's rebirth with as much tenderness and rejoicing as the father in the biblical parable of the prodigal son greeted the son's return: "Walden was dead and is alive again" (311).

To endow the pond with a separate, integral being is not to forgo appropriating it for human uses. It is also the hermit's "well ready dug" (183), a food source, a bathing spot. Thoreau admits to having slightly "profaned" the area (197). More abstractly, Walden serves as a multipurpose symbol: of steadfastness, calm, purity, and—most importantly—of the speaker's own better self, his soul's ideal. He looks at his reflection in the pond and asks, hopefully, "Walden, is it you?" (193). He avails himself of the pond to demonstrate his surveying credentials. Indeed, there is no limit to the clever uses Thoreau can make of this piece of real estate: they run the full gamut defined by Emerson in *Nature*—commodity, beauty, language, discipline.[88] Yet Thoreau's arresting rhetorical transformations of Walden are finally so much frothy effervescence compared to his deeply felt affection for the place, which is what provided the original incentive for his imaginative repossession of Walden from hundreds of different angles.

The chief mark of this affection is the personification of the pond. In the climactic passage of "The Ponds," Thoreau calls Walden a "character," as Carson did the sea, only more insistently. Walden is "perennially young," with "the same thought . . . welling up to its surface" as when he first visited it, "the same liquid joy and happiness to itself and its Maker" (*Wa* 193). I take it that this passage stretches beyond playful metaphor toward an almost animistic evocation of Walden as a living presence, not merely a "neighbor" but a mentor, a role model. The analogy between Thoreau's admiration of Walden's purity and his own sermon on chastity was no accident, nor was it probably just the convenience of proximity that led him to use Walden as the test case for establishing kinship between limnological contour and human character

(*Wa* 289–291). Not only transcendentalist dogma but also the felt sense of the pond's companionableness helped make Thoreau's moral formulations credible.

Thoreau's evocation of a nonhuman entity as a major presence, superior to any human being in the text, the narrator included, is an extraordinary event in the premodern American literary canon, matched only by Melville's white whale, whose interest to a much greater extent than Walden Pond hinges on its status as a figment of the quester's imagination. This is not to deny that Thoreau traveled with the usual Eurocentric baggage. "We can suspect a Transcendentalist leap into at least the borderland of idealism here," as Catherine Albanese says of Thoreau's personification of nature in general. Albanese rightly insists that although Thoreau moved further toward "spiritual paganism" than Emerson, "he never fully got there,"[89] at least not by the time *Walden* was completed. But the sense of personal intimacy with nature continued to grow, notwithstanding his increasingly scientific approach to nature study. It became axiomatic for Thoreau that "sympathy with nature is an evidence of perfect health" (*J* 10: 188), and further that "to insure health, a man's relation to Nature must come very near to a personal one . . . I cannot conceive of any life which deserves the name, unless there is a certain tender relation to Nature" (*J* 10: 252).

What exactly did Thoreau mean by that "certain tender relation"? One clue is his sensitivity to violence against nature as if it were violence against people. He upbraids himself for pelting chestnut trees with rocks in order to make the nuts fall: "It is worse than boorish, it is criminal, to inflict an unnecessary injury on the tree that feeds or shadows us" (*J* 7: 514). Indignant at a neighbor's felling of his hackberry trees, the only stand of its kind in Concord, Thoreau declares, "if some are prosecuted for abusing children, others deserve to be prosecuted for maltreating the face of nature committed to their care" (*J* 10: 51).

The hyperactivity of environmental conscience in cases like these was quickened by a combination of lococentrism and local knowledge not unique to Thoreau, although he felt it more keenly than most. In Gilbert White and Celia Thaxter, in Muir's knowledge of the Mariposa Grove sequoias, in Sue Hubbell's attachment to her Ozark farm, in Wendell Berry's affinity to Appalachian Kentucky, long commitment to place expresses itself in affectionate bonding to landscape particulars far deeper

than the proprietary motives that sometimes accompany it or the rhetorical uses made of it. Anglo-American celebrants of the bond to place
enact the rite of passage that Robert Frost made famous in "The Gift
Outright." "The land was ours before we were the land's," after which we
must learn how to belong to it.[90]

One of Thoreau's contributions to this literature of belonging, however, was to widen irretrievably the split between the communal bond to
place and the individual bond, a split already opening in the late colonial
period. (The contrast between Crèvecoeur's depiction of the middle-states
farmer and the community of Nantucket is an early example.) Thoreau
typically represents himself as Concord's sole ecological conscience. The
powers that be think his finickiness absurd; townspeople are indifferent;
the more environmentally sensitive country folk tend to be his informants
rather than his comrades. Thoreau frequently uses "neighbors" sarcasti-
cally when referring to humans; but when referring to plants and animals,
never.[91]

Thoreau's representation of himself as nature's solitary champion is
hyperbolic, albeit not without justification. From his mordant comments
on the dispatching of Concord's great elm ("I was the chief if not the
only mourner there"; J 8: 130), one would hardly appreciate how pervasive
throughout New England was reverence for elms as the emblematic
regional tree and the status of particular great elms in different communities as symbols of their history or welfare. Indeed, in some lyrical
accounts, elms (and occasionally other hardwoods) had a totemic status
in nineteenth-century New England not far distant from the position of,
say, the white spruce among the Koyukon of central Alaska.[92] Nor was
this sentiment an American invention. Communal expression of reverence for trees, especially particular famous trees, had long run strong in
old England, owing to the greater embeddedness of lococentrism and the
scarcity of woodland since the early seventeenth century, not to mention
more ancient symbolic associations attached to trees in western culture.[93]
So Thoreau's elegy was in form if not in detail an almost stereotypical
expression of Anglo-American sentiment, although he delivered it as a
lonely dissent. Thoreau might still with some justice have objected that
his grief was more passionate than most people's. The resurgence of New
England's woodlands during the late nineteenth century was due more
to the decline of agriculture and the rise of coal than to preservationism,

although Concordians started setting out white pine seedlings in the mid-1850s, to Thoreau's surprise and delight.[94] No other Concordian would have confessed to falling "in love with a shrub oak"; none would have claimed "all nature is my bride"; none would have imagined inconsequential copses as "little oases of wildness in the desert of our civilization" and been inspired by them to "believe almost in the personality of such planetary matter" (*J* 9: 146, 337, 44–45).

The intensity of these declarations may be "excessive," but it is churlish to carp about Thoreau's maladjustment without acknowledging the insight to which his obtuseness led him. He made disaffection productive by discovering through it an almost neopagan sense of the neighborliness of nature that only the Wordsworths among recent major writers had approached. Emerson wrote: "In the tranquil landscape, and especially in the distant line of the horizon, man beholds somewhat [*sic*] as beautiful as his own nature."[95] Thoreau wrote: "In the bare and bleached crust of the earth I recognize my friend" (*J* 11: 275). The affect, the implicit ethics, of these two statements could not differ more strongly. Through a combination of romantic literary sensitivity, a villager's fondness for countryside, hard-won knowledge of natural history, and a loyalty to Concord more akin to New England local boosterism than he acknowledged, Thoreau enlisted old-style pathetic fallacy rhetoric in the service of a sacred environmentalist cause that both echoed the ruralist nostalgia widespread in England and New England and radicalized it by demanding that it be taken seriously as a criterion for regulating social action.

It was partly on this account that Thoreau valued Native American culture, first as a romanticized image of a life close to nature, later for the richness of its ability to read, use, and (in its impressively discriminating vocabulary) express the natural environment. Though it took him some time to get past the platitudes of romantic savagism, he became the first major Anglo-American creative writer to begin to think systematically of native culture as providing models of environmental perception rather than as a mysteriously compelling vestige.[96] This aspect of native culture eminently appealed to a westerner deeply interested in rehabilitating an awareness of kinship between human and nonhuman realms. For one of the marks of traditional Native American culture, as for other aboriginal peoples, has been its understanding of the human-nature relation as a continuum or a monism rather than as a binary schism.

"Nature is not sharply set off as something different from man." "Other living things," as one Native American intellectual puts it, "are 'peoples' in the same manner as the various tribes of men are peoples." Even a casual reader of traditional Native American tales notices the frequency of conversations and identity exchanges between animals and humans, in contrast to western assumptions of a "mute" world "in which only humans speak."[97] Thoreau did not need Native American culture to teach him this basic idea, but his ethnological researches and his contacts with Indian guides during his last two trips to Maine began to give him a greater understanding than he ever had before of the cultural conditions and detailed environmental and linguistic competences that underlay this mentality. He never fully entered into it, however. For one thing, his relationship with the nonhuman realm remained largely a solitary affair, whereas in Native American spirituality "the possibility of conceiving of an individual alone . . . is ridiculous."[98] A second barrier was the aesthetic self-consciousness with which Thoreau appraised landscapes, from his first essay excursions to his late natural history lectures. No traditional Native American would intuitively think of nature "in the way the nineteenth century 'nature poets' thought of looking at nature and writing about it," writes Native American writer N. Scott Momaday, himself a specialist in American romantic literature. "They employed a kind of 'esthetic distance'" that "would be alien to the Indian." Anthropologist Äke Hultkrantz goes so far as to claim that "the aesthetic enjoyment of nature is a peculiar development of the white man's civilization," introduced by the likes of Rousseau and Thoreau. "The American Indians were practical people, nature was to them the means of subsistence, housing, dress, transportation, and so on."[99] Hultkrantz overstates the case, but the conception of the aesthetic as a distinct category of experience does seem to be a westernism. Thoreau's notion of nature's sacred space was similarly compartmentalized.

As his sense of the deep meaningfulness of the Concord landscape continued to grow, Thoreau did acquire something like a tribe member's sense of the sacrality of his ancestral ground, but not quite. The difference between the two perspectives is evident from his most memorable formulation of his new consciousness: two eloquent proposals, drafted late in his life, for the creation of public parks—one for the preservation of the banks of the Concord River as public lands, the other for "a primitive forest, of five hundred or a thousand acres," to be sequestered in every township, "where a stick should never be cut for fuel, a common posses-sion forever, for instruction and recreation." In this way "all Walden Wood," he continues, "might have been preserved for our park forever, with Walden in its midst" (*J* 12: 387).[100]

This is Thoreau's contribution to the nineteenth-century American passion for creating sacred places, as the town of Concord had done in the 1830s in erecting the battle monument celebrated in Emerson's already classic "Concord Hymn." Thoreau participates in, competes with, and seeks to redirect his compatriots' memorializing bent. It is an inspiring proposal. It has helped inspire the late twentieth-century campaign to save Walden Woods from developers and to define Walden ecosystemi-cally and not just in terms of the pond's perimeter and immediate vicinity. It reflects, however, a comparatively Euro-American vision of sacred space: what environmental theorists call the "sanctuary" or the "cathedral" concept, according to which sacred space is more distinctly marked off from the profane. Whether because of the surveyor in him, the post-Puritan, or just the pragmatist, Thoreau's notion of land appor-tionment follows the European settlers' practice of assigning explicit titles to specific parcels of land.[101]

An even more fundamental symptom of Thoreau's cultural distance from indigenous thinking was his envisagement of the Indian intimacy with nature that he so much admired and envied as a form of training rather than as a mode of spirituality. Native American spirituality did not greatly interest Thoreau as such; when he mused about "how much more conversant" were Indians "with any wild animal or plant than we," he had in mind such things as Indian woodsmanship and the fine distinc-tions of the Abenaki vocabulary respecting animals and plants (*J* 10: 294). There is a revealing moment during the third and last narrative in *The Maine Woods* when Thoreau's guide, Joe Polis, points out some mountains of forbidding look, which "my imagination personified," conjuring up the specter of "some invisible glutton" that "would seem to drop from the trees and gnaw at the heart of the solitary hunter who threaded those woods." Polis calmly tells Thoreau that he has been there several times and proceeds to give some anecdotes of his expert woodsmanship, which Thoreau at first chalks up to "instinct" but on second thought to "a sharpened and educated sense."[102] For the younger Thoreau, whose interest in nature was more aesthetic and theoretical, the romance of intimacy with nature was heightened by imagining himself as a symbolic Indian. For the older Thoreau, at least in this instance, an actual Indian's practical sagacity helped to counteract the imagination's excesses. If the younger Thoreau held the Indian in his mind's eye and imagined too much, the older Thoreau may have looked at his companion and imagined too little. No superstitious nonsense there, no mumbo-jumbo—just years of hands-on experience.

As this episode from "Allegash and East Branch" suggests, although Thoreau created in his characterization of Walden (and also of Mount Katahdin) a triumph of animistic feeling equaled among American writers of his day only by Melville's white whale, intimacy with nature in his case led ultimately to demythologization, which was confirmed and accelerated by his increasingly systematic study of Native American history and culture. By contrast, for many contemporary Euro-American ecocentric writers, including some who are more knowledgeable about Native American culture than Thoreau was, it is precisely the vision of humankind as belonging to a partnership of creatures within an animate environment—an awareness Thoreau himself felt but did not derive from his assiduous Indian research—that is most inspiring about Native American culture. Gary Snyder, for example, praises Inupiaq iconography as depicting "a panoply of different creatures, each with a little hidden human face. This," Snyder emphasizes, "is not the same as anthropocentrism or human arrogance. It is a way of saying that each creature is a spirit with an intelligence as brilliant as our own." Likewise, Barry Lopez, in a provocative essay calling for renegotiating the "contracts" between humans and animals, characterizes western exploitation of the nonhuman world as a massive "failure of imagination" that might be addressed, in part, by learning from the seriousness with which animals are taken ("as part of a coherent and shared landscape") in aboriginal narrative.[103]

Undoubtedly the commonest image, in both Euro-American and Native American traditions, for expressing the idea of an earth-humanity continuum has historically been the metaphor of "mother earth" or "mother nature." "Our Mother the Earth," one witness testifies, "is a reality in the cosmologies of virtually every native people in the world."[104] Perhaps its persistence in western discourse to this day is a sign of western culture's own vestigial aboriginality. We encountered mother earth in

Lucretius; we observed her in Muir; we find her in Thoreau's playful reference to "our great-grandmother Nature" (*Wa* 138); in Lovelock's Gaia she appears again. The spread of post-Enlightenment science and secularism did not eradicate her; on the contrary, the personification still tugs at the western sensibility. As one New Age ecological manifesto states, even if the Gaia hypothesis is only a name for "some highly technical chemical and geological analysis," "still, there clings to the image something of an older and once universal natural philosophy that quite spontaneously experienced the Earth as a divine being."[105] Indigenous discourse may itself have been affected by the awareness of this penchant among westerners. Sam D. Gill argues in a fascinating revisionist study that American Indian rhetoric since the first contact with whites has accentuated the place of mother earth in native cosmology beyond the place she originally occupied, partly with a view to playing on white primitivist nostalgia. His argument does not to my mind to refute the claim of a number of Native American intellectuals today that "the fundamental idea that permeates American Indian life" is that "the land (Mother) and the people (mothers) are the same," but it does suggest that Native American spokespersons may have historically accentuated the ancient earth-mother association in awareness of its cross-cultural appeal.[106]

But the persistence of the earth-mother personification in modern western thought can hardly be understood simply as a heroic resistance to its demystifying tendencies. As feminist historians have shown, the mother earth image has been used by western male writers since the Renaissance to underwrite the domination both of nature and of women. The ancient mythification of nature as a "benevolent female," Carolyn Merchant argues, "contained the implication that nature when plowed and cultivated could be used as a commodity and manipulated as a resource." With the scientific revolution, nature changed "from an active teacher and parent" into "a mindless, submissive body"—in the hands of the Baconian engineers of the modern world system, that is. Looking at the American situation, Annette Kolodny finds a persistent tendency emanating from the early literature of exploration and romance to imagine the land not merely as mother but also as "the female principle of gratification itself, comprising all the qualities that Mother, Mistress, and Virgin traditionally represent for men." Indeed, anthropologist Sherry B.

Ortner argues for the universality of the equation "man is to woman as culture is to nature" as an instrument of dominance worldwide.[107]

It is therefore all the more striking to see certain other contemporary feminists rehabilitate the metaphor, sometimes not only despite but even partially because of the very idea of nature as a figure of female oppression. "This earth is my sister," meditates Susan Griffin. "I love her daily grace, her silent daring, and how loved I am *how we admire this strength in each other, all that we have lost, all that we have suffered.*"[108] The most spectacular contemporary response of this kind has been the reemergence of feminist neopaganism in middle-class Euro-America, centering on the figure of the Goddess, associated with maternity, earth, female essence and spiritual strength.[109] Its advocates stress that the earliest form of human worship, which pictographic and archaeological evidence seems to date as far back as twenty millennia B.C.E., was of a female divinity. She seems to have been displaced during the Iron Age by patriarchal forms of worship (first in Babylonia, later by Judeo-Christian monotheism), persisting in official Christian-era religion only through the much reduced form of the cult of the Virgin Mary. Yet "the religion of the Goddess never completely died out"; at the folk level, she "was kept alive by a handful of the faithful who practiced their rituals in small bands and preserved their knowledge of nature's teachings."[110] Today the idea of the Goddess flourishes, variously, as a reference point in feminist theology; as a figure in worship practices ranging from witchcraft cults to spontaneous feminist support groups; as an idealized image of femaleness; as an inspiration for feminist literature, visual art, theater, and dance; and as an ethical metaphor for our proper relation to earth. All of these forms are more or less ecocentric. The appeal of this and other versions of the mother earth formation in western thinking, as noted earlier, helped ensure the astonishingly rapid popularization of the Gaia hypothesis, which was seen to be "a scientific update of the belief system of Goddess-worshipping prehistoric societies."[111]

Although goddess theology looks on Judeo-Christianity as the adversary, as part of the ancient patriarchal conspiracy to dethrone *magna mater,* comparable attempts have recently been made within it to reconnect it more closely to earth and femaleness, as in the metaphorical theology of Sallie McFague. She advocates a "*remythologizing* of the relationship between God and the world" by recourse to metaphors like the world as God's body and God as mother rather than father. These metaphors she presents as evolutions from rather than apocalyptic breaks with Christian theology.[112]

Only time can tell how far feminist neopaganism and more conservative forms of revisionist ecotheology will be taken and whether they will join forces. Most important for our purposes, they indicate the unquestionable, perhaps unshakable persistence of the repeatedly discredited dream of a living, sentient earth not only among pockets of aboriginal culture but even among well-educated, often thoroughly secularized denizens of a modernized world in which the official intellectual culture stands for demythologization. Whether one chooses to credit mother earth movements as enabling a politics of Native American or feminist spirituality or to decry them as a regression (and the latter remains the dominant position),[113] their upsurgence is one of many contemporary signs that the idea of an earth-humanity continuum of more than a material sort may be unsuppressible, that people cannot do without the idea of a "living earth," and that humanity is perhaps better off accepting it—some versions of it, anyhow—than trying to extirpate it. Who is more likely to treat other people as machines, a person who has trained herself to feel that plants and animals are fellow beings or a person who looks at them as convenient resources? If there is anything that can "stop the human species from poisoning the Earth or blowing it up," writes feminist ecotheologian Carol Christ, it is "a deeply felt connection to all beings in the web of life."[114] Of course a callous tyrant or entrenched bureaucracy is not likely to listen to a phalanx, even a nation, of people holding such attitudes. But a society that genuinely cherished these views might be less likely to breed such tyrants and bureaucracies.

The rhetoric of nature's personhood speaks merely to the nominal level; what counts is the underlying ethical orientation implied by the troping. "Mere projection or personification," as environmental ethicist John Tallmadge writes, signifies far less than the commitment to perceiving the nonhuman world not "as an object, but . . . as a presence."[115] Furthermore, it is not enough, as Snyder argues, "just to 'love nature' or to want to 'be in harmony with Gaia.' Our relation to the natural world takes place in a *place*, and it must be grounded in information and experience."[116] When Thoreau writes in painstaking but rather clinical fashion about the sensitivity of tender seedling oaks to frost, he may be closer to apprehending the nonhuman world as part of a community of concerned beings than when he composes, a page later, a metaphorical set piece about a stand of pines marching across a plain as on a field of battle, to extend their range (*J* 14: 149–150).[117] "The grand question remains whether most people actually *Want* hearts to be tenderer or harder," as Joseph Wood Krutch put it a generation ago. "Do we want a civilization that will move toward some more intimate relation with the natural world, or do we want one that will continue to detach and isolate itself from both a dependence upon and a sympathy with that community of which we were originally a part?"[118] From such an ecocentric standpoint, the promise of the image of nature's personhood lies in the extent to which it mobilizes what feminist ecological thinkers have come to call an ethics of care.[119] At its best, the ethics of care promises to quicken the sense of caring for nature and to help humans compensate for the legacy of mind-nature dualism while at the same time respecting nature's otherness. Clearly the rhetoric of nature's personhood does not always induce these results—no more than any other system. The ethics of care may be deflected back into narcissism instead (loving the goddess or green man in *oneself*), and always it must be taken for granted that benign principle may not translate into benign practice.[120] Yet to ban the pathetic fallacy— were such a thing possible—would be worse than to permit its unavoidable excesses. For without it, environmental care might not find its voice. For some, it might not even come into being.

CHAPTER SEVEN

Nature's Face, Mind's Eye: Realizing the Seasons

↜

These regular phenomena of the seasons get at last to be—they were *at first,* of course—simply and plainly phenomena or phases of my life. The seasons and all their changes are in me.

—Henry David Thoreau, *Journal*

There is no certainty vouchsafed us in the vast testimony of Nature that the universe was designed for man, nor yet for any purpose, even the bleak purpose of symmetry.

—Donald Culross Peattie, *An Almanac for Moderns*

ENVIRONMENTAL TEXTS MAY SEEK to order natural phenomena either as a perceiver might encounter them or as the environment manifests itself. Writing that stresses the former often adopts some sort of excursion narrative—the walk, the ramble, the exploration, the quest. The latter approach typically relies on some natural cycle: the day, the seasons, geologic epochs, evolutionary development, and so on. These are loose containers that admit of infinite gradients and combinations, since the experience of engaging the environment is always both "subjective" and "objective." Clarence King's *Mountaineering in the Sierra Nevada* (1872) reads like an adventure story relative to David Rains Wallace's *The Klamath Knot* (1983), in which Wallace describes a series of ecosystems in the northern end of the same range, discussing them in turn as an evolutionary history. Yet Wallace treats each ecosystem as he progresses on a faintly sketched trek upward into the mountains, while King's comparative egocentrism finally amounts to little more than a bit of dirt on the windowpane through which he glimpses the regional geology and geography.

The excursion format, then, is not by definition the less "environmentally oriented" choice, since the excursioner can efface himself to the point of becoming little more than a recording device, as in Thoreau's early essay "A Winter Walk" ("Now our path begins to ascend gradually to the top of this high hill").[1] Even the most protagonist-centered narratives can build to a culmination in which the speaker's egoism is overwhelmed or dissipated. In Peter Matthiessen's *The Snow Leopard* (1978), for example, what begins as a rather complacent *National Geographic*–style adventure in the remote Himalayas turns into an unexpectedly life-changing event in which resurfacing memory and powerfully defamiliarizing environment shatter and reform the secular ego.

Indeed a whole volume could be written on the excursion as a form of environmental interaction—or even on a single subgenre, as Jeffrey Robinson and Roger Gilbert have shown in their studies of the literary walk.[2] But having explored in Chapter 5 perhaps the most fundamental preoccupation of such writing, voluntary simplicity, I shall concentrate here on texts, or portions thereof, that purport to organize themselves in terms of the motions of the environment itself: texts that rely on nature's motions to provide the central organizing device. As such they shed further light on the central question of just how far the human imagination is prepared to be drawn away from anthropocentrism, to enter imaginatively into a realm where human concerns are no longer central.

In environmental prose, the seasons have been a particularly favored organizing principle. Among American books, Susan Cooper's *Rural Hours,* large portions of Thoreau's *Walden,* Celia Thaxter's *Among the Isles of Shoals,* John Muir's *My First Summer in the Sierras,* Henry Beston's *The Outermost House,* Rachel Carson's *Under the Sea Wind,* Part I of Aldo Leopold's *Sand County Almanac,* Joseph Wood Krutch's *The Twelve Seasons* and *The Desert Year,* Edward Abbey's *Desert Solitaire,* Annie Dillard's *Pilgrim at Tinker Creek,* David Rains Wallace's *Idle Weeds,* Sue Hubbell's *A Country Year* all follow a seasonal ordering in whole or part. This is not surprising. For the seasons, next to the alternations of day and night, are the environmental cycle most perceptible in everyday life. To observe their passage and take pleasure in it requires no formal training. Yet they are also tantalizingly elusive; even a lifetime of study, as Thoreau found, does not make one the master of their nuances. Hence the inexhaustible challenge, albeit the likelihood of falling into threadbare repetition, of reviewing their progress. Furthermore, insofar as the seasons condition, predict, and (in the popular imagination) symbolize human behavior, a comprehensive anthropology and cosmology can be constructed on their foundation. For every person, there is a season. The seasons traditionally symbolize stages of life. Every human activity, at least in the rhythm of preindustrial life, can be thought of as having its own season. Hence Susan Cooper, in the first and still the most ambitious seasonal compendium published by an American author, could use the daybook format of *Rural Hours* (1850) to furnish a complete anatomy of Cooperstown's cultural life as well as its natural history, updating and deepening her father's fictionalized portrait of the village's early years in *The Pioneers* (1823), likewise arranged in seasonal form. Yet since all such literary formulations are arbitrary, they are also the symbol of nature's resistance to symbolism: nature's endlessly intricate face or body, as well as the mind's construct. Whichever way one responds to them, they offer one of the first and commonest paths by which a human being may be teased into ecological consciousness.

Before Thoreau: Thomson's *Seasons*

The notion that the seasons structure life-rhythms or symbolize life's passage is ancient and ubiquitous—seasonal contours varying greatly by region, of course. It underlies the art of paleolithic cave drawings.[3] The most primitive form of seasonal writing, the almanac, dates back to Egypt of the third millennium B.C.E. Possibly the earliest work of developed literature basing itself on the idea of seasonal change, the Canaanite mythical *Poem of Aqhat* (fifteenth century B.C.E.), depicts the murder of the mythic hunter-hero and the resulting drought on the land, apparently symbolizing the coincidence of the disappearance of the constellation the Greeks knew as Orion and the dry season in the Middle East.[4] About eight centuries later, in what must be one of the first western examples of secular season poetry, Hesiod devoted 335 lines of his *Works and Days* to a calendar of advice to farmers, a genre that Virgil wrought to perfection in *The Georgics* (29 B.C.E.), but following a topical rather than chronological order (farming, arboriculture, stock raising, beekeeping). Seasonal poetry was also introduced at an early date in China (see the 154th lyric in the *Book of Songs*, a poem ascribed to the eleventh century

222 FORMS OF LITERARY ECOCENTRISM

B.C.E.). One of the early texts of Sanskrit literature (fourth century C.E.) was the *ṛtu-saṃhāra*, attributed to Kālidāsa. This poem of 140 stanzas imagines the blandishments and pangs of love from a male point of view, as they unscroll over the course of the *six* seasons into which the poet divides the Indian year. In the rainy season, for instance: "Clouds, bent down by the weight of water, are covering all the sides of the mountain. The fountains are filled with water and the peacocks are dancing in delight. With these objects of beauty the mountains are filling the minds of men with curiosity."[5] Season signs here become projections of eroticized desire, as the flowing fountains and dancing peacocks interact to sexualize the mountains. The poem achieves the kind of transformation that the early English imagination later wrought upon the innocent cuckoo, first emblematized on natural history grounds as "sumeres weard" in the Old English "Seafarer" and in the Middle English "Cuckoo Song," but subjectified as a mocking harbinger of the cuckolding season by Chaucer's time. In the fourteenth century, we first find a major work of English literature constructed in terms of the passage of the seasons: *Gawain and the Green Knight.*[6] Although often strikingly particularized, seasonal representation in English literature through the Renaissance tends to be regulated by theological and astronomical formulas.[7]

The foregrounding of the seasons as the central subject of a major work of English literature came only on the eve of the scientific and industrial revolutions, and partly in reaction to the experience of social displacement wrought by urbanization. This was James Thomson's four-part blank-verse epic *The Seasons* (1726–1740). Thomson seems to have gotten the idea for his protoeffort, a short descriptive poem on *Winter*, from Milton's briefer celebration of the course of the paradigmatic day in *Il Penseroso*, then to have transfused his style with Miltonic blank verse, georgic vignettes, Newtonian science, and descriptive set pieces from the emerging locodescriptive tradition on whose future course *The Seasons* became an important influence.[8]

Read respectfully by a century of Anglo-European literary naturists including Gilbert White, William Howitt and Mary Howitt, Susan Cooper and Henry Thoreau, Thomson's work crystallized a number of the fundamental conventions of the premodern season piece: its linkage of the natural, human, and divine estates; its serious contemplative, indeed reverential tone; its countertone of jocund playfulness (rendered slightly

elephantine by ponderous pentameters); its elevation of "trivial" phenomena to the status of important events; its humanitarian appeal to the
"higher" orders to respect the lower; its miscellaneous and encyclopedic
character. More than any previous long poem of merit in the language,
The Seasons leaves one with the impression that there is nothing, natural
or cultural, that might not somehow have found a place in it. An idyll of
fly fishing; a parody of fox hunting; a discourse on vegetarianism; a view
of the tropics in summer, of the Arctic in winter, of wolves in the
Pyrenees; a tender Ruth-and-Boaz story; a shuddering glimpse of a
suicide's grave; a comet viewed in the light of superstititon, then in the
light of science; a vignette of a lethal snowstorm conjoined with a vignette
of unjust imprisonment; a fantasy of "converse with the mighty dead";
close-up portraits of wasps, bees, and spiders; a hymn of praise to
commerce; sundry tributes to Britannia and compliments to patrons—all
this and more Thomson offers in a positive riot of metonymy.

Here is one case where polite culture coincided with popular culture.
The popular tradition of the almanac, a genre disseminated in Europe
almost from the dawn of printing in the late 1400s and by Thomson's
day read throughout America as well as in the old world, also thrived on
a congeries of seasonable agricultural lore, moral essays, aphorisms, and
affecting anecdotes. In 1786 a waggish American almanac compiler ety-
mologized the word as "an evident abbreviation of ALL MY KNACK, or ALL
MAN'S KNACK, plainly intimating, in the most expressive and laconic
manner, that ALMANACK was the *ne plus ultra* of human genius, that this
astonishing art engrossed all the powers and faculties of the mind."[9]

"The great defect of *The Seasons* is want of method," opined Samuel
Johnson. Yet Johnson also saw the virtues of "a mind that at once
comprehends the vast, and attends to the minute," causing the reader to
wonder "that he never saw before what Thomson shews him, and that
he never yet has felt what Thomson impresses."[10] These aphorisms begin
to get at the quiddity of the season book as Thomson established it. It is
an encyclopedic form, potentially inspiring as a kind of textual man-
dala—an epitome of the physical universe—and intriguing in its linkages
and juxtapositions. In "Winter," for example, a pretty vignette of a
redbreast given crumbs at a cottager's hearthside suggests a sermon to
shepherds on the proper care of disconsolate sheep, which suggests a
gruesome tale of a countryman frozen to death in a snowstorm, which

leads to a jeremiad addressed to the "gay licentious Proud" who overlook such things. Although he does not question the traditional ordering of God over humankind over the beasts of the field, compared to previous bards Thomson sets up an economy of creation that puts animals almost on the same footing of importance as people, giving animals nearly equal time. For the first time in English poetry, as Thoreau would have put it, "all the chinks in the scale of being are filled" (*Wa* 284).

The Seasons anticipates the fine networking of out-of-the-way ecological observations that is one of the pleasures of later environmental writing. "The dandelion tells me when to look for the swallow, the dogtooth violet when to expect the wood-thrush"; "in New York and in New England the sap starts up in the sugar maple the very day the bluebird arrives, and sugar-making begins forthwith."[11] I quote John Burroughs, whose works brim with such microlevel insights into nature's minute concurrences, beckoning us toward a lost ancestral wisdom— whether or not the individual reader's forebears ever had such. Even the least imaginative seasonal compendiums transmit an invigorating jolt to the armchair pastoralist, like the section of the Massachusetts Audubon Society bimonthly journal, *Sanctuary*, to which I always turn first: the "Outdoor Almanac" printed on the back cover, which for the week of 16 January 1994 contains these fascinating items:

16   In rocky outcroppings watch for growths of rock polypody fern.
18   A general warming trend known as the January thaw occurs about this time. Watch for flights of bees and other insects.
20 21 St. Agnes Eve. This night traditionally marks the change from the bitter chill of midwinter to the warming trends of late winter.[12]

To be sure, I dimly recall reading much the same in the previous year's almanac. But it is no mere tenderfoot susceptibility that makes me enjoy this juxtaposition of tidbits again; indeed, I find that people more weatherwise than I like to ponder (and recite) them also.

But to return to Thomson. Rather than focus on the interlacing of flower and bird, or on the rapid catalog of diverse phenomena, *The Seasons* generally operates at the level of the discrete phenomenon or cameo, not likely to surprise the reader by choice so much as by treatment. These vignettes become modular units in later season books also. One example may stand for all:

> When Autumn scatters his departing Gleams,
> Warn'd of approaching Winter, gather'd, play
> The Swallow-People; and, toss'd wide around,
> O'er the calm Sky in Convolution swift,
> The feather'd Eddy floats: rejoicing once,
> Ere to their wintry Slumbers they retire;
> In Clusters clung, beneath the mouldring Bank,
> And where, unpierc'd by Frost, the Cavern sweats.
> Or rather, into warmer Climes convey'd,
> With other kindred Birds of Season, there
> They twitter chearful, till the vernal Months
> Invite them welcome back: for, thronging, now
> Innumerous Wings are in Commotion all.
>
> ("Autumn," lines 836–848)

In the last line of "To Autumn," Keats skimmed the cream from this passage, picking out its one vernacular—and onomatopoetic—word: "And gathering swallows *twitter* in the skies" (my emphasis). By picking up on an image Thomson had taught two generations of poetry lovers to associate with the "departing gleams" of autumn, and by conflating the autumn prospect of the first lines (the gathering) with the swallow's off-season retreat (the twitter), Keats deepened the suggestion of the movement of the season into the seasons to come. In comparison to such briskness, Thomson's convolutions seem less swift. Yet he has his subtleties. The birds are imagined as an image and echo of autumn's scattering (scatter/twitter); a bit like the dallying swallows, Thomson plays with the superstition, from Pliny, of the swallows hibernating in a mudbank (which even Gilbert White believed), only to reject it after ostensible endorsement, in favor of the migration theory. This adds mystery to the transaction, as does the paradox of the passiveness of the birds' intense activity: the "feather'd Eddy floats" despite its swift churning; it is "toss'd" and "convey'd" as if the whole scene were puppeteered by Father Autumn.

We have come to expect such lingering visual and intellectual play of Thoreauvian writing also. In his wonderful passage on the Walden pickerel the ice fishermen have caught, the fish seem to possess a dazzling beauty that separates them by

> a wide interval from the cadaverous cod and haddock whose fame is trumpeted in our streets. They are not green like the pines, nor gray like the stones, nor blue like the sky; but they have, to my eyes, if possible, yet rarer colors, like flowers and precious stones, as if they were the pearls, the animalized *nuclei* or crystals of the Walden water. They, of course, are Walden all over and all through; are themselves small Waldens in the animal kingdom, Waldenses. It is surprising that they are caught here,—that in this deep and capacious spring, far beneath the rattling teams and chaises and tinkling sleighs that travel the Walden road, this great gold and emerald fish swims. (284–285)

There is almost no chance of direct influence here, so the parallels are all the more intriguing. As Thomson embodied late autumn's light in the form of the swallow's play, Thoreau encapsulates the wintry pond in the piscatory ice crystals. As Thomson both fixes the season through the image and transports us forward, so Thoreau's pickerel symbolizes winter and reminds us also of the "deep and capacious spring," which will melt forth again in the next chapter. Thomson might have been embarrassed by such extravagances as likening the pickerel to Protestant martyrs ("Waldenses") and the snipes at respectable New England commerce ("the cadaverous cod and haddock whose fame is trumpeted in our streets"), but the Thoreauvian program of impressing on oblivious towns-people the preciousness and centrality to the divine economy of ordinary creatures was Thomson's own program also. The most basic common denominator, however, is the building block technique: the extended look at the symptomatic seasonal item in such a way as to raise it from a quotidian nonevent to a key to the season.

Seasonal Givens, Seasonal Artifacts

The delight *and* frustration of seasonal vignettes is that an unlimited number of things can be singled out, for the moment, as the key image or symbol. As Emerson asserted, there is absolutely nothing, however contemptible, that cannot be seen as microcosmic. Thomson does not raise this issue as pointedly as Thoreau, because bird migration is a long-recognized autumn motif, whereas no one before Thoreau would have transformed a pickerel into an aesthetic object. Aldo Leopold, another temperamentally reserved man who preferred insinuation to polemics, seems deliberately to have created a problem of this kind in the "April" section of *Sand County Almanac.* It comprises four vignettes: of springtime floods, of the history and demise of natural prairie fires, of the sky dance of the woodcocks, and of draba: "the smallest flower that blows," which you must search on your knees in the mud to find (*SCA* 26). The tenacious reader can detect a rationale for the quartet as a casual parade of the traditional four elements—water, fire, air, earth. Leopold, with perversity prepense, creates an additional hazard for the reader by making the draba section as miniscule as the flower, fewer than twenty lines and ending in the anticlimax: "Altogether it is of no importance— just a small creature that does a small job quickly and well" (*SCA* 26). Accordingly, one member of Leopold's posthumous revising team pressed to delete the whole section as being "insignificant as the plant itself."[13] But it was spared, and Leopold was allowed the private joke of dramatizing the centrality of the unobtrusive unobtrusively. As a practicing applied scientist in the microscopic age, Leopold would have been even more aware of the endless number of possible overlooked centers to the creation than Thoreau and Emerson were. But it is the scientific amateur Annie Dillard who, among recent literary naturists, has made this point most eloquently. "That there are so many details seems to be the most important and visible fact about the creation"; "even on the perfectly ordinary and clearly visible level, creation carries on with an intricacy unfathomable and apparently uncalled for"—let alone the vertiginous proliferation of microforms that awaits you when you step inside a cell or an atom. "The point of the dragonfly's terrible lip, the giant water bug, birdsong, or the beautiful dazzle and flash of sunlighted minnows, is not that it all fits together like clockwork . . . but that it all flows so freely wild . . . in such a free, fringed tangle."[14]

For Thomson, it *did* fit like clockwork, as is especially evident from his eulogy "To the Memory of Isaac Newton" ("Nature herself / Stood all subdued by him, and open laid / Her every latent glory to his view"). What distinguishes Thomson's representation of the seasons from those of his romantic successors is his sense of the fixity of the seasonal round. He goes about his business without worrying whether what he is reporting is actually there or whether he can capture it adequately in print. "Inveterate tinkerer" though he was,[15] Thomson never questioned, as later naturists came to do, whether properly speaking a fourfold typology of seasons made best sense, whether each month or perhaps even each day might more properly be called a season in itself. "There is a bit of every season in each season," Dillard writes, choosing as her emblem of time an image at once traditional and modern: "the snakeskin with scales endlessly overlapping without beginning or end."[16] Thoreau was the first Anglo-American writer to question seasonal categorization rigorously. As H. Daniel Peck has shown, he questioned the traditional grid without giving up the idea of seasonality. He sought to free himself "from the tyranny of chronological time," to redefine November for example from "a calendrical unit" to a "phenomenological category of thought"—all the while somewhat systematically gathering and collating data on the first appearances of seasonal phenemona with a view to producing a master account of seasonal unfolding.[17] In devoting himself seriously both to empirical phenology and to seasonal perception as an epistemological issue, Thoreau went beyond even his more venturesome romantic contemporaries. Neither Shelley nor Keats, skeptics though they were, doubted for a minute in their respective odes "To the West Wind" and "Autumn" that "autumn" referred to a solid fact of natural history.

Far less did Thomson question whether most of the seasonal phenomena he reported were culturally conditioned artifacts, even though at a certain level of apprehension he knew perfectly well that there was no such thing as "winter" in the torrid zone, and he was probably aware of his own propensity for representing winter more in the image of his native Scotland than in its benigner English guise. It was self-evident to him that the "many-coloured woods" of autumn were "dusk and dun," ranging in hue "from wan declining green / To sooty dark." Such American literary naturists as Susan Cooper were quick to point out the "dull character" of autumn in English poetry and to celebrate the more spectacular fall colors of the American Northeast. "Scarce a poet of any fame among us," wrote Cooper, "who has not at least some graceful verse, some glowing image connected with the season."[18]

The history of seasonal representation in the United States could be studied as a test case of both the persistence of intellectual colonization and the rise of national literary difference. The same documents often illustrate both. An almanac produced in 1779 "by the Professor of Mathematics in Yale College," for instance, represents the months of February and November, respectively, as follows:

> FROM southren climes the faithful sun
> Returns to cheer us with his rays,
> Dissolving snows in rivlets run,
> While he his kindly pow'rs displays.
>
> The nymphs and swains their aking fingers blow;
> Soon loaded sleds glide smoothly o'er the snow.[19]

Obviously, the first vignette bears closer resemblance to England's milder climate than to February in New Haven, whereas the reverse is true of the almanac's November passage, with its reference to the typical means of cold season transport in the preindustrial Northeast. There is no evidence whatsoever that the author strove to play the cultural nationalist here, although his fellow collegian Timothy Dwight was almost at that very moment reading the telltale passage from the "Autumn" section of Thomson's *Seasons* (first published in the United States in 1777) and observing that Thomson "had entirely omitted" what to a New Englander was "often among the most splendid beauties of nature."[20] Dwight was one of the first literati in North America to celebrate this item of cisatlantic difference.

To the extent that American writers came to wonder about the adequacy and relativity of seasonal typologies, they responded not only or primarily to British lococentrism but to at least two other factors. One was the meteorological volatility of the northern United States. Thoreau in *Walden* remarks on the "seemingly instantaneous" transition from winter to spring: "Suddenly an influx of light filled my hours, though the evening was at hand, and the clouds of winter still overhung it, and the eaves were dripping with sleety rain. I looked out the window, and lo! where yesterday was cold gray ice there lay the transparent pond already calm and full of hope as on a summer evening, reflecting a summer evening sky in its bosom, though none was visible overhead, as if it had intelligence with some remote horizon" (*Wa* 312). The *Journal* original specifies "March 26th 1846" (*PJ* 2: 191). The passage gives a poetized rendition of the regional cliché: If you don't like the weather in New England, wait a minute.

A second factor was the variability of climate throughout the United States as a whole relative to Britain. A vast continental expanse subject to much more dramatic vicissitudes of weather, America was distressingly hard to generalize under any one set of seasonal rubrics. John Burroughs, after moving from the Catskills to Washington, D.C., observed with quiet satisfaction that "our calendar is made for this climate. March is a spring month"—implying that for his Yankee readers the nominal season and the real are perpetually disjunct. This disjunction has been the more typical American experience, as western writers have perhaps stated most emphatically. "In the great Central Valley of California," begins Muir's *My First Summer in the Sierra,* "there are only two seasons—spring and summer."[21] Joseph Wood Krutch, having confidently divided the natural year in southern Connecticut into months of distinct seasonal signs *(The Twelve Seasons),* boggled on the seeming transitionlessness of the Sonoran desert *(The Desert Year),* making light of his Yankee urge to find markers where none exist.

Yet Krutch insists in his later book on retaining the old categories. Although he is "hard put to say when either spring or summer began," he cannot give up the underlying symbolic framework: "I like to think that a renewal and a rebirth are natural even where the whole earth does not die a deep death." At the start of what Krutch is conditioned to believe ought to be autumn, he is relieved and delighted to find ants stashing away little piles of chaff: for "that, on the unimpeachable authority of John Keats, is one of the signs by which autumn may be recognized. His criteria are valid in a latitude for which he never intended them."[22] In this way, Krutch wryly shores up his wavering faith in seasonality. This combination links him closely to Thoreau. In the passage just quoted, Thoreau draws on an old-time Calvinist rhetoric of grace when it comes to imaging the "memorable crisis" of the season "which all things proclaim." Suddenly an "influx" of "light" though "evening" was "at hand"—and, lo! Spring as Irresistible Grace. In the last phrase, Thoreau hides under cover of the "as if," but the *Journal* version is more forthright: "There seemed to be some intelligence in the pond which responded to the unseen serenity in a distant horizon" *(PJ* 2: 191). In other words, a deep need to give shape to the season, to pin spring's advent to a decisive instant, to imagine spring as Spring—these override for the moment not only Thoreau's meterological empiricism but even to an extent his typical religious position.

Override but do not cancel. Thoreau remains keenly interested in phenological data, in reading seasonal signs at the physical level. Indeed, even the passage on the influx of spring has an empirical basis to it. It actually happened to him on a particular day. It even had some call to be considered representative—not a one-time event. For, as Thoreau remarked in his *Journal* a year before *Walden*'s publication, "It is evident that the English do not enjoy that contrast between winter and summer that we do . . . There is no such wonderful resurrection of the year" (*J* 5: 29). In one compartment of his mind, Thoreau may have thought of his chapter "Spring" as the proof of an equation (spring = Spring) that English writers had bandied about as a mere trope.

Peck characterizes Thoreau's way of shuttling between empirical evidence and associative play as a "categorical imagination" that sought "a structure to contain his explorations of phenomena," which would, "in some sense, sanction that exploration."[23] That might stand as an epitome of the way modern literary season books work. To begin with, the interplay between the objectively given and the latitude that imagination desires to maintain in its rendering of the object-world seems congruent with, indeed almost prophesied by, the flexible ineluctability of earth's diurnal round. The fickle environment seems to have given its imprimatur to a certain degree of poetic license when it comes to representing how the seasons work. Thus the seasons can serve both as a lens for interweaving an infinite number of environmental events in their minute particularity and as a set of counters in a game of the imagination from which the empirical content has largely been abstracted. Traditional eclogues and pastoral elegies operate at the latter extreme. The usual register of seasonal representation lies, however, in a middle ground where the writer transfuses the record of natural phenomena with meditation that uses seasonal categories as loose containers for reflective as well as for descriptive purposes. Aware of the looseness of the seasonal categories, the writer resolves to hang onto them anyhow as good public coinage and as comfortably canonized by precursors, the way Keats canonizes autumn for Krutch. Even if a particular seasonal template does not translate from one latitude to another, a writer can at least operate in the assurance that *some* sort of perodicity is inherent in the nature of things.

Season talk can thus either be the measure of an increasingly closer commitment to the environment, as with Thoreau's development of the autumn-to-spring sequence in the later stages of writing *Walden,* or signify what appears to be the very opposite of this commitment, such as the accommodationism Aldo Leopold felt pressured into. Leopold knew perfectly well how to create a seasonal calendar of short essays; he had already done so for several years in his regular column for the *Wisconsin Agriculturalist* (1939–1941). In fact, he at first seems to have wished precisely *not* to repeat this form in *Sand County Almanac,* to avoid making a pretty calendrical garland. He created the almanac portion only after prodding by publishers and colleagues to make his book more accessible. Fortunately, although Leopold as stylist was no Thoreau, he was incapable of writing without indirection. (This was true even of his magazine pieces.) His pabulum always has a hook in it, as the draba vignette does. But even the most recondite book that is calendrically organized must be read on the assumption that the author had at least some sense of the popularity of this method of organization. Not by accident was Thomson's *Seasons* the work at issue in the landmark lawsuit that established English copyright law.[24] Not by chance were Thoreau's manuscript journals first published in excerpt form, a generation after his death, as four season books *(Early Spring in Massachusetts, Summer, Autumn, Winter).*

Finally, whether considered as an empirical fact or an imaginative device, the seasons are infinitely elastic. They vary by region, and they refuse to repeat themselves exactly; transposed to texts, they can be as short as a stanza, long as a volume; they can be pondered as a durable presence, the triumph of the moment, or as a route of evanescence or perpetual transition. If one measure of able environmental writing about the seasons is the ability to generate cameos like Thomson's swallows and Thoreau's pickerel that will convince and surprise, a further measure of the higher skill we call genius is the ability to do at least as much strategic violence to the expected boundaries as any particular iteration of the seasons is bound to do. Programmatically calendrical books like Krutch's *Twelve Seasons* or Donald Peattie's *Almanac for Moderns,* which dutifully give equal time to the respective months, or days, risk gridlock. A look at some of the more venturesome cases will give us a better sense of some of the forces in the interest of which the circle of the seasons is invoked and bent, and this in turn will prepare us for a closer look at the most famous of all American season books, *Walden.*

Testing Limits: Thaxter and Dillard

Celia Thaxter's *Among the Isles of Shoals* (1873) is the first extended work of environmental nonfiction produced by the late nineteenth-century regional realist movement. Despite the feminist rediscovery of regionalist writers like Jewett, Kate Chopin, and Cather, the book has remained comparatively neglected.[25] In a hauntingly guarded way whose elegiac resonance emerges as one picks one's way through the somewhat uneven prose, it compresses decades of ambivalent bonding to the desolate islets off the New Hampshire coast where Thaxter grew up as a lighthouse keeper's daughter, and to which she later returned—first to visit, then to tend her mother (the time of writing), and finally to live as a widow. As for Thoreau, a life of (semi)voluntary simplicity paid off in the intensity of microvision.

> Each of these [seasonal] changes, and the various aspects of their little world, are of inestimable value to the lonely children living always in that solitude. Nothing is too slight to be precious: the flashing of an oar-blade in the morning light; the twinkling of a gull's wings afar off, like a star in the yellow sunshine of the drowsy summer after-noon; . . . every phase of the great thunder-storms that make glorious the weeks of July and August, from the first floating film of cloud that rises in the sky till the scattered fragments of the storm stream eastward to form a background for the rainbow,—all these things are of the utmost importance to dwellers at the Isles of Shoals.[26]

To be sure, this scene looks so far like a landscape by John Singer Sargent, rather than a grainy, textured Winslow Homer. Thaxter states a doctrine of particularity in prettified generic language: the "glorious" storms, the twinkle-star gull's wing. These are signs that Thaxter, like Leopold only more so, was a serious person attempting to write a book in a popular style. Instigated, for better and for worse, by the encouragement of John Greenleaf Whittier, a summer visitor to the Shoals who admired her descriptive gift, her book was published after serialization in the *Atlantic Monthly* partly with the tourist trade in mind. A cheap edition was issued concurrently with a prettily printed one "to be sold in railroad stations." Thaxter told James T. Fields that her chief desire was "to have Osgood's check in my pocket"; and she prefaced the book with an apology for "these fragmentary and inadequate sketches," which would not have seen the light of day "except that some account of the place, however slight, is so incessantly called for by people who throng these islands in summer." [27]

Thaxter was sincere in refusing to consider *Shoals* her best work; she thought of herself as a poet. Yet we should not take her apologies at face value. This passage, from a March 1874 letter (six months after *Shoals* was published), shows why.

> It takes Thoreau and Emerson and their kind to enjoy a walk for a walk's sake, and the wealth they glean with eyes and ears. I cannot enjoy the glimpses Nature gives me half as well, when I go deliberately seeking them, as when they flash on me in some pause of work. It is like the pursuit of happiness: you don't get it when you go after it, but let it alone and it comes to you. At least this is my case. In the case of the geniuses (now is that the proper plural?) aforesaid, it is different. So I industriously filled my basket with the pretty, wet, transparent clusters lying all strewn about the beach; but I didn't fail to see how the dampness brought out the colors of stone and shell, and to be glad therefor; and I heard the living ripple of the swiftly rising tide among the ledges and boulders, and saw how it bubbled and eddied up close to the shore, for the fog pressed in so close one could not see a rod across the calm surface. And I even paused long enough to address the flood as it rushed and sang almost round my feet. "O everlasting, beautiful old eternal slop!" I said, and the force of language could no farther go. And, my basket being full, I selected a formidable club from the heaps of driftwood strewing the beach, and went to the end of the outermost ledge and began beating off the thick, white shining girdle of salt-water ice that partially clasps each island yet. I loosened large ponderous masses, that fell with a great splash into the sea and sailed off slowly to annihilation. "Go, go," I cried, "and never come back again! I hate you!" and I assailed it with wrath till I had beaten the rock quite free, and I was tired enough to be glad to sit down and watch the floating fetters I had cast loose as they swam heavily away.[28]

Clearly we have here the familiar Victorian pattern of the woman writer creating a space for feisty assertion within the parenthesis of "deference" to "Thoreau and Emerson and their kind" and casual chattiness to her correspondent. Underneath, the passage shrewdly reflects on the resistances to nature that frustrate direct pursuit—for which she clears her way, again with Victorian feminist mock-insouciance, by alleging (with arch disregard for their own expressed scruples) that Thoreau and Emerson were happily untroubled walkers. Thaxter implies that they were such obstinately purposive significance-mongers that they did not know the more spontaneous pleasures of nature encounter that she does (and other sensible, practical people do as well, the passage suggests). Even if Thaxter did rank her writing below that of Thoreau and Emerson, she shows an equally keen awareness of the slippage between perception and articulation. "O everlasting, beautiful old eternal slop!" could stand as Thaxter's comment not only on the perceptual inadequacies of her own purple passages but on the rarefactions of the transcendentalists'. Yet all the while the passage has been conveying, quite perspicaciously and poignantly, how early spring feels in a place where spring always seems unconscionably late.

Shoals shows a similar acuity of seasonal vision. About half of it is loosely organized in terms of the seasonal cycle. The book's fundamental structure was blocked out in the four *Atlantic* serial chunks: (1) the islands' basic appearance, topography, pattern of settlement; (2) cultural history and sociology; (3) autumn to winter; (4) winter to summer, with a coda on island supernatural lore. The momentum and proportioning are such as to make winter dominate, as befits the time when *Shoals* was composed (a long winter visit to Thaxter's widowed mother) as well as the spirit of the place: "these lonely rocks," "this thin soil," "the vast loneliness," "the bleakness."[29] Thaxter's starting point is Melville's "Encantadas." To Melville's claim that the Galapagos must be the most godforsaken place on earth, Thaxter replies, "their dark volcanic crags and melancholy beaches can hardly seem more desolate than do the low bleached rocks of the Isles of Shoals to eyes that behold them for the first time."—Although, she teasingly adds, they "are enchanted islands in a better sense of the word than are the great Gallipagos [*sic*]." In the third section of the book as serialized, the emptying of the year from fall to stormy winter culminates in a tableau of white on blue: salt mist, white sails, white gulls ("no bird so white,—nor swan, nor dove, nor mystic ibis"), against the blues of sky and sea, "with nothing between you and the eastern continent across its vast, calm plain." In the spirit of her reply to Melville, Thaxter wants to acknowledge both the season's increasing forbiddingness and the unique pleasures to be derived from that: "A whole conservatory, flushed with azaleas, and brilliant with forests of camellias and every precious exotic that blooms, could not impart so much delight as I have known a single rose to give, unfolding in the bleak bitterness of a day in February, when this side of the planet seemed to have arrived at its culmination of hopelessness, with the Isles of Shoals the most hopeless speck upon its surface." Or, if you prefer an outdoor scene: "It is exhilarating, spite of the intense cold, to wake to the brightness the northwest gale always brings . . . The sea is deep indigo, whitened with flashing waves all over the surface; the sky is speckless; no cloud passes across it the whole day long; and the sun sets red and clear, without any abatement of the wind." But this center does not hold. As the paragraph unfolds, the storm returns, and the speaker gets stir-crazy in her "prison." She turns to description of winter fauna only to veer from pretty gulls and snow buntings to "the spectral arctic owl" and from there to the plague of rats that afflicts the island.[30] Winter challenges the author's resources as islander and as author, setting up a battle between the will to acknowledge hardship and the will to pastoralize it.

Perhaps this conflict causes the ensuing provocative disruption of chronology. Rather than continue into the fourth quadrant of her original work, which begins with a long doleful section on shipwrecks, Thaxter interpolates a 6,000-word retrospect of early childhood on the Shoals, starting (like the second section) in autumn, but moving back to and centering on summer. The imagistic color and emotional register of this section are striking. Apropos girlhood marigold growing, for instance, Thaxter insists that Keats never felt the beauty of flowers "more devoutly than the little, half-savage being who knelt, like a fire-worshipper, to watch the unfolding of those golden disks." These reminiscences done, Thaxter returns to her manuscript and finally gets us on from winter to spring to summer. But the swerve has had its effect. Thaxter has made the seasons reverse themselves—the seasons of the year and the seasons of life. On the one hand, Thaxter has achieved a small victory over nature's dominance, similar to her epistolary curse on winter, as she kicks the late-winter ice from the shore. Of course she has already been playing fast and loose with the seasons, loading the dice in favor of winter and forcing us to wait interminably for spring and summer, but time-travel is more disruptive. On the other hand, the flashback suggests that as with the deliberately childish language of Thaxter's curse, winter can be exorcised only through acts of regression, like Dylan Thomas remembering in "Fern Hill" the days when the boy felt himself nature's master, in happy ignorance of bondage to time. Yet the fruits of regression are manifest on every page of *Shoals*. The most portentous events are not the great storm of X or the shipwreck of Y, but events that recur, that are awaited, that are absorbed through iteration and familiarity, like the constellations assuming "the faces of old friends looking down out of the awful blackness," so that in summer when "great Orion disappears, how it is missed out of the sky!"[31] One-time anomalies and the contrasts between youth and maturity exercise *their* magic against this background of constant repetition of predictable phenomena. Even some no-longer-recurring events (like kneeling to the marigold god) take on power as rituals once repeated although long done with. The imagination's triumphs over the iron law of season take place within a Wordsworthian reverence for the infinite depth of minute phenomena made luminous by repeated experience.

Annie Dillard's *Pilgrim at Tinker Creek* (1974) makes Thaxter's liberties with time management look like modest departures from staid documentary realism, however. No American environmental writer, as Peter Fritzell affirms, "is more resistant to the processes and methods of conventional explanation, or more disposed to the wild and extreme, the manifestly unexplainable."[32] Dillard's prose is a rushy kaleidoscope of perceptual and intertextual fragments, precariously contained by a basketry of image motifs. The solid middle ground of environmental reportage on which Thaxter, Burroughs, Muir, Austin, Beston, Leopold, Krutch, and even Thoreau much more heavily depend is constantly dissolving into free-floating aphorisms, philosophical and religious quotations, and bits of natural history gleaned from experts. Somewhat like *Moby-Dick* with its extracts and folio whales, *Tinker Creek* advertises its indoor circumstances of composition, from a stack of note cards put together in a library.[33]

Applying to Dillard her own dictum that postmodernity is evolution, not revolution, we could say that the grab bag texture, the bookishness, the collaging of science and theology, all of these Thomson anticipated. Dillard, however, underscores the structural jumble and epistemological precariousness of this type of work. ("There is no epistemological guarantee between *any* subject and *any* object," she insists in another context.)[34] We see this self-consciousness especially, perhaps, in Dillard's multiplication and scattering of perceptual angles, a trait she (and many others) have identified as a hallmark of "contemporary modernism," as she prefers to call it. "The world is the fabrication of a billion imaginations all inventing it at once."[35] This description of the riotously anarchic climax of Robert Coover's story "The Babysitter" fits *Tinker Creek*'s vision of the state of the world. Dillard's way of imagining "the intricacy of the created world," for instance, is to start by imagining multiple centers:

> You are God. You want to make a forest . . .
> You are a man, a retired railroad worker who makes replicas as a hobby. You decide to make a replica of one tree . . .
> You are a starling . . .
> You are a sculptor . . .
> You are a chloroplast moving in water heaved one hundred feet above ground. Hydrogen, carbon, oxygen, nitrogen in a ring above magnesium . . . You are evolution; you have only begun to make trees.
> You are God—are you tired? finished?[36]

No more than any other trait of style can this perspectival shiftiness be ascribed to a single cause. It may register a temperamental preference for an aesthetic fugacity as much as a reasoned conviction of what good "contemporary modern" writers do. But it certainly reflects among other things Dillard's conviction that taking modern science seriously has serious experiential and philosophical consequences.

Microscopy and the proliferation of specialized expertise create a world in which there is much more to perceive, in which it is much harder to know where and how to begin to perceive anything. One of Dillard's striking innovations as an environmental writer is her dexterity in conveying how it feels to be an amateur in the field observing nature in an age of esoteric science. Unlike most artists, who do not even try to learn much science, and unlike most scientists when they try to communicate outside the tribe, Dillard tries to make her reader feel as well as notionally understand the combination of exhilaration, bafflement, and inadequacy that can beset the contemporary autodidact.

> Specialists can find the most incredibly well-hidden things. A book I read when I was young recommended an easy way to find caterpillars

to rear: you simply find some fresh caterpillar droppings, look up, and there's your caterpillar . . .

If I can't see these minutiae, I still try to keep my eyes open. I'm always on the lookout for antlion traps in sandy soil, monarch pupae near milkweed, skipper larvae in locust leaves. These things are utterly common, and I've not seen one.[37]

And these barriers to becoming the complete naturalist do not compare to the challenges of noting, let alone comprehending, the microscopic results of comparative anatomy (the caterpillar's 228 head muscles), of human biology (the two million Henle's loops in each kidney), of bacteriology, of parasitology.

At a more philosophical level, Dillard's perspectivalism expresses the sense of being overwhelmed by a post-Heisenberg awareness of the world's radical unobservableness and a post-Darwinian awareness of the universe as dominated by life-forms of insect size and below that elude ordinary notice and defy commonsense standards of probability and ethics. The seasons have a particularly crucial role to play in both dramatizing and regulating this vision. At first Dillard seems to invoke seasonality in support of the necessary indeterminacy of perception and the cosmos itself. "Yesterday I set out to catch the new season, and instead I found an old snakeskin," knotted in a loop with no beginning or end. This sentence opens the winter-to-spring chapter. Spring and the snakeskin both form a continuous loop; you cannot catch either by the tip or the tail: the transition is ungraspable, and seasons are after all as filled with unseasonable moments as not. Dillard uses this circle motif as a way of talking about "the power we seek," a "divine power" that in pantheistic peripeteia "travels about the face of the earth as a man might wander," rolling "along the mountain ridges like a fireball": Ezekiel's wheel. "This is the arsonist of the sunny woods: catch it if you can." Here the chapter ends.[38] The nervous metamorphoses as the circle motif whirls through the chapter dramatize the fugacity of season, demiurge, perception, everything.

Yet mainly the seasons counter, not further, the vision of a chancy indeterminate universe. They are the formal elements that stand most clearly for structure rather than anarchy. The endlessly chased hoop is a stable concept, a variant of an age-old emblem of time reconfigured as eternity: the serpent with its tail in its mouth. The concept of the seasons as a somehow meaningful cycle is the book's fundamental premise. Dillard explains this in a 1981 interview. *Tinker Creek,* she says, turns on the Christian distinction between *via positiva* and *via negativa,* the soul's approach to God through good works, loving God, loving the creation, versus the soul's approach "by denying anything that can be said about God . . . Language deceives, the world deceives. God is not perfectly good, perfectly powerful, perfectly loving; these words apply to beings, and God is not a being." This distinction underlies *Tinker Creek's* structure.

> The first half of the book represents the *via positiva;* the second half, the *via negativa.* The book has bilateral symmetry; opposite chapters are paired.
>
> The first and last chapters form a simple frame. The second chapter, "Seeing," keys the *via positiva* . . . The newly-created soul looks around at the world and finds it good.
>
> Each subsequent chapter zigzags along, mixing good and evil, but essentially building a vision of the world as good. The vision culminates in a chapter titled "Intricacy"—in which the world is seen in all its detail, and loved. This can't last. The center is a little "Flood" chapter—a narrative break between "Intricacy" and its twin, "Fecundity." In "Fecundity" the downhill journey begins—the rejection of the world. The soul gags on abundance; the mind quarrels with death.
>
> The second half of the book moves downward into realms of greater and greater emptiness, culminating in the next-to-last chapter (twin of the "Seeing" chapter), the "Northing" chapter. The time is late fall, Advent. The soul empties itself of the world in order to prepare for the incursion of God at Christmas. Some of the Advent psalms are quoted. Narratively, everything empties; the caribou pour out of the hills, the monarch butterflies migrate through the valley, the leaves and birds, like the caribou and butterflies, vamoose. All this suggests prayer, the soul's emptiness and receptivity.
>
> Then of course the last chapter repeats the first; it reiterates the same incident with, one hopes, a year's wisdom in between.[39]

"The same incident" is actually plural: the pet tomcat splotches her with his bloody paw, in an ambiguous act of either pollution or purification; and the giant waterbug eats the frog by sucking out its juices, which raises the theodicy question that gives the first chapter its title: Were the heavens and earth made in jest? Eventually Dillard treats this as a rhetorical question, but the answer itself is an acceptance of unanswerability and the need to keep pilgrimaging. In another return to the first chapter, which associates itself with Pascal, Dillard ends up reaffirming both the *deus* and the *absconditus.*

Dillard's outline indicates how the seasons supply a macronarrative framework for her pilgrimage, which goes from January to winter solstice, just before Christmas. The summer solstice (the very day of "Flood") is the turning point, when nature conceived as plenitude (amid some misgivings) starts to become nature as excess, causing the pilgrim to gag on the nightmare vision of fecundity. It is the end of June; "creatures extrude or vent eggs; larvae fatten, split their shells, and eat them."[40] The catalog of swarming, dying things goes on interminably. Query leads to anticipation leads to plenitude leads to decadence leads to "realms of greater and greater emptiness," as the pilgrim feels herself beset and faces with resignation, but also relief, the onset of cold weather and the symbolic harsh but maybe purifying north of being. More insistently than in any other major work of American environmental writing the seasons encode a succession of moods, which conspire with nature and myth to sacramentalize the year into a paradigmatic pilgrimage.

Tinker Creek relies on the embedded presumption that the calendar year *is* a determinate order so that the reader will be charmed into experiencing as a regulated process what otherwise might come across as an unsettling hodgepodge. At the close, the speaker pictures herself bravely proceeding "in and out of Shadow Creek, upstream and down, exultant, in a daze, dancing, to the twin silver trumpets of praise." What is it that gives such a sentence more depth than its manic effervescence might suggest, apart from its touches of solemnizing biblicism—the shadow of death allusion, the twin silver trumpets?[41] Why, the expectation of ongoingness nurtured by conflating a single lifeline with Life as cycle. Dillard's shattering of narrative line and consciousness abets this reassuringly traditional vision by making the protagonist's individual life story less consequential. The speaker becomes a choric figure and thereby a model for the reader of praiseful witness to the miraculous, scary confusion of a phenomenal flow utterly baffling in its particulars but reassuringly predictable in its basic sequence of events.[42]

Finally, then, *Tinker Creek* manages the difficult feat of affirming the already deconstructed, by virtue of this paradox. Seasonality is an ideal artifact that cannot be held at any moment to the classic form in which we like to formulate it, cannot be located except through manifestations too multiple and raggedy to be recorded. But seasonality is also bedrock, not just the cultural vocabulary of whatever ethnoregion but in some sense an obstinate objective given, underlying whatever clash of ethnic vocabularies and formalisms we may use to chart it—and of course Dillard's Protestant formulation would differ from the Cherokee. Though her dominant patterns of imagery reflect a particular theological and liturgical standpoint, her subtle awareness of how seasonality pervades human experience is anything but tribal—a major reinvention of an ancient genre.

Walden's Seasonal Agenda

Working from *Tinker Creek* backward to its predecessor, *Walden*,[43] can keep us from succumbing to the banality that easily overcomes critical thinking about the work the seasons perform for Thoreau. We have so often been told, as the Q.E.D. of the old formalist proof of *Walden*'s organic unity, that *Walden*'s timeline follows the circle of the year from spring to spring and that this temporal unfolding symbolizes the spiritual renewal wrought by the experiment. *Tinker Creek* reminds us by contrast of how comparatively little, and how obliquely on the whole, *Walden* is "about" the seasons. In this respect, *Tinker Creek* is more like the book formalist criticism imagined *Walden* to be than *Walden* itself is. Indeed, even at the height of the new critical dispensation, one finds a certain discomfiture about pressing the seasonal argument, a disclaimer that seasonal succession is "more a device for maneuvering than a strict form."[44] Yet it is equally true of Thoreau, as Scott Slovic remarks of his *Journal*, that "every natural observation he made was . . . a note regarding a seasonal landmark, or timemark. 'On *this* day at *this* hour at *this* location, I saw *this* plant or animal doing *this* or having *this* done to it.'"[45] In a less picky but more fundamental way, most of Thoreau's published works are obsessed with temporality in general and with natural cycles particularly. So we should not abandon but rather shift the mode of traditional *Walden* inquiry and recenter it on Thoreau's decision to make use of the seasons in a deliberately eccentric way.

The most obvious case is *Walden*'s long summer, about which every

Thoreauvian remarks. Contrary to Thaxter, not to mention regional actuality, Thoreau makes summer last virtually two-thirds of the book. He gets to it as early as "Economy" (*Wa* 45, 54), after brief vignettes of cabin building, and he does not verge decisively into autumn until the loon encounter toward the end of "Brute Neighbors" (233). For Thoreau's reader, as for Keats's bees, it feels as if warm days will never cease. This "endlessly prolonged summer" serves perfectly Thoreau's discourse on simplicity: "The summer, in some climates, makes possible to man a sort of Elysian life. Fuel, except to cook his Food, is then unnecessary; the sun is his fire, and many of the fruits are sufficiently cooked by its rays; while Food generally is more various, and more easily obtained, and clothing and Shelter are wholly or half unnecessary" (13–14). *Walden's* reconfiguration of the seasons forces nature to corroborate this pastoral logic.

Thoreau does not banish the harsher seasons from this portion of the book but incorporates them into the sweet endless-seeming summer. "Economy" repeatedly draws exempla from cold-weather scenes; the Tierra del Fuegian or Australian aborigine going "naked with impunity, while the European shivers in his clothes" (13); the Laplander snugly tented in his head-and-shoulder bag of fur (27); the Penobscots securely camped amid a Concord snowstorm (28–29); the old-time Massachusetts Indians residing in winter-proof lodges (29–30). Winter's privations are thus neutralized. "Sounds," from the embryonic first draft onward, has two passages a few paragraphs apart that pinpoint their respective scenes on "this summer afternoon" and "this winter morning" (114, 117)—an absolute clash of immediacies. In the first, the speaker watches the lazily circling hawks; in the second, he admires the punctuality of the iron horse, fair weather or foul. Yet no critic has complained about this incongruity. The detour into winter is not sustained enough to puncture the illusion of easeful summer, and the nominal subject is not after all seasons but sounds. Topicality overrides seasonality. The same applies to "The Ponds," which incorporates imagery from every season and even contains a three-paragraph sequence covering September through December. The prevailing imagery and larger context sustain the impression of summertime continuing.

Another sign of Thoreau's success in hoodwinking us into imagining the protagonist in a state of still time is our not noticing when events repeat themselves. Thoreau celebrates July 4 thrice: in "Economy," in

"Where I Lived," and—most elaborately although also most obliquely—in "The Bean-Field." He forages twice for September chestnuts in the town of Lincoln, in "The Ponds" and in "House-Warming." And he repeats the late-summer huckleberry supper on Fair Haven Hill with which he celebrated his release from prison (171) almost verbatim at the start of the next chapter. These repetitions do not attract notice as violations of decorum, if they attract notice at all, because dramatically speaking no seasonal time elapses for two hundred or so pages. Yet time has not been forgotten: in each of these three examples, the incident is assigned a definite point in the year. These reiterations relate to another kind of temporal manipulation I have discussed elsewhere: the manipulation of tenses. Sometimes Thoreau writes like an on-the-spot reporter of a particular experience as it is happening ("this winter morning"), sometimes as the reporter of habitual action (his auroral bathing ritual), sometimes in retrospect (as the sojourner in civilized life again), sometimes in awareness of many different experiences of the same event (statistics on the tardiness of Walden's unfreezing).[46] The net effect is another sort of elongation: of the two-year Walden experience extending far beyond itself, like the elongated summer.

Starting at the end of "Brute Neighbors" the situation changes. Fall arrives with the loons and the ducks. From now until spring, seasonality dominates. To some extent this change makes the latter third of *Walden* a more conventional logbook. In other ways, the appearance of straightforwardness increases the opportunities for deviance. Thoreau's treatment of autumn exemplifies that deviance. *Walden*'s conspicuous lack of a bona fide autumn chapter may be due, in part, to the extensive treatment of the subject in *A Week*. Thoreau ordered that voyage so as to lead into fall at the end. On the last night, the season abruptly seems to change ("We had gone to bed in summer, and we awoke in autumn"),[47] and this shift ushers in a certain elegiac resignation. Elegiac resignation was not the note Thoreau wanted to strike in *Walden*. Yet he could have found other uses for autumn here. The northeastern autumn, with its spectacular visual effects was, we have seen, a source of aesthetic delight and nationalist pride. Susan Cooper devoted many pages to it. In "Autumnal Tints," Thoreau does the same: and his unfinished "The Fall of the Leaf," from which that undelivered lecture-essay came, might have been the American *summa* of that subgenre. But in *Walden* he knocks off the subject of fall foliage in one short paragraph of "House-Warming" (239–240). Thoreau's main topic here is domestic preparation for winter, with attendant reflections on architecture, wood, and fire: an elaboration of some of the concerns of "Economy" with a stronger conservationist motif.[48] Even at that, the chapter leaves the impression that Thoreau wants to skip lightly over autumn in order to get to winter. By the middle of the chapter, ice has started to form on the pond. The next three chapters ("Former Inhabitants," "Winter Animals," "Pond in Winter") chart a frozen landscape. Thaw does not get the upper hand until midway through "Spring."

The disjunction between *Walden* and the *Journal* is clear. Although during the 1850s Thoreau became increasingly attentive to all the transitions of all the seasons, in *Walden* only the transition between winter and spring deeply interested him. "One attraction in coming to the woods to live was that I should have leisure and opportunity to see the spring come in" (302). Originally, this read "*The* attraction."[49] This is *Walden*'s exuberant climax, exuberant from the start and additionally so as Thoreau mythified it further ("the coming in of spring is like the creation of Cosmos out of Chaos and the realization of the Golden Age" [313]) and introduced into the last drafts the extended conceit of the sand-lava metamorphoses. The transitions from spring to summer, summer to fall, fall to winter are much briefer. Compared to Dillard's, Thoreau's natural year is violently misshapen: an outsized summer, a cursory fall, a long and only gradually attenuating winter, and a brief intense blaze of spring.

The difference, of course, partly reflects the difference in latitude between Virginia and Massachusetts. Thoreau records the icebound northeasterner's experience of deferred gratification at the end of April. This deferral heightens the long anticipation process: "Every incident connected with the breaking up of the rivers and ponds and the settling of the weather is particularly interesting to us who live in a climate of so great extremes" (303). This representation of a late, resurrecting spring was a happy coincidence of the local truth and the symbolic reality enforced throughout Euro-America by setting the Christian Easter (the Resurrection of Jesus) on the Sunday following the first full moon following the vernal equinox. But on the way to celebrating this correspondence between the Yankee ecosystem and the Yankee cosmos, Thoreau deviated in at least three ways.

First, regarding autumn Thoreau resisted not only the self-congratulatory Yankee piety about autumn's beauty but also the older Anglo-American piety linking autumn to death, a motif exploited by Yankee preachers and poets including Thoreau himself in *A Week*. Others, like Ellery Channing (the "poet" referred to in *Walden*), tied the motif to literary nationalist celebrations of autumn by such devices as linking bright foliage to the extinction of the Indian on the one hand (one of the popular pseudoexplanations for the term "Indian summer") and to death by tuberculosis on the other (the great regional killer, one of whose symptoms was "the hectic flush"). Thoreau ignores these conventions, though they form the infrastructure of many works of northeastern autumnal art.[50]

Second, Thoreau exaggerated winter's chilly whiteness. This was perhaps true to the psychological facts,[51] but not to meteorology. As I draft this passage, Thoreau country happens to be experiencing a proverbial January thaw (see the snippet from *Sanctuary* magazine, quoted above), notwithstanding the month's unusual severity this particular winter. "This is an event in which no well-brought-up New-Englander will for a moment abandon faith," remarked Wilson Flagg more than a century ago.[52] In fact, Thoreau's famous "spring" meditations on the sandbank drew on periods of thaw that took place in December, January, and February (*J* 3: 164–165, 235; 6: 100). But Thoreau tolerates no such interruptions to *Walden*'s winter, during which "the snow had already covered the ground since the 25th of November" (249) and does not melt off until mid-March. Thoreau's stylized deep freeze is reinforced by his reluctance to transgress seasonal limits during these chapters, and such transgressions as occur are more conspicuous as deviances from chapters whose subjects are explicitly *winter* visitors, *winter* animals, the pond in *winter*. *Walden* differs in this respect from the early essay "A Winter Walk," in which Thoreau emphasized to an extreme how, "in the midst of the arctic day, we may trace the summer to its retreats."[53]

Yet, third, Thoreau also pastoralizes winter. "No weather interfered fatally with my walks" (265); the owl's cry is "forlorn but melodious" (271); the soaked ice cutters quickly revive in front of Thoreau's stove (295). Thoreau's is not the spirit-threatening, shipwreck-bringing, bone-chilling winter from which Thaxter must wrest her delicate epiphanies, nor is it even Dillard's winter, whose onset is the objective correlative of the *via negativa*. Thoreau would not have complained like Krutch that "the most serious charge which can be brought against New England is not Puritanism but February."[54] On the contrary, Thoreau seems to be trying to make a case for winter. With regard to the "antique" effect of frozen grasses, for example, he remarks that "many of the phenomena of Winter are suggestive of an inexpressible tenderness and fragile delicacy. We are accustomed to hear this king described as a rude and boisterous tyrant; but with the gentleness of a lover he adorns the tresses of Summer" (310). Here we see Thoreau availing himself of a convention from contemporary (and modern) popular literary naturism, which later became (as in Thaxter and Austin) a convention of regional realist writing generally: the axiom that intense microvision compensates for a dearth of blandishment. Since "long deprivation of any kind of pleasure increases our susceptibility and magnifies our capacity for enjoyment," therefore "in winter the mind possesses more sensibility to rural charms than during the seasons of vegetation and flowers." So reasoned Wilson Flagg, with characteristic gravity.[55] Thoreau himself commented on how winter brought clarity and acuity of vision. Snow served as "a great revealer" of faint tracks and paths, which it "reprints . . . in clear white type, alto-relievo" (*J* 6: 124–125).

Within this pattern of doublethink regarding winter, Thoreau orchestrates the adventures of his protagonist as follows. At first he shields himself, by nesting in with cabin refurbishment and fuel preparation, then by populating his solitude with dead former neighbors and visits from live ones. Then he increasingly ventures outward, first mainly as observer (of winter animals), then as actor, in the chapter centering on the enterprise of pond measurement, which rivals the commercial activity of the ice harvesters. The deliberateness of this shift from withdrawal to activity is demonstrated, if further proof be needed, by its reversal of the "plot" of Thoreau's early winterpiece, "A Winter Walk," which ends a day of outdoor rambling with a retreat indoors before "the surly night-wind," and the reflection that "in winter we lead a more inward life. Our hearts are warm and cheery, like cottages under drifts . . . from whose chimneys the smoke cheerfully ascends. The imprisoning drifts increase the sense of comfort which the house affords, and in the coldest days we are content to sit over the hearth and see the sky through the chimney-top, enjoying the quiet and serene life that may be had in a warm corner by the chimney side."[56] In *Walden*, Thoreau gets past this hibernation phase during the first parts of the winter sequence, after which the protagonist bestirs himself. Thoreau thereby reinforces the direct opposite of the ethos ultimately commended by the essay—not a more inward life, but one more preoccupied with logging exterior detail. This exteriority is the main reason why the winter chapters are the least admired, least taught major section of *Walden*.[57] The best defense is not to defend but explain their presence. The explanation seems to be this. For Thoreau's economic and spiritual experiment to seem to succeed, winter had to be coped with and not merely endured. Thoreau "overcame" the challenge of winter by getting through the indoor phase first, then venturing more actively out into winter, a process that starts with his beech-tree appointments (265) and climaxes in the *tour de force* of surveying, which makes "The Pond in Winter" a wintertime counterpart of both "The Bean-Field" and "The Ponds." The key to the exuberance of "Spring" is the protagonist's earlier "rebirth" after short hibernation into a state of more attentive rapport with natural things. He can watch winter animals without the self-consciousness of "Brute Neighbors"; he has reached a level of environmental responsiveness that will allow him to register the anticipated spring changes minutely and sensitively.

The emphasis on winter and the transition to spring ostensibly pulls *Walden* away from its original purpose as a treatise on living, a critique of political economy, reflecting the irresistible expansion of Thoreau's natural history projects in the 1850s more than his original intent for the book. Nature-resistant readers tend to be vexed by this change. Yet the belated seasonal emphasis fits the treatise. If the experiment works even in winter, the most starkly demanding season—if even an exaggeratedly cold, snowy winter can feel satisfactory—then the experiment in voluntary simplicity through adaptation to nature has succeeded. If in the face of these conditions, one's sense of place and rapport with the environment deepens, then the experiment has been a triumph. The intensified sensitivity to seasonal microphenomena registered by presenting first winter and then spring as dominant rather than background events shows that the experiment has worked the desired magic. If, as some readers contend, we leave the book imagining Thoreau still in the woods rather than sojourning back in civilized life, then the magic has worked on us.

Of course *Walden* does not literally end in the woods. By adding the "Conclusion," Thoreau left Walden rhetorically, as he did in life, returning to the treatise level, the more deliberately intersocial plane at which he had begun. This return creates a double closure—the conclusion of the narrative and of the sermon—similar to but more pronounced in its internal contrast than the double introduction of the first two chapters:

first the disquisition on economy, then the personal glimpse of the more intangible, spiritual motives and pleasures of the experiment. It is important to read the last two chapters also as a matched pair and to entertain the thought—which can never be proven or disproven—that the divergent foci and, even more, the clashing tones (lyrical exuberance versus jeremiad) were a quite intentional effect on Thoreau's part.

Considered as a social text, "Spring" is accommodationist, despite its pantheistic excrescences, whereas "Conclusion" is confrontational, however familiar the jeremiad form was to Thoreau's fellow New Englanders. Even with his relatively modest experience as a lecturer and magazine writer, Thoreau would doubtless have been aware that the joyous lyricism of "Spring" brought it pretty close to standard magazine and giftbook fare. Yet in truth the position of living through spring in a shack at the town's fringe was identical in point of marginality to the disaffection registered in "Conclusion." "Spring" may seem a more sociable essay, but the lifestyle that underlies it is every bit as cranky. Thoreau used the comparative conventionalism of season writing here to accomplish these different purposes: to meet the reader halfway, so as to dramatize attractively some of the aesthetic and spiritual fruits of the experiment; to set up a contrast between the pleasurable-seeming life in nature versus the irritable mood that the "Conclusion" reinstates with its return to the intersocial (a no-longer-friendly speaker advising us that we cannot feel fulfilled as we did in the previous chapter); and, finally, to enjoy a kind of private joke at the expense of most readers, who fail to see that the seemingly sudden return to standoffishness in "Conclusion" was really the fruit of the experience of "Spring" itself, the experience of having been more fully weaned than most people from conventional entanglements. That Thoreau could capitalize so fully on both the accommodationist and the oppositional faces of literary naturism is one of *Walden's* greatest achievements as a season book.

The Seasons as a Discipline in Environmental Awareness

What, then, can be said by way of conclusion about the function of the seasons as a literary device? They can be a way of establishing common ground, as strangers negotiate the awkwardness by chatting about the weather. By the same token, the seasons can be a placebo, or a way of pursuing touchier subjects under safe cover. They are so malleable as to give enough leeway to broach just about anything the writer might wish. No one will object if Mary Oliver decides, in a sequence of summertime poems, to deal with bats, horses, and sharks in that particular order, or to devote another poem to the biography of her great aunt.[58] No one will object to a poem that stresses how one particular writer's seasons do not match the standard grid, how April is the cruellest month, and so forth. On the contrary, as prosody becomes piquant by quarreling with the metronome, so here.

Yet the metronome ticks on. The seasons are also an aesthetic discipline that enforces a certain sense of shape and continuity. More to the present point, they can be, although they not necessarily are, a discipline in environmental structure and process: a loose discipline, which either writer or reader is free to ignore for sizable intervals, but which can become rigorous, intricate, and deeply significant for those who choose to follow it. The track of the seasons is easy to follow up to a point, but quickly one realizes that a lifetime of pursuit will not suffice. The sheer obviousness of seasonality, and its janus-faced epistemological status as both a plastic mental construct and an environmental imperative, make it the most accessible path for luring nature novices into thinking about the environment as a holism involving many intricate interrelations. The question then becomes the degree to which one is prepared to follow along that path from subject to object, fancy to perception, self-centeredness to self-refashioning in the light of an awakened environmental sense.

Environmental writers write in the expectation that there will be a motivational as well as an information gap between themselves and most readers in this respect. When beekeeper-essayist Sue Hubbell reports a January walk to inspect her hives, she leaves the reader free to respond to it as a picturesque excursion into "one of those clear bright days that we often have here in winter in the Ozarks," although for her (especially in "real life" but also as author) it is a much more portentous affair: to make sure her bees are still alive and well. As writer, she fudges this purposefulness by sounding casual and dotting the path with animal tracks and pleasant recollections of wild turkeys and hawks sighted recently. (Lingering on these also makes the point that the walk was something more than a business trip.) At the same time, she plays the initiator, offering to share her competence to those who care through a vignette of environmental reading. The external signs "tell about the health of the colony within." The vital signs may seem counterintuitive to a novice: corpses and stains. Bees in healthy hives have "been tending to sanitation, flying out to defecate, spattering the snow with their yellow droppings, and carrying out . . . sister bees who had died of age or cold."[59] We are free to sniff at this passage and leave it behind with the other rural imagery, as part of an ephemeral winter morning's bouquet. Or we can absorb it as part of a hitherto unknown branch of environmental knowledge. Or, likelier than either extreme, we may take the passage as an exemplum in the craft of environmental reading, which (though perhaps it does not deeply affect us at the time) may jog us in the direction of wanting to make ourselves more aware of how phenomena signify and how, beyond that, even our suburbanized, attenuated lives are subtly regulated—maybe even constituted—by the elements. If not bees, then trees, clouds, humidity, heat, light. In such ways, seasonal representations tease us toward awareness of ourselves as environmental beings.

CHAPTER EIGHT

Place

✧

In the moral (the ecological) sense you cannot know *what* until you have learned *where*.

—Wendell Berry, "Poetry and Place"

It is not down in any map; true places never are.

—Herman Melville's Ishmael, in *Moby-Dick*

I describe my location as: on the western slope of the northern Sierra Nevada, in the Yuba River watershed, north of the south fork at the three-thousand-foot elevation, in a community of Black Oak, Incense Cedar, Madrone, Douglas Fir, and Ponderosa Pine.

—Gary Snyder, *The Practice of the Wild*

THIS IS THE CHAPTER most conspicuously missing so far: the one on place. How could a book on environmental writing not give pride of place to place?[1] Is it not more fundamental than seasonality, or even relinquishment? Judging from the multitudinous testimonials by and on behalf of writers, ancient and modern, as to the importance of the sense of place in their work, it might seem that place ought to be central to anyone's theory of environmental imagination. If the visions of relinquishment and of nature's personhood are to be realized concretely, if the face of nature's seasonality is to be perceived, surely these events must happen some*where*. Some would even argue that environmental steward-ship requires a personal commitment to a specific place. "Without a complex knowledge of one's place, and without the faithfulness to one's place on which such knowledge depends," warns Wendell Berry, "it is inevitable that the place will be used carelessly, and eventually destroyed."[2]

Yet grounding in place patently does not guarantee ecocentrism, place being by definition perceived or felt space, space humanized, rather than the material world taken on its own terms.[3] "The meanings of places may be rooted in the physical setting and object and activities," geographer Edward Relph observes, "but they are not a property of them—rather they are a property of human intentions and experiences."[4] "Place thus comes to being," as Edward Soja concurs, "from the 'short circuits' inherent in the horizontal experience" of a thinking subject.[5] If we idealize the sense of place as a panacea for the disaffections of modern uprootedness, we run almost as great a risk of cultural narcissism as when we accept the myth of place-free, objective inquiry. For place-sense may actually "connect" us with actual environments in such a way as to insulate us from critical apprehension of them, so that they instill a form of "amnesia" that allows us "to forget our separateness and the world's indifference."[6] Thus Berry distinguishes sharply between unself-conscious, insular regionalism and *"local life aware of itself,"* which "would tend to substitute for the myths and stereotypes of a region a particular knowledge of the life of the *place* one lives in and intends to *continue* to live in."[7] Even this might be thought restrictive. To be environmentally sensitive must one commit to living one's entire life in a particular place, as Berry has? Must a writer write only about his or her home place? Does the vision of "local life aware of itself" guarantee respect for natural environment as a value independent of the values assigned to it by the community of human inhabitants? In each case, the answer is, clearly not. One can be lococentric and homocentric, peripatetic yet environmentally responsive. At the same time, it seems indisputable that the self-conscious commitment to place that Berry celebrates would more likely produce or accompany environmental responsiveness than would atopia or diaspora. What we require, then, is neither disparagement nor celebration of place-sense but an account of those specific conditions under which it significantly furthers what Relph calls environmental humility, an awakened place-awareness that is also mindful of its limitations and respectful that place molds us as well as vice versa.[8]

Place as a Utopian Project

Anyone looking for place-sense in literature had better start with modest expectations, bearing in mind Yi-fu Tuan's dictum that "topophilia is not the strongest of human emotions" and Neil Evernden's definition of *Homo sapiens* as "the natural alien," the creature without a proper habitat.[9] As an Emily Dickinson poem has it, to make a prairie requires only a clover, a bee, and reverie—and "revery alone will do, / If bees are few."[10] Consider how sparse a representation of place we find tolerable even in so-called realistic fiction. William Dean Howells starts *A Modern Instance* with a charmingly illustrated four-paragraph map of a rural New England village, its mountains and fields and elms, its architecture, its main street. Then he turns to the affairs of his characters, rarely to look at this villagescape again, letting it stand once and for all as a sufficient "composition of place" and implied statement about the bearing of environment on behavior. Here and elsewhere in fiction, writers typically regulate the evocation of setting according to a few simple rules: prefatoriness (each new location briefly described), dramatic intensification ("It was all wild and lonesome"), and symbolic doubling ("the silence in which the house was wrapped was another fold of the mystery which involved him").[11] Perhaps this formula explains the durability of the term "setting": that is, mere backdrop. In any case, it is striking how easily readers accept what is absurdly untrue to actual experience. Do most people look attentively at landscapes only when looking at them for the first time? Does the rhythm of the occasional highlighted cameo correspond to the rhythm of our actual attention to our environment? Yet we do not complain about having to make these accommodations; they quickly seem self-evidently right. Even some of the most place-respectful people do not complain. Eudora Welty, for example, who holds that "establishing a chink-proof world of appearance" is "the first responsibility of the writer," begins her great essay "Place in Fiction" by conceding that "place is one of the lesser angels that watch over the racing hand of fiction . . . while others, like character, plot, symbolic meaning, and so on, are doing a good deal of wing-beating about her chair, and feeling, who in my eyes carries the crown, soars highest of them all and rightly relegates place into the shade."[12]

A more promising instance than *A Modern Instance* of setting's potential in fiction of the realistic sort is Thomas Hardy's *Return of the Native*. Hardy would likely have demurred at Welty's subordination of place to the role of handmaiden. It has been said, with little exaggeration, that every Hardy novel "seems to focus upon some form of organic life in terms of which the characters themselves are described."[13] Nowhere is this more evident than in his portrayal of Egdon Heath, which Hardy realizes in fine visual detail, endows with an aboriginal personhood ("singularly colossal and mysterious in its swarthy monotony"), intermittently evokes throughout the novel as a leitmotif, and uses as a potent force that molds the character and behavior of those who come into association with it. Hardy's hero, Clym Yeobright, "might be said to be its product": "His eyes had first opened thereon; with its appearance all the first images of his memory were mingled; his estimate of life had been coloured by it; his toys had been the flint knives and arrow-heads which he found there, wondering why stones should 'grow' to such odd shapes; his flowers, the purple bells and yellow furze; his animal kingdom, the snakes and croppers; his society, its human haunters."[14] It is hard to imagine more forthright testimony to environmental influence in shaping human affairs. But by the same token the passage makes it clear that the heath is in the long run ancillary to Clym's story, however vital to the direction it takes. *Return of the Native* is about people in place, not about place itself. Measured against the totality of what might have been said about the Wessex ecosystem, even on the basis of biology's still rudimentary state, Hardy barely scratched the surface. He and Welty agree that the function of place is to define character by confining it, to act as "the ground conductor of all the currents of emotion and belief and moral conviction that charge out from the story in its course."[15]

Such cases as Howells, Hardy, and Welty show how hard it is for writers to do justice to place, even when they respect it. Undoubtedly this holds more for fiction than for nonfiction, since a more or less pandemic ingredient of the novelistic contract is that novels feature human affairs. Still, it can be said of all genres that place is something authors find easier to name and praise than to present. Although Berry justifiably claims that he would not be the writer he is if not for his home base on an Appalachian Kentucky farm, he may need more than a lifetime to articulate what that sense of place feels like, what its ingredients are. Much will remain tacit, unapprehended, and—possibly—censored by the commitment to a certain kind of lyric or meditation or satire. William Least Heat Moon sets out to write a book about a single county in Kansas: *Prairy-Erth*, perhaps the most ambitious literary reconstruction of a small portion of America ever attempted in a single volume. It turns out to be three times as long as he expected: roughly two hundred thousand words. Yet "ninety-nine-point-nine to the ninth decimal of what has ever happened here isn't in the book."[16]

Even if Least Heat Moon had devoted a lifetime of research to his project and arrived at something like an omniscient command of oral and archival history, it still might not have sufficed to articulate the sense of place. "What must a man do to be at home in the world?" a Berry poem muses.

> It must be with him
> as though his bones fade beyond thought
> into the shadows that grow out of the ground
> so that the furrow he opens in the earth opens
> in his bones, and he hears the silence
> of the tongues of the dead tribesmen buried here
> a thousand years ago.[17]

But how likely is that to happen? And if it did, would it not pull a person over into a state of dreamtime unconsciousness far removed from the sphere of reading and writing? While reading E. O. Wilson's essay "The Right Place," I was struck by its account of the three ingredients of humanity's putative primal habitat and their persistence in shaping the taste for landscape. "It seems that whenever people are given a free choice," Wilson observes, "they move to open tree-studded land on prominences overlooking water."[18] Before my Thoreauvian eyes immediately flashed an image of the Walden cabin site. Did Thoreau himself sense this? Could such an idea have occurred to him? Was historical anthropology far enough along in his day to have permitted him to think it? Even if so, Wilson implies that the human sense of place—such as it is, whether or not it happens to be one of the strongest human emotions—is so deeply embedded, so instinctual, that no one will ever be able to bring it to full consciousness in all its nuanced complexity. John Haines, a contemporary poet and essayist exceptional for self-conscious attentiveness to the importance of place as a shaping influence in his writing, is one of the few writers I know to claim to have fulfilled the dream of his youth "to find a specific place and be born over again as my own person." Yet he confesses that he cannot fully explain why the place he found in Richardson, Alaska, so appealed to him except that it gave him a sense of freedom, of openness, of primality.[19]

Of course Haines made it hard on himself by relocating in a dream place—in the tradition of the new world aesthetics of the not-there (see Chapter 2). He would have started with a richer place-sense had he been an Alaskan aborigine or had he recommitted himself, like Berry, to his former home place. Immediately a landscape of much richer personal and social memory, both mythic and secular, might have suggested itself: landmarks with Wordsworthian traces of childhood encounters many times layered over and magnified in the memory. A Spoon River Anthology of houses with multigenerational histories attached to them, so that as one dream-walks through the neighborhoods, long, intertwined family histories rise up before the mind. The extraordinary events in the community's history, its redundant social rituals, persistent moth-eaten scraps of local gossip, and the infinite series of intense and painful and joyous relationships of childhood. Indeed, for some home places, whether of aboriginal peoples or of more recent settlers banded in place long enough to have become as good as aboriginal, the sense of the sacred converts place into shrine and history into myth and binds all together in a single plenum. "Thus the sight of virtually every landmark, no matter how insignificant it may seem to the foreign visitor passing through the desert, brings deep emotional satisfaction."[20] This observation was made about Australian aborigines, but a version of it would apply also, even if with reduced force, to long-established settler cultures where a sense of history as sacred memory is evoked by certain spots: trees, commons, churches, cemeteries.

But for all cultures, the art of bringing to full personal consciousness and articulating a sense of place is arduous, and for new world settler cultures especially so, given the relative shortness of their history in place. These cultures face the uphill battle of jump-starting the invention of place-sense by superimposing imported traditions and jerry-building new ones—Anglo-American wholesale borrowings and fabrications of Indian stories being a conspicuous example of this kind. The very year Thoreau

graduated from Harvard, 1837, the town of Concord was zealously engaged in just such an endeavor, dedicating the completed Battle Monument commemorating "the shot heard round the world" in 1775, when
the local minutemen resisted the British in the first skirmish of the
American Revolution. The ceremony came just two years after an equally
significant social ritual, Concord's bicentennial, at which Emerson, who
wrote the poetic inscription on the monument from which I have just
quoted, delivered a "Historical Discourse" in which he assured his townspeople that "we hold by the hand the last of the invincible [Puritan] men
of old" in the persons of those selfsame, now aged veterans.[21] This
village-oriented sense of place was ultimately a much less richly interesting phenomenon to Emerson, however, than the mysterious "something"
in the "fields and woods" that he found "more dear and connate than"
what he felt "in streets and villages."[22] His disciple Thoreau, albeit himself
an avid regional history buff, felt so even more keenly; and it fell to him
to try to articulate on behalf of nineteenth-century New England settler
culture what this sense of the place of exurban space might be.

Indeed, nowhere is the struggle to articulate the proper place of nature
to a person's overall sense of place more visible and absorbing than in
Thoreau's literary career. He wanted, we have seen, to write a Book of
Concord, and had he lived long enough he might have produced one.
Certainly he gathered a huge amount of material. But in the literary result
Concord remained, on the one hand, a territorial and conceptual gestalt
and, on the other hand, a welter of different niches, semicoordinated
botanical and meteorological details, a few densely realized tracts like
Walden Pond, sundry historical anecdotes, and thousands of personal
encounters with fellow inhabitants, human and nonhuman. The richer
Thoreau's store of knowledge, the more "Concord" fissured into constituent items, like the different kinds of berries and seeds that are the topics
of his late unfinished natural history manuscripts. This specialization of
focus, I have come to believe, bespoke not a shrinkage of creative energy
but, as Emerson perceived, the fact that "the scale on which his studies
proceeded was so large as to require [a] longevity" that could not be
granted him.[23] His one completed Concord book, *Walden,* at times conveys a marvellously intricate sense of place. But how selective and idiosyncratic and fitful it seems if we ask it to tell us what the town of

Concord looks like, what kind of people and plants grow there, what their history has been, specializing as it does in the play of phenomena through a particular chapter of a particular person's life.

Indeed the net result of Thoreau's environmental observations during the dozen years when he plied them most systematically, was so fragmentary as to make one wonder about his powers of synthesis. Certainly, some modern environmental writing, especially when assisted by modern microscopy, expresses itself with a far greater comprehensiveness and assurance. I have in mind especially documentary work that concentrates intensively on the play of natural phenomena occurring in a delimited place, including: Rachel Carson's *Under the Sea-Wind,* Sally Carragher's *One Day at Beetle Rock,* Edwin Teale and Mildred Teale's *The Life and Death of a Salt Marsh,* and David Rains Wallace's *Idle Weeds: The Life of an Ohio Sandstone Ridge.* Here is an exemplary passage from the last:

> In the spring pool there were two levels of food-producing green plants. At the first level silver maple and white ash leaves fell into the pool, decomposed, and formed a nourishing broth for diverse populations of bacteria, aquatic fungi, protozoans, mites, copepods, amphipods, and other tiny organisms. The nutrients released by their decay also fertilized the second level—growths of filamentous green algae and freshwater diatoms. Algae and animalcules served in their turn as food for larger animals.[24]

When Robert Frost looks into such vernal pools, he sees only their beautiful surfaces as they briefly "reflect / The total sky almost without defect" before the thirsty tree roots dry them up in early summer,[25] but Wallace renders a succinct exposition of the entire food chain without blinking. In one sense, Wallace's narrative of the interplay of flora and fauna at Chestnut Ridge throughout the seasons handsomely supplies within a mere 180 pages what Thoreau never felt ready to supply even after logging thousands and thousands of *Journal* entries about Concord ecology. In another sense, however, the Wallace passage and the Frost poem illustrate mirror-opposite limitations of environmental perception: in Frost's case, the illusion of transparency, whereby space is reduced to a mental construct; in Wallace's case, the illusion of opacity, whereby (as Soja puts it) "spatiality is comprehended only as objectively measurable appearances."[26] If the tendency to relegate landscape items to the status of symbols or reflectors is the occupational hazard, environmentally speaking, of fictive writing, then the tendency to fall into stolid documentary that deletes the traces of human interest and presence from its landscapes is the occupational hazard of nature writing.[27] All things considered, Thoreau's incompletion is more complete than Wallace's incompletion, especially if, like Sharon Cameron, we take the incompletion of Thoreau's *Journal* as a sign of the seriousness with which he took nature's refusal to conform to the system of correspondences between environmental and moral realms that he sought to find there.[28] Altogether, it seems that place-consciousness in literature, and most especially the consciousness of the nonhuman environment as a network enfolding human inhabitants, ought to be considered a utopian project that realizes itself, in its more instructive forms, not as a *fait accompli* but as an incompletion undertaken in awareness that place is something we are always in the process of finding, and always perforce creating in some degree as we find it, so as to make it a perpetual challenge to compensate for the different kinds of reduction I have described. Most especially is this true of modern westerners, who are much more nomadic than aborigines and more buffered from the exigencies of their physical environments by technological aids like central heating and freeway systems.

To concentrate on this line of thinking in the discussion below, I shall intentionally avoid certain standard ways of discussing the sense of place. I shall not review "archetypal" images like houses, nests, and other enclosures as Gaston Bachelard does in *The Poetics of Space,* nor try to define various paradigmatic frames of reference in terms of which place can be formulated, as D. W. Meinig does in "The Beholding Eye";[29] nor attempt to classify different kinds of space (home, region, sacred space, and the like), as Tuan and Relph do. Nor shall I dwell on how mythography and folklore help establish a sense of place by defining a regional or tribal ethos. Nor shall I survey canonical literature's famous imagined countries, like Faulkner's Yoknapatawpha, the Nebraskas of Willa Cather and Wright Morris, the deserts of Austin and Abbey. Instead I shall proceed by focusing on certain memorable ways in which literature provokes environmental reflection by expanding preconceived understandings of the nonhuman environment as a dimension of personal and communal sense of place.

Reperceiving the Familiar

Perhaps the commonest attraction of environmental writing is that it increases our feel for both places previously unknown and places known but never so deeply felt. The activation of place-sense that comes with this vicarious insidership is apt to subside quickly, however, unless it is repeatedly jogged. Whether from laziness or a desire for security, we tend to lapse into comfortable inattentiveness toward the details of our surroundings as we go about our daily business. Place is related to complacency psychologically as well as etymologically; we reassure ourselves by converting abstract space into familiar place and subsisting in the unconsciousness of its familiarity.[30] We thus face the constant challenge of keeping the familiar fresh, so that we do not reach a level of complacency where place-sense dwindles into a caricature of itself. This is true for both writer and reader.[31] Therefore, rather than concentrate on place's role in holding psyche and society together by supplying a deeply satisfying sense of home base or home range, I want instead to take this for granted as an important dimension of many human lives and artistic works and concentrate instead on the more delicate issue of how the sense of place can be kept alert and sensitive rather than left to lapse into dogmatic slumber in some cozy ethnocentric alcove.

Environmental literature launches itself from the presumption that we do not think about our surroundings, and our relation to them, as much as we ought to. "We" often includes the writer as well. "There is smugness in knowledge like that," writes John Janovy, Jr., as he muses about the prospects for research on grasshopper parasites. "There is smugness in knowing that a valuable jewel lies in the grass of the Ackley Valley Ranch, and all someone has to do is go pluck it up with an insect net. There is a smugness in knowing that thousands of others could walk those fields day after day and never see that jewel; its security is in its simplicity and obviousness."[32] In this case, one suspects that the speaker feels confident of his power to make the familiar come newly alive for us but that he trusts to the writing process itself to keep himself invigorated. In revving up "smugness" to a pitch of exuberance, he can excite both parties by celebrating the banal grasshopper as a hidden jewel, so that complacency will give way to wonder. The best environmental writers continually recalibrate familiar landscapes (sometimes familiar to reader as well as writer) in such ways, so as to keep alive the sense of the "undiscovered country of the nearby," as John Hanson Mitchell calls it.[33] The writing process itself, as for Janovy if I read him rightly, does not equate with the moment of discovery as the writers experienced it; but the rhetorical energy points backward to the prior experiences of discovery that provoked them to their present plateaus of environmental consciousness and commitment to place.

Thoreau's *Journal*, being a (nearly) private register of thought composed (nearly) at the times of occurrence, provides an almost perfect record of this process. Consider Thoreau on the subject of muskrat houses, "singularly conspicuous for the dwellings of animals" (*J* 5: 440). Their regular appearance in autumn he always looked forward to and seldom failed to note, often at length. Thoreau had an engineer's interest in the details of muskrat construction, but more noteworthy is his stylization of the inert data so as to enliven it with place-sense. Muskrat nests are not *things* but habitats, dwellings remotely like one's own that provide a basis for erasing the line between village and outback and seeing both as variant forms of settlement in place.[34] ("There is a settler whom our low lands and our fogs do not hurt" [*PJ* 4: 129]. "A more constant phenomenon here than the new haystacks in the yard, . . . they were erected here probably before man dwelt here and may still be erected here when man has departed" [*J* 12: 389].) Muskrat houses resemble Thoreau's cabin ("They have reduced life to a lower scale than Diogenes" [*PJ* 4: 129]), as well as Eskimo igloos, boat houses, and Indian lodges.

Thoreau keeps environmental perceptiveness activated by shuttling back and forth between standard reportage that objectifies the dens and whimsical twists that transform them into places, between transforming muskrats into members of the human community and transforming people into muskrats. "For thirty years," he declares, "I have annually observed, about this time or earlier, the freshly erected winter lodges of the musquash along the riverside, reminding us that, if we have no gypsies, we have a more indigenous race of furry, quadrupedal men maintaining their ground in our midst still. This may not be an annual phenomenon to you. It may not be in the Greenwich almanac or ephemeris, but it has an important place in my Kalendar" (*J* 12: 389). The sequence is typical of him: the author's familiar calendrical routine ("I have annually observed") transfused by defamiliarizing exotica (muskrat-gypsies) produces readjustment of the familiar as socially defined ("my Kalendar" displaces the conventional one). Thoreau's sense of Concord as a distinct place over time depends equally on loving, on habituated familiarity with its phenomena—we might call this the Wendell Berry part of Thoreau—and on keeping alive a sense of strangeness about them. Without novelty, place would lapse into banality; but without the element of repetition, Thoreau would not have thought so consciously about the muskrats as part of the spirit of place. Here as always in Thoreau the key rhetorical devices are analogy (switching reference frames from Concord to the [European?] gypsies and classical antiquity) and synecdoche (local phenomenon set in macrocosmic context).

Here Thoreau also shows the environmentally restorative side of the exotica with which he habitually overlays his landscape descriptions. Ultimately it was not alienating but immensely enriching to the place-sense to see the humble ground-nut not merely as a botanical item but "the potato of the aborigines," introduced perchance by "some Indian Ceres or Minerva," destined or so he hopes to outlast "the tender and luxurious English grains" and (self-fulfilling prophecy) to "be represented on our works of art" when "the reign of poetry commences here" (*Wa* 239). The ability to exfoliate whole cultural histories out of local minutiae was the rhetorical correlate of the heightened perceptual sensitivity with which Emerson credited him.

Thoreau found it invigorating to see things newly; but to see new things he found positively thrilling. A fascinating passage from the late *Journal* sheds light on Thoreau's gift for keeping place-sense alive and on his perceptual limits. He rejoices at having discovered what he takes to be a new species of bream in Walden Pond. Apparently he was wrong (see *J* 11: 349n), but that is not the point so much as the thoughts to which his pseudodiscovery gave rise after he described the creature's appearance meticulously and carried around for several days "in my mind's eye those little striped breams poised in Walden's glaucous water."

> They balance all the rest of the world in my estimation at present, for this is the bream that I have just found, and for the time I neglect all its brethren and am ready to kill the fatted calf on its account. For more than two centuries have men fished here and have not distinguished this permanent settler of the township . . . When my eyes

first rested on Walden the striped bream was poised in it, though I
did not see it . . . —the miracle of its existence, my contemporary
and neighbor, yet so different from me! . . . The bream, appreciated,
floats in the pond as the centre of the system, another image of God.
(*J* 11: 358–359)

This is the ultimate extension of the romantic dictum of discovering
greater truths within particulars: the universe from the grain of sand,
thoughts too deep for tears prompted by the meanest flower that blows.
His sense of the immense significance of the minute life-form is remarkable. It propels him to set the obscure minnow on the same ethical and
spiritual footing as his townspeople, as contemporary and neighbor and
image of God. "Every fact," as Emerson justly said, "lay in glory in his
mind, a type of the order and beauty of the whole."[35] What especially
quickens Thoreau's excitement here is of course the sense of a common
habitat as the bond joining fish to human and of the whole place as
enriched by the previously unknown species.

A typically homocentric bias for the contemplation of the discrete
item channels Thoreau's excitement as well.[36] Although he has been
credited with being the first person to study a body of water systematically, in this passage the question of how the bream fits into the pond's
"economy" (the closest prescientific synonym for "ecology," a term not
coined until 1866) scarcely interests him compared to the bream's unique-
ness. A very few years after Thoreau wrote this passage, young John Muir
was converted to the study of botany as a University of Wisconsin
undergraduate when an older student showed to his amazement that the
pea and the locust tree belonged to the same genus.[37] Although Thoreau
would have been intrigued by this discovery, his background first as a
transcendentalist and then as a botanist yoked him to synecdoche: to the
contemplation of the individual fact in relation to whatever truth seemed
to flower from it. His two major late integrative projects, the study of
seasonal phenomena and the dispersion of seeds, confirm by their belat-
edness and inchoate state how hard it was for Thoreau, lacking a modern
understanding of ecological theory, to shift from reasoning "vertically"
(from individual fact to ulterior truth) to thinking "horizontally." Thus
the drift of Thoreau's meditation on the bream runs counter to the
precept of the first important American scientific treatment of pond

ecology, published a quarter of a century after his death: "If one wishes to become acquainted with the black bass . . . he will learn but little if he limits himself to that species."[38] Not that Thoreau was guilty of the kind of specialized myopia this article was really indicting. As *Walden*'s "Ponds" chapter attests, Thoreau certainly had an ecological *sense* even if he generally preferred, until late in life, to formulate it in terms of a series of luminous defamiliarizing perceptions of this and that phenomenon.

The more conventional but no less environmentally informed descriptions of Thoreau's contemporary Susan Fenimore Cooper show more systematic unfolding of place consciousness than Thoreau attempted in print. A longish July entry from her literary daybook *Rural Hours,* which complements the passages we have just scanned, surveys village topography and history from the standpoint of a unique nearby "remnant" of old pine woods on a hillside. After sketching where this "monument of the past" is situated, Cooper imagines the pines, with a bit of quiet irony, as "silent spectators of the wonderful changes that have come over the valley," from pre-Columbian wilderness to the present. She ends with a plea that the grove be spared; for "this little town itself must fall to decay and ruin . . . ere trees like those, with the spirit of the forest in every line, can stand on the same ground in wild dignity of form like those old pines now looking down upon our houses."[39] In effect, Cooper reinvents the whole cultural ecology of Cooperstown within the space of a half-dozen pages as falling under the aegis and tutelage of the ancient pine grove. She repeats the epochal events of public memory: the Europeans' arrival, the naming of the local lake by George Washington, the Revolution, the gradual retreat of the Mohawks, the march of settlement. Her historical recitation articulates the sense of a community emerging over time, but it puts human history under the gaze of the pines in order to redefine it as accountable to natural history as a higher authority than its own parochial institutions. Cooper would not have approved of *Walden*'s more aggressive remapping of Concord history from the social margins, according to which ex-slaves like Brister Freeman and down-at-the-heel dipsomaniacs like Hugh Quoil are recalled to public memory as notable former inhabitants while the glorious Concord Fight of 1775 is relegated to a comic aside during the Battle of the Ants (*Wa* 257–258, 261–262, 230). But as a reinterpretation of place, Cooper's essay is a *tour de force* of the same sort: the ecological transformation of a somewhat stolid Yankee community by seeing it from the woods, seeing it indeed as if it were properly part of the woods, rather than seeing the woods as ancillary to itself. What chiefly differentiates Cooper's vision from Thoreau's is her insistence on the "we"; even in her deviance she represents the scenes in front of her as "our" village. The comparative transparency of her style reflects this sense of her eye as public, not merely idiosyncratic. But this sociable posture belies the significance of the mental readjustment that she requires of her readers when they take her seriously.

What Cooper does to town history, Wendell Berry does on a more personal scale in writing about the "marginal farm" he and his wife bought and moved to 4 July, 1965. The longest of the sequence of poems Berry apparently composed as a public statement of dedication to this place is a poem about the history of the property. To a great extent, it tells a painful story of mismanagement, yet such is the price of vision, which Berry holds up (in the next poem) "against the false vision / of the farm dismembered, sold in pieces on the condition / of the buyer's ignorance."[40] The long view of the place as tended and mis-tended by generations of precursors allows him to inhabit it with awareness and care. For Berry this is both good practical sense and good inspiration. Berry would presumably agree with Leopold's valuation of husbandry as the highest form of ecological aesthetics (*SCA* 175).

Seeing things new, seeing new things, expanding the notion of community so that it becomes situated within the ecological community—these are some ways in which environmental writing can reperceive the familiar in the interest of deepening the sense of place. These examples make clear not only that such devices *dis*place in order to *re*place, but also that they depend heavily on metaphor, myth, and even fantasy to put readers in touch with place. Thus "in Thoreau's writing," as one discussion of his "anti-geography" puts it, "static 'areas' start to metamorphose into shifting cognitive profiles and perspectives, and topographical features that seem arrested and fixed remain in subliminal flux."[41] Muskrats montage into gypsies, grasshoppers transform into jewels. But far from alienating the reader from the physical environment, these defamiliarizations seem meant to return us there with a new understanding and enthusiasm in accordance with Paul Ricoeur's rule of metaphor: its representations both warp us away and return us to the world.[42] This doubleness is a fact not just of linguistic representation but also of actual place-experience, insofar as place always implies active reciprocal relation between inhabitant and context. All creatures process their environment subjectively and seek to modify it in the process of adapting to it. It is not a question of whether we can evade this ground condition but of how to make it subserve mutuality rather than proprietary self-centeredness.

To transpose from literary terms to those of practical environmental reform, Thoreau's, Cooper's, Berry's, and Janovy's work as literary place-creators can be compared to contemporary environmental restoration-ism. Unlike the conservationist resource-management tradition, unlike the preservationist approach of protecting environments in their present state, the restorationist project seeks "to repair the biosphere, to recreate habitat." According to its premise, "humans must intervene in nature, must garden it, participate in it."[43] It extends beyond Leopold's transpo-sition of the stewardship ethic in *Sand County Almanac*: "whoever owns land has thus assumed, whether he knows it or not, the divine functions of creating and destroying plants" (*SCA* 67). For all practical purposes when you are living in a place, you are constructing it, whether you like it or not. So when a person wields an axe, he or she should do so "humbly aware that with each stroke he is writing his signature on the face of his land" (*SCA* 68).[44] Environmental restorationism, likewise, assumes that we have no alternative but to alter the landscape; there is no return to primordialness, if indeed such a state existed; and it further holds up as its goal, like Leopold himself in renewing his Sauk County place, modifi-cations that replenish biodiversity. Now, environmental writing does not literally repair the biosphere, does not literally do anything directly to the environment. But in the ways I have described it tries to practice a conceptual restorationism in reorienting the partially denatured reader not to a primordial nature, which we cannot recover either in fact or in fantasy, but to an artifactual version of environment designed to evoke place-sense. "Reverdure / is my calling," Berry writes. He refers directly to his farmer's vocation: "to make these scars grow grass."[45] But this is his mission as poet also.

Environmental texts, then, practice restorationism by calling places into being, that is, not just by naming objects but by dramatizing in the process how they matter. Inevitably certain reductions occur: no one can realize (in the full sense) anywhere near the totality of what can be realized about the environment; to set anything down in an essay or a book, one must be rigorously selective (compare Thoreau's copious lists of *Journal* observations on a good afternoon walk with any passage in his published works); and one's selections will express personal and culturally mediated preferences that others may not share. But these are niggling objections to an effective result, like the section of *Walden* that initially establishes place sense: "Sounds" through "Solitude." The first of these chapters begins with the most leisurely evocation of the cabin setting yet (*Wa* 111–114), then proceeds through a haphazard-seeming inventory of sounds heard on the spot: a sumach branch breaking (114), the railroad whistle and whiz (114–122), church bells filtered through the wood, the lowing of cows (123), whipporwills (123–124), owls (124–126), the rumbling of wagons and the croaking of frogs (126). Thoreau savors each sound, often for a long time. Frequently the passages become highly subjective, even rarefied; Thoreau seems to have been a positive epicure of auditory experiences ("All sound heard at the greatest possible distance produces one and the same effect, a vibration of the universal lyre, just as the intervening atmosphere makes a distant ridge of earth interesting to our eyes by the azure tint it imparts to it" [123]). Selective though it is, however, Thoreau's catalog of sound effects is so unhurried and pro-tracted as to create a certain plenitude. From this time forth Walden is solidly established as place, and we are prepared for the next chapter's insistence that solitude does not mean isolation, that nature itself is neighborhood (132).[46] "The externality of the world," observes Stanley Cavell, "is articulated by Thoreau as its nextness to me."[47] Nature remains other but connected, meaningful albeit not fully known: not terrain, but place. In the process of perceiving this place-sense for himself, the speaker creates it for the reader also.

Map Knowledge and Place-Sense

Places are by definition bounded, but human-drawn boundaries usually violate both subjectively felt reality and the biotic givens. The truism that one learns much about a subject by focusing on its border disputes was never truer than here. Where does a place start or end? Janovy thinks of Keith County as his place. Fine. But to the reader it is a confusing patchwork of scattered niches: a farm here, a bridge there with a swallow's nest underneath, a dam here, a marsh there, as the chapters swerve

whimsically around. Annie Dillard's *Pilgrim at Tinker Creek* is less peripatetic: the speaker hangs out mostly around a rustic cabin of some sort,
with the creek nearby. But the locale is not specified or even much
described, not even as sketchily as *Walden* describes where things are
around Concord. Edward Abbey's *Desert Solitaire* provides more conventional geography, but as the book unfolds the sense of sacred ground
extends outward across southern Utah for thousands of square miles. Can
we still think of this huge region as "a place"? Perhaps Mary Austin had
the right idea when she called her territory the Country of Lost Borders
and admitted to not feeling at home within it notwithstanding the bond
she felt to it.

Clearly there is no point trying to stipulate the precise territory
comprised by the there to which the what of an author's (or community's)
place-sense is meant to refer, since "territoriality is always socially or
humanly constructed in a way that physical distance is not."[48] But since
there is always a more or less localized physical there, and since jurisdic-
tional units never correspond faithfully to reality, we should expect that
place-sense will define itself partly in acquiescence to and partly in
resistance to or evasion of official boundaries. Environmental writing
approaches this antinomy by pitting map knowledge against empirical
knowledge. In ancient times, there was not perhaps much difference
between chorography and diagrammatic representations in point of subjectiveness. The perfection of orthogonally sectioned mapping, however,
opened the way for a "desubjectified" cartography wildly at variance from
the perceived reality of the more impressionistic and ethnocentric mapping practices of prescientific cultures.[49] Nowhere has this been more
obvious for a longer period of time than in the United States, for "no
previous paradigm of government ever took the notion of boundary so
seriously as did the young American republic."[50] As is well known, much
of the credit goes to Thomas Jefferson. A modified version of his system
of dividing territories into rectilinear townships and sections ("a model
example of Enlightenment abstraction," John Stilgoe rightly calls it) was
approved by Congress in 1785 as the template for defining the American
hinterland and thereby, in time, also what Philip Fisher has termed
"democratic social space."[51] The spatial physiognymy of American egalitarianism, entrepreneurialism, and privatism was rolled into one diagram.
The most obvious significance of such a legally mandated mapping system

in America and elsewhere, as colonial discourse studies and American ethnic studies have pointed out, is that it was part of a strategy for consolidating control over "unsettled" regions. From this standpoint, the challenge of present-day interpretation is to deconstruct the official map.[52] Set the white man's maps against each other. Oppose the official version with the map of Indian claims.[53] Or set ethnogeographical narrative against legally sanctioned agrarian geography, as Leslie Marmon Silko does in *Ceremony* when she has her protagonist recover his manhood by rustling back his own cattle as part of a ceremonial journey to the sacred mountain that has been cordoned off with wire fences by the occupying forces of the Floyd Lee ranch. My own chief concern here, however, is not with mapping or official geography as the site of clashing political or cultural systems. I am more concerned with its role as a provoker of environmental consciousness on account of the oscillation in the mind between "mental maps" and scientific maps (both procrustean, yet both having their own explanatory power), a tension that could only have arisen from the rigorous pursuit of standards of objectification that marks modern western culture.[54] From this perspective, official maps look more complexly productive than when seen merely as agents of cartographical imperialism.

Among the fruits of the contemporary renaissance in American environmental nonfiction that dates back to the 1940s and the work of Aldo Leopold, Rachel Carson, Loren Eiseley, and Joseph Wood Krutch, two of the most intricate achievements so far have been Barry Lopez's *Arctic Dreams* (1986) and William Least Heat Moon's *PrairyErth* (1991). No apology whatsoever needs to be made for these works on the score of belonging to a "minor" genre like "nature writing." In point of thematic and formal sophistication, they fully equal the classics of American autobiography and narrative fiction. If their stature is not recognized for awhile, and it probably won't be, that is because we have not learned how to read them. Cartography is one way in.

Both authors rely heavily on maps of their respective places: the North American Arctic and a single county in Kansas. Lopez ends with a scholarly section of panoramic maps, a gazetteer of places (with a latitude and longitude key), and a bibliography. Least Heat Moon sets identical facing maps of the county watersheds and road and rail system (which are remarkably symmetrical) at front and end. Subsectional maps occur throughout both books, and Lopez intersperses a series of special maps as well (of the distribution of the region's Eskimo population, for instance). The two authors both distrust maps and rely on them. "I traveled everywhere with maps," as Lopez recalls, but they were never entirely accurate; "they were the projection of a wish that the space could be this well organized." He recognizes the superiority of aboriginal place-sense to western cartography in this respect: "the evidence of continued intimacy with a local landscape—a practical knowledge of it, a sensitivity toward it, a supplication of it."[55] Throughout he is careful to honor the sophistication of Eskimo feats of land-memory, eyesight, technological inventiveness and thrift, attention to individual members of a species, and ecological understanding of the relations between weather and season and animal behavior. He also takes care to affirm the validity of indigenous mythic narrative as a way of reinforcing community stewardship of the environment.[56] Moreover, he tries to imagine nonhuman perception—how an island looks to a loon or land terrain to a fox. Lopez devotes separate chapters to muskoxen, polar bears, and narwhals, and in them tries to get inside the creature's heads and reconstruct how its range looks from its own standpoint. No work of settler literature ever dramatized more conscientiously the aboriginal principle that "the animals one encounters are part of one's community, and one has obligations to them." This indeed has been a major theme running throughout all of Lopez's work.[57] In *Arctic Dreams*, it makes for a multiperspectival representation of region in the course of which the western lay narrator and the finds of western science on which he also extensively draws are repeatedly calibrated against or corrected by the knowledge of native culture and animal behavior that Lopez painstakingly gleans from personal encounters and scientific studies.

Notwithstanding, neither the status of maps as keys to place nor their status as imaginative artifacts is undermined for Lopez. Whatever doubts his commentary may raise about maps, Lopez presents them as bibliographical apparatus without suggesting that they might not be reliable guides. What is more, he takes pleasure in Eskimos' adeptness at this genre, noting that Eskimos with no western education "were making and using maps long before they met Europeans" and have shown the ability to read European maps of their home range with ease, to produce maps of almost equal sophistication.[58] Lopez's thinking is inconsistent here; his temptation to vindicate Eskimo science by showing that it almost meets western standards of objectivity is at cross-purposes with his tendency elsewhere to contrast the two different forms of knowing. If Lopez had more fully entered into the spirit of aboriginal thinking about cartography, he might have written an account like Hugh Brody's description of the hearing at which representatives of the Indian tribes of northeastern British Columbia, who had produced reams of orthodox maps of their hunting territories (quite accurate, it seems) in connection with a late 1970s land-use survey, rolled out for the astonished whites a ceremonial "dream map" of their region representing its spiritual reality.[59] But it would be fairer to say that Lopez looks upon *both* western and Eskimo ways of knowing as indispensable approximations, each needing to be supplemented by the other. The text's voice defines its place as that of a mediator between local and scientific forms of knowledge, expert in neither, respectful but not uncritical of each.

Perhaps what especially makes Lopez relish convergences of native and outsider forms of landscape apprehension is that he writes from the standpoint of an outsider who wants to become more of an insider. To this end, it is important both to contrast the two modes of knowing and to imagine bridges from the one to the other. Maps afford one such bridge. Eskimo alacrity with western maps points to a key trait of indigenous culture: its successful adaptation to territorial imperatives and the need, in the harsh Arctic climate, "to pay attention to the smallest [visual] clues."[60] Conversely (as Lopez's grateful reader comes to realize), westerners' charts, limited though they are, are essential if one is to get past the tenderfoot stage and begin making contact with the subtler navigational clues that Eskimos and other Arctic aboriginals in practice steer by. Western maps register a shallow sense of place, but despite their superficiality they can guide one toward deeper understanding. At times they can even lend to place-sense a perspective that local knowledge cannot, as when Lopez muses that the Arctic region "turns on itself like any nation. It is organized like Australia around an inland desert sea, with most of its people living on the coastal periphery. It is not vast like the Pacific. It is vast like the steppes of Asia. It has the heft, say, of China, but with the population of Seattle."[61] This is a wonderfully inventive *and* objectively compelling passage. It could only have been written with the aid of a globe or an atlas, however. Local knowledge by itself would never have thought it up. In a way the passage is blatantly presumptuous: What arrogance to conflate Arctic with Australia with Asia with Pacific—not to mention the conflation of all Arctic peoples with each other into an imitation-western "nation." Why then is Lopez, usually so sensitive to cultural difference, completely unfazed? Clearly because he is using cartography to unmoor his readers from their own provincial embeddedness by taking them on the verbal equivalent of a plane ride over the territory he will soon immerse them in. The panorama, the area map, cannot substitute for a sense of place, but it can provide a stage of basic reconfiguration that may induce the wonder, openness, and perplexity needed to make a more comprehensive Arctic training program work.

Lopez sidesteps some hard questions. He does not, for example, take note of the relation between cartography and the culturally insensitive division of Arctic terrain into Russia, the United States, Canada, and Greenland (Denmark), although he devotes a chapter to European Arctic expeditions that chronicles their blundering rapacity and histrionic pathos at some length. I suppose that Lopez never makes geography the villain as such, except for easy shots at the foolishness of Northwest Passage fantasies, because is broadly interested in bioregional knowing and because cartographical knowledge has, in the long run, assisted rather than impeded that knowledge, at least for those westerners aware of the limitations of graphs. William Least Heat Moon, by contrast, writes about a place whose sense of itself has been much more violently shaped by cartographic practices than the Arctic, where with the partial exception of the Bering Straits area the political borders of settler culture marked on maps seem to have determined the cultural forms to a lesser degree. Chase County, Kansas, was carved out during the nineteenth century according to Jefferson's grid. *PrairyErth* follows the same grid in seeking to invent a way of thinking about county landscape, culture, and history that will express both the durability and the arbitrariness of this legacy. So Least Heat Moon maps his book as twelve equal-size chunks (each with a set of six more or less symmetrically arranged chapters), in recognition of the county's twelve Jeffersonian "quadrangles."

He offers the quadrangles both as a profound reality of the county's topographical and cultural life and as a sign of what has to be transcended to grasp the "deep map" (the book's subtitle) underlying the surface one. The speaker observes the impress of rectilinearity in land parcel patterning, in the orientation of the region's settlements, in the design of farmscapes, even in the way individual houses were situated on lots. These are givens of settler culture that, in turn, have become part of the communal spirit of place to which he must be faithful. At the same time, there is something raucous and campy about his "fidelity." As it protracts, it becomes an ostentatiously gymnastic exercise calculated to undermine the neoclassical rationalism it purports to observe—and which, indeed, it overstates by so underscoring (for surely it would never have occurred to a resident to formulate his or her place-sense in the mathematicized form that Least Heat Moon renders it). Sure enough, when the traveler gets to the ninth quadrangle and finds it *too* gridlike, "lying as it does with all the mystery of a checked tablecloth," he is repelled, "baffled with the imaginary become real, inked lines turned to cut-in roads." He dislikes "that perfect scotching of the prairie which imprisoned the place and fenced me out; it was a net to ensnare the land and haul dark mysteries like a load of pilchards into the light."[62] It comes as no surprise, then, and not just because Least Heat Moon is part-Osage on one side, that the book ends with a coda imagining the county's shape and pathways very differently, from the standpoint of the remnant Kaw population. The author does not expect or particularly want settler culture to evaporate. It is, he admits, the presenting sociogeographical reality and likely to remain so; something like 95 percent of the book follows its construction of place. Furthermore, he clearly relishes pointing out cases where symbiosis of land and settlement has occurred, as in the planting of osage orange trees as natural hedgerows or the adaptation of the hardy cottonwood, now the totem tree of the state of Kansas. When settlers modify regional ecology in such a way that nature flourishes and the people intertwine with it, that is not imperial imposition; for the grid itself is modified, biologized. The author is not at all disposed to deny bona fide deeply rooted place-sense to the "countians" because of their culture's gridlike inception, least of all when the grid begins to soften and dissolve.

Two levels of self-consciousness affect *PrairyErth*'s account of the imposition of design on terrain: self-consciousness not only about the imposed design of settler culture but also about the artifice of the book's own design.[63] The reason for *PrairyErth*'s various omissions, the author confesses near the end, is not just that "a book can't include everything . . . but rather because my explorations quite early began forming into a gestalt that seems to control what I am capable of writing about."[64] This awareness may help account for his decision to start each new section with a series of several dozen "Commonplace Book" quotations, like the "Extracts" preamble to *Moby-Dick*. (He quotes Thoreau, Berry, and Lopez, among others, in the very first batch.) Many of these are prescriptive assertions like "You must not be in the prairie; but the prairie must be in you," and "Except by the measure of wildness we shall never really know the nature of a place."[65] Each batch is a heterogeneous cacophony of other peoples' landscape designs: of all sorts of places but particularly of Kansas, with Kansan voices liberally represented. Each batch says in effect: (1) Don't trust me; (2) I am the only way in. This ambiguous message advertises the bibliographical minefield that the author has had to pick his way through more openly than Lopez's more conventional list of sources at the end of his volume; and it warns us in advance that the book itself may be nothing more than a potpourri of self-contradictory crotchets. In this way *PrairyErth* generates more ironic self-reflexivity about anybody's perception of place than does *Arctic Dreams*, which reposes a deep trust in the validity and holism of aboriginal place-sense, by and large respects the explanatory power of western science, and treats the perceptual flaws of well-meaning westerners as educable rather than intractable. Although both books treat the two levels of cartography—as literal mapping and as authorial design—with ambivalence, sometimes as neglecting place-sense and sometimes as producing it, they clearly sit at different points on this continuum, *PrairyErth* standing relatively for the principle that grids impose a false or foreshortened consciousness and *Arctic Dreams* for grids and local place-sense as complementary ways of seeing. Again, I am not suggesting that Least Heat Moon denies his countians place-sense. Theirs may be more intersocial and less comprehensively biotic than that of Lopez's Eskimos; theirs may also be more personal and neighborly than tribal (in the sense of ethnic and sacral). But although Least Heat Moon interposes more of confessional and of abstruse meditation between the land and the reader, the reader of *PrairyErth* likely comes away with the distinct impression of how much more complex and profound a shared sense of interaction with region persists in this county than one would have expected from prairie stereotypes, the sterile-looking atlas map of Kansas, and the flyover at 35,000 feet. This fruition, such as it is, the grid has impeded but also produced.

The ambivalent relation of map knowledge to place-sense that Lopez and Least Heat Moon elegantly unfold operates on one frequency or another to help define the sense of place in much environmental writing. The better we understand its operation, the better we can understand environmental mimesis. To prepare the way for some final reflections, let us turn once more to *Walden*.

Thoreau is the only major American writer to have earned a living from defining and measuring tracts of land. This experience, on top of a strong positivist streak that uneasily coexisted with his transcendentalist bent, gave him an unusually firm—although ambivalent—command of official geography and made him very likely the most skillful cartographer who ever penned a literary classic.[66] These endeavors inspired the map of Walden Pond that he inserted into *Walden* (*Wa* 286). Visually, it comes as an unexpected and slightly bizarre interruption—the sole illustration in the main body of the text—as an accompaniment to Thoreau's narrative of sounding the pond. Like the map itself, this narrative shows the author at his most pickily meticulous. ("I can assure my readers that Walden has a reasonably tight bottom at a not unreasonable, though at an unusual, depth. I fathomed it easily with a cod-line and a stone weighing about a pound and a half" [285–286].) Thoreau completely suspends the "poetic" dimension of *Walden* for the nonce and lets geometry take over. Indeed, he seems flatly to disown fancy's vagaries ("the imagination, give it the least license, dives deeper and soars higher than Nature goes" [288]). Has Prospero, then, forsaken his rod for the cod-line and stone? By no means: for as the statistics accumulate, Thoreau weaves them into his most extravagant conceit yet, the ethical law he deduces from the pond's dimensions: "draw lines through the length and breadth of the aggregate of a man's particular daily behaviors and waves of life into his coves and inlets, and where they intersect will be the height or depth of his character" (291). Thus Thoreau applies Emerson's dictum in *Nature:* "The axioms of physics translate the laws of ethics."[67] Thoreau commentators have rightly hesitated to take seriously this *jeu d'esprit,* as one calls it.[68] Fair enough. Yet the mock-serious pedantry of the long passage in which this declaration occurs seems explicable only as Thoreau's way of coping with the impossible dream of a synthesis of poetry and science that will put qualities on as firm an objective ground as quantities.[69] The transcendental deduction does this. Significantly, the passage winds down by bemoaning the divorce between the modes of thinking: that either we "are conversant only with the bights of the bays of poesy, or steer for the public ports of entry, and go into the dry docks of science, where they merely refit for this world, and no natural currents concur to individualize them" (292). Despite this conclusion, however, the speaker proceeds, as it were, to reiterate his commitment to putting moral truth on an objective footing with two more paragraphs of factual reportage.

Thoreau's attempt in this section first to banish fancy and then to drive it over to the side of objectification by reintroducing it as ethical science is encapsulated by the map, which is both the Q.E.D. of the moral geometry exercise and a nice piece of professional work that establishes the section as one half of a diptych of "enterprise" scenes—the other half being the seriocomic narrative of the ice cutters that immediately follows. The map genre presumes the validity of a proper kind of appropriation of the pondscape for civic uses; it then becomes the implicit standard used to measure the capitalist enterprise in ice harvesting (which imposes its own sort of mathematics).

The pond-sounding episode both squares and competes with the accumulating place-sense in *Walden* generally. Up to this point, Thoreau has constructed the pondscape seemingly without much system. The early glimpses are sketchy and metaphor-laden (for example, pp. 86–87). "The Ponds" chapter stands out chiefly for its narratives, its legendizing, and its dreamy imagery ("It is a soothing employment . . . to sit on a stump on such a height as this, overlooking the pond, and study the dimpling circles which are incessantly inscribed on its otherwise invisible surface amid the reflected skies and trees" [187–188]). The sketch of White Pond, Walden's lesser twin, consists of little more than a garrulous story about a waterlogged tree (198–199). From this accumulation of imagery and anecdotalism a strong, compelling, but nebulous sense of place builds: delicious, inviting, mystical, leafy, limpid, refreshing, and secluded despite the railroad. The reader may have to exert a self-conscious effort to notice the amount of data crammed into many of these passages because Thoreau's fussy precision, for example on changing pond levels ("now, in the summer of '52" [180]), tends to dissolve in fancy ("It licks its chaps from time to time" [181–182]). One mark of Thoreau's success at lyricizing, although also of the obstinacy of disciplinary paradigms, is the insistence with which literary critics have wanted to interpret the pond as a symbol of something rather than as a meditation about and arising from a particular body of water. But while Thoreau abets this reading, he refuses to let the pond remain at the subjectified level of an intensely felt green world, a pastoral gem. He must give an exact, proportional account of it (the map). He must disenchant the legend of its bottomlessness. However many false bottoms *Walden* has, Thoreau must find and chart the bottom of Walden Pond.[70] The facts are not to be ignored.

His triumph is slightly rueful. After reciting the definitive sounding results, the speaker adds: "I am thankful that this pond was made deep and pure for a symbol. While men believe in the infinite some ponds will be thought to be bottomless" (287). Disenchantment whets the desire to remystify and no doubt partly drives the correspondential fantasy a few pages later, not to mention the lyrical effervescence of the next chapter, "Spring."

Thoreau represents the pond, then, by building on a counterpoint between a surveyor's deference to verifiable truth and a denizen's sense of place as subjectively felt. I mean "subjective" in the sense of affect-laden yet not entirely idiosyncratic, inasmuch as it is mediated and thereby rendered intersocial by the various interlocking topoi that Thoreau has internalized: romantic pastoralism, the aesthetics of relinquishment, the vision of nature's personhood, seasonality, maybe even (if E. O. Wilson is right) an atavistic sense of humanity's primal habitat. The kind of text that emerges from the interaction between map knowledge and experiential place-sense in *Walden*—and in *Arctic Dreams* and *PrairyErth* as well—can help us refine the theory of environmental nonfiction's "dual accountability" to imagination and to the object-world, developed in Chapter 3. All the nonfictions I have discussed operate, in different degrees, with due respect for the way experiential place-sense can connect up with actual environments but also with respect for its perceptual limits; all recognize in map knowledge both a potential standard against which to measure the vagaries of place-sense and an alternative form of perceiving valid only insofar as it has the power to connect one with lived reality or to impress itself on the environment so as to create the environment in its own image. In the interplay of map knowledge and place-sense, then, environmental writing affirms the alterity of the ground that is felt or mapped and thereby also the relativity of all visions of place, be they cartographic or intuitive; but at the same time it activates and validates (within limits) both "subjective" and "objective" modes of knowing that otherness. In the interplay of these alternatives the possibility both of a heightened consciousness of place-sense and of a self-critical resistance to sleepily centripetal place-embeddedness is quickened. In the betweenness of mapmaking and place-bonding environmental writing locates itself. Both official and intuitive knowledge are ultimately directed toward expressing its topophilia, its commitment to rendering a textual equivalent of an actual or virtual place.

Wendell Berry sums up the most fundamental principle that underlies this commitment when he insists that "it is vain to think either that the mind can *be* a place, or that the mind alone can *find* a proper place for itself or for us. It must look out of itself into the world."[71] Self-evident though Berry's assertion might seem, in practice it is not so easy to hold in the mind. The discourse of epistemology is conventionally atopic; even Heidegger has trouble getting from the theory of being's situatedness to the realization of that situatedness as a particularity. When *qua* epistemologist one tries to imagine what the "objective self" might be—a way of seeing that transcends personal idiosyncracies—one may conceivably talk about stepping outside ego and "considering the world as a place in which these phenomena [the personal experiences of other people] are produced by interaction between these beings and other things," but one may all the while have in mind rather the transmission of abstractions between minds. We can step out of ourselves if we are lucky; but if we do, we will find no world there. The "objective self," at least in the exposition of it I follow here, does not have anything to do with a world of objects.[72] Of course everyone knows that there is no such actual being, that an unplaced intersubjective self is no more possible than an isolated *cogito*. But when we are constructing arguments, or texts (such as this book) it is all too easy to think as if being *were* decontextualized. Ethnic and feminist revisionism provide one check to this misconception to the extent that they insist on keeping us from forgetting that every human being inhabits a particular kind of body. Place-consciousness provides another sort of check by insisting that every body occupies a bounded physical space. That limitation can be irksome; but although it circumscribes our horizons, it also helps to make possible what we can know.

At best, the placedness of experience provides humankind with a way of offsetting, if not altogether overcoming, its inheritance of "natural alienness" described by Evernden.[73] If the perception of seasonality is the commonest avenue toward fuller understanding of nature's motions, so the experience of place may be the commonest avenue toward experiencing relinquishment as ecocentrism.

CHAPTER NINE

Environmental Apocalypticism

✦

When I submit these thoughts to a printing press, I am helping to
drain a marsh for cows to graze, and to exterminate the birds of
Brazil. When I go birding in my Ford, I am devastating an oil field,
and re-electing an imperialist to get me rubber.

—Aldo Leopold, "Game and Wild Life Conservation"

There was no end to it; it knew no boundaries; and he had arrived
at the point of convergence where the fate of all living things, and
even the earth, had been laid. From the jungles of his dreaming he
recognized why the Japanese voices had merged with Laguna
voices, with Josiah's voice and Rocky's voice; the lines of cultures
and worlds were drawn in flat dark lines on fine light sand,
converging in the middle of witchery's final ceremonial sand
painting. From that time on, human beings were one clan again,
united by the fate the destroyers planned for all of them, for all
living things; united by a circle of death that devoured people in
cities twelve thousand miles away, victims who had never known
these mesas, who had never seen the delicate colors of the rocks
which boiled up their slaughter.

—Leslie Marmon Silko, *Ceremony*

MY PREOCCUPATION with seasonality and place as types of experience has kept me from reckoning with the diverse array of paradigms of
natural order in terms of which phenomena like place and seasonality
have historically been conceived. In western culture, the order of nature
has been variously imagined as, for example, an economy (from the Greek
oikos, household), a chain or scale of being, a balance, a web, an organism,
a mind, a flux, a machine.

Master Metaphors

The pervasiveness of these phenomena warrant our thinking of them as "master metaphors," of centuries-long, sometimes millennia-long persistence.[1] We cannot begin to talk or even think about the nature of nature without resorting to them, whether or not we believe they are true; and our choice of metaphors can have major consequences. That Darwin favored the trope of natural *selection*, for example, made his account of evolution more palatable to mid-Victorian readers, although Darwin himself did not mean to ascribe purposefulness to nature.[2] It would be worthwhile to reread *Walden* in light of the fact that Thoreau aggressively introduces, but then largely abandons "economy" metaphor;[3] or to reread George Perkins Marsh's nearly contemporary *Man and Nature* (1864) in light of Marsh's inability to choose among the images of home, stewardship, cooperation, and struggle when trying to state the proper relation between his two master terms.

My emphasis on the universality of seasonalism and place-sense has also led me to understate nature's own instability over time, in particular its susceptibility to human modification. Because seasonal succession, for example, has not (yet) been so affected more than marginally, to take it as a central point of reference is to risk perpetuating an old-fashioned picture of nature as a homeostasis that humanity can ignore but not change. Likewise, even though we may recognize great differences in place-sense according to whether we live as indigenes or as settlers, and even though those differences obviously point to a pattern of human destabilization of the environment that modernization has intensified, the persistence of *some* sort of place-sense as an inevitable aspect of human experience can convey a lulling impression of physical environment as eternal constant and the natural order as balance. But if we switch the paradigmatic image of natural order to one that dramatizes its constructedness and historicity more openly—"mind" for instance—then the creations of the topophiliac imagination and the penchant for subjectifying play in the treatment of seasonal representation begin to look quite different, no longer so auspiciously ecocentric and maybe even ominous—symptoms, perhaps, of an incipient desire to reshape the environment that in unrestrained hands might have more disruptive results.

A pretty fair sense of how the natural order has been conceived by western culture during the past two centuries can be obtained by juxta-posing the images of the web and the machine. As Donald Worster shows in his intellectual history of ecological thought, these and cognate images have competed with one another since the late Renaissance (the Newto-nian mechanization of the world picture versus the vitalism of the Cam-bridge Platonists) and up to the present (the "ecosystem" of normative ecological science after Arthur Tansley versus the "biotic community" of environmental ethics after Aldo Leopold).[4] This is not quite the straight-forward Manichaean antithesis it might seem. Both terms stress func-tional unity at the expense of temporal evolution;[5] and their connotations were once more similar than they now are. Before the Industrial Revolu-tion gave "machine" its negative connotation and as long as "web" also meant snare, they seemed not as morally polarized as they do to us but rather like variant ways of imagining artisanship and design. The *Oxford English Dictionary* gives "fabric" as the oldest denotation of web in English. Still, the differences between flexible web and rigid machine, between an art shared with spiders and an art exclusive to humanity, were evident from the start.

For that reason, the more organic metaphor has always been preferred by those wishing to stress the subtle, delicate intricacy of the world's body over its efficient operation.[6] Thus John Bruckner, in his *Philosophical Survey of the Animal Creation* (1768), imagined the vital energy coursing through nature as "a web of curious contexture, wrought with soft, weak, fragile, delicate materials, forming all together a piece admirable in its construction and destination, and for this very reason subject to ten thousand accidents."[7] And in the next century Darwin, while preferring the image of the (genealogical) tree as the epitome of the history of speciation, when it came to characterizing the affinities among "plants and animals, remote in the scale of nature" imagined them as being "bound together by a web of complex relations."[8] Thus a century after that Rachel Carson, drawing on Darwin's study of earthworms, wrote of the "soil community" as consisting "of a web of interwoven lives, each in some way related to the others."[9] And a few years after that Wendell Berry wrote of the apparent distinctions between body and soul, body and other bodies, body and world that "these things that appear to be distinct are nevertheless caught in a network of mutual dependence and influence that is the substantialization of their unity."[10] These affirmations, however, do not stand cleanly in opposition to the ostensibly contrasting overtones of machine metaphors; they can also be seen as benign expressions of the idea of a constructed universe that in another mood might be looked at as ominously deterministic. Plants and animals are, after all, *bound* together; bodies and world are *caught* in a network of dependence. Carson makes this complementarity very clear when she turns to the impact of pollution "the web of life—or death—that scientists know as ecology." [11] It is not just the omnipresence of DDT traces throughout the world's life-forms that allows Carson, in an instant, to transform life into death but also the suppleness of the metaphor itself. Her way of decrying the unintended consequences of the chemical industry's intervention into natural systems unintentionally makes a point about the unintended consequences of metaphor.

The same could be said about other master metaphors used to characterize nature's structure and process. Malleable to start with, they are made more so by the vicissitudes of cultural history. The great chain of being once provided a stable hierarchy, but it proved plastic enough to become thought of as a temporal succession and thus prepare the way for evolutionist thinking in the nineteenth century. [12] The obsolete metaphor of nature as "economy" has been revived in the twentieth century both by ecological science, which has used the vocabulary of production and consumption to transform "nature into a reflection of the modern corporate, industrial system" as Worster puts it, and by environmentalists stressing the ancient understanding of economy as the manifestation of divine order in the form of local stewardship precisely in order to assail the industrial economy. [13] The former camp alters the meaning of the original metaphor by defining a different economy from what the ancients had in mind; the latter alters it by reintroducing an economy radically opposed to the status quo. A particularly striking case of slippage in a master metaphor of natural ordering is the trope of natural selection. Darwin came to regret that he had not used "natural preservation" instead, to avoid creating the impression of teleology rather than simply a rule of procedure. He had in fact derived the term from the field of stock breeding, where it was used to denote forces outside the sphere of human control. [14] Yet on another level, by introducing the subject of artificial breeding, Darwin made it impossible not to think of evolution as rationally engineered. Indeed, he relied more heavily on the history of breeding experiments than on any other source for demonstrating that species over the course of time can transmute by small alterations. Though Darwin wrote with the sense of a quantum gap between the powers of artificial and natural selection, in the light of modern history it is easy to conceive of genetic engineering as having been anticipated by his vision of species as malleable and improvable, even if he did not yet imagine the degree of control that humans could exert over the process. The metaphor of selection, then, carries a different force in our time than in his. In Darwin's century, it could suggest either (to the pious) a comforting providentialism operating through historical change or (to the secularized) the survival of the fittest. Now that the technology of recombinant DNA has put humanity more firmly in the creator's position, it seems especially to suggest the discipline of artificial speciation.[15]

The way I have just been discussing metaphors of natural order like web, machine, economy, and selection—as a welter of disparate possible rubrics each subject to creative redirection and historical change—might seem unnatural except in a cultural climate where the nature of the natural order seemed precarious and contested. That is certainly true of late twentieth-century environmental thinking, which since the invention of nuclear weaponry has been forced to confront more seriously than ever before the possibility of the imminent end of life as we know it. "None of us can be sure that at any second we will not be killed in a nuclear attack," states one best-selling apocalyptic book of the 1980s, Jonathan Schell's *The Fate of the Earth*.[16] In the 1990s nuclear holocaust looks less likely, but what about pollution? global warming? genetic mutation? "A rabbit may be a rabbit for the moment, but tomorrow," writes Bill McKibben in *The End of Nature*, "'rabbit' will have no meaning. 'Rabbit' will be a few lines of code, no more important than a set of plans for a 1940 Ford. Why not make rabbit more like dog, or like duck?"[17] These and many other contemporary works of both "nonfiction" and "fantasy" face the challenge of imagining the remote consequences of the transformation of environment that seem to follow from the unprecedented instability widely perceived to mark both the actual state of physical nature, as human power over it increases, and the understanding of what the natural order (if any) inherently is and what the human relation to it should be.

Just as the metaphor of the web of interdependence is central to the ethical force of the contemporary ecocentric critique of anthropocen-trism, so is the metaphor of apocalypse central to ecocentrism's projection of the future of a civilization that refuses to transform itself according to the doctrine of the web. Apocalypse is the single most powerful master metaphor that the contemporary environmental imagination has at its disposal. Of no other dimension of contemporary environmentalism, furthermore, can it be so unequivocally said that the role of the imagi-nation is central to the project; for the rhetoric of apocalypticism implies that the fate of the world hinges on the arousal of the imagination to a sense of crisis. It presupposes that "the most dangerous threat to our global environment may not be the strategic threats themselves but rather our perception of them, for most people do not yet accept the fact that this crisis is extremely grave."[18] Some go even further and claim that environmental concern will be activated only by actual apocalypse ("It will probably take a Great Ecological Spasm to convince people that something is wrong"); but this kind of remark is, after all, only a permu-tation of the first: in both cases, the imagination is being used to antici-pate and, if possible, forestall actual apocalypse.[19] Hence my decision to devote an entire chapter of this book to examine the pervasiveness, history, and cultural force of environmental apocalypticism. In the next section, I shall approach the subject by way of two examples: Leslie Marmon Silko's novel *Ceremony*, which I take to be one of the major works of contemporary American environmental fiction, and Rachel Carson's *Silent Spring*, the book that inaugurated "the literature of eco-logical apocalypse" and played a significant part in inspiring the radicali-zation of environmental activism since the 1960s.[20]

Imagining Ecocatastrophe: Silko and Carson

This chapter's second epigraph is the climax of Silko's novel.[21] Her GI-protagonist, Tayo, a casualty of the Bataan death march that killed his cousin and foster-brother, Rocky, has been trying to work his way toward mental health following the regime of his medicine man, who foresaw the fatefulness of this night of the autumnal equinox. Tayo has arrived at the abandoned uranium mine on tribal land, from which the ore for Hiroshima and Nagasaki had been quarried and on which his traitorous buddies are about to converge with the intent of turning him over to the authorities as a lunatic. Everything suddenly clicks. Tayo realizes how the global reach of destructive forces connects up everything in his life experience: his reservation to the Pacific Rim, by reason of the bomb, and American Indian to Japanese. What he had experienced as insanity, as the uncontrollable montaging of impressions (seeing the face of his Japanese "enemy" as the face of his Uncle Josiah, for instance), is sanity. "He was not crazy. He had only seen and heard the world as it always was: no boundaries, only transitions through all distances and time." This insight helps give Tayo the strength to resist the "witchery" that has overtaken his similarly damaged peers. He remains hidden and self-restrained despite his urge to attack the man who has been his chief tormentor, while his peers turn their violence against each other.

One of the most remarkable features of this remarkable book is its fusion of regionalism and globalism, its assertion that "the fate of all living things" hinges on a minor transaction taking place in a remote cultural niche, a smallish Pueblo tribe of marginal influence within an already marginalized race. Silko capitalizes brilliantly on the historical facts that uranium was mined on Laguna land and that the Laguna—including both Tayo and Silko herself—are an extensively hybridized people. These contingencies allow her to develop a fiction of Tayo's cure both as an intensely particularized story of a reservation lad's retribalization and as a case study of a sickness of global scope. Tayo cannot be cured until he realizes that "his sickness was only part of something larger, and his cure would be found only in something great and inclusive of everything" (125–126). This realization is forced on him not only in his capacity as a hybrid or world citizen but also as a Laguna: the realization that individual and social pathologies are coextensive. The elders traditionally think of the world as a place-centered continuum of human and nonhuman beings subsisting in the fragile "intricacies of a continuing process, and with a strength inherent in spider webs woven across paths through sand hills where early in the morning the sun becomes entangled in each filament of web" (35). In Laguna myth, poetically evoked at the start of *Ceremony,* the creator is Spiderwoman.[22]

Thus *Ceremony* becomes a work of ecological ethnopoetics. Although seemingly about people rather than about the environment as such, its vision of human affairs is governed by a sense of their reciprocity with the land. The geography is precise; Silko later affirmed that "the writing was my way of re-making that place" in compensation for her absence from it;[23] her ordering of physical terrain conforms to the ordering of Laguna sacred geography.[24] Every place signifies; every place, every creature has a story connected with it that forms a web of significance (always in process, not a constant) within which human thought assumes form and meaning.[25] To look at a particular hill or spring, to see it rightly, is to realize where it stands in relation to family history and tribal myth; to look at an insect, rightly, is to connect it with a folktale about the insect's contribution to tribal welfare. This web of associations, which Silko renders schematically through the ceremonial sand painting within which Tayo's mentor performs the first healing ritual, is the antithesis of "witchery's final ceremonial sand painting," the antiweb of "the destroyers," of which European conquest and technological transformation are the symptoms.

Ceremony's innovations with cosmic metaphor equal in importance its traditional elements. Its Laguna-style ecocentrism stays very much in the spirit of Tayo's Navajo healer, Betonie, who believes that in a world thrown out of balance ceremonies must evolve in order to remain strong. Simply by incorporating World War II into a mythical narrative, making it part of Laguna ceremonial grammar by absorbing it into a plot of purification, Silko updates the practice of incorporating stories of European (and Mexican) contact into "traditional" storytelling, which was obviously well in place before the first anthropologists took notes on Laguna culture.[26] Nor does Silko refrain from tinkering with what would seem to be purely autochthonous motifs. Take the opening invocation:

> Ts'its'tsi'nako, Thought-Woman,
>   is sitting in her room
> and whatever she thinks about
>   appears.

Relative to "the dynamic, all-comprehensive nature of Thought Woman" in Laguna myth, this image domesticates her, limits her ability to transgress gender, makes her more the magnified image of the writer.[27] The world-web metaphor is another revisionary touch. It makes perfect sense as a consolidation of the image of a Spiderwoman-creator "who weaves us together in a fabric of interconnection," in Paula Gunn Allen's words;[28] but judging from the anthropological record it is not inevitable for metaphors of weaving and web to be ascribed to Spiderwoman or Thought-Woman, logical though that extension might seem. The revisions produce a somewhat ecofeminized image of the Laguna cosmos that purifies it of certain patriarchal encrustrations introduced by Christianity and in other respects modernizes it to accord even more strikingly with feminist and environmentalist presuppositions.[29]

But I want to turn more directly to how Silko's revisionary storytelling leads her to construct a kind of ecological apocalypse. A bit like the protean speaker in *The Waste Land,* one of the first canonical works of modern Anglo-American literature to envision a dying society in the aftermath of world war, Tayo is an initially impotent and inchoate figure who epitomizes and perpetuates the sickness of his culture in a time of aftermath, when the old order of pastoral agrarianism, knit together by the common understandings of ritual and story, has been broken. He has returned home to a drought for which he feels personally accountable. The curse on him, on the land, and on the tribe (whose other young men are also war-damaged) is linked. Only his transformation, as symbolic representative of his generation, by a year-long ceremonial process that simultaneously reintegrates him psychically and retribalizes him can instigate the redemption of the people and the land.[30] Significantly, he recovers his sexuality when reinitiated by the mysterious Ts'eh Montaño (literally "water mountain"), at one level a personification of the land, who offers him reintegration with it. Ts'eh is an avatar of Spider/Thought-Woman and also of the equally mysterious Mexican woman who first initiated him into sex during a symbolic rainstorm that Tayo had "caused" by an ad hoc prayer ceremony—the first sign in the book that Tayo has the capacity to become a shamanistic hero.[31] (Silko's improvisational multiplication of Spiderwoman's avatars, two of whom are ethnic outsiders, is one of the book's prime examples of her redirection of traditional materials in the interest of a hybridized vision.)[32]

Silko is certainly cosmopolitan enough to have been aware of both *The Waste Land* and its scholarly precursor, Jessie Weston's *From Ritual to Romance.*[33] But whatever the facts of that matter, she also had ready to hand, in the repertoire of Laguna stories, many of the motifs for her rebirth-of-the-hero narrative. One such story is that of Sun Youth, who with the aid of Old Woman Spiderwoman recovers from Kaup'ata' the Gambler the clouds that he stole from the people, causing a three-year drought during which "the earth and the whole ground cracked."[34] Silko interpolates this story into *Ceremony* at a crucial moment (170–176), when Tayo appears to have recidivized by falling back under the influence of his drunken buddies after his encounter with Betonie. Thereby she both counterpoints Tayo's failure with the mythic hero's success, underscoring in the process the present disjunction between sacred and profane worlds, and foreshadows what Tayo will eventually become.

As in the story of Sun Youth, the fate of the earth is made to hang on Tayo's fate. Silko justifies the portentousness of this burden by investing his saga with mythic, prototypical elements, and by presenting her vision of the inextricable tie between individual and community. *Ceremony*'s culminating section oscillates wildly between world as web and world as machine. As Tayo staggers irresolutely toward the mine, he moves through a no-man's-land of barbed wire, another antiweb, the sandstone and dirt extracted by the laborers "piled in mounds, in long rows, like fresh graves" (245). As a sudden sense of convergence hits him, he becomes aware of "the delicate colors of the rocks" and utterly antithetical master images collide:

> He knelt and found an ore rock. The gray stone was streaked with powdery yellow uranium, bright and alive as pollen; veins of sooty black formed lines with the yellow, making mountain ranges and rivers across the stone. But they had taken these beautiful rocks from deep within earth and they had laid them in a monstrous design, realizing destruction on a scale only *they* could have dreamed.   (246)

In rapid succession, Tayo sees the world as pristine ecodesign and as "monstrous design." A few pages later, the victory of the former gets written in the pattern of the sunrise that ushers him home, the sun "pushing against the gray horizon hills, sending yellow light across the clouds, and the yellow river sand . . . speckled with the broken shadows of tamaric and river willow" (255). The hill/river, yellow/gray, schematic/kinetic interweave make this epiphany a macrocosmic sequel to the microcosmic rock—a glorious melodrama of human and cultural redemption as a state of ecological grace.[35]

By building on traditional Laguna storytelling Silko thus brings world crisis to an almost utopian closure, at least at the local level. Tayo assumes a place of honor within his family, his domineering aunt no longer disdaining him as her younger sister's half-breed bastard, who ought to have been the one killed in the war instead of her more promising son, Rocky. The place is the one left vacant by Josiah, his uncle and father figure, his first teacher of ceremonial wisdom and of the cattle herding that Tayo will presumably take full charge of. His sick companions either die or flee; the elders are satisfied that Tayo is healed and that "we will be blessed again" (257). After such a narrow escape ("It had been a close call. The witchery had almost ended the story according to its plan" [253]), the outcome is almost too idyllic. Perhaps Silko herself realized this, for her second full-scale fictional recreation of the southwestern borderlands, *Almanac of the Dead* (1991), is a massive chronicle of social perversions that spares nobody. The continent's modern dispensation began, the text suggests, with an occult collaboration between Montezuma and Cortes, "members of the same secret clan"; "Montezuma and his allies had been sorcerers who had called or even invented the European invaders with their sorcery." Cross-cultural cartels of corrupt entrepreneurs who deal in drugs, arms, and erotica largely control economies and politics. The counterforce, such as it is, resides in a fragmentary native "almanac" that might contain within it "a power that would bring all the tribal people of the Americas together to retake the land," but its inheritors are incapacitated.[36] In an echo of *Ceremony*, *Almanac* ends with one character's return to the Laguna community from which he had been exiled, but he is only one of dozens of figures on Silko's movable stage, and his homecoming is an antiromantic affair compared to Tayo's triumphant return from his ordeal at the uranium mine. On the whole, *Almanac* reads like *Ceremony*'s counterpoint: a dystopian anatomy of the profane, as if *Ceremony* had been redone so as to make the bars of Gallup or the psychiatric ward of the Los Angeles veterans' hospital the center of the novel. The contrast again shows the ease with which utopian thinking can become its opposite. The same is true of Rachel Carson's work.

Carson's first ambition was to be a creative writer; in college she became a biologist; after receiving her master's degree she combined both, working as a science writer until the success of *The Sea around Us* (1950) allowed her to write full-time.[37] "Intensely fond of anything pertaining to outdoors and athletics,"[38] the young Carson was drawn to the sea, which later became the subject of her first three books, long before she first saw it. The idea of the sea attracted Carson, as the idea of wilderness had attracted Thoreau, as a mysterious domain beyond human control.

"What human mind can visualize conditions in the uttermost depths of the ocean?" she asked rhetorically in her first published article.[39] "Man," she observed with relish in *The Sea around Us*, "has returned to his mother sea only on her own terms. He cannot control or change the ocean, as in his brief tenancy of earth, he has subdued and plundered the continents."[40] Written in this spirit, her first three books are all evocatively descriptive prose poems that approach their subjects as an intricate green world of beautiful integrity.

"But I was wrong," she came to think. "Even these things that seemed to belong to the eternal verities are not only threatened but have already felt the destroying hand of man," she lamented in a commencement speech at Scripps College given late in life, in the year of the publication of her fourth and most famous book, *Silent Spring* (1962).[41] It is Carson's least "literary" book, being a relentlessly documented exposé of the consequences of indiscriminate use of pesticides, rather than a work of descriptive art. But the creative imagination is central to its effect. Carson began her previous book, *The Edge of the Sea*, with a charming vignette of a seaside grotto, a little enchanted world of its own, accessible only at the lowest of low tides. *Silent Spring* starts with a chilling "Fable for Tomorrow" of an American town in which the animals and vegetation are dead and the people are dying. Antithetical microcosms, yet closely linked—as in Silko. The rage that underlies the second arises from the shock of awakening from the first, awakening to the realization that not only is there no sanctuary but all is infected. For pesticides "have entered and lodged in the bodies of fish, birds, reptiles, and domestic and wild animals so universally that scientists carrying on animal experiments find it almost impossible to locate subjects free from such contamination. They have been found in fish in remote mountain lakes, in earthworms burrowing in soil, in the eggs of birds . . . They occur in the mother's milk, and probably in the tissues of the unborn child."[42] Such evidence drives Carson to conclude that the web of life has become a web of death: "It is not possible to add water anywhere without threatening the purity of water everywhere" (42). This being the case, all nature threatens to turn monstrous:

> The world of systemic insecticides is a weird world, surpassing the imaginings of the brothers Grimm . . . It is a world where the enchanted forest of the fairy tales has become the poisonous forest

in which an insect that chews a leaf or sucks the sap of a plant is doomed. It is a world where a flea bites a dog, and dies because the dog's blood has been made poisonous, where an insect may die from vapors emanating from a plant it has never touched, where a bee may carry poisonous nectar back to its hive and presently produce poisonous honey.   (32–33)

Without trivializing the catastrophic disruptions of physical health portrayed by Carson and the disruptions of social and psychic health portrayed by Silko, we can better understand the horror of such passages as Silko's on "the destroyers" and Carson's on the poisonous forest by imagining them in the terms that anthropologist Mary Douglas imagines the perception of defilement: as anomalies that violate a culture's deeply embedded ordering categories.[43] In Carson's case, a polluted universe seemed *so* perverse partly because the idea of nature as an integral realm, long sanctioned as we have seen by the American pastoral tradition, seemed so profoundly right. That Carson knew herself to be suffering from terminal cancer during the latter stages of working on *Silent Spring* must have intensified her rage at the suffering inflicted on others' bodies, and on earth's body.

This analysis still does not do justice to Carson's sophistication. Carson was not a naïf awakening belatedly at mid-life to the problem of environmental degradation. Five years before *The Sea around Us*, a decade before she even thought of *Silent Spring*, she had proposed (unsuccessfully) an article on pesticides to *Reader's Digest*. A subtle but firm critique of homocentrism, more particularly a critique of "man," runs throughout all her work. Woman is rarely, if ever, nature's adversary in Carson's work, but "man" often is. Carson adeptly exploits the protective coloring of the generic pronoun—a satirical obliquity no longer open to enlightened discourse. Carson's favorite nature book was Henry Williamson's *Tarka the Otter*, a poignant tale of an animal beset by hunter's dogs. *Under the Sea-Wind* includes a bitter description of fish strangling in a gill net. *The Sea around Us* mordantly reflects on man's mistreatment of the edenic places of the earth and how "he has seldom set foot on an island that he has not brought about disastrous changes."[44] Nevertheless, until *Silent Spring* Carson, like her near-contemporary Aldo Leopold, deferred more often than she preferred to middlebrow nature book decorums. When her future editor for *Silent Spring* approached Carson with the idea of doing a book aimed at preserving the rapidly vanishing unspoiled shoreline, at a time when she was crafting a nature essay for a popular magazine, she warmed to the notion "as giving me a chance to *do* something and a place to say what I want to say, for certainly I can give only a small part of the *Holiday* piece to being a Cassandra."[45] This comment by no means implies a disdain for the feeling of reverence for nature that underlay the decorums at which Carson chafed—far from it. It was precisely because she felt that sentiment so keenly that Carson criticized the doublethink bound up with those conventions: the assumption of nature's actual inviolateness, the assumption that we are not responsible for that violation, the assumption that reverence for nature is a feeling to be indulged chiefly when engaged in vacation reading of books like *The Sea around Us.*

In the mythical landscape of *Silent Spring* World War II plays almost as important a part as it does in *Ceremony.*[46] Carson identifies the pesticide industry as "a child of the Second World War" (16). Certain insecticides, she notes, were developed out of the German nerve gas program (28). She points to a worldwide rise in "malignant diseases of the blood-forming tissues"(227) starting with the leukemia contracted by Hiroshima survivors. One of the worst cases she reports of poisoning by chemicals spread through groundwater systems emanated from the Rocky Mountain Arsenal of the Army Chemical Corps, which manufactured war materials in the 1940s, then sold out to a private oil company (42–44). Such cause-and-effect links between war and pollution lead Carson to draw a moral analogy between the two. ("We are rightly appalled by the genetic effects of radiation; how, then, can we be indifferent to the same effects in chemicals that we disseminate widely in our environment?" [37].) Carson's prose bristles with imagery borrowed from military holocaust reportage: weaponry, killing, victimage, extermination, corpses, massacre, conquest. "Under the philosophy that now seems to guide our destinies," she declares sardonically, "nothing must get in the way of the man with the spray gun" (86). Like Silko, Carson thus draws on the apocalyptic frame of reference that high-tech militarism and years of Cold War consciousness have implanted in her readers' minds,[47] but Carson uses this framework to focus exclusively on an environmentalist argument.

Despite the obvious difference in genre from *Ceremony* (no hero, no cast of characters, no narrative plot), *Silent Spring*'s disenchantment with the pesticide industry's witchery has a novelistic momentum to it, building from considerations of earth, water, and plants (Chapters 4–6) to wildlife (7–11) to people (11–14), culminating in the chapter on cancer. Then comes a counterthrust (two chapters on the resistance pests develop to pesticides), followed by a chapter of possible solutions. Like Silko, Carson takes us to the edge of catastrophe and then offers "The Other Road"—without, however, offering much hope that it will be taken. It is again partially a measure of the difference in genres that Silko, who comes close to embracing neoprimitivism and rejecting modernized society altogether, can emerge as the greater optimist, whereas Carson, who countenances after all a pretty strong degree of managerial control over nature, as long as it is the right kind of control,[48] is driven nearly to despair. Silko's comparative lococentrism may be another reason for her relative optimism. Renewal at the level of the subculture seems a much likelier possibility for her than it is for Carson. Although Silko gives full play to Betonie's philosophy that contemporary healing practices must reckon with the history of the world beyond the reservation, it seems that for purposes of the novelistic denouement once the purification is effected for Tayo the Laguna borders can be secured and witchery declared "dead for now" (261). *Silent Spring* recognizes no such borders; it is localized in no place; the problem is ubiquitous. The difference is not just in the nature of the problem, for Silko's witchery and Carson's are felt to have a common root in runaway military-industrial proliferation. The difference lies more fundamentally between two modes of environmental imagination: a bioregionalist commitment, which looks to "the solution," if any there be, at the level of community; and a globalist commitment, which focuses on pervasive environmental systems or attitudes rather than regional variants.

At a certain level of abstraction, these modes are yin and yang. Global culture theory bears this dichotomy out. Ulf Hannerz schematizes global culture into a concourse of "locals" identified with territories and transnational "cosmopolitans" who subsist in relation to "a plurality of cultures understood as distinctive entities."[49] As the work of James Clifford and other students of third world–first world imbrication makes clear, such a distinction is too crude to apply to real persons like the biographical Silko and the biographical Carson.[50] But it applies better to roles; and certainly the voice Carson assumes for *Silent Spring* is that of the "cosmopolitan," relative to her more place-identified *The Edge of the Sea,* whereas Silko's voice in *Ceremony* (not to mention her next book, *Storyteller*) is much more that of the spokesperson for local knowledge relative not only to *Silent Spring* but also to her own later achievement, *Almanac of the Dead*. Perhaps the "cosmopolitan" perspective more or less automatically predisposes one to greater pessimism. Bill McKibben suggests so in a gloomy comment on how much more inherently unmanageable the 1990s problem of global warming is than the pesticide problem Carson attacked: "Carbon dioxide and the other greenhouse gases come from *everywhere,* so they can be fixed only by fixing everything."[51] His statement eerily echoes Tayo's awestruck realization that "his sickness was only part of something larger, and his cure would be found only in something great and inclusive of everything" (125–126). Yet the psychic health of an individual in a relatively self-contained subculture, and the health of that subculture as a whole, can be altered more easily than the rate of global CO_2 emissions or the trace levels of noxious elements in the bodies of wildlife all over the world.

Ironically, Carson's presentation of the insoluble led to some solutions. Though commentators disagree on how radical and how long-lasting an impact *Silent Spring* had on the production and use of environment-degrading chemicals, the book manifestly precipitated both immediate legislative action and organized environmentalist radicalism, with its accompanying "rhetoric of scientific activism," as Jimmie Killingsworth and Jacqueline Palmer term it.[52] Others had portrayed doomsday by bomb and holocaust; Carson invented doomsday by environmental genocide. In the process, despite anticipating failure, Carson succeeded in making herself heard in the public arena to as great an extent as any creative writer can expect to be.

That posture of anticipation cannot of course be taken at face value. As Jonathan Schell suggests, "maybe only by descending into this hell in imagination now" can we "hope to escape descending into it in reality at some later time."[53] We create images of doom to avert doom: that is the strategy of the jeremiad, and partly on that account Sacvan Bercovitch diagnoses the traditional American jeremiad as having an optimistic, even self-congratulatory aspect to it. (It brings us together in the consciousness that we *are* after all the chosen people.)[54] Whether the same logic applies to the rhetoric of environmental apocalypse, however, is less clear. For one thing, we can no longer count on the traditional motif of apocalypse threatening an elite community that has enjoyed God's special favor and may enjoy it again if it forswears its evil ways. The motif began to vanish in the nineteenth century. In *Ceremony* it is still potent, but in *Silent Spring* it is nearly extinct. For Carson, the salvific potential of industrialized society resides in nothing better than its scientific know-how, which can generate good products to replace the bad. But to understand better this and related matters, we must delve further into the history of American apocalypticism.

The Roots of American Apocalypticism

Apocalypticism is an old American tradition. A look at American literary history confirms its persistence through three centuries of American writing. As is well known, the best-selling work of seventeenth-century New England belles lettres was Puritan poet Michael Wigglesworth's *The Day of Doom*. The most polished American neoclassical poem remains Timothy Dwight's "The Triumph of Infidelity." Among nineteenth century fiction, the vision of the world or microcosm thereof coming to a cataclysmic end governs Cooper's *Crater,* Poe's *Eureka,* Melville's *Moby-Dick,* Twain's *Connecticut Yankee,* and Donnelly's *Caesar's Column,* to name but a few examples. Borderline cases like Stowe's *Uncle Tom's Cabin* swell the list immensely. In early modern America the roster continues with London's *Iron Heel,* Faulkner's *Absalom, Absalom,* and West's *Day of the Locust.* The links among such works have been studied at length.[55] For our purposes, a few major points will suffice.

To begin with, two largely unrelated developments during the seventeenth century permanently affected apocalyptic thinking in America. One was the impact of the Copernican and Newtonian revolutions on Christian cosmology, threatening the belief that the world must end in a divinely ordained catastrophe. Scientific developments precipitated in the short run a panicky series of revisionary sacred histories and forced in the long run a separation of thinking about "the moral judgment . . . from the physical."[56] The other, specific to Puritan America, was the late seventeenth-century apotheosis of the first generation as what Theodore Dwight Bozeman calls a primordium, an image of the state of primitive

Christianity Puritanism had for more than a century sought to recover.[57] The first development began to convert eschatological thinking from a game of deductive logic into a form of speculative free play; the second set the key precedent for visualizing the American state in millennial terms and for regulating the imagery of ultimate hope or destruction, as the case may be, as a function of the relationship between the state of contemporary secular society and an idealized historical antecedent. In the eighteenth and nineteenth centuries, the sense of the United States as a unique, unprecedented sociopolitical experiment conduced to opposite mood swings of national fantasy (millennial promise, despair at imminent ruin) that ensured the diffusion and persistence of eschatological thinking, both secular and religious, long after Puritanism itself attenuated. As Ernest Tuveson notes in one of the best studies of premodern American millennialism, this period saw the crystallization of the oft-remarked American tendency "to expect each crisis to be final, to think each must be solved by a permanently decisive conflict."[58] American Protestants' response to approaching Civil War is a good case in point. Although the majority had by this time abandoned premillennialism (the doctrine that world destruction will precede the establishment of God's kingdom on earth), it nonetheless seemed that the denouement of "the plot of the world's great drama" was imminent. Harriet Beecher Stowe, in *Uncle Tom's Cabin,* warned of a day of wrath if something was not done about slavery. Julia Ward Howe's "Battle Hymn of the Republic" envisioned the Lord trampling out the vintage where the grapes of wrath were stored. Northern "Protestants were convinced that failure to uphold the Union would set in motion centrifugal tendencies that would not halt until the nation and its cherished freedom were in ruins."[59] The image of the nation in ruins was fed by nontheological sources as well, particularly romantic classicism, which during the antebellum period had inspired what one scholar has called "the American school of catastrophe" in literature and art.[60] Thomas Cole's epic sequence of five paintings, *The Course of Empire,* remains the most lasting monument of this romanticism.

Nor did apocalypticism cease to flourish in the United States after the Civil War. American catastrophism has repeatedly renewed itself under pressure of public events (at the turn of the century, Ignatius Donnelly's *Caesar's Column;* after World War I, Eliot's *Waste Land*); and it has also

thrived in a more continuous, ongoing way as a theological passion—
from the eighteenth century down to this day—within American sectar-
ian thought. It has reappeared again and again as a form of secular
imaging, applied to racial and class struggles, to the modernist revolution
in technology and the arts, to economic depression, to world wars.
Although Perry Miller professed bemusement at the resurgence of apocalypticism in 1945, nothing was more logical than its return for such an
occasion. The most comprehensive history of popular American premillennialism finds that the crises of the twentieth century have strengthened, not diminished, its appeal both as a theological force and as a
"secular apocalyptic."[61]

The historicization of the eschatological trivializes it, in a sense, in
tying it to this or that secular matrix or event. The grandeur of the divine
design is diminished when the great work of redemption is made to hinge
on this or that puny time-bound experiment. Conversely, however, "the
crude product of nature, the object fashioned by the industry of man,
acquire their reality, their identity, only to the extent of their participation
in a transcendent reality. The gesture acquire[s] meaning, reality, solely
to the extent to which it repeats a primordial act."[62] So secular events
gain immensely in significance when the eschaton is felt to be immanent
in the historical process—as long as the apocalyptic frame of reference
maintains its power. The impending American Civil War looks grander
when partisans imagine the storm to come as God's day of wrath. Indeed
a temporalized conception of apocalypse allows us to declare at any
moment that on that moment the fate of the creation depends. It allows
Silko to say at the climax of *Ceremony* and us to indulge the possibility
that "this was the last night and the last place, when the darkness of night
and the light of day were balanced" (247).

Douglas Robinson, in the most searching book to date on American
literary apocalypticism, notes that the idea that nuclear weaponry "has
rendered the theological sense of apocalypse obsolete . . . is rapidly
becoming a critical commonplace."[63] Robinson does well to hold that
claim at arm's length, first, because as he goes on to show contemporary
millennarians have demonstrated a remarkable ability to fit nuclear holocaust into traditionally religiocentric paradigms; and, second, because the
obsolescence process was already two centuries old by the time the atomic
age began. The image of nuclear holocaust helped reactivate apocalyptic

thinking precisely by providing a more convincing secular frame of reference for the apocalyptic paradigm than had been available since the so-called Enlightenment started to undermine the credibility of Christian sacred history. In fact, apocalyptic thinking has evolved along a kind of path leading to nuclear-age images of world destruction according to an inner logic obscured by the supposition, plausible though it might seem, of a sharp break. First, the ancient Greco-Oriental myth of eternal return was displaced by the Judeo-Christian scheme of cosmic history moving from an origin to a close.[64] Second, cosmic history was displaced by secular history and more specifically by the history of the nation-state (for example, the myth of American exceptionalism). Third, the scientific-industrial revolution further changed the meaning of time by making social change permanent, so that generations and individuals could more readily conceive of themselves as occupying ultimate and unique positions in history. (Henry Adams's portentous contrast between his obsolete generation and the present age of the dynamo is an obvious example.) Then, fourth, the nuclear dispensation intensified this mentality by building its self-definition around the idea that *its* technology contained more history-annihilating power than any generation before it. The nuclear generation probably does differ from its forebears in its emphasis on *annihilative* apocalypticism (the "prediction of an imminent end to history controlled by no God at all and followed by the void," Robinson succinctly defines it),[65] but it is a change of emphasis and not a new conception. The concept of annihilative apocalypse itself is as old as Lucretius.

By intensifying the theme of imminent annihilation, the advent of a more plausible scenario for secular apocalypse than the world has ever seen aggravates traditional oscillations between hope and despair, vehemence and dispassion, credulity and cynicism. Nothing is more serious than nuclear holocaust, yet many have found it hard to take seriously, even at the height of the Cold War. The justification and the challenge of nuclear alarmism has been that "the world we could destroy is not destroyed."[66] The possibility of total destruction is enough to sustain a high level of vehemence; the moral absurdity of it actually happening is enough to provoke skepticism toward apocalyptic discourse. Opposite attitudes can easily coexist within the same person or text, for example Miller's brilliant post-Hiroshima *tour de force* "The End of the World."

Miller obviously considers his subject both of great historical and moral importance as a theme and absurd as a literal script for history. His essay (archly positioned at the end of his volume) parodies the jeremiad, arguing that eschatological discourse has unraveled since Puritanism. Miller maintains as great an aesthetic distance from Puritan quaintness as he does from nuclear-age secularism. If the urbanity of tone is merely a concession to a scholarly audience that does not share his quasi-Calvinist commitments, Miller makes no sign.

Scholarship now ranks Miller among the great American literary artists, and with reason. The metanarrative irony with which he retails the history of apocalypse theology is identified by Robinson as one of the hallmarks of American literary apocalypticism itself: "apocalyptic confrontations in American literature tend almost invariably toward self-conscious explorations of the validity of literary creation. It is the American attempt to have things both ways: to tell compelling stories that compel by offering powerful metaphors for the interpretation of reality, and at the same time to remain cognizant of the necessary failure of those metaphors to *accomplish* an interpretation."[67] Robinson's immediate reference is to John Barth, but he is prepared to make the same argument about Poe, Faulkner, and Nathanael West. Clearly, both Miller and (especially) Robinson show presentist bias in treating apocalypse as metafiction (Robinson) or ratiocinative fantasy (Miller); but in doing so they speak for many creative writers. In the era of *Cat's Cradle, Doctor Strangelove,* and *Star Wars* it is hard for apocalypticism to keep a straight face.

Was it then a mistake to select as our central examples texts like Silko's *Ceremony* and Carson's *Silent Spring,* neither written in the postmodern manner, both works of high seriousness lacking in the self-reflexivity about the possible fantasticalness of one's discourse that we would expect of Barth, Kurt Vonnegut, Thomas Pynchon, Ralph Ellison, or Margaret Atwood? By this criterion, Edward Abbey would have been a better choice: Abbey, who imagines a final confrontation in the West between the forces of machine culture and old-style cowboys or new-style environmental activists, but with a raffish panache that unsolemnizes his jeremiads.[68] The high seriousness of texts like Silko's and Carson's, however, brings out more strikingly the pastoral logic that undergirds environmental apocalypse, which rests on the appeal to the moral superiority of an antecedent state of existence when humankind was not at war with nature in the way that prevails now. Silko grounds that appeal in the liberal traditionalism of Tayo's maternal Uncle Josiah (the matriarchal society of Laguna's equivalent of the father figure)—liberal, because Josiah, like Betonie, is a nonfundamentalist believer in the efficacy of tribal wisdom and ceremonies. Carson grounds her appeal in a vision of the mythical American small community, the desecration of whose integral leafy exurban bliss is portrayed in her introductory "Fable of Tomorrow."

These are both prime examples of the doubleness of American pastoral ideology discussed in Chapter 2: activist appeals to nostalgia, accomplishing their interventions by invocations of actual green worlds about to be lost. It should not be assumed that either Carson or Silko believe that their portrayals of those about-to-be-lost worlds say all there is to be said about them; they only intended to create moral antitheses that would force readers to confront the possibility that history has reached a turning point where the extinction of a land-centered culture *(Ceremony)* or even nature itself *(Silent Spring)* is imminent.

American Environmental Apocalypticism

For the first two centuries of settlement, American environmental thought remained millennial rather than apocalyptic, driven by the vision of wilderness as an inexhaustible resource waiting to be transformed into productive farms, towns, and cities, in the spirit of the biblical promise that the desert shall blossom as the rose. Only by gradual degrees, during the nineteenth century, did the sense of environmental endangerment gather force and begin to challenge this gospel of plenty; indeed, only during the past two or three decades, and scarcely even then, have larger numbers of Americans declared themselves willing to curtail their taste for abundance to alleviate pressure on the environment. The story of this slow, partial, and still only incipient change in public attitudes has been told by others.[69] I shall concentrate on the discourse rather than the social history of environmental apocalypticism.

It emerged in the mid-nineteenth century, in George Perkins Marsh's *Man and Nature; or, Physical Geography as Modified by Human Action* (1864), the first full-scale diagnosis of impending environmental disaster to be published in the English-speaking world. Marsh surveyed the entire geographical history of the northern hemisphere, with special reference to the American situation. He wrote with the cosmopolitan scope of one widely traveled and conversant with a score of different languages, ancient and modern, but also with a particular urgency lest growth-addicted America ignore the negative lessons of past disregard for nature's limits and the positive lessons of European conservationist thought. Though not immediately influential, Marsh's warnings had a long-range impact on both conservationists and preservationists, beginning with John Muir and Gifford Pinchot.[70] For the purpose of grasping the nature of eco-catastrophical metaphor, however, to dwell on the landmark status of *Man and Nature* or, for that matter, *Silent Spring* is less important than to examine the structures of environmental perception that shape these and other such works. Five ingredients I now want to stress especially.

The first and most obvious of these is the dramatization of networked relationships: environmental reality seen and mapped in terms of the metaphor of the web and its cognates. What most horrifies Carson about pesticides is their diffusion through the food chain, the water cycle, the circulation of the atmosphere. These arenas of biological interdependence can of course be talked about in wholly clinical ways devoid of political or affective content. Such is the discourse of scientific ecology. But the totalization of phenomena in terms of concepts like biotic community and ecosystem is readily adaptable to apocalyptic ends by concerned individuals like Carson who understand the discourse and its more ominous findings. Undoubtedly for many specialists thinking about issues of "ecological interdependence" the concept is so attached to professional routine, to formal laboratory procedures, that there is nothing insurgent, let alone apocalyptic, about it at all. Yet as the first epigraph to this chapter suggests, even hardheaded professionals, when they tease out the implications of their own categories of analysis, may begin to see them in strangely decentered ways.

The passage occurs in an article Leopold wrote in 1932 as a reply to a preservationist critique of his proposal for regulating hunting as a way of managing game populations. He actually intended the passage as a *reductio ad absurdum* of purist thinking, his point being that it is not worth worrying over whether, for instance, birding in a Ford would deplete an oil field. Yet Leopold plainly feels queasy about having done his research in the employ of the Sporting Arms and Ammunitions Manufacturers' Institute. He goes on to characterize himself as trying "surreptitiously" to set up "within the economic Juggernaut certain new cogs and wheels whereby the residual love of nature, inherent even in Rotarians, may be made to recreate at least a fraction of those values which their love of 'progress' is destroying."[71] Here we see Leopold wriggling on the hook of his own ecological conscience, sensitized not only by his critic but also by anxieties he has been feeling for some time about the juggernaut's baleful power. After landing his professorship the next year, Leopold felt more at liberty to pursue the ethical correlates of ecological knowledge that he here hesitates to press. His great project in those later years was to reinvent the study of biotic interrelationships as an ethics of conservation. The apocalyptic theme became part of his repertoire. Two years before his death, Leopold delivered a jeremiad to the Midwest Wildlife Conference in Des Moines on the problem of Wisconsin's excess deer population, caused, he thought, by the state's failure to correct it in time. What especially enraged Leopold was "the ethical degradation" of deer hunters resulting from the ecological problem of too many deer: "the average deer hunter loses his scruples in the woods" and runs amok. Leopold concluded that the problem extended nationwide, that "we have not learned from other states, nor will other states learn from us. All will end up with impoverished herds, and depleted forests."[72] What had changed for Leopold between 1932 and 1946 was not so much his view of the ethics of hunting *per se* or even the legitimacy of intervening to control ecological imbalances, as much as his fear of interventions perpetrated by the wrong people with the wrong motives. This fear rested, in turn, on his increasingly keen sense of the rift between institutional self-interests, be they economic or hedonistic, and the interests of community, by which he meant "the soil, waters, fauna, and flora, as well as people."[73]

As Leopold's definition of community suggests, interrelatedness implies also equality of members, the second key ingredient of environmental apocalyptic vision. If like Thoreau one imagines animals as neighbors; if like Muir or traditional Native Americans one imagines life-forms as plant people, sun youths, or grandmother spiders, then the killing of flies becomes as objectionable as the killing of humans. In an early section of *Ceremony,* Tayo remembers being gently reprimanded by Josiah for killing flies, because the greenbottle fly "way back in the time immemorial" interceded for the people at a point of dire need. With this biotic egalitarianism Josiah undermines the reservation schoolteacher's hygiene lesson (flies "are bad and carry sickness," Tayo recites [101]), and this new view adds to the adult Tayo's burden of guilt at remembering how, as a prisoner of war in the Philippines, he cursed and killed the flies torment-ing the wounded Rocky. That incident becomes the basis for the story Tayo, during his period of "sickness," comes to tell about himself to explain why he is responsible for the drought on the land. Silko implies both that Tayo is too hard on himself and that the ethical standard that drives him to be so is superior to the western rationalism that would see his guilt as nothing more than hallucination.

Nothing dramatizes biotic egalitarianism so poignantly as the myth of the personhood of nonhuman beings. To the extent that westerners teach themselves to reimagine earth as Gaia, people and nonhuman primates as reciprocals, and life-forms of all sorts as having *umwelten,* the extinction of a large nonhuman population begins to feel like a holocaust. That is precisely how parasitologist John Janovy, Jr., imagines the impact on a certain snail of flooding the cattail marshes of Nebraska's Keystone Lake with ice-cold water by manipulating a certain dam: as a "multiple murder" comparable to the local mass murder Truman Capote depicted in *In Cold Blood.*[74] Carson goes so far as to suggest that human life without birds and trees is not worth living. Some environmental writers, like David Rains Wallace, go even further, turning the anthropo-centric sense of holocaust against itself, as it were, and imagining that a world purged of humans by human-engineered environmental apoca-lypse would not be so apocalyptic after all because wildness in some form would be sure to endure.[75]

The intensity with which Janovy contemplates snail, termite, and protozoa could not have happened before cellular biology, but the basic shape of his contemplation goes back doctrinally to Darwin and formally to Thoreau. Two related modes of Thoreauvian perception are involved here, both Emersonian legacies: the aggrandizement of the minute and the conflation of near and remote. Thoreau's friend and biographer Ellery Channing was the first to collect a large array of examples and comment on them. "The translucent leaves of the *Andromeda calyculata,*" Channing writes, seemed "like cathedral windows; and he spoke of the cheeks and temples of the soft crags of the sphagnum. The hubs on birches . . . might be volcanoes in outline," distant lightning "like veins in the eye." "A large, fresh stone-heap, eight or ten inches above water," was "like Teneriffe. These comparisons," Channing emphasizes, "to him were realities, not sports of the pen."[76] *Walden* shows their importance. Magnification of scale and collapse of distance are two of its major motifs. The passage of the railroad cars montages into "a celestial train beside which the petty train of cars which hugs the earth is but the barb of the spear" (117); a contemporary snowstorm becomes the prototype of all New England storms, the "Great Snow" of 1717 (119); an Irish ice cutter is revealed to be the servant of the antipodal as well as the local "Brahmin," with whom Thoreau holds converse by drinking from the same source (298). One reason *Walden* makes such strenuous reading is that every moment, or so one often feels, is made to seem the ultimate moment; every object is the transfiguration of itself; nothing, however small, is small.

Unlike some of the analogies recorded by Channing, these examples from *Walden* do not reveal great environmental perspicacity. They are largely efforts of wit and reading. But *Walden* points in the direction of what became more distinctive about Thoreau's magnifications of scale and conflations of near and distant. He transformed these structures of perception, as he internalized them more and more deeply, from the mythmaking devices that they primarily are in *Walden* into the apparatus of environmental perception described by Channing: an apparatus that functioned for Thoreau, as for Janovy and Carson, both as magnifying glass and analogue.

So far I have identified four modes of perception that can subserve environmental apocalyptic ends: interrelatedness, biotic egalitarianism, magnification, conflation. Yet these would not interact to that end without an additional ingredient, the sense of imminent environmental peril. That is why Thoreau, jealous guardian of the landscape though he was, only by fits and starts filled the role of apocalyptic naturist. Though he knew the New England forests were endangered, though he knew that a number of species had disappeared from the region, though he knew agriculture and commerce could not be trusted to respect the land, though he profoundly distrusted technological fixes, he was too committed to demonstrating the proximity of a nearby nature almost as good as wilderness to make the abuse and endangerment of nature his main theme. Only when confronted by the rapidity of deforestation in Maine did Thoreau fully acknowledge how denuded his own Middlesex landscape had become since the first settlement, how distressing the whole history of environmental practice in the region had been to that date— and even then he felt impelled to counter this admission with a tribute to "the partially cultivated country" over wilderness ("the raw material of all our civilization").[77] It made sense, then, that not Thoreau but Marsh, whose early life in Vermont enabled him to witness a more vertiginous pace of environmental degradation, became the first American prophet of environmental disaster.

The most elaborate and passionately argued chapter of Marsh's *Man and Nature*, "The Woods," ends with a jeremiad on the instability of American life, which Marsh sees as basic to environmental negligence. This "restless love of change" that "makes us almost a nomad rather than a sedentary people" Marsh considers the characteristic American defect, responsible for the appalling denudation of the American landscape. "Let us restore this one element of material life [the forests] to its normal proportions," urges Marsh, "and devise means for maintaining the permanence of its relations to the fields, the meadows, and the pastures."[78] Thoreau would have agreed; indeed, he might have read this statement in a more fundamentalist way than Marsh intended, as a mandate to freeze America forever in a paleotechnic state. But Marsh reacted more sharply than Thoreau did against the ethos of environmental transformation that had dominated American thinking since John Winthrop had advised his fellow colonists to avail themselves of the Lord's garden.[79] It was Marsh, with eyewitness knowledge of the scars it had left on the landscapes of Europe and the Middle East as well as greater first-hand experience of its effects at home, who was in the better position to appreciate that it might be possible for nature to suffer irretrievable damage at the hands of humankind.[80] In the most searching study of apocalypticism as a rhetorical form, Stephen O'Leary identifies it with three "topoi": an image of actual evil, a theory of time as epochal, and a sense of irrefutable authority.[81] The documentary thoroughness, prophetic zeal, and sense of imminence with which Marsh decried human despoliation of earth's resources brought the rhetoric of environmental concern into the apocalyptic era.

That today's environmental activists more often honor Thoreau than Marsh testifies not only to Thoreau's greater literary skill but also to the greater fit between contemporary preservationism and Thoreau's vision of the relation between humankind and nature as one of reciprocal interchange, as against Marsh's more managerial approach. "The establishment of an approximately fixed ratio," Marsh concludes, "between the two most broadly characterized distinctions of rural surface—woodland and plough land—would involve a certain persistence of character in all the branches of industry . . . and would thus help us to become, more emphatically, a well-ordered and stable commonwealth, and, not less conspicuously, a people of progress."[82] Here Marsh seems to promote the techno-fix, despite his reference to "character." Thoreau is more continuously aware of culture's dependence for its health on environmental health, even though this awareness inhibits him from being as apocalyptic about the subject as he doubtless would have been if reincarnated in the late twentieth century. Later generations have had to draw this connection for him, in his name. The fact that Thoreau's early pastoralism, like Carson's a century later, both sensitized his environmentalist instincts and blunted for the nonce his environmentalist zeal suggests that the promise of pastoral aesthetics as a stimulus to ecocentrism can fulfill itself completely only when pastoral aesthetics overcomes its instinctive reluctance to face head-on the practical obstacles to the green utopia it seeks to realize. Only then can it mature as social critique.

What is especially striking, however, about the pioneer-era expansionist gospel that Marsh was the first to indict systematically from a conservationist standpoint is its structural similarity to the specter of environmental apocalypse he pitted against it. Both views promote nature in terms of its capacity for being changed with amazing swiftness into its opposite through human agency. Indeed, republican "course of empire" thinking sometimes linked the two states directly without being fully aware of it. One nineteenth century booster of American hinterlands development prophesied, for example, that "before many cycles shall have completed their rounds sentimental pilgrims from the humming cities of the Pacific coast will be seen where Boston, Philadelphia, and New York now stand, viewing in moonlight contemplation, with the melancholy owl, traces of the Athens, the Carthage, and the Babel of the Western hemisphere."[83] This author clearly *meant* to stress the magnificence of the natural resources of the West and their complete malleability to entrepreneurial control, that is, the romance of real estate. Today's prairie is tomorrow's metropolis. Just as the American government magisterially quartered the land into rectilinear sections, we can build our own world. But the author also suggests that today's efforts of civilization are tomorrow's (environmental) disasters—not his intended meaning, but an inference that Marsh would have drawn in an instant. To turn utopia into dystopia we need only deny the environment's malleability. If there are land-imposed limits to growth and resistance to human tampering, or if the environment can resist our control, then attempts to control it will produce the death or the revolt of nature.

These are the bases of late twentieth-century environmental dystopianism: (1) the vision of exploitation leading to "overshoot" (excessive demands on the land) or interference producing irreversible degradation, (2) the vision of a tampered-with nature recoiling against humankind in a kind of return of the repressed, and (3) the loss of all escape routes. Carson voices all these fears. We are poisoning ourselves irretrievably; we are producing pesticide-resistant insects our poisons cannot control; we are all infected.[84] Since the old dream of bending nature to our will (through genetic technology, for instance) also continues to run strong in late twentieth-century American culture, we may expect the oscillation between utopian and dystopian scenarios that began in the last century to continue unabated into the next as the switch flicks back and forth depending on whatever scientific breakthrough or technological foul-up dominates public attention. That is both a burden and a blessing. Already Carson's strikingly original updating of environmental apocalypticism begins to look somewhat hackneyed. But then so are stories about the rites of passage, star-crossed lovers, cross-generational misunderstandings, and the like. Nothing can seem more threadbare, if handled ineptly, than the issues most fundamentally important to us. By the same token, the rapid assimilation of environmental apocalypticism as a pervasive nightmare for western and—increasingly—world culture suggests that there is no question of its disappearing anytime soon as a plot formula. The question is whether it will rise to the occasion. As ecocatastrophe becomes an increasingly greater possibility, so will the occasions for environmental apocalyptic expression and the likelihood that it will suffuse essay, fiction, film, sculpture, painting, theater, and dance in unprecedentedly powerful, mind-haunting ways. Can our imaginations of apocalypse actually forestall it, as our fears of nuclear holocaust so far have? Even the slimmest of possibilities is enough to justify the nightmare.

*Environmental
Sainthood*

CHAPTER TEN

The Thoreauvian Pilgrimage

The consciousness of the sacred character of the locality that has
once been chosen is . . . always retained.

> —Gerardus van der Leeuw,
> *Religion in Essence and Manifestation*

We need both Waldens, the book and the place. We're not all spirit
any more than we're all clay; we are both and so we need both—as
in: You've read the book, now see the place.

> —E. L. Doctorow, Remarks at the Walden Woods Project
> press conference, Boston, 25 April 1990

I advanced upon the trail of the oak leaves. We were all the eye of
the Visitor—the eye whose reason no physics could explain.
Generation by generation the eye was among us . . . I had emerged
on the path as followed by the author of *Walden*. The eye was
everywhere, and as for Walden it too was everywhere that the eye
existed.

> —Loren Eiseley, *The Lost Notebooks*

ONLY A FEW DAYS after his death in 1862, Thoreau began (as Auden
said of Yeats) to become his admirers when Emerson delivered the address
at his funeral that still stands as the most influential portrait. Well before
his full-scale canonization two generations later as one of America's
leading writers, he was enshrined by admiring coteries: by religious
liberals and literary naturists in America and by social reformers in
Britain. Their differing versions of him suggest the range of posthumous
appropriations to which he has been subjected in our century. Like the

body of Osiris, Thoreau's spirit has been scattered and transplanted in a thousand forms through his transmutation into cultural property.

How does Thoreau's canonization shed light on the history, present state, and future potential of the environmental imagination as a literary and cultural force? That is the central question pursued in the next three chapters. I attach great importance to the phenomenon of canonization for several reasons. First, most people need role models as points of reference for constructing their lives. Thoreau has had a history of changing peoples' lives, at least by their own say-so, or of confirming changes on which they had resolved. His admirers have occasionally been known to follow his example even to the point of death.[1] Figures seen as "major" or "great" have the potential, if like Thoreau they are associated with the idea of cultural change, to further that process by virtue of their iconic status, despite the risk that canonicity also brings of co-opting the maverick into a guardian of the standing order—as defenders of the "canon" often try to do. Conversely, one cannot understand any historical actor's significance without confronting posterity's repossession of him or her.

I admit also to being drawn to study canonization because of an intra-tribal issue of interest chiefly to literary scholars yet with much broader implications as well: the issue of how closely a writer's influence and cultural significance should be seen as bound to his or her texts. Most literary specialists understandably would say, quite closely. Yet clearly some authors are as likely to be remembered, and more likely to exert widespread influence, in the form of gestalts based not only on their writings but also on actual or supposed events of their lives, the totality of which converges to yield myths of authorial stance and voice that are shaped by the cultural climates of succeeding generations. Many literary scholars would retort that personality-tinctured myths are extraneous popularizations and that legitimate scholarship ought to hold the line and focus rigorously on the textual evidence. In response one could argue that custodianship of Thoreau's or another author's reputation does not nec-essarily fall to scholars alone—and, moreover, that biographical facts and inferences affect literary scholars whether they admit it or not, and rightly so. Sexual orientation is an obvious example. It cannot help affecting most people's readings of the work at hand to think that Thoreau might have been gay, or that Emily Dickinson might have had lesbian tendencies.

The question becomes, to what sort of rereading does this possible fact point us?—not, can it be bracketed?[2]

For writers like Alexander Pope or Henry Adams, who are almost unread today outside the academy, custody rights will devolve upon academics by default. Historian of science Lynn White remarks of *The Education of Henry Adams* that such a book can be reckoned "a classic in the proper sense that, while it is read by few, it has helped to shape the notions and emotions of millions of Americans who have never even heard of it."[3] I agree that a canonical work's influence circulates beyond its readership or even its name recognition, even as those who study it minutely remain within the academy. But it would be shortsighted to think that, except when interpretation has been very tightly controlled by academicians, a book's circulation has been exclusively or even primarily regulated by the "great traditions" of scholarly midrash or the later classics it directly influenced rather than by the "little traditions" generated by, for example, autodictats, amateur enthusiasts, journalists, and other arbiters of popular culture, spottily informed and partially attentive college students governed more by extracurricular imperatives than those of their instructors, and broad-based political and ideological ferments. All these arenas must be taken into account if we are to come to terms with the cultural significances of Thoreauvian writing, and the impact of Thoreau himself is the obvious place to start.

Thoreau as Cultural Icon

To understand the impact of the green Thoreau, we must bear in mind that this aspect is only one of his legacies. His admirers have mirrored and amplified his combination of motives by transfusing it with their own. The smorgasbord of resulting Thoreaus is jauntily presented in a 1985 article in the middlebrow history magazine *American Heritage,* which profiles *Walden* as the first of "ten books that shaped the American character," owing to its breadth of appeal. "From libertarians to the civil rights marchers, the right wing to the vegetarians, almost every organized (and unorganized) American *ism* has found something to its taste in *Walden,* so wide is the net it casts."[4] A quick scan of Thoreauviana at almost any point during the last half-century bears out this claim. During one ten-year span from the mid-sixties through the mid-seventies, for instance, Thoreau was acclaimed as the first hippie by a nudist magazine, recommended as a model for disturbed teenagers, cited by the Viet Cong in broadcasts urging American GI's to desert, celebrated by environmental activists as "one of our first preservationists," and embraced by a contributor to the John Birch Society magazine as "our greatest reactionary."[5] American astronauts named a moon site after Walden; a Thoreau button was sold in San Francisco; several housing developments were named after him; the Kimberley-Clark Corporation marketed a new grade of paper as "Thoreau vellum"; a rock opera and a black comedy were written about him, as well as the highly successful play *The Night Thoreau Spent in Jail.* A Boston paper considered it news when a *Playboy* girl of the month confessed her love for Thoreau, and the journal *Medical Aspects of Human Sexuality* printed a page of quotations entitled "Thoreau on Sex." Allen Ginsberg, Martin Luther King, Jr., B. F. Skinner, and Rod McKuen all paid homage to him.[6]

Although any famous figure may be appropriated by clashing interest groups, this spread of responses is extraordinary. It reflects two related facts about Thoreau's reputation that make his case an unusually good one for raising questions about standard notions of how canonicity works. First, he has steadily gained fame as a folk hero as well as a specialist's hero, unlike his mentor Emerson (whose popular fame dwindled after 1900), unlike his friend Hawthorne (who rightly supposed his own audience to be a choice but restricted one), unlike Margaret Fuller (who despite her revival as the American Mary Wollstonecraft remains a cynosure of scholars rather than of laypersons), unlike even Walt Whitman (whom the "young mechanic" has never understood as well as Whitman liked to think). Among Thoreau's contemporaries, only Louisa May Alcott has anything like the uniform strength of appeal among both academics and nonacademics that Thoreau does. Among later creative writers currently deemed "major" by academics, only Mark Twain and Ernest Hemingway do. The Thoreau Society, which in 1991 celebrated its sesquicentennial with an exuberant two-week jubilee featuring symposia ranging from Thoreau and music to the geological history of Concord,[7] is by no coincidence the largest and most diverse of all American author societies, with more than a thousand members nationwide. One of its first annual meetings was attended not only by academics but also by a naval lieutenant, a letter carrier, two advertising men, a rabbinical student, and a "hobo philosopher." The same pattern persists to this day.[8]

Related to Thoreau's appeal across lines of occupation and class has been the diversity of basis for that appeal. He has been canonized as natural historian, pioneer ecologist and environmentalist, social activist, anarchistic political theorist, creative artist, and memorable personality combining some or all these roles. The result has been a more than ordinarily contested imaging process that presents itself to a striking extent both as a barometer of cultural history and as a means by which cultural values have been defined. Although it is Thoreau's American fame and influence that concerns me especially in this book, the subject is really global in scope, more so than for any other American renaissance writer except Whitman; for within a century after his death Thoreau has gained admirers and interpreters in Japan, Australia, India, South Africa, Russia, and eastern and western Europe, as well as in the United Kingdom and the United States.

In the next three chapters I discuss three aspects of Thoreau's fame: the most distinctive public ritual of commemoration, namely, the pilgrimage to Concord and Walden; the history of Thoreau's canonization as a "green" writer: the birth, eclipse, and rebirth of the image(s) of Thoreau as an environmental hero; and how *Walden,* his most widely read work, discloses itself as a book that gives encouragement to biographical myth building by reason of its apparent character as a personal testament—and what, finally, is to be made of that testament. My choice of these particular ways of getting at Thoreau's impact reflects, as I have indicated, somewhat unorthodox convictions as to how authors make history, such as my conviction that professional readers underestimate the importance of myths about authors' lives and personalities. Admittedly, these are popular simplifications; but instead of dismissing them on that account we need to take them seriously as pointing to how literary greatness becomes transmuted into an active ingredient in the minds of its audience. I suspect that most people would be more likely to respond at an emotional level to an unknown work if they approached it taking for granted that it was a deliberate, or at least a heartfelt, act than as if they approached it predetermined to conceive of it as a textual construct.[9] The former approach is likely to assume too much (that the author was in complete control of the medium), but the latter is likely to lead to a skeptical, often even adversarial, response to the work that fails to take into account the basis of its appeal to actual people. The classic version of this impasse, familiar to all specialists, is the case of the naively enthusiastic student and the coolly analytical professor. S comes to class burning with enthusiasm about Thoreau's eloquent testament of resistance. P deftly shows how it comprises rhetorical stratagems, none of which can be ascribed to the "real" Thoreau, only to a "persona." P does well to complicate S's vision but would also do well to recognize the simplicity of his own.

Let us start, then, by imagining Thoreau *in situ* as he and it have seemed over the years to devoted Thoreauvians. Concord, Massachusetts, is America's most sacred literary place. Hundreds of thousands of tourists visit it annually: some to see the Revolutionary battle monument, some to see the haunts of the Concord authors, most to see both. Of all the shrines associated with Concord's literary figures, Walden Pond gets the most visitors, partly because it is a recreation area. Many of the bathers and hikers think about Thoreau little or not at all. But Walden has also attracted thousands of more serious Thoreauvians. This chapter is especially about them. Looking at what they wrote about their experiences over more than a century of recorded visits, and also more briefly at the symbolic Thoreauvian pilgrimages recorded by those who have attempted Walden experiences of their own, I shall try to give some indication of the cultural importance of Walden as a site of pilgrimage and as a prototype for imitation.

At intervals throughout I recur to a particular devotee, John Muir. His testimony is extensive; it illustrates Thoreauvian iconography at an early stage in its formation; it has a special historical importance given Muir's own naturist achievements as well as Muir's efforts to perpetuate Thoreau's memory; and it exhibits also some of the complication, even self-division, of motives that we shall see in other pilgrims as well.

John Muir's Pilgrimage

On Thursday 7 June 1893, John Muir visited Concord, during his first trip east after achieving fame as writer, conservationist, naturalist, and pastoral solitary of Yosemite Valley. Muir was almost exactly the same age as Thoreau when he died. The Concord visit came as part of a strenuous round of introductions and visitations orchestrated by Muir's editor, Robert Underwood Johnson. "Mr. Johnson is making me go to all the pretty & famous places & people whether I will or no," wailed Muir in mock exhaustion after his return to Boston.[10] But in truth Muir had enjoyed himself hugely.

The trip to Concord was one of the highlights of his visit. He "wandered through the famous Emerson village"; saw the Concord Bridge of Revolutionary (and Emersonian) fame; visited the houses of Emerson, Hawthorne, and Thoreau; and laid flowers on the graves of both Thoreau and Emerson, admiring Emerson's rugged unmarked granite monument. "I did not imagine I would be so moved at sight of the resting-places of these grand men," he confessed in a long letter to his wife that records the Concord visit in great detail, even by Muir's voluble standard as a producer of chatty letters home during his many long excursions. "I could not help thinking how glad I would be to feel sure that I would also rest here." From there Muir and Johnson walked to Walden Pond, "a beautiful lake about half a mile long, fairly embosomed like a bright dark eye in wooded hills of smooth moraine gravel and sand, and with a rich leafy undergrowth of huckleberry, willow, and young oak bushes, etc., and grass and flowers in rich variety." Struck by its peaceful beauty, Muir thought it "no wonder Thoreau lived here two years. I could have enjoyed living here two hundred years or two thousand."[11] Before leaving, Muir picked a bouquet of flowers and sent them to his daughter Helen, later to be followed by pictures of Emerson and Thoreau, and of Walden Pond. "Some day," he wrote his other daughter, Wanda, "you & Mama & Helen will go there & see where Thoreau lived & Emerson so much greener & fresher & calmer than Martinez [California, their home,] is & so many good & great people lived there."[12]

The visit to Concord concluded with dinner at the home of Edward Emerson, who seemed to Muir to look just like his father, whom Muir had met during a memorable encounter in Yosemite Valley a dozen years before. He was especially delighted when the younger Emerson's father-in-law, "a college mate of Thoreau who knew Thoreau all his life," greeted him, when they were introduced, "as if I were a long lost son. He declared he had known me always, and that my name was a household word."[13]

Although the Concord visit may have started as a forced excursion, it clearly became a pilgrimage for Muir, partly because it fit into a larger ritual of induction into Brahmin culture, leading during the next few years to a close friendship with Muir's Boston host and fellow botanist Charles Sprague Sargent, an honorary degree from Harvard, and—ironically for R. U. Johnson of New York's Century Publishing Company—the capture of Muir's literary talents for the *Atlantic Monthly* and Houghton, Mifflin.

Muir's visit to the Northeast completed a process begun many years before during his meeting with Emerson in 1871. Characteristically overcoming his country-boy bashfulness with an excess of bravado, Muir had invited the old man for a two-week camping trip with himself as guide. Emerson's eastern escort headed Muir off, but not before he had charmed the sage into an initial acceptance and a permanent enthusiasm for Muir. Back home, Emerson inconsistently but typically issued a ringing invitation to him to leave his hermitage, come east, and stay with him, insisting that Muir would find this cosmopolitan environment more invigorating than his own. Muir responded in the Thoreauvian vein, urging that Emerson revisit the Sierras, professing not to "understand the laws that control you to Concord," reassuring the sage in psalmic tones that "I know smooth places on the mountains & you will never be wearied."[14] But finally it was Muir who accepted Concord's terms. Three years after his eastern visit, when he was offered the Harvard degree, Muir's first thought was again to resist by parading the persona of the California rustic, but on second thought he accepted because "from the very beginning of my studies it was Harvard men," starting with Emerson, "who first hailed & cheered me."[15]

So Muir was no ordinary Concord pilgrim. He was returning, as it were, Emerson's previous invitation, moreover as a dignitary in his own right on whom the master had bestowed a sonship that was confirmed by the actual son's own father-in-law. In other fundamental ways, however, his experience was typical of the hundreds of records left by the millions of pilgrims that have come to Concord from the mid-nineteenth century to the present.

The Pilgrimage Structure

The most fundamental common thread has been the theme of pilgrimage itself. Among all American places made famous by literary associations, Concord had already long been and still remains today the most visited and the most luminous. Its sacrality, to be sure, was not wholly self-generated. Concord's nineteenth-century enshrinement depended partly on the broad proliferation of American picturesque tourism, partly on a regional tradition of sanctifying townships as organic units that was intensified during Muir's lifetime by the rise of such institutions as filiopietistic historiography, local historical societies, and town (bi)centennials.[16] Yet among New England towns, Concord stood preeminent as the first inland settlement, the cradle of American liberty, and the home of Emerson and his circle.[17]

I use the term "sacred" with entire seriousness. Customary though it has become to speak of the American literary "canon" and the process of "canonization" by which writers become recognized as major, the full extent to which the forms of hagiography have come to invest some of these figures has not been recognized. One starts to appreciate the implications of this investiture when one takes note of the similarities between the pilgrimage to Concord and the findings of historical and anthropological students of religious pilgrimage as ritual process.

In particular, I follow Victor Turner and Edith Turner's analysis of Christian pilgrimage, both ancient and modern. The Turners see pilgrimage as a "liminoid" experience offering a temporary "liberation from profane social structures" and spiritual renewal at the journey's end through the exchange of these structures for a sacred realm of significant symbols (in the form of shrines, icons, and the life) that usher the pilgrim imaginatively "into the culturally defined experiences of the founder." Within the Christian tradition, the example par excellence is the *via crucis,* the reenactment by the pilgrim of Jesus' procession to the cross. Such symbolic actions express what the Turners call root paradigms, that is, "cultural models for behavior" that express fundamental assumptions underlying the human societal bond.[18]

When we compare Muir's account with that of other Concord travelers and with the model I have begun to unfold, it becomes clear that his visit was at least a borderline example of pilgrimage in this sense. We can read the telltale signs in the way he envelops Concord and environs in an atmosphere of holy calm: he portrays Sleepy Hollow and Walden Pond as attractive final resting places; he conveys a sense of treading in the footsteps of the "great men" (he vicariously self-inters beside the transcendentalists, he vicariously enacts a grander version of Thoreau's Walden sojourn); he concentrates his attention and reverence on the famous shrines (including even the younger Emerson's household, a

mandatory stop for the well-connected); and he acquires iconic memen-
tos, the flora and the photographs.

The selectivity of Muir's account in the interest of sacralization is especially apparent in the celebration of Walden Pond. He makes no mention
of the busy railroad at the west end or of the commercialization of the
adjacent pond area, which was more meretricious in the 1890s than it is
today. "You cannot get away from the Walden Fourth-of-July picnic
feeling," wrote a visitor just two years after Muir, "not even in Thoreau's
own cove"; there "great beams" projected out into the water where once
a bathhouse stood. Two years later, another pilgrim was disconcerted to
see a "gaily draped pleasure-craft filled with . . . picnickers" floating on
the lake and "gaudy signs inscribed 'Walden lake Picnic Grounds.'"[19] Muir
apparently saw Walden later in the afternoon, when the activity might
have subsided; still, there must have been a number of blemishes, compromising to his vision, that he chose not to see or at least not to record.
It is notable that Muir, unlike some more citified visitors of the day for
whom Walden looked genuinely primitive, was under no illusion that this
was wilderness. "It is only about one and a half or two miles from
Concord, a mere saunter, and how people should regard Thoreau as a
hermit on account of his little delightful stay here I cannot guess," writes
the ex-hermit of Yosemite. Yet even here Muir makes the point not that
Walden bears the marks of civilization but merely that it is near civilization.[20]

This will to pastoralize Walden has persisted in the face of staggering
visitation statistics (thirty thousand Concord pilgrims annually by World
War I, a half million to the pond alone in the late 1970s)[21] and in the face
of protest, starting at least as early as the 1890s, against the exploitation
of the pond area. On the centenary of Thoreau's experiment, naturalist
Edwin Way Teale found Walden "wilder in 1945 than it was . . . in 1845,"
despite the incursion of as many as ten thousand picnickers and bathers
a day. In 1969, a writer for *American Forests* found Walden "as beautiful,
wood-fringed, and satisfying to escapees from today's urbanization as
Henry David Thoreau described its environs nearly 125 years ago." Even
in 1979, another visitor supposed that "the place seems pretty much as it
must have been when Thoreau quit the cabin and went back to Concord."[22] These reactions, like Muir's, attest as much to the perceiver's
power to see the landscape through Thoreauvian eyes as to the literal
state of Walden at the time of viewing—or at the time Thoreau lived

there, when in fact it was much less woodsy than it is today.[23] As Chapter 4 showed, Thoreau himself initiated the tradition of viewing Walden through green spectacles. Partly as a result—despite such enterprises as the Concord and Fitchburg Railroad's development of the pond as a recreation area in the late nineteenth century, despite such subsequent incursions as the advent of a trailer park and a town landfill less than a quarter mile away and a busy commuter highway just beyond that—the threats to pastoral tranquillity have been controlled to the extent that it is still possible for many pilgrims (especially if they choose the right time of day, year, weather) to see the environment in a more natural state than might have been expected. The contrary evidence is not (yet) so over-whelming as to prevent the resolute from making the transition to the liminoid, sacralized vision.

The three visitors' accounts just cited differ from Muir's in being preoccupied solely with Walden Pond. They ignore the rest of the town of Concord, whereas for Muir the visit to Walden was only one of several high points. Muir, however, exemplifies the shift in the central focus of the Concord pilgrimage then in process. During Thoreau's life and for some time thereafter, Emerson and Hawthorne were the great literary figures one came to see or track. They and the lure of Concord's Revolutionary fame kept the tourist's or pilgrim's interests focused more on the village than on the woods.[24] Even as late as the turn of the century, some tourist guidebooks made no mention, or scant mention, of Walden Pond ("too far from the center of town for the average tourist to visit," judged one in 1895), though they inevitably cited Thoreau as a local author. A typical promotion piece, issued on the occasion of the Emerson Centenary (1903), placed Emerson first (as probably "the best known of anyone who has ever lived here"), followed by Hawthorne. In 1904, the decade's most famous literary pilgrim, Henry James, strayed as far from the village center as the Concord River but, while paying Thoreau tribute in a hasty parenthetical phrase, insisted on associating even the sylvan places of Concord with Emerson's genius: "not a russet leaf fell for me, while I was there, but fell with an Emersonian drop."[25]

But Thoreau's disciples had already begun to predict in the 1890s that "Thoreau will continue to grow, while Emerson will become more and more of a back number." Franklin Benjamin Sanborn—the last surviving member of the antebellum Concord transcendentalist group, and its most officious memorializer—had begun prudently to tip the scales of his praise so as to give Thoreau more play, Emerson less. In 1897, a villager in the literary souvenir business told a visitor that Thoreau items were selling better than Emerson and Hawthorne memorabilia. In 1898, Thomas Wentworth Higginson observed that Thoreau's manuscript letters were fetching the same as Hawthorne's ($17.50) and nearly four times Long-fellow's. In 1904, an enterprising Concordian advertised in a Boston paper that he owned some of the remaining timbers of Thoreau's cabin, pre-sumably displayable at a price. In 1906 *Good Housekeeping* noted that Thoreau hatpins, made from the nuts of a tree he supposedly once sowed, were being sold in Concord. More important, that same year Thoreau became the first American man of letters to have his private journal published in full—with a few judicious deletions, of course. Reappraising Concord culture in 1919, forty years after having been a student in the Concord School of Philosophy, Henry Beers of Yale University confessed that Thoreau was interesting him more and more, Emerson less, and registered little surprise at Sanborn's recently quoted statement that Thoreau was the Concordian most likely to endure.[26] These signs of the times coincided with the more conventional mark of literary canonization: Thoreau's promotion, by 1900, to major figure status in the majority of surveys of American literature (which I will discuss in the next chapter).

Beers's estimate reflects the trajectory of Muir's thought and that of a number of his contemporaries. Muir and the other most prominent literary naturist of the period, John Burroughs, follow a parallel course here. For both, Emerson was the first American literary star to fill their firmaments. Both were Emersonians before they were Thoreauvians, and both became what posterity has called Thoreauvians without original intent to follow Thoreau as model, even though their mature writing often echoes his. Burroughs, or so he claimed, turned from Emersonian essays to nature writing in order to establish his individuality from the master; and all his life he was irritated by what he insisted was the false conception of his discipleship to Thoreau, whereas in point of fact he came to Thoreau after he had charted his course with Thomas Wentworth Higginson's *Out-Door Papers* (1860) his only transcendentalist model for nature writing. (Higginson himself, though, was confessedly influenced by Thoreau and mentions him honorifically in almost every essay.)[27] Although Muir may have been introduced to Thoreau as early as college and eventually became an ardent proselytizer, Muir probably did not absorb Thoreau deeply until after he had established his life as hut-dwelling Yosemite naturist and met Emerson.[28] So the Concord pilgrimages of both Muir (1893) and Burroughs (1883) were as much visits to the village honoring Emerson as visits to Walden, although the cumulative accomplishments of both pilgrims, combined with Thoreau's rising prestige, caused posterity to align them both especially with him.

The rise in Thoreau's prestige increased the tendency to envisage Concord as an oasis of pastoral felicity and Walden as its spiritual center. Considering that nineteenth-century mainstream accounts generally cited Concord's Revolutionary fame as its greatest historical significance, the Waldenization of the Concord pilgrimage is striking.[29] This tendency had prior roots in the Concord transcendentalists' highly self-conscious rusticity as they defined themselves over and against the culture of Boston and Cambridge, a legacy reinforced by Concord's ability to maintain the appearance of a small village in the face of nearby urban growth. Both earlier and later images were somewhat illusory. Far from being simple rustics, those associated with the Concord group were cultured intellectuals, and Concord itself was linked to greater Boston by the railroad and other economic institutions.[30] The emotional fact of the matter, if not the literal truth, is that from the very start of the transcendentalist movement Concord was poised to become a spot to which literary pilgrims might repair in the sense of having forsaken the profane metropolis for the sacred grove; the attraction of Thoreau's haunts as a magnet for pilgrims was an intensification of a liminoid structure extant from the time Margaret Fuller started visiting the Emersons in the 1830s, long before Thoreau became famous. Thoreau, indeed, can be said to have realized the Emersonian vision and gone beyond it.

The first canonical work outside the transcendentalist ranks that celebrated Concord as a place of notable bucolic philosophers and literati was the title essay of Hawthorne's *Mosses from an Old Manse* (1845), which renders in a droller and more ruminative way the epistolary lyricism expressed, especially by Sophia Hawthorne, during the Hawthornes' honeymoon period in the house where Emerson composed *Nature*. In "Mosses," too, we see the start of the tradition of urbanite self-consciousness about entering this liminal world and falling under its spell. Hawthorne achieves a certain distance from it by poking fun at the mystics as well as at his own self-rustication during this interval of lotus-eating. In time, the Hawthornian formula of mythic pastoralism made more earthy or plausible through a bemused detachment became the well-worn formula of popular journalistic reports of Concord visits. Though it is impossible to set an exact date, the late 1860s seems to have been a point of transition. "A more peaceful village you can find nowhere," writes one tourist of these years. "You may walk a mile on the main road without meeting a single human being." Concord "is a very quiet place," another agrees, revealingly adding: "a place, above all others, where one would think poets, dreamers, and philosophers would live." "A little rural world curtained off for slumber and drowsy dreams," writes another in 1870.[31] These travelers came expecting to find elysium, and that made elysium all the easier to find.

Hence, in descriptions of Walden Pond from the same period, we find illogically but understandably two opposite messages. First, we read that Walden had become "a pleasure resort," "a famous place for pic-nics." One reporter, interviewing latter-day hermit Edmond Hotham, ingenuously quoted him as complaining about the number of visitors who interrupted his solitude. Already Walden was no longer such a good place to set up a hermitage. But other reporters insisted just as strongly as Thoreau had on Walden's unspoiled character—that it was no mundane spot but fully as special and magical as Thoreau had averred: "a beautiful lakelet," "a picture of delight," a body of water exceptionally "Mediterranean in its kaleidoscopic tints."[32] In short, Walden was being transformed from Thoreau's sacred place into the reading community's sacred place: "Tourists who know the dreamer of Walden Pond look upon it as a shrine." By the early 1870s, even an antitranscendentalist nature writer could affirm that "every student of nature or admirer of poetry as exemplified in life and action, who should make a visit to Walden Pond, would seek the spot which was made sacred by the two years' solitary residence of Henry D. Thoreau."[33]

Concerning the history of the rituals that began at this point to build up around the pond site, a book in itself could be written,[34] simple and informal though they were compared to the pilgrimages studied by the Turners. The devotee has always been expected to stroll a bit in the woods, to look at the pondscape as if through the eyes of Thoreau himself, and to let his or her imagination "saunter." Muir did all this. Starting in 1872, pilgrims have brought stones to a cairn near the cabin site. This Muir apparently did not do, perhaps because he visited at a time when the area was so denuded of rocks that another visitor complained about the amount of foraging required to find a suitable offering.[35] Since 1945, when the exact cabin site was discovered, thoughtful inspection of it is also de rigueur; and so, of late, is a look at the cabin replica in the parking lot across Route 126 to the east of the lake. Conversely, some marks of homage have fallen out of favor. "He who would know Thoreau's Walden will do well to bathe in it," recommends one 1911 pilgrim, who proceeds to depict the experiences of both spiritual and bodily refreshment in detail. Today serious Thoreauvians may well consider swimming in Walden a form of pollution rather than a ritual cleansing.[36]

Indeed, the boundaries of the sacred ground have themselves changed, as the consciousness of Thoreau's admirers has been raised by the principles of ecology. Within the last decade, Thoreau's Walden has increasingly been felt to extend beyond the pond and its perimeter, the tract covered by Thoreau's surveyor's map (*Wa* 286), to include the entire 2,680-acre ecosystem: Walden Woods.[37] "Walden Woods," as former Massachusetts Senator Paul Tsongas put it, "is the buffer that protects the pond and provides the ambience that makes the Walden Pond experience meaningful. The drive to preserve Walden Woods is the precondition for preserving Walden Pond."[38]

More important than undertaking a literal visit to Walden, however, more important even than preserving it as an oasis, is the enactment in whatever place or mode of Thoreau's own disassociation from organized society. Like Muir, the devotee may feel energized by having visited the spot of Thoreau's experiment and having imagined him or herself in Thoreau's place but, perhaps partly because of Thoreau's own aggressive lococentrism and warnings against literal imitation of his example, serious pilgrims are bound to see any act of virtue accomplished by the literal pilgrimage as trivial compared with whatever they can achieve in their own lives by way of parallel.

Hence we find a proliferation of homesteading experiments during the past century that claim Thoreau as inspiration, directly or obliquely. These started about a generation after Thoreau's death, not right away. I have already alluded to what might seem to be the first of these: a shanty-dwelling project at Walden Pond itself in 1869, by Edmond Hotham, who built his hut very close to Thoreau's site. Hotham, however, did not claim Thoreauvian ancestry, despite the fact that he too sought Emerson's patronage.[39] As Thoreau's fame grew, it became increasingly common to see each new experiment in pristine solitary living framed in terms of the Walden experience as prototype. In the 1880s, British utopian socialists like Edward Carpenter and Henry Salt began to take Thoreau's gospel of simplification seriously and act it out in modified form. In 1889 appears the first elaborate literary account of a retreat to rusticity that claims Thoreau as model: a Long Island venture undertaken by journalist Philip G. Hubert, Jr., who followed his autobiographical record with a passionate defense of the feasibility of Thoreau's experiment. By 1901, Paul Elmer More could not resist seeing his brief outing in the Maine woods as a Thoreauvian experience, even though (as More soon came to realize) he and Thoreau were temperamentally incompatible. Meanwhile, in Holland, Frederick van Eeden had started a Christian Socialist commune named after Walden, and at the antipodes Australian writer Edmund James Banfield was about to embark on a twenty-five-year Walden experiment of his own on a Pacific island.[40] A generation later, it seemed self-evident that American retreat literature like Henry Beston's *Outermost House* (1928) and Aldo Leopold's *Sand County Almanac* (1949) should be seen as Thoreauvian documents even though they make little reference to Thoreau.[41] Whether in fact it was Thoreau or some entirely different constellation of forces that prompted these "Thoreauvian" experimenters is ultimately less important than how his image as pastoral hermit gave public shape and articulation to other such ventures, whatever their actual impetus.[42]

The greatest outpouring of biographical and autobiographical narratives of people who have lived portions of their lives with Thoreau's example in mind has come since World War II, since the centennial of the Walden experiment: Edward Abbey's *Desert Solitaire* (1968, Utah); Charles Seib's *The Woods: One Man's Escape to Nature* (1971, North Carolina); Annie Dillard's *Pilgrim at Tinker Creek* (1974, Virginia); George Sibley's *Part of a Winter* (1978, the Colorado mountains); Gilbert Byron's *Cove Dweller* (1983, Maryland's eastern shore); and Anne LaBastille's *Beyond Black Bear Lake* (1987, the Adirondacks).[43] The central plot of such works, the plot of relinquishment, I discussed in Chapter 5. Its establishment as an American master narrative has called into existence a literature of parody, and occasionally also (as in Abbey and Sibley) a vein of self-parody interacting with more serious elements in the same piece. Among lighter treatments, among the best and best-known are E. B. White's occasional essays, such as "Walden—1954," which contains a seriocomic description of the boathouse workshop ("that, through no intent on my part, is the same size and shape as his own domicile on the pond"), where the author's essay is being written. "I have learned," White continues, with mock-Thoreauvian solemnity (or is it Thoreauvian mock-solemnity?) "that in most respects it shelters me better than the larger dwelling where my bed is, and which, by design, is a manhouse not a boathouse."[44] Here and elsewhere White gently mocks modern sylvan gestures, as well as the owlish rhetoric of the guru himself. White is well aware of living on the threshold of an era in which the man who discovered Thoreau's cabin site and built the first replica would be flooded by mail orders when he advertised Thoreau cabin kits for $4,000. But neither the kits nor White's essay would have sold without the moral authority that had come to invest Thoreau's experiment. The mainstream of Walden imitation continues to be borne by accounts like *At Home in the Woods: Living the Life of Thoreau Today,* by a Bostonian couple who became homesteaders in Hudson Hope, British Columbia, with *Walden* as their scripture. Their first sentence reads: "We went to the wilderness because 100 years ago a man wrote a book."[45]

The decentralization of the Walden pilgrimage manifest in the experiments of Seib, Byron, Sibley, and the Angiers has come about not only as a result of Thoreau's transcendentalist dicta against conformity but also because devotees have rightly sensed Thoreau's own retreat to be the enactment of a more fundamental ritual of which not even he was the originator. In the Turners' typology, Walden excursions like Muir's represent a combination of "prototypical pilgrimages"—that is, those established by the founder of the cult, or by the first disciples of important evangelists—and "archaic pilgrimages," those which bear traces of older beliefs and symbols.[46] Although Thoreau's Walden retreat has become the most memorable American example of the civilized person's withdrawal to a simpler state of spiritual refreshment, its authority derives not only from its own originating power but from the fact that versions of it date back several millennia, in both western and oriental culture, and had begun to take on new authority from the time New England settlement became conceived as an errand into the wilderness. Thoreau's experiment had a wealth of American precedents, from the near at hand (like that of his college classmate Charles Stearns Wheeler a few years earlier) to the long ago (the first settlement of the town of Concord); and the narrative he published about it had its precursors too: John Filson's chronicle of Daniel Boone; *The Pioneers* and various other romances by James Fenimore Cooper, who repeatedly created isolated, often beleaguered wilderness huts and homesteads; and Joel T. Headley's *The Adirondack; or, Life in the Woods.*

That the Concord pilgrimage has increasingly been seen as culminating at Walden is therefore symptomatic not merely of the rise of Thoreau's personal reputation but, more broadly, of an American apotheosis of green retreat from urban entanglements that was itself a heightened form of a root paradigm manifested in many world cultures, east and west.

Yet shrines also require saints. Walden should be thought a shrine, as Wallace Stegner has written, "not just because it is a pretty wood surrounding a little pond in suburban Massachusetts, or because any pretty little wood or pond saved is a step gained on a bearable future, but because this little pond is a glowing spot in the American memory, and because Thoreau made it so by living a couple of years on its shore."[47] Furthermore, state the Turners categorically, "All sites of pilgrimage have this in common: they are believed to be places where miracles once happened, still happen, and may happen again. Even where the time of miraculous healings is reluctantly conceded to be past, believers firmly hold that faith is strengthened and salvation better secured by personal exposure to the beneficent unseen presence of the Blessed Virgin or the local saint, mediated through a cherished image or painting."[48] Though the Walden pilgrimage might not have evolved without the sense that Thoreau's retreat was culturally representative, neither would it have evolved at Walden had not a particular charismatic individual dwelt there. Let us see how the figure of Thoreau became invested with pastoral sainthood.

Most crucial to the hagiographical process was doubtless the book *Walden* itself: a central source of the mediating images through which traditional pilgrims experience the local saint as saint. Their magic has arisen in good part from Thoreau's ability to invest even small gestures with ritual significance. His morning bath is a religious exercise, his hut a hermitage. In "Higher Laws" he espouses a sadhu-like asceticism; in "Spring" he experiences the renewal of the season as a resurrection from the dead.[49] In *Walden*'s companion piece, "Walking," Thoreau charges his reader or devotee to think of the whole process of nature rambling as "sauntering" in the sacred sense—as a kind of pilgrimage to the Holy Land.[50]

Nowhere does Thoreau actually *claim* sainthood, of course. On the contrary, anticipating E. B. White, he often treats his solemn aspirations lightly, as in the hermit-poet dialogue following "Higher Laws," where the hermit's pious resolve evaporates when he is invited to go fishing. Thoreau's friends and followers, however, were quick to make bigger claims for him, and his own penchant for homily has helped to make them stick. Emerson and the Alcotts thought of him as the Concord Pan, the flute-playing god of nature. It was repeatedly alleged in the nineteenth century that Thoreau was the model for the Pan-like Donatello in Hawthorne's *Marble Faun*.[51] Both friends and casual visitors told stories about Thoreau's mysterious ability to charm the forces of nature. "I am sure he knew the animals one by one," declared Bronson Alcott; "the plants, the geography, as Adam did in his Paradise, if, indeed, he were not that ancestor himself."[52] The most striking of these testimonials, reported in almost identical form by two independent witnesses, concerns how Thoreau liked to entertain children of acquaintances who visited him at Walden. Here is one version of the story as remembered in adulthood by one of the delighted children.

He was talking to Mr. Alcott of the wild flowers in Walden woods when, suddenly stopping, he said, "Keep very still and I will show you my family." Stepping quickly outside the cabin door, he gave a low and curious whistle; immediately a woodchuck came running towards him from a nearby burrow. With varying note, yet still low and strange, a pair of gray squirrels were summoned and approached him fearlessly. With still another note several birds, including two crows, flew towards him, one of the crows nesting upon his shoulder. I remember it was the crow resting close to his head that made the most vivid impression upon me, knowing how fearful of man this bird is. He fed them all from his hand, taking food from his pocket, and petted them gently before our delighted gaze; and then dismissed them by different whistling, always strange and low and short, each little wild thing departing instantly at hearing its special signal.[53]

In "Brute Neighbors," Thoreau refers to making friends with mice and birds; but it was chiefly by report of those who had known him that his reputation for occult mastery over nature became established, especially through an oft-quoted passage of Emerson's funeral tribute: "Snakes coiled round his legs; the fishes swam into his hand, and he took them out of the water; he pulled the woodchuck out of its hole by the tail, and took the foxes under his protection from the hunters."[54] Today we know that Thoreau's woodland miracles can be duplicated by other sufficiently patient nature watchers, and that Native American sages could probably do all Thoreau could and more centuries before he learned to do it. But that is not the point: the point is the sense of wonderment that Thoreau's woodsmanship aroused in his friends and visitors. Here was a man of essentially their own background, who had crossed a threshold into a new realm of being of which they had no knowledge whatsoever.

Emerson qualifies the tone of his list of wonders by his usual mixture of envy and condescension toward all forms of practical ability and perhaps also his awareness of a certain histrionic quality in Thoreau himself. But the net effect was to mysticize Thoreau and set the stage for further mythification by his biographers. Ellery Channing came first, insisting in his appendix of verses on the curative powers of Thoreau's writing:

> For thoughtful minds in Henry's page
>   Large welcome find, and bless his verse,
> Drawn from the poet's heritage,
>   From wells of right and nature's source.
>
> Fountains of hope and faith! inspire
>   Most stricken hearts to lift this cross,
> His perfect trust shall keep the fire,
>   His glorious peace disarm the loss![55]

Here and elsewhere in his poetry, Channing bears out what Emma Lazarus said of him: that he "actually worships" the memory of Thoreau.[56] Although, like Emerson, Channing was not above amusing himself at Thoreau's expense, he typically portrays Thoreau as a holy hermit, a beneficent spiritual influence, and so on. In short, when Channing (the model for the interlocutor in Thoreau's hermit-poet dialogue) came to writing his side of the story, the drollery tended to evaporate and the solemnity to be heightened.

The same was even truer of Thoreau's second biographer, A. H. Japp, an English gentleman reformer who knew Thoreau exclusively through the medium of his writings and published testimony. It was Japp who first propagated the comparison between Thoreau and Saint Francis of Assisi, on the strength of their reverence for fellow creatures and their uncanny power over the animal kingdom.[57] Japp's hagiography was dismissed by some reviewers, and no later Thoreauvian critic has taken it as seriously as its perpetrator; but it has often been repeated, and the Thoreau-as-Saint Francis image is still alive today. Indeed, Joseph Wood Krutch compared the two figures to Thoreau's advantage, seeing Saint Francis as anthropocentric in forcing Christian doctrine on the birds and Thoreau as imbued with a more truly ecological gospel of reverence for fellow creatures as equals.[58] This was a historic recasting. In effect, Krutch sought to define a new dispensation of ecological consciousness in which humankind would be emancipated from the anthropocentrizing way Christianity traditionally had dealt with the environment.[59]

The Saint Francis analogy is only one of the forms that the apotheosis of Thoreau has taken. Many of those who have thought about him during the past century have liked to envisage him as a larger-than-life being. Sometimes the magnification of Thoreau reaches improbable heights. The Angiers, for instance, take him as the infallible guide. The one moment when their faith falters, after returning to civilization (as Henry did) and finding themselves unhappy about it, is especially striking. Brad sadly opines that Thoreau "must have been wrong in leaving the woods when all that meant so much to him. Yet he was so right in everything else." To which Vena, fortunately, is able to make this bright reply: "'But he was never really wrong, not in real life. That's where we made our mistake.' I managed to smile, and I lifted my face. His questioning lips touched mine, warm and alive. 'Thoreau left his cabin, yes. He didn't mention the rest of it in that book we have, but . . . He spent the rest of his time roaming about the same woods, the same fields, and the same Walden Pond.'"[60] This realization gives the couple the needed reassurance. Here as many times before they solve their problem by invoking their patron. It is not so much the specific doctrinal formulation of Thoreau as saint that counts as the elevation of Thoreau to the status of model or prototype of whatever sort. When the Reverend Jesse Jackson endorsed the Walden Woods Project on the ground that we must "respect the sacred places of our civilization, and preserve them so that we might become a better nation," he did well to blend together Thoreau the abolitionist and Thoreau the environmentalist into a single image of an admirable spirit "that has helped so many of us do what we know to be right."[61]

Canonization as a Cultural System

Having made this point, however, I must repeat that the patron is the center of an ideological system but not the whole system. And the system itself varies. For Channing it is the ethos of the romantic poet-prophet; for Japp, Christian asceticism; for Krutch, modern ecological conscious-ness; for Jackson, doubtless more the cause of equal rights than the environment per se; for the Angiers, the homesteaders' way; for Seib and Sibley, a temporary release from the work ethic. But in each case there is a larger symbolic system. To return to the case of John Muir, we can see at least two such systems at work. One merges the perspectives of Chan-ning and Japp: a late-romantic, secularized Christianity that saw nature as a primary revelation, displacing scripture and worship service. Muir's description of his own first months of cabin living in Yosemite is most revealing here:

> I am sitting here in a little shanty made of sugar pine shingles this Sabbath evening. I have not been at church a single time since leaving home. Yet this glorious valley might well be called a church, for every lover of the great Creator who comes within the broad overwhelming influences of the place fails not to worship as he never did before. The glory of the Lord is upon all his works; it is written plainly upon all the fields of every clime, and upon every sky, but here in this place of surpassing glory the lord has written in capitals.[62]

What authorizes Muir's experience of subsistence living in this natural paradise, which from a practical standpoint looks unproductive and antisocial, is the sense of holiness within nature, to which he can appeal as an extension of the paradigm of piety shared by his Christian-reared and also nature-sensitive siblings. Clearly not just the figure of Thoreau, whose masterpiece Muir had not yet read, but also the sense of something like a shared paradigm, as well as a shared literal experience of retreat, enabled Muir to respond as he did when he visited Concord. (Muir, incidentally, was just as capable as Thoreau of editing the bald facts to make his symbolic world luminous. The passage just quoted fails to indicate that his hut is not freestanding out in nature but is attached to a sawmill.) When Muir's published prose echoes Thoreau's, Muir has not so much deliberately remade himself in Thoreau's image as used Thoreau's vocabulary as a kindred expression of the holiness of the pristine places of the earth.

The other paradigm that made Muir's Concord visit resonate was the system of cultural accreditation that had drawn William Dean Howells to the town thirty-three years before to pay homage to local shrines and personalities. After mid-century, Concord came to stand not only for pastoral retreat but also for the cultural establishment on whose margins the largely self-educated outlander Muir felt himself to be. Whether or not we credit his insinuation that he visited Concord because Johnson dragged him there, Muir's way of broaching the point shows his awareness of Concord as an established shrine. The ease with which Johnson later overcame Muir's resistance to the bother of trekking east to receive a degree at Harvard in the kind of ceremonial display from which he habitually shied reveals how susceptible this ex-farmboy was to the prospect of becoming an institution himself. *Atlantic Monthly* editor Walter Hines Page knew his man when he stressed in his courtship of Muir that his magazine and the press that then owned it (Houghton, Mifflin) published the most prestigious list of authors in America—backing the appeal to prestige with a better contributor's wage and royalty contract than Muir had received from Johnson.[63]

Clearly, the sense that "great men" rested at Sleepy Hollow heightened Muir's experience of natural piety there. The bucolic moment at Walden probably afforded no pleasure more delicious than Edward Emerson's father-in-law welcoming him like "a long lost son." And the whole ensuing stay in greater Boston was rendered even more delightful for being hosted by his well-to-do Brahmin botanist friend Sargent at his elegant Cambridge home—"the finest mansion and grounds I ever saw."[64]

Students of Emerson's and Thoreau's reputations are normally solicitous, and with reason, to distinguish the two men's relative status in nine-teenth-century Concord: between the genteel Emerson, for whom all was forgiven in view of his pedigree and good manners, and the prodigal son Thoreau, borderline gentry to start with and downwardly mobile by his own perverse intent. But to most late-century outlanders, Concord pre-sented a global impression of portentousness: "the biggest little place in America," as James wryly expressed the local self-image.[65] That settled, finer distinctions could then be made, of course. Above all, even by the time of the Civil War, Concord was, as the journalists liked to say, "classic ground": a cultural reference point, whose collective literary achievement emanated a certain power.

The subsequent correspondence between *Atlantic* editor Page and favored contributor Muir is a gloss on that power. "The greatest single compact body of American literature of permanent value that exists anywhere is put forth by this firm," Page—a fellow outlander—reminds Muir. "This single fact gives the firm an advantage that no other one has in putting writings which have sufficient merit first alongside of this compact mass of permanent literature and finally into it—thus bringing about not simply such a sale of a book as can be made so long as it is a new publication, but in addition thereto such a continual nurture of it as a piece of literature as will keep it alive as long as it has any vitality whatsoever."[66] In his genial, florid, confident, relentless way, Page harped on this same string again and again. In actual fact, the Houghton-*Atlantic* establishment had passed its peak of prestige; but from a contributor's perspective in the 1890s, given the firm's long track record of success, Page's argument looked strong and understandably impressed Muir. The Ticknor and Fields publishing empire that evolved into Houghton, Mifflin was in fact the single literary institution most responsible for forming the first national canon and for sponsoring the work of the majority of the premodern American writers widely considered "major" even today.[67] Henry Thoreau was a case in point. Ticknor and Fields helped make his reputation with *Walden,* with Fields keeping Thoreau before the public in the 1860s in a series of *Atlantic* articles (not to mention reviews of Thoreau's posthumous books and references to Thoreau in many other articles). It was Houghton, Mifflin that eventually brought out Thoreau's *Journal,* first in excerpts during the 1880s and 1890s, then almost in its entirety (1906); and it was Houghton, Mifflin that published the author-ized collected editions of his work.

Concord, then, represented the intertwined forces of American natur-ism and American literary culture, as the hundreds of touristic guide-books that began to appear in the late nineteenth century eagerly stressed. Concord, "our literary Mecca," attracted by the 1890s if not before "more pilgrims than any other place of equal size upon the continent," not only because of its Revolutionary fame but also because the transcendental coterie "helped the village of Concord do more for American literature than has any great metropolis of the nation."[68] Yet it and particularly Walden retain their pastoral charm withal. "Commercialism is a thing of which Concord does not boast" (1902); "Much of the Pond's natural beauty is still present" (1929); "Thoreau's cove, and the woods surround-ing it, are still peaceful, and the lover of Thoreau will not find here too great interruption of his thoughts" (1936).[69] Of course these statements convey what the writers wanted their readers to notice, rather than provide documentary descriptions of the locale. The point is not to haggle over their precise degree of accuracy but to recognize their desire to associate Concord with both nature's power and culture's power. Thoreau's reputation benefited from that association more than it suffered from the initial disadvantage of being cast in Emerson's shadow. Increasingly, since the turn of the twentieth century, he has become the principal *raison d'être* for Concord's continued existence as a literary shrine. As long as Thoreau continues to be seen as an American cultural hero—that is, as long as the interlinked values of pastoralism and counterculturalism remain cherished parts of the American cultural heritage—the present configuration is likely to remain.

What, then, can we conclude from this Janus-faced aspect of the Concord pilgrimage? For one thing, it confirms that canonization is assisted by good connections and by larger ideological patterns that direct us to interpret the author's life and work as having a patterned significance. This process clearly can have a conventionalizing, embalming effect, co-opting the saint into what looks like a kind of conspiracy of com-modification. We have seen, for example, the tendency of the pilgrimage literature examined above to crystallize into prefabricated genres: the Concord guidebook and the narrative essay or epistle. As such writings multiplied around the turn of the century, the intensity of the represented experience became muffled in cliché. Even debunking narratives written in attack against touristic commercialization—a thriving minority sub-genre I have regretfully given short shrift here—become themselves routi-nized reverse-stereotypes of the straight-faced accounts. These conven-tionalizations doubtless both reflect and produce a routinization of the pilgrim's experience, such as to make one wonder how many Thoreauvian pilgrims deserve the name. An eminent transcendentalist scholar once remarked to me that the *true* Concord pilgrims are those who visit the Alcott house in memory of Louisa May Alcott's *Little Women* and other children's writings; for these books (still) have no high canonical status, and there is (as yet) no special cultural capital to be derived from proclaiming oneself a devotee. This shrewd perception is important as a check on the temptation to take Thoreauvian pilgrimages at face value.

By way of both concession and rebuttal to this side of the account, it should be reiterated that the literal pilgrimage of Concord visitation obviously counts for less in the long run than the symbolic pilgrimage of putting Thoreau to work in one's life. The more original and promi-nent among those who have paid homage to Thoreau are figures like van Eeden, Gandhi, and Martin Luther King, who have been less interested in visiting other saints' shrines than in enacting their own independent pilgrimages. This independence can be seen in Muir's life as well, in his comparative hesitancy at being drafted into literary tourism in contrast to the enthusiasm with which he acted out his own Thoreauvian role at Yosemite. As far as the history of the environmental imagination is concerned, what counts is not that Muir, Burroughs, and Loren Eiseley visited Concord but that they inscribed in their work variants of the Thoreauvian narrative of departure from town to Walden, works that have sometimes inspired Walden-style pilgrimages in their turn: to Muir's Yosemite, to Burroughs's Slabsides, to Leopold's Wisconsin shack, to Beston's outermost house on Cape Cod.

Yet a far greater simplification than taking the Concord pilgrimage at face value would be to write it off as amounting to nothing more than a routine or normalizing device. To visit Thoreau's retreat (or Burroughs's, or Leopold's) has always offered a chance to emulate Thoreau's own gesture of shaking the dust of urbanity and materialism from one's feet, as with Muir's daydream of a 2,000-year sojourn by the pond. In this inclination we see not only the capacity for pilgrimage to promote cozy smugness but also its capacity to promote reflective detachment. If Thoreau's reputation has benefited from his connection with the literary and pub-lishing power centers, it has benefited at least as much from the societal desire to free ourselves from quotidian entanglements that threaten to compromise us much more than they did him. To the extent that Muir's belated discovery of Thoreau as an inspirational force helped equip him with a rhetoric and an ethos of empowerment on behalf of the unpopular doctrine of wilderness preservationism, we see in Muir's "discipleship" also the potential of the canonized figure, by definition an extraordinary person, to instigate resistance to normalization, especially when that figure is linked in the public mind to a story of secession from norms. A pilgrimage, be it literal or vicarious or symbolic, that one takes seriously undoubtedly may express or instigate transformative experiences that produce life-long results. For some pilgrims, contact with Walden the place has been the means of making the book itself live for the first time.[70] This experience applies especially to environmentally directed readers. For to connect the literature of place with the actual place that gave rise to the literature can deepen not only one's sense of the book itself but one's sense of what it means to be in communion with place.

Finally, and closely related to the previous point, the phenomenon of canonical investment, instanced by the pilgrimage, confirms that the imaginative bond of devotee to writer probably operates less exclusively at the level of the reading experience than literary specialists normally think. The consequences of canonization should be measured less exclu-sively than we normally do in terms of texts (or criticism) engendered, and more broadly in terms of the author's lifework and the impact of that lifework on those who come in contact with it. Thoreau's case forces us to take seriously the question of whether the Angiers, for all their sentimental naïveté, are closer to understanding the kingdom of Henry than those who have concentrated mainly on his rhetorical sophistication. It is notable that at least some Thoreauvians, like Anne LaBastille, have actually found Thoreau's text repellent until they awakened to a sense of voice behind the text. In her case, the experience of hearing *Walden* read offset the sense of the textual Thoreau as "a cold idol," and Thoreau the ecologist in action offset Thoreau the somewhat misogynist writer.[71] Maybe she was not Thoreau's ideal reader. But neither are most English professors.

Not for all writers, but certainly for some and most certainly for a writer like Thoreau, imagination and practical action are continuous in a way that makes arbitrary our attempts to confine them to either arena or to insist that the literary level of their legacy is the only one that matters. Even if we imagine Thoreau as primarily a writer, the same applies. Environmental restorationist William R. Jordan III finds, for instance, an "imaginative and performative element in Thoreau's thought that is directly related to the business of ecological restoration," an element that Jordan locates precisely in Thoreau's capacity for imaginative redemption of "a partly despoiled landscape" in *Walden*. Here Jordan sees a possible prototype: "we can turn every neighborhood park, every schoolyard, vacant lot, abandoned field or right-of-way into a Walden Pond."[72] Jordan's point loses no power from its basis in the commentator's own vocation. For Thoreau's writings positively lend themselves to this. By "this" I mean not just ecological restorationism but more broadly an ethos of repossession through practical action as well as through restatement.

CHAPTER ELEVEN

The Canonization and Recanonization of the Green Thoreau

We cannot perceive what we canonize.

—Edward Dahlberg,
"Thoreau and Walden," in *Bones*

    If you can't put
two and two together, you must throw up
a house by guesswork and by paradox.
His sermons and economies obtain:
to add, you must subtract; to stay, get lost.
Thoreau is the most gone. None of his books
makes much of where. Away. Some few hide out
with him. Turtles, adream in a dome. Frogs.

—Paul Monette, "Come Spring," in *No Witnesses*

THIS CHAPTER REVIEWS the story of Thoreau's canonization and subsequent fame. Since the attainment of canonization means being subjected to the disparate mental universes of one's readers, this story cannot be told without vacillation, indistinctness, and equivocation. For the saint's promoters may be muddleheaded or self-serving; their influence and pertinacity may seem as responsible for the canonization as the saint's merits; and the traits held up for reverence by some may repel others. Canonization therefore is always contingent, though it seems permanent when it is in place. Some classic American writers have been decanonized (Washington Irving and Henry Wadsworth Longfellow), some elevated after falling into limbo (Melville and Margaret Fuller), some recanonized on entirely different bases by later generations (Hawthorne). Since the second and third of these outcomes befell Thoreau, can we be altogether certain the first will not? As George Orwell said of Gandhi, perhaps saints should be "judged guilty until they are proved innocent."[1]

In the present age of canonical revisionism, the traditionally upbeat story of the great writer's recognition may be easily inverted into a story of competition for cultural power and dominance, with success coming at the cost of repression. ("Within our culture, Shakespeare is enormously powerful. Power corrupts and disfigures.")[2] In Thoreau's case, we sometimes encounter a quite un-transcendental atmosphere of vanity, bickering, possessiveness, and commodification in the orchestration of his fame. Yet the tendency to celebrate Thoreau as a reproach to ignoble forms of self-interest has outweighed whatever obsessions his advocates have had with their own versions of him. Whether the same is true of other cases of canonization, of Alexander Pope or Henry James for example, I would not venture to assert. But I have come to believe it necessary to envisage the canonization of Thoreau as being driven both by the desires of individuals and institutions to create and manipulate self-serving images and by the need to find some sort of ideal to steer by, even at the cost of self-indictment.

Thoreau's Canonization as a Marketing Event

Thoreau often complained about the commodification of art and the neglect of the serious artist. These complaints, like his famous denunciation of the failure of "my publisher, falsely so called" to promote his first book (J 5: 259), both contradict themselves—expressing conflicted views of the value he set on having his say and making a living—and mislead us as to his lack of success. The myth that Thoreau was unlucky in his contacts with the publishing industry survives, although the reverse was actually more true. The timing of his sorties into the marketplace may have sometimes been unfortunate and his business judgment faulty, but Thoreau benefited throughout his professional lifetime from the goodwill and interventionary efforts not only of his original patron, Emerson, but also of two of America's most enterprising literary promoters: journalist Horace Greeley of New York and publisher James T. Fields of Boston, both of whom were far more supportive of Thoreau's work than his commercial track record warranted.[3] After his death, the Houghton,

Mifflin Company, successor to the firm of Ticknor and Fields, which farsightedly bought up all the Thoreau copyrights for a modest sum during the 1870s, played a major role in bringing about his canonization. During the next quarter century, the firm's resourceful use of its publishing distribution machine in the service of a speculative, as yet unremunerated faith in Thoreau's destiny again shows the same combination of idealistic enthusiasm and hardheaded business maneuvering exhibited by Greeley and Fields.[4]

The start and close of the most decisive part of the story goes like this. Around 1880, when Houghton, Osgood reorganized and renamed itself Houghton, Mifflin, Thoreau was accorded a distinctly second-rank status. "Our book list," reads an 1879 circular, "includes the works of the most eminent and popular of American writers," among whom nine are identified, including Longfellow and other leading poets of the New England group (James Russell Lowell, Oliver Wendell Holmes, John Greenleaf Whittier), as well as Harriet Beecher Stowe and Bret Harte, but not Thoreau.[5] Indeed, there was no reason to name him; Thoreau's seven volumes were selling a total of less than a thousand copies a year. By 1903, however, the company's head, George H. Mifflin, was declaring that "Thoreau should be our next great author after Emerson."[6] This decision inaugurated the twenty-volume edition of Thoreau's collected writings, published in 1906—a historic event commonly taken as the point of Thoreau's canonization. The inclusion of the *Journal* in fourteen volumes made Thoreau the first American person of letters to have his diary published in full.

Some aspects of this success story have been well chronicled, notably the heroic efforts of Thoreau's disciples to promote his reputation.[7] Thoreau was not canonized, however, until he became respectable and his canonization was finally effected more by establishment forces than by an insurgent group.

Contemporary readers, who accept Thoreau's "greatness" as a given (whatever emotions of pleasure, excitement, distrust, or boredom that self-evidency inspires), may find it hard to understand Mifflin's affirmation as anything other than inevitable. Yet the investment he contemplated, and for which he spared as little expense as possible, was less economically justified than was the omission in 1879 of Thoreau's name from the firm's circular. Between 1880 and 1903, the sales of Thoreau's books had indeed quadrupled, but his annual thousands were dwarfed by Emerson's ten thousands, not to mention Longfellow's hundred thousands. As it turned out, the 1906 edition apparently brought more renown than profit to the firm. Less than two thousand copies were printed, counting both the deluxe "manuscript" edition and the plain gray-blue "Walden" edition that one chiefly finds today in open library stacks; although these seem to have sold out (by subscription) within five years or less, the edition was not reprinted for almost half a century, nor did the firm's sales of other Thoreau works measurably benefit from the venture. In fact, sales were actually starting to taper off at the moment the 1906 edition came on the market, since all of Thoreau's books except his *Journal* entered the public domain between 1891 and 1905 and competing editions by other publishers, especially of *Walden,* had begun to appear. (In 1910 American readers could choose among at least eight different publishers' editions of *Walden* and at least two of *A Week, Cape Cod,* and *The Maine Woods.*) As far as narrowly commercial motives and benefits are concerned, therefore, I can interpret Houghton, Mifflin's backing of Thoreau in no other way than as a calculated risk taken in the confidence of Thoreau's greatness, a risk that was by any reasonable standard significant even when one allows the interconnectedness of his work with other titles on the Houghton, Mifflin list (as I shall detail below).

What caused George Mifflin's decision is not, however, a mystery, although his exact motive remains mysterious. He was influenced strongly by *Atlantic Monthly* editor and Harvard professor Bliss Perry, the successor to Walter Hines Page, whose wooing of John Muir I described in the previous chapter. In his autobiography, published in 1935, Perry remembered "sometimes cajoling the House against its better judgment to risk something upon a new poet or to try once more a book by some veteran whose prose was savory and yet hitherto unsalable." In particular, Perry was "inordinately proud" of persuading the firm to publish first Thoreau's *Journals* and then Emerson's.[8]

May we conclude, then, that enthusiastic intervention on behalf of artistic greatness by the forward-looking intellectual broke down the cautious, pragmatic resistance of the boss and his senior staff? Likely so, for Mifflin's private correspondence with his partners also credits Perry with the initiative. But Mifflin himself cannot be presumed a Thoreauvian convert: indeed, he may never even have read Thoreau. It is entirely possible that Mifflin's zealousness to establish Thoreau's greatness resulted from his frustration at the sag in profits elsewhere on the firm's literary list. Just two days before he announced his position, Mifflin had acknowledged to a partner: "I note what you say about the Whittier copyright. We have known for some time that the amount we were paying as an annuity was an extravagant one. The truth is that the sale of Whittier is steadily declining and has been during the past ten years, and instead of increasing our rate ten years ago from $1500 to $2500 as we did, we ought to have reduced it by $1000, and then we should have been about right." Fortunately, it would be up for renegotiation in August.[9]

It is hard to resist positing a causal link between the decision to downgrade John Greenleaf Whittier and the decision to upgrade Thoreau, an intention Mifflin announced in the very next letter bound in the company letter book. Surely this signifies the displacement of the old genteel order that formed what might be called America's first canon of great authors by the new order that formed its second, whose ranks included other comparatively marginal or oppositional figures like Walt Whitman and Mark Twain as well as redefined versions of originally canonized figures like Hawthorne and Emerson. Thoreau's turn-of-the-century disciples, away from the literary power centers, were at that very moment claiming such a shakeout was in process. Yet Whittier continued to outsell Thoreau in raw numbers; and Houghton, Mifflin continued to advertise Whittier as one of the great American writers. It is by no means clear, then, that the cases of Whittier and Thoreau would have been connected in Mifflin's mind by any other principle than the desire to keep on top of the market. His decision certainly did reflect a confidence in Thoreau's stature that none of his predecessors would have been so bold as to assert, but he probably did not see an aesthetic paradigm shift in the making; more likely, he simply put Thoreau in the preexisting category of "American writers worth promoting."

But what about Bliss Perry? His interpretation is much more significant than Mifflin's, since Mifflin relied on Perry's expertise as "literary adviser." As a vigorous promoter of Walt Whitman's literary reputation during the same era, Perry seems to have solid credentials as a canonical revisionist. Yet his championship of Thoreau does not seem to have been driven by a desire to call established theories of American literature into question. Neither then nor later does Perry seem to have considered that Thoreau's canonization might significantly readjust the general view of what was coming to be known as the American Renaissance.

Perry outlined his ideas in a historical sketch entitled *The American Spirit in Literature*, published shortly after World War I. With obvious pride, he notes that "our literature has no more curious story than the evolution of this local crank into his rightful place of mastership"—a pronouncement that, as Perry must have known, had already become formulaic in American criticism. Significantly, he finds the event no more than "curious," something to cherish as a wonder rather than to try to explain—and definitely not a turn of events that would threaten Emerson's position. For Perry, Thoreau achieved greatness by fulfilling Emerson's vision: "to the student of American thought Thoreau's prime value lies in the courage and consistency with which he endeavored to realize the gospel of Transcendentalism in his own inner life." In effect, this means that Thoreau exemplifies good old American individualism, whose patriotic rather than oppositional flavor Perry stresses in the way he describes Thoreau's support for John Brown as the culmination of Thoreau's life: "Once, toward the close of his too brief life, Thoreau 'signed on' again to an American ideal, and no man could have signed more nobly."[10]

Perry's treatment of Thoreau in this textbook literary history is in keeping with what is known about his professional activities two decades before. We have seen him link the Emerson and Thoreau journal projects in his autobiography. In 1903 Mifflin, presumably with Perry's encouragement, also linked them in suggesting to his partners that current public interest in the much publicized centennial of Emerson's birth (marked by the firm's publication of Emerson's *Complete Writings* in twelve volumes) "will spread itself to Thoreau, and that there would be a good market for a thoroughly good edition of Thoreau." To the extent that Perry induced Mifflin and his staff to think in a radically new direction, his contribution was apparently to stress (just as he later did in the case of Emerson) the unpublished journals as an unusual literary find. "It is almost unique," continues Mifflin, "for writers to leave so full Journals and so interesting Journals as Thoreau has left." "Mr. Perry's theory is that the publication in full of the Journals will only add to the interest of the writings, and that lovers of Thoreau and his writings would attach all the more value to the completed journals, which, as I say, contain matter of the utmost interest according to his report."[11]

Perry seems, then, to have been advocating little more than a completion of the Thoreau canon, on the ground that more is better: having the full text in print promised to attract interest and enrich understanding. In so doing, he took a historic step in moving the standards of American literary publishing in a more "scholarly" direction, but this effort did not in itself advance the interpretation of Thoreau or of American culture generally. It comes as no surprise to find Perry delivering a concurrent public tribute to Longfellow's enduring importance. His recommendation to publish Thoreau in full was a bold stroke, and his esteem for Thoreau as Emerson's peer was ahead of its time, but the basis of his interest in Thoreau was apparently not. Significantly, one of Perry's next steps in negotiating with E. H. Russell, who owned the *Journal* manuscripts and eventually received $3,000 for their use, was to inquire about the possible publication of the manuscript of a fifth book of season-inspired perceptions ("Late Spring and Early Summer") quarried by Thoreau's literary executor H. G. O. Blake out of the *Journals*.[12] Houghton, Mifflin had published the first four in the 1880s and the 1890s, along with still another Blake compendium entitled *Thoreau's Thoughts*. In imagining a continuation of the series, and in advocating full publication of the *Journals* from which they came, Perry sought to continue in the same vein of Thoreau promotion that the firm had been employing for the past two decades to ride the crest of the modest Thoreau revival.

Not until Houghton, Mifflin issued the 1906 edition as part of its library of deluxe collected editions of major American authors' works did the firm decisively promote Thoreau as a member of the first-rank pantheon. Before that, the sextet of Emerson, Hawthorne, Longfellow, Lowell, Holmes, and Whittier got top billing as "the six great representatives of American literature."[13] Starting as early as the 1880s, however, Houghton, Mifflin made increasingly aggressive attempts to market Thoreau's work in various ways.

One was the series of season books assembled by Blake, the first of which *(Early Spring in Massachusetts)* appeared in 1881. Next, starting in 1889, the firm began issuing *Walden* in multiple editions. Within a decade, patrons could chose from among five different Houghton, Mifflin editions of *Walden*, and sales in the late nineties momentarily surpassed those of the seven editions of Hawthorne's *Scarlet Letter*. The house also issued *Cape Cod* in a deluxe, illustrated edition in 1896.

Even more important for ensuring that Thoreau would become a household word, Houghton, Mifflin began anthologizing his writings as early as 1881, in a collection, *American Prose*, edited by the firm's own Horace Scudder. Scudder selected "Sounds" and "Brute Neighbors" from *Walden* and "The Highland Light" from *Cape Cod*. (Emerson was represented by "Behavior" and "Books.") These three pieces, all relatively accessible, emphasize descriptive portraiture; and they feature a mild, whimsical, generally noncombative persona. With this selection, the trend of editing Thoreau for classroom use began. Although at first omitted from mid-1880s advertisements of Houghton, Mifflin "Out-Door Books," Thoreau's "A Winter Walk" appeared in the Emerson Little Classics volume, and in 1888 he was chosen as the first nature author to be represented in the Riverside Literature Series, a pedagogical project designed to make available "the best and purest" writing in order to effect "the formation of a taste in the reader for the best and most enduring literature."[14] The Thoreau volume comprised the late natural history essays "Wild Apples" and "The Succession of Forest Trees," as well as Emerson's eulogy on Thoreau (later distributed as part of a free promotional package to attract interest in the "Walden" edition). Over the next two decades, this book was the biggest Thoreau seller next to *Walden*, although its sales were miniscule compared to, say, the *Evangeline* volume, which in 1906 sold 60,000 copies as compared to Thoreau's 2,500.

Thus Thoreau would have become first known to American readers growing up in the late nineteenth and early twentieth centuries as the author of comparatively descriptive and scientific, nonmystical, and nonpugnacious essays, and through Emerson's representation of him as "the bachelor of thought and Nature."[15] Students not assigned the Riverside Thoreau volume might encounter "Wild Apples" in the firm's 1892 school textbook *Masterpieces of American Literature*, along with Bryant's "Thanatopsis," Holmes's "The Chambered Nautilus," Emerson's "Behavior," Longfellow's *Evangeline* and Whittier's *Snowbound*. This mode of anthologizing helped ensure Thoreau's canonization in the normalizing terms later expressed in Perry's literary history and in the spirit of Emerson's affirmation in 1862 that "no truer American existed than Thoreau."[16] It followed predictably from this centrist promotion that the Thoreau volume containing his political essays (including "Civil Disobedience") consistently sold the least well in America through the turn of the century.

Houghton, Mifflin also promoted Thoreau's reputation by recirculating critical tributes to Thoreau as the effective founder of modern American nature writing—in connection, of course, with puffing new titles by contemporary writers, thus hatching two birds from the same egg. One Houghton, Mifflin promotional piece quoted an allusive review of Charles Dudley Warner's *In the Wilderness* ("as fresh and fragrant of the woods as anything that Thoreau ever wrote"); in others, Frank Bolles's *The Land of Lingering Snow* was said to "reveal a power of minute observation as remarkable as Thoreau's"; John Burroughs was promoted as "the same breed as Gilbert White of Selborne, as Audubon, as Thoreau"; and John Muir was touted as "the Thoreau of the Far West." Reciprocally, potential subscribers to the "Walden" edition were informed that the type was "the same as in the Riverby Edition of Burroughs's works."[17] In short, Houghton, Mifflin used its name-droppable authors to market the works of newer authors, who if all went well became name-droppable themselves. The publishers thereby built the image of an emerging canon of literary nature writing with Thoreau at its head. This policy proved especially effective given the firm's investment in the overlapping categories of "local color" and "out-of-door" literature of different kinds. In addition to Thoreau, Houghton, Mifflin published Burroughs, Muir (after 1900), Mary Austin (until World War I), Celia Thaxter, Sarah Orne Jewett, Bret Harte, Bradford Torrey, Andy Adams *(Log of a Cowboy),* popular ornithologist Olive Thorne Miller, and the nature-oriented works of Charles Dudley Warner and James Russell Lowell, not to mention other figures less well known. The contents for the same period of the firm's magazine organ, the *Atlantic Monthly,* in which many future books appeared in serial or excerpt form, also shows a strong tilt toward literary nature writing and sketches of rustic or backwater life.

In its sponsorship of environmental writing, which extended to the publication of natural history field guides, the firm was of course responding to the perceived climate of opinion among the reading public (a climate that its books and *Atlantic* articles had influenced): it attempted to capitalize on (and help direct) such contemporary movements as back-to-naturism (the rise of scouting and wilderness camping), conservationism and preservationism, and the emergence of the "nature essay" as an established, respectable genre. Yet the firm's behavior probably also reflected more particular tastes among the editors, who to this day have included such staunch naturists as Francis Allen and Paul Brooks. As with the decision to go ahead with the "Walden" edition, the role of individual intervention in publishing (and other corporate) achievements cannot be ignored. The same applies to Brooks's role in publishing Rachel Carson's *Silent Spring* (1964).[18]

Houghton, Mifflin's marketing strategies reflected and undoubtedly perpetuated a very different view of Thoreau's "official canon" than has generally prevailed in modern times.[19] The late nineteenth-century view of Thoreau was much less *Walden*-centered and also less text-centered than the average view a century later. To be sure, *Walden* was always Thoreau's most popular book; and by the turn of the century textbook histories of American literature had begun to recognize it as the one Thoreau volume "that can strictly be called a classic, or at least a probable classic."[20] But *Walden* did not emerge as quickly or dramatically as one might think. In 1880, all-time sales of *Walden* stood at 3,695, as against 3,528 for *Cape Cod* and 3,263 for *The Maine Woods*.[21] Long after that, commentators stressed the overall unity and interest of Thoreau's writing as a whole. The first full-length interpretative history of American literature declared a slight preference for *Walden* and *Cape Cod* among Thoreau's books but emphasized that he was "a remarkably even writer; his chapters were like his days, merely parts of a serene and little-diversified life." "Open his works almost anywhere," affirmed another critic, "there are ten volumes of them now,—and even in the philosophic passages you will find loving precision of touch." (The "even" tips us off to the American Victorian interest in Thoreau as a naturist, distinct from the greater contemporary European interest in Thoreau as a social critic.) In other words, not just *Walden* but the entire Thoreau canon could be counted on to provide the kind of inspiration for which Thoreau was noted. "If your lot be ever cast in some remote region of our simple country," writes the same critic, "he can do you, when you will, a rare service, stimulating your eye to see, and your ear to hear, in all the little commonplaces about you."[22] From this standpoint, Thoreau looms not as author of a series of texts between covers but as a voice, indeed as a companion, sharing his love of nature with the reader through all his volumes. Even a reader who, like this one, recognized that *Walden* was Thoreau's best book was not likely to argue that it dwarfed the rest.

The American Image of Thoreau at the Turn of the Century

My emphasis on publisher promotion of Thoreau might suggest that Houghton, Mifflin was solely responsible for the late-century Thoreau revival and the terms under which Thoreau was revived. That is hardly so. To be sure, publishers then and now exert influence over what the public reads (if a book isn't available, it isn't read) and the terms under which a new book is discussed (the reviews scholars most often cite to demonstrate "public" reception have always been subject to publisher manipulations). Yet rather than infer a publishing conspiracy theory whereby Houghton, Mifflin arranged for Thoreau's canonization, it would be fairer to surmise that despite such backing he almost did not make it. Before 1880, no book by Thoreau achieved an average sale of more than 200 copies annually; in the 1890s, the firm sold only 310 copies of its first edition of Thoreau's collected works, the ten-volume Riverside edition; and the "Walden" edition of 1906 was not reprinted for decades. In short, while the support of a prestigious publisher certainly did not hurt Thoreau's cause, it hardly guaranteed his success.

An alternative theory, traditionally preferred by Thoreauvians, credits Thoreau's late-century disciples with the crucial role, particularly such figures as: Blake, whose editorial contributions have been noted and who also popularized Thoreau's work by giving public readings at the Concord School of Philosophy and elsewhere; British reformer Henry Salt, who wrote the first important biography; and the raspish, indefatigable Michigan doctor and professor Samuel A. Jones. Yet one also must beware of overcrediting the Thoreau vanguard. Yes, Salt had a lot to do with raising sympathetic consciousness of Thoreau as culture critic, especially abroad. Yes, Blake's nature- and philosophy-oriented presentation of Thoreau as journalizer helped to establish Thoreau as a sage and spiritual pilgrim. Yet contemporaries like Emerson and Thomas Wentworth Higginson had been playing fundamentally similar tunes for a quarter of a century; and their literary connections and prestige were for a generation after Thoreau's death much greater than his. So even though the continued entrepreneurialism of true believers was important in pushing Thoreau to the fore, it does not explain why he emerged when he emerged, or even why the critical establishment ever accepted his claims to greatness. If we lean too hard on a disciple-promotion theory, we risk falling into a kind of simplification no better than alleging that Thoreau had to emerge because he was great. It is more reasonable to assume that Thoreau's advocates, be they individual disciples or editorial staff (and people like Allen and Torrey combined these roles) could not have succeeded if history had not already been running their way—meaning that the inchoate complex of social habits and attitudes we call culture was reorienting itself toward the end of the nineteenth century in such a way as to redound to Thoreau's benefit. To understand Thoreau's canonization, we finally have to drag the whole of American civilization in.

When we do *that,* we risk error of still another sort: overgeneralizing on the basis of abstractions like "history" or "America." As a way of containing the risk, we need to sift further through the presentations of Thoreau in the several dozen textbook codifications of American literary history published between the Civil War and World War I, with a view to highlighting the prevailing strategies of justification supporting the upgraded view of Thoreau's achievement at the turn of the century. Here if anywhere, in these standardized compendiums often designed for school and college use, one might hope to find a codification of the middle-of-the-road consensus of the educated about who the major American authors are and why. This analysis still does not get at the grass roots reaction—the reaction, for example, of students who might have resisted these assigned readings and the teachers who assigned them. But it does present the official turn-of-the-century version of Thoreau.

My study of publisher behavior has paradoxically shown that at the heart of the Houghton, Mifflin juggernaut, the discretionary role of the individual actor was crucial. As we look at the testimonies to follow, we may seem to see the reverse: the spectacle of voices blending together to create a composite late Victorian discourse of Thoreau. Yet dominant motifs there certainly were, the main one being the increasing tendency of these histories, after 1895, to accord Thoreau major figure status, in the form of an individual chapter or section devoted exclusively to him, comparable to the treatment of the previously canonized authors Houghton, Mifflin had long been promoting.

Five specific arguments were most often advanced to justify this revaluation of Thoreau—the fact of revaluation itself typically singled out for special comment as a most unusual phenomenon, in the manner of the Perry's astonishment at the apotheosis of the local crank. For in the early 1900s the idea that an author's reputation could abruptly shift seemed strikingly new. The chief arguments justifying Thoreau's promotion were: (1) that his originality relative to Emerson's was greater than had been supposed; (2) that Thoreau was America's best and most influential nature writer; (3) that he soared above mere nature writing into higher (more spiritual) realms; (4) that he was a good conscientious citizen and person, contrary to the charges of civic dereliction and misanthropy; and (5) that he was great in the courage and the character of his dissent.

The internal contradictions are obvious. More on them as we proceed.

Those who stressed Thoreau's originality reversed the debunking of the earliest literary histories, which pigeonholed Thoreau as Emerson's disciple, of narrower range than the master, whose chief claim to originality was "in the minutiae of description, only appreciable by professed naturalists." That assessment neatly stratified Thoreau as mediocre and confined him to a minor genre, whose achievement had only a coterie appeal. As another history condescendingly put it, "His poems of observation were good, and, like a pointer-dog, he could fix his gaze upon an object for a long time at a stretch." This remained a minority position. But in the more apologetic commentary of the 1890s and the years after, it gets recast in the form of tributes to Thoreau's difference from Emerson: "No one has lived so close to nature and written of it so intimately, as Thoreau." The influence of Emerson on Thoreau, argued another historian, went in the other direction as well: "Emerson was blind to obvious processes of nature until Thoreau opened his eyes." Thoreau now seemed "the parent of the out-of-door school of writers represented by John Burroughs" and a number of other figures this same scholar goes on to list. Yet "not the best of his disciples," continues another commentator, "can reach his upper notes."[23]

These commentators held up Thoreau's status as the father of a genre to his credit rather than as a sign of his minor status. This change reflected the increase in production, sales, and critical praise of nonfiction nature writing in America in the late nineteenth century, which in turn reflected the rise of preservationist and (more broadly) anti-industrialist sentiment, not to mention the influence of what has been called the heyday of natural history writing in Britain, from Gilbert White to Charles Darwin and (in a more specifically literary vein) Richard Jefferies. A combination of international literary fashion and future shock seems to have helped stimulate a following for the brand of artful meditative observation featured in middle and late Thoreau and highlighted in Blake's season books. The late Victorian era saw the "invention" of the wilderness vacation, scouting, and summer camps; the rise of markets of all sorts for camping and woodcraft items; the proliferation of outing and garden clubs; the acceleration of previously fitful efforts at wildlife protection. These and other forms of organized naturism were characteristic symptoms of ambivalence toward modernism (medievalism and orientalism being two other forms of recoil) that made late nineteenth-century American thought more internally divided about the question of "progress" than any previous era.[24] Out-of-door literature spoke eloquently to this condition.

In this respect, the agenda of the American literary establishment at the turn of the century differed from all other epochs of American literary history since its emergence as an autonomous force during the antebellum period. From the standpoint of mid-nineteenth-century American literary critics, the genres of the nature essay and the nature book did not exist, although nature poetry did. From a mid-twentieth-century literary historian's standpoint, they no longer existed in the sense that the ordinary business of literary analysis had become more focused on the fictive modes of poetry, prose fiction, and drama. At the turn of the century, however, readers were readier than in the previous or next generation to take seriously Thoreau's credentials as the founder of what later came to look like a mere enclave canon.

The ascription of a Thoreau-founded legacy was historically simplistic (as I argue in the Appendix), but it fit the agreed-upon facts. Especially among the northeastern practitioners, the politics of quotation makes it very clear that Thoreau had become the key precursor. William Bartram, Thomas Jefferson, John James Audubon, Alexander Wilson, indeed all the colonial and early national natural history writers had largely faded from memory—as creative writers, anyhow. A generation after Thoreau, John Burroughs, America's leading nature essayist at the turn of the twentieth century, wrote about Thoreau almost as eighteenth-century and romantic poets wrote about Milton: as the imposing precursor whose shadow he must disown or destroy to establish his own legitimacy. Lesser literary naturalists paid Thoreau great deference, as in the following passage from Joseph Jackson's book of essays *Through Glade and Mead* (1894):

> Thoreau led the way, and the number of his disciples is increasing, though they follow the master with unequal steps. Where a hundred persons read one of Thoreau's books on their publication, a thousand have now learned to look forward with pleasure to a new outdoor book by Burroughs . . .
> . . . What White did for Selbourne and Jefferies for Coate was done as effectually, but entirely in his own way, by Thoreau. As Aias stood preeminent among the Argives by the measure of his head and broad shoulders, so stands Thoreau among men who have loved Nature. He stands alone, not to be compared with others, for he is incomparable.[25]

Just what it was that put Thoreau in a different category from his successors was never precisely identified. Commentators referred to his dexterity as a verbal artist, to his mysticism, to his bookishness, to his cantankerous tone. They groped to define the Thoreauvian difference without, as yet, having a refined enough critical apparatus to make the necessary distinctions. No one defined the metaphorical structure of *Walden* until 1941, when F. O. Matthiessen pointed out, in *American Renaissance,* the correlation between images of seasonal change and the theme of spiritual metamorphosis.[26] By comparison, turn-of-the-century commentators praised Thoreau impressionistically for possessing "the power of making sentences and paragraphs artistically beautiful," but exactly how Thoreau accomplished that effect remained opaque to them.

In defense of Thoreau as more than simply a nature essayist literary historians resorted to the final strategies of justification listed above: the resolute normalization of Thoreau as a good citizen and respectable figure, and the praise of Thoreau as a social conscience. Literary historians pursuing both these arguments clearly had to dwell up to a point on Thoreau's closeness to nature—those arguing the former stressing the charm and coziness of his rapport and portraiture, those arguing the latter, Thoreau's wildness as antisocial hermit. But having done that, it was also in the interest of both to turn Thoreau away from nature, again for different reasons. All this we can easily see by comparing the work of two quite different Thoreauvians.

Thomas Wentworth Higginson, mentioned earlier as a younger transcendentalist and admiring friend of both Emerson and Thoreau, sought to make Thoreau look appealing to establishment literati and mainstream readers in a series of critical writings extending over almost half a century. In 1903 he coauthored with Henry Walcott Boynton a textbook history of American literature. Predictably, the Thoreau discussion starts by challenging James Russell Lowell, whose critique of forty years earlier still stood as the most imposing disparagement, being from the pen of America's most eminent critic.[27] "Lowell accepts throughout," the authors state, "the popular misconception . . . that Thoreau hated civilization, and believed only in wilderness." In truth, however, Thoreau was never "really banished from the world," nor did "he seek or profess banishment." He earned "an honest living by gardening and land-surveying"; furthermore, "his home life—always the best test—was thoroughly affectionate and faithful."[28] Higginson and Boynton saw the Walden experiment's significance in its being a test of simple living and a means to execute the task of producing a literary classic. This interpretation might be called the "bourgeois reduction of Thoreau": Thoreau as thrifty latter-day Puritan who follows what all sensible readers of his enduringly absorbing work will recognize as a legitimate and productive calling.

By contrast, John Macy's *Spirit of American Literature* (1913) sought to make Thoreau look appealing precisely because of his opposition to genteel norms. Macy seems to echo Higginson and Boynton when he says, "Thoreau does not, as some people imagine, argue the case for the wilderness against the town; on the contrary, he loves best the cultivated land with people on it. He merely uses the wilderness to try himself in." But Macy intends by pulling Thoreau back into society, not to legitimate him but to strengthen his credentials as a social radical, as "the one anarchist of great literary power in a nation of slavish conformity to legalism." Macy, indeed, was the first American critic to put Thoreau's "Civil Disobedience" on the same plane of importance as *Walden*. And he was very conscious of this innovation, noting impatiently for example that Thoreau's essays "Wild Apples" and "The Succession of Forest Trees" had been schoolbook anthology pieces for a quarter of a century, whereas "the ringing revolt of the essay on 'Civil Disobedience' is still silenced under the thick respectability of our times." Macy praised *Walden* as

Thoreau's masterpiece, but as a social gospel rather than for its skill at representing nature, which he commended perfunctorily. Macy repeated the Higginson-Boynton diagnosis that Thoreau "merely uses the wilderness to try himself in," but to the end of subordinating Thoreau the nature writer to Thoreau the social critic.[29]

Thus the early twentieth century saw efforts both to rehabilitate Thoreau as a good mainstream American and to promote him as a radical dissenter. Often these antithetical arguments commingled, as in Bliss Perry's analysis of Thoreau's support for John Brown, quoted earlier. Macy, however, refused to play the juggler and pushed the image of a radical Thoreau farther than any of his colleagues. The divergence of views is one infallible sign that an author has achieved canonical status: sharply differing codifications of history seek to claim him or her. Macy's appraisal is also notable as a foretaste of the next epoch in American Thoreau criticism. Higginson and Boynton did nothing more than embroider on the original ground of defense established by Emerson in his 1862 essay on Thoreau (the other influential mid-century evaluation, along with Lowell's): namely, that Thoreau was an exceptional naturist who had his crotchets yet remained a loyal American withal. Macy's argument was not wholly original either, being already current in radical circles.[30] But Macy was the first to locate "the spirit of American literature" in the quarrels of selected great figures with established American institutions. In him we see the origin of the so-called antinomian theory of American literature—the theory that the major American writers have been visionary dissenters—that came to dominate American scholarship between the 1920s and the 1960s. This shift had a great deal to do with changing public impressions of who the great American writers were (thus Melville became canonized, Longfellow decanonized), how to interpret their works (thus a Kafkaesque vision of Hawthorne superseded the earlier Jamesean vision of Hawthorne as an urbane stylist), and which of their works seemed important (hence the rise of academic if not popular interest in Melville's most nihilistic work, *The Confidence-Man*).

Thoreau as Critic and Artist

Higginson's opinions typified the turn-of-the-century consensus that produced Thoreau's acceptance into the first American canon. In terms of that consensus, Thoreau had gained in stature relative to 1860 because his eccentricities seemed forgivable if not positively wholesome to this era of back-to-naturism, his books had measurable influence, the nature essay was more esteemed and widely practiced in America than during his own lifetime, and his obvious though indescribable excellence within that genre made Thoreau look more like Emerson's complement than his imitator. The Emerson connection now worked in Thoreau's favor rather than to his detriment. Bliss Perry gave a clear sense of the way the wind was blowing when he advised his boss that sales of Thoreau would benefit from the piggyback effect of the Emerson centenary, as did the firm itself when it offered to distribute Emerson's 1862 essay on Thoreau as a pamphlet, free of charge, to anyone inquiring about purchase of the "Walden" edition. Nina Baym has shown that the first American canon was based on a vision of the canonized writers as a kind of family group rather than as isolated individual geniuses.[31] That same logic certainly applies to how both publishers and literary historians initially treated the Thoreau-Emerson link. This close affiliation of the two transcendentalist geniuses—first through biography and later through a combination of publisher monopoly and collective memory shaped by a half-century of critical essays, literary histories, anthologies, advertisements, and other publisher manipulations—may indeed have been more important than any other factor in ensuring Thoreau's canonization at an early date, compared to other American Renaissance figures now considered major who still languished in doubtful repute at the turn of the century.

Yet even as Thoreau won his place in the first American canon alongside the traditional New England pantheon, the second canon that would displace it was in the process of being formed. To a larger degree than the first, this canon was based on a great artist theory of literary history (the isolated genius, qualitatively different from the herd, who goes against the grain), a canon whose nineteenth-century heroes would include such figures as Edgar Allan Poe, Walt Whitman, and Mark Twain. This newer vision eventually had major consequences for how Thoreau was read. Macy's work anticipates this effect. Macy suspected that framing Thoreau as a literary naturist was a strategy of sanitization. Had Macy read everything Higginson had ever written on Thoreau's behalf he might well have said "aha!"—because what drew Higginson to Thoreau and what kept him there was the image of Thoreau as the perceiver of beautiful, unexpected, microscopic truths about the flora and fauna of his own backyard. To do Higginson justice, the one-time fire-breathing abolitionist also admired Thoreau the dissenter; but that is not what he chiefly talked about when he talked about Thoreau in public. Macy, however, unencumbered by Bostonian proprieties, was quick to perceive an alignment between the second, third, and fourth of the turn-of-the-century justifications for elevating Thoreau: Thoreau the naturist, Thoreau as something loftier than mere nature writer, and Thoreau as good citizen.[32]

Just what caused the gradual displacement of the first "genteel canon" by the conception of an "oppositional canon" is a question too complex and incompletely excavated to be answered fully here.[33] Undoubtedly the change was quickened, on the one hand, by the emergence of an American radical intellectual establishment and, on the other hand, by the prestige of modernist experimentalism in literature and criticism, both of which took root early in the twentieth century, and each of which set a high value on certain forms of dissenting expression: American traditions of protest for the former, and the stylistic and conceptual individuality of major American authors for the latter. In the long run, this reconception of the representative, admirable American writer as a dissenting genius certainly furthered the growth of Thoreau's prestige, although in the short run his acceptance into the first canon was, ironically, a stumbling block for some insurgents. The most careful study of Thoreau's political reputation argues that Thoreau criticism until the late 1920s remained deadlocked in a redundant controversy over whether or not he was primarily a nature writer.[34]

The autobiographies of two of the architects of what I have called the second or oppositional canon shed light on this problem. Van Wyck Brooks recalled the overbearing nostalgic anecdotalism of a local schoolteacher who had a sentimental friendship with H. G. O. Blake ("they walked together to Thoreau's grave and rowed on Walden Pond, which was desecrated already by human innovation. For there were boat-houses on the beach and boats full of noisy girls profaned the spot where Thoreau had once embarked"). Young Brooks was forced to view Thoreau through a lens of prissy, fastidious respectability that must have reinforced his trenchant indictment of New England culture's thinness in *The Wine of the Puritans* (1909) and *Coming of Age in America* (1915). It was not until the 1920s that Brooks took Thoreau seriously as a major, positive force in the history of American literature and thought, and then only because his interest was aroused by praise of Thoreau by Irish writer George Russell ("AE"), for whom Thoreau had served as a model of cultural naturalism.[35] Likewise, Waldo Frank came to think of Thoreau as America's first great writer only after long prejudice to the contrary. "When we were boys," reminisced Frank, "we all had tedious uncles who professed to be very fond of Thoreau. They said that Thoreau was a great naturalist; that he wrote delightfully of butterflies and mushrooms. These uncles were typical good citizens of old America: altogether dull—mindless and sober paragons. We decided that their favorite author could be no favorite of ours. We took it for granted that Thoreau also was a stuffy bore."[36] The converted Frank found the "real" *Walden* of course not in the *Walden* of "Sounds" and "Brute Neighbors" but in the *Walden* of "Economy."

If Brooks and Frank read Thoreau's naturism as insipidly respectable, their reading owed more to historical circumstances than to the actual nature of his writing, as became clear a half-century later, when environmental activists advanced a green Thoreau. Indeed, even by the turn of the century, if not before, a pastoral anarchist version of Thoreau was being advanced in the utopian novels of William Lloyd, who invented America's first band of fictional hippies, led by a cultivated pagan named Forrest Westwood, who reads Greek and Latin but makes his own clothing and cites Thoreau as inspiration.[37] That this version of Thoreau did not prevail testifies to the institutional control of interpretation wielded by his more powerful late-century constituencies: his aging transcendentalist admirers, his editors, and fellow natural history enthusiasts. As things stood, the disaffections of Brooks and Frank presaged a long concerted attempt during the 1920s and 1930s to pry Thoreau loose from naturism. For Thoreau to "take his due place as one of the three or four most original men of letters America has produced," declared Odell Shepard in 1920, it must be made clear "that he was not a naturalist, and did not even wish to be one."[38] In that spirit, Vernon L. Parrington, in the most important American history of American letters before World War II (1927), defined Thoreau as a radical "economist," the heir of Rousseau and William Godwin, whose "one concern, that gave to his ramblings in Concord fields a value as of high adventure, was to explore the true meaning of wealth." Thoreau "was the completest embodiment of the *laissez-faire* reaction against a regimented social order, the severest critic of the lower economics that frustrate the dreams of human freedom." In this reading, which "firmly established Thoreau's reputation as a social thinker" as Meyer rightly says, Thoreau's naturism counted as a vehicle of social satire, nothing more.[39]

This populist version of Thoreau turned out to be well suited for the decade of the Depression, when "Thoreau first really came into his own" as an American popular hero, chiefly on the basis of his social disaffection.[40] Sometime literary naturist Henry S. Canby, author of the best American prewar biography of Thoreau, had to admit in 1939 that the naturist image was outdated ("already Burroughs and Muir fade"), that the basis for what Canby took to be Thoreau's burgeoning fame was the reformist image that had originated more in Britain than in America, where "in my own youth he was known to us as a man who wrote about birds and animals for children." Thoreau's prestige had dramatically risen, Canby thought, because he had been discovered to be "perhaps . . . the greatest critic of values among modern writers in English."[41] In a later, strongly Parringtonian article, Canby compared Thoreau and Whitman as anticapitalist rebels who "each in his way constantly maintained that the prime evil was not in the unequal distribution of this new-world wealth (though that was bad enough) but in the destruction of all true values for happiness, when the best energies of a country were geared to money-making."[42]

Meanwhile, Thoreau's artistic conscience started to seem as crucial a subject as his social conscience, for academics if not for ordinary citizens. Matthiessen made the major breakthrough, equivalent to Macy's in boldness and Parrington's in influence. Matthiessen aimed to intertwine social with literary criticism, raising both to a higher plane of sophistication than had yet been reached; but he ended up, as far as Thoreau Studies was concerned, bringing new critical formalist analysis to bear in a major revaluation of Thoreau as artist that established *Walden* as a triumph of form and defined the succession from Emerson to Thoreau not as a succession from master to disciple or model to enactment but from literary promise to "actual glory." More aggressively than any precursor, Matthiessen made the case for Thoreau as a better writer than Emerson, as the one transcendentalist to compose a classic work. In the process, Matthiessen carefully paid tribute to Thoreau's social message (*Walden* "became a bible for many of the leaders of the British labor movement after Morris"), and he tried to ward off rarefaction by comparing Thoreau's masterpiece to fine artisanal labor, like clipper ships and Shaker cabinetry. But finally what he celebrated was the aesthetics of the literary text, its "organic form," its "structural wholeness."[43] He set the tone for the academic Thoreauvians of the next generation. It is evident in the other critical reading of Thoreau from the 1940s that has endured, Stanley Edgar Hyman's "Henry Thoreau in Our Time" (1946), a tribute to "Civil Disobedience" which enlists that essay, indeed the whole reformist aspect of Thoreau, under the heading of art. "Thoreau's political value, for us," is as an exemplum of "the honest artist struggling for terms on which he can adjust to society *in his capacity as artist.*"[44]

This containment of Thoreau's challenge to society within a vision of him as artist, accompanied by concurrent depoliticization of Thoreau the dissenter into a solitary spiritual quester who turned away from the public arena, became hallmarks of what is now referred to as the Cold War criticism of the late 1940s and 1950s.[45] Commentators did not eradicate the image of Thoreau the dissenting thinker (the 1950s was also the decade of George Hendrick's study of Thoreau's influence on Tolstoy and Gandhi),[46] but they sublimated and subdued it. Thoreau was "a very reluctant crusader" who "never supposed that social organization itself was an interesting subject"; for him "social ethics were personal ethics, and the only valuable reform was self-reform." I quote from Joseph Wood Krutch and Sherman Paul, the foremost Thoreau biographers of the period.[47] In general, apoliticism and consensus myths of cultural continuity dominated American literary and historical studies for the nonce. "Thoreau was popular in the United States during the 1950s," remarks Meyer in a pardonable hyperbole, "largely because he was perceived as apolitical rather than political."[48]

Yet Thoreau commentary was hardly a mere reflex of public events. On the contrary, to at least as great an extent the academic professionalization of American letters that had been underway since the 1920s drove the conventions of literary criticism. Both Parrington and Matthiessen contributed indispensably to that movement, but Parrington was an extraordinarily ambivalent pioneer, with a pragmatist's distrust of belletristic criticism, whereas Matthiessen, while also distrusting academic establishments, had a more Jamesean and also a more "professorial" sensibility, relishing complex aesthetic form and practicing a rhetoric of indirection and intricacy. These preferences made him a convenient model—beyond what he would have wished or anticipated—for more specialized formalist exercises, culminating in 1968 in Charles Anderson's celebration of *Walden* as a linguistic artifact whose figural richness and motival networks constitute its greatest interest.[49] The academic professionalization of the 1950s also led to J. Lyndon Shanley's publication, with historical commentary, of the earliest draft of *Walden,* a harbinger of the more intensively specialized industry of Thoreau textual studies that has followed.[50]

The development of technical vocabularies within academic Thoreau criticism created a rift between Thoreau specialist and Thoreauvian, sometimes within the same individual, that has steadily widened since the 1940s.[51] Nevertheless, a shareable version of Thoreau as sturdy individualist—whether radical, conservative, or apolitical—remained a ground on which professors and laypeople could continue to communicate, as for instance at the annual meetings of the diverse constituency of the Thoreau Society, founded serendipitously in 1941, the year of *American Renaissance,* the book in which the professionalization of Thoreau Studies may also be said to have come of age.[52]

The stratification of Thoreauvian commentary had become irreversible by the late 1960s, with the revival, on the one hand, of the radical Thoreau to a height of public prominence never before attained, alongside the burgeoning, on the other, of increasingly specialized academic study of Thoreau's thought and literary craftsmanship.[53] Since then, Thoreau Studies has become such a large and balkanized operation that even most specialists do not try to follow it all, while the popular enshrinement of Thoreau as a countercultural icon has taken on a life of its own that no establishment will likely ever be able to control—if indeed it ever did. But rather than trace all the branches of these subplots I want to turn back to the subject of the green Thoreau, who seems to have atrophied sometime during the 1920s.

Whatever their differences, the Parringtonian economist shared with the Matthiessenian craftsman a tendency to minimize Thoreau's interest in physical nature. It was Thoreau's conversion of the Walden experience into a social product that excited them (into a gospel of political economy, into an aesthetic design that marked American literary culture's coming of age) rather than the experience of environmental immersion or awakening. This emphasis applied even to the Thoreaus invented by a number of contemporaries with formidable naturist credentials of their own. Canby is a case in point. Likewise, Sherman Paul, whose conviction and amplitude on the subject of green American writing has been exceeded by no Thoreau scholar, in his interpretation of *Walden* as a symbolic poem stated that nature was "only the middle term in the progression from a lower to a higher society: nature was not Thoreau's final goal, but rather the place of renewal."[54] This summation implies that nature could not have been a primary object of interest for him, that it must have interested him for ulterior reasons, for some higher use to which it could be put. Canby's psychobiographical theory of Thoreau's naturism as driven by disappointment in love implied the same. As Krutch dryly observed, "Thoreau himself would have been astonished at the suggestion that a passion for nature was inexplicable except on the theory that it substituted for some other passion which had been frustrated."

Yet Krutch himself, though he recognized more clear-sightedly than most Thoreauvians of the era the central importance of Thoreau's bond to nature as a motivational force in his life and work, nonetheless hesitated to press this line of thought vigorously in his biography. Of the late *Journal,* Krutch remarked that "the delight which Thoreau took in nature is no more explicable to those who cannot share his pleasure . . . than the delight of a Pepys or a Boswell is explicable to those who do not share their interest in a different sort of social intercourse."[55] If Krutch shared Thoreau's crochet, he was too sheepish to confess it openly here, even though he was at that very moment in the process of being inspired by Thoreau to begin his own second career as a distinguished literary naturist with *The Twelve Seasons* (1949). So for the present Krutch went on to the safer ground of Thoreau as individualist thinker and as literary artist. Such was the incubus of the old nature-watcher image. Yet as it happened, that old image was soon to take on new life, and Krutch himself was to be one of the agents of transformation.

The Revival of the Green Thoreau

Two years later, Krutch made Thoreau the centerpiece of his anthology *Great American Nature Writing,* prefaced by the most elaborate history of the premodern phases of the genre that had yet been written. Here and in a series of concurrent articles, he sought to define the distinctive contribution that entitled Thoreau to be granted pride of place as the "real inventor" of modern nature writing. Krutch cited in particular Thoreau's genuine sense of intimate "fellowship" with the natural world, a more reciprocal ethos than that of Saint Francis, who chiefly preached to other creatures.[56] His praise of Thoreau's work as a reproach to anthropocentrism exemplified and helped to further the most distinctive of the three principal ways in which Thoreau's naturism has been revived during the past several decades.

One has been the revived interest in Thoreau as a natural scientist. Although local ornithologists and botanists had continued to make use of Thoreau's field observations, starting in the 1940s, with the rise of ecological biology, stronger claims began to be made on Thoreau's behalf. Both historians of science and literary scholars asserted that despite his lack of formal training and lack of influence on the course of scientific research, he ought to be reckoned a pioneer ecologist on the strength of his studies in limnology and forest succession.[57] Since then, to a much greater degree than formerly, Thoreau's observations have been drawn upon in mainstream scientific literature. In a survey of Thoreau references in the *Science Citation Index* from the mid-1950s to 1983, Robin McDowell found that during the last seven years of this period, "Thoreau was cited over four times per year, which compares favorably with 8.2 times per year for the average working scientist"—a level sustained throughout the 1980s. In the index Thoreau runs even with Muir and surpasses George Perkins Marsh. Some of these citations are passing references ("Since Thoreau's observation was made, there has been little improvement in our understanding of shoreline vegetation"), but many rely on Thoreau's findings as support for their own: for example, a 1972 article on the behavior of white-breasted nuthatches, a 1986 study of forest succession, and a 1988 discussion titled "Character and Distribution of American Chestnut Sprouts."[58] This increased interest in Thoreau's empirical observations has been reflected in literary scholarship also. Two of the major Thoreau biographies of the 1980s provide good examples. William Howarth, in *The Book of Concord* (1982), gives unprecedented emphasis to Thoreau's late natural history investigations; Robert Richardson, Jr., in *Henry David Thoreau: A Life of the Mind* (1986), stresses Thoreau's seriousness as a reader of science, his contacts with scientists at Harvard, and the comparative foresightedness of his receptivity to

Darwin's *Origin of Species*. Howarth notes that the Concord town clerk, recording Thoreau's death, listed his occupation as "natural historian"; Richardson points out that Thoreau was appointed in 1859 to the Harvard Committee for Examination in Natural History, charged with the oversight of Asa Gray's department.[59]

The revisionary push to validate Thoreau's scientific credentials is bound to continue as editors of the Princeton edition of his works reedit the later volumes of Thoreau's *Journal* and as more of his late natural history manuscripts are published, particularly "The Dispersion of Seeds," of which "The Succession of Forest Trees" was a kind of digest or interim statement.[60] However, most modern Thoreauvians, whether literary scholars or scientists or laypeople, have been and no doubt will continue to be more interested in the philosophical, intellectual, and historical aspects of Thoreau's naturism.

A second modern emphasis, accordingly, has been on Thoreau's epistemology of nature. Joel Porte portrayed Thoreau as an empiricist, reacting against Emerson's idealism, an approach Victor Friesen developed in his study of Thoreau's sensuousness. James McIntosh treated Thoreau's "shifting stance toward nature" against the background of traditions of romantic self-consciousness. Stanley Cavell represented *Walden* as a post-Kantian recovery of the thing-in-itself by apprehending nature's "nextness to me"; Sharon Cameron approached Thoreau's *Journal* as a heroically quixotic attempt to render "the wholeness of nature" in a text; H. Daniel Peck explored the phenomenology of the perceptual structures in terms of which Thoreau saw nature. These six studies derive partly from Krutch's and Paul's understanding of Thoreau as an intellectual quester insofar as they also emphasize the importance of defining a central unfolding Thoreauvian sensibility or mental orientation or intellectual project. What distinguishes them is the decidedness and the increasing descriptive specificity with which they locate that central project in Thoreau's transactions with the physical environment. In the eighties John Hildebidle and Joan Burbick went so far as to define Thoreau's entire intellectual and literary aspiration as a kind of revisionary natural history project.[61] None of these scholars have any doubt that the natural environment was of the first importance in Thoreau's thought; none make any apologies for the seriousness of Thoreau's interest in it.

The third, most assertive note in modern discussions of Thoreau's naturism, however, has been the one struck in the passages of Krutch's essays noted above, the preemption of Thoreau as an environmentalist prophet. This image certainly did not originate in 1950; it can be traced back to Emerson's backhanded tribute to him as the attorney of the indigenous plants.[62] Various intervening commentaries mention Thoreau's preservationism; in their biographies, Canby and Krutch note in passing that he would have opposed the later desacralization of wilderness. But whereas issues like preservationism and ecological ethics are tangential to most precontemporary Thoreau commentary, today they are more central; and they tend to yield an image of his naturism different from both the green Thoreau of his first canonizers and the two kinds of commentary just discussed. At the turn of the century, discussions of Thoreau as naturist, as we have seen, generally neutralized his more confrontational tendencies. This mentality persisted for a long time. In 1935 botanist and literary naturist Donald Culross Peattie, a Thoreau admirer, had to admit that Thoreau's "view of the natural world will not answer to our needs today. He has no sense of problem. But," Peattie added, "if he had known what we know—space expanding, elements no longer elemental, life as a battle—he would, I venture, have come out of his thicket and joined the fight."[63] In the last third of the twentieth century, Thoreau has in fact been enlisted; and his allegiance to nature is more regularly linked to the element of oppositionalism in his thought that used to be disassociated from it. Thoreau "saw that American capitalism was set on a course that would ultimately ravage all wild nature on the continent—perhaps even in the world." He "sympathized with nature and criticized human society for destroying it." He "saw unchecked profiteering set on a collision course that ultimately would devour all wild nature on the continent." "Nothing less than a conviction as passionate as Thoreau's can resist the process which, unless determinedly arrested, will end in the elimination of every animal except man (and presently man himself) from the terrestrial globe."[64] These typically vehement statements from the early 1970s (the first by Thomas Merton, the last by Krutch) reflected the prior invocation of Thoreau, during the 1960s, by Sierra Club and other environmental activists, who circulated and recirculated such Thoreauvian dicta as "What is the use of a house if you haven't got a tolerable planet to put it on?" and "In wildness is the preservation of the world" (which in 1962 supplied the title for a popular Sierra Club publication of a sheaf of Eliot Porter color photographs, with an introduction by Krutch, each photo captioned by a Thoreau quotation).[65] The scholarly works most influential in promoting this image of Thoreau were perhaps Leo Marx's *Machine and the Garden* (1964), which emphasized Thoreau's pastoralist critique of emerging industrial capitalism; Roderick Nash's *Wilderness and the American Mind* (1967, 1973, 1982), which credited Thoreau with making "the classic early call for wilderness preservation"; and Donald Worster's *Nature's Economy* (1977), the first and still the most comprehensive intellectual history of Anglo-American ecological thought, which honored Thoreau as one of its greatest harbingers.[66]

Edward Abbey's revision of the closing words of Emerson's eulogy to Thoreau, in his own defense of the subversive potency of Thoreau's naturism, epitomizes the contrast between early and late images of green Thoreau. Emerson had written, "Wherever there is knowledge, wherever there is virtue, wherever there is beauty, he will find a home."[67] Abbey rewrote as follows: "Wherever there are deer and hawks, wherever there is liberty and danger, wherever there is wilderness, wherever there is a living river, Henry Thoreau will find his eternal home." Emerson gathered Thoreau up into the higher reaches of moral idealism; Abbey reinterpreted Thoreau's love of nature as a counterestablishment stance. In the same spirit as Emerson, Barrett Wendell, the most sophisticated of the early literary historians, capped his discussion of Thoreau by citing the "well-known" last paragraph of "Spring" ("Early in May, the oaks, hickories, maples, and other trees . . . imparted a brightness like sunshine to the landscape" [*Wa* 318]) as a model of Thoreau's "delicate sensitiveness." Abbey, by contrast, took as *his* quotation from the end of "Spring" the portion of the previous paragraph where Thoreau recalls the "dead horse in the hollow by the path to my house" and "the assurance it gave me," despite the stick, "of the strong appetite and inviolable health of Nature" (*Wa* 318).[68] What William Blake wrote about the Bible applies to Thoreauvian scripture: "Both read the Bible day & night, / But thou readst black where I read white."[69]

Not all contemporary environmental historians, ecophilosophers, and environmental activists worship at Thoreau's shrine; even those that do sometimes genuflect perfunctorily. Not everyone would agree with the prominence accorded Thoreau as a patron saint of ecologism by Nash and especially by Worster.[70] Not everyone would assent to the political valence of Thoreau the environmentalist. Leo Marx, for example, has tended to locate Thoreau's oppositionalism in his economic and social criticism much more than in his pastoralism per se, whereas for Max Oelschlaeger Thoreau's pastoralism opens onto a radical wilderness ethic that Marx, who emphasizes Thoreau's commitment to the "middle land-scape" of traditional pastoral as a literary ideal rather than as a social program, per se, declines to associate with him.[71] Some Thoreauvians would strongly resist the idea that the green Thoreau is the "essential" Thoreau. But it has become much harder in the 1990s than it was a half-century ago to insist that nature was "at bottom" a nominal concern for Thoreau and that his devotion to nature can be separated from his reform interests. It is no accident that the published proceedings of the 1991 Thoreau Jubilee commemorating the fiftieth anniversary of the founding of the Thoreau Society allotted the most space to collections of papers under the headings "The Ecology of Walden Woods" and "Thoreau and the Tradition of American Nature Writing."[72] The "Deep ecologists," in particular, have questioned whether political and social engineering can cope with environmental issues in the absence of more fundamental attitudinal change and advocated reverence for nature and a life of self-restrained simplicity as keys to political and social change. Their position may be contested but not dismissed out of hand.[73] It reinforces radical environmentalist history's image of Thoreau "as the spiritual founder of the modern crusade to preserve what is left of our wilderness," as a recent popular account puts it.[74] It has made Thoreau's naturism a more widely attractive formation among Thoreauvians. Its centrality as a touchstone for understanding Thoreau, and his place in American culture, is at this point likely to be enhanced rather than repressed by disagreements among contemporary naturist readings of Thoreau, for example on the question of whether his naturism was regressive or progressive. It is no coincidence that one of the main sections of the first issue of the first major scholarly journal specializing in what is coming to be called ecocriticism was a symposium on feminist approaches to Thoreau evaluating his work from diametrically opposite standpoints.[75] If literary history is to be reimagined under the sign of environment, Thoreau will certainly continue to be one of the key points of reference, even by those who expose his feet of clay.

Although the rise of environmental concern worldwide suggests that

the green Thoreau will continue to seem an important model and historical reference point, after the path we have traversed it is impossible
to imagine that public memory will not continue to evolve in ways we
cannot foresee. This much, however, can be said about the reinvention
of the old first-canon image of him in contemporary times. First, what
is most distinctive about it has primarily been defined not by literature
specialists but by cultural and social historians, by ecophilosophers and
concerned scientists, and by creative, journalistic, and environmental
activists responding to public events. Literary scholars, who compose the
majority of professional Thoreauvians, have by and large responded to
rather than led this wave of reinterpretation, as was also the case in the
late 1960s and 1970s with regard to the placement of Thoreau within the
history of American radical protests against statism and infringement of
civil rights. No doubt we have been relatively slow to respond for a variety
of reasons, including the discipline's long-standing commitment to textual analysis and the stigma attached to the old tradition of Thoreau the
naturist. It would be interesting to study the autobiographies of those
who eventually become Thoreau scholars to see how many of them fit
the profile of one whose "interest in Thoreau grew initially out of my
feeling for woods and fields and streams" but who went on to complete
a dissertation on Thoreau and abolitionism and write little about Thoreau's
nature interests.[76] Nothing would be more logical than for such a person
to become socialized into the same apprehension that Thoreau had of
the Greeks, that bonding to nature pertains to the childhood phase of
social existence, not to what society considers the serious pursuits of one's
own—or Thoreau's—maturity. Certainly I myself have felt such pressure.

For one disposed to regard naturism as atavistic, the reviving image
of the green Thoreau muddies the waters, by holding up as avant-garde
what seems no better than an adolescent fantasy. One who reckons the
romance of continuous technosocial development a more obnoxious kind
of fantasy will welcome this return of the repressed. But only an extreme
partisan of either view with a dogged disinterest in history could fail to
take a keen historical interest in how contemporary thinking about the
green Thoreau seems to have put in contact with one another avatars of
Thoreau previously set more at odds: the naturalist, the rebel, the artist.
If an such an image appears Janus-faced and opportunistic (setting
Thoreau on the latest bandwagon), it may by the same token help us

more than its predecessors to understand, retrieve, and benefit from both Thoreau and the company of Thoreauvians in all eras—both specialists and nonspecialists—who have directed our thinking to a greater degree than we might like to acknowledge. In particular, it may move us toward a vision of Thoreau that is more "ecological," not only in the sense of associating him more solidly with the history of environmental history but also in the more fundamental sense of contributing to the explanation of how to overcome the traditional opposition between the "naturist" and the "social protester." The hypothesis of Thoreau as "deep ecologist" helps us, for example, to bring into the open the sublimated social valences of Thoreau's late-life documentary notes on the environment by directing our attention to how "private" transactions with nature may be animated, at least in part, by the will to effect transformation of humankind's social identity and indeed the whole fabric of the social.

CHAPTER TWELVE

Text as Testament:
Reading Walden for the Author

⌇

What would his fame have been if he had attributed the pastoral retreat enacted in *Walden* to an avowedly fictive narrator?

—Leo Marx, "The Two Thoreaus"

The author: an imaginary person who writes real books.

—Edward Abbey, *A Voice Crying in the Wilderness*

EVEN IF THE PREVIOUS two chapters have been partly wrong, it seems certain that we literature scholars must unlearn some things in order to grasp the extent of Thoreau's reach. Here is a writer who neither before nor after death stayed put within the ordinary bounds of the literary, a writer the events of whose writings have been so interwoven with the events of actual existence on the one hand and cultural mythography on the other that at this distance the lines between text and life, text and culture, blur irretrievably. I suspect we could say the same of other literary heroines and heroes who have been, as we now oddly put it, "institutionalized" by posterity, although like Thoreau at the start of *Walden* (*Wa* 3), I shall try to bear in mind that the narrowness of my focus tempts me to overgeneralize from a single case. Yet Thoreau's case seems ground enough for suggesting that literary eminence depends on a wider and more complicated sense of what a text does than its linguistic and ideational properties, essential as those are. Furthermore, it is striking how shrewdly and self-consciously Thoreau's work itself reflects on these issues a century in advance of the professionalization of literary criticism and theory. *Walden* seems to define itself as aspiring literary classic in the form of self-reflexive personal testament. That makes it a work of considerable pertinence to contemporary critical theory, though in such a way as to raise a major question about Thoreau's credentials as an environmentalist prophet, a question we shall have to confront squarely if this book is to arrive at a happy ending.

Texts as Authorial Acts

Thoreau, we have seen, has become a canonical author; but what has been canonized? To what exactly do we refer when we use that term with reference to a literary figure? Certainly not to the entire body of his or her writing equally, as if *A Yankee in Canada* were as canonical as *Walden,* even though our overall sense of Thoreau's importance to American literary history causes scholars to take *Yankee* more seriously than the run of mid-nineteenth-century magazine excursion narratives from which *Yankee* is barely distinguishable. "Emily Dickinson" means, effectively, one or two hundred lyrics; "Frederick Douglass" still means his *Narrative* rather than the two later versions of his autobiography; *Leaves of Grass* means a small fraction of the poems in that bulky volume. As far as Thoreau is concerned, it is still unclear whether any of his works besides *Walden* and "Resistance to Civil Government" are canonical.

   Nor do we canonize whole works equally, except for short stories and lyrics. What about the whaling chapters in *Moby-Dick?* the denouement of *Huckleberry Finn?* Not only is it obvious that some parts of *Walden* are more canonical than others ("Where I Lived and What I Lived For" more than "Winter Animals") but also that the canonicity of Thoreau in the eyes of many rests on a Bartlett's *Quotations* smattering of obiter dicta like "The mass of men lead lives of quiet desperation" and "In Wildness is the preservation of the world."

   But a more fundamental question about canonicity is the extent to which it rests on a myth of the written text as against a myth of the author. Do we take a "Catholic" view of canonization and think "Thoreau," or a "Protestant" view and think *Walden, sola scriptura?* Literary theory favors the latter. T. S. Eliot, who saw literary history as a museum of great objects, imagined the creative act as a catalytic process in which the personality of the author was extinguished in the production of the text.[1]

Roland Barthes cautions us not to reinstate his ghost. To read a text as belonging to its nominal author is to impose a principle of authority that enslaves reader response.[2] Jacques Derrida stresses that the author is already displaced by text, so that even the signature is nothing more than a textual function.[3] Michel Foucault locates authors as nodal points within networks of discursive practices.[4] All finally discredit the notion of authoring as a proprietary fiction. But deauthorization then becomes a tyrannizing fiction in its turn, as Henry Louis Gates, Jr., observes:

> We started with a realization that the cogito . . . isn't simply a given, a subjectivity existing prior to, and independently from, language, from *écriture*. But the next thing you know, we're insisting that because of its factitious pedigree, the reflexive actor is simply epi-phe-nomenal, just an effect of linguistic or structural determination. And that, of course, is a *non sequitur* . . . Once we see the subject as imbricated in the broader matrix of social practices, the flux of social life, we find that the subject isn't only an effect of language, but a participant in an articulated realm of social practices that, far from constraining its agency, are its very conditions of possibility.[5]

Disjoin text from author and you lose, among other things, history. You lose the text as productive work, the text as act. You sacrifice the order of the body to the order of the text.[6]

In the case of a writer so autobiographical and rhetorical as Thoreau, yet also so bookishly convoluted and reluctantly disclosing, the questions of the relation between authorial *cogito* and textual persona take on special weight—all the more so in a study of the environmental imagination. Environmental history demonstrates the fallaciousness of imagining environments without agents responsible for influencing them. To imagine a literary history comprised of textual objects, or discursive practices, without responsible individual agents is as problematic from an environmentalist perspective as imagining a beautiful landscape without the traces of human shaping that have tailored it to the standards of the picturesque. Of course the opposite simplification, the reduction of textual representation to authorial intention or biography, is no more fruitful. In that event, text (or landscape) is in danger of being reduced to nothing more than an act of authorial will. In this chapter, then, I want to affirm that it is entirely legitimate for the terms of Thoreau's canonization to be shaped in no small degree by presuppositions about authorial agency, while not losing sight of the considerable dependence of one's construction of the figure of Thoreau on the evidence of his texts, and to affirm the importance of approaching his texts as authorial works, while not losing sight of their considerable dependence on conventions of discourse, ideology, and literary marketplace forces for their original utterance and continued circulation.

All Americanists know the stereotypical distinction between the Emersonian and the Thoreauvian personae. The figure we call Emerson has typically been defined as a set of memorable pronouncements, philosophical distinctions, and rhetorical moves. To that set of motifs Harold Bloom attaches the name of Emerson as the primal ancestor of all strong American poets. Thoreau, relatively speaking, has been seen much more as a great American *character,* on similar legendary and historical footing as Daniel Boone, Benjamin Franklin, and Abraham Lincoln.

Literary scholars know that this contrast is overdrawn. Stanley Edgar Hyman rightly claimed that Thoreauvian civil disobedience became historically influential not through Thoreau's biographical act but through his ability to write it up. On text rather than on the act prior to it Thoreau's activist credentials depend.[7] Nevertheless, although Thoreau's stature would not be what it is today had he not written eloquently, to a marked extent his stature depends not on his image *as* writer so much as on the image of Thoreau as a certain kind of person who led a certain kind of life. Especially for laypeople, but also for scholars to some degree, a myth of personality invests Thoreau and causes many to want to picture him as a living presence, to hear him as a voice, and to think of his significance in terms of an exemplary life. Pretty clearly this response to Thoreau is one of the main reasons for the old parlor game of praising Henry at Waldo's expense. Whereas Henry impresses himself on one's mind as a person-in-the-flesh, Waldo seems alongside Henry a mere recording consciousness.

Thus we find apocryphal tales about the biographical Henry, like the story of him and Emerson talking through the jailhouse window (Henry, what are you doing there? Waldo, why aren't you in here with me?), not only lingering as anecdotal residue but assuming for many the status of touchstone encapsulations of the quintessence of Thoreauvianism, despite our best pedagogical efforts to quash them. Thus a modern author like Edward Abbey, who we see from the second epigraph to this chapter perfectly well knew the difference between authors and texts, remembers his precursor in the rompish essay "Down the River with Henry Thoreau" less as a writer than as a character, whose personality Abbey forms from a combination of haphazard quote snatching and a memory stocked with odd bits of biographical knowledge and misinformation. Thoreau comes alive for Abbey not as a literary influence that might suffuse his own prose (although Thoreau does) but as "the village crank" who became "a world figure"—the "Johnny Appleseed" who "sows the seeds of liberty around the planet."[8]

Even in academic writing, this disposition can be found, though kept under more restraint. One of the many charms of Stanley Cavell's *Senses of Walden* is the judicious grace with which his essay crosses the boundaries between "the book," "the writer," and "Henry Thoreau"—whatever the formal terms he happens to be using. Here is part of Cavell's gloss on the riddlesome passage about the three losses, of hound, bay horse, and turtle dove: "The writer comes to us from a sense of loss . . . Everything he can list he is putting in his book; it is a record of losses . . . Like any grownup, he has lost childhood; like any American, he has lost a nation and with it the God of the fathers. He has lost Walden; call it Paradise; it is everything there is to lose. The object of faith hides itself from him."[9] "The writer" composing "his book" becomes movingly personalized here, when Cavell retrieves *Walden* from the antiseptic operating room of textuality to become *work,* the labor of a complicated living person about whose losses we are required to think as we imagine him conjuring them up and trying to lay them to rest.

Cavell's preference for envisaging Thoreau's achievement in terms of a work and not a textual construct fits, of course, with Thoreau's generally autobiographical style of writing, a style emphasized by his early memorializers, first among them Emerson. In his essay on Thoreau, which (as we have seen) became Houghton, Mifflin's primary instrument for promoting Thoreau's work in the late nineteenth century, Emerson overwhelmingly stressed Thoreau the man, the "bachelor of thought and Nature,"[10] treating his writing almost as an afterthought, and then only as a batch of arresting fragments and unpublished manuscripts. The occasion itself partly dictated this approach: Emerson first presented the essay as a funeral address, in the midst of the Civil War, before a crowd of Concordians acutely aware of Thoreau's eccentricity. It was proper for Emerson to dwell on Thoreau's personhood and on what made him a memorable neighbor and citizen. But he suppressed the literary Thoreau for more than circumstantial reasons. Although in the relationship between Emerson and Thoreau, Thoreau had a stronger impact on Emerson than is generally realized, that impact came mostly through his person rather than through his writing, notwithstanding Emerson's consistent support of Thoreau's literary career. Thoreau's woodsmanship, self-sufficiency, mechanical dexterity, and repartee ultimately seemed more salient traits of Thoreau's character, whether as virtues or as limitations, than his identity as a writer.[11] This was an entirely logical result of their old mentor-tutee relation. Not until Emerson himself was past mid-life did Thoreau write anything that would mark him as more than a likely lad. But Emerson's substitution of the biographical Thoreau for the archive of his works is also predictable culturally, apart from the nature of their relationship. For we see throughout Emerson's career the romanticist penchant for imaging favorite writers, indeed whole movements, in terms of hypostasized personality types: the philosopher, the mystic, the skeptic, the transcendentalist. Emerson fitted Thoreau into this gallery as another representative figure.

Some would say "representative caricature." Julie Ellison, for one, sees Emerson's penchant for personality classification as a covertly aggressive move that puts the great in their places even as it establishes that greatness.[12] Emerson's ingrained skepticism toward authority, added to the sober worldly wisdom of middle age, led him to the settled conviction by the mid-1840s that people "appear to us as representatives of certain ideas, which they never pass or exceed."[13] Thereafter all of Emerson's profiles at some level extract from their subject's writings and career a neat-to-the-point-of-grotesque abstraction, which also characterizes his essay on friend Henry. But certainly grotesquification was not Emerson's main intent.

Emerson's biographicalist memorialization was also at odds with the actual thrust of Thoreau's own work in some respects. Consider these facts about *Walden*. In its stages of composition, it moved from the order of the body to the order of the text, that is, from oral lecture to printed book. In the process, it became less narrative and more depersonalized by mythical embellishment on the one hand (the addition of the Orientalia, for instance) and by the expansion of environmental data on the other hand. Furthermore, the theory of reading Thoreau embeds within *Walden* is based on the premise that great writing and reading requires self-distancing. The writer forsakes his mother tongue, the vernacular, for what Thoreau called the "father tongue" (*Wa* 101), referring here to the classics specifically (then as traditionally identified with the genteel male curriculum) but by extension all challenging literary art. The reader, likewise, must recognize that "the noblest words are commonly as far behind or above the fleeting spoken language as the firmament with its stars is behind the clouds" (102). The two parties communicate with each other through the medium of "a reserved and select expression, too significant to be heard by the ear, which we must be born again in order to speak" (101). This sense of the necessarily alien character of good textual intercourse was for Thoreau the first requisite of great writing and great reading. All the biographical evidence suggests that Thoreau found the distanced relation between communicating parties that obtained within the order of the text more comfortable than the order of the body.

But this realization does not entitle us to conclude that Thoreau meant for *Walden* to function as a text in the contemporary sense. A notion of intersubjective communion lay at the bottom of his theory of reading. Thoreau's idea seems to be that the truest ground of communication lies in the distanced obliquity of writing as opposed to the immediacy of speech.[14] Whereas for Emerson, the successful lecturer, the immediacy of oral eloquence provided the model against which writing was to be tested, for Thoreau, the much more recessive individual who confessed to his *Journal* that he would rather write than lecture, the medium of writing (the father tongue) allowed the more authentic means of expression precisely because of its more alienated nature: because it acknowledges the inherent gap between author and audience. *Walden* points again and again to this gap through vignettes of imperfect communication: the protagonist and the woodchopper, the protagonist and John Field, the anonymous flute player (a Thoreau disguise) and John Farmer at the end of "Higher Laws," Homer and the speaker himself, who confesses that he reads the ancient Greek laboriously and seldom. This motif culminates in the book's last paragraph when Thoreau expresses his doubts that either John or Jonathan will understand him, meaning either the British or the American reader, meaning most of us.

Yet these gestures of aloofness also point to a ground of intersubjective rapport, just as Thoreau claims in "Visitors" that conversation flows better when our chairs are farther away. The occlusion of the author is offset by the constant hovering of the persona and by the text's refusal altogether to abandon the rhetorical mode of address. By this I mean especially places where an "I" speaks to an auditor (variously identified as my townsmen, poor students, people of New England, or just "you"), but also the many additional cases where Thoreau uses the imperative mood: for example, "beware of all enterprises that require new clothes" (*Wa* 23). No author figure distinctly emerges at such a moment, but the command implies a commander. This being so, Emerson's memorialization of Thoreau as a figure seems less obtuse and the subsequent personalized repossessions of Thoreau make sense in terms of how *Walden* reads.

What is most intriguing about how Thoreau situates "himself" in relation to his book is the way he playfully lays down and erases the boundary between extratextual author and on-the-spot experiencer. Thoreau evinces a disconcerting readiness to break the dramatic illusion and advance from behind the curtain *in propria persona.* "I desire to speak somewhere *without* bounds," he exclaims in "The Conclusion"—as if all that he has written has been a claustrophobic exercise he is impatient to put behind him (*Wa* 324). Such moments, as Cavell says, leave one wondering whether we should finish *Walden* or ditch it and just go there. Again, after detailing his expenses in "Economy," Thoreau observes: "The reader will perceive that I am treating the subject rather from an economic than a dietetic point of view, and he will not venture to put my abstemiousness to the test unless he has a well-stocked larder" (*Wa* 61). Of course technically both the dutiful record keeper and the sly commentator exist within the text as personae; but the distinction Thoreau draws between the two here is more schismatic than, say, Saint Augustine writing about his unregenerate self from the standpoint of having received grace. For the point of the passage is to offset the text's "normal" persona with a persona that has nothing to do with it, and thereby to point to a disjunction between "textual" I and "real-life" I. This distinction Thoreau has of course warned us of very plainly on the first page, telling us that these pages reflect a stage of his existence now over and done with.[15] The later asides, then, bespeak both unusual theatricalization and unusual sincerity. Somewhat the same can be said of the deadpan puns strewn throughout the book, unless one assumes that Thoreau is just trying to catch the reader off guard. When he jolts us out of lyricism by hinting that one of his tender pastoral ministrations to the Concord flora—"I have watered the red huckleberry, the sand cherry," etc., "which might have withered else in dry seasons" (*Wa* 18)—was urinating on them, the turn to laughter (or dismay?) ejects us from the narrative. This mood fades when Thoreau resumes as if nothing had happened, and most readers apparently find it easy to mesmerize themselves back into a state of rapt solemnity (otherwise commentators would have written more before the 1960s about Thoreau's wordplay); but the possibility of drawing back at any moment from the experience to an immense critical and emotional distance remains.[16]

The tonal shift from "Spring" to "Conclusion" illustrates this distance most forcibly. Suddenly the speaker seems dissatisfied with where he has been. Restlessly he circles the globe for images and metaphors: Canada, Yellowstone, Tierra del Fuego, South Africa, Zanzibar. Instead of shooting game, he tells us, it's better "to shoot one's self" (*Wa* 319), whatever that means: the alternatives of suicide and canoeing grate against each other. Is Thoreau like Melville's Ishmael suggesting that what he's just written is merely his substitute for pistol and ball? In any case, Thoreau's text continually expresses what the speaker says about himself in "Solitude": "However intense my experience, I am conscious of the presence and criticism of a part of me, which, as it were, is not a part of me but a spectator, sharing no experience, but taking note of it" (*Wa* 135). Thoreau keeps alive the sense of an "author" standing apart from the autobiographical text.

Yet the opposite is also true: the narrative can become so all-encompassing as to absorb even the author's supposed detachment of mood and temporality. "The Fitchburg Railroad touches the pond about a hundred rods south of where I dwell" (*Wa* 115); "This is a delicious evening, when the whole body is one sense, and imbibes delight through every pore" (*Wa* 129); "I have occasional visits in the long winter evenings . . . from an old settler and original proprietor" (*Wa* 137); "I cherish them, I hoe them, early and late I have an eye to them; and this is my day's work" (*Wa* 155). At its most ambitious, *Walden*'s reach dissolves centuries of time ("On this morning, of the Great Snow, perchance" [*Wa* 119]) and thousands of miles of space ("I meet the servant of the Brahmin . . . who still sits in his temple on the Ganges reading the Vedas" [*Wa* 298]). At these moments it seems that Thoreau wants to negate authorial distance, conflate the observing self with the acting self, and use his book to prolong the Walden sojourn forever. Like the Yeatsean speaker in "Sailing to Byzantium," Thoreau wants to be gathered into "the artifice of eternity"—except that he demands it not be artifice, not Yeats's golden nightingale or "gold mosaic of a wall," but a non-artifice: Walden as actual life rather than Walden as immortal book.

It would seem that these two types of boundary violations must work against each other, that the metanarrative aspect of *Walden* ought to be at cross-purposes with the self-mystifying aspect. But mainly they reinforce each other as symptoms of a hyperactive authorial consciousness. Prepared at any moment to abandon his project or totally immerse himself in it, Thoreau is like Whitman: sometimes insisting that his text is alive—an extension of his body, even; sometimes playing the quizzically distanced observer viewing his poems as impromptu fabrications that he casually throws behind him. A period-specific "American" malaise or ferment partially drives him: a romanticist combination of self-abandoning zest for the inspired visionary creative moment and restlessness at being bound by it, heightened and complicated by postcolonial uncertainty at whether to genuflect at art or spurn it as effete artifice.[17] But it trivializes the issue to "historicize" Thoreau's or Whitman's textual self-presentations in summary terms as a "cultural formation" called something like "American Romantic ideology" and leave the matter there without inquiring more closely into what that formation meant to them.

Respecting Thoreau, none has probed more sensitively than Frederick Garber. For Thoreau, Garber argues, writing was part of a larger field of "inscribings" that might also include ploughing, cabin building, surveying, tracing Indian trails, and observing loggers' marks. He wished to connect writing with deeds, from which perspective "words take on an inescapable secondariness," for Thoreau must recognize that writing in fact never equals deed, only "the record of a deed." This commitment to a never fully realizable act-centered program of writing, as opposed to a logocentric or scriptocentric program, ensured that Thoreauvian writing would continually strive to index and make present antecedent extratextual objects and actions yet acknowledge "the otherwhereness of the original context, its necessary and permanent absence from us." In effect,

Garber imagines a "proto-Heideggerean" Thoreau who wishes for build-ing, dwelling, thinking, and writing to be concentric if not coextensive domains.[18] Although I would take issue with Garber on certain points, it seems to me that he has splendidly characterized Thoreau's desire to approach writing as a mode of action, more specifically of environmental *inter*action, and the tensions with his medium (also sources of endlessly interesting convolution) that resulted from Thoreau's not being able to dodge recognition that a book is not an act in the same sense as the activities it records.[19] The author-text boundary violations I described a moment ago seem to me well described by Garber's elegant explanation of Thoreau's lover's quarrel with his medium. They reflect a by turns passionate and skeptical commitment to text-making as work: as enact-ment of a biographical self in historical moment in a real place alongside and in combination with other tangible forms of work. Thoreau is too scrupulous to identify hunting and carpentry with the printed words "hawk" and "handsaw," but he will not fall into the opposite error and alienate the workman from his textual labor, as if the discipline of writing were any more out of his hands than the discipline of cabin building. He did not yearn to stamp "Thoreau fecit" on all his products or especially crave literary immortality, but he recognized with exceptional clear-sight-edness that writing is one among various things people do that, like it or not, bears the irretrievable stamp of who they are. This I take to be the basic justification for the "Catholic" approach to canonizing Thoreau.

In an important revisionary study of the idea of labor in antebellum writing, Nicholas Bromell pursues the subject farther with special refer-ence to *Walden,* showing the great extent to which it is a book about the nature of labor and exemplary among literary labors of its era for the intensity of its worrying about what labor means. *Walden* begins, of course, with the unacknowledged paradox of the "labor of my hands" with which the speaker says he supported himself (*Wa* 3). He thereby both hints at and conceals the status of literature as labor, complicating the question of what labor means. Thoreau goes on to try to arrive at a satisfactory theory of labor by contemplating successively the labor of building, the labor of farming, and the labor of nature (in bringing forth spring, especially the famous sandbank passage). This last is Thoreau's greatest effort to imagine artistic creativity as immanent—an activity of body and earth as well as mind; and he cannot quite conceptualize it. He resorts to God language, and to the parable of the detached artist of Kouroo in the "Conclusion." *Walden* is generated, Bromell concludes, "by Thoreau's inability to commit himself to either labor or work, expression or artifice, earth or world, body or mind; its most successful moments are those in which this dialectic is most fully dramatized."[20]

Thoreau's self-consciousness about whether and how art might be considered a form of work equivalent to earthier forms of labor was quickened by his historical situation as a would-be intellectual in an emerging nation where art, as opposed to artisanship, was not yet considered to be a legitimate life-labor.[21] That hardly makes his case irrelevant for our purposes, however. On the contrary, it enables us, through his case, to see more clearly what is easily obscured by the curtaining effect of print transmission: that art is always laboriously produced by real people. Homer and Shakespeare are well-nigh invisible, but here is Thoreau in his shirtsleeves moiling around wondering (throughout *Journal*, essay, and book) just what sort of produce his pen is producing. An awareness of his agitation helps to free the reader from the false hypostasis of the AUTHOR that Eliot and Barthes in their respective ways seem to fear. Indeed, whether this effect has caused it or not, it is a matter of record that Thoreau has not functioned as the intimidating monitor one might expect of a "major figure" given what is sometimes alleged to be the repressive impact of such a figure. This paradox is all the more intriguing in light of Thoreau's capacity for self-righteous hectoring: the frequency with which he appears before the reader "so sternly virtuous, so inexorably in earnest, so heart-set upon perfection" as Bradford Torrey put in his editorial introduction to the first edition of Thoreau's *Journal* (*J* 1: xlvii–viii).

Perhaps it is partly because Thoreau started out his posthumous career with an underdog reputation that still lingers, perhaps because Thoreau self-consciously writes as a social outsider, but also it is because Thoreau seems to write so transparently as a character. "We smile," Torrey continues, "when he brags, in early February, that he has not yet put on his winter clothing, amusing himself the while over the muffs and furs of his less hardy neighbors, his own 'simple diet' making him so tough in the fibre that he 'flourishes like a tree;' and then, a week later, writes with unbroken equanimity that he is down with bronchitis, contenting himself to spend his days cuddled in a warm corner by the stove." This from an admirer of Thoreau, not a debunker. Torrey presents Thoreau's peccadilloes not as deductions from his greatness but as warts and bumps that humanize him, encouraging "a pleasant feeling of brotherly relationship. He is one of us, after all" (*J* 1: xlviii). The supposition of a complex, vulnerable, sometimes even slightly absurd human behind the stiff textual gestures makes this reaction possible. The myth of the author in this case does not invite a specious pedestalization of the text as having a strict authority over us never to be called into question; rather it liberates reading by turning it into a fuller communication in which the reader becomes a legitimate partner, feels freer to make what he will of Thoreau, and ultimately digests Thoreau's texts more fully now that the word has been made flesh.

Torrey's experience of Thoreau was a common one. Throughout the history of his memorialization, we find the same motif, beginning with Emerson's wry but compassionate funeral tribute, whose wryness Thoreau would have understood howevermuch he might have resented its condescension, wryness being also a Thoreauvian hallmark. To leaven the superseriousness of Thoreau's owlish gravity about small matters with a bit of light irony is both a self-protective distancing device and a tribute-by-reflection to Thoreau's own capacity for irony. Emerson's critical astringency also expresses the private rapport between the two of them. In this same vein, many of Thoreau's most discerning admirers have revered him with a dash of veneration and slight chuckling reserve: Ellery Channing, Torrey, E. B. White, Annie Dillard, Edward Abbey; scholars like Henry Seidel Canby, Joseph Wood Krutch, Walter Harding, Taylor Stoehr. Nor is the wry and playful quality of their admiration for Thoreau a unique case in the annals of literary remembrance. Walt Whitman, for example, presents an even more striking instance, as in Allen Ginsberg's Whitmanesque fantasy of the guru as "childless, lonely old grubber, poking among the meats in the refrigerator and eyeing the grocery boys." [22]

If the cost of such remembrance is that the hard textual facts may become encrusted in biographicalist legend, the benefit is that the literary work may be retrieved as complex human product. This trade-off may not hold for every work, but certainly it does for those of Thoreau and Whitman that personalize "authorial" selves in one way or another, reach out to actual readers by anticipating hypothetical ones, and scatter throughout their books hints that they are hardly seamless webs but interim statements. The author must labor over these statements to bring under control and finally acknowledge at last that he has not managed to contain all that could have been said, all his possible moods or avatars. I should be inclined to argue that most works at least incipiently do this, although works like *Walden* and *Leaves of Grass* express unusual self-consciousness about trying to achieve a mix of scriptural authority and human partnership in relation to their readers. As such works become remembered as the work of flesh-and-blood persons, whether or not we imagine those persons aright, their capacity to work for us is enhanced. To the extent that this is so, it is certain that the (figure of the) author has at least as much capacity to enrich reading as to constrain it; and if Barthes thought otherwise that was either because he mistakenly assumed that the concept of "author" must needs eventuate in some pedagogical codification, or—more likely on the evidence of his own autobiography— because he was concerned, as an author, to avoid becoming frozen into a single attitude, to keep from putting "my present expression in the service of my previous truth," to "abandon the exhausting pursuit of an old piece of myself."[23] Thoreau would immediately have understood this: he who had many lives to live, he who wished us not to imitate his present lifestyle lest he already have found another, he of the multilayered innuendo, the perpetually oscillating tone. ("Deeply confessional tones of voice assert truths, often with messianic force, which subsequent tones of voice retract, undercut, or rebut"—as one reader sums up an astute comparison of Thoreau to another premodern proto-Barthesian ironic lyricist, Søren Kierkegaard.)[24]

This fugacity offers an invitation to the reader to partake in the admixture of serious assertiveness and ironic skepticism that the author brings to his projects. The partially self-deauthorizing turn Thoreau gives to what otherwise might seem self-righteous dogmatism cues in the tone of affectionately ironic respect evinced by Thoreauvians like Torrey and White and Abbey. If we take seriously, as readers, the Thoreauvian notion that there is always a part of us watching from a distance what we are doing (*Wa* 135), we are less likely to become paralyzed by Thoreau's authority as canonical figure or by his text as verbal icon, and less likely in our role as readers to imitate authorial authority in the domineering sense by insisting on what would have horrified Thoreau, Barthes, and

Foucault almost equally—namely, the will to pin meaning and authors down. Certainly Thoreau wrote *Walden* in such a way as to help us to this liberated form of discipleship, unless we have a very low tolerance for indefiniteness, in which case we had better look elsewhere for heroes.

A book that expresses and generates work belongs, then, to an order of textuality in which the order of the body figures also: an order in which author and reader can be imagined as flesh-and-blood participants, not merely as textual functions, even though perforce they must operate and cooperate within the realm of textuality as a limit condition of their exchange.[25] In ascribing an almost totalitarian regulatory power to discursive institutions, Foucault left himself unable to explain the potency of dissenting or subversionary writers, even though he certainly believed that there were such writers (De Sade, Nietzsche, himself). There is no place for Foucault in Foucault's system—quite an irony, since nothing is more striking about his rhetoric than the utter self-confidence of its generalizations: for example, the three, four, or five considerations he continually and peremptorily tells his readers follow from or are inherent within this or that condition. (The desubjectified mode of address, which perhaps intends to honor discourse by excising the person of the author, seems in the long run a lofty platform from which the supreme commander can pass judgment unimpeded.)[26] Now, it is hardly clear that restoring a messy intersubjective model of writing and reading will solve all the problems of the world. But we are more likely to make progress if we imagine texts as emanating in the first instance from responsible agents communicating with other responsible agents than if we imagine texts without agency inhabiting discursive force fields.

Canonization versus Ecocentrism

These remarks about text and authorial agency may look like parochial, in-group concerns when set alongside another concern of far more pressing magnitude from an ecocritical standpoint. Is not the canonization of Thoreau on whatever terms directly counter to the path of self-relinquishment that I have ascribed to him, and that I have seen as crucial to the critique of anthropocentrism generally? If it is true that Thoreau became less interested in himself as he became more interested in nature, if ecocentrism means becoming less egocentric—then it would seem that to linger on Thoreau as person, as agent, or even as persona either misconstrues his true nature or compromises its integrity beyond repair. When one further considers that the material text of *Walden* as a copyrighted enterprise of literary entrepreneurialism is doubly implicated in the ethos of individualism (as patented commodity and as a celebration of the romantic idea of individual genius that helped set modern copyright law in place),[27] *Walden* starts to seem hopelessly self-divided—and the canonizer of Thoreau even more so. The visitor to Walden who goes there to enjoy the pond is arguably more Thoreauvian than the visitor who goes there to find Thoreau's cabin site and muse about him. Professional Thoreauvians may fall into a sophisticated equivalent of the cultist's shortsightedness when reading his prose as autobiographical discourse. This shippage can happen even in thoughtfully environmentalist readings, like one that reflects as follows on a series of such observational passages from the *Journal* (as "June 30. 2 p.m.—thermometer north side of house, 95; in river one foot deep, one rod from shore, 82": "Even in the absence of the first-person singular pronoun there is a distinctive personality dictating the content and language of these entries, a characteristic tone which identifies the origin of these bits of observation as a specific human inspector of nature."[28] I certainly would not disagree with this observation outright; I made a similar point a moment ago. What *is* at issue is how much primacy should be attached to "personality" as a trait of Thoreauvian writing. Ironically, modern critical theory invites this identification in the same breath with which it banishes the figure of the author. As a surrogate, it supplies the concept of the persona, the "I"-function of the text, which then becomes a central category of analysis in lyric and nonfiction. Though we are forbidden to identify persona with author, we continue to be given the option of imagining texts suffused with simulated personalities. Indeed, personality in this rarefied sense has, if anything, become a more favored subject of criticism since the days when we considered texts strategized lenses of perception rather than transparencies through which authorial thought is rendered directly. We are more likely to personify an anonymous third person "narrator," more likely to speak of a lyric or essayistic voice as if it were a character, more likely to think of *all* of Thoreau's writing as a species of autobiographical discourse.[29]

There is, of course, an important theoretical difference between imagining *Walden* as about "the Thoreauvian persona" and imagining it to be about "Thoreau" the person. Yet the difference, on second thought, is not so great as it might seem. Ecocritically speaking, these positions have a certain interchangeability as human subject-centered approaches to literary texts. The persona, at least in the case of documentary nonfiction, remains in such close dialogue with the biographical person that the insistence on disjoining them, from an ecocritical standpoint anyhow, signifies little more than a literary-critical incest taboo anxiety. The Thoreauvian persona is not coexistensive with the historical Thoreau, but it can legitimately be thought of as a provisional identity that the author has imagined for himself. Such a provisional identity may never have been a historical reality, but it cannot be kept from becoming one, as Whitman became during the Civil War in his capacity as male nurse the healer he imagined the "I" to be in "Song of Myself." Still less can a provisional identity be prevented from becoming a historical force, as with Thoreau's civilly disobedient persona, or—it now seems—contemporary environmentalists' reinvention of the figure of Thoreau the green advocate. Given the ease with which a literary persona can circulate back into biography and into history, we should be all the more concerned if there seems to be something "ecologically" problematic about a reading of an author's work in terms of its speaker or its *cogito*.

My best answer to this concern is the same sort of response Chapter 6 gave to Chapter 5: that the path to biocentrism must lead through humanitarianism. Human denizens of the modernized world are most likely to move toward ecocentric ways of thinking when the sympathetic bond is activated. It may be true, as Edward O. Wilson argues, that "biophilia" (an affinity with other organisms) is genetically encoded.[30] But to activate the altruism that Wilson takes to be one ingredient of this affiliative bond some projection of empathy from self to other is necessary. This projection requires reinstating a myth of agency. Thus, as Robert Sayre astutely points out, Aldo Leopold's land ethic arises out of, although ultimately in critique of, bourgeois liberalism, insofar as it begins in the state of empathetic, refined sensibility that was second nature for Leopold by reason of his bourgeois individual heritage.[31] Perhaps it is potentially consoling as well as disturbing that Adam Smith was the philosopher of both capitalism and moral sentiments.[32] Similarly, subject-centered readings and author-centered remembrances have the power to exercise ecocentric influences insofar as it is true that "for the most part, people get their standards not from ethical treatises or even scriptural texts or homely sayings, but by idealizing and following the examples of some living persons or persons."[33] Some would go so far as to claim "that there is no new image of the future without a corresponding new image of the individual."[34] What makes this true, to the extent it is true, is identified quite pointedly by Charles Taylor: the "objective" order of public reality "is only accessible through personal . . . resonance."[35] These personalized models may be locally supplied, from family members for instance, or they may be more distant public or historical figures, who come to play the role of moral prototypes for others. These "paradigmatic individuals," as moral philosopher A. S. Cua calls them, function either "as a source of retrospective justification for moral agents" or as a "prospective task to be accomplished."[36] Cua has in mind the examples of great religious and philosophical teachers: Socrates, Buddha, Confucius, and Jesus. But at least a modified version of the paradigm of the paradigmatic individual could apply to canonical writers also, especially writers who, like Thoreau (or Emerson, Whitman, Milton, Tolstoy, or Ñgugĩ wa Thiong'o), stand not only for "artistic excellence" but also for some moral or social vision. The question then becomes a matter of appraising just what sort of example they offer.

In Thoreau's case, we have seen, the paradigm is not one of achieved wisdom or settled doctrine but of striving to achieve a state of being that the author is in the process of defining for himself. By no means does this paradigm undermine his exemplary potential, however. I do not know if Gabriel Josipovici's assertion about authorial voices applies categorically, but it certainly holds for Thoreau: "Out of the writer's renewed attempts to say 'I' and renewed refusal to come to rest in any position in which 'I' is less than his whole self, out of his perpetually repeated failure to find that fullness of voice for which James and Virginia Woolf longed, a certain voice does emerge . . . This fullness of voice is something *we* register as we read, but it always eludes the writer himself. He who thinks he has it, loses it; he who goes on searching, releases it."[37] In other words, Thoreau was a Virgil, not a Beatrice, and he knew it; yet at the same time, both despite and because of his restless and exploratory disposition as a writer his work has the capacity to project itself to readers as stamped with a more distinctive and coherent impress than he himself would have felt at ground level. I find this particularly the case with regard to Thoreau's ecologism. His life was a long, slow, painstaking, intermittently successful process of reeducation. Yet this experimental odyssey-aspect of his naturism, as it developed from an essentially bourgeois upbringing and a fairly standard formal education, and from his lover's quarrels with those, makes Thoreau an especially useful prototype for readers of this book, most of whom have started from similar positions. If Thoreau had been brought up as a land-wise aborigine, he would command more respect of a certain kind, but his example might be less pertinent and instructive.

Perhaps a more worrisome aspect of Thoreau as a candidate for the status of paradigmatic Virgilian guide is the high degree of social disaffection that his environmental responsiveness reflected. If the cornerstone of ecologism is community, as Leopold held, then there is something presumptively ironic in Thoreau's having felt more at ease communing with nonhuman species than with his own. Doubtless it was a character flaw that he was so severe on ordinary mortals and so grudging in his acknowledgment of his dependence on them.[38] Yet without that flaw he might not have managed to become a memorable critic of anthropocentrism, and he might not have pursued his self-transformative quest with such energy. He might not have been able to imagine humanity as part of a larger ecological community if he had been altogether at ease within the confines of the human community. Besides, if we believe the deep ecologists, then environmental reorientation requires transformation at the level of (every) individual in the face of an unreceptive social order. A degree of what passes for misanthropy may be necessary to attain this.[39] If political philosopher George Kateb is right, as I think he is, what fundamentally distinguishes the "democratic individuality" of Emerson, Thoreau, and Whitman from the ideology of possessive individualism that is easily conflated with it in broad generalizations about the liberal tradition is precisely that the former begins with an antisocial gesture, in order to clear the mind of the tyranny of intellectual and political conventionalism, only to culminate in affirmation of the worth of others. It fulfills itself in what Kateb calls impersonal individuality, whereby not only oneself but all persons are seen as beautiful and worthwhile and the individual subject is freed from "a sickly self-interest and blinding anxiety for success."[40] Where Thoreau arguably is most innovative, relative to his

Emersonian auspices, is in the extension of this democratic principle to nonhuman as well as human entities. That he did so imperfectly is less important than the fact that he did so at all. We see the process at work in *Walden*'s "plot" of relinquishment: the protagonist in the act of becoming weaned from the project of a solely individual fulfillment as his primary subject of interest.

More problematic about Thoreau's individualism than its bringing him into collision with community is its potentially escapist element. Using pastoralism to rebuke the work ethic Thoreau risked playing into the hands of the emerging consumer culture and reinforcing the image of nature, sponsored by the fast-emerging American leisure industry, as a picturesque space of escape where one's needs can readily be gratified with little or no austerity required.[41] Clearly this travesties—and occludes—the "strenuous and continual effort at self-cultivation" that Tu Wei-ming rightly advises us to expect if we wish to enter into "the aesthetic experience of mutuality and immediacy with nature." Tu refers specifically to Taoist aesthetics, but the point applies broadly. Any sort of conversion from anthropocentrism to ecocentrism cannot take place without a rigorous discipline of "unlearning and forgetting as well as remembering."[42]

Roderick Nash's *Wilderness and the American Mind,* after relating what looks like a success story of the American public's belated recognition of the wilderness as a priceless treasure, ends with chilling reflections on the likelihood that wilderness will be "loved to death" by eager visitors in search of Thoreauvian experiences.[43] Although we cannot blame Thoreau for there not being land available for more than a few million Americans at a time to replicate his homesteading experiment, he does bear some responsibility for abetting the memorialization of what he stood for as a leisure-time activity. At least ostensibly, precious little work gets done at *Walden* once he builds the cabin. Most often we encounter the protagonist rambling, idling, swimming, conversing, spectating: nature's *flâneur.* Thoreau makes the activities of cabin building, bean farming, plastering, and foraging sound like casual pastimes. For a latter-day Thoreauvian, nothing is easier than to absorb him within the space of one's leisure. Yes, I shall build that weekend cabin. Yes, I shall pay a little more heed to my surroundings, and the meaning of those surroundings, when I take my morning or afternoon walk. Yes, I shall think again about my workaholism, about whether I should work less and meditate more.[44] In this way, I compartmentalize the problem and reduce it to a plaything for my idle hours.

Such glimmerings of dissatisfaction are not necessarily trivial. Who can tell where they will lead? Yet the space in which they occur is more a space of escape than of confrontation. "Such spaces," Henri Lefebvre remarks, "appear on first inspection to have escaped the control of the established order, and thus, inasmuch as they are spaces of play, to constitute a vast 'counter-space.' This is a complete illusion . . . leisure is as alienated and alienating as labour; as much an agent of co-optation as it is itself co-opted; and both an assimilative and an assimilated part of the 'system' (mode of production)."[45] To the extent that this is so, it threatens to turn devotion to Thoreau into a parody of itself. If the pilgrimage to Walden, however seriously undertaken, leads to nothing more than a Sunday jaunt, if *Walden* is reserved for a backpack item alongside the gorp and the jerky, if we save Thoreau for reading aloud at campfires like a once-a-year family-circle reading of the Christmas story, that is a sad diminution of his hopes for his life, his sojourn, his book. Thoreau becomes part of the apparatus of what Herbert Marcuse calls the "institutionalized desublimation" of late industrial society, which like Huxley's brave new world enlarges the scope of libidinal satisfaction but reduces its force by depriving it "of the claims which are irreconcilable with the established society" and by defining incipient opposition as merely "libidinal," a "pleasure principle."[46]

Thoreau opened himself up to such a reduction by advertising the Walden experience as a short-term experiment and by the degree to which he pastoralized it—pastoral, being as we have seen, a double-edged ideological instrument. Consequently, from the first, many readers have been tempted to ingest *Walden* as little more than piquant titillation. "Abounds in exquisite sketches and many fine thoughts"; "full of beauty, poetry and entertainment"; "redolent of the woods, and brings all their pleasant sights and sounds graphically before the reader's senses"—these were typical verdicts by *Walden*'s first reviewers.[47] This impression of *Walden* as a pleasant junket can be countered only by opposing to it the myth of it as a serious "enterprise," the counterpart of the work ethic as well as its underminer. One quick, decisive way to make this case is simply to note that to read *Walden* the book attentively is hard. As Cavell points out, the chapter "Reading" supplies instructions as to how Thoreau probably wanted his book to be approached, in the passage where he describes the effort required to engage the Greek classics in the original: "we must laboriously seek the meaning of each word and line, conjecturing a larger sense than common use permits out of what wisdom and valor and generosity we have" (*Wa* 100).[48] Certainly anyone can whiffle through *Walden* in a cursory pleasure tour of well-wrought passages, but such an excursion hardly counts as reading in any legitimate sense of the word.

But let us not shirk the more circuitous route of building the case in terms of the content of Thoreau's exposition. His critique of conventional strenuousness (of hard labor directed at the acquisition of property or at clearing it from debt), when this critique takes the form of a playful indulgence of leisure, belies the intensity of Thoreau's resistance to commodification and the challenge of living up to the morally superior standard he wants to enjoin. The ideology of the simple life, of spartan virtue, for Thoreau refines and validates expression; and, despite certain appearances, he knows how hard it is to maintain. Thus, as Bromell shrewdly points out, Thoreau scarcely rejects work, he merely "disburdens" it of its propertarian purpose so that "it becomes an end in itself."[49] Thoreau's critique of conventional farming, for example, incorporates an ecological-georgic ideal of respect for the kind of labor that values the land-wisdom above the material product to be extracted from land.[50] But nowhere in the book does the importance Thoreau attaches to a non-propertarian understanding of labor emerge more clearly than in "Higher Laws." This chapter of *Walden,* more explicitly than any other, makes clear the insufficiency of pastoral *otium,* the space of leisure, as an explanation of what the turn to nature properly means. It declares full allegiance to the ideal of rigorous self-discipline, which produces the intense "deliberateness" that Thoreau throws into each multilayered sentence and into the contemplation of each minute item in his daily routine or field of vision. "Higher Laws" moves abruptly from the celebration of play to the celebration of work: from the childhood of the hunter stage of precivilization to the adult stage of moral awakening and exertion. ("From exertion come wisdom and purity; from sloth ignorance and sensuality" [*Wa* 220]).

Not many modern readers can follow this move without falling into vexation or snickering. For nowhere else in *Walden* does Thoreau so blatantly advertise his "Victorian prudery" as here, in his praise of chastity and his strictures against hydra-headed "sensuality." ("When the reptile is attacked at one mouth of his burrow, he shows himself at another" [220].) Furthermore, this prudishness seems blatantly inconsistent, for suddenly it appears that nature has become the enemy. Thoreau may start by insisting "I love the wild not less than the good" (*Wa* 210), but a few pages later the "animal" nature has become "reptile and sensual" and Thoreau declares, "He is blessed who is assured that the animal is dying out in him day by day, and the divine being established" (219, 220). Even without the historical-cultural gap that causes the late twentieth-century reader to set much less store by temperance and chastity than Thoreau did, "Higher Laws" would still be a confusing performance; for the "finished" version incorporates a major switch of emphasis from the first draft, a kind of playful valediction to the pleasures of fishing now outgrown, to a much more severe homily on the desirability of vegetarianism in particular, abstemiousness in general, all this informed by the cosmic drama of the perennial war between virtue and vice.[51] No doubt the chapter switches too peremptorily from indulgence to austerity. Indeed, Thoreau recognizes his abruptness, after the fact, when he ends the chapter with a comic vignette of a perplexed auditor figure (John Farmer, listening to a flute player [guess who?]) and starts the next with the droll hermit-poet dialogue in which the high-minded ascetic poet immediately relapses into angling. But "Higher Laws" is not really so paradoxical as it seems. It may *look* as if Thoreau has forsaken nature in his quest for moral purity, especially when we quote sentences out of context ("Nature is hard to be overcome, but she must be overcome" [221]). But the point of the chapter is not that we should turn our backs on nature but that we must imagine the ulterior benefits of the original turn *to* nature in the spirit of economy, both fiscal and ethical.[52]

"Higher Laws" is not, in other words, about ascending to a spiritual state in which the body is left behind, but about reforming the bodily life through a homemade asceticism so that even the seemingly ignobler functions are purified. It converts the gospel of simplification in "Economy" into a moral system, albeit a homocentric one. Thoreau makes no bones about the superior moral potential of the ethically awakened human to both nonhuman animals and unawakened humans, who can at times be charming (like the woodchopper) but remain as far as Thoreau is concerned in a sort of animal state. But despite the rhetorical ferocity of his bestialization of the natural world, combat with it is the farthest thing from his mind. On the contrary, his reluctance to eat meat and fish stems from his aversion to being a predator and his preference for simple fare, from the thought that one's bodily demands can become so regulated and thereby subtilized "that some berries which I had eaten on a hill-side had fed my genius" (218). Thoreau's vision of an abstemiousness schooled by life within nature, which—thanks to humankind's ethical sense—can in principle measure up to a higher standard than we hold nonhumans to, is not a platform most modern ecocentrists could endorse without qualification; but it may be a platform from which we can look farther and more clearly than otherwise toward the promised land.[53]

In the next chapter, then, Thoreau does not simply follow the logic of comic antithesis when he re-imbeds himself, as protagonist, within the economy of nature, as neighbor to the brutes, in a degree of immersion greater than we have seen before. To be sure, he still maintains a spectator's distance: taxonomizing the mice, recording the mock-heroic ant battle, drolly confessing the gap between the loons and him. The narrative sequence, though, has meanwhile implicitly established these experiences as the fruits of the disciplined sensibility portrayed in "Higher Laws," indeed as a further definition of that sensibility as one in the process of defining and strengthening itself by its replacement from the economy of the village to the economy of nature.

In this way the domains of work and leisure blur and redefine, as Thoreau—that "most unplayful playful man," as one historian of American play calls him—converts what started as leisure into what increasingly looks like ethical work.[54] Thoreau was hardly alone among American writers of his day. Writers of the period typically offered what looked like images of leisure and then tried to use those images seductively to prod their readers into forms of moral effort that would permanently disable them from doing business as usual.[55] Whitman's "Song of Myself" invites readers to loaf with him, then introduces them to an entirely new vision of reality. Melville's "Typee" offers a leisurely sojourn with Polynesian natives as an antidote to missionary zeal. Margaret Fuller turns the ostensible record of a touristic junket into a serious discussion of frontier society. In light of such examples, Lefebvre's dismissal of the oppositional possibilities of the space of leisure seems doctrinaire. Doubtless it applies to the type of worst case he has in mind, contemporary resort hotels, but hardly across the board. It could just as truthfully be said that the space of leisure is the only position from which one can get a clear enough view of the working world to allow one to go about the business of trying to change it. In some ways, Thoreau's generation was uniquely situated to make the most of leisure as an oppositional space, because the institutionalization of such leisure pursuits as pleasure journeys and home-grown belles lettres were relatively new phenomena, at least for the middling classes, and could not be looked on as simple releases by many writers and readers schooled in the canons of republican simplicity and the protestant work ethic.[56] A figure like Thoreau predictably both resisted these procrustean canons in the name of leisure and strove to put the leisure he found back to work.

"Once the Land Ethic becomes as familiar and ingrained as the Work Ethic is now, the very definition of work will have changed." So writes Sayre, and wisely, about Aldo Leopold. Thoreau's importance as an environmental saint lies in being remembered, in the affectionate simplicity of public mythmaking, as helping to make the space of nature ethically resonant. He went a certain distance in *Walden;* he went farther thereafter. "Work will be 'right,'" Sayre adds significantly, quoting Leopold, "'when it tends to preserve the integrity, stability, and beauty of the biotic community.'"[57] Thoreau moved toward this biocentrist awareness. Later admirers of the green Thoreau, in their imagination of him, have completed his quest for him by imagining him in place, forever at Walden, refusing quite to believe that he ever left there. Thoreau is the wanderer always at rest, the Ulysses always in his Ithaca. Thoreauvians who form their image of him on the basis of this paradox of the always-restless but always-situated being distort history, of course, but the problem with this is not the transgression against external fact, inasmuch as the paradox is profoundly true to Thoreau's self-conception. The problem, if it is such, lies, as noted before, in the susceptibility of the Thoreauvian, of the modern human, to become overly caught up in the figure as opposed to the ground: to reduce ecological self to detached autonomous self, to read *Walden* for the autobiographical narrative alone. To the extent *Walden* tempts us to do that, it must be offset by an ampler vision of the environmental imagination that includes, for example, Thoreau's contemporary Susan Cooper, also the detached and somewhat judgmental observer, but who for literary purposes reckoned Cooperstown more interesting than herself. Or we must refer to Leopold, who wrote the kind of self-effacing book about *his* space of leisure that Thoreau perhaps would have written had he lived to the age Leopold was when he finished, or virtually finished, *Sand County Almanac.* So the environmental imagination cannot live by Thoreau alone. But with him as a point of reference, we can move in all the necessary directions.

Nature's Genres:
Environmental Nonfiction at the Time
of Thoreau's Emergence

IN THIS BOOK I have repeatedly referred to "environmental nonfiction" as an entity, whereas nothing is more striking than its variegated character. *Walden*, for example, belongs to many genres. It can be read as a poem, a novel, an autobiography, a travel narrative, a sermon, a treatise.[1] Sometimes the text positively flaunts its diversity, fragmenting into multigeneric collage. "Brute Neighbors" begins with dialogue, shifts to natural history vignettes, shifts again for the heavily stylized mock-epic narrative of the ant fight, and climaxes with an autobiographical narrative of an encounter with a loon. It is as if Thoreau had designed the chapter to dramatize, not answer, the question with which the main section begins: "Why do precisely these objects which we behold make a world?" (*Wa* 225). This puzzlement gets expressed by the stylistic breaks, which create a world of discursive chunks that can never be welded into a seamless whole, any more than Thoreau can capture the evading loon. Nor does Thoreau really want such closure, which might exaggerate his power to formulate and control nature.[2]

   Walden's discursive instability does not arise merely from incorporating genres like Platonic dialogue and homeric epic into a book that was "properly" a work of environmental nonfiction. The field of environmental nonfiction as Thoreau knew it was itself a patchwork, in some ways more "polyphonic," more "heteroglossic," than that of the novel.[3]

Before Thoreau

American environmental nonfiction predates Thoreau by a longer span than he predates us, going back at least as far as such inventories of

American resources by seventeenth-century observers as John Smith's *Generall Historie of Virginia, New-England, and the Summer Isles* (1632), William Wood's *New England's Prospect* (1639), and John Josselyn's *Account of Two Voyages to New England* (1673), to name some of the early texts Thoreau most liked to cite.[4] The late colonial period saw a flowering of prose about the natural phenomena of the American regions, particularly the south and west: for example, by Mark Catesby, Jonathan Carver, Thomas Jefferson, and the two Bartrams, all of whose work Thoreau knew, as he also did that of Alexander Wilson and John J. Audubon in the early nineteenth century. William Bartram was the first to achieve transcontinental literary fame.[5] In ornithology especially, Wilson, Audubon, and Thomas Nuttall brought the aesthetics as well as the precision of environmental reportage to a pitch of considerable sophistication by 1850.[6]

Yet a mere generation after Thoreau it began to seem as if nothing had preceded him. Late nineteenth-century readers began to forget that Audubon, Wilson, and the Bartrams had existed, at least as literary figures; they derived Thoreau from Emerson, then marked Thoreau as the effective start of the nature essay.[7] They exaggerated both Thoreau's originality and Emerson's influence on the genre; indeed, they exaggerated more grossly than had they claimed there was no American fiction worth mentioning before Irving and Cooper, or no American poetry worth mentioning before Freneau and Bryant. But the mythical reduction of history also reflected the practice of later environmental writers themselves, who tended not to look back before transcendentalism in pursuit of ancestors, as well as the societal realities of American authorship during the early period. Until Thoreau's youth, the conditions did not exist to enable literary naturism to flourish in America. For environmental nonfiction to seem an important literary enterprise, three developments had to take place: a specialization in the branches of natural science to the point that exposition for laypersons seemed necessary; a degree of urbanization sufficient to produce substantial numbers of readers regretful about being cut off from nature; and a sufficient array of literary media (lecture forums, magazines, book production and distribution networks) to provide belletristic writers with a decent hearing if not a fortune. In America, these several conditions did not develop until the second third of the nineteenth century. Consequently, before

Thoreau few American artists chose environmental prose as their special province. The first of any note was Alexander Wilson, who was a competent poet before he won recognition as an ornithological writer and illustrator. The first American to produce a nonspecialized book of environmental essays seems to have been John Godman of Philadelphia, whose *Rambles of a Naturalist* was serialized, then gathered as a collection, without commercial success.[8] The first clear case of commercially successful American literary nonfiction about the environment was Washington Irving's frontier trilogy on the prairies and the fur trade: *A Tour of the Prairies* (1835), *Astoria* (1836), and *Adventures of Captain Bonneville* (1837) (*TR #758*). The only professional writer specializing in environmental nonfiction during Thoreau's lifetime to make anything like a real go of it financially was British-born William Henry Herbert ("Frank Forester"), "the Shakespeare of sporting literature," the genteel progenitor of *Field and Stream*–style reportage.[9]

This maturing body of American naturist description was by no means the only source from which Thoreau and his successors drew. They would have been aware of a burgeoning array of contemporary books and articles in the process of making nature a centrally important subject for the serious writer of creative prose. Such writers were even more active in Britain, where the interrelated developments of modernization, romanticist aesthetics, and popular natural history were at least a generation ahead.[10] In the sections that follow I shall give an inventory of representative texts and types of environmental prose in which Thoreau is known to have taken interest.

Literary Almanacs

The first book about nature that we know Thoreau read seriously was William Howitt's *The Book of the Seasons* (1831) (*TR #729*), on which he wrote a laudatory college essay in the spring of 1836.[11] Howitt's *Seasons* is a gently moralistic compendium of environmental wit and pious wisdom, interspersed with descriptive sketches, organized by month and following a predictable agenda: the characteristic traits of the month defined and its etymology sketched, followed by information about "rural occupations" proper to the month, angling tips, seasonal bird migrations, flora, and insects, with accompanying charts to illustrate the last three.

Howitt sprinkled poems by himself and his sister Mary throughout. The book is a medley of exposition, narrative, poetry, charts, and lists.

Howitt professedly aimed to respiritualize an increasingly commercial people through restitution of contact with nature, in the assurance that once nature's influence is implanted, a person will never "become utterly debased in sentiment, or abandoned in principle." In short, he wrote for the urban bourgeoisie. The lyrical anthropology of the rural occupations section underscores this intention ("In farm-kitchens, in spring, we perpetually hear a chirping of chickens, ducklings, goslings, etc.")[12]

Howitt achieved at best a homely eloquence, as Thoreau the collegian affirmed ("We have here a book calculated to do all that books can do to excite a spirit of attachment to Nature"),[13] and as attested also by Thoreau's mentor Emerson. Emerson condescended to Howitt but also imitated him; "The Snow-Storm" was a blank-verse rendition of Howitt's January vignette, right down to the final metaphor of snow architecture.[14] The famous exordium of Emerson's Divinity School Address ("In this refulgent summer, it is a luxury to draw the breath of life") probably drew on Howitt's celebration of the "carnival of Nature" in June—and therefore may be a less scandalous gesture than Emersonians like to think, given Howitt's unexceptionable piety. ("It is a luxury to walk abroad, indulging every sense with sweetness," exudes Howitt, dramatizing the idea of "luxury" by repeating it over and over.)[15]

The design of seasonal arrangement would have appealed strongly to the young Thoreau, whose first preserved essay, possibly written before his teens, is a chronicle of the seasons:[16] a foreshadowing of his later attempt to create a meticulously calibrated objective and subjective account of seasonal change and phenomena. His college essay on Howitt quickly metamorphoses into a semi-independent seasons essay of his own—a declaration of independence. Howitt's ordering was too procrustean to serve Thoreau for long, nor was *The Book of the Seasons* the only "season book" he knew. Thanks to the popularity of almanacs and the prestige of James Thomson's gigantic locodescriptive poem *The Seasons* (1726–1740) (*TR* #1333), the seasonal *omnium gatherum* was a recognizable literary mode well before Howitt wrote.[17]

During the composition of *Walden* itself, the books dealing with seasonal topics that meant most to Thoreau were the writings of the

Roman agriculturists, especially Virgil's *Georgics* (TR #1390), which Robert Richardson, Jr., rightly calls "the great poem of earth" for Thoreau, but also Varro, Columella, and Cato (*TR* numbers 1380, 337, 271).[18] But the scope and historical position of Howitt's *Seasons* made it a closer if not more directly influential precedent, as a romantic pastoral intervention seeking to return the age of enterprise to the natural world it had lost and thereby promote moral transformation. Howitt would have reinforced the Thoreauvian penchant for dignifying preindustrial labor by appeal to its "timeless" character, that is, its capacity to allow the observer to revoke or suspend the erosions of modernity. For Howitt, the English grain harvest was an aesthetic treat, feasting the mind "with the pleasures of antiquity. The sickle is almost the only implement which has descended from the olden times in its pristine simplicity—to the present hour neither altering form, nor becoming obsolete amid all the fashions and improvements of the world." Howitt bolstered this new with scriptural citations, which he embellished with Keats's image of Ruth standing amid the alien corn. Thoreau, too, loved to be reminded of the antiquity of "modern" farming practices, noting with pleasure that the farmers of Concord carried out their autumn manuring in accord with Cato's prescriptions (Thoreau quotes the Latin); "Before Christianity was heard of this was done" (*PJ* 4: 32). By pitting classicism against Christianity, Thoreau swerved from the more conventional Howitt, but they practiced a similar enameling of the mundane, thereby testifying, of course, to the foreignness of those rustic pursuits that they sought to perpetuate. Howitt's fastidiousness ("*almost* the only implement") and categorical insistence ("*neither* altering its form, *nor* becoming obsolete") are Thoreauvian mannerisms also.[19] But above all, it is the luminous significance of the unobtrusive rustic item, the sickle and the dunghill, that binds passages like these together. "When we read 'Walden,'" wrote Virginia Woolf in a centenary tribute to Thoreau, "we have a sense of beholding life through a very powerful magnifying glass. To walk, to eat, to cut up logs, to read a little, to watch the bird on the bough, to cook one's dinner—all these occupations when scraped clean and felt afresh prove wonderfully large and bright."[20] Howitt scraped less cleanly and felt less freshly, but this kind of retrieval was exactly what he had in mind.

Howitt's *Seasons,* and *Walden* as well, reflected a growing market for seasonally oriented art in various media from poetry to genre painting and prints. Later in the nineteenth century the vogue reached a culmination of sorts with Oscar Fay Adams's twelve-volume anthology of season poems, one book for each month, and the publication of excepts from Thoreau's own journals in four volumes covering early spring, summer, autumn, and winter.[21] Howitt himself attempted to cash in with a "companion" volume, *The Year-Book of the Country*, which Thoreau may not have known, although he would have been interested by its comparative political radicalism.[22]

Homiletic Naturism

The strong homiletic undertones of Howitt's season books resonate with a much larger body of nineteenth-century writing about nature: the secular sermon or didactic essay. Both the religious and the secular press generated during the nineteenth century a vast amount of "natural theology" for laypersons designed to show, or at least to celebrate, natural phenomena as the manifestation of some coherent spiritual plan or design. Emerson's *Nature* (*TR #476*) is the one work of the sort that has become a literary classic, but in the context of antebellum religiophilosophical naturism generally, that rhapsodic treatise seems a recognizable avatar of liberal protestant homily, cousin to more respectable liberal sermons like Cyrus Bartol's "Autumn" and N. L. Frothingham's "Cold," and the middlebrow ministerial journalism of Henry Ward Beecher's *Star Papers* (1855), an immensely popular book of (largely) country ruminations, ranging from a decorous "Discourse on Flowers" to a jaunty, unbuttoned fishing idyll ("Trouting").[23] This clerical literature always contains at least a modicum of empirical observation. Sometimes it becomes the dominant ingredient, as in Beecher's *Plain and Pleasant Talk about Fruits, Flowers, and Farming* (1859), or in texts designed to provide instruction in science from a properly orthodox standpoint. Liberal Boston minister F. W. P. Greenwood, sometime officer of the Boston Society of Natural History, sponsored one ambitious project of this kind, a reprinting of a four-volume Scottish school compendium, *Sacred Philosophy of the Seasons: Illustrating the Perfections of God in the Phenomena of the Year*, which furnished a course of natural history lessons with a pietistic twist.[24] A more original seasonally oriented work of didactic scientism, a brisk mid-century seller, was *Religious Lectures on Peculiar*

Phenomena in the Four Seasons . . . Delivered to the Students in Amherst College (1849), by Amherst president Edward Hitchcock, better known to Thoreau as the erstwhile state geologist (*TR* #951–952).

A pillar of the Connecticut Valley evangelical establishment, friend of the Dickinson family, Hitchcock "epitomized American attempts to harmonize geology and revelation in the second quarter of the century." In *Religious Lectures,* he puts on both his professorial hats to weave four sermonettes, each prettily illustrated by a seasonal lithograph: "The Resurrections of Spring," "The Triumphal Arch of Summer," "The Euthanasia of Autumn," and "The Coronation of Winter." Each has a religioscientific agenda. Hitchcock seeks, for example, both to celebrate spring as a season of spiritually significant natural beauty and to demonstrate the plausibility of the scriptural doctrine of resurrection by appeal to scientific principles.[25]

This agenda does not make for the kind of book that would have appealed to Henry Thoreau any more than the life of Chalmers that his aunt wanted him to read instead of watching frogs (*J* 5: 58). Even those doctrinally disposed collegians who overcame the sense of being captive auditors would have had their powers of deferred gratification severely tested by the antique text-doctrine-application format of Hitchcock's first discourse, on spring, which lingers for thirty pages on such thorny questions as the chemical composition of the spiritual bodies we receive upon being resurrected.

Yet in dramatizing the pervasiveness of mid-nineteenth century Protestant America's linkage between close observation of nature and theism, *Religious Lectures* exposes the cultural significance of the providential subtext of Thoreau's thought better than Emerson's *Nature* does. Thoreau's vision of the March snake in "Economy" as a symbol of human emergence from moral torpor, the metamorphosis of the beautiful bug in "Conclusion," the imagery of returning spring interlaced with quotations from I Corinthians (*Wa* 41–42, 333, 317)—these are also Hitchcock's stock in trade. Their styles strikingly converge when we look closely at Hitchcock's summer sermon, which he builds around the image of the rainbow (God's biblical promise to Noah and perpetual emblem of God's glory and human hope). Hitchcock caps his predictable homily with an anecdote of seeing a magnificent rainbow after a late afternoon summer thunderstorm. The time of day is important, one of Hitchcock's larger points being that the rainbow in evening (the hour that conventionally symbolizes death) is more portentous than the rainbow at dawn.[26] Thoreau builds an identical construct in "The Baker Farm" chapter of *Walden*. Upon leaving the cottage of the hapless Irish laborer John Field, to whom he has unsuccessfully preached his gospel of economy while taking refuge from the rain, the speaker runs "down the hill toward the reddening west, with the rainbow over my shoulder" and suddenly hears the voice of his "Good Genius" empowering him to "grow wild according to thy nature" (*Wa* 207). Thoreau does not specify the season, but circumstantial evidence makes clear that it is high summer (the *Journal* antecedent occurs 23 August 1845 [*PJ* 2: 175–179]). The phenomenon, the season, the time of day, the message of divine favor—everything matches Hitchcock with tolerable exactness except, of course, for Thoreau's classicizing of the sacral experience.[27]

It is tempting to reduce "Baker Farm" to its classism and xenophobia.[28] Hitchcock's *Lectures* help show what else was at stake, at least from Thoreau's perspective. The rainbow trope makes the chapter a climax to *Walden*'s summertime sequence, which begins in earnest with "Sounds," for it dramatizes the protagonist's chosenness more openly than any other part of the book. Those two contiguous chapters, "The Ponds" and "Baker Farm," are complementary explorations of the countryside (the first extrospectively descriptive, the second protagonist-centered), each offering visionary culminations, that of "The Ponds" being the famous doggerel hymn to Walden. In "The Ponds," however, the visionary moment is a supplication, whereas in "Baker Farm" it is a mandate from the Almighty, rendered both less and more scandalous by its paganization. The imagistic vehicle is the rainbow, which appears unobtrusively in the passage I have mentioned (another Thoreauvian strategy being avoidance of showy homiletic effects), but which is announced pointedly toward the start of the chapter as the climax to come. "Once it chanced that I stood in the very abutment of a rainbow's arch," the speaker declares, remarking on the "halo of light" that he saw around his shadow at that time (*Wa* 202). So in differentiating himself from poor Field, Thoreau filches the apparatus of evangelical natural theology. If we miss the significance of the rainbow manifesting itself late on a summer afternoon, well, that goes to show that we too belong to the race of unchosen bogtrotters.

Thoreau included the rainbow image only as an afterthought. In the

Journal original, the shower occurs, the Good Genius speaks, but no rainbow is mentioned. The decision to embroider in the process of going public seems a clear proof that Thoreau wanted to tap into conventional religiocentric nature discourse. Though he twisted that discourse, he drew on it as a framework, especially in the "Spring" chapter. Altogether, Thoreau's seasonal symbolism was thoroughly steeped in Christian troping, displayed more overtly in sermons like Hitchcock's.

Literary Bioregionalism

The notion of writing a book of local travels did not originate with Thoreau. In the early national period, neoclassical locodescriptive poetry had flourished in America, giving rise to Timothy Dwight's *Greenfield Hill* (1794) and many more ephemeral works. The period of American literary emergence proper, the antebellum period, was strongly influenced by the village portraiture of the native tales in Washington Irving's *The Sketch-Book* (1817) and in the much more ambitious *Our Village* (1824–1832) of Irving's British contemporary and acquaintance, Mary Russell Mitford. From these precedents arose, under the auspices of British writers like Elizabeth Gaskell and American writers like Catharine Maria Sedgwick, Lydia Sigourney, and Harriet Beecher Stowe, the largely female-identified genre that Sandra Zagarell has called the narrative of community. Sarah Orne Jewett's *The Country of the Pointed Firs* is the most distinguished nineteenth-century American example.[29] Meanwhile, the book of local natural history was becoming familiar through the example of Gilbert White's *Natural History of Selbourne* (1789) (*TR* #1418), which had inspired such British successors, also known to Thoreau, as John L. Knapp's *Journal of a Naturalist* (*TR* #811) and W. J. Broderip's *Leaves from the Notebook of a Naturalist* (*TR* #199). Early national writers, furthermore, had regularly included natural history as part of regional chronicle and reportage, as in the *History of New-Hampshire* by Jeremy Belknap (1791–1792) and Dwight's massive four-volume *Travels in New-England and New York* (1820).

 Walden draws on all these traditions. Thoreau was anticipated in this, however, by Susan Fenimore Cooper, the novelist's daughter and literary executor, who published an American edition of Knapp's *Journal* and an undeservedly forgotten book of her own, *Rural Hours* (1850, abridged

1887). Thoreau consulted its information about loons (*J* 4: 380). *Rural Hours* is the first major work of American literary bioregionalism, a vein developed more fully in works by such mid- to late-century natural historians as Wilson Flagg and John Burroughs, but more particularly by those writers within the much better known and related local color or regional realist movement who had strong interests in natural history— Celia Thaxter and Mary Austin especially. (This is a significant point at which "male" and "female" literary traditions crisscross and blend.)[30]

The botany, zoology, ornithology, and ichthyology of Otsego county Cooper assiduously records, along with a series of genre sketches of country housekeeping, maple sugaring, the annual cattle show, the general store, and so on. She exhibits a finely calibrated environmental sense; she distinguishes, for instance, the behavior of the individual tree from the species and keeps track of the changing ratio, year by year, between the time maple sap runs and the tree blossoms. Her apprehension of natural *history,* like George Perkins Marsh's, seems to have come more quickly and become more ingrained than it was for Thoreau because of the rapid ecological transformation her region had undergone in her lifetime. Glancing over one stretch of agricultural landscape, Cooper could differentiate at least four stages of cultivation, from the just-chopped to the long-tilled.[31]

Like *Walden, Rural Hours* shows an encyclopedic passion for bringing bibliographical resources to bear on one's native township. Observation of the local grain harvest, for example, inspires a long essay on comparative gleaning practices in the old world: France, Germany, Switzerland, and (of course) ancient Israel. Her underlying point is Thoreauvian: a sermon on economy. She considers gleaning thrifty and begging shiftless, although her compatriots find begging more acceptable than gleaning.[32] Herein lies the fundamental similarity between Thoreau and Cooper: the ability to let one's imagination play whimsically but tenaciously and indeed sometimes almost interminably over some element of local landscape, lingering over nuances and making unexpected leaps. Any subject will do, the odder and more out of the way the better: a rumor (which proves true) of a panther sighting in the county, the question of whether old-fashioned village graveyards should be broken up, the types and habits of swallows native to the region—or, as in Thoreau, the fantasia of frog choruses on summer evenings, the colors of water bodies from different vantage points, an anecdote of fox and hounds.

Like Thoreau, Cooper writes out of a passionate attachment to her locale combined with distress and contempt for provincialism, which like him she seeks to correct through practicality, erudition, and assertion, although Christian domesticity makes her persona tamer than Thoreau's. She directs some of her sharpest thrusts against ignorance of nature. "As a people," she wrote in another work, "we are still . . . half aliens to the country Providence has given us," leading lives largely unaware of "the creatures which held the land as their own long before our forefathers trod the soil." It was Cooper, not Thoreau, who among all antebellum writers wrote the most comprehensive short treatise on the history of environmental consciousness in world cultures from ancient times to the present.[33] More even than he, she deserves the title of attorney for the indigenous plants, on whose displacement by invading species she continually remarks. The prettiest flowers are native; weeds are old world imports. Cooper strikes the nationalist chord on many other topics also: the beauties of sharp seasonal change, the bird species unique to America, the difference between the condition of women in America and in Europe.

The delight Cooper takes in "natural" over artificial charms, and her pain even at small violations or displacements of that charm, are fully as keen as Thoreau's. Both of them would have agreed that "a fine tree near a house is a much greater embellishment than the thickest coat of paint that could be put on its walls." Nay, she adds, "a large shady tree in a door-yard is much more desirable than the most expensive mahogany and velvet sofa in the parlor." But Cooper praises nature over artifice not because nature is wild rather than tame, but because it "marks a farther progress" in civility than the axe-wielding phase of frontier living.[34] The shade tree and the sofa are not enemies but alternative forms of cultivation.

It comes as no surprise, therefore, to find that Cooper was more self-consciously in touch with "the literary world" than Thoreau was: more decorous about venting personal opinions, she was also more anxious to show herself current on fashions in the nature-writing line. Thoreau did up his lecture "Autumnal Tints" as if he had invented the subject laboriously out of his journal observations. "October has hardly tinged our poetry," Thoreau claims.[35] Cooper would have smiled at such naïveté. As she discourses on the same subject, she knowingly remarks that "just now allusions to beautiful 'autumnal tints' have become very much the fashion in English books," whereas the older writers do not praise autumn for its colors. (The reason, she theorized, had to do less with the rise in the standard of realism in descriptive writing than with the way that "the American autumn has helped to set the fashion for the sister season of the Old World.")[36] Now, Thoreau would have known about this trend, too: he sometimes read *Harper's* and *Putnam's* magazines; he knew perfectly well that his friend and walking companion Ellery Channing wrote poetry about fall colors. And certainly Thoreau would not have chosen to lecture and essay on autumnal tints without some dim sense of the subject's potential appeal. But he never could have brought himself to think that he was doing so *because* the topic had become fashionable. Yet precisely for that reason Cooper helps establish a context for Thoreau that he tends to suppress, and the success of her book (which Putnam promoted vigorously and which quickly went into a second printing) helps explain how Thoreau's own local book and his later nature essays came to be, and came to be received. The same publisher that brought forth *Rural Hours* and Cooper's later anthology, *The Rhymes and Reason of Country Life,* also published four installments of *Cape Cod* in *Putnam's Magazine* and included two of those same items in anthologies of "*Putnam's* best" designed for the mass market.

On the issue of wildness versus civility, then, Cooper and Thoreau stand closer than we might have thought, as will become even clearer when we consider the next genre.

The Picturesque

Though he complained about its mannerisms, Thoreau was an attentive reader in the field of landscape aesthetics. He ransacked William Gilpin's writings (*TR* #576–583), looked into Uvedale Price (*TR* #1120), and in the later 1850s read Ruskin with testy but sincere interest (*TR* #1196–1198). The high-water mark of mid-century American environmental writing influenced by theoretical work on landscape by artists and architects was *The Home Book of the Picturesque* (1852), a Putnam coffee-table book combining essays and illustrations culled from a who's who of the period's notable writers and painters: Irving, Bryant, James Fenimore Cooper, N. P. Willis, Bayard Taylor; Daniel Huntington, Jasper Cropsey, John Frederick Kensett, and Asher B. Durand (one of Ruskin's foremost American devotees, to whom the volume was dedicated).[37] Most of the essays evoke vistas ("West Rock, New Haven," "Schroon Lake," "The Valley of the Housatonic"), which the artwork visualizes with tasteful, soothing glimpses of rills, trees, and bridges.

That Thoreau neither contributed to nor, so far as we know, even looked at this volume is symptomatic of the contrast between him and Susan Fenimore Cooper, who wrote one of its best essays. In *Rural Hours* we already find Cooper holding forth on how current theory of landscape representation is moving in a more realist direction, with Ruskin presumably in mind, while Thoreau's great authority at this juncture is still the late neoclassicist Gilpin.[38] Yet Thoreau himself helped carry out the very revolution in taste that Cooper discusses even though he would certainly not have described himself as ushering transcendentalist prose from its romantic phase to the representational density and fidelity to "isness" commended by Ruskin. His style of writing in *Walden* was already more "modern" than those of the contributors to the *Home Book,* most of whom were constrained by ponderous classical symmetries. ("When we meditate in plains, the globe appears youthful and imbecile; among crags and mountains, it exhibits energy and the gravity of age.")[39] So Thoreau might have disdained *The Home Book* as a production that, however current its topical references and its dedication, was already dated.

It is a major ingredient of the Thoreauvian intertext nonetheless. Both it and Thoreau are obsessed with how land is seen aesthetically: as landscape, as scenery.

> The scenery of Walden is on a humble scale, and, though very beautiful, does not approach to grandeur. (*Wa* 175)
> [Compare Susan Cooper: "Our own highland lake can lay no claim to grandeur; . . . yet there is a harmony in the different parts of the picture which gives it much merit."][40]

> The beech, which has so neat a bole and beautifully lichen-painted, perfect in all its details. (*Wa* 201)

> Gradually from week to week the character of each tree came out, and it admired itself reflected in the smooth mirror of the lake. Each morning the manager of this gallery substituted some new picture, distinguished by more brilliant or harmonious coloring, for the old upon the walls. (*Wa* 240)

> Thus for sixteen days I saw from my window a hundred men at work like busy husbandmen, with teams and horses and apparently all the implements of farming, such a picture as we see on the first page of the almanac. (*Wa* 297)

The first passage manipulates the "right" art vocabulary to describe his hermitage; the third and fourth self-consciously convert event into artifacts; the second imitates—and corrects—*Remarks on Forest Scenery* (*TR* #582), in which Gilpin complains that the beech tree's attractive trunk is spoiled by a "very deficient" "skeleton."[41] That Thoreau did not produce these passages merely for publication purposes is clear from the frequency with which the later *Journal* records aesthetic pleasure at points when the day or the landscape seemed to organize itself as a composition: sunsets, distant views, vegetational patterns, and so on. No less than John Denham, John Dyer, Thomas Gray, and Susan Cooper did Thoreau favor lovely hilltop views.[42]

Thoreau extends the cultural nationalist project of *The Home Book* using the dual strategy of discovering wildness near home and stylizing the mundane, like the Irish ice harvesters (in contrast to Emerson's complaint that the mess they made might prompt him to sell his Walden holdings, especially since the march of progress had increased the land's resale value).[43] Thoreau manipulated picturesque cliché with gusto even as he put it under pressure. "Former Inhabitants," for example, pretends to give short shrift to the picturesque passion for ruins. "Deliver me," the speaker cries, "from a city built on the site of a more ancient city, whose materials are ruins, whose gardens cemeteries" (*Wa* 264). But this plea comes only after he has played the ruined cottage motif to the hilt ("Still grows the vivacious lilac a generation after the door and lintel and the sill are gone, unfolding its sweet-scented flowers each spring, to be plucked by the musing traveller" [*Wa* 263]). Susan Cooper executes her contribution to *The Home Book* (a distant Indian summer prospect of a certain American village) in a more conventionally picturesque way by flashing forward in time to an epoch when the comparatively unstylized landscape might effuse a certain antique old world charm, the burgeoning town replaced by "low picturesque, thatched cottages," with a "half-ruined convent" somewhere in the middle distance.[44] Thoreau would have scorned this image, but the will to stylize scenes otherwise banal or philistine ran equally strong in him.

The title page illustration to *The Home Book* is a splendid bridge over the New York and Erie Railroad, viewed from the gorge below. The scenic pleasures of travel along that line are effusively celebrated in an essay by Bayard Taylor ("wonder beyond the tales of Scheherazade!—our superb train carried a heart of luxury into that savage realm").[45] The essay and the accompanying illustration show how intricately symbiotic was modernization in *all* its branches with the business of writing about nature: beyond providing a creative stimulus or irritant, the transportation revolution fed the taste for such writing by making the originals accessible in comfort, as an indispensable part of the marketing and distribution process, as an instance of the technological sophistication that enabled the production of such beautifully illustrated American books, and as a manifestation of the national wealth that made them salable.[46] Railroads threatened the landscape but increased the taste for nature writing and the incentives to produce it; trains even enhanced aesthetic pleasure when perched on trestles athwart deep romantic chasms. The railroad, as much in *Walden* as in the *The Home Book,* is the predominant, polymorphous industrial leitmotif. It was symbolically right that Thoreau moved to Walden just after the Concord and Fitchburg Railroad pushed through— maybe even historically determined if we suppose (although this is pure guesswork) that Emerson's purchase of acreage at the pond stemmed from speculative farsightedness as well as natural piety. Not only did the railroad inspire the ambivalent responses to technology that Leo Marx has disentangled;[47] it also provided Thoreau with whimsical sound effects, the romance of commerce, and the "natural" spectacle for the climactic sandbank passage in "Spring." In the long run, the railroad also helped ensure Thoreau's canonization; for during the half-century following Thoreau's death by far the easiest way to make the Walden pilgrimage was by train from Boston.

Walden resembles the picturesque essay more in its aesthetic self-consciousness than in its tone. In the average contribution to the *Home Book* and the endless issues of popular illustrated magazines that stand behind it, the two sides of the rhetorical coin are effusion ("it seemed as if seraphic music might breathe from that dreamy mist")[48] and genial

urbanity verging on flipness (Taylor's "wonder beyond the tales of Scheherazade"). Though they try to sound like devotees of rural simplicity,
the authors are all men and women of the world, whatever their literal
places of residence, writing for readers who might be interested in renting
an exurban villa or going on a luxury excursion to a major beauty spot.

The result is a kind of chronic stylized levity to which Thoreau tried
at intervals to adapt himself ("The Landlord," written specifically for
popular magazine consumption, was his most concerted effort of this
sort), but only occasionally managed to assimilate on anything like his
own terms. His wit was too waspish, his enthusiasm unsupple. These
tendencies formed the basis of James Russell Lowell's famous criticism of
A Week on the Concord and Merrimack Rivers, that "we were bid to a
river-party, not to be preached at." In effect, Lowell indicted Thoreau for
breach of generic contract.[49] Lowell's own understanding of appropriate
picturesque excursion discourse is well illustrated by his version of "The
Maine Woods," titled "A Moosehead Journal" and serialized by *Putnam's
Magazine* the year before *Walden* appeared. Addressed in a bantering tone
to a German academic friend, it contains a maximum of chatter and a
minimum sense of place. ("There is very little about Moosehead Lake in
it," Lowell confesses in the last entry. "I did not profess to give you an
account of the lake, but a journal.")[50] Yet Lowell's perplexity over *A Week*
was more pardonable than in his later, harsher dismissal of Thoreau's
whole career. Thoreau's apprentice work in environmental nonfiction
followed the picturesque excursion format closely enough to make a
person who liked and even wrote in this genre wonder at the violation
of what seemed an obvious decorum.[51]

Natural History Writing

During Thoreau's lifetime, "science" in the modern sense was introduced
into English usage and became irreversibly professionalized. Concurrently
natural history writing for nonscientists reached a new standard of literary and empirical sophistication. Thoreau read widely both in manuals
and monographs like Gray's *Botany* (*TR* #617) and Lyell's *Geology* (*TR*
#902) and in popularizations like the geological lectures of Hugh Miller
(*TR* #980–981) and the charming melanges of Philip Henry Gosse (*TR*
#609). "I would keep some book of natural history always by me as a

sort of elixir," he exudes in an early essay.[52] Indeed, Thoreau's first published work of environmental nonfiction, the one just quoted, was a "review" of state reports on the natural history of Massachusetts, given over to displaying his own experiential knowledge in a series of descriptive rambles; in "Ktaadn" (1848) and *A Week* (1849), botanical, geological, and ichthyological observations at times dominate the text. One common type of natural history writing that particularly attracted Thoreau from the first was the profile, or profile series, of individual species and genera: the portrait of the fox in "Natural History," the catalog of fishes in "Saturday" of *A Week,* the owls in "Sounds" and "Winter Animals," the mouse and loon in "Brute Neighbors." A staple of natural history books and magazines to this day, it was fully established by the 1840s. Wilson and Audubon had set the standard in American ornithology (*TR* #70–71, #1439–40), and J. J. Audubon and John Bachman had begun to carry that same standard into mammalology, with their volume *The Viviparous Quadrupeds of North America* (1846) (*TR* #72). Their observations were embroidered and extended by more self-consciously literary magazinists of the middle third of the century, including Wilson Flagg (birds and trees), Thomas Wentworth Higginson (flowers), and John Burroughs (birds).[53]

Within the company of literary naturalists, from the start Thoreau ranked high, higher indeed than in any other literary coterie during his lifetime. He was remembered in the annals of the Boston Society of Natural History as an "unrivalled" "observer of the habits of animals." Thoreau's first literary disciple of any importance, Higginson, also credited Thoreau with "unerring eyes." He "camps down by Walden Pond, and shows us that absolutely nothing in Nature has ever yet been described." Flagg was hurt by Thoreau's criticism of his phlegmatic writing style but paid tribute to him after his death; Burroughs delighted in exposing Thoreau's errors, bridled at being likened to him, but fought a losing battle against conceding that Thoreau was the more pungent writer of the two.[54]

Literary natural history writing normally required a more sober tone than the picturesque narrative or sketch. Minute facts had to be got straight; it was crucial for the public to know that the eye sockets of day owls lack "that extreme prominence and mobility . . . which give to the nocturnal species so rare a power of sight in the glimmer of the gloaming, or even in the rayless gloom of midnight." It was equally important, or so thought this same *Putnam's* contributor, to defend the owl tribe against the perfidy of superstition, as a protector of humankind against the "deadly devastators" of dovecote and granary; important not simply to list but to celebrate the owl's advantages of anatomy, such as "his powerful retractile talons, wherewith" he seizes "the lithe and sinewy weasel, or the slippery and reluctant snake."[55]

Not that levity is banished from such accounts; it hardly could be, caught as the writers often felt between niggling experts and bored laypeople scorning naturalists as a race of pedants, like Obed Bat in Cooper's *The Prairie.* So the owl defender must resort to awkward pleasantries like "Signor Owl" the "occasional pullicide or columbicide" and emphasize in a footnote that he "aims only, while amusing, to induce others to observe, and contribute their mite, however humble." Thoreau was entirely typical of nineteenth-century literary naturists in knowing his passion for nature to be thought eccentric. "Even among our literary classes," declared fellow New England naturalist Wilson Flagg, "if you speak of trees and woods, there is only an occasional individual of eccentric habits who seems capable of taking any other than an aesthetic view of their relations to human wants."[56] Thoreau's response in *Walden* to this kind of perception was to use natural history cameos sparingly and infuse light touches into a number of them (the "aldermanic" frogs, the "Jonsonian" or Macbethish screech owls, the epic ant fight [*Wa* 124–126, 228ff.]) without sacrificing either his zest for detail or for pushing toward grand thoughts: thoughts of the screech owls, for instance, as "the low spirits and melancholy forebodings, of fallen souls that once in human shape night-walked the earth and did the deeds of darkness, now expiating their sins with their wailing hymns or threnodies in the scenery of their transgressions" (*Wa* 124). Here Thoreau infuses the playfulness of "Signor Owl" with a version of the magazine writer's zeal to establish the owl, all kidding aside, as "rarely . . . adapted by the hand of the All-wise Artificer to the purposes for which he is intended."[57] Only Thoreau's owl is at once more whimsical and more metaphysically hypercharged than the pedantic magazinist's.

The natural history profile of Thoreau's day did not much encourage metaphysical flights. But it did license what by today's standards would seem a great degree of subjectified, asymmetrical, and idiosyncratic treat-

ment, including the introduction of an almost unlimited array of anecdotes and asides, so that even writers of relatively austere imagination
could fashion their cameos into little heterocosms. Even among submis-
sions to avowedly scientific publications, an "Enumeration of the Fishes
of Brookhaven, Long Island" might include helpful hints on how to catch
bluefish, and an inventory of birds observed in Florida might recall the
problems of fighting off alligators to retrieve the specimens the author
shot.[58] The *Viviparous Quadrupeds* of Audubon and Bachman, a book
Thoreau knew well (*TR* #72), is a more pertinent case, being a serious
work of natural history intended to pass muster with zoologists. Certain
portions of their entries are cut-and-dried: on description, color, dimensions, range. But the sections on "habits" and "general remarks" stretch
out to what seems a delightful infinity. For example, under "Habits" of
mus leucopus (compare *Wa* 225–226) we learn how white-footed mice
climb up and down vines from their refuge in cedar trees in New Jersey,
how their nests in New York hay sheaves rival the Baltimore oriole's in
intricacy, how the authors once raised a female who had several litters in
quick succession, how an eminent botanist "unfortunately killed in the
Florida war" was once kept awake by frisky mice in his cabin, how
white-footed mice are timid and gentle and seldom bite when taken into
the hand, how *mus leucopus* has been slandered unfairly by farmers. This
account makes for a fascinating (to some) welter of detail, like Charles
Lamb on old china perhaps, alongside which Thoreau's sketch of his
dealings with the same creature looks like quite the regular naturalist's
account.[59] Although Thoreau hardly designed the short sketches in "Brute
Neighbors" and "Winter Animals" of his dealings with Concord fauna as
substitutes for formal expositions, the intermixture of fact, narrative, and
autobiography, even the tonal interweave of reportage and playful mock-
epic pedantry, did not differ in kind from many natural history publications designed for general audiences. Conversely, amateur literati like
Higginson could imagine their work making a contribution to the botanical record as well as dramatizing nature. ("I have formerly found the
hepatica in bloom at Mount Auburn, for three successive years, on the
twenty-seventh of March; and it has since been found in Worcester on
the seventeenth, and in Danvers on the twelfth.")[60] His detailed observations suggest, in turn, that the "general reader" of the day's literature was
really interested in being told these facts. The taste for detail increased in

the late nineteenth century, influenced not only by popular interest in knowing about the natural world but also by the aesthetic movement we inadequately call realism. Neither then nor later would Thoreau's *Journal* make pleasant reading for large audiences, but by the 1880s generous selections from it could sell as many copies as *Walden* had sold during Thoreau's lifetime. Thoreau's awareness of this emerging public taste undoubtedly explains in part why he closed his publishing career on the note with which he began: as a writer of literary natural history.[61]

As it gained in popularity in the later nineteenth century,[62] literary natural history writing tended to raise its standard of precision in matters of detail, as per Higginson's punctilious reportage, and to narrow its field of concentration. A literature of garden, farm, and estate sprung up, for instance, influenced as much by picturesque aesthetics as by natural history and exemplified by certain among Henry Ward Beecher's *Star Papers* (1855), *Country Living and Country Thinking* (1862) by Mary Abigail Dodge ("Gail Hamilton"), and *My Farm of Edgewood* (1863) by Donald G. Mitchell ("Ik Marvell"). From this line descended a large family of American country writing on which Thoreau's influence was almost nil. His impact has been much greater on literary field naturalism of byway, edgeland, and wilderness of the sort also practiced by Flagg, Burroughs, and Muir.

Travel Narrative

Thoreau's favorite form of environmental prose, travel narratives appealed to him more than any other kind of contemporary writing. He is known to have read nearly two hundred books in the genre, most in their entirety.[63] The category of "travel narrative" merges with the previous two, of course: some travel accounts are picturesque essays (such as Bayard Taylor's aforementioned paean to the railroad), and "most travelers were naturalists in some degree."[64] Such works supplied Thoreau with data, metaphors, and formal models. For example, *The Commerce of the Prairies* (*TR* #627), a memoir of the Santa Fe trade by entrepreneur-adventurer Josiah Gregg, supplied Thoreau with information about ruthless, wasteful slaughter of buffalo for their tongues and about prairie dog "towns" (a description Gregg laced with urban metaphors and accompanied by a somewhat whimsical illustration).[65] These tidbits Thoreau then worked into *Walden* (238, 167), using them to satirize rapacious farmers and vacuous villagers, respectively, and in the case of the prairie dogs to sustain a metaphor of travel—picturing himself trekking from one "horizon" to another, as if across a vast open expanse, from the demesne of muskrats to the "village of busy men, as curious to me as if they had been prairie dogs, each sitting at the mouth of its burrow, or running over to a neighbor's to gossip." The countless analogies of this sort between near and distant that Thoreau drew on the basis of his travel reading, throughout the *Journal* and all his published works, kept his powers of observation alive, his sense of local drama keen, and his lococentrism from stodginess. Finally, *The Commerce of the Prairies* served Thoreau as a model of mixed-mode prose, being at once a narrative anatomy of a heroic enterprise with the author as hero, a discussion of natural history (with chapters on the geography and the fauna of the prairies), and an anthropological account (with six chapters on the Indians).

No contemporary travel book interested Thoreau more than the one that became most enduringly famous: Charles Darwin's *Journal of Researches . . . during the Voyage of HMS Beagle* (1839) (*TR* #384). Unlike Gregg, Darwin does not organize his account into discrete sections of narrative and scholarship but arranges it chronologically, alternating topographical, botanical, and geological description with micronarratives in a daybook. This journal format was doubtless a part of his popularizing strategy, announced in the preface to the second edition (1845): to sketch the history of the voyage and such "observations in Natural History and Geology, which I think will possess some interest for the general reader." Darwin refers those looking for rigorous specialized analysis to his monographs on coral reefs and volcanic islands.[66]

One striking feature of Darwin's work, common to most travel literature then and now, is his conflation of natural and human phenomena under the traveler's appraising eye, so that he can throw together observations of *Homo sapiens,* nonhuman species, and landscape panoramas into a tossed salad of perceptions. In the reading experience if not in the narrative analysis, boundaries between species become porous. On the one hand, this approach instilled something like an "ecological" vision of human and natural history as parts of a single environment, a vision common to Susan Cooper's bioregional chronicle as well. On the other hand, the same approach might also authorize the imperial gaze of the Olympian observer, especially when the traveler focused on "primitive" peoples. The Fuegians, for instance, struck Darwin as more like animals than men. ("One of our arms being bared, they expressed the liveliest surprise and admiration at its whiteness, just in the same way in which I have seen the ourang-outang do at the Zoological Gardens.")[67]

Thoreau's response to travel-book ethnonaturalism was complex. To a considerable extent he adopted the convention or ideology of the gaze, in the process "otherizing" figures like the Irish laborer John Field and the French Canadian woodchopper (in "Visitors"), of whom Thoreau complacently notes "in him the animal man chiefly was developed" (*Wa* 146). Yet Thoreau also reversed the gaze, making Darwin testify, for example, against himself by praising savages' capacity to thrive in the savage state. Significantly, Thoreau's single overt citation of Darwin in *Walden* refers to one of Darwin's few concessions to the Fuegians' superior powers, their adaptation to the cold climate (*Wa* 12–13). This is but one among many spots where *Walden* undermines the hierarchies of civilization/barbarity (the villagers as bizarre penance-performing Brahmins) and humanity/animal (the villagers as prairie dogs, himself competing with squirrels for fall forage).[68]

Such instances of undermining do not reflect Thoreau's attempt to quarrel with Darwin as much as Thoreau's desire to accentuate tendencies already present in Darwin and other travelers' accounts. Take for example a passage from the Australian section of *Journal of Researches,* notable for its anticipation of Darwin's mature theory of natural selection and for the social Darwinist edifice later reared on his thought, in which Darwin reflects that

> Wherever the European has trod, death seems to pursue the aboriginal . . . Nor is it the white man alone that thus acts the destroyer; the Polynesian of Malay extraction has in parts of the East Indian archipelago, thus driven before him the dark-coloured native. The varieties of man seem to act on each other in the same way as different species of animals—the stronger always extirpating the weaker. It was melancholy at New Zealand to hear the fine energetic natives saying that they knew the land was doomed to pass from their children. Every one has heard of the inexplicable reduction of the population in the beautiful and healthy island of Tahiti since the days of Captain Cook's voyages.[69]

Anyone looking for evidence that naturalists, equally with missionaries, served as lackeys of conquerers can obviously find it here. The Caucasianist magisterialism is blatant. Equally obvious, though, are the countercurrents within Darwin's reduction of sociology to ethology ("the varieties of man seem to act on each other in the same way as different species of animals") and his desire to give "the fine energetic natives" a certain hearing. No simple celebration of the triumph of white civilization over barbarity, this passage acknowledges the subjection of all races to biological givens whose implications trouble him. Tonally, the passage sounds as much like that of late twentieth-century ecological colonization theory as that of late nineteenth-century social Darwinism.[70] So Darwin, like Thoreau albeit to a lesser degree, was prepared to relativize moral distinctions between "advanced" and "backward" cultures and between human and animal estates.

Ethnonaturalist conflation did not impress itself as a distinct idea on Thoreau as he read the *Journal of Researches*. Thoreau reacted in curious wonderment at the plenitude of the strange new life-forms he found recorded there. He was struck, for instance, by a passage on a species of kelp, "worthy of a particular history," which because of its enormous size functions as a habitat for a universe of tiny creatures.[71] Thoreau comments: "Number of living creatures of all orders whose experience seems to depend on the kelp—a volume might be written on them. If a forest were destroyed anywhere so many species would not perish as if this weed were—& with the fish would go many birds & larger marine animals, and hence the Fuegian himself perchance" (*PJ* 3: 258). The sense of vast "numbers of living creatures" comes first; then comes the intimation of interdependence of creatures; but in the long run, Thoreau carries the latter point farther than Darwin does. To tuck the Fuegian (on whom Darwin has just commented pungently and on whom Thoreau has just taken notes) into this ecological daydream was Thoreau's extrapolation.

The Upshot

Darwin has been said to have achieved a breakthrough in Victorian prose by expressing through his rhetoric the vision of the insubstantiality of formal categories that constitutes the revolutionary element of his philosophy of evolution. "By involving the reader in a perceptual chaos that parallels the organic chaos of the entangled bank, Darwin demonstrates the formlessness of evolutionary nature and the artificiality of a theory of distinct species," James Krasner observes. Some typical marks of this "perceptual chaos" are the rapid, unprocessed profusion of imagery in some of Darwin's responses to the tropics and his catalogs of animal parts near the start of *Origin of Species:* "Hairless dogs have imperfect teeth; long-haired and coarse-haired animals are apt to have, as is asserted, long or many horns; pigeons with feathered feet have skin between their outer toes; pigeons with short beaks have small feet, and those with long beaks large feet." Of such descriptions Krasner notes that "the swiftness of the images, their minute precision, and their almost surreal disassociation combine to create a welter of whirling animal parts that constricts the possibility of imaging a whole form."[72] This is an attractive argument— that the Darwinian moment in intellectual history brings with it a new order in environmental prose by contrast to the comparative linearity and structuredness of Paley, Malthus, and Lyell. If it were wholly accurate, it would make a wonderful culmination to this chapter. For in Thoreau we can find similar tendencies, which together with his late-in-life approval of *Origin of Species* (a book he had read soon after it became available in America) might warrant our placing him as an anticipator of the great Darwinian revolution in environmental prose as well as biological theory.[73] One thinks immediately of the climactic sandbank passage in the "Spring" chapter of *Walden,* where Thoreau decomposes the human body into a paratactic series of supposedly analogous forms: "Is not the hand a spreading *palm* leaf with its lobes and veins? The ear may be regarded, fancifully, as a lichen, *umbilicaria,* on the side of the head, with its lobe or drop . . . The nose is a manifest congealed drop or stalactite" (*Wa* 307–308).

We cannot so easily pin down the genealogy of the rhetoric of perceptual chaos, however. That of Thoreau's passage is arguably more post-Emersonian than pre-Darwinian. Its intellectual roots are in romantic philology and *naturphilosophie.*[74] Indeed the vision of unstable forms and an accompanying rhetoric of perceptual disorientation could arise during the mid-nineteenth century from causes having nothing whatever to do with the theory of species. In the work of Susan Cooper, it can be traced to her sense of the vertiginous pace of American environmental transformation, such that to look afield was to see not an integral pasture but a strange botanical patchwork: "The shepherd's purse . . . is common in China, on the most eastern coast of Asia. One kind of mallows belongs to the East Indies; another to the coast of the Mediterranean. The Jimson weed, or Datura, is an Abyssinian plant, and the Nicandra came from Peru." In her "Dissolving View" essay for *The Home Book of the Picturesque,* Cooper disintegrates the same landscape in another way, fast-forwarding it through several stages of development.[75]

But an even more fundamental aspect of the instability of form thematized and evinced by the environmental writing we have surveyed is its rudimentary and uncertain grasp of appropriate forms for rendering an environmental plenum. From the genres we have examined can be extracted three primary ways of organizing environmental material, all seemingly inchoate: as seasonal chronicle, as episodes in an excursion, and as items in an inventory. Each approach invites atomization: a catalog of spring events, a series of things seen, a bestiary. The fragmentation is compounded for a writer like Thoreau who is pulled in several different discursive directions simultaneously, as in this sentence from "Spring":

> I am particularly attracted by the arching and sheaf-like top of the wool-grass; it brings back the summer to our winter memories, and is among the forms which art loves to copy, and which, in the vegetable kingdom, have the same relation to types already in the mind of man that astronomy has. (*Wa* 310)

What's going on here? What sort of discourse is this? In the taxonomy this chapter has created, the passage belongs by turns to natural history (the precisely visualized knotgrass detected by Thoreau's botanizing eye comes at the end of a catalog of spring-appearing plants), to the literary almanac (but disrupting the genre by splicing seasons together), to the picturesque ("among the forms which art loves to copy"), to homily (the wool-grass typologically considered). In other words, there is an instability of form built into Thoreauvian prose by reason of its multi-discursiveness, apart from any theory that Thoreau might or might not be entertaining here about the instability of bioforms as such. On the contrary, with respect to its biological vision the passage suffuses a most un-Darwinian stolidity, for Thoreau hardly questions the fixity of wool-grass as a species; indeed, at this moment he is not even at the stage of protoevolutionary consciousness Emerson reached by the second edition of *Nature,* which he introduced with the ditty of the worm, "striving to be man," mounting "through all the spires of form."[76] Indeed, Thoreau positively glories in the immutability of the wool-grass as a seasonal marker. Certainly he does want to blur and unfix nature's categories nonetheless; to redefine spring as a legacy of winter, which sculpted the grass form, to summer; to make the material object form metamorphose into art form and then into a relation so abstruse it can no longer even be imagined. (What in the world *is* the figural resemblance between astronomy and wool-grass, anyway?)[77] And this analysis does not begin to address the fragmentation at the chapter level that results from having created a more or less freestanding paragraph nominally on the subject of "the first tender signs of the infant year," which turns into a fantasia on this single plant, whose relation to the pondside setting of the previous paragraph or the cabinside location of the next is never stated.

Altogether, it would be as valid to credit nineteenth-century environmental prose with creating an auspicious climate for the destabilizing practices of Thoreau and Darwin as to credit either of them with having destabilized environmental prose. But it remains true that Darwin's ideas and Thoreau's art have influenced not only the course of modern science and modern environmental writing, respectively, but also the rewriting of history, so that we now imagine nineteenth century thought as leading up to Darwin and early American environmental writing as an antedeluvian phase "before Thoreau." That this assessment is more true poetically than literally is not to deny that the power that their writings continue to exert.

But does this conclusion not refute my defense in Chapter 12 of the author as responsible agent? There I represented the canonical work *(Walden)* as authorial act and the figure of the author as a paradigmatic individual, exerting influence on readers by reason of his inferred personhood. In this appendix I have characterized Thoreau as a negotiator among a menu of preexisting environmental discourses and chiefly stressed *Walden*'s imbrication with these, not its status as unique testament. I consider these perspectives, however, to be mutually illuminating, not antithetical. Thoreau's standing as an independent agent is calibrated, not confuted, by the realization that his literary masterpiece was an intricate nest woven idiosyncratically out of materials gathered from diverse sources. Indeed, only if one starts from an impossibly puristic conception of independent agency, such as Emerson's vision of an original relation to the universe, can the record of Thoreau's borrowings fail to deepen one's respect in the long run for the complexity of the task he set himself and for having arrived at a distinctive synthesis even as his style of thought and writing continued to be molded by discursive conventions from so many quarters. Even if we cannot resist feeling some romantic disappointment at the spectacle of his dependence on his culture, our awakening to Thoreau's degree of cultural embeddedness can help us ultimately to repossess him as a more pertinent, usable exemplar of the quest for environmental—indeed, any sort of—enlightenment, which even the most brilliant and imaginative individuals must conduct amidst, with, and against sociocultural forces that set the initial terms of inquiry.

By that standard, Thoreau remains both securely enshrined as an extraordinary figure and immediately accessible as a creature of his era, whose conventionalisms, confusions, and opacities afford as useful an admonishing mirror for his readers as do his triumphs of art and perception. Properly understood, the former do not compromise the latter; if anything, a lively awareness of the limitations quickens one's respect for the achievements. Thoreau affirmed as much when, in another context, he held up as the goal and mark of effective expression that "the volatile truth of our words should continually betray the inadequacy of the residual statement" (*Wa* 325). He took it for granted that a text's original power consisted in being able partially to resist its inertial tendencies. Indeed, who could reasonably ask more than this of a book—or of a life?

Notes

Introduction

1. "Ecocentrism" is defined succinctly by Timothy O'Riordan as follows: "Ecocentrism preaches the virtues of reverence, humility, responsibility, and care; it argues for low impact technology (but is not antitechnological); it decries bigness and impersonality in all forms (but especially in the city); and demands a code of behavior that seeks permanence and stability based upon ecological principles of diversity and homeostasis" (*Environmentalism*, 2d ed. [London: Pion, 1981], p. 1). I propose two amendments: (1) that ecocentrism may in fact be antitechnological, and (2) that it need not adhere to a dogma of homeostasis. Otherwise the definition suffices. O'Riordan distinguishes two, often intersecting, modes of ecocentrism, that of "bioethics" (committed "to protect the integrity of natural ecosystems" [p. 4]), and that committed to "the establishment of small, self-sustaining communities where nature still [was] very much in evidence" (p. 7). This accords with the best historical study of western "ecologism" as a political force, Anna Bramwell's *Ecology in the Twentieth Century: A History* (New Haven: Yale University Press, 1989). The premodern origins of ecologism and ecocentrism Bramwell locates in holistic biology and energy economics, while O'Riordan finds *the* "root" of both modes of modern (western) ecocentrism in American transcendentalism (p. 3). Donald Worster's *Nature's Economy: The Roots of Ecology* (1977; rpt. Garden City, N.Y.: Doubleday, 1979), the most ambitious survey of the history of modern western ecological thinking, also attaches great historical importance to the "arcadian" tradition represented by Henry Thoreau but sees its modern origins in post-Renaissance thinking from the Cambridge Platonists through Gilbert White. Some scholars, like political theorist Robyn Eckersley, would distinguish more strenuously than O'Riordan and Bramwell do between strictly "ecocentric" and relatively "anthropocentric" forms of ecologism, restricting "ecocentric" for approaches that regard "the question of our proper place in the rest of nature as logically prior to the question of what are the most appropriate social and political arrangements for human communities" (*Environmentalism and Political Theory: Toward an Ecocentric Approach* [Albany: State University of New York Press, 1992], p. 28), though as Eckersley admits this distinction is hard to apply.

2. The number of environmental thinkers who have stressed the need for new paradigms for envisioning the relation between human and nonhuman is far too great to begin listing here. Two exemplary recent presentations are Freya Mathews, *The Ecological Self* (New York: Barnes and Noble, 1991), and Neil Evernden, *The Social Creation of Nature* (Baltimore: Johns Hopkins University Press, 1992). Mathews develops an ecological metaphysics on the basis of relativity theory and Spinozan philosophy; Evernden traces the collapse of post-Renaissance episte-mology, as he sees it, from dualism into "materialistic monism" and looks for the clues to an alternative within the comparatively unmediated vision of early childhood. I cite these studies not so much for their specific arguments as for their eclectic pursuit of the idea that a reinvention of vision and values is the key to environmental amelioration (or failure). My own arguments do not derive from any one school or model of ecocentric thinking. Some would consider my emphasis on environmental crisis as a crisis of "vision" or "attitude" a version of "deep ecology" (for an overview of which, see Andrew McLaughlin, *Regarding Nature: Industrialism and Deep Ecology* [Albany: State University of New York Press, 1993], pp. 169–196); but I see my approach rather as broadly humanist and eclectic; and I shall not for the most part classify the literature I discuss in terms of categories taken from this or that branch of environmental studies, "conser-vationist" or "preservationist," for example. I should say of most of the green writers treated in this book what philosopher Bryan G. Norton sensibly says about environmentalists generally (apropos two of my own cases in point, Aldo Leopold and Rachel Carson): that "most activist environmentalists will operate . . . with systems that are not closed" (*Toward Unity among Environmentalists* [New York: Oxford University Press, 1991], p. 68).

3. Gérard Genette, *Narrative Discourse: An Essay in Method,* trans. Jane E. Lewin (Ithaca: Cornell University Press, 1980).

4. Albert Gore, *Earth in the Balance: Ecology and the Human Spirit* (Boston: Houghton Mifflin, 1992), p. 269.

5. Victor B. Scheffer, *The Shaping of Environmentalism in America* (Seattle: University of Washington Press, 1991), p. 113. This is a readable introductory history. See also Samuel P. Hays, *Beauty, Health, and Permanence: Environmental Politics in the United States, 1955–1985* (Cambridge, Eng.: Cambridge University Press, 1987), a detailed study of public policy and opinion that argues, persua-sively to my mind, that notwithstanding the conservative administrations of the 1980s the post–World War II era deserves to be called the Environmental Era.

6. Worster, *Nature's Economy*, p. 22.

7. Among the important discussions of the need to set limits to growth as a global priority, see for example Donella H. Meadows, Dennis L. Meadows, Jørgen Randers, and William W. Behrens III, *The Limits to Growth: A Report for the Club of Rome's Project on the Predicament of Mankind* (New York: Universe Books,

1972); the recent revision and reaffirmation by the first three authors, *Beyond the Limits: Confronting Global Collapse, Envisioning a Sustainable Future* (Post Mills, Vt.: Chelsea Green Publishing, 1992); and William Ophuls, *Ecology and the Politics of Scarcity: Prologue to a Political Theory of the Steady State* (San Francisco: Freeman, 1977). For a wry appraisal of some of the fiendish complications involved in forming a bona fide global culture on the basis of ecocentrism, see for example Andrew Ross, "Is Global Culture Warming Up?" *Social Text,* 28 (1991): 3–30.

8. On the psychological and social influence of metaphor, see for example Sallie McFague, *Metaphorical Theology: Models of God in Religious Language* (Philadelphia: Fortress, 1982); George Lakoff and Mark Johnson, *Metaphors We Live By* (Chicago: University of Chicago Press, 1980); Johnson, *The Body in the Mind: The Bodily Basis of Meaning, Imagination, and Reason* (Chicago: University of Chicago Press, 1987); and Lakoff, *Women, Fire, and Dangerous Things: What Categories Reveal about the Mind* (Chicago: University of Chicago Press, 1987). A shorter treatment that focuses specifically on the social power of metaphors of the environment (the book as nature, "man" as microcosm, and nature as machine) is William J. Mills, "Metaphorical Vision: Changes in Western Attitudes to the Environment," *Annals of the Association of American Geographers,* 72 (1982): 237–253. See also, however, the critique of Lakoff and Johnson by Naomi Quinn, "The Cultural Basis of Metaphor," in *Beyond Metaphor: The Theory of Tropes in Anthropology,* ed. James W. Fernandez, (Stanford: Stanford University Press, 1991), in which Quinn argues that "particular metaphors are selected by speakers, and are favored by these speakers, just because they provide satisfying mappings onto already existing cultural understandings" (p. 65). This seems an important qualification but not a decisive refutation of the cultural power of metaphor.

9. See the contributions of Edmund Schofield and Don Henley to *Heaven Is under Our Feet,* ed. Henley and Dave Marsh (New York: Berkley, 1991), pp. 9–36; D. C. D. Pocock, "The Novelist's Image of the North," *Transactions of the Institute of British Geographers,* 4, n.s. (1979): 62–76; and especially Kenneth Robert Olwig, "Literature and 'Reality': The Transformation of the Jutland Heath," in *Human-istic Geography and Literature: Essays on the Experience of Place,* ed. Douglas C. D. Pocock (London: Croom Helm, 1981), pp. 47–65, elaborated in Olwig, *Nature's Ideological Landscape: Preservation on Denmark's Jutland Heath* (London: Allen and Unwin, 1984). Olwig's is the most fully documented study I know of the impact of literary art on environmental policy.

10. The seminal contemporary formulation of this idea is Herbert Marcuse, *One Dimensional Man: Studies in the Ideology of Advanced Industrial Society* (Boston: Beacon, 1966). It has lately, somewhat serendipitously but very force-fully, resurfaced in American "new historicist" criticism. For an exemplary dis-cussion, see Myra Jehlen, "The Novel and the Middle Class in America," *Salma-*

428 ❖ Notes to Pages 4–5

gundi, 36 (1977), reprinted in *Ideology and Classic American Literature* ed. Sacvan Bercovitch and Jehlen (Cambridge, Eng.: Cambridge University Press, 1986), pp. 125–144.

11. On American suburbanization, see Kenneth T. Jackson, *Crabgrass Frontier: The Suburbanization of the United States* (New York: Oxford University Press, 1985), which prophesies that "no other nation . . . is likely ever to be as suburban as the United States is now, if only because their economic resources and prospects are even more limited than those of the American republic" (p. 304). Although Jackson is right that antiurbanism is a strong and distinctive motif in American culture (see also Peter Rowe, *Making a Middle Landscape* [Cambridge: MIT Press, 1991]), and that the relative affluence and low density of the U.S. population make suburbanization an easier option in the United States than elsewhere, comparative study of suburbanization worldwide has found it relatively uniform in its process, "despite the properties of any social system, be it uncontrolled capitalist urban sprawl, the centralized planned environment of the East Bloc, or the political consensus of quasi-capitalist nations of western Europe" (Donald N. Rothblatt and Daniel J. Carr, *Suburbia: An International Assessment* [London: Croom Helm, 1986], p. 244).

12. Darwin's visit to the archipelago in 1835 is reported in Chapter 17 of his *Journal of Researches into the Natural History and Geology of the Countries Visited during the Voyage of HMS Beagle* (1839). Melville's more casual visits of 1841 and 1842 were not written up until 1854, and then of course in a much more deliberately fictionalized way. For the circumstances of composition and an indication of the range of sources on which Melville drew, see *The Piazza Tales and Other Prose Pieces, 1839–1860*, ed. Harrison Hayford, Alma A. MacDougall, and G. Thomas Tanselle (Evanston: Northwestern University Press; Chicago: Newberry Library, 1987), pp. 602–605. In short, I have loaded the dice somewhat in drawing this contrast. But the general point holds that homocentrism is aggravated by genre and other literary institutions, as will be discussed more fully below.

13. Edward O. Wilson, *On Human Nature* (Cambridge: Harvard University Press, 1978), p. 17. In this book I use both "homocentrism" and "anthropocentrism" to refer to human-centered biases of perception, although I generally prefer the former as being more unequivocally species-specific.

14. No one has made this point more eloquently than Edward Said, in the two initial essays of his collection *The World, the Text, and the Critic* (Cambridge: Harvard University Press, 1983), pp. 1–53, one of the several books (including Said's own *Orientalism* [New York: Pantheon, 1978]) responsible for changing the dominant paradigm in American literary theory from 1970s poststructuralism to 1980s historicism. But by "world" Said of course means "social world" (p. 4), and by the "plain empirical realities" (p. 35) he means ideological-historical context.

I agree with his critique of textuality but would revise his definition of what counts as "world."

15. On the ecological colonization of the western hemisphere, see Alfred Crosby, *Ecological Imperialism: The Biological Expansion of Europe, 900–1900* (Cambridge, Eng.: Cambridge University Press, 1989).

16. Throughout this book, I prefer "environmental nonfiction" or "environmental prose" to "nature writing," which is restrictive both in its implied identification of "nature" as the writer's exclusive field of environmental vision and in its tendency to exclude borderline cases like eclectic travel and autobiographical and sermonic material. For a genre map that identifies most of the discursive strands that seem important to me, see Thomas J. Lyon, "A Taxonomy of Nature Writing," part of the editorial introduction to his anthology, *This Incomperable Lande: A Book of American Nature Writing* (Boston: Houghton Mifflin, 1989; rpt. New York: Penguin, 1991), pp. 3–7. See the Appendix to this book for a fuller discussion of the range of genres that "environmental prose" encompassed in Thoreau's day.

17. See especially John Tallmadge, "Anatomy of a Classic," in *Companion to "A Sand County Almanac:" Interpretative and Critical Essays,* ed. J. Baird Callicott (Madison: University of Wisconsin Press, 1987), pp. 110–127.

18. The guide is *Teaching Environmental Literature: Materials, Methods, Resources,* ed. Frederick O. Waage (New York: Modern Language Association, 1985). Recent anthologies include *This Incomperable Lande: A Book of American Nature Writing* (1989, 1991); *The Norton Book of Nature Writing,* ed. Robert Finch and John Elder (New York: Norton, 1990); *Sisters of the Earth: Women's Prose and Poetry about Nature,* ed. Lorraine Anderson (New York: Vintage, 1991); *Reading the Environment,* ed. Melissa Walker (New York: Norton, 1994); and *Green Perspectives: Thinking and Writing about Nature and the Environment,* ed. Walter Levy and Christopher Hallowell (New York: HarperCollins, 1994).

19. Modern studies of American environmental prose start with Philip Marshall Hicks's doctoral dissertation, *The Development of the Natural History Essay in American Literature* (Philadelphia: University of Pennsylvania Press, 1925), and approach sophistication with Joseph Wood Krutch's editorial introduction to his anthology, *Great American Nature Writing* (New York: Sloane, 1950). Only in the last few years, however, has the field started to come alive. Among monographs, see Peter Fritzell, *Nature Writing and America: Essays upon a Cultural Type* (Ames: Iowa State University Press, 1990); Scott Slovic, *Seeking Awareness in American Nature Writing* (Salt Lake City: University of Utah Press, 1992); and Sherman Paul, *For Love of the World: Essays on Nature Writers* (Iowa City: University of Iowa Press, 1992). In addition, a number of critical symposia have recently appeared, e.g., *On Nature: Nature, Landscape, and Natural History,* ed. Daniel Halpern (San Francisco: North Point, 1987), which also includes creative writing;

and "Nature Writers/Writing," ed. Sherman Paul and Don Scheese, *North Dakota Quarterly,* 59, no. 2 (Spring 1991). The best sources of information about current creative and scholarly work are *Interdisciplinary Studies in Literature and Environment* and *Orion Nature Quarterly.*

20. "Ecocriticism" might succinctly be defined as study of the relation between literature and environment conducted in a spirit of commitment to environmentalist praxis. The most illuminating published discussions of aims and relevant scholarship to date are two articles by Glen A. Love in *Western American Literature:* "Revaluing Nature: Toward an Ecological Criticism," 25 (1990): 201–215; and "*Et in Arcadia Ego:* Pastoral Theory Meets Ecocriticism," 27 (1992): 195–207. Love identifies as the effective start of contemporary ecocriticism Joseph Meeker's neglected revisionary genre study *The Comedy of Survival: Studies in Literary Ecology* (New York: Scribner's, 1974), an appraisal which accords with that of America's first scholar to hold a professorship of literature and environment, Cheryl Burgess Glotfelty, whose research is in progress (cf. her pedagogical article "Teaching Green," *Interdisciplinary Studies in Literature and Environment,* 1, no. 1 [Spring 1993]: 151–166). Perhaps the single most intellectually venturesome monograph so far is John Elder's *Imagining the Earth* (Urbana: University of Illinois Press, 1985), a study of contemporary American poetry in light of Whiteheadean process philosophy. Some interested observers have expressed reservations about ecocriticism as too doctrinaire (e.g., Slovic, *Seeking Awareness,* pp. 169–171); but if one thinks of it—as I am inclined to do—as a multiform inquiry extending to a variety of environmentally focused perspectives more expressive of concern to explore environmental issues searchingly than of fixed dogmas about political solutions, then the neologism becomes a useful omnibus term for subsuming a large and growing scholarly field, albeit cultivated as yet (for obvious reasons) more intensely to date in regional rather than metropolitan centers. In this broader sense of the term, the sense in which I shall use it, this book would certainly count as an ecocritical project.

21. Joseph Wood Krutch, *The Great Chain of Life* (1956; rpt. Boston: Houghton Mifflin, 1978), p. 162.

22. Lynn L. Merrill, *The Romance of Victorian Natural History* (New York: Oxford University Press, 1989), p. 22, may be contrasted with John Hildebidle, *Thoreau: A Naturalist's Liberty* (Cambridge: Harvard University Press, 1983), p. 56. For the MLA survey, see Bettina J. Huber, "Today's Literature Classroom: Findings from the MLA's 1990 Survey of Upper-Division Courses," *ADE Bulletin,* no. 101 (Spring 1992): 53.

23. I have in mind Gillian Beer, *Darwin's Plots: Evolutionary Narrative in Darwin, George Eliot, and Nineteenth-Century Fiction* (London: Routledge, 1983); George Levine, *Darwin and the Novelists: Patterns of Science in Victorian Fiction* (Cambridge: Harvard University Press, 1988); and James Krasner, *The Entangled*

Eye: Visual Perception and the Representation of Nature in Post-Darwinian Narrative (New York and Oxford: Oxford University Press, 1992).

24. Wendell Berry, "On the Hill Late at Night," in *Collected Poems, 1957–1982* (San Francisco: North Point, 1985), p. 113. Here is the poem:

> The ripe grassheads bend in the starlight
> in the soft wind, beneath them the darkness
> of the grass, fathomless, the long blades
> rising out of the well of time. Cars
> travel the valley roads below me, their lights
> finding the dark, and racing on. Above
> their roar is a silence I have suddenly heard,
> and felt the country turn under the stars
> toward dawn. I am wholly willing to be here
> between the bright silent thousands of stars
> and the life of the grass pouring out of the ground.
> The hill has grown to me like a foot.
> Until I lift the earth I cannot move.

25. Norman Foerster, *Nature in American Literature* (New York: Macmillan, 1923), pp. 10–11.

26. Jonathan Bate, *Romantic Ecology: Wordsworth and the Environmental Tradition* (London: Routledge, 1991), p. 4.

27. Leo Marx, *The Machine in the Garden; Technology and the Pastoral Ideal in America* (New York: Oxford University Press, 1964), pp. 264.

28. Throughout this book "literary naturism" will be my preferred term to designate an interest in representation of literal nature as a substantial if not exclusive part of one's literary project. I prefer "naturism" to "naturalism," since "naturalism" and "naturalist" suggest a more restrictively (proto)scientific approach, and they have the additional disadvantage of being associated with the tradition of social representation in fiction, drama, and documentary exemplified by the novels of Emile Zola and Theodore Dreiser, the early plays of August Strindberg, and the journalism of Jacob Riis. Some works by William Wordsworth and Dorothy Wordsworth clearly qualify as naturist but none clearly as naturalist (in the sense of belonging to the natural history tradition). My preference for the latitudinarian term is of course consonant with my latitudinarian definition of the environmental text.

29. Norman Lacey, *Wordsworth's View of Nature and Its Ethical Consequences* (Cambridge, Eng.: Cambridge University Press, 1948), p. 124.

30. Friedrich von Schiller, *Naive and Sentimental Poetry,* trans. and ed. Julius A. Elias (New York: Ungar, 1967), pp. 102–117.

31. Thoreau, "Ktaadn," in *The Maine Woods,* ed. Joseph J. Moldenhauer (Princeton: Princeton University Press, 1972), pp. 70–71.

32. Max Oelschlaeger, *The Idea of Wilderness: From Prehistory to the Age of Ecology* (New Haven: Yale University Press, 1991), p. 149.

33. On "Ktaadn" in relation to other popular excursion essays, see Steven Fink, *Prophet in the Marketplace: Thoreau's Development as a Professional Writer* (Princeton: Princeton University Press, 1992), pp. 164–187. Fink observes that "while many critics have insistently characterized Thoreau's account of the mountain as a record of his confrontation with the 'reality' of nature as opposed to his earlier 'romanticism' . . . it is actually at this point in his essay that Thoreau is his most literary and allusive" (p. 176). On Thoreau and the sublime, see also Ronald Wesley Hoag, "The Mark on the Wilderness: Thoreau's Contact with Ktaadn," *Texas Studies in Literature and Language,* 24 (1982): 23–46. On Thoreau's observance of the romantic conventions of exploration narrative, see Bruce Greenfield, *Narrating Discovery: The Romantic Explorer in American Literature, 1790–1855* (New York: Columbia University Press, 1992), pp. 189–192.

34. This position is formulated partly as a response to Henri Lefebvre's influential theory of the "double illusion," which he sees as occluding our apprehension that space is socially produced: the "illusion of transparency" (the myth of the possibility of perfect vision) versus the "realistic illusion" (the myth that the object is more real than the subject). See Lefebvre, *The Production of Space* (1974), trans. Donald Nicholson-Smith (Oxford: Blackwell, 1991), pp. 27–30. This dichotomy I find most suggestive, but the notion of socially produced space as Lefebvre goes on to develop it becomes another form of the transcendental illusion (the myth of total control of nature by architectonic humankind), although Lefebvre's witheringly ironic view of the triumph of *techne*—and his deliberately antisystematic method of argument—are important counters to his analytical monolith-building tendencies. Notwithstanding any conceptual limitations, *The Production of Space* is one of the most brilliantly suggestive theoretical discussions of environmental imagination to date.

35. Leo Marx, "The Puzzle of Anti-Urbanism in Classic American Literature" (1962), reprinted in *The Pilot and the Passenger: Essays on Literature, Technology, and Culture in the United States* (New York: Oxford University Press, 1988), p. 210. In contrast to Marx, British cultural historian Raymond Williams was of rural background, with a relish for the material textures of landscape and rural life and an affection and loyalty to his working-class origins that verges on pastoral nostalgia. Yet the class-consciousness that developed as Williams matured as a Marxist within and against genteel Oxbridge culture led him in his best-known work, *The Country and the City* (New York: Oxford University Press, 1973), to be far more severe on pastoral mystification—to emphasize the myopia of literary representations of environment as artifacts of leisure-class illusion-building above their capacity for environmental retrieval. See for example Williams's discussion of the writer toward whom he is most sympathetic, the working-class

poet John Clare (*Country and City,* pp. 133–141). Clare's particularity of vision delights Williams but finally amounts to nothing more than "the culmination, in broken genius, of the movement which we can trace from a century before him: the separation of Nature from the facts of the labour that is creating it, and then the breaking of Nature, in altered and now intolerable relations between men" (p. 141).

36. Both "Euro-American" and "Anglo-American" are more or less unsatisfactory omnibus terms. "Euro-American" is extremely misleading for premodern America, when Irish, Italian, and other non-English European American groups were discriminated against; but "Anglo-American" is pedantically narrow. If applied puristically, it could be used to eliminate Leopold, John Muir, John Burroughs, even Thoreau. So I opt for the less unsatisfactory term.

37. Morton White and Lucia White, *The Intellectual versus the City: From Thomas Jefferson to Frank Lloyd Wright* (Cambridge: Harvard University Press, 1962).

38. Irving Howe, "Robert Frost: A Momentary Stay," in *Selected Writings, 1950–1990* (New York: Harcourt, 1990), p. 181.

39. Irving Howe, *A Margin of Hope: An Intellectual Autobiography* (New York: Harcourt, 1982), p. 142. Howe commented with great explicitness on his youthful sense of the alienness of the Emersonian-Thoreauvian emphasis on individualism and nature in an interview on National Public Radio (8 November 1990). For calling it to my attention, and for other insights into the disjunctions between "mainstream" American environmental discourse and Jewish cultural traditions, I am indebted to Susanne Klingenstein, whose monograph, *Jews in the American Academy, 1900–1940: The Dynamics of Intellectual Assimilation* (New Haven: Yale University Press, 1991), sheds further light on these matters.

40. Alfred Kazin, *A Writer's America: Landscape in Literature* (New York: Knopf, 1988).

41. The key first-wave feminist revisionary studies were Nina Baym, "Melodramas of Beset Manhood: How Theories of American Fiction Exclude Women Writers" (1981), reprinted in *Feminism and American Literary History* (New Brunswick: Rutgers University Press, 1992), pp. 3–18; Annette Kolodny, *The Lay of the Land: Metaphor as Experience and History in American Life and Letters* (Chapel Hill: University of North Carolina Press, 1975); and Kolodny, *The Land before Her: Fantasy and Experience of the American Frontiers, 1630–1860* (Chapel Hill: University of North Carolina Press, 1984). See also Susan Armitage, "Through Woman's Eyes: A New View of the West," in *The Women's West,* ed. Armitage and Elizabeth Jameson (Norman: University of Oklahoma Press, 1987), pp. 9–18; and Melody Graulich, "'O Beautiful for Spacious Guys': An Essay on the 'Legitimate Inclinations of the Sexes,'" in *The Frontier Experience and the American Dream: Essays on American Literature,* ed. David Mogen, Mark Busby, and Paul

Bryant (College Station: Texas A & M University Press, 1989), pp. 186–201. Their revisionism is itself in the process of being refined and revised—e.g., by Vera Norwood's *Made from This Earth: American Women and Nature* (Chapel Hill: University of North Carolina Press, 1993)—but Baym's critique of academic misogyny and the reconstruction by Kolodny and her successors of the frontier as imagined by American women writers are likely to stand as landmark achievements. Another important revisionary appraisal of masculinist frontierism, from a psychohistorical rather than a feminist perspective, is Richard Slotkin's trilogy beginning with *Regeneration through Violence: The Mythology of the American Frontier, 1600–1860* (Middletown, Conn.: Wesleyan University Press, 1973).

42. Baym, "Melodramas," p. 12: "I find women students responsive to the myth insofar as its protagonist is concerned." The central precontemporary studies of the male wilderness imagination remain Leslie Fiedler, *Love and Death in the American Novel* (1960, rev. New York: Dell, 1966), Richard Slotkin's trilogy, and Edwin Fussell, *Frontier: American Literature and the American West* (Princeton: Princeton University Press, 1965).

43. Annis Pratt et al., *Archetypal Patterns in Women's Fiction* (Brighton: Harvester, 1982), pp. 16–24; and Baym, "Melodramas," p. 14.

44. See in this last regard Irene Neher, *The Female Hero's Quest for Identity in Novels by Modern American Women Writers* (Frankfurt am Main: Peter Lang, 1989); and Dana A. Heller, *The Feminization of Quest-Romance* (Austin: University of Texas Press, 1990). Both seek to complicate the distinction between "male" and "female" responses to nature, frontier, wilderness. Quotation from Carol Fairbanks, *Prairie Women: Images in American and Canadian Fiction* (New Haven: Yale University Press, 1986), p. 71, a more historically informed and sophisticated although also more narrowly focused study, which very carefully appraises and modifies Kolodny's account of women's frontier discourse (pp. 50–67 passim).

45. In this regard the recent revisionary histories of women in the outdoors are a particularly notable cultural symptom. See for instance Kate H. Winter, *The Woman in the Mountain: Reconstructions of Self and Land by Adirondack Women Writers* (Albany: State University of New York Press, 1989); Janet Robertson, *The Magnificent Mountain Women: Adventures in the Colorado Rockies* (Lincoln: University of Nebraska Press, 1990); Marcia Myers Bonta, *Women in the Field: America's Pioneering Women Naturalists* (College Station: Texas A & M University Press, 1991); and especially Norwood, *Made from This Earth*. These texts all participate in a late twentieth-century feminist project of reviving a tradition of American women's historical experience of nature distinct from (but parallel to) the male wilderness adventure. The naturalist-writer Anne LaBastille, author of *Woodswoman* and other books about cabin living in the Adirondacks, is a good example of the recent emphasis on woman as outdoorsperson. See LaBastille's informal history *Women and Wilderness* (1980) and her autobiographical essay

on the history of her developing interest in Thoreau, "Fishing in the Sky," in *New Essays on Walden,* ed. Robert F. Sayre (Cambridge, Eng.: Cambridge University Press, 1992), pp. 53–72.

46. See George Dekker, *James Fenimore Cooper the Novelist* (London: Routledge, 1967), pp. 20–63; and Dekker, *The American Historical Romance* (Cambridge, Eng.: Cambridge University Press, 1987), pp. 29–98.

47. Melvin Dixon, *Ride Out the Wilderness: Geography and Identity in Afro-American Literature* (Urbana: University of Illinois Press, 1987).

48. Rachel Kaplan and Stephen Kaplan, in *The Experience of Nature: A Psychological Perspective* (Cambridge, Eng.: Cambridge University Press, 1989), p. 100, report that when asked to react to photographs, whites tend to prefer "scenes of dense forests," whereas African Americans tend to prefer more open, managed landscapes. On African Americans and environmentalist issues, see for example Eric Jay Dolin, "Black American Attitudes toward Wildlife," *Journal of Environmental Education,* 20, no. 1 (1988): 17–21. In a global context, however, there appears to be no clear correlation between, say, environmental activism and race, although—as would be expected on grounds of comparative national wealth alone—institutional activism is predominantly funded by western sources. See for example the multiethnic group of individuals profiled in Aubrey Wallace, *Eco-Heroes: Twelve Tales of Environmental Victory,* ed. David Gancher (San Francisco: Mercury House, 1993).

49. Quotations from Lebert Bethune, "Harlem Freeze Frame," and Norman Jordan, "Black Warrior," in *Black Fire: An Anthology of Afro-American Writing,* ed. LeRoi Jones and Larry Neal (New York: Morrow, 1968), pp. 382, 389.

50. A more skeptical theory would be that African American as well as white writers have realized the market appeal of rural folk culture. Certainly African American writers from Frederick Douglass to Charles Johnson have a long history of manipulating ruralist pieties satirically (see Chapter 1). With respect to the shifting positions of Wright and Hurston in critical esteem, it may not be accidental that both this shift and the popularity of literature and history about black culture's preurban roots (Alex Haley's *Roots* is another spectacular example) owe something to the comparative institutionalization of African American Studies in the academic as well as the literary marketplace during the past dozen years.

51. Simon Ortiz, quotations from *Harper's Anthology of Twentieth Century Native American Poetry,* ed. Duane Niatum (New York: Harper Collins, 1988), pp. 143, 141–142.

52. Ortiz, interview with Laura Coltelli, in *Winged Words: American Indian Writers Speak* (Lincoln: University of Nebraska Press, 1990), p. 112. I do not mean to underestimate the tensions inherent in negotiating between different cultural identities. See for example Louis Owens's sensitive discussion of the challenge

faced by Native American novelists in adjusting to print genres alien to oral tradition (*Other Destinies: Understanding the American Indian Novel* [Norman: University of Oklahoma Press, 1992], pp. 9–12).

53. See for example Guillermo Gómez-Peña, "From Art-Mageddon to Gringo-Stroika," *High Performance,* Fall 1991, 22: "We now inhabit a social universe in constant motion, a moving cartography with a floating culture and a fluctuating sense of self. We do not understand that we can speak two or more languages, have two or more identities and/or nationalities and not necessarily be in conflict with ourselves and others. Hyphenated, transitional and multiple identities are no longer just theories of radical anthropologists, but familiar pop cultural realities." For a perspective on some of the literary manifestations of ethnic crossing, see William Boelhower, *Through a Glass Darkly: Ethnic Semiosis in American Literature* (New York: Oxford University Press, 1987). An almost quintessential example of a contemporary literary work based on the idea of multiple ethnic roles would be Anna Deavere Smith's *Fires in the Mirror* (1992), a multivocal monodrama based on the Crown Heights (Brooklyn) incident in which Smith (an African American) impersonates twenty-seven figures in succession. It should go without saying, however, that the appeal of cultural hybridization as an idea or ideal will differ greatly according to subject position: for Native American and other intellectuals of color it may be a fact of genealogy; for whites it may be a romantic sentimentalism; for Mexican Americans the prospect of a Hispanic-Indian continuum (e.g., *Atzlánismo*) must seem quite different from the way it would to Native Americans.

54. I quote from ecocritic John Tallmadge, untitled review essay, *Orion,* 9, no. 3 (Summer 1990): 64; and from cultural theorist Bruno Latour, *The Pasteurization of France,* trans. Alan Sheridan and John Law (Cambridge: Harvard University Press, 1988), p. 150.

55. See for example Calvin Martin, *Keepers of the Game: Indian-Animal Relationships and the Fur Trade* (Berkeley: University of California Press, 1978).

56. See particularly Sherry Ortner, "Is Female to Male as Nature Is to Culture?" in *Woman, Culture, and Society,* ed. Michelle Rosaldo and Louise Lamphere (Stanford: Stanford University Press, 1974), pp. 67–87; Carolyn Merchant, *The Death of Nature: Women, Ecology, and the Scientific Revolution* (New York: Harper and Row, 1980); and Christopher L. Miller, *Blank Darkness: Africanist Discourse in French* (Chicago: University of Chicago Press, 1985).

57. The possible influence of "aboriginal" culture is reflected in the estimate that although somewhere between two-thirds and five-sixths of the world's cultures might be considered "indigenous," not more than about 10 percent of the world's population is (Alan Thein Durning, "Supporting Indigenous Peoples," in *State of the World, 1993: A Worldwatch Institute Report on Progress toward a Sustainable Society,* ed. Linda Starks [New York: Norton, 1993], p. 81). Whatever

one might wish, the influence of these mostly small, widely dispersed, and politically disempowered population groups seems sure to be limited. This of course does not mean that America, or "the west," is going to *dictate* global environmental policy and practice; if China, for example, continues to fuel its economic boom with coal-powered energy, no emission control laws in the west will keep atmospheric quality from deteriorating.

58. The alternatives I seek to coordinate are elegantly described in the two initial essays of *Canons,* ed. Robert von Hallberg (Chicago: University of Chicago Press, 1984): Barbara Herrnstein Smith, "Contingencies of Value," pp. 5–40, and Charles Altieri, "An Idea and Ideal of a Literary Canon," pp. 41–64. I do not mean to minimize the force of John Guillory's deconstruction of canonicity as an institutional form developed by modern scholastic culture to regulate distribution of cultural capital (*Cultural Capital: The Problem of Literary Canon Formation* [Chicago: University of Chicago Press, 1993]). But I am more optimistic than he about canonicity's potential to redistribute a culture's energies, not just to rigidify them.

59. See Annette Kolodny, *The Land before Her,* for an overview of the female frontier canon as emanating from Rowlandson. Since Kolodny, Rowlandson's *Narrative* (1678) has been used as the master text around which to orient even more ambitious (and somewhat conflicting) revisionary maps of literary history, Nancy Armstrong and Leonard Tennenhouse identifying it as an *ur*-text in the formulation of the ideology of family-based civility in English domestic fiction ("The American Origins of the English Novel," *American Literary History,* 4 [1992]: 386–410), Susan Howe identifying it as the quintessential subversion of the standing order (*The Birth-mark: Unsettling the Wilderness in American Literary History* [Hanover, N.H.: Wesleyan University Press for University Press of New England, 1993]). The other frontier narratives I refer to are Eliza Farnham, *Life in Prairie Land* (1846), ed. John Hallwas (Urbana: University of Illinois Press, 1988), and Caroline Kirkland, *A New Home, Who'll Follow?* (1839), ed. Sandra Zagarell (New Brunswick: Rutgers University Press, 1990).

60. See Marcia B. Kline, *Beyond the Land Itself: Views of Nature in Canada and the United States* (Cambridge: Harvard University Press, 1970), and Fairbanks, *Prairie Women.*

61. "Ktaadn" was serialized in Kirkland's *Sartain's Union Magazine* in five installments, from July to November 1848.

62. See for example Josephine Donovan, *New England Local Color Literature: A Woman's Tradition* (New York: Ungar, 1983); John L. Idol, Jr., "Mary Russell Mitford: Champion of American Literature," in *Studies in American Renaissance, 1983,* ed. Joel Myerson (Charlottesville: University Press of Virginia, 1983), pp. 313–334; and Sandra A. Zagarell, "Narrative of Community: The Identification of a Genre," *Signs,* 13 (1988): 498–527.

63. Douglas Anderson, in *A House Undivided: Domesticity and Community in American Literature* (Cambridge, Eng.: Cambridge University Press, 1990), pp. 72–86, observes that *Walden* is permeated by the rhetoric of domesticity. See also the four extremely disparate contributions to the symposium "Ecology, Feminism, and Thoreau," *Interdisciplinary Studies in Literature and Environment*, 1, no. 1 (Spring 1993): 121–150.

64. Norwood, *Made from This Earth*, pp. 25–53, calls attention to the existence of the rich but neglected vein of environmental nonfiction by American women writers starting with Susan Fenimore Cooper in the mid-nineteenth century, pertinently remarking that "although female nature essayists consistently pose women's images of nature as a critique of certain male behaviors, they have done so in the full confidence that they and their male compatriots ultimately share the same public stage and often have the same goals" (p. 53).

65. Marjorie Pryse's edition of two of Austin's most powerful books (*Land of Little Rain* and *Lost Borders*) in the American Women Writers Series, under the title *Stories from the Country of Lost Borders* (New Brunswick: Rutgers University Press, 1987), may have been a turning point in this regard, judging from the reissues of other Austin works that have since appeared. The confident tone of the introduction to Esther Lanigan Stineman's biography, *Mary Austin: Song of a Maverick* (New Haven: Yale University Press, 1989), pp. 1–5, is another sign of the times—as is the biography itself.

1. Pastoral Ideology

1. The scholarship on pastoral is copious, and no one treatment is authoritative. Western pastoral's 2,500-year history is so long and diverse that specialists predictably diverge. Two short treatments that strike me as especially effective though necessarily self-limited attempts to define pastoral by locating one deep structure amidst its various forms are Paul Alpers, "What Is Pastoral?" *Critical Inquiry*, 8 (1982): 437–460; and Frederick Garber, "Pastoral Spaces," *Texas Studies in Literature and Language*, 30 (1988): 431–460. (Most important previous scholarship, particularly that of a formalist cast, is noticed in their footnotes.) For Alpers, the key is "the central fiction that shepherds' lives represent human lives" (p. 459). For Garber, pastoral is a means of spiritual reorientation that "always implies that we are returning, in the fiction, to where we used to be" (p. 455). These attempts to isolate an archetype, however, illuminating though they are, have been less central to my own project than discussions of pastoral in relation to historical and environmental actualities of the past two centuries or so. In this respect the two most influential works, on my work and on others', have unquestionably been Leo Marx, *The Machine in the Garden: Technology and the Pastoral Ideal in America* (New York: Oxford University Press, 1964), and (for

British literature) Raymond Williams, *The Country and the City* (New York: Oxford University Press, 1973).

2. William Empson, *Some Versions of Pastoral* (London: Chatto and Windus, 1935).

3. A recent work of comparative cultural geography (Britain, Australia, the United States) that treats some manifestations of this trend, but does not trace its history and coherence with the rigor that one would wish, is John Rennie Short, *Imagined Country: Environment, Culture, and Society* (London: Routledge, 1991). "In most countries," Short asserts, "the countryside has become the embodiment of the nation, idealized as the ideal middle landscape between the rough wilderness of nature and the smooth artificiality of the town, a combination of nature and culture which best represents the nation-state" (p. 35). This statement overgeneralizes, but it applies to the transmigration of country mythography to the British colonies.

4. By "ideology" I mean the literary text's implicit position of dissent from or consent to the prevailing political system. "Pastoral" I use henceforth in an elastic sense, to refer not to the specific set of largely obsolete classical conventions that started to break down in the eighteenth century, but broadly to all literature that celebrates an ethos of rurality or nature or wilderness over against an ethos of metropolitanism. This domain includes for present purposes all degrees of rustication, temporary or longer term, from the greening of cities through metropolitan park projects to models of agrarianism and wilderness homesteading. Consequently, I may blur certain distinctions that some scholars would wish to press: between pastoral and georgic, between Eurocentric romanticism and new world frontier or wilderness writing, between nonfictional so-called nature writing and fictive genres. My justifications for doing so, such as they are, are fourfold. (1) It is sanctioned by the eclecticism of critical practice. (2) It is sanctioned by the messiness of literary history; for by the time American literary culture had taken root, traditional genre distinctions had already become porous: for instance, "pastoral" had begun to merge with "georgic." (3) It calls attention to the status of American environmental literary mythography as an outgrowth from a point of origin principally in European literary culture (see next chapter). (4) It allows one to put on a continuum different forms of "naturism" (a term I favor over pastoralism as having less ideological and aesthetic baggage and as referring unequivocally to the material nonhuman environment—see note 28 to the Introduction). For the "middle landscape" imagined by centrist versions of American pastoral unfolded by Leo Marx and others is commonly, and with justice, thought of by different commentators and at different times by the same commentator either as enfolded within urban or suburban settings or as leading off toward wilderness settings unimagined by Theocritus and Wordsworth. Examples of the former kind of thinking would be James L. Machor's *Pastoral Cities:*

Urban Ideals and the Symbolic Landscape of America (Madison: University of Wisconsin Press, 1987) and Peter G. Rowe's study of contemporary suburban planning, *Making a Middle Landscape* (Cambridge: MIT Press, 1991). Examples of the latter would be Edwin Fussell, *Frontier: American Literature and the American West* (Princeton: Princeton University Press, 1965), although Fussell does not favor the term "pastoral" itself; Roderick Nash, *Wilderness and the American Mind,* 3d ed. (New Haven: Yale University Press, 1982); and contemporary ecocritics who would argue, as Glen A. Love says, that "wild nature has replaced the traditional middle state of the garden and the rural landscapes as the locus of stability and value, the seat of instruction" ("*Et in Arcadia Ego:* Pastoral Theory Meets Ecocriticism," *Western American Literature,* 27 [1992]: 203).

5. D. H. Lawrence, *Studies in Classic American Literature* (1923; rpt. Garden City, N.Y.: Doubleday, 1951). Perry Miller's "Nature and the National Ego" (1955), reprinted in *Errand into the Wilderness* (Cambridge: Harvard University Press, 1956), pp. 204–216, remains an eloquent short statement on the place of nature in American cultural nationalism. The most searching treatment of the Lawrentian impress on American criticism is Michael Colacurcio's review essay, "The Symbolic and the Symptomatic: D. H. Lawrence in Recent American Criticism," *American Quarterly,* 27 (1975): 486–501, although my present concern differs from that of Colacurcio's critique, which focuses on the inadequacy, as historical analysis, of psychohistorical interpretations.

6. Before Leslie Fiedler, *Love and Death in the American Novel* (1960; rev. New York: Dell, 1966), Richard Chase had advanced the romance hypothesis in *The American Novel and Its Tradition* (Garden City, N.Y.: Doubleday, 1957); and the way for Chase had been suggested by Lionel Trilling's "Reality in America," in *The Liberal Imagination* (New York: Viking, 1950).

7. See also Charles Sanford, *The Quest for Paradise: Europe and the American Moral Imagination* (Urbana: University of Illinois Press, 1961), as well as Fussell, *Frontier;* and John Seelye, "Some Green Thoughts on a Green Theme," in *Literature in Revolution,* ed. George Abbott White and Charles Newman (New York: Holt, 1972), pp. 576–638, which eloquently states the case for the "revolutionary" potential of the American (male) pastoral tradition. Marx, however, is unquestionably the most influential formulator of the ideology of American naturism. The limitations of his model, to my mind, are these: a relative disinterest in the literal environment as opposed to the environment as cultural symbol; an acceptance of the persistence of a sharp distinction between middle landscape and wilderness that does not do full justice to the flexibility of American literary thought, particularly western American literature (cf. Fussell and Love); and a canonicalist perspective that leads Marx to distinguish too cleanly between a few discerning major writers and culture critics who are credited with "complex pastoral" and a mass of conformists who accepted a facile

doublethink of pastoral values and industrial progress. Notwithstanding, *The Machine in the Garden* remains an invaluable resource—the most durable of the landmark "myth-symbol" studies that marked the first mature phase of the American Studies movement. No one has more pungently diagnosed the schizophrenia of American naturism. For an important retrospect, suggesting that he might have framed his argument somewhat differently if he had composed it twenty years later, see Marx's "Pastoralism in America," in *Ideology and Classic American Literature,* ed. Sacvan Bercovitch and Myra Jehlen (Cambridge, Eng.: Cambridge University Press, 1986), pp. 36–39. This same collection also contains a retrospect by Henry Nash Smith on his *Virgin Land,* pp. 21–35, acknowledging the need to be more critical of westward expansionism in light of the newer ideological criticism I mention below. But Marx's position has altered less than Smith's, partly no doubt because it was more critical of pastoralism to start with than Smith was critical of agrarianism. Indeed, Marx's collected essays, *The Pilot and the Passenger* (New York: Oxford University Press, 1990), are remarkable for their consistency and coherence of critical perspective over a thirty-year period.

8. Annette Kolodny, *The Land before Her: Fantasy and Experience of the American Frontiers, 1630–1860* (Chapel Hill: University of North Carolina Press, 1984), p. 226. See also Kolodny, *The Lay of the Land: Metaphor as Experience and History in American Life and Letters* (Chapel Hill: University of North Carolina Press, 1975); and Nina Baym, "Melodramas of Beset Manhood: How Theories of American Fiction Exclude Women Writers" (1981), reprinted in *Feminism and American Literary History* (New Brunswick: Rutgers University Press, 1992), pp. 3–18.

9. Kenneth S. Lynn, "The Regressive Historians," *American Scholar,* 47 (1978): 480–489; Bernard Rosenthal, *City of Nature: Journeys to Nature in the Age of American Romanticism* (Newark: University of Delaware Press; London and Toronto: Associated University Presses, 1980).

10. Myra Jehlen, *American Incarnation: The Individual, the Nation, and the Continent* (Cambridge: Harvard University Press, 1986). Another revisionary project of major importance is Richard Slotkin's "post-Vietnam" thesis that the frontier experience afforded a catharsis for the violent impulses of American civilization: see his *Regeneration through Violence: The Mythology of the American Frontier, 1600–1860* (Middletown, Conn.: Wesleyan University Press, 1973); *The Fatal Environment: The Myth of the Frontier in the Age of Industrialization, 1800–1890* (New York: Atheneum, 1985); and *Gunfighter Nation: The Myth of the Frontier in Twentieth-Century America* (New York: Atheneum, 1992). Race rather than gender is Slotkin's key variable.

"New historicism," first introduced during the 1980s into Renaissance studies by Stephen Greenblatt, quickly became an omnibus phrase to denote a shift in the premises of literary study from poststructuralism's somewhat ahistorical preoccupation with textuality in the 1970s to an approach that would once again concentrate on the sociohistorical context of literary production while at the same time resist what was taken to be the naive empiricism of traditional historiography. In practice this has meant focusing on literary text and history as ideological construct. For good symposia with critical introductions, see *The New Historicism,* ed. H. Aram Veeser (London: Routledge, 1989), and *New Historical Literary Study,* ed. Jeffrey N. Cox and Larry J. Reynolds (Princeton: Princeton University Press, 1993).

11. Donald Pease, "Sublime Politics," in *The American Sublime,* ed. Mary Arensberg (Albany: State University of New York Press, 1986), p. 46. One of the striking developments in 1980s Americanist criticism, exemplified by this essay, was the politicization of the theory of the American sublime, originally put into critical circulation by Harold Bloom to account for what he saw as American poetry's distinctive way of converting the challenge of American landscape to the imagination. The "new historicist" revision was to reread the American sublime as a resource of and mandate for expansionist technological power. See also Rob Wilson, *The American Sublime: The Genealogy of a Poetic Genre* (Madison: University of Wisconsin Press, 1991).

12. See the exhibition catalog *The West as America: Reinterpreting Images of the Frontier, 1820–1920,* ed. William H. Truettner (Washington: Smithsonian Institution Press, 1991). I should emphasize that important scholarship pursuing the older view of America's spokespersons for nature as social critics continued to be produced during the 1980s. See especially the three editions of Roderick Nash, *Wilderness and the American Mind* (New Haven: Yale University Press, 1967, 1973, 1982); and Lee Clark Mitchell, *Witnesses to a Vanishing America: The Nineteenth-Century Response* (Princeton: Princeton University Press, 1981); both works demonstrate that in art, politics, and social theory gentry-class nostalgia for America's vanishing wilderness has had a reformist impact. Nash in particular valuably supplements Marx's presentation of American social history in *Machine in the Garden,* which tends to presume that the battle against rampant industrialism was irretrievably lost in the early nineteenth century. Nash's and Mitchell's characterization of the social and intellectual relationships between the spokespersons for wilderness and the American establishment seems to me, however, in keeping with Marx's model of pastoral ideology; and so I have used Marx as my central example in this brief summary.

13. For Geoffrey Hartman's influential interpretation, see his *Wordsworth's Poetry, 1787–1814* (New Haven: Yale University Press, 1964), pp. 31–69. The culmination of the formalist tradition in *Walden* criticism is Charles Anderson, *The Magic Circle of Walden* (New York: Holt, 1968). The shortcoming I have pinpointed is exemplified by Hartman's summation: "Nature and Poetry matter only as they quicken regeneration" (p. 68). The "only" too relentlessly dematerializes and thereby oversimplifies the relation between poet and nature.

14. Scholarship on European pastoral has shown itself capable of making finer ideological discriminations. See for example Annabel M. Patterson's *Pastoral and Ideology: Virgil to Valery* (Berkeley: University of California Press, 1987), which examines the history of the repossession of Virgil's *Eclogues*—the greatest pre-text of western pastoral—through imitations and commentaries from the early middle ages to the near-present. Patterson shows that pastoral's ideological valence has oscillated astonishingly over these two millennia, according to the writer's historical position: some have used it as an instrument of oppositional critique, others as a means of dramatizing competing positions, still others as a way to purge pastoral of political reference and completely aestheticize it—to re-Theocritize it, as it were. Patterson reveals both the historical logic of these dissonant outcomes and their limits of plausibility, by stressing, following Paul Alpers's *The Singer of "The Eclogues"* (1979), that they are built on the interplay of positions represented in Eclogue 1 by the unhappy shepherd Meliboeus (dispossessed by Augustus) and the happy shepherd Tityrus (exempted by Augustus's special favor). In the area of intellectual and political history, a comparable work is Anna Bramwell's *Ecology in the Twentieth Century: A History* (New Haven: Yale University Press, 1989), which is especially astute on a question broached in her previous book, *Blood and Soil: Richard Walther Darré and Hitler's "Green Party"* (Abbotsbrook: Kensal, 1985), namely, whether "ecologism" (by which Bramwell essentially means holistic biology and energy economics) is somehow irretrievably tainted by its having been developed both as a discourse and as a movement to its highest levels of precontemporary sophistication under the Nazis. Although Bramwell finally rejects "today's ecological movement" as impracticable neoprimitivism (*Ecology*, p. 248), she argues resourcefully and carefully that the link with fascism was historically contingent rather than inherent (e.g., ecologism largely fell out of favor with Hitler's regime during World War II), and that ecologism cannot be categorically identified with any one political position. A recent study of pastoral ideology in American art history that exhibits a similar flexibility of perspective is Angela Miller, *The Empire of the Eye: Landscape Representation and American Cultural Politics, 1825–1875* (Ithaca: Cornell University Press, 1993). See also Peter Rowe's analysis of pastoral ideology as a progressive though bounded force in contemporary suburban design, *Making a Middle Landscape*, pp. 217–247.

15. Andrew Ettin, *Literature and the Pastoral* (New Haven: Yale University Press, 1984), pp. 75–95.

16. Thoreau, *Reform Papers*, ed. Wendell Glick (Princeton: Princeton University Press, 1973), pp. 108–109.

17. Ibid., p. 84.

18. Emerson, "Thoreau," in *The Complete Works of Ralph Waldo Emerson*, ed. Edward W. Emerson (Boston: Houghton Mifflin, 1903–1904), 10: 480.

19. *The Heart of Burroughs's Journals,* ed. Clara Barrus (Boston: Houghton Mifflin, 1928), pp. 36–37.

20. Thoreau's relation to the farmers of Concord is more complex than can be fully explored here. It and other dimensions of Thoreau's loyal opposition to Concord's social norms have been astutely explored in a series of articles by historian Robert A. Gross. Two are devoted to agricultural issues: "Agriculture and Society in Thoreau's Concord," *Journal of American History,* 69 (1982): 42–61; and "The Great Bean Field Hoax: Thoreau and the Agricultural Reformers," *Virginia Quarterly Review,* 61 (1985): 483–497. Gross shows that Thoreau treated his rural pursuits in *Walden* with one eye on the goal of echoing and parodying the efficiency-minded agricultural reformist thinking of his day. "What radically divided Thoreau from the agricultural improvers," Gross states, "was his refusal of intensive cultivation. Thoreau was appalled at the improvers' vision of a tame, polite landscape of apple orchards and market gardens" ("Hoax," p. 490). The passage just quoted (which Gross does not discuss) might be read, in other words, not as a social dropout's pleasant fantasy but as a satire on the fetishization of agricultural efficiency.

21. David Shi, *The Simple Life: Plain Living and High Thinking in American Culture* (New York: Oxford University Press, 1985). Shi concludes that "though a failure as a societal ethic, simplicity has nevertheless exercised a powerful influence on the complex patterns of American culture," serving as "the nation's conscience" in such a way as to entitle us to expect it "will persist both as an enduring myth and as an actual way of living" (pp. 278–279). These formulations appropriately straddle the issue of its orthodoxy, typing the simple life as both consensual and deviant.

22. *Narrative of the Life of Frederick Douglass, an American Slave* (New York: New Signet, 1968), p. 33; Richard Wright, *Uncle Tom's Children,* in *Early Works,* ed. Arnold Rampersad (New York: Library of America, 1991), pp. 239–275. The point about African American pastoral could be ramified further by taking into account a case like Zora Neale Hurston's *Their Eyes Were Watching God,* whose protagonist's adventures start with rebellion against confinement in the role of the farmer's wife to which her grandmother consigns her for the sake of protection and security. Janie's subsequent move into an increasingly unsocialized and increasingly natural environment oddly echoes the social secessions depicted by Cooper and Thoreau and Twain. Escape from farm (and later town) means escape from (black) patriarchy.

23. Sterling Brown, "Old King Cotton," in *Collected Poems,* ed. Michael S. Harper (New York: Harper and Row, 1980), pp. 64–65.

24. See especially Wilson J. Moses, "Writing Freely? Frederick Douglass and the Constraints of Racialized Writing," in *Frederick Douglass: New Literary and Historical Essays,* ed. Eric J. Sundquist (Cambridge, Eng.: Cambridge University

Press, 1990), pp. 66–83. By contrast, Houston Baker identifies Douglass's mastery over mainstream ideological rhetoric as the sign of intellectual independence, in *Blues, Ideology, and Afro-American Literature: A Vernacular Theory* (Chicago: University of Chicago Press, 1984); and Valerie Smith, in *Self-Discovery and Authority in Afro-American Narrative* (Cambridge: Harvard University Press, 1987), sees the very act of expression on the part of slave narrators as tantamount to self-realization.

25. See Eric J. Sundquist, *To Wake the Nations: Race in the Making of American Culture* (Cambridge: Harvard University Press, 1993), for a sophisticated discussion of these and related matters in "Grapevine" (pp. 361–365) and Chesnutt's fiction generally (Chapter 4 passim); Sundquist emphasizes to a greater degree than I do the status of the story as more a register of Chesnutt's anxieties than an indication of intellectual control.

26. For example, Douglass recalls the "parks" of the plantation, "where—as about the residences of the English nobility—rabbits, deer, and other wild game, might be seen, peering and playing about, with none to molest them or make them afraid." "These all belonged to me," he asserts, "as well as to Col. Edward Lloyd, and for a time I greatly enjoyed them" (*My Bondage and My Freedom* [1855; rpt. New York: Dover, 1969], pp. 67–68). Passages like this establish that the relative paucity of attention to landscape in Douglass's *Narrative* and other slave narratives has to do more with the constraints of the genre than with any lack of susceptibility to the charms of pastoral. Unquestionably the pastoral insets in *My Bondage* are partly designed to appeal to the sensibilities of white readers; but even more unquestionable is that Douglass, to a greater degree than in the *Narrative*, was this time writing to suit himself. Indeed, evidence of independent pastoral sensibility can be found within slave narrative itself, e.g., in Solomon Northup's recollection, in *Twelve Years a Slave* (1853; rpt. in *Puttin' on Ole Massa*, ed. Gilbert Osofsky [New York: Harper and Row, 1969]), of a certain bayou, a "little paradise in the Great Pine Woods," "towards which my heart turned lovingly, during many years of bondage" (p. 304).

27. See especially Wendell Berry, *The Unsettling of America: Culture and Agriculture* (San Francisco: Sierra Club, 1977). Since my exemplary pastoral passage in this section has been an antiagrarian excerpt from Thoreau, I may seem to be playing fast and loose by including within my purview at this point a figure like Berry, the leading voice of contemporary literary agrarianism. Indeed Berry *has* differentiated himself from Thoreau with respect, for example, to his individualism as opposed to communitarianism, which is a characteristic fault line between pastoralism and agrarianism as those terms are narrowly construed (cf. Berry, "Writer and Region," in *What Are People For?* [San Francisco: North Point, 1990], pp. 86–87). Still, Berry has aligned himself with Thoreau on such other key points as his lococentrism and his refusal to separate body and spirit (cf. Berry's "A

Secular Pilgrimage," in *A Continuous Harmony: Essays Cultural and Agricultural* [New York: Harcourt, 1971], pp. 8, 28–29).

28. The more important contributors include Sarah Orne Jewett, Celia Thaxter, Edith Thomas, Olive Thorne Miller, and Sophia Kirk.

29. For bibliographical guidance to late nineteenth-century Thoreau criticism, see Gary Scharnhorst, *Henry David Thoreau: An Annotated Bibliography of Comment and Criticism before 1900* (New York: Garland, 1992). Elizabeth Wright's *Lichen Tufts, from the Alleghanies* (New York: Doolady, 1860) is discussed below. For the early society, see Walter Harding, "An Early Thoreau Club," *Thoreau Society Bulletin,* 77 (Fall 1961): 3–4. The first Thoreau dissertation, since lost, was by Ella A. Knapp, the published monograph by Annie Russell Marble (1902). For a more astringent view of Thoreau by a literary naturalist-feminist who is also a Thoreauvian, see Ann Zwinger's presidential address to the Thoreau Society, "Thoreau and Women," *Thoreau Society Bulletin,* 164 (Summer 1983): 3–7, which starts by noting Thoreau's misogyny and then measures his writing against ten passages by nature-observing women from Dorothy Wordsworth to Rachel Carson.

30. Clara Barrus, *The Life and Letters of John Burroughs* (Boston: Houghton Mifflin, 1925), 1: 333–334; 2: 294, 319. For the influence of mothers on Muir and Burroughs, see William Frederick Badè, *Life and Letters of John Muir* (Boston: Houghton Mifflin, 1924), 1: 16; and Edith Burroughs Kelley, *John Burroughs: Naturalist* (New York: Exposition, 1959), pp. 49–50. The story of Marian Parsons's being denied an important role in Muir's literary affairs is told in the correspondence between Badè and Houghton Mifflin editors (Houghton Mifflin Papers, Houghton Library, Harvard University), especially Badè to Ferris Greenslet 7 January 1915, Greenslet to Badè, 12 January 1915, and Badè to Roger L. Scaife, 12 May 1915. Respecting posthumous editions of Muir's works, Badè declared to Greenslet that Muir "would have had a fit if any one had suggested to him that a woman was to edit his work." Greenslet replied: "I share your distrust of a female editor for a work of this character. No doubt Mrs. Parsons can do a fairly workmanlike job on the Alaska book, but the production of a definitive edition is unquestionably a man's job."

31. C——y, "Study of Botany," *Maine Monthly Magazine,* 1 (1837): 491, 492.

32. Joseph Kastner's *A Species of Eternity* (New York: Knopf, 1977), p. 23, is one of several general histories of premodern American natural history, all of which mention Jane Colden. For a short profile, see Marcia Myers Bonta, *Women in the Field: America's Pioneering Women Naturalists* (College Station: Texas A & M Univ. Press, 1991), pp. 5–8. This book documents an extensive array of women botanists, entomologists, and ornithologists working in premodern America. For further background on nineteenth-century botanizing by women in America, see Elizabeth B. Keeney's chapter "Gender and Botany," in her book *The Botanizers*

(Chapel Hill: University of North Carolina Press, 1992), pp. 69–82; and Vera Norwood, *Made from This Earth: American Women and Nature* (Chapel Hill: University of North Carolina Press, 1993), pp. 1–24. While recognizing that genteel constraints against, for example, free-ranging specimen collecting limited women from botanizing fully, Keeney is more optimistic about botanical pursuits as a way of extending women's sphere than is Ann B. Shteir, "Linnaeus's Daughters: Women and Botany," in *Women and the Structure of Society*, ed. Barbara J. Harris and Jo Ann K. McNamara (Durham: Duke University Press, 1984), pp. 67–73. Shteir argues that botany in the eighteenth century "served, and in some quarters was intended to serve, as a form of social control, substituting innocuous activities and attitudes for others more threatening to conventional views of womankind" (p. 73). She goes on, however, to underscore the seriousness of the women botanizers she has studied and the importance of their neglected contributions to botanical science.

33. See Anne T. Trensky, "The Saintly Child in Nineteenth-Century American Fiction," in *Prospects 1*, ed. Jack Salzman (New York: Burt Franklin, 1975), pp. 389–413.

34. Annis Pratt, with Barbara White et al., *Archetypal Patterns in Women's Fiction* (Sussex: Harvester, 1981), p. 17. For the importance of the green world to identity formation in childhood, see Edith Cobb, *The Ecology of Imagination in Childhood* (New York: Columbia University Press, 1977), a pioneering work of interpretative developmental psychology based on autobiographies of childhood as well as on analytical observation.

35. Wright, *Lichen Tufts*, pp. 9, 11, 16, 51.

36. Ibid., p. 81.

37. Norwood, *Made from This Earth*, pp. 25–41, argues persuasively that Cooper's appearance "sets the stage for women nature essayists" by "conjoining women's roles as domesticator and the American landscape's new image as home" (pp. 26, 28), from which unassailable basis she proceeds to address herself to a mixed-sex public on such issues of public significance as environmental protection.

38. Susan Fenimore Cooper, *Rural Hours* (New York: Putnam, 1850), pp. 182, 202–218. Cooper certainly reveals herself to be her father's daughter, in that here and elsewhere *Rural Hours* shows a protectionist sensibility rather like that of *The Pioneers* by developing a wide range of environmental concerns (e.g., wasteful ways of logging, fishing, and game hunting) from a combination of moral, utilitarian, and aesthetic perspectives. In *Rural Hours*, however, all dimensions of the environmental critique are more systematically amplified except for the legal aspect, concerning which *The Pioneers* is especially masterful in weaving the latter part of its plot around the violation of Judge Temple's game laws.

39. Cooper, *Rural Hours*, p. 120.

40. Edith Thomas, *The Round Year* (Boston: Houghton, Mifflin, 1886), p. 73.

41. Baker, *Blues, Ideology, and Afro-American Literature*, e.g. pp. 11–12, 24, 66–67 (on railroads, jeremiads, and "America" as sign).

42. I borrow the phrase from Jehlen, *American Incarnation*, p. 21.

43. Marx, "Pastoralism in America," p. 66; and "Does Pastoralism Have a Future?" in *The Pastoral Landscape*, ed. John Dixon Hunt, Center for Advanced Study in the Visual Arts Symposium Papers 20 (Hanover, NH: University Press of New England, 1992), p. 222.

44. Donald Worster, *Nature's Economy: The Roots of Ecology* (1977; rpt. Garden City, N.Y.: Doubleday, 1979), pp. 340–349.

45. Jean Hersey, *The Shape of a Year* (New York: Scribner's, 1967), p. 27; Josephine Johnson, *The Inland Island* (1969; rpt. Columbus: Ohio State University Press, 1987), p. 153.

46. Gary Snyder, "By Frazier Creek Falls," in *Turtle Island* (New York: New Directions, 1974), p. 41. This collection is an excellent example of a contemporary enlistment of pastoral (with a strong transfusion from Amerindian and, to a lesser extent, Asian thought) for the purpose of ecocentric manifesto.

2. New World Dreams and Environmental Actualities

1. I favor the neologism "post-European" over "postcolonial" for two reasons. First, "post-European"—in my intended usage, anyhow—points specifically and restrictively to the circulation of Europhone language and print forms without implying that this is the totality of what comprises "emerging" national culture. And second, "post-European" avoids awkward and impossible attempts to distinguish between "colonial" and "postcolonial" phases.

2. See Angela L. Miller, *The Empire of the Eye: Landscape Representation and American Cultural Politics, 1825–1875* (Ithaca: Cornell University Press, 1993), pp. 21–64, for a careful discussion of Cole's *Course of Empire* and other paintings with regard to this problematic. Miller distinguishes judiciously between Cole and such Cole followers as Frederick Church as well as between different Cole canvases that seem to evince different positions toward and different degrees of critical awareness about the nineteenth-century transformation of American landscape that Cole decried *ex cathedra*.

3. Wolfgang Iser, "Pastoralism as Paradigm of Literary Fictionality," in *The Fictive and the Imaginary: Charting Literary Anthropology* (Baltimore: Johns Hopkins University Press, 1993), p. 24. So far as Renaissance Studies is concerned, Iser's argument is both anticipated and historicized by Harry Berger, Jr., *Second World and Green World: Studies in Renaissance Fiction-Making*, ed. John Patrick Lynch (Berkeley: University of California Press, 1988).

4. J. H. Elliott, in his seminal lectures, *The Old World and the New, 1492–1650*

(Cambridge, Eng.: Cambridge University Press, 1970), remarks briefly on the arcadianization of the New World by certain Renaissance humanists (pp. 25–27). The process began with Columbus, in whose *Diario*, as José Rabasa observes, "the *locus amoenus* of classical literature congeals into an empirical region"—a departure from prior European travel writing, wherein "paradisiacal landscape is a legendary phantasm, but not an actual locus given for description" (*Inventing America: Spanish Historiography and the Formation of Eurocentrism* [Norman: University of Oklahoma Press, 1993], p. 71). In *Marvelous Possessions: The Wonder of the New World* (Chicago: University of Chicago Press, 1991), Stephen Greenblatt shows how the rhetoric of wonder comes to subserve an ideology of conquest. In American Studies scholarship, the classic discussion of the European imagination as a context for understanding American pastoral tradition is Leo Marx's chapter "Shakespeare's American Fable," in *The Machine in the Garden: Technology and the Pastoral Ideal in America* (New York: Oxford University Press, 1964), pp. 34–72. The pertinence of Marx's central proof-text, *The Tempest*, to the history of discovery and colonization of the Americas has, however, been the subject of countless previous and subsequent analyses by Renaissance specialists. One of the most recent and sophisticated is Jeffrey Knapp's *An Empire Nowhere: England, America, and Literature from Utopia to "The Tempest"* (Berkeley: University of California Press, 1992), which is especially illuminating in the present context (1) for its attentiveness to how the political implications of pastoral form in *The Tempest* and other texts are complicated by the traditional association of the pastoral mode with fictive rarefaction (cf. Iser and Berger); and (2) for its discussion of English new world representation in light of the tradition of imagining England itself as a utopian space apart.

5. I do not deny, of course, the capacity of old world cultures to generate or reinvent autochthonous mythical ecologisms of their own: e.g., English legends of the Green Man and the symbolic importance of the Black Forest in Germany.

6. "Heterotopia" is a Foucaultian term, referring to actual places within society that function as countersites, where opposition to the predominant culture is located. This insight has been usefully applied to green utopianism in William Chaloupka and R. McGreggor Cawley, "The Great Wild Hope: Nature, Environmentalism, and the Open Secret," in *In the Nature of Things: Language, Politics, and the Environment,* ed. Jane Bennett and Chaloupka (Minneapolis: University of Minnesota Press, 1993), pp. 6–21.

7. Quotations from Wendell Berry, *A Continuous Harmony* (New York: Harcourt, 1972), pp. 80, 72; *The Unsettling of America: Culture and Agriculture* (San Francisco: Sierra Club, 1977), p. 14. Berry might object to my lumping his agrarianism together with other traditions that represent America as countryside, although they share the consignment of (sub)urban landscapes to the status of American epiphenomenon.

8. As Larzer Ziff points out, the epistolary fiction of Farmer James writing to Mr. F. B. "broadens the actual contrast between Crèvecoeur, the cultured farmer, and his European readership," although it also vernacularizes the literary convention of gentlepersons' correspondence (through the creation of an unsophisticated farmer-writer); see Ziff, *Writing in the New Nation: Prose, Print, and Politics in the Early United States* (New Haven: Yale University Press, 1991), p. 25.

9. Roderick Nash, *Wilderness and the American Mind,* 3d ed. (New Haven: Yale University Press, 1982), p. 67.

10. Anne Farrar Hyde, *An American Vision: Far Western Landscape and National Culture, 1820–1920* (New York: New York University Press, 1990), p. 18; Barbara Packer, "'Man Hath No Part in All This Glorious Work': American Romantic Landscapes," in *Romantic Revolutions: Criticism and Theory,* ed. Kenneth R. Johnston et al. (Bloomington: Indiana University Press, 1990), p. 259.

11. For discussion of postcolonial anxiety in "The American Scholar," see my "American Literary Emergence as a Postcolonial Phenomenon," *American Literary History,* 4 (1992): 422–423, and "Emerson in His Cultural Context," in *Ralph Waldo Emerson: A Collection of Critical Essays,* ed. Buell (Englewood Cliffs, N.J.: Prentice-Hall, 1993), pp. 51–52.

12. See, however, the more complex analysis of antebellum African American writing in Chapter 1, which takes note of pastoral elements that go well beyond the mandatory degree of ruralism in setting.

13. *The Oxford Book of Canadian Verse,* ed. Wilfred Campbell (Toronto: Oxford University Press, 1913), pp. 1–2; *A Book of Australian Verse,* ed. Judith Wright (London: Oxford University Press, 1956), p. 15; *South African Poetry: A New Anthology,* ed. Roy MacNab and Charles Gulston (London: Collins, 1948), p. 198; John Greenleaf Whittier, "Sunset on the Bearcamp," in *The Poetical Works of Whittier* (Boston: Houghton Mifflin, 1975), p. 162.

14. John Povey, "Landscape in Early South African Poetry," in *Olive Schreiner and After: Essays on Southern African Literature in Honour of Guy Butler,* ed. Malvern Van Wyk Smith and Don MacLennan (Capetown: David Philip, 1983), pp. 116–123.

15. Bruce Clunies Ross, "Landscape and the Australian Imagination," in *Mapped but Not Known: The Australian Landscape of the Imagination,* ed. P. R. Eaden and F. H. Mares (Netley: Wakefield, 1986), p. 226. To my knowledge there has been no comprehensive comparatist study of literary representation with regard to internalization of or resistance to European landscape aesthetics among settler cultures. In this connection, I have been helped not only by the works cited elsewhere in this chapter's notes but also by the following sources in particular: the classic study by Australian art historian Bernard Smith, *European Vision and the South Pacific,* 2d ed. (New Haven: Yale University Press, 1985); *The Iconography*

of Landscape, ed. Denis Cosgrove and Stephen Daniels, (Cambridge, Eng.: Cambridge University Press, 1988); and John Rennie Short, *Imagined Country: Environment, Culture, and Society* (London: Routledge, 1991).

16. Marx, *Machine in the Garden,* p. 42, makes this point with regard to the United States, but it is applicable to other new worlds as well. G. A. Wilkes remarks, for instance, that "the conception of Australia as a promised land vies with the conception of it as a desolate and melancholy expanse" (*The Stockyard and the Croquet Lawn* [Victoria: Edward Arnold, 1981], p. 13). More sophisticated recent work on (post)colonialism has complicated the discussion with more scrupulous analysis of the variety within, as well as the intersections between, old and new world perspectives on the new world as utopia. See for example Lemuel A. Johnson, "Inventions of Paradise: The Caribbean and the Utopian Bent," *Afro-Hispanic Review,* 10, no. 2 (1991): 3–15.

17. However, Alan Heimert, in "Puritanism, the Wilderness, and the Frontier," *New England Quarterly,* 26 (1953): 361–382, shows that the "howling wilderness" topos was generated only after the actual challenges of frontier living in New England had disabused the Puritans of their original "land of Canaan" imagery.

18. Northrop Frye, "Conclusion" to *A Literary History of Canada* (1965), reprinted in *The Bush Garden: Essays on the Canadian Imagination* (Toronto: Anansi, 1971), p. 225. Margaret Atwood, "Nature the Monster," in *Survival: A Thematic Guide to Canadian Literature* (Toronto: Anansi, 1972), p. 49. The relationship between Frye and Atwood was one of mutual esteem. Atwood, Frye's student, used his phrase as one of her chapter's epigraphs; Frye took his title for *The Bush Garden* from Atwood's first collection of poems, *Journals of Susanna Moodie*—Moodie being for both Frye and Atwood one of the founders of Canadian wilderness gothic. Atwood's poetic rendition gothicizes her further. Frye's pronouncement, coming from Canada's most eminent critic at the conclusion of the landmark history of English Canadian writing (the Canadian equivalent of the *Literary History of the United States*), was widely influential. For a more extended, systematic presentation of the gothic wilderness theory of Canadian writing, see Gaile McGregor, *The Wacousta Syndrome: Explorations in the Canadian Langscape* (Toronto: University of Toronto Press, 1985). McGregor starts by contrasting the vision of a "regenerative" nature that she ascribes to Fenimore Cooper with what she takes to be the deliberate absence of landscape from *Wacousta,* by John Richardson (Cooper's Canadian counterpart), an absence McGregor attributes to a "garrison" mentality (pp. 3–25).

19. *The Puritans in America: A Narrative Anthology,* ed. Alan Heimert and Andrew Delbanco (Cambridge: Harvard University Press, 1985), pp. 45–50, 52–58. Mary Lu MacDonald, in "The Natural World in Early Nineteenth-Century Canadian Literature," *Canadian Literature,* 3 (1986): 48–65, argues that "before 1850,

with few exceptions, all the evidence points to an essentially positive literary view of the Canadian landscape" (p. 48). T. D. Maclulich, "Reading the Land: The Wilderness Tradition in Canadian Letters," *Journal of Canadian Studies*, 20 (1985): 29–44, is of the same persuasion. See also Patricia Hunt, "North American Pastoral: Contrasting Images of the Garden in Canadian and American Literature," *American Studies*, 23 (1982): 39–67; Hunt is more deferential to the position of Frye and Atwood while aware of its simplifications. An older study that is helpful in its insistence on the difficulty of resolving Canadian landscape vision into a single image is D. G. Jones, *Butterfly on Rock* (Toronto: University of Toronto Press, 1970).

20. Coral Lansbury, *Arcady in Australia: The Evocation of Australia in Nineteenth-Century English Literature* (Carlton, Victoria: Melbourne University Press, 1970), pp. 30, 157, 160. The poetic quotation is from Bernard O'Dowd, *The Bush* (1912). Other cultural historians of nineteenth-century Australia have been somewhat more hospitable to the nationalist possibilities of pastoral modes of expression and dated their internalization earlier: cf. Geoffrey Searle, *The Creative Spirit of Australia: A Cultural History*, rev. ed. (Victoria: Heinemann, 1987). Some of these scholars, predictably, draw sharp distinctions between modes of literary naturism Lansbury tends to conflate: G. A. Wilkes, in *The Stockyard and the Croquet Lawn*, for example, contrasts genteel pastoralism and masculinist visions of bushranging.

21. Brian Elliott, *The Landscape of Australian Poetry* (Melbourne: Cheshire, 1967), p. 29.

22. Stephen Gray's *Southern African Literature: An Introduction* (New York: Barnes and Noble, 1979) focuses on the creation and recent questioning of South African myths of the savage and the frontier; J. M. Coetzee's, *White Writing: On the Culture of Letters in South Africa* (New Haven: Yale University Press, 1988) concentrates more on landscape representation per se. Like Lansbury and Elliott, both Gray and Coetzee discuss the transition from travelers' and visitors' writing to settlers' literature. Coetzee draws helpful distinctions between writing about rurality in English and Afrikaans, noting the former's interest in landscape description as opposed to the latter's agrarian emphasis.

23. Raymond Williams, *The Country and the City* (New York: Oxford University Press, 1973). For works influenced by Williams, see John Barrell, *The Dark Side of the English Landscape: The Rural Poor in English Painting, 1730–1840* (Cambridge, Eng.: Cambridge University Press, 1980); and Ann Bermingham, *Landscape and Ideology: The English Rustic Tradition, 1740–1860* (Berkeley: University of California Press, 1986). Sarah Burns, in *Pastoral Inventions: Rural Life in Nineteenth-Century American Art and Culture* (Philadelphia: Temple University Press, 1989) argues, I think soundly, that owing to the strength of democratic

ideology "American images of the ideal farm and the agrarian dream" did not "uphold the social order in quite the same way" as their British counterparts (pp. 78ff.), although she too represents American painting as a genteel institution that underrepresented poverty and squalor except when engaging in caricature.

24. Williams, "Country and City," p. 281.

25. The imperial tendencies within American pastoral representation have of late been discussed most intensively by art historians. See *The West as America: Reinterpreting Images of the Frontier, 1820–1920,* ed. William H. Truettner (Washington: Smithsonian Institution Press, 1991), and Albert Boime, *The Magisterial Gaze: Manifest Destiny and American Landscape Painting, c. 1830–1865* (Washington: Smithsonian Institution Press, 1991). For literary history, see especially Myra Jehlen, *American Incarnation: The Individual, the Nation, and the Continent* (Cambridge: Harvard University Press, 1986), and Rob Wilson, *American Sublime: The Genealogy of a Poetic Genre* (Madison: University of Wisconsin Press, 1991). The most recent scholarship seems to be revising the imperial argument in a way somewhat congruent with the multivalence that I have attributed to pastoral. In art history, see Miller, *The Empire of the Eye;* and in literary criticism, Bruce Robert Greenfield, *Narrating Discovery: The Romantic Explorer in American Literature, 1790–1855* (New York: Columbia University Press, 1992). Both hold that the story of continental conquest became the master narrative for most nineteenth-century commentators; but both carefully locate sources of contradiction and resistance within this history. Greenfield calls attention to how the "close cooperation with local peoples" required of Lewis and Clark "opened up a mode of relationship with the west that contradicted the authority of the legal and scientific" (p. 101), although the explorers' interpreters and successors ignored and overrode this particularity.

26. Mary Louise Pratt, *Imperial Eyes: Travel Writing and Transculturation* (London: Routledge, 1992), pp. 33, 56, and pp. 15–107 passim.

27. Charles Hose, *The Field-Book of a Jungle-Wallah: Being a Description of Shore, River, and Forest Life in Sarawak* (1929; rpt. Singapore: Oxford University Press, 1985). ("My friend, the late Robert Shelford, in his book, 'A Naturalist in Borneo,' repeats an amusing Malay legend [which may or may not be true] . . .")

28. Quotation from Charles Darwin, *Voyage of the Beagle* (New York: Collier, 1909), p. 471. Both the range and the outer limits of Bartram's ability to stretch beyond the standard perceptions of settler culture are well illustrated by his reflections on a marriage between a white trader and a Seminole woman whose kin disapproved of her behavior (*Travels* [1791; rpt. New York: Dover, 1928], pp. 110–111). The anecdote plays to a stereotype (the topic of Indian degeneracy) but only to demolish it by holding up the trader's wife as the exception that proves "savage" is a misnomer, since the "impartial observer, who resides but a

little time" among the natives must perceive their civility, must perceive "that it is from the most delicate sense of the honour and reputation of their tribes and families, that their laws and customs receive their force and energy." It is finally much less interesting in a case like Bartram's, and Darwin's also, to stress their imprisonment within cultural parochialism than it is to stress their ability to see far enough beyond it to become somewhat aware of its limits and of the inner coherence and integrity of cultures far different from their own. For an opposite perspective on Bartram, which overstresses to my mind his confinement within preexisting literary, spiritual, and natural history discourses, see Pamela Regis, *Describing Early America: Bartram, Jefferson, Crèvecoeur, and the Rhetoric of Natural History* (DeKalb: Northern Illinois University Press, 1992), pp. 40–78. Myra Jehlen, however, rightly points to the influence of noble savagism on Bartram's pro-Indian stance, in "The Literature of Colonization," *Cambridge History of American Literature*, ed. Sacvan Bercovitch (Cambridge, Eng.: Cambridge University Press, 1994), pp. 135–136.

29. Observance of "basic grammar" at the level of form, however, does not mean that *Ceremony* is an easily comprehensible text for the non-Indian reader in all respects. In drawing on native storytelling traditions and on Laguna myth and sacred geography, *Ceremony*, as Louis Owens rightly says, "challenges readers with a new epistemological orientation while altering previously established understandings of the relationship between reader and text" (*Other Destinies: Understanding the American Indian Novel* [Norman: University of Oklahoma Press, 1992], p. 171). Thus in some respects its very "familiarity" may have a defamiliarizing effect on the historically informed reader.

30. Léopold Sédar Senghor, *Prose and Poetry*, ed. and trans. John Reed and Clive Wake (London: Heinemann, 1976), p. 99, from *Pierre Teilhard de Chardin et la politique africaine* (1962). "More has been written on Negritude, perhaps, than on any other single concept concerning African literature," writes Rand Bishop, in *African Literature, African Critics: The Forming of Critical Standards, 1947–1966* (Westport, Conn.: Greenwood, 1988), p. 141. Bishop's chapter on the subject, pp. 142–167, identifies the basic positions and many of the key players, Francophone and Anglophone, pro and con, in good handbook fashion. On Senghor, the fullest study is Sylvia Washington Bâ's highly sympathetic appraisal, *The Concept of Négritude in the Poetry of Léopold Sédar Senghor* (Princeton: Princeton University Press, 1973). *Colloque sur la négritude* (Paris: Editions Présense Africaine, 1972) is a valuable symposium including much insider testimony. For two useful short expositions, see Albert Gérard, "Historical Origins and Literary Destiny of Negritude," trans. Victor A. Velen, *Diogenes*, 48 (1965): 14–38; and Abiola Irele, "Negritude or Black Cultural Nationalism," *Journal of Modern African Studies*, 3 (1965): 321–348. V. Y. Mudimbe has provided important astrin-

gent critical judgments in "Psychiologie de la negritude," *Etudes Congolaises*, 10, no. 5 (1967): 1–13; and *The Invention of Africa: Gnosis, Philosophy, and the Order of Knowledge* (Bloomington: Indiana University Press, 1988), pp. 83–87. For a sense of the variety of political positions Negritude could occupy, see Omafume F. Onoge, "The Crisis of Consciousness in Modern African Literature: A Survey (1974)," reprinted in *Marxism and African Literature*, ed. Georg M. Gugelberger (Trenton, N.J.: Africa World Press, 1985), pp. 21–30.

31. In addition to the articles by Gérard and Irele, see Mbulamwanza Mudimbe-Boyi, "African and Black American Literature: The 'Negro Renaissance' and the Genesis of African Literature in French," trans. J. Coates, in *For Better or Worse: The American Influence in the World*, ed. Allen F. Davis (Westport, Conn.: Greenwood, 1981), pp. 157–169.

32. Sol Plaatje's *Mhudi*, ed. Stephen Gray (London: Heinemann; Washington: Three Continents, 1978), is a melodramatic rewriting of early nineteenth-century South African history that focuses on a young Barolong couple who survive the genocidal vengeance of the Zulus, whom they and their decimated peoples drive northward with the aid of the Afrikaner pioneers just then trekking north over the Transvaal. Plaatje highlights a romance of the forest (the noble African couple overcoming all obstacles) and what superficially seems a naively mystified Afro-centric redreaming of history (interblack struggle shown as the era's great event, with European conquest remaining a side issue)—all of which is in line with the stated purpose of preserving Sechuana "folk-tales, which with the spread of European ideas, are fast being forgotten" (p. 21). But these elements then become cover for an indictment of white racism.

33. Aimé Césaire, *The Collected Poetry* (bilingual edition), ed. and trans. Clayton Eshleman and Annette Smith (Berkeley: University of California Press, 1983), p. 72: "my race that no ablution of hyssop mixed with lilies could purify / my race pitted with blemishes / my race a ripe grape for drunken feet." I have been assisted in developing an understanding of Césaire's *Cahier* and of Negritude by Abiola Irele's gracious willingness to share with me in typescript his scholarly edition of the *Cahier* (Ibadan: New Horn, 1994). Here and below in this chapter I have deliberately preferred literary to literal translations so as to preserve some equivalence of affect.

34. Christopher L. Miller elegantly defends the complexity of *L'enfant noir* in *Theories of Africans: Francophone Literature and Anthropology in Africa* (Chicago: University of Chicago Press, 1990), pp. 114–180. Miller claims that the work should be read as a bicultural *kunstlerroman* (though he does not use this term) about becoming a writer or griot, and that it does this by its evocation of the Mande ethos of the griot, which in Mande terms was a metier "interchangeable" with the protagonist's father's vocation of goldsmithing. This intricate and (to

me) generally persuasive argument does not, however, do away with the fact that *L'enfant noir* unfolds in a more limpidly, comfortingly straightforward and unabrasive narrative than anything in Soyinka.

35. Derek Walcott, *The Star-Apple Kingdom* (New York: Farrar, Straus, 1979), pp. 46, 48, 49, 51, 56, 58.

36. Léopold Sédar Senghor, *Selected Poems/Poems Choisies* (bilingual text), trans. and ed. Craig Williamson (London: Rex Collings, 1976), "Nuit de Sine," pp. 28–29:

> Woman, lay on my forehead your hands of balsam, your hands
> softer than fur,
> High above, the balancing palms hardly rustle in the high
> Nightwind. Not even a cradlesong.
> Let it rock us, the rhythmic silence.
> Listen to its song: listen to the beating of our dark blood,
> listen
> To the beating of the dark pulse of Africa in the haze of
> forgotten villages.

37. Charles Baudelaire, *Les fleurs du mal* (bilingual text), trans. and ed. Richard Howard (Boston: Godine, 1982), pp. 208, 30:

> Take me, tousled current, to where men
> as mighty as the trees they live among
> submit like them to the sun's long tyranny;
> ebony sea, you bear a brilliant dream
> of sails and pennants, mariners and masts
>
> a harbor where my soul can slake its thirst
> for color, sound and smell—where ships that glide
> among the seas of golden silk throw wide
> their yardarms to embrace a glorious sky
> palpitating in eternal heat.

Senghor's enthusiasm for this poem is noted in Janet G. Vaillant, *Black, French, and African: A Life of Léopold Sédar Senghor* (Cambridge: Harvard University Press, 1990), pp. 80–81. For a discussion of Baudelaire's Africanism, see Christopher L. Miller, *Blank Darkness: Africanist Discourse in French* (Chicago: University of Chicago Press, 1985), pp. 69–138. For a comparison of the aesthetics of Baudelaire and Senghor, see Bâ, *Senghor*, pp. 104–108.

38. I. Allen Jack, "The Academy and the Grove in Canada" (1878), reprinted in *The Search for English-Canadian Literature,* ed. Carl Ballstadt (Toronto: University of Toronto Press, 1975), p. 130.

39. Kwame Anthony Appiah, "The Postcolonial and the Postmodern," in *In My Father's House: Africa in the Philosophy of Culture* (New York: Oxford University Press, 1992), p. 149.

40. See Barbara Novak, *Nature and Culture: American Landscape Painting, 1825–1875* (New York: Oxford University Press, 1980), which also makes clear (in Part IV) the continuing dependence of ninteenth-century American artists on European models.

41. Senghor, "Masque négre," in *Selected Poems,* p. 34. On the European definition of the primitive and western circulation of primitive commodities, see Marianna Torgovnick, *Gone Primitive: Savage Intellects, Modern Lives* (Chicago: University of Chicago Press, 1990).

42. Thoreau, "Natural History of Massachusetts" (1842), in *Excursions and Poems,* ed. Bradford Torrey and Francis H. Allen (Boston: Houghton, Mifflin, 1906), p. 103.

43. The first draft of *Walden* includes the Catskill reminiscence as part of the first full glimpse of the cabin in the section that later became "Where I Lived and What I Lived for" (J. Lyndon Shanley, *The Making of Walden* [Chicago: University of Chicago Press, 1957], p. 138).

44. Bruce Greenfield comments shrewdly on the conventionalism of this emptying process in "Ktaadn" as an example of the tradition of new world discovery narratives, which Thoreau knew well (*Narrating Discovery,* pp. 189–195).

45. Ann Ronald remarks in her critical study of Abbey that *Desert Solitaire* "lovingly pursues the fulfillment of [Abbey's] desire. That he succeeds is due primarily to his skill as a writer of romance, for only by reshaping his own desert universe into a mythic place can he finally know, possess, embrace the real one" (*The New West of Edward Abbey* [Albuquerque: University of New Mexico Press, 1982], p. 65). Although I think Ronald somewhat underestimates the importance of the element of environmental documentary in *Desert Solitaire,* I agree that it is Abbey's postpastoral dream that gives focus to that factical substrate. See also Scott Slovic, "'Rudolf the Red Knows Rain, Dear': The Aestheticism of Edward Abbey," in *Seeking Awareness in American Nature Writing* (Salt Lake City: University of Utah Press, 1992), pp. 93–114.

46. Edward Abbey, *Desert Solitaire: A Season in the Wilderness* (New York: Ballantine, 1968), pp. 2, 7, 6.

47. Ibid., pp. 200, 219. This account of Abbey is admittedly one-sided, not doing justice to his powers of description and polemic, nor to his hard-bitten aggressiveness of tone. But I believe that the self-consciousness of his persona and his literary allusiveness are traits that need stressing. Abbey's self-consciousness regarding Thoreau is a matter of record. See his lively "Down the River with Henry Thoreau" (in *Slumgullion Stew: An Edward Abbey Reader* [New York: Dutton, 1984], pp. 272–307), which suggests after the fact that "Down the River" should be read as a kind of competition with Thoreau.

48. Annie Dillard, *Pilgrim at Tinker Creek* (New York: Harper and Row, 1974), p. 83.

49. Annie Dillard, "Walden Pond and Thoreau" (master's thesis, Hollins College, 1968).

50. Paul Carter, *The Road to Botany Bay: An Exploration of Landscape and History* (Chicago: University of Chicago Press, 1987), p. 83.

51. Peter Fritzell, *Nature Writing and America: Essays upon a Cultural Type* (Ames: Iowa State University Press, 1990), pp. 16–35 and passim. Fritzell indicts the ruck of nature writers for turning "away from the potentially exhausting effects of self-consciousness" (p. 17) and opting for what he takes to be a naively "positivistic and representational" stance (p. 16), which he sees as a colonizer's stance: "The vast majority of American nature writing has functioned almost solely to settle the country—to compose it and delineate it . . . to establish . . . names and classifications, to fix (or attempt to fix) the terms of the nonhuman environment." (p. 19). My reservations about Fritzell's argument are chiefly that he sorts the washed from the unwashed too hastily (he has to admit that the differences are less of kind than of degree: p. 34) and that his antirepresentationalism is too eager an attempt to jump on the postmodern bandwagon. But *Nature Writing and America* is, withal, an important albeit often redundant book. For a roughly parallel discussion of the self-reflexive turn in contemporary American environmental fiction, see Linda Anne Falkenstein, "The Simulated Wilderness in the Contemporary American Novel" (Ph.D. diss., Harvard University, 1991); and (with emphasis on feminist deconstructions of wilderness fiction like Jean Stafford's *Mountain Lion* [1947]) Melody Graulich, "'O Beautiful for Spacious Guys': An Essay on the 'Legitimate Inclinations of the Sexes,'" in *The Frontier Experience and the American Dream: Essays on American Literature,* ed. David Mogen, Mark Busby, and Paul Bryant (College Station: Texas A & M University Press, 1989), pp. 186–201.

52. *Audubon,* 93, no. 6 (November–December 1991): "Preserving Paradise," pp. 41, 50. For a critical analysis of this sort of rhetoric, see Lisa Lebduska, "How Green Was My Advertising: American Ecoconsumerism," *Interdisciplinary Studies in Literature and Environment,* 1 (1993): 5–17.

53. Harry Thurston, "Power in a Land of Remembrance," *Audubon,* 93, no. 6 (November–December 1991): 59.

54. On this point, a helpful discussion is Edward W. Soja's chapter on "spatialized ontology" in *Postmodern Geographies: The Reassertion of Space in Critical Social Theory* (London: Verso, 1990), pp. 118–137.

55. Packer, "American Romantic Landscapes," pp. 263–264; and Wilson, *American Sublime,* p. 128. For the text of "The Prairies," see *Norton Anthology of American Literature,* 3d ed., ed. Nina Baym et al. (New York: Norton, 1989), 1: 894n and 896. The editors point out that the literary nationalist note was a

belated (and therefore more than ordinarily self-conscious?) substitution. The original line replaced by "For which the speech of England has no name" was "And fresh as the young earth, ere man had sinned"—a similitude that discloses the Eurocentric root of the pastoral impetus to which Bryant later gives a more specifically postcolonial expression.

56. See especially Leah Dilworth, "Rhythm Nation: Modernism, Primitivism, and *The American Rhythm*," pp. 242–301 of Dilworth's Ph.D. dissertation, "Imagining the Primitive: Representations of Native Americans in the Southwest, 1880–1930" (Yale University, 1992). For a more sympathetic perspective, see Lois Rudnick, "Re-Naming the Land: Anglo Expatriate Women in the Southwest," in *The Desert Is No Lady: Southwestern Landscapes in Women's Writing and Art*, ed. Vera Norwood and Janice Monk (New Haven: Yale University Press, 1987), pp. 12–26. Austin's expertise, such as it was, was recognized; she authored the chapter on Native American aesthetics for the *Cambridge History of American Literature* (1917–1921).

57. On Austin's life, the most illuminating sources are Esther Lanigan Stineman, *Mary Austin: Song of a Maverick* (New Haven: Yale University Press, 1989), and Austin's own *Earth Horizon: Autobiography* (New York: Literary Guild, 1932). For Austin's early trials in California, despite her enthusiasm for the country itself, see Stineman, pp. 31–43, and Austin, pp. 192–194.

58. Guy Rotella, in *Reading and Writing Nature* (Boston: Northeastern University Press, 1991), writes sensitively about this poem's (admittedly limited) capacity to open itself up to recording nature's motions (pp. 9–10) and, throughout his study, of the tendency of the Puritan epistemology to encourage observation of nature even while circumscribing it within a providentialist paradigm. Although Puritanism could produce a rationale of land appropriation and transformation (cf. Cecelia Tichi, *New World, New Earth: Environmental Reform in American Literature from the Puritans through Whitman* [New Haven: Yale University Press, 1979]), it could equally, indeed much more self-consistently, justify the stance of suspending all human desire for the sake of devoted contemplation of the structure of God's handiwork. See also in this connection Elisa New, *The Regenerate Lyric: Theory and Innovation in Amerian Poetry* (Cambridge, Eng.: Cambridge University Press, 1993).

59. Bradstreet, "Contemplations," line 7, in *The Norton Anthology of American Literature*, 1: 97; Bartram, *Travels*, p. 126.

60. Austin, *Earth Horizon*, p. 195.

3. Representing the Environment

1. See for example Yi-fu Tuan, "Common Traits in Perception: The Senses," in *Topophilia: A Study of Environmental Perception, Attitudes, and Values* (1974;

rpt., with new preface, New York: Columbia University Press, 1990), pp. 5–12; E. V. Walter, *Placeways: A Theory of the Human Environment* (Chapel Hill: University of North Carolina Press, 1988), pp. 132–145 and passim; and Hans Jonas's classic essay "The Nobility of Sight" (1953), in *The Phenomenon of Life: Toward a Philosophical Biology* (1966; rpt. Chicago: University of Chicago Press, 1982), which points out that "since the days of Greek philosophy sight has been hailed as the most excellent of the senses" (p. 135).

2. Samuel A. Jones to A. W. Hosmer, 16 April 1903, in *Toward the Making of Thoreau's Modern Reputation*, ed. Fritz Oehlschlaeger and George Hendrick (Urbana: University of Illinois Press, 1979), p. 387.

3. Sharon Cameron, *Writing Nature: Henry Thoreau's Journal* (New York: Oxford University Press, 1985), p. 44. In "A Crisis in My Mental History," Mill explains why reading Wordsworth helped him get through his breakdown: "In the first place, these poems addressed themselves powerfully to one of the strongest of my pleasurable susceptibilities, the love of rural objects and natural scenery" (John Stuart Mill, *Autobiography* [New York: Columbia University Press, 1924], p. 103). See also Jonathan Bate, *Romantic Ecology: Wordsworth and the Romantic Tradition* (London: Routledge, 1991), pp. 14ff., for thoughtful reflections on the current unfashionableness of Mill's response and the need to take it more seriously.

4. For a sophisticated anatomy of contemporary debates about the viability and politics of representation from a perspective professedly neither for nor against mimesis, see Christopher Prendergast, *The Order of Mimesis: Balzac, Stendhal, Nerval, Flaubert* (Cambridge, Eng.: Cambridge University Press, 1986), a study deeply informed by poststructuralist and antecedent literary and philosophical theory. To make an elegant story extremely short, Prendergast finds more problems with "a wholesale rejection of the idea of mimesis" than with retention of some version of mimesis, although all versions seem problematic (pp. 252–253). For my purposes, the utility of his discussion is limited by his concentration on fiction and his understanding of mimesis as a textualized internalization of social norms; but I have found his intricately lucid presentation most enlightening.

5. Leonard Lutwack, *The Role of Place in Literature* (Syracuse: Syracuse University Press, 1984), p. 24. At the outset, Lutwack declares that "a concern for time rather than place is the mark of civilization . . . the maturation of an individual is a process of growing away from nature" (p. 4).

6. Carolyn Porter, "History and Literature: 'After the New Historicism,'" *New Literary History*, 21 (1990): 257.

7. This deconstructive process effectively began with *American Realism: New Essays*, ed. Eric Sundquist (Baltimore: Johns Hopkins University Press, 1982). Among subsequent books, perhaps the most pertinent here are two by contribu-

tors to that collection: Amy Kaplan, *The Social Construction of American Realism* (Chicago: University of Chicago Press, 1988), and Michael Davitt Bell, *The Problem of American Realism: Studies in the Cultural History of a Literary Idea* (Chicago: University of Chicago Press, 1993). The confident tone of Kaplan's opening statement indicates how quickly the revisionary reading has taken hold: "from an objective reflection of contemporary social life, realism has become a fictional conceit, or deceit, packaging and naturalizing an official version of the ordinary" (p. 1). A third contributor's study, Philip Fisher's *Hard Facts: Setting and Form in the American Novel* (New York: Oxford University Press, 1985), gives much more attention to the quality of thingness as such in realist representation (see "The Life History of Objects: The Naturalist Novel and the City," pp. 128–178), though his major concern is the symbolic properties of things as psychograms, socio-logical gestalts, commodity forms, etc. At least as influential as any Americanist work in the reinterpretation of realism, however, have been more general Marxist and Marxoid treatises like Fredric Jameson's *The Political Unconscious: Narrative as a Socially Symbolic Act* (Ithaca: Cornell University Press, 1981).

8. Michael Fried, *Realism, Writing, Disfiguration* (Chicago: University of Chicago Press, 1987). Fried finds realism a "blandly normalizing bias" that confuses cause with effect and by limiting intention "to an initial choice of subject and point of view plus a general will to realism . . . implies a prejudicial conception of the realistic project as merely photographic" (pp. 64, 10–11). If this "exact transcription" model of realism were the best that a theory of realism's realism could manage, then one could understand Fried's displeasure.

9. Christopher Salter, "John Steinbeck's *The Grapes of Wrath* as a Primer for Cultural Geography," in *Humanistic Geography and Literature: Essays on Experience of Place,* ed. Douglas C. D. Pocock (London: Croom Helm, 1981), pp. 156–157. Salter and William J. Lloyd's coauthored *Landscape in Literature* (Washington: Association of American Geographers, 1977) reflects on the limits of realist assumptions while defending their viability within limits. I by no means wish to suggest that all cultural geographers are empirical mimeticists. The contemporary interest in "reading" place as text has also drawn geographers to poststructuralist and Marxist theory; see, for example, J. Duncan and N. Duncan, "(Re)reading the Landscape," *Society and Space,* 6 (1988): 117–126; and especially Edward W. Soja, *Postmodern Geographies: The Reassertion of Space in Critical Social Theory* (London: Verso, 1989). The broader point is that a number of contemporary humanistic geographers have turned to literary sources to tell them things about landscape that "scientific" geography seems not to register. In approaching literature as a supplementary resource, geographers are never so naive as to take it to be a distortion-free mirror of the object-world, nor are they unanimous in their methodologies of reading. As a group, however, their work emphasizes the ways in which literature seeks to engage and reveal actual landscapes. For further

illustration of the range of perspectives brought to bear in this body of scholar-ship, see "Focus: Literary Landscapes—Geography and Literature," ed. L. Anders Sandberg and John S. Marsh, *The Canadian Geographer*, 32 (1988): 266–276.

10. George Levine, "Scientific Realism and Literary Representation," *Raritan*, 10, no. 4 (Spring 1991): 23, 21. See also Levine's editorial introduction to the symposium *Realism and Representation: Essays on the Problem of Realism in Relation to Science, Literature, and Culture* (Madison: University of Wisconsin Press, 1993), which is helpful for bibliography as well as commentary. (As Levine notes, however, "strong" realism is scantly represented in the collection.) In humanistic fields outside literature, some of the recent work of Hilary Putnam is pertinent, especially *The Many Faces of Realism* (LaSalle, Ill.: Open Court Press, 1987) and the papers collected as *Realism with a Human Face*, ed. James Conant (Cambridge: Harvard University Press, 1990). What to me is most interesting about Putnam's project is his attempt to establish a ground for realism that frees it from having to meet standards of "scientific" objectivity.

11. O'Sullivan's photographs, remarks Barbara Novak, "seem to arise without the intervention of ideas about 'art,' from a one-to-one encounter of camera and nature. The artist's control, though convention-free, is of course present, but often in the most informal way, as if the photographs were taking themselves" ("Landscape Permuted: From Painting to Photography," in *Photography in Print: Writings from 1816 to the Present*, ed. Vicki Goldberg [New York: Simon and Schuster, 1981], p. 176).

12. I wish to dodge the vexed question of whether surrealism and avant-gard-ism generally are hegemonic or insurgent. My inclination, as on the subject of pastoral's ideological valence, is to say: either or both.

13. John Burroughs, "Nature and the Poets," in *Pepacton* (Boston: Houghton, Mifflin, 1881), pp. 93, 104, 94–95, 106.

14. Ibid., p. 127.

15. John Burroughs, *Ways of Nature* (Boston: Houghton, Mifflin, 1905), p. 208, quoted by Lynn L. Merrill, *The Romance of Victorian Natural History* (New York: Oxford University Press, 1989), p. 139, in the course of a chapter on Burroughs that clarifies the point helpfully.

16. Ralph Lutts's *The Nature Fakers: Wildlife, Science, and Sentiment* (Golden, Colo.: Fulcrum, 1990) gives a detailed historical account and analysis of this controversy.

17. Burroughs, *Pepacton*, p. 155.

18. See Lutts, *The Nature Fakers*, p. 44.

19. Charles Taylor, *Sources of the Self: The Making of the Modern Identity* (Cambridge: Harvard University Press, 1989), pp. 53–90.

20. An obverse but also, I think, very fruitful approach is taken by James

Krasner, in *The Entangled Eye: Visual Perception and the Representation of Nature in Post-Darwinian Narrative* (New York: Oxford University Press, 1992), which examines as its subtitle indicates visual perception and representation of nature in British fiction and nonfiction from Richard Jefferies and Hardy through D. H. Lawrence. Krasner shows by recourse to the history of perception theory during this period that there is a link between the sense conveyed by Darwin's writing of the perceiver's inability to grasp and formulate landscape and the inward turn of modern narrative. Although Krasner's account of the literature of this period as science-responsive is subtle and persuasive, it seems to me more urgent, being more scandalous to current critical orthodoxy, to stress writerly interest in fidelity to the world of objects as against fidelity to perception theory.

21. Ruskin, *Modern Painters*, in *The Works of John Ruskin*, ed. E. T. Cook and Alexander Wedderburn (London: George Allen, 1903–1912), 3: 137, 616.

22. Ibid., 3: 584. Ruskin affirmed, "I have never known one whose thirst for visible fact was at once so eager and so methodic" (*Praeterita*, in *Works*, 35: 51.)

23. George Eliot, review of Ruskin, *Modern Painters*, vol. 3, in *Westminster Review*, 9, n.s. (1856), reprinted in *Ruskin: The Critical Heritage*, ed. J. L. Bradley (London: Routledge, 1984), pp. 180–181. For Ruskin's influence on American art and art criticism, see Linda S. Ferber and William H. Gerdts, *The New Path: Ruskin and the American Pre-Raphaelites* (Brooklyn, N.Y.: Brooklyn Museum and Schocken Books, 1985); and Roger B. Stein, *John Ruskin and Aesthetic Thought in America, 1840–1900* (Cambridge: Harvard University Press, 1967). A concise study of the rise of literalism in nineteenth-century British aesthetics is Patricia M. Ball, *The Science of Aspects: The Changing Role of Fact in the Work of Coleridge, Ruskin, and Hopkins* (London: Athlone Press, 1971).

24. Leslie Marmon Silko, "Landscape, History, and the Pueblo Imagination," *Antaeus*, no. 57 (1986): 85.

25. Barry Lopez, *Arctic Dreams: Imagination and Desire in a Northern Landscape* (1986; rpt. New York: Bantam, 1987), p. 84. For critical discussion of *Arctic Dreams* and other Lopez works, see particularly Sherman Paul, "Rereading Barry Lopez," in *For Love of the World: Essays on Nature Writers* (Iowa City: University of Iowa Press, 1992), pp. 67–107, and Scott Slovic, "'A More Particularized Understanding': Seeking Qualitative Awareness in Barry Lopez's *Arctic Dreams*," in *Seeking Awareness in American Nature Writing* (Salt Lake City: University of Utah Press, 1992), pp. 137–166.

26. Linda Hutcheon, "Metafictional Implications for Novelistic Reference," in *On Referring in Literature*, ed. Anna Whiteside and Michael Issacharoff (Bloomington: Indiana University Press, 1987), p. 9. In a revised version of this discussion in her book *A Poetics of Postmodernism: History, Theory, Fiction* (London: Routledge, 1988), pp. 155–157, Hutcheon adds a fifth dimension of reference to

allow for reader response and, somewhat ominously from my point of view, attenuates the notion of outer mimesis by rebaptizing it as "the textualized extratextual kind of reference," thus according primacy to textualization.

27. For the first draft, see J. Lyndon Shanley, *The Making of Walden* (Chicago: University of Chicago Press, 1957), pp. 192–193.

28. Ronald Earl Clapper, "The Development of *Walden*: A Genetic Text," (Ph.D. diss., UCLA, 1967), p. 605.

29. For the reference to Thoreau's marginalia and the identification of the "distinguished naturalist" as Louis Agassiz, see Philip Van Doren Stern, *The Annotated Walden* (New York: Clarkson Potter, 1970), p. 353.

30. John Burroughs, *Riverby* (Boston: Houghton, Mifflin, 1894), p. 35.

31. For exemplification, see Francis Ponge's collection of prose-poems, *The Voice of Things*, ed. and trans. Beth Archer (New York: McGraw-Hill, 1974); for analysis of Ponge's critical position (which is finally somewhat more idealist than I myself am comfortable with), see Ian Higgins, *Francis Ponge* (London: Athlone Press, 1979), pp. 51–66; and Paul, *For Love of the World*, p. 19 and passim, to which I am indebted for first calling Ponge's work to my attention.

32. *Gerard Manley Hopkins: A Selection of His Poems and Prose*, ed. Helen Gardner (Hammondsworth: Penguin, 1953), "Pied Beauty," p. 30.

33. For the association between modernism and spaces of accumulation, see Henri Lefebvre, *The Production of Space*, trans. Donald Nicholson-Smith (Oxford: Blackwell, 1991), pp. 48–49 and passim. On Hopkins's aesthetics, see for example Ball, *Science of Aspects*, and Carol T. Christ, *The Finer Optic: The Aesthetics of Particularity in Victorian Poetry* (New Haven: Yale University Press, 1975). "Insensitivity to particularity," Christ states, "becomes [for Hopkins] the measure of man's corruption . . . Renewed sensitivity to particularity heals this corruption" (pp. 98–99). See Tom Zaniello, *Hopkins in the Age of Darwin* (Iowa City: University of Iowa Press, 1988), for discussion of Hopkins's scientific interests.

34. Catherine Belsey, *Critical Practice* (London: Methuen, 1980), p. 128. Belsey's succinct, straightforward presentation of her version of Althusserian poststructuralism contains a helpful panoramic survey of resistance to realism as developed in various recent schools of literary theory from new critical formalism on.

35. Josef Maria Eder, *History of Photography*, trans. Edward Epstein (New York: Columbia University Press, 1945), pp. 523–524; Miles Orvell, *The Real Thing: Imitation and Authenticity in American Culture, 1880–1940* (Chapel Hill: University of North Carolina Press, 1989), pp. 100–101. For comparisons of Austin's art to photography, see Esther Lanigan Stineman, *Mary Austin* (New Haven: Yale University Press, 1989), pp. 183–187; and Vera Norwood, "The Photographer and the Naturalist: Laura Gilpin and Mary Austin in the Southwest," *Journal of American Culture*, 5 (1982): 1–28.

36. John James Audubon and John Bachman, *The Viviparous Quadrupeds of North America* (New York: Audubon, 1846), pp. 302–305.

37. John Janovy, Jr., *Keith County Journal* (New York: St. Martin's, 1978), p. 105.

38. Annie Dillard, *Living by Fiction* (New York: Harper and Row, 1982), p. 71.

39. Ralph Waldo Emerson, *Nature, Address, and Lectures,* ed. Robert E. Spiller and Alfred R. Ferguson (Cambridge: Harvard University Press, 1971), p. 36.

40. Wendell Berry, "The Specialization of Poetry," in *Standing by Words* (San Francisco: North Point, 1983), p. 8; Berry, "Poetry and Place," in ibid., p. 140.

41. George Eliot, *Adam Bede,* Book 2, Chapter 17, par. 5; William Carlos Williams, *Paterson* (New York: New Directions, 1963), p. 14; John Ruskin, *The Elements of Drawing,* in *The Works of John Ruskin,* ed. E. T. Cook and Alexander Wedderburn (London: George Allen, 1903–1912), 15:116; Francis Bacon, *The Great Instauration,* in *Works,* ed. James Spedding, Robert Leslie Ellis, and Douglas Denon Heath, 14 vols. (London, 1857–1874), 4: 32–33.

42. For Bacon's influence on Dutch painting, see Svetlana Alpers, *The Art of Describing: Dutch Art in the Seventeenth Century* (Chicago: University of Chicago Press, 1983). For an environmentalist critique of the way Baconian empiricism entraps realist painters into a reduction of nature to surface, see Neil Evernden, *The Social Creation of Nature* (Baltimore: Johns Hopkins University Press, 1992), pp. 78–80. In Evernden's widely shared view, the Renaissance introduced a technology of surface realist aesthetics (cf. Samuel Y. Edgerton, Jr., *The Renaissance Rediscovery of Linear Perspective* [New York: Basic, 1975]) that created a "purified *alternative* to the external world, a new 'Nature' whose genesis is within the individual" (e.g., the dominance, in painting, of a particular point of perspective) "and which is subsequently used to make sense of external objects" (p. 67). Prior to the Renaissance, as Evernden puts it in a previous work, "the painter represented the world as he experienced it, not just as he saw it"; but "with his mastery of perspective" he was "forced into a placeless world by virtue of the technique he has embraced" (*The Natural Alien* [Toronto: University of Toronto Press, 1985], pp. 49, 50. Both of Everenden's books are brilliantly suggestive throughout, first-rate pieces of environmental reflection; but I think his justifiable criticism of the hazards of realist procedures when crystallized into a system causes him to overstate realism's capacity to become a technology for displacing the world and to underestimate its capacity for expressing and inducing the kind of awe and wonder at the sense of objects realized in their "isness."

43. Hopkins, "As Kingfishers Catch Fire," in *Gerard Manley Hopkins,* p. 51.

44. Norman Bryson, *Looking at the Overlooked: Four Essays on Still Life Painting* (Cambridge: Harvard University Press, 1990), pp. 63, 64, 60.

45. Ibid., p. 64.

46. Charlotte M. Porter, in *The Eagle's Nest: Natural History and American Ideas, 1812–1842* (University, Al.: University of Alabama Press, 1986), pp. 81–82,

125–134, and passim, describes the privations and professional slights experienced by field naturalists as they became increasingly upstaged by the rise of organized science. On Bartram's nickname, see his *Travels* (1791; rpt. New York: Dover, 1928), p. 200. See Mary Louise Pratt, *Imperial Eyes: Travel Writing and Transculturation* (London: Routledge, 1992), p. 56, for a discussion of the oddly (and to her deceptively) innocent and impotent persona in traditional natural history writing.

47. Henry Salt, *Richard Jefferies: A Study* (London: Swan Sonnenschein; New York: Macmillan, 1894), p. 10.

48. Thoreau, "Wild Apples," in *Excursions and Poems*, ed. Bradford Torrey and Francis H. Allen (Boston: Houghton, Mifflin, 1906), pp. 317–318.

49. Christ, *The Finer Optic*, pp. 19, 63.

50. Walt Whitman, "Song of Myself," in *Leaves of Grass*, 1855 edition, line 1040.

51. John Canady, *Mainstreams of Modern Art* (New York: Simon and Schuster, 1959), p. 293.

52. Walt Whitman, "To Think of Time," in *Leaves of Grass*, 1855 edition, lines 131–132.

53. I owe this analogy to Joseph Wiesenfarth, who is not to be held accountable for the inferences I draw from it.

54. Three particularly suggestive discussions of environmental awareness as a form of culture are John Elder, *Imagining the Earth: The Poetry and the Vision of Nature* (Urbana: University of Illinois Press, 1985); Gary Snyder, "The Etiquette of Freedom" and subsequent essays in *The Practice of the Wild* (San Francisco: North Point, 1990); and the title essay and several other discussions in David W. Orr, *Ecological Literacy: Education and the Transition to a Postmodern World* (Albany: State University of New York Press, 1992).

55. See for example Elder, *Imagining the Earth*, pp. 40ff.

56. Wendell Berry, *Recollected Essays*, quoted by Elder, *Imagingin the Earth*, p. 60.

57. The most intelligent bioregionalist statement I have seen is Snyder, *The Practice of the Wild*; for a popular account of the history and nature of the idea, see Kirkpatrick Sale, *Dwellers in the Land: The Bioregional Vision* (San Francisco: Sierra Club, 1985).

58. Henry Wadsworth Longfellow, *The Complete Poetical Works* (Boston: Houghton, Mifflin, 1893), p. 297.

59. T. S. Eliot, "The Metaphysical Poets" (1921), in *Selected Essays* (New York: Harcourt, 1950), p. 247. A lively history of the loss of experiential reciprocity with nature is Keith Thomas, *Man and the Natural World: A History of the Modern Sensibility* (New York: Pantheon, 1983). The two losses are related. Although Eliot concentrates on what he takes to be the divorce of sensuous and intellectual sensibility among the literary classes and Thomas focuses on English social history from the Renaissance through the early stages of industrialization, both chart a divorce of cognitive knowledge from sensuous apprehension.

60. "Aftermath" and "rowen" were used figuratively as early as the Renaissance but the primary connotation was agricultural until modern times, according to the *Oxford English Dictionary*. In fairness to contemporary readers, I should concede that Longfellow can be held partially responsible for presentist under-reading of his poem. After all, he did choose to construct his tableau from highly generalized typic images. If his ghost were to accuse us of premature metaphorizing, we could reply that he asked for it. We might further chide him, as Raymond Williams chides most British pastoralists, for being almost as alienated as ourselves from the labor he represents, since the work of mowing is never described.

61. In an interview, Barry Lopez explains his interest in the relation between language and landscape on similar grounds: "What I am striving to do is to assist the reader in the quest to understand landscape as not only something that is living but something that includes us and upon which we are subtly dependent" (Kenneth Margolis, "Paying Attention: An Interview with Barry Lopez," *Orion*, 9, no. 3 [Summer 1990]: 50).

62. Pierre Bourdieu, *Outline of a Theory of Practice,* trans. Richard Nice (Cambridge, Eng.: Cambridge University Press, 1977), p. 89.

63. Eric Gullichsen and Randal Walser, "Cyberspace: Experiential Computing," quoted in Howard Rheingold, *Virtual Reality* (New York: Simon and Schuster, 1991), p. 191.

64. Jean Baudrillard, *Simulations,* trans. Paul Foss, Paul Patton, and Philip Beitchman (New York: Semiotext[e], 1983), pp. 88, 141, 140. See also Albert Borgmann's critique of VR as "instrumental hyperreality" in *Crossing the Postmodern Divide* (Chicago: University of Chicago Press, 1992), pp. 82–86.

65. Fredric Jameson, *Postmodernism: or, The Cultural Logic of Late Capitalism* (Durham: Duke University Press, 1991), pp. 38–39 and passim.

66. "Virtual Reality: How a Computer-Generated World Could Change the Real World," *Business Week,* 5 October 1992, 98.

67. Baudrillard, *Simulations,* p. 86.

68. Hence Ruskin's third law of drawing, "that nothing is ever seen perfectly, but only by fragments, and under various conditions of obscurity" (*Elements of Drawing,* in *Works,* 15: 120). What I have claimed for writing can also, however, be claimed of still photography; see for example Wright Morris, *Time Pieces: Photographs, Writing, and Memory* (New York: Aperture, 1989), in which Morris assuages his recurring worries about the photographic image's power to displace reality by stressing "what continues to elude us" (p. 140).

4. Walden's *Environmental Projects*

1. Thoreau's first problem as a would-be reader of nature, Robert Milder notes, "was that Thoreau in the 1840s lacked the skills to do it" (*Reimagining Thoreau*

[Cambridge, Eng.: Cambridge University Press, forthcoming 1994], p. 82). He did imbibe an enthusiastic amateur interest in natural history from his parents, however. At least one Concord resident claimed that Thoreau's "nature-love was a direct transmission from the Thoreau father and mother to the children" (Horace Hosmer, according to a letter dated 16 September 1890 from Samuel A. Jones to Henry S. Salt, in *Toward the Making of Thoreau's Modern Reputation,* ed. Fritz Oehlschlaeger and George Hendrick [Urbana: University of Illinois Press, 1979], p. 81); see also Hosmer to Jones, in *Remembrances of Concord and the Thoreaus,* ed. George Hendrick (Urbana: University of Illinois Press, 1977), pp. 84, 93. Thoreau's early biographer Franklin Benjamin Sanborn, an always interesting but dubious authority, claimed that Thoreau knew the flowers of Concord while he was still a schoolmaster, shortly after his graduation from Harvard ("Thoreau at the Concord Lyceum," 1904–1905 manuscript lecture, Concord Free Library).

2. "The wild apple," as Steven Fink observes, "is the European who, like himself or the backwoodsman, has reattached himself and adapted to the natural environment" (*Prophet in the Marketplace: Thoreau's Development as a Professional Writer* [Princeton: Princeton University Press, 1992], p. 278). When Thoreau contemplated moving to the western frontier in 1850, he had to admit that he saw "less difference between a city & . . . some dismallest swamp than formerly," and that he preferred "a more cultivated place, free from miasma & crocodiles" (*PJ* 3: 97).

3. H. Daniel Peck, "Better Mythology: Perception and Emergence in Thoreau's Journal," *North Dakota Quarterly,* 59, no. 2 (Spring 1991): 40.

4. For basics on the excursion genre with reference to Thoreau, see my *Literary Transcendentalism: Style and Vision in the American Renaissance* (Ithaca: Cornell University Press, 1973), pp. 188–203.

5. J. Lyndon Shanley, *The Making of Walden* (Chicago: University of Chicago Press, 1957); Linck C. Johnson, *Thoreau's Complex Weave* (Charlottesville: University Press of Virginia, 1986). An essential supplement to Shanley is Ronald Earl Clapper, "The Development of *Walden:* A Genetic Text," (Ph.D. diss., UCLA, 1967), which provides all variant readings from all drafts of the book. Another important study of Thoreau's redrafting practices is Stephen Adams and Donald Ross, Jr., *Revising Mythologies: The Composition of Thoreau's Major Works* (Charlottesville: University Press of Virginia, 1988). I am grateful to Professor Ross for furnishing me with his checklist of *Journal* passages used in *Walden.* For an excellent concise narrative and interpretative account of *Walden*'s genesis, see Robert Sattelmeyer, "The Remaking of *Walden,*" in *Writing the American Classics,* ed. James Barbour and Tom Quirk (Chapel Hill: University of North Carolina Press, 1990), pp. 53–78. See also Milder, *Reimagining Thoreau.*

6. All Thoreau's commentators remark on this; but perhaps the two prior

treatments most congruent with this chapter's approach to *Walden* are Paul Schwaber, "Thoreau's Development in 'Walden,'" *Criticism*, 5 (1963); and H. Daniel Peck, *Thoreau's Morning Work* (New Haven: Yale University Press, 1990), pp. 117–133: "The Worlding of *Walden*."

7. In 1855 *Putnam's* published the first four chapters of *Cape Cod* (1864). As for *The Maine Woods* (1864), "Ktaadn" (the first of its three parts) appeared in *Sartain's Union Magazine* in 1848, and "Chesuncook" in the *Atlantic* in 1858, although Thoreau may have written it as much as five years earlier. He continued to work on the third part, "Allegash and the East Branch," until his death; *Cape Cod*, Adams and Ross surmise, was complete by 1857 though published posthumously. See Adams and Ross, *Revising Mythologies* pp. 253–265, for chronologies of the composition and publication of Thoreau's works.

8. On Thoreau's literary interests, see Robert Sattelmeyer's excellent *Thoreau's Reading: A Study in Intellectual History with Bibliographical Catalogue* (Princeton: Princeton University Press, 1988), as well as the biography of Robert D. Richardson, Jr, *Henry David Thoreau: A Life of the Mind* (Berkeley: University of California Press, 1986), which is outstanding on the subject of Thoreau's intellectual sources and on the particular issue of Thoreau's growing interest and sophistication in natural history, landscape aesthetics, and related topics. Richardson takes the "late," post-*Walden* Thoreau very seriously, as do the other two important Thoreau biographers of the last decade: William Howarth, *The Book of Concord: Thoreau's Life as a Writer* (1982; rpt. New York: Penguin, 1983), and Richard Lebeaux, *Thoreau's Seasons* (Amherst: University of Massachusetts Press, 1984), both of whom draw heavily on the later *Journal*. Richardson, Howarth, and Lebeaux all insist, rightly to my mind, on reading Thoreau's career as a process of continuous intellectual and literary growth, rather than, as traditionally suggested, as a process that stopped after *Walden*. Although I concentrate mainly on *Walden* in this book, as my discussion of it will make clear I heartily concur with the "continuous growth" reading, which is now the majority position among Thoreauvians, though some hold to the traditional view (cf. Adams and Ross, *Revising Mythologies*, p. 241).

9. On Emerson's theory of correspondence, see especially Sherman Paul, *Emerson's Angle of Vision* (Cambridge: Harvard University Press, 1952). The most detailed study of the relationship between Emerson and Thoreau is Joel Porte, *Emerson and Thoreau: Transcendentalists in Conflict* (Middletown, Conn.: Wesleyan University Press, 1966), which, however, somewhat overstates the contrasts between the two. For a more balanced view, v. Richardson's biography, *Henry David Thoreau*. The first chapter of Sherman Paul's *The Shores of America: Thoreau's Inward Exploration* (Urbana: University of Illinois Press, 1958) is very insightful on the subject of how Emerson's ideas and example initially defined the terms of Thoreau's existence, as is Robert Milder, "An 'Errand to Mankind': Thoreau's

Problem of Vocation," *ESQ*, 37 (1991): 91–105. A searching article on the cooling of the friendship between them is Robert Sattelmeyer, "'When He Became My Enemy': Emerson and Thoreau, 1848–49," *New England Quarterly*, 62 (1989): 187–204. For Emerson on science and technology, see Leonard Neufeldt, *The House of Emerson* (Lincoln: University of Nebraska Press, 1982), pp. 75–99, and David M. Robinson, "Fields of Investigation: Emerson and Natural History," in *American Literature and Science*, ed. Robert J. Scholnick (Lexington: University Press of Kentucky, 1992), pp. 94–109. For Thoreau on science, the classic article is Nina Baym, "Thoreau's View of Science," *Journal of the History of Ideas*, 26 (1965): 221–234; but see also Walter Harding, "*Walden*'s Man of Science," *Virginia Quarterly Review*, 57 (1981): 45–61; Robert D. Richardson, Jr., "Thoreau and Science," in *American Literature and Science*, (cited above), pp. 110–127; and the several essays on Thoreau as scientist in *Thoreau's World and Ours: A Natural Legacy*, ed. Edmund A. Schofield and Robert C. Baron (Golden, Colo.: North American Press, 1993), pp. 39–73.

10. Ralph Waldo Emerson, *Nature, Addresses, and Lectures*, ed. Robert E. Spiller and Alfred R. Ferguson (Cambridge: Harvard University Press, 1971), p. 81.

11. Franklin Benjamin Sanborn, *The Personality of Emerson* (Boston: Goodspeed, 1903), p. 63.

12. Gordon G. Whitney and William Davis, "From Primitive Woods to Cultivated Woodlots: Thoreau and the Forest History of Concord, Massachusetts," *Journal of Forest History*, 30 (April 1986): 70–81.

13. H. Daniel Peck, "The Crosscurrents of *Walden*'s Pastoral," in *New Essays on Walden*, ed. Robert F. Sayre (Cambridge, Eng.: Cambridge University Press, 1992), p. 90. In a careful discussion of the same sequence I am examining here, Peck rightly diagnoses Thoreau's mood swings both as inherent within the pastoral mode and as particular to his own "historical memory, which contains both reverie and loss" (p. 90).

14. Lebeaux speculates that "the pond . . . was a motherly presence associated with fondest childhood memories, nurturing breast and womb, and continuity with the 'golden age' that preceded the driving of Adam and Eve out of Eden" (*Thoreau's Seasons*, p. 37). Although this characterization genders the pond more unequivocally than Thoreau himself did, certainly Walden and the memory of childhood were linked in Thoreau's mind. To the extent this was the case, he must have felt any violation of it on a deeply personal level. But by the same token it is interesting that Thoreau did not express more direct outrage at such violations than he did. When the ice cutters invaded his precincts in the winter of 1846–47, Thoreau's response was quite restrained compared to that of Emerson, who was prompted by the invasion of privacy to consider selling his tract (*The Letters of Ralph Waldo Emerson*, ed. Ralph L. Rusk [New York: Columbia University Press, 1939], 3: 383).

15. In "Thinking Like a Mountain," one of the most cited sections of *SCA* (pp. 129–133), Leopold recalls killing a wolf years earlier, believing that "fewer wolves meant more deer, that no wolves would mean hunter's paradise," but then being unsettled by the "fierce green fire dying in her eyes." Slowly he realizes the shallowness of the conventional dichotomy between "good" animals and varmints. "I now suspect that just as a deer herd lives in mortal fear of its wolves, so does a mountain live in mortal fear of its deer," which overbrowse the woods and eventually die for want of forage. Human inclinations need to be tempered by the mountain's nonhuman wisdom. This narrative encapsulates a lifelong process of environmental self-education; see Susan L. Flader, *Thinking Like a Mountain: Aldo Leopold and the Evolution of an Ecological Attitude toward Deer, Wolves, and Forests* (Columbia: University of Missouri Press, 1974), on the evolution of Leopold's thinking about biocentrism and especially about respect for predators.

16. We cannot know this for certain, since the text of the first manuscript version is not complete. But the relevant sections that do survive—e.g., early drafts of descriptions of the railroad's incursion in "Solitude" and the ice cutters' incursion in "The Pond in Winter"—seem to be written in a droll and jaunty manner that disguises any dismay at the alteration of the landscape.

17. George Barrell Emerson, *Report on the Trees and Shrubs Growing Naturally in the Forests of Massachusetts* (Boston: Dutton and Wentworth, 1846), p. 2. For Thoreau's reading of this work, see Sattelmeyer, *Thoreau's Reading*, p. 173. For the history of Concord's woods, see Whitney and Davis, "From Primitive Woods to Cultivated Woodlots." During the first half of the nineteenth century, the percentage of Concord land tilled also declined steeply as dairy and meat became the town's major agrarian pursuits. On this point, see Carolyn Merchant, *Ecological Revolutions: Nature, Gender, and Science in New England* (Chapel Hill: University of North Carolina Press, 1989), p. 189. Merchant provides the best general ecological history of the larger region during Thoreau's lifetime, together with Theodore Steinberg, *Nature Incorporated: Industrialization and the Waters of New England* (Cambridge, Eng.: Cambridge University Press, 1991). For the Concord area specifically, see also two essays by Brian Donahue: "The Forests and Fields of Concord: An Ecological History," in *Concord: The Social History of a New England Town, 1750–1850*, ed. David Hackett Fischer (Waltham, Mass.: Brandeis University Press, 1983); and "Henry David Thoreau and the Environment of Concord," in *Thoreau's World and Ours*, pp. 181–189.

18. See for example Hopkins's poem "Binsley Poplars," in *Gerard Manley Hopkins: A Selection of His Poems and Prose*, ed. Helen Gardner (Hammondsworth: Penguin, 1953), p. 39.

19. Even before the Walden experience, Thoreau occasionally evinced an environmentalist sensibility. Steinberg begins the introduction to *Nature Incor-*

porated, pp. 2–9, with an inventive synthesis, extrapolated from the history of technologizing on the one hand and from *A Week on the Concord and Merrimack Rivers* (1849) on the other hand, of how Thoreau would have seen the degraded landscape with a jaundiced eye as he paddled. Overall, however, the environmental critique in *A Week* is muted. The most striking passage is his protest (probably drafted in 1844) against the Middlesex Canal dam at Billerica, which prevented the migration of anadromous fish and caused severe flooding upstream on the Concord and Sudbury rivers, ruining hay crops and leading to a poorer mix of meadow grass. Thoreau, characteristically, seems to have been relatively unconcerned by the problems of local farmers (*PJ* 2: 126) compared to the plight of the "poor shad" condemned to wander "the sea in thy scaly armor to inquire humbly at the mouths of rivers" (p. 107); and, just as characteristically for his earlier writing, to have equivocated by resorting to the language of mock-heroic pathos apropos the shad. For the history of the controversy, including Thoreau's involvement as surveyor for some of the aggrieved farmers, see Brian Donahue, "'Damned at Both Ends and Cursed in the Middle': The 'Flowage' of the Concord River Meadows, 1798–1862," *Environmental Review,* 13, nos. 3–4 (1989): 47–68.

20. Robert Pogue Harrison, *Forests: The Shadow of Civilization* (Chicago: University of Chicago Press, 1992), p. 227. Harrison comments with special reference to the extraordinary passage from "Sounds" in which the speaker contemplates the look of his household effects when they are transported outdoors (*Wa* 112–113). Harrison sees this passage as a turning point from Thoreau's initial focus on domestic economy.

21. Tabulations derived from Marlene A. Ogden and Clifton Keller, *Walden: A Concordance* (New York: Garland, 1985).

22. Emerson, *Nature, Addresses, and Lectures,* p. 106.

23. Clapper, "The Development of *Walden,*" pp. 827, 831–832.

24. The best extended studies of Thoreau's natural history interests are John Hildebidle, *Thoreau: A Naturalist's Liberty* (Cambridge: Harvard University Press, 1983), and Howarth's biographical study, *The Book of Concord.* For the centrality of natural history as a key to Thoreau's thinking generally, see also Joan Burbick, *Thoreau's Alternative History: Changing Perspectives on Nature, Culture, and Language* (Philadelphia: University of Pennsylvania Press, 1987). For Thoreauvian landscape aesthetics, see Peck, *Thoreau's Morning Work.* For the development of Thoreau's thinking about nature as concept and as literary image against the background of romantic tradition, see James McIntosh, *Thoreau as Romantic Naturalist: His Shifting Stance toward Nature* (Ithaca: Cornell University Press, 1974).

25. Clapper, "The Development of *Walden,*" p. 158n.

26. See especially the peroration of Thoreau's late, unpublished natural history

essay "Huckleberries," which calls for the preservation of riverbanks as public walks and the sequestration of tracts of 500 to 1,000 acres in every township "for instruction and recreation." First edited as a book in 1970 by Leo Stoller (published by Windhover Press of the University of Iowa and the New York Public Library), "Huckleberries" is most widely available in Robert Sattelmeyer's edition of *The Natural History Essays* (Salt Lake City: Peregrine Smith, 1980). See pp. 252–262.

27. Sharon Cameron, *Writing Nature: Henry Thoreau's Journal* (New York: Oxford University Press, 1985), pp. 3–26: "The *Journal* against *Walden*." Cameron's argument has attracted a mixed response. For an important recent study that in good part concurs with Cameron's but builds on hers in such a way as to complicate her distinction usefully, see Henry Golemba, *Thoreau's Wild Rhetoric* (New York: Columbia University Press, 1990), especially Chapters 2 and 4. Although I would take issue with Cameron's dismissal of *Walden* and also her representation of the *Journal* as devoted to a single project, her conception of Thoreau as engaged in an admirably quixotic endeavor to fathom nature has invigorated my own reading of his work.

28. As further demonstration, see the Appendix to this book, an outline of the various discursive strands that Thoreau synthesized in *Walden* and that partly as a result might be said to constitute a genealogy of American environmental nonfiction.

29. For example, the network of classical pastoral and epic allusions developed in *Walden* was strongly present in his *Journal* record of the first summer there. See Ethel Seybold, *Thoreau: The Quest and the Classics* (New Haven: Yale University Press, 1951), pp. 48–63. For the romanticist idealization of ancient Greece as (comparatively) a state of nature, see Friedrich von Schiller, *Naive and Sentimental Poetry*, trans. and ed. Julius A. Elias (New York: Ungar, 1967), pp. 102–106.

30. Stanley Cavell, in *The Senses of Walden* (1972; rpt. San Francisco: North Point Press, 1981), pp. 51–53 and passim, is particularly sensitive to the resonances of temporal layering, as is Barbara Johnson, in "A Hound, a Bay Horse, and a Turtle Dove: Obscurity in *Walden*," in *A World of Difference* (Baltimore: Johns Hopkins University Press, 1987), pp. 49–56. Johnson concludes "that it is never possible to be sure what the rhetorical status of any given image is . . . because what Thoreau has done in moving to Walden Pond is to move *himself*, literally, into the world of his own figurative language. The literal woods, pond, and bean field still assume the same classical rhetorical guides in which they have always appeared, but they are suddenly readable in addition as the non-figurative ground of a naturalist's account of life in the woods" (pp. 55–56).

31. Leo Marx, *The Machine in the Garden: Technology and the Pastoral Ideal in America* (New York: Oxford University Press, 1964), pp. 73–144.

32. Peter Fritzell, in *Nature Writing and America: Essays upon a Cultural Type* (Ames: Iowa State University Press, 1990), pp. 153–171, stresses this point strongly.

33. Thoreau's first draft, printed in Shanley, *The Making of Walden*, p. 139; cf. *Wa* 88–89.

34. Cf. Shanley, *The Making of Walden*, p. 199, and *PJ* 2: 240. For a discussion of this passage (*Wa* 285–293), see Chapter 8.

35. Already suggested in his early essay "Of Insects," this linkage is perhaps best illustrated by Jonathan Edwards's *Images and Shadows of Divine Things*.

36. Quotation from Merchant, *Ecological Revolutions*, p. 256. See especially, however, David M. Robinson, "'Unchronicled Nations': Agrarian Purpose and Thoreau's Ecological Knowing," *Nineteenth-Century Literature*, 48 (1993): 326–340, a careful and persuasive reading of the experience and text as a critique of conventional farmwork and the work ethic, in the interest of a reformed conception not only of farming specifically but also of work generally according to a more ecological vision.

37. For Thoreau's interest in the Roman agriculturalists, see Richardson, *Henry David Thoreau*, pp. 248–252. For Thoreau's bean farming in the context of Concord's agricultural history, see Robert Gross, "The Great Bean-Field Hoax: Agriculture and Society in Thoreau's Concord," *Virginia Quarterly Review*, 61 (1985): 483–497.

38. Tamara Plakins Thornton, *Cultivating Gentlemen: The Meaning of Country Life among the Boston Elite, 1785–1860* (New Haven: Yale University Press, 1989), especially Chapters 1–2.

39. "Biologist" is technically anachronistic; the term did not come into common usage until the late nineteenth century; but the phrase "amateur field biologist" captures Thoreau's role pretty well in late twentieth century parlance. On Thoreau's specific natural history interests, see—in addition to Peck, Richardson, Howarth, Harding, and Hildebidle (notes 6, 8, 9, and 24 above)—the following important specialized discussions: Philip Whitford and Kathryn Whitford, "Thoreau: Pioneer Ecologist and Conservationist," *Science Monthly*, 73 (1951): 291–296; Kathryn Whitford, "Thoreau and the Woodlots of Concord," *New England Quarterly*, 23 (1950): 291–305; Leo Stoller, "A Note on Thoreau's Place in Phenology," *Isis*, 47 (1956): 172–181; R. S. McDowell, "The Thoreau-Reynolds Ridge, a Lost and Found Phenomenon," *Science*, 172 (1971): 973; Donald G. Quick, "Thoreau as Limnologist," *Thoreau Journal Quarterly*, 4, no. 2 (1972): 13–20; Ray Angelo, "Thoreau as Botanist: An Appreciation and a Critique," *Arnoldia*, 45 (Summer 1985): 13–23; and Parts II and VI of *Thoreau's World and Ours: A Natural Legacy*. This scholarship conclusively establishes three points about Thoreau's prowess and commitment as a naturalist, quite apart from the more ulterior and metaphysical or aesthetic motives that regulated his interest in the scientific study of nature. First, his interest in various branches of natural history became increasingly serious and systematic after 1850. Second, his skills as an observer of phenomena were remarkably good, especially in botany. Third,

he achieved several historic firsts as a naturalist: e.g., he was the first to study a body of water systematically and the first to discover the principle of forest succession. For a broader contextual sense of mid-nineteenth century amateur scientific activity that helps to put Thoreau in perspective, see Elizabeth B. Keeney, *The Botanizers: Amateur Scientists in Nineteenth-Century America* (Chapel Hill: University of North Carolina Press, 1992).

40. See especially Stoller, "A Note on Thoreau's Place in Phenology," and Peck, *Thoreau's Morning Work*, pp. 47–48, 90–106, 163–165.

41. Shanley, *The Making of Walden*, p. 202.

42. For Haeckel's significance, see Anna Bramwell, *Ecology in the Twentieth Century: A History* (New Haven: Yale University Press, 1989), pp. 39–63.

43. "The Dispersion of Seeds" has been published, together with several of Thoreau's other late natural history manuscripts, as *Faith in a Seed: The Dispersion of Seeds and Other Late Natural History Writings,* ed. Bradley P. Dean (Washington: Island Press, 1993).

44. Peck, *Thoreau's Morning Work*, pp. 84, 95, 81.

45. In this connection, see (in addition to Peck's work on Thoreau's aesthetics) Richard Grusin's essay "Thoreau, Extravagance, and the Economy of Nature," *American Literary History,* 5 (1993): 30–50, in which Grusin provocatively argues that the image of Thoreau as a frugality-espousing embracer of nature in rejection of a prodigal commodity culture occludes one from perceiving Thoreau's awareness of and relish for the vision of nature's economy as based on extravagance, not frugality. No Thoreauvian, however, has been more attuned to the mixture of sensuous and intellectual excitement Thoreau took in nature's prodigality than Sherman Paul, in *The Shores of America.*

46. Thoreau's minute attention to local niches was a prime example of turning what Yi-fu Tuan calls segmentation bias (the propensity to see the environmental field in terms of discrete units) to constructive use. For illuminating analysis of Thoreau's conceptual mapping of Concord places, see William Howarth, "Travelling in Concord: The World of Thoreau's Journal," in *Puritan Influences in American Literature,* ed. Emory Elliott (Urbana: University of Illinois Press, 1979), pp. 143–166; and J. Walter Brain, "Thoreau's Poetic Vision and the Concord Landscape," in *Thoreau's World and Ours*, pp. 281–297.

47. For discussions of the verbal, imagistic, and tonal intricacy of this celebrated passage, see for example Gordon E. Bigelow, "Thoreau's Melting Sandbank: Birth of a Symbol," *International Journal of Symbology,* 2 (November 1971): 7–13; Michael West, "Scatology and Eschatology: The Heroic Dimensions of Thoreau's Wordplay," *PMLA,* 80 (1974): 1043–1064; Philip F. Gura, *The Wisdom of Words: Language, Theology, and Literature in the New England Renaissance* (Middletown, Conn.: Wesleyan University Press, 1981), pp. 132–137; Gordon Boudreau, *The Roots of Walden and the Tree of Life* (Nashville: Vanderbilt University Press,

1990), pp. 105–134; and Nicholas K. Bromell, *By the Sweat of the Brow: Literature and Labor in Antebellum America* (Chicago: University of Chicago Press, 1993), pp. 234–238.

48. See especially Cameron, *Writing Nature,* and McIntosh *Thoreau as Romantic Naturalist.*

49. See my discussion "Lococentrism from Dwight to Thoreau," in *New England Literary Culture* (Cambridge, Eng.: Cambridge University Press, 1986), pp. 323–325.

50. Roland Wells Robbins, *Discovery at Walden* (Concord: Roland Wells Robbins, 1947).

51. Leo Marx appraises this duality from a point of view slightly, but necessarily, different from my own: "As he settles into his life at the pond . . . the problems of ordinary people recede from his consciousness," thereby "dissipating the radical social awareness" generated "at the outset. Considered as a single structure of feeling," however, "Thoreau's masterwork may be described as superbly effective in transmuting incipiently radical impulses into a celebration of what Emerson calls 'the infinitude of the private man'" ("Henry Thoreau: The Two Thoreaus," in *The Pilot and the Passenger* [New York: Oxford University Press, 1988], p. 98). Marx's strict notion of what counts as "political" discourse (argument explicitly engaging social issues) leads him, in short, to read the discursive shift in *Walden* simply as withdrawal from the political. A looser interpretation of what counts as political would, I think, do more justice to the aims and impact of Thoreau's "celebration" (Marx's equivocal term) of solitary fulfillment within nature, though part of that justice must involve recognition of its ideological multivalence, as argued in Chapter 1.

52. To take a specific example, the long first paragraph of "House-Warming" (*Wa* 238–239), a late addition to the manuscript (in 1852–1853), reports Thoreau's autumn activity as he satirically observes market-oriented cranberry harvesters, forages for nuts in the forest, and fondly recalls the ancient aboriginal dispensation that he wishfully prophesies may someday return: "let wild Nature reign here once more, and the tender and luxurious English grains will probably disappear before a myriad of foes, and . . . the crow may carry back even the last seed of corn to the great cornfield of the Indian's God in the south-west" (p. 238). This passage pictures the speaker in a series of locations: river meadows, cranberry bogs, barberry-studded scrubland, chestnut woods near and distant, and the unnamed place where he finds the ground-nut, the "potato" and totem fruit of the aborigines, that inspires the meditation on once and future Native American culture. A careful reader will detect a narrative line to this series (from river to upland to deep woods to the primordial time and space evoked by discovering the ground-nut), but it takes much effort to grasp because the persona tends to fade into the scenery and the main clues of his movement are supplied by the vegetable world itself. Clearly Thoreau expects to lose all but the

most environmentally aware reader, who is already "lost" in what Thoreau would consider the right way.

53. Thoreau could not have been aware of Marsh's environmental researches, nor was Marsh more than idly interested in Thoreau, if that. I have found no substantive references to Thoreau in the Marsh Papers at the University of Vermont. As Roderick Nash notes in *Wilderness and the American Mind*, 3d ed. (New Haven: Yale University Press, 1982), pp. 104–105, Marsh's approach to environmental issues was by and large utilitarian, not romantic.

54. For a discussion of the relation of "The Succession of Forest Trees" to the ambitious unfinished project, "The Dispersion of Seeds," of which it was a part, see Howarth, *The Book of Concord*, pp. 192–199, and Robert D. Richardson, Jr., "Introduction" to *Faith in a Seed*, pp. 3–17. Another late unfinished ecological manuscript, excerpted in *Faith in a Seed*, pp. 177–203, was "Wild Fruits" (cf. Howarth, *The Book of Concord*, pp. 199–202), from which "Huckleberries" was quarried as a (never delivered) lecture. Thoreau's last illness cut short these projects.

55. For "Succession" as a contribution to scientific ecology, see Kathryn Whitford, "Thoreau and the Woodlots of Concord." The most widely available discussion of Thoreau's overall contribution to modern ecological thought is Donald Worster, "Thoreau's Romantic Ecology," in *Nature's Economy: The Roots of Ecology* (1977; rpt. Garden City, N.Y.: Doubleday, 1979), pp. 57–111. Worster paints in broad brushstrokes and accords Thoreau a prominence that is truer to his retrospective canonization than to the facts of the history of ecological theory. For correctives, by historians of science, see Frank Egerton, "The History of Ecology: Achievements and Opportunities, Part One," *Journal of the History of Biology*, 16 (1983): 259–260; and Hunter Dupree, "Thoreau as Scientist: American Science in the 1850s," *Thoreau's World and Ours*, pp. 42–47. To be fair to Worster, he is less interested at this point in his study in tracking scientific discourse than in detailing the rise of what has come to be called "deep ecology," i.e., a commitment to environment based on a holistic affirmation of the symbiosis of all life-forms (see "Thoreau's Romantic Ecology," p. 76). Furthermore, it *is* true that Thoreau's credentials as a pioneer ecological scientist have been sustained by a number of scholars, including practicing scientists. See, in addition to the sources listed in note 39, two bibliographical articles both entitled "Thoreau in the Current Scientific Literature" by Robin S. McDowell, *Thoreau Society Bulletin*, 143 (1978): 2 and 172 (1985): 3–4, calling attention to the frequency of Thoreau citations in the *Science Citation Index*. My check of more recent volumes of the index bears out McDowell's claim that "real" contemporary scientists are taking Thoreau seriously.

56. Thoreau, "The Succession of Forest Trees," in *Excursions and Poems*, ed. Bradford Torrey and Francis H. Allen (Boston: Houghton, Mifflin, 1906), p. 204.

57. See note 26 above.

58. For Thoreau in the context of the history of environmentalism, see for example Worster, *Nature's Economy;* Nash, *Wilderness and the American Mind,* pp. 84–96; Max Oelschlaeger, *The Idea of Wilderness: From Prehistory to the Age of Ecology* (New Haven: Yale University Press, 1991), pp. 133–171; and Philip Shabecoff, *A Fierce Green Fire: The American Environmental Movement* (New York: Hill and Wang, 1993), pp. 51–55. All four writers see Thoreau as a vanguard figure. The subject, however, has been more sketchily explored than the subject of Thoreau's scientific credentials, perhaps because environmentalism in America as an organized movement did not begin until the end of the nineteenth century. Certainly Thoreau's park system proposal was forward-looking but not unique. The municipal park idea, developed in England in the early part of the century, had caught hold in the United States by the 1850s; and the notion of American state and national parks had been in the air for some time and would be begin to be realized not long after Thoreau's death. See for example John Stilgoe, "Parks," in *Borderland: Origins of the American Suburb, 1820–1939* (New Haven: Yale University Press, 1988), pp. 49–55; and Alfred Runte, *National Parks: The American Experience,* rev. ed. (Lincoln: University of Nebraska Press, 1987).

59. For Thoreau's natural history writing as a strategy of audience and marketplace accommodation, see especially Fink, *Prophet in the Marketplace.*

60. Thoreau, *The Maine Woods,* ed. Joseph J. Moldenhauer (Princeton: Princeton University Press, 1972), p. 121.

61. Ibid., p. 156.

62. From examination of Muir's marginalia in his personal library, Muir collection, University of the Pacific, Stockton, Calif.

63. This is not to say that Thoreau was fully aware of the elements of classism and ethnocentricity in his environmentalist attitudes.

64. I do not list surveying here among the occupations; although Thoreau took pride in his skill and success at it, his actual contract work as a surveyor generally seems to have disaffected him and left him with the impression that he had compromised himself by having to anesthetize his proper sensitivities while pursuing the trade. One suspects that the survey that gave him most satisfaction was the one he did for literary purposes, the survey of Walden Pond (*Wa* 286).

65. W. H. Auden, "In Memory of W. B. Yeats," in *The Collected Poetry of W. H. Auden* (New York: Random, 1945), p. 50; T. S. Eliot, "Gerontion," in *The Complete Poems and Plays, 1909–1950* (New York: Harcourt, 1950), p. 22.

5. The Aesthetics of Relinquishment

1. *The Complete Works of Ralph Waldo Emerson,* ed. Edward Waldo Emerson (Boston: Houghton, Mifflin, 1903–1904), 9: 125.

2. Wendell Berry, "Work Song," in *Clearing* (New York: Harcourt, 1977), p. 33.

3. Holmes Rolston III, "Is There an Ecological Ethic?" in *Philosophy Gone Wild: Environmental Ethics* (Buffalo: Prometheus, 1986), p. 23.

4. Duane Elgin, *Voluntary Simplicity: Toward a Way of Life That Is Outwardly Simple, Inwardly Rich* (New York: Morrow, 1981), p. 37.

5. Thoreau's distinct if unspectacular success during the late 1840s in lecturing on his Walden experiment, the difference between publishers' interest in *Walden* as against *A Week*, and the efforts of Thoreau's most vocal promoter, Horace Greeley, to help him advertise and commodify his homesteading experiment are discussed in Steven Fink, *Prophet in the Marketplace: Thoreau's Development as a Professional Writer* (Princeton: Princeton University Press, 1992), pp. 139–141, 193–206.

6. The intellectual backgrounds and cultural history of the simplicity ethic are presented in David E. Shi, *The Simple Life: Plain Living and High Thinking in American Culture* (New York: Oxford University Press, 1985), which includes a short discussion of Thoreau (pp. 139–149). For analysis of the dominant materialistic ethos, see David Potter, *People of Plenty: Economic Abundance and the American Character* (Chicago: University of Chicago Press, 1954); *The Culture of Consumption*, ed. T. J. Jackson Lears and Richard Fox (New York: Pantheon, 1983); and Jack Greene, *Pursuits of Happiness: The Social Development of Early Modern British Colonies and the Formation of American Culture* (Chapel Hill: University of North Carolina Press, 1988).

7. Shi, *The Simple Life*, p. 278.

8. See Leonard Neufeldt, "*Walden* and the Guidebook for Young Men," in *The Economist: Henry Thoreau and Enterprise* (New York: Oxford University Press, 1989), pp. 101–110, the most detailed study ever made of the relation between *Walden* and the various genres of nineteenth-century self-improvement literature.

9. For an amusing bestiary of profiles, see Carl Sifakis, *American Eccentrics* (New York and Bicester, Eng.: Facts on File, 1984). His roster includes Francis Phyle, "the hermit of Mount Holly"; Sarah Bishop, "the atrocity hermitess"; Albert Large, "the hermit amidst the wolves"; and many more. For specific discussion of Thoreau's case in the context of other transcendentalist experiments in voluntary simplicity, see Taylor Stoehr, *Nay-Saying in Concord: Emerson, Alcott, and Thoreau* (Hamden, Conn.: Archon, 1979).

10. On the relationship between Muir and Thoreau, the authority is Richard F. Fleck, "John Muir's Homage to Henry David Thoreau," *Pacific Historian*, 29, nos. 2–3 (1985): 55–64. Fleck overstates Thoreau's influence, I think, in identifying Thoreau as Muir's "spiritual and literary mentor" (p. 55), but he is right that Muir "carefully read Henry Thoreau cover to cover" (p. 58). Muir owned, marked, and indexed all the volumes of both the Riverside and the Walden editions of Thoreau's works, as well as individual copies of all his major books. For Thoreau's impact on Burroughs, the best appraisal is Perry Westbrook, *John Burroughs* (New York: Twayne, 1974), pp. 57–63.

11. Henry Beston, *The Outermost House* (1928: rpt. New York: Ballantine, 1985).

12. "Ever since a childhood spent near New York City," Anne LaBastille states at the outset of one of her lively autobiographical, how-to narratives of homesteading in the Adirondacks, "I had wanted to live in a Thoreau-style cabin in the woods" (*Woodswoman* [New York: Dutton, 1987], p. 7). A more recent statement shows that her interest was not quite so long-standing: see LaBastille, "Fishing in the Sky," in *New Essays on Walden,* ed. Robert F. Sayre (Cambridge, Eng.: Cambridge University Press, 1992), pp. 53–72. Thoreau did not have so formative an influence on Leopold (see note 70 below) nor, probably, on Beston. Beston did write an appreciative introduction to a 1951 edition of *Cape Cod* (New York: Norton, rpt. New York: Bramhall House, 1965), in which he praised Thoreau as "the first American to write a completely modern prose," without Victorian "unctuous and moralistic fustian" and evincing "the modern ease with the reader, and even the modern touch of structural austerity" (pp. 8–9). But as Sherman Paul tactfully puts it, Beston "had difficulty in acknowledging filiation" with Thoreau ("Coming Home to the World: Another Journal for Henry Beston," in *For Love of the World: Essays on Nature Writers* [Iowa City: University of Iowa Press, 1992], p. 113).

13. *The Collected Poems of William Butler Yeats* (New York: Macmillan, 1956), p. 39; Helen Nearing and Scott Nearing, *Continuing the Good Life: Half a Century of Homesteading* (New York: Schocken, 1979), pp. 95, 109, 149, 159, 169. The Nearings tend to use Thoreau more as a commodity (as grist for their epigraphs) than as inspiration; but in so doing they obviously invite comparison. Their earlier book, significantly, makes no reference to Thoreau: *Living the Good Life: How to Live Sanely and Simply in a Troubled World* (New York: Schocken, 1954).

14. Roger Payne, *Why Work? or, The Coming "Age of Leisure and Plenty"* (Boston: Meador, 1939); Charles B. Seib, *The Woods: One Man's Escape to Nature* (Garden City, N.Y.: Doubleday, 1971), pp. 2, 39.

15. Stoehr is surely right in observing that Thoreau's "account of his own self-marooning at Walden has always appealed to the same type of imagination as *Robinson Crusoe*" (*Nay-Saying in Concord*, p. 114), although I see Thoreau as bending that imagination in different directions from Defoe.

16. Mayne Reid, *The Desert Home; or, The Adventures of a Lost Family in the Wilderness* (Boston: Ticknor and Fields, 1853), p. 399.

17. Wright Morris, *The Territory Ahead: Critical Interpretations in American Literature* (New York: Atheneum, 1963), p. 46.

18. Beston, *Outermost House*, p. 174; Joseph Wood Krutch, *The Twelve Seasons* (New York: Knopf, 1949), pp. 3, 188; Barry Lopez, *Arctic Dreams: Imagination and Desire in a Northern Landscape* (New York: Bantam, 1987), pp. xvii, 371–372; Annie Dillard, *Pilgrim at Tinker Creek* (New York: Harper and Row, 1974), pp. 5–7, 271.

19. Michael Warner, "*Walden*'s Erotic Economy," in *Comparative American*

Identities: Race, Sex, and Nationality in the Modern Text, ed. Hortense J. Spillers (London: Routledge, 1991), pp. 162, 169, 172.

20. Shi remarks on this in *The Simple Life,* p. 143.

21. Warner ("*Walden's* Erotic Economy," p. 173) pertinently remarks that "it is child's play to show the limits of Thoreau's critique" of capitalism, that what counts is his ability to redirect its terms of discourse rather than his ability to achieve an impossible extrication from its confines.

22. Thoreau, *Early Essays and Miscellanies,* ed. Joseph J. Moldenhauer and Edwin Moser, with Alexander C. Kern (Princeton: Princeton University Press, 1975), pp. 19–21.

23. Cf. Payne: "I was educated at a university, that of Cambridge, England, where work is looked upon as something only fit for the working class to do" (*Why Work?* p. 24). Edward Carpenter, one of Thoreau's early British admirers, was particularly impressed by his finding that he needed labor only six weeks a year (*England's Ideal and Other Papers* [London: Swan Sonnenschein, 1887], p. 13). Henry Salt, who heard about Thoreau from Carpenter and wrote one of the first and best biographies of Thoreau, was influenced by Thoreau to resign his teaching post and live exclusively on his independent income (George Hendrick, *Henry Salt: Humanitarian Reformer and Man of Letters* [Urbana: University of Illinois Press, 1977], p. 26).

24. *Anniversary Memoirs of the Boston Society of Natural History* (Boston: Society of Natural History, 1880), pp. 90–91.

25. See Robert Pogue Harrison, *Forests: The Shadow of Civilization* (Chicago: University of Chicago Press, 1992), pp. 112–113, for a short but perceptive comment on this passage, which he rightly considers pivotal to the development of environmental consciousness in *Walden.*

26. William Carlos Williams, "The Red Wheelbarrow," in *Collected Earlier Poems* (New York: New Directions, 1966), p. 277; Martin Heidegger, "The Thing," in *Poetry, Language, Thought,* trans. and ed. Albert Hofstadter (New York: Harper and Row, 1971), pp. 163–186; Matoko Eeda, *Matsuo Bashō* (Tokyo: Kodansha International, 1970), p. 62.

27. Ralph Waldo Emerson, *Nature, Addresses, and Lectures,* ed. Robert E. Spiller and Alfred R. Ferguson (Cambridge: Harvard University Press, 1971), p. 9.

28. Dennis Ribbens, "The Making of *A Sand County Almanac,*" in *Companion to "A Sand County Almanac": Interpretive and Critical Essays,* ed. J. Baird Callicott (Madison: University of Wisconsin Press, 1987), p. 105.

29. Gilbert Byron, *Cove Dweller* (Trappe, Md.: Unicorn Book Shop, 1983), pp. 78, v.

30. Among literary critics, the pathology of American individualism has been most vigorously assailed by Quentin Anderson, *The Imperial Self* (New York:

Knopf, 1971); and, from a feminist standpoint viewing it as a masculinist formation, by Joyce W. Warren, *The American Narcissus: Individualism and Women in Nineteenth-Century American Fiction* (New Brunswick: Rutgers University Press, 1984). Both discuss Thoreau dismissively. Sacvan Bercovitch has undertaken the most elegant analysis of individualism as social ritual, in *The Puritan Origins of the American Self* (New Haven: Yale University Press, 1975) and subsequent essays collected in *Rites of Assent* (London: Routledge, 1993). See also Myra Jehlen, *American Incarnation: The Individual, the Nation, and the Continent* (Cambridge: Harvard University Press, 1986), as well as Jehlen's and Bercovitch's contributions to their coedited collection, *Ideology and Classic American Literature* (Cambridge: Harvard University Press, 1986).

31. Neil Evernden, *The Natural Alien* (Toronto: University of Toronto Press, 1985), p. 38. As Evernden goes on to remark, "there is nothing particularly subversive about ecology" as a set of normative disciplinary procedures; indeed, quite the reverse. "But its most basic premise, that of interrelatedness, could be subversive, if taken seriously." The concept of evolution, too, "implies a plasticity of being which can be disconcerting to orderly minds."

32. David Rains Wallace, *The Klamath Knot: Explorations of Myth and Evolution* (San Francisco: Sierra Club, 1983), p. 132.

33. Evernden, *The Natural Alien*, p. 40.

34. Martin Heidegger, *Being and Time*, trans. John Macquarrie and Edward Robinson (New York: Harper and Row, 1962), p. 100.

35. John Janovy, Jr., *Keith County Journal* (New York: St. Martin's, 1978), p. 186.

36. Freya Mathews, *The Ecological Self* (Savage, Md.: Barnes and Noble, 1991), p. 93. Whereas Evernden's model of interdependence derives from ecological biology, Mathews's doctrine of "substance monism" derives from relativity theory, which in her judgment would make Spinoza rather than Locke the central figure in premodern philosophy of mind.

37. Wendell Berry, "Notes from an Absence and a Return," in *A Continuous Harmony: Essays Cultural and Agricultural* (New York: Harcourt, 1972), p. 49; "Poetry and Place," in *Standing by Words* (San Francisco: North Point, 1983), pp. 168, 143; *The Unsettling of America: Culture and Agriculture* (San Francisco: Sierra Club, 1977), p. 30.

38. Wendell Berry, *Collected Poems, 1957–1982* (San Francisco: North Point, 1985), p. 159.

39. Berry, *Unsettling*, p. 111; "Poetry and Place," p. 169.

40. Berry, *Unsettling*, pp. 20, 14, 143; cf. Thomas Jefferson, *Notes on the State of Virginia*, in his *Writings*, ed. Merrill D. Peterson (New York: Library of America, 1984), p. 290.

41. J. Hector St. John de Crèvecoeur, *Letters from an American Farmer* (New York: Dutton, 1957), p. 40.

42. I am indebted to Howard Horwitz's discussion of *O Pioneers!* in his *By the Law of Nature: Form and Value in Nineteenth-Century America* (New York: Oxford University Press, 1991), pp. 218–238, as well as to William Conlogue's paper "Industrializing Agriculture: Willa Cather's *O Pioneers!* as a Modern Georgic," presented at the MLA meeting, December 1993, Toronto.

43. Berry, *Unsettling,* p. 13.

44. Raymond Williams, *The Country and the City* (New York: Oxford University Press, 1973), pp. 9–12.

45. See especially the chapter "The Body and the Earth," in *Unsettling,* pp. 97–140.

46. Berry, "Poetry and Place," p. 168.

47. My thinking about the strategic deemphasis or excision of the persona in modern poetry was originally stimulated by David Walker's study of Wallace Stevens and William Carlos Williams, *The Transparent Lyric* (Princeton: Princeton University Press, 1984), although I do not follow Walker to the extent of agreeing that the persona is absent altogether from the lyrics he discusses. See also J. Hillis Miller, *Poets of Reality: Six Twentieth-Century Writers* (New York: Atheneum, 1974). This is not to say that either Walker or Miller are interested in ecologism, nor that the modernist experiment with the desubjectification of personae be ascribed to this or any other single motive. On the contrary, in some cases it is quite clear that the primary motive is more often, for example, epistemological doubt about the validity of individual perception (e.g. Stevens) or the sense of the self's impotence within technologized mass culture (e.g. Dos Passos in the "Camera Eye" sections of *U.S.A.*). But this does not concern me, for it seems to me that the task of overriding importance for present purposes is not to reconstruct the precise intellectual genealogies behind the series of poems I am about to discuss as much as to apprehend how twentieth-century lyric discourse has, by whatever means, generated a mode of desubjectification that has the capacity to situate its personae more ecocentrically than, say, the greater romantic lyric did.

48. Robinson Jeffers, "Signpost," in *Selected Poetry* (New York: Random, 1959), p. 574.

49. Max Oelschlaeger, *The Idea of Wilderness: From Prehistory to the Age of Ecology* (New Haven: Yale University Press, 1991), pp. 252–253.

50. Williams, *Collected Earlier Poems,* p. 332.

51. William Carlos Williams, "Spring and All," in *Imaginations* (New York: New Directions, 1970), p. 117. A helpful gloss on what Williams might have had in mind, for obviously he means to distinguish between the mere illusion of external reality and the poetic expression of it, is Lois Oppenheim, "An Inheritance of Poetic Referentiality," *Comparative Literature Studies,* 20 (1983): 329–345.

52. A. R. Ammons, *Collected Poems, 1951–1971* (New York: Norton, 1972), p. 162.

53. Theodore Roethke, "Cuttings *(later),*" in *Collected Poems* (Garden City, N.Y.: Doubleday, 1966), p. 37.

54. Gary Snyder, *Myths and Texts* (New York: Totem Press, 1960), p. 37.

55. In *Literary Transcendentalism: Style and Vision in the American Renaissance* (Ithaca: Cornell University Press, 1973), p. 302, I argued that Thoreau places his persona "solidly before the reader," then proceeds to present himself as a kind of (mock-)epic hero. The classic essay on the rhetorical strategizing of the persona in *Walden* also situated him in terms of a single formation, as an *eiron* facing an *alazon*, the witty, ironic trickster versus the stolid, disapproving, moralistic establishment: Joseph Moldenhauer, "Paradox in Walden," *Graduate Journal*, 6 (1964): 132–146. Following Stanley Cavell's *Senses of Walden* (1972), more recent critics have developed a finer sense of the precariousness of *meaning* in *Walden*; cf. Walter Benn Michaels, "*Walden's* False Bottoms," *Glyph*, 1 (1977): 132–149; and Henry Golemba, "The Voices of *Walden*," *ESQ*, 31 (1985): 243–251. But that the "I"-function itself, as distinct from this or that avatar or voice, is a more or less stable category has not been questioned as vigorously as it might have been. It is assumed even by the interpretation of *Walden* that most assertively presses the idea of the book as a kind of conversion narrative with a movement from assertive didacticism to the protagonist's greater responsiveness "to the ripe world about him" (Paul Schwaber, "Thoreau's Development in 'Walden,'" *Criticism*, 5 [1963]: 77).

56. Richard J. Schneider, "An Overview of the Forthcoming *Approaches to Teaching Thoreau*," paper presented at the MLA meeting, December 1991, San Francisco. Schneider's survey of professorial assignment of *Walden*, chapter by chapter, indicated that "Winter Animals," "House-Warming," and "Former Inhabitants" were the chapters assigned least.

57. Steven Fink, *Prophet in the Marketplace: Thoreau's Development as a Professional Writer* (Princeton: Princeton University Press, 1992), p. 139.

58. Sharon Cameron, *Writing Nature: Henry Thoreau's Journal* (New York: Oxford University Press, 1985), p. 89.

59. Robert Milder, in the course of an admirably meticulous presentation of *Walden's* unfolding, wisely observes that "even in its final, published version, *Walden* is never quite the harmonious 'afterthought' of a fully controlled, fully conscious intention, in part because Thoreau's development was so singularly 'frayed'—not a steady linear progress but a dynamic interplay of moods and tendencies, some advancing, some retreating, yet nearly all live enough to assert themselves at a given moment against the general tide of months and years"; see *Reimagining Thoreau* (Cambridge, Eng.: Cambridge University Press, forthcoming 1994), p. 119.

60. Andrew Marvell, "Upon Appleton House," in *Poems*, ed. Hugh MacDonald (Cambridge: Harvard University Press, 1952), p. 107.

61. Wallace, *Klamath Knot*, p. 132.

62. Quoted in Kurt Meine, *Aldo Leopold: His Life and Work* (Madison: Uni-

versity of Wisconsin Press, 1988), p. 419. The publication history of *SCA* is also carefully traced by Ribbens (in "The Making of *SCA*"). For information about Leopold's life and the genesis of *SCA*, I rely not only on these and other printed sources but also on the Leopold Papers in the Steenbock Archives, University of Wisconsin, which include correspondence concerning *SCA*, drafts, editorial comments, and reviews.

63. Ribbens, "The Making of *SCA*," p. 96.

64. Ibid., p. 97.

65. Meine, *Aldo Leopold*, p. 461.

66. The Leopold Papers include several annotated copies of Leopold's typescript. After Oxford accepted *SCA* just a week before Leopold's death, he dictated a memo to a half-dozen family members and associates asking for help in making the final revisions he intended to complete during the upcoming summer of 1948.

67. See especially Leopold's 1947 address "The Ecological Conscience," in which he defines the title phrase as "the ethics of community life" and sharply criticizes self-interest as a criterion of value in both land-use ethics and social ethics; in Leopold, *The River of the Mother of God and Other Essays,* ed. Susan L. Flader and J. Baird Callicott (Madison: University of Wisconsin Press, 1991), p. 340.

68. Meine, *Aldo Leopold*, p. 403.

69. Marti Kheel, "Ecofeminism and Deep Ecology," in *Reweaving the World: The Emergence of Ecofeminism,* ed. Irene Diamond and Gloria Feman Orenstein (San Francisco: Sierra Club, 1990), p. 135.

70. Ever since the publication of *SCA* Leopold and Thoreau have been compared. Oxford University Press quickly lifted a tribute for advertising purposes from Lewis Gannett's review (*New York Herald Tribune,* 27 October 1949): "He wrote like Thoreau and Muir at their best" (clipping, Series 6, Box 5, Leopold Papers). Scholars today regularly pair them. The relationships, such as they are, are a matter of affinity rather than influence, however. Thoreau's direct impact on Leopold was slight (as was Muir's). Leopold's "Personal Notebook" of quotations (Leopold Papers, Series 10–7, Box 1) contains just two Thoreau quotations, one from *Walden* ("A man sits as many risks as he runs"—*Wa* 153), the other from "Walking," the famous passage starting "In Wildness is the preservation of the World" (in *Excursions and Poems,* ed. Bradford Torrey and Francis H. Allen [Boston: Houghton, Mifflin, 1906], p. 224), later used in "Thinking Like a Mountain" (*SCA* 133). (The notebook contains many more quotations from John Burroughs and John Muir.) Meine notes that when recovering from a severe illness in his mid-twenties, Leopold "leafed through Thoreau's *Journals,* a wedding gift from his mother" (*Aldo Leopold,* p. 128), but notes no other specific instance when Leopold read Thoreau.

71. Mary Austin "Woman Alone," *Nation*, 124 (1927): 228. Austin is at last getting the critical attention she deserves. A good, short critical appraisal is Marjorie Pryse's introduction to *LLR*, pp. vii–xxxv, after which follows a helpful bibliography. The best biography is Esther Lanigan Stineman, *Mary Austin: Song of a Maverick* (New Haven: Yale University Press, 1989).

72. Elizabeth Ammons suggests that the chapter title "My Neighbor's Field" (discussed below) is taken from *Walden* with intent to contrast (*Conflicting Stories: American Women Writers at the Turn into the Twentieth Century* [New York: Oxford University Press, 1991], p. 96). Austin's chapter on Seyavi, the Indian basket maker, may respond to Thoreau's in-passing treatment of a similar subject (*Wa* 19). See below for other suggestions. In general, however, it seems to me that Austin alludes much more frequently to Emerson than to Thoreau—usually without the kind of irony she directs toward Harte. This assessment is borne out also by her autobiography *Earth Horizon*.

73. Edward Abbey, *Desert Solitaire* (New York: Ballantine, 1968), p. 6.

74. Thoreau, "Ktaadn," in *The Maine Woods*, ed. Joseph J. Moldenhauer (Princeton: Princeton University Press, 1972), p. 70.

75. There is no comprehensive monograph, to my knowledge, on traditions within women's environmental writing, which is usually treated as part of studies focused more on specific regions or broader issues of feminist theory; but Chapters 2, 5, and 6 of Vera Norwood, *Made from This Earth: American Women and Nature* (Chapel Hill: University of North Carolina Press, 1993), afford a helpful overview. Women's frontier writing has been the branch most studied; see especially Annette Kolodny, *The Land Before Her: Fantasy and Experience of the American Frontiers, 1630–1860* (Chapel Hill: University of North Carolina Press, 1984). On Austin's environmental representation, see also Lois Rudnick, "Re-Naming the Land: Anglo-Expatriate Women in the Southwest," in *The Desert Is No Lady*, ed. Vera Norwood and Janice Monk (New Haven: Yale University Press, 1987), pp. 10–26.

76. Perry Westbrook treated the issue of the "impoverishment" of the regional realists' backwater countries of the imagination in a descriptive, nonjudgmental fashion in his *Acres of Flint: Sarah Orne Jewett and Her Contemporaries*, rev. ed. (Metuchen, N.J.: Scarecrow, 1981). Ann Douglas, in "The Literature of Impoverishment: The Women Local Colorists of America, 1865–1914," *Women's Studies*, 1 (1972): 3–45, saw in regional realism a disturbing retreat from the sentimentalists' willingness to represent mainstream American life and speak out on public issues. Josephine Donovan, in *New England Local Color Literature: A Woman's Tradition* (New York: Ungar, 1983), stressed the local colorists' feminist achievement of turning a marginalized social position to account. Donovan's is clearly the view that prevails today.

77. By all accounts, Mary Austin, for example, had a more aggressive, domi-

nating ego than *Land of Little Rain* manifests. Although it is impossible to say for certain whether she was held in check by what she took to be generic proprieties, it seems clear that some of her more protagonist-centered works were at least as indicative of her temperament: e.g., the quasi-autobiographical feminist *kunstlerroman A Woman of Genius* (1912), whose heroine has an almost Cowperwood-like dynamism, and her autobiography *Earth Horizon* (1932). On the development of modern narratives by and about women, see for example Dana A. Heller, *The Feminization of Quest-Romance: Radical Departures* (Austin: University of Texas Press, 1990), one of several studies (cf. Heller's bibliography) that reimagine the female "hero" (her term) as a figure of mobility and independence without the baleful aggressivity that marks a number of American male heroes (though American androcentrism is hardly monolithic). I have also found helpful the introductory essay in *The Voyage In: Fictions of Female Development,* ed. Elizabeth Abel, Marianne Hirsch, and Elizabeth Langland (Hanover, N.H.: University Press of New England, 1983). As the editors remark, feminist scholars seem to concur "that the novel of development has become, in Ellen Morgan's words, 'the most salient form of literature' for contemporary women writing about women" (p. 13). Central to both Heller's and this book's conception of what differentiates, or at least ought to differentiate, the female "plot" of development is the theory of Carol Gilligan, who in her book *In a Different Voice: Psychological Theory and Women's Development* (Cambridge: Harvard University Press, 1982) argues that female upbringing conditions women to practice a relational ethics of mediation rather than to engineer a rules-based ethics of moral arbitration. But the anthology edited by Abel, Hirsch, and Langland judiciously opens with this epigraph from Gilligan: "There seems at present to be only partial agreement between men and women about the adulthood they commonly share."

78. John Burroughs, "A Sharp Lookout," in *Signs and Seasons* (Boston: Houghton, Mifflin, 1886), p. 5.

79. Sue Hubbell, *A Country Year* (New York: Harper and Row, 1987), p. 77.

80. Peter Fritzell, *Nature Writing and America: Essays upon a Cultural Type* (Ames: State University of Iowa Press, 1990), pp. 181–182.

81. Ibid., p. 189.

82. It is important to formulate this point so as not to go to the opposite extreme from homocentric individualism, i.e. what has been labeled "environmental fascism"—the view that the interest of the biota, or individual species, ought always to take precedence over the interests of human beings. As the environmental ethicist Lawrence E. Johnson asserts, "What we must not do is fall into the trap of thinking that we must choose between accepting individual values or accepting holistic values. Not only can we have it both ways, we *must* have it both ways" (*A Morally Deep World: An Essay on Moral Significance and*

Environmental Ethics [Cambridge, Eng.: Cambridge University Press, 1991], p. 178). I amend Johnson only slightly, as follows: we can't *really* have it both ways, but we must adopt the approach of mediating between these two competing goods. Johnson later espouses a version of this revised view that strikes me as judicious: "there is more than one level of interest," and "all interests are morally significant." He adds that with respect to the values of the individual as opposed to those of the community, the claims of individual entitites are to be considered relative both to the claims of communities (e.g., ecosystems) and, within individual communities, to the degree of self-identity of which the individual entity is capable (243–244).

6. Nature's Personhood

1. *The Collected Poems of Wallace Stevens* (New York: Knopf, 1961), pp. 137, 162, 218, 506, 373.

2. Stevens, *Collected Poems,* p. 70.

3. Edward Abbey, *Desert Solitaire* (New York: Ballantine, 1968), pp. 6, 23–24.

4. Lynn White, Jr., "The Historical Roots of Our Ecologic Crisis," *Science,* 155 (1967): 1203–1207, reprinted in *Machina ex Deo* (Cambridge: MIT Press, 1968), pp. 75–94. White's essay has perhaps attracted more endorsement than its skeletal and one-sided treatment deserves. The leading intellectual history of Euro-American ecological thought builds on it: Donald Worster, *Nature's Economy: The Roots of Ecology* (1977; rpt. Garden City, N.Y.: Doubleday, 1979), pp. 27ff. Theologians writing from a Christian perspective have worried repeatedly over it, sometimes with justifiable testiness at White's oversimplifications. See for example A. R. Peacocke, *Creation and the World of Science* (Oxford: Clarendon Press, 1979), pp. 275–278. Ethicist Robin Attfield, in *The Ethics of Environmental Concern,* rev. ed. (Athens: University of Georgia Press, 1991), not only criticizes White sharply, pp. 20–23, but also shows that a version of biblical stewardship theology undergirds a viable environmental ethics. But as ecotheologian James A. Nash writes in a judicious analysis entitled "The Ecological Complaint against Christianity," which discusses both Worster and White, White should at least be given credit as "a prime provocateur" more responsible than anyone else for goading Christian theologians to reflect more deeply on environmental issues (*Loving Nature: Ecological Integrity and Christian Responsibility* [Nashville: Abingdon Press, 1991], p. 71).

5. The most extensive theological treatise I have seen on the biblical theology of land seems to me to support this view while arguing for the consistent importance of land (in a symbolic sense) throughout the Hebrew and Christian scriptures: Walter Brueggemann, *The Land* (Philadelphia: Fortress Press, 1977).

6. Classicism was not, of course, unequivocally more environmentally sensitive than Judeo-Christianity. Greco-Roman civilization was, for example, responsible for deforesting the Mediterranean (see, *inter alia,* Robert Pogue Harrison, *Forests: The Shadow of Civilization* [Chicago: University of Chicago Press, 1992], pp. 52–58); and it accelerated the process of exploitation of animals that began with agricultural domestication (see, for example, James Serpell, *In the Company of Animals: A Study of Human-Animal Relationships* [Oxford: Blackwell, 1986], pp. 171ff.). In fact Christianity did away with some "pagan" abuses like animal sacrifice. In short, in both Greco-Roman and Judeo-Christian formations, principles were not monolithic, nor did principle and practice always align (nor were the two formations wholly distinct).

7. Lucretius, *On the Nature of Things,* 5: 795–796, trans. William Ellery Leonard (London: Dent, 1921), p. 220 ("ut merito maternum nomen adepta terra sit").

8. James Sambrook, *English Pastoral Poetry* (Boston: Twayne, 1983), pp. 4–5.

9. Quotations from William Collins, "Ode to Evening" (1746), lines 2, 11–12, in *The Poems of Thomas Gray, William Collins, Oliver Goldsmith,* ed. Roger Lonsdale (London: Longman, 1969), pp. 463–464.

10. Keith Thomas, *Man and the Natural World* (New York: Pantheon, 1983), p. 149. In his chapter "Compassion for the Brute Creation" (pp. 143–191) Thomas argues that the basic (theological) values admonishing against mistreatment of animals, particularly domestic animals, had long been in place, but that "a combination of religious piety and bourgeois sensibility" intensified them during this period (p. 159). Dix Harwood's documentary monograph, *Love for Animals and How It Developed in Great Britain* (New York: Columbia University, 1928), considers 1700 a more pivotal turning point (p. 74) but seems to accord with Thomas as to eighteenth-century trends. Among Thomson's precursors, seventeenth-century women poets are cited by both Harwood (Anne Finch, pp. 186–187) and Thomas (Margaret Cavendish, p. 170).

11. Virgil, *Georgics,* 4: 153–155, trans. H. Ruston Fairclough (Cambridge: Harvard University Press, 1960). Quotations from James Thomson's *The Seasons* are from James Sambrook's edition (Oxford: Clarendon Press, 1981).

12. Quotation from Thomas, *Man and the Natural World,* p. 98; cf. 137–142 and Harwood, *Love for Animals,* pp. 145–160, for discussion of animal souls. See John Greenleaf Whittier's poem "Telling the Bees," for a nineteenth-century reminiscence of the folk belief.

13. Harwood, *Love for Animals,* p. 193.

14. *The Poems of Samuel Taylor Coleridge,* ed. Ernest Hartley Coleridge (London: Oxford University Press, 1931), pp. 74, 75.

15. *The Poetry and Prose of William Blake,* rev. ed., ed. David B. Erdman (Garden City, N.Y.: Doubleday, 1970), pp. 482, 23. Harwood, *Love for Animals,*

p. 336, points out the Blakean inversion of Gloucester's lines in *King Lear:* "As flies to wanton boys are we to th' gods: they kill us for their sport" (IV.i.37–38). The poem's overall thrust, however, is not to ennoble flies to the dignity of people but to suggest that a person is no better than a fly if the universe functions as thoughtlessly as the fly-killing boy persona.

16. Josephine Miles, *Pathetic Fallacy in the Nineteenth Century* (1942; rpt. New York: Octagon, 1965), p. 113.

17. Miles sums up the major contrast between the pair: "In the Darwinian world the shared emotions were, partially, workable as if mechanisms; in Blake's they were infused like sunshine" (*Pathetic Fallacy,* p. 15).

18. Michel Foucault, *The Order of Things: An Archaeology of the Human Sciences* (New York: Random House, 1970), p. 161. Against Foucault's sweeping characterization of eighteenth-century natural history as a Linnaean monolith can be set, as a partial corrective, Donald Worster's contrast between "imperial" and "arcadian" strains in *Nature's Economy,* pp. 3–55, although Worster, ultimately, takes a somewhat similarly baleful view of Linnaeus as an imperial projector. For a much more concise, but also more complex and nuanced view of Linnaeus and of the environmental theories of his age, still the best resource is Clarence J. Glacken, *Traces on the Rhodian Shore: Nature and Culture in Western Thought from Ancient Times to the End of the Eighteenth Century* (Berkeley: University of California Press, 1967), pp. 510–512 and Part IV passim.

19. Gilbert White, *The Natural History and Antiquities of Selborne* (London: Bensley, 1789), pp. 172, 193–194, 240–243, 193, 149.

20. Wilson's and Audubon's essays are conveniently reprinted and juxtaposed in *This Incomperable Lande: A Book of American Nature Writing,* ed. Thomas Lyon (Boston: Houghton, Mifflin, 1989; rpt. New York: Penguin, 1991); quotations from pp. 123, 133. In his study of eighteenth-century natural history writing, *In the Presence of Nature* (Amherst: University of Massachusetts Press, 1978), David Wilson calls attention to anthropomorphism as a common style in botanical, entomological, and zoological description: pp. 31–32, 109–110, 134.

21. The choice of hermit thrush was suggested to Whitman by his literary naturist friend John Burroughs (Perry Westbook, *John Burroughs* [New York: Twayne, 1974], pp. 17–19). Although Burroughs became sharply critical of personification later on (see below), in the 1860s he would have supported Whitman's anthropomorphisms. In *Wake-Robin,* his first book, Burroughs described the hermit thrush's song as a "hymn" that "suggests a serene religious beatitude as no other sound in nature does," and seems to say, "O spheral, spheral . . . O holy, holy! O clear away, clear away! O clear up, clear up!" (Boston: Houghton, Mifflin, 1871), p. 51.

22. James Engell, *Forming the Critical Mind: Dryden to Coleridge* (Cambridge: Harvard University Press, 1989), pp. 204–205. An excellent short discussion of

the neoclassical premises from which developed the transitional state Engell describes is Earl R. Wasserman, "The Inherent Values of Eighteenth-Century Personification," *PMLA,* 65 (1950): 435–463.

23. William Wordsworth, "Essay Supplementary to the Preface" (on Thomson) and "Prose Diction" (on Cowper), in *Prose Works of William Wordsworth,* ed W. J. B. Owen and Jane Worthington Smyser (Oxford: Clarendon Press, 1974), 3: 73; 1: 163–164; "The Ruined Cottage," manuscript D, lines 74–82, in *The Ruined Cottage and the Pedlar,* ed. James Butler (Ithaca: Cornell University Press, 1979), pp. 49, 51. In *Personification and the Sublime: Milton to Coleridge* (Cambridge: Harvard University Press, 1985), Steven Knapp elegantly sums up Wordsworth's transitional position from the standpoint of one interested in personification's richness as a self-reflexive device rather than as a way of defining one's relation to the object-world: "Wordsworth largely abandons the practice of explicit personification (thus jettisoning much of the self-conscious theatricality of a poet like Collins), while on the other hand, he allows his sublime agents to retain enough of their allegorical heritage to prevent them from comfortably inhabiting their naturalized roles" (pp. 120–121). See also Knapp's ensuing discussion of Wordsworth's "Yew-Trees."

24. John Ruskin, *Modern Painters,* in *The Works of John Ruskin,* ed. E. T. Cook and Alexander Wedderburn (London: Longmans, 1903–1912), 3: 25, 616; 5: 205. Ruskin allowed the exceptional case when an artist faced a subject so overwhelming that it "*ought* to throw him off his balance." Prophecy was the example Ruskin specifically had in mind: "the language of the highest inspiration becomes broken, obscure, and wild in metaphor, resembling that of the weaker man, overborne by weaker things" (5: 209).

25. Miles, *Pathetic Fallacy,* pp. 40, 33–34.

26. Edgar Allan Poe, "The Fall of the House of Usher," in *Collected Works of Edgar Allan Poe: Tales and Sketches, 1831–1842,* ed. Thomas Ollive Mabbott (Cambridge: Harvard University Press, 1978), p. 408. The narrator stresses that "other men have thought thus," but that in Roderick Usher "the idea had assumed a more daring character, and trespassed, under certain conditions, upon the kingdom of inorganization." I interpret this passage as showing that nineteenth-century scientism made it easier to think of this fancy as pathology, hence to create figures like Usher.

27. Ralph Waldo Emerson, *Nature, Addresses, and Lectures,* ed. Robert E. Spiller and Alfred R. Ferguson (Cambridge: Harvard University Press, 1971), p. 10.

28. Charles Darwin, *The Descent of Man* (1871; rpt. Princeton: Princeton University Press, 1981), pp. 104, 105. Two excellent discussions focusing on *Origin of Species* emphasize Darwin's self-conscious prudence and wariness in personifying nature and at the same time the attractions that personification held for him: the title essay of Robert M. Young, *Darwin's Metaphor: Nature's Place in*

Victorian Culture (Cambridge, Eng.: Cambridge University Press, 1985); and Gillian Beer, "'The Face of Nature': Anthropomorphic Elements in the Language of *The Origin of Species*," in *Languages of Nature: Critical Essays on Science and Literature*, ed. L. J. Jordanova (London: Free Association Books, 1986), pp. 212–243.

29. See note 37 below and Burroughs, "An Egotistical Chapter," in *Indoor Studies* (Boston: Houghton, Mifflin, 1899), pp. 243–259.

30. Burroughs, *Ways of Nature* (Boston: Houghton, Mifflin, 1905), p. 238; Clara Barrus, *The Life and Letters of John Burroughs* (Boston: Houghton, Mifflin, 1925), 2: 336; 1: 212, 247.

31. Burroughs, manuscript journal, 1 March 1899 (Vassar College Archives); *Wake-Robin*, pp. 44, 45–46; *Ways of Nature*, p. v; "Real and Sham Natural History," *Atlantic*, 91 (1903): 298–309. Burroughs's no-nonsense realism was probably even more a product of his experience as a field naturalist than of his reading (for which, see Westbrook, *Burroughs*, pp. 100–126), although the latter empowered him to raise observational realism to a higher plane of importance as an artistic criterion than he would have felt entitled to do in his early Emersonian days.

32. Burroughs, *Under the Maples* (Boston: Houghton, Mifflin, 1921), p. 179; *Ways of Nature*, pp. 77, 109, 110, 64.

33. Burroughs, *Ways of Nature*, p. 128.

34. Burroughs, *Ways of Nature*, p. 229; *Leaf and Tendril* (Boston: Houghton, Mifflin, 1908), p. 267.

35. Burroughs, *The Summit of the Years* (Boston: Houghton Mifflin, 1913), p. 49; *Accepting the Universe* (Boston: Houghton Mifflin, 1920), p. 97.

36. Burroughs, *The Light of Day* (Boston: Houghton, Mifflin, 1900), p. 226; *Accepting the Universe*, pp. 90, 305.

37. *The Heart of Burroughs's Journals*, ed. Clara Barrus (Boston: Houghton Mifflin, 1928), pp. 192–193. After Muir's death, Burroughs drew this comparison: "I have more intellect than character, while such a man as John Muir had more character than intellect. Muir was a child in dealing with the nature of things, and the reason of things; his strength came out when he met men, or explored the mountains and glaciers" (see *Life and Letters of John Burroughs*, 2: 320). Barrus documents their relationship well from Burroughs's point of view. For a short comparative overview, see Paul Brooks, "The Two Johns," in *Speaking for Nature* (Boston: Houghton Mifflin, 1980), pp. 1–32.

38. *John of the Mountains: The Unpublished Journals of John Muir*, ed. Linnie Marsh Wolfe (1938; rpt. Madison: University of Wisconsin Press, 1979), pp. 138, 92.

39. Ibid., pp. 438, 436–437. As Muir's first biographer, William Frederic Badè, pointed out, Muir reconciled "the alleged antagonism between natural science and the Bible" by ascribing it "to the accumulated lumber of past generations of

faulty Bible teaching" rather than by throwing the baby out with the bathwater (*The Life and Letters of John Muir* [Boston: Houghton Mifflin, 1924], 1: 146). No doubt his early immersion in scripture helped him both internalize and revise the Bible: Muir recalled in old age that by age eleven he had been whipped into memorization of "about three fourths of the Old Testament and all of the New" (*The Story of My Boyhood and Youth* [Boston: Houghton Mifflin, 1913], pp. 31). Muir's formal education at the University of Wisconsin would have consolidated for him a sense of continuity between religion and science, as Steven Holmes has shown in his forthcoming dissertation (Harvard University) on the psychosocial underpinnings of Muir's understanding of nature.

40. John Muir, *Travels in Alaska* (Boston: Houghton Mifflin, 1915), pp. 93, 24; *Mountains of California* (1894; rpt. New York: Penguin, 1985), pp. 26, 12, 59, 112; *John of the Mountains*, p. 170.

41. John Tallmadge, "John Muir and the Poetics of Natural Conversion," *North Dakota Quarterly*, 59, no. 2 (Spring 1991): 73.

42. Muir, *A Thousand Mile Walk to the Gulf*, ed. William Frederic Badè (Boston: Houghton Mifflin, 1916), pp. 138–139, 140.

43. Max Oelschlaeger rightly calls Muir's ecotheology "animistic" in his analysis of Muir's wilderness theology and its consequences, in *The Idea of Wilderness: From Prehistory to the Age of Ecology* (New Haven: Yale University Press, 1991), p. 185. I think Oelschlaeger goes too far, however, in asserting that Muir eventually arrived at "a conception of God as entirely incarnate" (p. 190) and that his "completed wilderness paradigm thus represents a theological antithesis of orthodox Judaeo-Christianity" (p. 192). This is at once a modernization and a sentimentalization of Muir's neopagan aspect at the expense of his complexity. Michael P. Cohen's analysis of Muir's theocentrism in *The Pathless Way: John Muir and American Wilderness* (Madison: University of Wisconsin Press, 1984) is more complex. Cohen agrees that Muir grew partially away from the theocentric model of his boyhood, argues persuasively that his later writings use the rhetoric of transcendence strategically ("Muir found it necessary to argue in terms that Christian people might understand," p. 126), but also points out that Muir adhered to the end to a belief in an intelligence prior to evolution and "was evasive on the confrontation of pantheistic faith and scientific skepticism" (p. 163).

44. Muir, *Mountains of California*, pp. 40–41.

45. Muir, *Travels in Alaska*, p. 146. Robert U. Johnson unwittingly diagnosed the proprietary aspect of Muir's relation to nature when he wrote that Muir loved the Yosemite region "as a mother loves a child" (*Remembered Yesterdays* [Boston: Little, Brown, 1923], p. 281).

46. Muir, *Mountains of California*, p. 77.

47. Judging from Muir's annotated copies of *Walden* in his personal library

(now at University of the Pacific, Stockton, Calif.), "Higher Laws" was one of Muir's favorite chapters. A "good Victorian" in this respect, Muir was especially interested in Thoreau's remarks on the necessity of self-purification.

48. Muir, "An Adventure with a Dog and a Glacier," *Century*, 54 (September 1897): 773, 774, 770. Published in book form as *Stickeen*, included five years later in Houghton, Mifflin's Riverside Literature Series of school textbooks, finally cannibalized for *Travels in Alaska*, pp. 246–257. By 1940, *Stickeen* had sold 125,000 copies and was still selling at the rate of 1,000 yearly (Manley H. Jones to Eugene Armfield, 31 July 1940, Houghton Library, Harvard University). Stickeen was indeed a kind of collaborative popular culture product from the start, having been elicited from Muir by his friend *Century* editor Robert U. Johnson, who had heard Muir tell it several times and who pruned the manuscript's "digressions" freely. "Remember that this is my story as well as yours," Johnson told Muir; and Muir agreed that "I would never have written the story had you not urged me to do so" (Johnson to Muir, 9 July 1897, Muir to Johnson, 16 July 1897, University of the Pacific.) Muir should not have been as bemused and dismayed as he later was to get propositioned in 1902 by a representative of the Victor Talking Machine Company (the original RCA Victor), asking Muir's permission to reprint the story as a book with the company emblem on the cover: a dog peering into a victrola, with "His master's Voice" as the caption (J. E. Powers to Muir, 29 March 1902, University of California, Berkeley). For an excellent historical analysis of the genesis of *Stickeen* and its cultural significance, see Ronald H. Limbaugh, "Stickeen and the Moral Education of John Muir," *Environmental History Review*, 15, no. 1 (1991): 24–45.

49. Ralph Lutts, *The Nature Fakers: Wildlife, Science, and Sentiment* (Golden, Colo.: Fulcrum, 1970), p. 22.

50. For general treatments of the genre, see "The Animal Story," *Edinburgh Review*, 214 (July 1911): 94–118; Alec Lucas, "Nature Writers and the Animal Story," in *Literary History of Canada*, 2d ed., ed. Carl F. Klinck (Toronto: University of Toronto Press, 1976), pp. 380–404; and Lisa Mighetto, *Wild Animals and American Environmental Ethics* (Tucson: University of Arizona Press, 1991), pp. 9–26.

51. Charles C. D. Roberts, *The Kindred of the Wild* (Boston: Page, 1902), pp. 23, 24; Williamson cited by Eleanor Graham in the foreword to *Tarka the Otter* (Hammondsworth: Penguin, 1937), p. 7.

52. Limbaugh, "Stickeen and the Moral Education of John Muir," p. 26.

53. Ernest Ingersoll, *The Wit of the Wild* (New York: Dodd, Mead, 1906), pp. 48, 196, 16; Lutts, *Nature Fakers*, p. 202.

54. I should add that the perplexities of literary representation reflected the exploratory state of research on animal intelligence. In 1894 C. Lloyd Morgan had announced the principle "that we should not interpret animal behaviour as the outcome of higher mental processes, if it can be fairly explained as due to

the operation of those which stand lower in the psychological scale of development"; but though he and other psychological researchers drew sharp lines between human and animal intellection, he was "far from wishing to assert dogmatically that in no animals are there even the beginnings of a rational scheme," and he ascribed to animals "the perceptual germs" of both "aesthetic appreciation" and "ethical approbation" (Morgan, *Animal Behaviour*, rev. ed. [London: Edward Arnold, 1900], pp. 270, 155, 281). Limbaugh ("Stickeen and the Moral Education of John Muir," p. 35) points out that Muir was much impressed with an earlier book called *Animal Intelligence* (New York: Appleton, 1883) by George J. Romanes, which suggested, in a passage Muir underscored in his personal copy, that just as humans reason about the Divine Mind from the analogy of the human, "so with 'inverted anthropomorphism' we must supply a similar consideration to the animal world" (p. 10).

55. Harriet Ritvo, *The Animal Estate: The English and Other Creatures in the Victorian Age* (Cambridge: Harvard University Press, 1987), pp. 39–41.

56. Ritvo sheds valuable collateral light on Jack London's fascination with crossing the border between pet and wild animal and between human and animal counterparts; see *The Animal Estate*, Chapters 2 (on pets), 4 (on fear of rabies), and 6 (on hunting wild beasts). A later London novel, *White Fang* (1906), crosses the border from the opposite direction, telling the story of a one-quarter-part dog, born as a wolf, who becomes semidomesticated. For a critical discussion of London's animal stories that deals with them *inter alia* as proletarian fiction, see Mary Allen, *Animals in American Literature* (Urbana: University of Illinois Press, 1983), pp. 77–96.

57. Another mode of post-Darwinian modernism that focuses on humanity's bestial nature is surveyed in Margot Norris, *Beasts of the Modern Imagination: Darwin, Nietzsche, Kafka, Ernst, and Lawrence* (Baltimore: Johns Hopkins University Press, 1985). Norris sees her writers' protagonists as engaged in a project of "biocentric" expressionism designed "to extricate the animal body from its Gothic matrix by decoding the pornological functions in which culture entraps it" (p. 235). ("Pornology" is glossed as "the hypocritical investment of libido in cultural forms" [p. 11].) In my view, both movements are more accurately characterized as antihumanist rather than antianthropocentric: they are not so much biocentrist, let alone ecocentric, as preoccupied with undermining the view of *Homo sapiens* as a rational animal. But in their efforts to blur the line between human and nonhuman, these movements certainly are related to the work that primarily concerns us here.

58. Lisa Mighetto, "Science, Sentiment, and Anxiety: American Nature Writing at the Turn of the Century," *Pacific Historical Review*, 54 (1985): 35.

59. Roberts, *Kindred of the Wild*, p. 112.

60. James Turner, *Reckoning with the Beast: Animals, Pain, and Humanity in*

the Victorian Mind (Baltimore: Johns Hopkins University Press, 1980), pp. 74 and 15–95 passim.

61. Sarah Orne Jewett, "The White Heron," in *The Country of the Pointed Firs and Other Stories* (Garden City, N.Y.: Doubleday, 1956), p. 165.

62. Muir, *Our National Parks* (1901; rpt. Madison: University of Wisconsin Press, 1981), pp. 335, 364.

63. On the nature and history of the older paradigm, see Samuel P. Hays, *Conservation and the Gospel of Efficiency* (Cambridge: Harvard University Press, 1959). In a later study, Hays succinctly defines the conservation movement as "an effort on the part of leaders in science, technology, and government to bring about more efficient development of physical resources" (*Beauty, Health, and Permanence: Environmental Politics in the United States, 1955–1985*, in collaboration with Barbara D. Hays (Cambridge, Eng.: Cambridge University Press, 1987), p. 13. On the history of American preservationist thinking, the tradition of intellectual and cultural ferment most hospitable to ecocentrism, see Roderick Nash, *Wilderness and the American Mind*, 3d ed. (New Haven: Yale University Press, 1982). Authorities of course differ as to when, if ever, conservationism was displaced as the dominant ideology (Hays sets World War II as the time), and as to just how ecocentric, or coherent in any respect, preservationism is. In *Beauty, Health, and Permanence*, Hays is also admirably clear-sighted about the shallowness of much contemporary pronature sentiment.

64. Worster, *Nature's Economy*, p. 318.

65. James Lovelock, *Gaia: A New Look at Life on Earth* (1979; rpt. with new Preface, New York: Oxford University Press, 1987), p. 9. For the scientific reception, see *Scientists on Gaia*, ed. Stephen H. Schneider and Penelope J. Boston (Cambridge: MIT Press, 1991), a number of whose contributors see promise in aspects of Lovelock's work without, however, endorsing the teleology implicit in the mythical rhetoric. Gaia theory has also precipitated more radical calls to reinvigorate academic ecology in terms of a holistic paradigm; e.g., Edward Goldsmith, "Gaia: Some Implications for Theoretical Ecology," *Ecologist*, 18 (1988): 64–74. For a popular history of Gaia's gathering momentum, see Lawrence E. Joseph, *Gaia: The Growth of an Idea* (New York: St. Martin's, 1990), especially pp. 223–247.

66. Lovelock, *Gaia*, pp. xii; Joseph, *Growth of an Idea*, pp. 87–93. 118.

67. Lovelock, *Gaia*, pp. 24, 36, 44, 46, 61, 92. In his follow-up study, *The Ages of Gaia: A Biography of Our Living Earth* (1988; rpt. New York: Bantam, 1990), Lovelock is more cautious in his personifications but no less intent on "humanizing" his concept: e.g., "In no way do I see Gaia as a sentient being, a surrogate God. To me Gaia is alive and part of the ineffable Universe and I am part of her" (p. 218).

68. Lovelock, *Gaia*, pp. 124, 121, 145; Joseph, *Growth of an Idea*, p. 68 and

passim. Some examples of Lovelock's warm popular reception: American feminist shaman Starhawk (Miriam Simos) welcomes growing scientific attention to Lovelock's theory in *Dreaming the Dark: Magic, Sex, and Politics,* rev. ed. (Boston: Beacon, 1988), p. xv; popular ecotheologian Thomas Berry expresses pleasure that "personal designation of the earth as Gaia is no longer unacceptable in serious discussion," in *The Dream of the Earth* (San Francisco: Sierra Club, 1988), p. 18; ecophilosopher Warwick Fox credits Lovelock's theory as "the main inspiration" for "ethical emphasis on the ecosphere," in *Toward a Transpersonal Ecology* (Boston: Shambala, 1990), p. 177.

69. For an example of the widely circulating modern goddess discourse prior to the publication of Lovelock's book, see Part I of the feminist anthology *The Politics of Women's Spirituality,* ed. Charlene Spretnak (Garden City, N.Y.: Doubleday, 1982). Interestingly, "Gaia" is not one of the avatars of the Goddess that the contributors stress, apropos Greek mythology, even though the goddess-earth association is seen as central. Lovelock has clearly helped popularize a specific avatar of the Goddess, but the modern revival of the Goddess predates his rise to public notice.

70. On this general subject, see Stephen Toulmin, *The Return to Cosmology: Postmodern Science and the Theology of Nature* (Berkeley: University of California Press, 1982). Toulmin emphasizes, however, the prevailing insouciance or discomfort evinced by modern scientists about the bearing of their findings on religious and ethical issues of public interest.

71. Donna Haraway, *Primate Visions: Gender, Race, and Nature in the World of Modern Science* (London: Routledge, 1989), pp. 185, 247, 249.

72. For example, Japanese misogyny poses problems for Haraway's thesis, which she does not fully address (*Primate Visions,* pp. 255ff).

73. See for example Daniel B. Botkin, *Discordant Harmonies: A New Ecology for the Twenty-First Century* (New York: Oxford University Press, 1990), particularly Chapter 3, which focuses on predator-prey studies done on Isle Royale, Lake Superior. Interestingly, Botkin's reflections on "the individuality of the wolves and the moose" (p. 31) prove to be a springboard for an argument on behalf of the advantages of computer modeling (with its capacity to digest many variables and thus allow for chance variation) in the science of environmental prediction.

74. The pioneer figure was Jacob von Uexküll; see especially his development of the concept of animal *umwelt* in "A Stroll through the World of Animals and Men: A Picture Book of Invisible Worlds" (1935), trans. and ed. Claire H. Schiller, in *Instinctive Behavior: The Development of a Modern Concept* (New York: International Universities Press, 1957), pp. 5–80. For a short account, illustrative of Uexküll's appeal to contemporary holistic ecological thought, see Neil Evernden, *The Natural Alien* (Toronto: University of Toronto Press, 1985), pp. 79–83. For an example of the literary influence of the *umwelt* concept, see Barry Lopez, *Arctic*

Dreams: Imagination and Desire in a Northern Landscape (New York: Bantam, 1987), pp. 240–241, 281. Uexküll, an antievolutionist of somewhat mystical tendencies, is not well regarded by historians of science today; Ernst Mayr does not mention him in *The Growth of Biological Thought* (Cambridge: Harvard University Press, 1982). But he has had some influence on the course of modern ethology as the teacher of Konrad Lorenz, (author or coauthor of the other papers collected in *Instinctive Behavior*). The depth of this influence is especially clear in Lorenz's theoretical paper "Kant's Doctrine of the A Priori in the Light of Contemporary Biology" (1941), trans. Charlotte Ghurye and ed. Donald T. Campbell for Richard Evans, *Konrad Lorenz: The Man and His Ideas* (New York: Harcourt, 1975), pp. 181–217. Uexküll has also been claimed as a pioneer semiologist by Thomas A. Sebeok, in *The Sign and Its Masters* (Austin: University of Texas Press, 1979), pp. 187–207.

75. Quoted in Roderick Nash, *The Rights of Nature: A History of Environmental Ethics* (Madison: University of Wisconsin Press, 1989), p. 23.

76. Michael J. Bean, *The Evolution of National Wildlife Law,* rev. ed. (New York: Praeger, 1983), pp. 329–383; Leopold, *SCA* 225–226: "A thing is right when it tends to preserve the integrity, stability, and beauty of the biotic community. It is wrong when it tends otherwise."

77. Christopher Stone, *Should Trees Have Standing?* (1972; rpt. Palo Alto, Calif.: Tioga, 1988), pp. 5, 42, and Stone's 1988 preface to this volume, pp. v–xi.

78. Nash, *Rights of Nature,* p. 177; Bean, *Evolution,* p. 343; 639 *Federal Reporter,* 2d ser. (1981): 496. My thanks to Norma Brach for clarifying this distinction. It is interesting, parenthetically, that legal protection has so far been extended more vigorously to species than to habitats or ecosystems. This may reflect the persistence of what Yi-fu Tuan calls segmentation bias in environmental perception (see Tuan's *Topophilia: A Study of Environmental Perception, Attitudes, and Values* [1974; rpt. New York: Columbia University Press, 1990], pp. 15–16).

79. In a more recent and more elaborate work of environmental legal philosophy, *Earth and Other Ethics: The Case for Moral Pluralism* (New York: Harper and Row, 1987), Stone maintains his original antianthropocentrism but backs away from his former equivalence of human and nonhuman individuals, espousing the more complex and capacious notion of "legal considerateness" in place of a straightforward rights-of-nature position (p. 44 and passim).

80. John Passmore, "The Treatment of Animals," *Journal of the History of Ideas,* 36 (1975): 212.

81. The distinction between moral subjects and moral agents is discussed in Paul W. Taylor, *Respect for Nature: A Theory of Environmental Ethics* (Princeton: Princeton University Press, 1986), pp. 14–47. On category mistakes, see for example Holmes Rolston III, *Environmental Ethics: Duties to and Values in the Natural*

World (Philadelphia: Temple University Press, 1988), p. 181. Lawrence E. Johnson, in "Toward the Moral Considerability of Species and Ecosystems," *Environmental Ethics,* 14 (1992): 145–158, argues that species and ecosystems as well as organisms should be considered as having moral interests (he stops short of saying "agency") and are therefore morally "considerable."

82. Rachel Carson, *Under the Sea-Wind* (1941; rpt. New York: Oxford University Press, 1952), pp. 222–223.

83. Philip Booth, "Heron," reprinted in *Relations: Selected Poems, 1950–1985* (New York: Penguin, 1986), p. 19.

84. A more developed example is David Rains Wallace, *Idle Weeds: The Life of an Ohio Sandstone Ridge* (Columbus: Ohio State University Press, 1980), which chronicles the natural history of a year on "a crouching resistant groundhog of wildness with enemies too powerful and numerous to afford it much ease or generosity" (p. 10). Wallace approaches this task, however, from the view that the physical environment's capacity to sustain itself in some form, albeit mutated, is stronger than the human capacity to control nature, human life itself being dependent on the biosphere (pp. 165–169). This vision figures in the text in the way humans are humbled or frustrated by the landscape (a mower breaks his tractor, a turtle eats a clandestinely planted marijuana crop, etc.).

85. Carson, preface to 1941 edition of *Under the Sea-Wind,* quoted in Paul Brooks, *The House of Life: Rachel Carson at Work* (Boston: Houghton Mifflin, 1972), p. 34.

86. Brooks, *The House of Life,* pp. 32, 8.

87. Darwin, *The Descent of Man,* p. 101.

88. For example, "The Bean Field" extracts commodity; "Sounds" purports to record "the language which all things and events speak without metaphor" (*Wa* 111); "Higher Laws" approaches the relation to nature in terms of (ethical) discipline. In all these cases Thoreau both absorbs and answers Emerson.

89. Catherine Albanese, *Nature Religion in America: From the Algonkian Indians to the New Age* (Chicago: University of Chicago Press, 1990), pp. 92–93.

90. Robert Frost, "The Gift Outright," in *Complete Poems* (New York: Holt, 1958), p. 467.

91. Thoreau's relation to the town of Concord was one of loyal opposition rather than of outright separatism, however. His satire can keep the casual reader from appreciating the degree of interdependence. For more on this point than is covered in the present chapter, see my *New England Literary Culture* (Cambridge, Eng.: Cambridge University Press, 1986), pp. 319–334. See also Robert Gross's invaluable reconstructions of the intersections and disjunctions between the town's agendas and Thoreau's, beginning with "'The Most Estimable Place in All the World': A Debate on Progress in Nineteenth-Century Concord," in

Studies in the American Renaissance, 1978, ed. Joel Myerson (Boston: Twayne, 1978), pp. 1–15; and "Agriculture and Society in Thoreau's Concord," *Journal of American History,* 69 (1982): 42–61.

92. Richard K. Nelson, *Make Prayers to the Raven: A Koyukon View of the Northern Forest* (Chicago: University of Chicago Press, 1983), pp. 49–50; Buell, *New England Literary Culture,* pp. 307–308. Thoreau's personal favorite was the white pine (*J* 10: 33). "The pines impress me as human," he once wrote; "Nothing stands up more free from blame in this world than a pine tree" (*PJ* 4: 212). A famous instance of Thoreauvian hypersensitivity on this point that takes on new resonance in light of his dendrophilia was his excoriation of *Atlantic* editor James Russell Lowell for deleting from "Chesuncook" the declaration that the pine tree "is as immortal as I am, and perchance will go to as high a heaven, there to tower above me still" (*Correspondence of Henry David Thoreau,* ed. Walter Harding and Carl Bode [New York: New York University Press, 1958], pp. 515–516).

93. On English tree worship, see Thomas, *Man and the Natural World,* pp. 212–222. On the crisis of deforestation during the early modern period, see John Perlin, *A Forest Journey: The Role of Wood in the Development of Civilization* (Cambridge: Harvard University Press, 1991), pp. 211–227. On the history of myths of the forest considered as symbols of humanity's other, see Douglas Davies, "The Evocative Symbolism of Trees," in *The Iconography of Landscape,* ed. Denis Cosgrove and Stephen Daniels (Cambridge, Eng.: Cambridge University Press, 1988), pp. 32–42, and especially Robert Pogue Harrison, *Forests: The Shadow of Civilization* (Chicago: University of Chicago Press, 1992). Harrison includes a sensitive brief discussion of *Walden* (pp. 220–232), which seems to me somewhat weakened, however, by the claim that "Thoreau goes into nature to be brought out of nature" (p. 230). See too Harrison's meditation on John Constable's *Study of the Trunk of an Elm Tree* (ca. 1821), which says beautifully of the impression of Constable's chiaroscuro what I should also say of Thoreau's work: that it suggests that "human presence in the world belongs most intimately to nature's manner of being" (*Forests,* p. 208).

94. On the reforestation of New England, see John Brinckerhoff Jackson, *American Space: The Centennial Years, 1865–1876* (New York: Norton, 1972), pp. 88–90; on the development of coal-burning stoves, see A. William Hoglund, "Forest Conservation and Stove Inventors: 1789–1850," *Forest History,* 5, no. 4 (1962): 1–8.

95. Emerson, *Nature, Addresses, and Lectures,* p. 10.

96. See especially Robert Sayre, *Thoreau and the American Indian* (Princeton: Princeton University Press, 1977), which judiciously defines the range of interest and the limits of his evolving grasp of Native American cultures.

97. Robert Redfield, *The Primitive World and Its Transformations* (Ithaca: Cornell University Press, 1953), p. 105; Vine Deloria, Jr., *God Is Red* (New York:

Dell, 1973), p. 103; Christopher Vecsey, "American Indian Environmental Religions," in *American Indian Environments* ed. Vecsey and Robert M. Venables (Syracuse: Syracuse University Press, 1980), p. 36.

98. Deloria, *God Is Red,* p. 201.

99. N. Scott Momaday, "Native Attitudes to the Environment," in *Seeing with a Native Eye: Essays on Native American Religion,* ed. Walter Holden Capps (New York: Harper and Row, 1976), p. 84; Äke Hultkrantz, *Belief and Worship in Native North America,* ed. Christopher Vecsey (Syracuse: Syracuse University Press, 1981), p. 125. Hultkrantz reports that a Seneca once told him that a white man, moving to a new region, "is impressed by the appearance of the landscape and meditates over its beauty, whereas the Indian first of all asks, where are my medicines?"

100. Both the Walden and the river park proposal Thoreau included in the peroration of a lecture he drafted but did not survive to deliver, "Huckleberries" (ed. Leo Stoller, 1970; reprinted in *The Natural History Essays,* ed. Robert Sattelmeyer [Salt Lake City: Peregrine Smith, 1980], pp. 255–260).

101. See J. Donald Hughes and Jim Swan, "How Much of the Earth Is Sacred Space," *Environmental Review,* 10 (1986): 247–259 (for the basic distinction between white "sanctuary" preservationism and the Indian view); Hultkrantz, *Belief and Worship,* pp. 118–122 (for a more nuanced view of Native American land sacrality); and Fox, *Toward a Transpersonal Ecology,* pp. 155–156 (for the "cathedral" concept).

102. Thoreau, *The Maine Woods,* ed. Joseph J. Moldenhauer (Princeton: Princeton University Press, 1972), pp. 184, 185.

103. Gary Snyder, *The Practice of the Wild* (San Francisco: North Point, 1990), p. 20; Barry Lopez, "Renegotiating the Contracts," *Parabola* (1983), reprinted in *This Incomperable Lande,* p. 384.

104. José Barriero, "Indigenous Peoples Are the 'Miners' Canary,'" in *Learning to Listen to the Land,* ed. Bill Willers (Washington: Island Press, 1991), p. 200.

105. Theodore Roszak, *Person/Planet: The Creative Disintegration of Industrial Society* (Garden City, N.Y.: Doubleday, 1978), p. 39.

106. Sam D. Gill, *Mother Earth: An American Story* (Chicago: University of Chicago Press, 1987); Paula Gunn Allen, "The Feminine Landscape of Leslie Marmon Silko's *Ceremony,*" in *The Sacred Hoop: Recovering the Feminine in American Indian Traditions* (Boston: Beacon, 1986), p. 127. Gill may carry his revisionism too far, but he persuasively documents the ironic collaboration and competition between Anglo-American savagist motives and Native American cultural nationalism; see especially pp. 128, 151–158. In Gill's account, the whites mistook a metaphor for a goddess; Native Americans responded in kind as a means of solidarity and as a polemic argument against white oppression; these cultural assertions were accompanied by changes of emphasis in native theology

and ritual. For a typical contemporary "mainstream" endorsement of the authenticity and therapeutic value of the mother earth concept, see Thomas Berry's popular ecotheological manifesto, *The Dream of the Earth*, p. 187.

107. Carolyn Merchant, *The Death of Nature: Women, Ecology, and the Scientific Revolution* (San Francisco: Harper and Row, 1980), pp. 8, 190; Annette Kolodny, *The Lay of the Land: Metaphor as Experience and History in American Life and Letters* (Chapel Hill: University of North Carolina Press, 1975), pp. 4, 150; Sherry B. Ortner, "Is Female to Male as Nature Is to Culture?" in *Woman, Culture, and Society*, ed. Michelle Zimbalist Rosaldo and Louise Lamphere (Stanford: Stanford University Press, 1974), pp. 67–87.

108. Susan Griffin, *Woman and Nature: The Roaring inside Her* (New York: Harper and Row, 1978), p. 219.

109. See for example *The Politics of Women's Spirituality;* Carol Christ, *Laughter of Aphrodite: Reflections on a Journey to the Goddess* (San Francisco: Harper and Row, 1987); Elinor W. Gadon, *The Once and Future Goddess: A Symbol for Our Time* (San Francisco: Harper and Row, 1989); and Anne Baring and Jules Cashford, *The Myth of the Goddess: Evolution of an Image* (London: Viking, 1991). There is also a male earth-figure tradition and revival; see for example, William Anderson, *Green Man: The Archetype of Our Oneness with the Earth* (London: HarperCollins, 1990).

110. Gadon, *The Once and Future Goddess*, p. 233.

111. Riane Eisler, "The Gaia Tradition and the Partnership Future," in *Reweaving the World: The Emergence of Ecofeminism*, ed. Irene Diamond and Gloria Feman Orenstein (San Francisco: Sierra Club, 1990), p. 26.

112. Sallie McFague, *Models of God: Theology for an Ecological, Nuclear Age* (Philadelphia: Fortress Press, 1987), pp. xi, 69–123.

113. For a representative statement, see Catherine Roach, "Loving Your Mother: On the Woman-Nature Relation," *Hypatia*, 6, no. 1 (Spring 1991): 46–59.

114. Carol P. Christ, "Rethinking Theology and Nature," in *Reweaving the World: The Emergence of Ecofeminism*, ed. Irene Diamond and Gloria Feman Orenstein (San Francisco: Sierra Club, 1990), p. 68.

115. John Tallmadge, "Saying *You* to the Land," *Environmental Ethics*, 3 (1981): 353–354.

116. Snyder, *The Practice of the Wild*, p. 39.

117. An old (1657) definition of "volunteer," however, is "a flower or tree which grows spontaneously" *(Oxford English Dictionary)*; thus botanical nuances are not so easily separated from the military.

118. Joseph Wood Krutch, *The Great Chain of Life* (Boston: Houghton Mifflin, 1956), pp. 165–166.

119. See especially Karen Warren, "The Power and Promise of Ecological Feminism," *Environmental Ethics*, 12 (1990): 125–146; and two contributions to

the 1991 *Hypatia* symposium "Ecological Feminism," edited by Warren (6, no. 1 [Spring]): Val Plumwood, "Nature, Self, and Gender: Feminism, Environmental Philosophy, and the Critique of Rationalism," 3–27; and Deane Curtin, "Toward an Ecological Ethic of Care," 60–74. For a dissent, see Roger J. H. King, "Caring about Nature: Feminist Ethics and the Environment," in the same issue of *Hypatia,* 75–89. The notion of an "ethics of care" was of course not invented by ecofeminists. For one important precedent, see Carol Gilligan, *In a Different Voice: Psychological Theory and Women's Development* (Cambridge: Harvard University Press, 1982), pp. 62–63 and passim. Nor is this ethics unique to feminism, as is clear from Attfield's *The Ethics of Environmental Concern,* which derives its own notion of caring from other sources.

120. On this problem of ubiquitous slippage, see Yi-fu Tuan's short discussion of western and Asian environmental ethics, "Our Treatment of the Environment in Ideal and Actuality," *American Scientist,* 58 (May–June 1970): 244–249.

7. Nature's Face, Mind's Eye

1. Thoreau, "A Winter Walk," in *Excursions and Poems,* ed. Bradford Torrey and Francis H. Allen (Boston: Houghton, Mifflin, 1906), p. 173.

2. Jeffrey C. Robinson, *The Walk: Notes on a Romantic Image* (Norman: University of Oklahoma Press, 1989); Roger Gilbert, *Walks in the World: Representation and Experience in Modern American Poetry* (Princeton: Princeton University Press, 1991). Thomas J. Lyon, in the editorial introduction to his anthology *This Incomperable Lande: A Book of American Nature Writing* (Boston: Houghton Mifflin, 1989; rpt. New York, Penguin, 1991), remarks on the importance of the "ramble" as a traditional subspecies of natural history writing (pp. 5–6).

3. Alexander Marshack, *The Roots of Civilization: The Cognitive Beginnings of Man's First Art, Symbol, and Notation* (New York: McGraw-Hill, 1972), pp. 169–234.

4. Theodor H. Gaster, *Thespis: Ritual, Myth, and Drama in the Ancient Near East* (New York: Schuman, 1950), pp. 57, 265.

5. Society for the Resuscitation of Indian Literature, *Ritu-Samhara; or, An Account of the Seasons* (Calcutta: H. C. Das, 1901), pp. 7–8.

6. On *Gawain* and the broader context of medieval seasonal representation, see the chapter "The Landscape of the Seasons," in Derek Pearsall and Elizabeth Salter, *Landscapes and Seasons of the Medieval World* (Toronto: University of Toronto Press, 1973), especially pp. 147–154; for a more detailed analysis of seasonal representation through Spenser, see Rosamund Tuve, *Seasons and Months: Studies in a Tradition of Middle English Poetry* (Paris: Librairie Universitaire, 1933).

7. See for example Patrick Cullen's account of the design of Edmund Spenser's *The Shepheardes Calender* as regulated by the trope of mutability and the stylized

contrast of procreative and destructive impulses: *Spenser, Marvell, and Renaissance Pastoral* (Cambridge: Harvard University Press, 1970), pp. 122–148.

8. For an account of some of the intellectual influences on *The Seasons*, see A. D. McKillop, *The Background of Thomson's Seasons* (Minneapolis: University of Minnesota Press, 1942). For the most authoritative version of this much revised text, I rely on James Sambrook's edition (Oxford: Clarendon Press, 1981).

9. Quoted in Marion Barber Stowell, *Early American Almanacs: The Colonial Weekday Bible* (New York: Burt Franklin, 1977), p. 7.

10. Samuel Johnson, *Lives of the English Poets*, ed. George Birkbeck Hill (London: Clarendon Press, 1905), 3: 299.

11. John Burroughs, *Wake-Robin* (1871; rpt. Boston: Houghton, Mifflin, 1904), 3, 206.

12. *Sanctuary*, 33, no. 3 (January/February 1994).

13. Quoted in Dennis Ribbens, "The Making of *A Sand County Almanac*," in *Companion to "A Sand County Almanac": Interpretive and Critical Essays*, ed. J. Baird Callicott (Madison: University of Wisconsin Press, 1987), p. 107.

14. Annie Dillard, *Pilgrim at Tinker Creek* (New York: Harper and Row, 1974), pp. 129, 131, 137.

15. From Sambrook's "Preface" to Thomson's *Seasons*, p. xciv.

16. Dillard, *Pilgrim at Tinker Creek*, pp. 75, 76.

17. H. Daniel Peck, *Thoreau's Morning Work* (New Haven: Yale University Press, 1990), pp. 92, 95.

18. Susan Fenimore Cooper, *Rural Hours* (New York: Putnam, 1850), pp. 325, 336.

19. *The Connecticut Almanack for the Year of Our Lord 1779* (Hartford: Watson and Goodwin), n.p.

20. Timothy Dwight, *Travels in New-England and New-York*, ed. Barbara Miller Solomon (Cambridge: Harvard University Press, 1969), 2: 101.

21. John Burroughs, "Spring at the Capital," in *Wake-Robin*, p. 140; Muir, *My First Summer in the Sierra* (1911; rpt. New York: Penguin, 1987), p. 3.

22. Joseph Wood Krutch, *The Desert Year* (1951; rpt. Tucson: University of Arizona Press, 1985), pp. 199, 207, 157.

23. Peck, *Thoreau's Morning Work*, p. 88.

24. See Mark Rose, "The Author as Proprietor: *Donaldson v. Becket* and the Genealogy of Modern Authorship," *Representations*, 23 (Summer 1988): 51–85.

25. An excerpt from *Among the Isles of Shoals* appears, with a concise and judicious editorial introduction, in *American Women Regionalists, 1850–1910*, ed. Judith Fetterley and Marjorie Pryse (New York: Norton, 1992), whose eight-item selected bibliography (p. 646) includes everything of scholarly importance so far published about Thaxter.

26. Celia Thaxter, *Among the Isles of Shoals* (1873; rpt. Boston: Houghton, Mifflin, 1888), pp. 169–170.

27. Rosamund Thaxter, *Sandpiper: The Life and Letters of Celia Thaxter* (Francestown, N.H.: Marshall Jones, 1963), pp. 102, 215; Thaxter, *Shoals*, p. 5. For Whittier's encouragement, see Rosamund Thaxter, *Sandpiper*, pp. 207–214.

28. *Letters of Celia Thaxter*, Annie Fields and Rose Lamb (Boston: Houghton, Mifflin, 1895), pp. 54–55. My understanding of this passage, and much else in this chapter, has been helped by H. Daniel Peck.

29. Thaxter, *Shoals*, pp. 8, 28, 14, 24.

30. Ibid., pp. 7, 119, 100–101, 105, 106.

31. Ibid., pp. 133, 99.

32. Peter A. Fritzell, *Nature Writing and America: Essays upon a Cultural Type* (Ames: Iowa State University Press, 1990), p. 218.

33. On the composition of *Tinker Creek*, see Annie Dillard, *The Writing Life* (New York: Harper and Row, 1989), pp. 25–37.

34. Annie Dillard, *Living by Fiction* (New York: Harper and Row, 1982), p. 131.

35. Ibid., pp. 36–44.

36. Dillard, *Tinker Creek*, pp. 129–131.

37. Ibid., p. 17.

38. Ibid., pp. 72–73, 76.

39. Karla M. Hammond, "Drawing the Curtains: An Interview with Annie Dillard," *Bennington Review*, no. 10 (April 1981): 32.

40. Dillard, *Tinker Creek*, p. 161.

41. Ibid., p. 271. On the twin trumpets, see Numbers 10.10 and Stan Goldman, "Sacrifices to the Hidden God: Annie Dillard's *Pilgrim at Tinker Creek* and Leviticus," *Soundings*, 74 (1991): 210.

42. Scott Slovic remarks of another work by Dillard: "Not only does the external world shift and vanish when the narrator attempts to study it, but the character herself becomes less and less substantial as she undergoes the experience of awareness; her very senses . . . are transferred to the nonhuman surroundings, where she becomes 'weightless,' translucent—an abstraction, a 'prayer'" (*Seeking Awareness in American Nature Writing* [Salt Lake City: University of Utah Press, 1992], pp. 68–69). This is very like what happens as *Tinker Creek* unfolds. The attitude Slovic describes is broadly "religious"; more specifically it expresses a kind of gospel of seeing (particularly in the chapters "Seeing" and "Stalking") that aspires to an ideal of attentive self-effacement such that every environmental stimulus will be perfectly and intensely registered on the psyche.

43. For more specific calibration of the Dillard-Thoreau connection, see for example Gary McIlroy, "*Pilgrim at Tinker Creek* and the Social Legacy of *Walden*," *South Atlantic Quarterly*, 85 (1985): 111–122; Judy Schaaf Anhorn, "Lines of Sight:

Annie Dillard's 'Purified Nonfiction Narration,'" in *Cross-Cultural Studies: American, Canadian, and European Literatures, 1945–1985,* ed. Mirko Jurak (Ljubljana: Edvard Kardelj University, 1988), pp. 141–149; and Marc Chénetier, "Tinkering, Extravagance: Thoreau, Melville, and Annie Dillard," *Critique,* 31 (1990): 157–172.

44. Charles Anderson, *The Magic Circle of Walden* (New York: Holt, 1968), p. 39. Indeed, Anderson's qualification is characteristic of the whole formalist project, which in discussions of work, if not in the same scholar's discussions of biography and politics, sets more store by artistic patterning than by the biographical figure's engagement with material reality. See also *The Magic Circle*'s two key precursors: the interpretation of Thoreau that inaugurated formalist criticism of *Walden,* with its emphasis on the seasonal theme, F. O. Matthiessen, *American Renaissance* (New York: Oxford University Press, 1941), pp.166–175; and Sherman Paul, "Walden; or, The Metamorphoses," in his *The Shores of America: Thoreau's Inward Exploration* (Urbana: University of Illinois Press, 1958), the most important precontemporary study of Thoreau's imagination. One of the most striking traits of the work of both Matthiessen and Paul is the disparity between their intellectual capaciousness and the comparatively restrictive "new critical" paradigm of interpretation which Matthiessen introduces and Paul elaborates.

45. Slovic, *Seeking Awareness in American Nature Writing,* p. 23.

46. See my *Literary Transcendentalism: Style and Vision in the American Renaissance* (Ithaca: Cornell University Press, 1973), pp. 308–309, for further reflections on manipulations of tense in *Walden.*

47. Thoreau, *A Week on the Concord and Merrimack Rivers,* ed. Carl F. Hovde, William L. Howarth, and Elizabeth Hall Witherell (Princeton: Princeton University Press, 1980), p. 334.

48. An intriguing psychobiographical complication here, well known to Thoreauvians, is his reference to his own great crime against nature: "I was interested in the preservation of the venison and the vert more than the hunters and the woodchoppers, and as much as though I had been the Lord Warden himself; and if any part was burned, though I burned it myself by accident, I grieved with a grief that lasted longer and was more inconsolable than that of the proprietors" (*Wa* 250). This passage obliquely refers to Thoreau's accidental burning of three hundred acres of Concord woodland in the unusually dry spring of 1844, when a campfire he and a companion built spread out of control. (Fortunately for Thoreau, his companion was the son of the town's leading citizen.) For an account of this incident, see the most comprehensive factual biography, Walter Harding's *The Days of Henry Thoreau* (1965; rpt. Princeton: Princeton University Press, 1982), pp. 159–162. Thoreau seems to have written nothing about it until bursting forth six years later in a long, very defensive *Journal* entry (*PJ* 3: 75–78), which makes clear how much animosity was directed at him. ("For years," observes Harding [*Days of Thoreau,* p. 161], "Thoreau had to endure the whispers

of 'woods-burner' behind his back.") Two years after the *Journal* entry, Thoreau interpolated into the draft of *Walden* the laconic, indeed cryptic, passage I have quoted—also defensive but more chastened. My sense is that although it drags along much more personal baggage than Thoreau confessed, his conservationism here is not subservient to his guilt or defensiveness but rather a sign of his desire to turn these to productive account by doing right by the land hereafter.

49. Ronald Earl Clapper, "The Development of *Walden:* A Genetic Text," (Ph.D. diss., UCLA, 1967), p. 799.

50. In his poem "Wachusett," lines 325ff, Ellery Channing imagines the Indian fading like Indian summer "into the white snows of that winter race/ Who came with iron hands and pallid face." "Their only monument, a fading week,/ The Indian summer, like the hectic cheek/ Of a consumptive girl who ere her time,/ In some gay anguish half renews her prime" (in *Collected Poems,* ed. Walter Harding [Gainesville, Fla.: Scholars' Facsimiles and Reprints, 1967], pp. 255–256). Wilson Flagg, next to Thoreau and Susan Fenimore Cooper the most observant mid-nineteenth-century American literary naturist, decouples autumn foliage and Indian summer in his calendrically arranged book of literary dendrology, *The Woods and By-Ways of New England* (Boston: Osgood, 1872), pp. 243–251 and 315–319. Indian summer, Flagg insists, takes place "immediately after the entire denudation of the forest" (p. 319). Flagg traces the origin of Indian summer to the Indian belief that the "fall summer" is a special providence ordained by the Great Spirit as the time to go to one's hunting ground. Whatever the exact origin of the term, it seems clear that the equation of frostbitten red leaf and vanishing Indian was a persistent white man's fancy that took a sturdy effort on Flagg's part to combat.

51. H. Daniel Peck reflects on a passage in Thoreau's 1852 *Journal* that divides the year into four months of green, four of white, and two apiece of transition (*Thoreau's Morning Work,* pp. 94–95). Such a passage suggests both that *Walden*'s scheme ought to be considered one among many experimental seasonal schemes Thoreau played with over the years, and that the notion of an elongated summer and winter, more stable than the intervening seasons, appealed to him.

52. Flagg quoted in Charles Goodrich Whiting, *The Saunterer* (Boston: Ticknor and Fields, 1886), p. 246. The idea of midwinter thaw is a staple of many literary season books from the frostbelt: e.g., Leopold's *Sand County Almanac,* David Rains Wallace's *Idle Weeds,* etc.

53. Thoreau, "A Winter Walk," p. 170.

54. Joseph Wood Krutch, *The Twelve Seasons* (New York: Sloane, 1949), p. 157.

55. Wilson Flagg, *The Birds and Seasons of New England* (Boston: Osgood, 1875), p. 449.

56. Thoreau, "A Winter Walk," p. 182.

57. Richard Schneider, "An Overview of the Forthcoming *Approaches to Teach-*

ing Thoreau," paper presented at the MLA meeting, December 1991, San Francisco.

58. Mary Oliver, *Twelve Moons* (Boston: Little, Brown, 1979), pp. 16, 30–33.

59. Sue Hubbell, *A Country Year: Living the Questions* (New York: Harper and Row, 1987), pp. 149, 150.

8. Place

1. Some theorists of environmental perception seem to use "environment" and "place" synonymously: e.g., David Canter, *The Psychology of Place* (London: Architectural Press, 1977), pp. 9–10. I follow the more common practice of using "environment" to apply, in principle, to the world outside the observer regardless of how it is perceived, and to reserve "place" for environment as subjectively located and defined.

2. Wendell Berry, "The Regional Motive," in *A Continuous Harmony: Essays Cultural and Agricultural* (New York: Harcourt, 1972), pp. 68–69.

3. This fundamental point is made clear in Edward Relph, *Place and Placelessness* (London: Plon, 1976), and Yi-fu Tuan, *Space and Place: The Perspective of Experience* (Minneapolis: University of Minnesota Press, 1977), two of the best short expositions of the concept of place by humanistic geographers. See also E. V. Walter, *Placeways: A Theory of the Human Environment* (Chapel Hill: University of North Carolina Press, 1988), which sums the point up usefully: "People do not experience abstract space; they experience places. A place is seen, heard, smelled, imagined, loved, hated, feared, revered, enjoyed, or avoided" (p. 142). Although it is certainly possible to desire to relocate to an "empty" space and to experience it as healing, the sense of location bonding that ensues from this seems to convert what these geographers call space into place; see for example the title essay of Gretel Ehrlich, *The Solace of Open Spaces* (New York: Penguin, 1986), pp. 1–15.

4. Relph, *Place and Placelessness*, p. 47.

5. Edward Soja, *Postmodern Geographies: The Reassertion of Space in Critical Social Theory* (London: Verso, 1989), p. 134.

6. Yi-fu Tuan, "Place and Culture," in *Mapping American Culture*, ed. Wayne Franklin and Michael Steiner (Iowa City: University of Iowa Press, 1992), p. 44. This collection is a good starting point for the multidisciplinary study of place in American literary culture. In *Topophilia: A Study of Environmental Perception, Attitudes, and Values* (1974; rpt. New York: Columbia University Press, 1990), Tuan shows both that environment shapes culture and that culture can shape perception of the environment even to the extent of prompting people to "see" things that don't exist (pp. 59–91).

7. Berry, "The Regional Motive," p. 67.

8. Edward Relph, *Rational Landscapes and Humanistic Geography* (London: Croom Helm; Totowa, N.J.: Barnes and Noble, 1981), pp. 161–164.

9. Tuan, *Topophilia*, p. 93; Neil Evernden, *The Natural Alien* (Toronto: University of Toronto Press, 1985), pp. 103–124. As Evernden puts it: "paradoxically, we are an exotic organism even in our place of origin, wherever that might be. We are exotic in any environment, for in a sense we did not evolve *in* any existing habitat. I say 'in a sense,' for of course we were part of local ecosystems during most of our history. But in our minds we may have fallen out of context a very long time ago" (p. 109).

10. Emily Dickinson, poem 1755, in *The Complete Poems of Emily Dickinson*, ed. Thomas Johnson, (Boston: Little, Brown, 1960), p. 710.

11. William Dean Howells, *A Modern Instance*, ed. William Gibson (Boston: Houghton Mifflin, 1957), pp. 43, 230.

12. Endora Welty, "Place in Fiction," in *The Eye of the Story* (1942; rpt. New York: Random House, 1970), pp. 125, 116.

13. John Alcorn, *The Nature Novel from Hardy to Lawrence* (New York: Columbia University Press, 1977), p. 10.

14. Thomas Hardy, *The Return of the Native*, ed. James Gindin (New York: Norton, 1969), pp. 4, 137.

15. Welty, "Place in Fiction," pp. 122, 128.

16. William Least Heat Moon, *PrairyErth: (a deep map)* (Boston: Houghton Mifflin, 1991), p. 615.

17. Wendell Berry, "The Silence," in *Collected Poems* (San Francisco: North Point, 1985), pp. 111–112.

18. E. O. Wilson, *Biophilia* (Cambridge: Harvard University Press, 1984), p. 110. This same line of speculation, deriving modern taste in landscapes from an atavistic proclivity for the primal savanna, has also been used to explain aesthetic preference for open spaces and for large grass lawns: see for example Tony Hiss, *The Experience of Place* (New York: Knopf, 1990), p. 37; and Winifred Gallagher, *The Power of Place* (New York: Poseidon Press, 1993), p. 219.

19. John Haines, "The Writer as Alaskan: Beginnings and Reflections," in *Living off the Country: Essays on Poetry and Place* (Ann Arbor: University of Michigan Press, 1981), pp. 5ff. By contrast, another sensitive outlander who found a special place in Alaska, anthropologist Richard Nelson, in *The Island Within* (San Francisco: North Point, 1989), makes much more specific and stronger claims for his ability to enter into deep understanding of and communion with that place; see especially the title chapter, which outdoes Thoreau and Muir and Gary Snyder for pantheistic exuberance: "There is nothing in me that is not of earth, no split instant of separateness, no particle that disunites me from its surroundings" (p. 249).

20. Richard Gould, *Yiwara*, quoted in Walter, *Placeways*, p. 138.

21. *The Complete Works of Ralph Waldo Emerson,* ed. Edward Waldo Emerson (Boston: Houghton, Mifflin, 1903–1904), 11: 76.

22. Emerson, *Nature,* in *Nature, Addresses, and Lectures,* ed. Robert E. Spiller and Alfred R. Ferguson (Cambridge: Harvard University Press, 1971), p. 10.

23. Emerson, "Thoreau," in *Complete Works,* 10: 484.

24. David Rains Wallace, *Idle Weeds: The Life of an Ohio Sandstone Ridge* (Columbus: Ohio State University Press, 1980), p. 94.

25. Robert Frost, "Spring Pools," in *Complete Poems of Robert Frost* (New York: Holt, 1961), p. 303.

26. Soja, *Postmodern Geographies,* p. 122. Soja goes on to discuss the illusion of transparency also. This notion of mirror-opposite fallacies derives from Henri Lefebvre, *The Production of Space* (1974), trans. Donald Nicholson-Smith (Oxford: Blackwell, 1984), pp. 27–30.

27. Peter Fritzell, *Nature Writing and America: Essays upon a Cultural Type* (Ames: Iowa State University Press, 1990), is particularly severe on the epistemological limitations of "impersonal description" in nature writing (p. 27 and passim).

28. Sharon Cameron, *Writing Nature: Henry Thoreau's Journal* (New York: Oxford University Press, 1985), pp. 44–48.

29. D. W. Meinig, "The Beholding Eye: Ten Versions of the Same Scene," in *The Interpretation of Ordinary Landscapes,* ed. Meinig (New York: Oxford University Press, 1979), pp. 33–48.

30. See Tuan, *Space and Place,* p. 199 and passim, on the comforting nature of the sense of place.

31. For example, in his essay "Landscape and Character," Lawrence Durrell assures us that "ten minutes" of quiet introspective rumination while sitting on the omphalos at Delphi "will give you the notion of the Greek landscape which you could not get in twenty years of studying ancient Greek texts" (*Spirit of Place* [New York: Dutton, 1969], p. 158). Maybe so, especially if one feels excited and alert. What is unsatisfactory about Durrell's advice is its promise of a once-for-all shortcut to insidership with the essential Greece.

32. John Janovy, Jr., *Keith County Journal* (New York: St. Martin's, 1978), p. 79.

33. John Hanson Mitchell, *Ceremonial Time: Fifteen Thousand Years on One Square Mile* (New York: Warner Books, 1984), p. 9.

34. Thoreau's interest in habitation in the broadest sense was so keen and persistent that Frederick Garber has made it central to his second book on Thoreau, *Thoreau's Fable of Inscribing* (Princeton: Princeton University Press, 1991), a sensitive and sophisticated study contending that Thoreau's work and life ought to be seen in the light of a quest to explore and realize the meaning of being in the world. Garber's analysis owes much to Martin Heidegger, par-

ticularly Heidegger's late essay "Building Dwelling Thinking" (see Heidegger, *Poetry, Language, Thought,* trans. Albert Hofstadter [New York: Harper and Row, 1971], pp. 145–161). Some contemporary humanistic geographers have also been strongly influenced by Heidegger, to the point of making habitation the center of *their* projects; see for example the essays collected as *Dwelling, Place, and Environment: Towards a Phenomenology of Person and World,* ed. David Seamon and Robert Mugerauer (Dordrecht: Martinus Nijhoff, 1985), particularly the four essays in Part III, "Place and Dwelling."

35. Emerson, "Thoreau," in *Complete Works,* 10: 471.

36. Tuan, *Topophilia,* pp. 15–16. The tenacity of segmentation bias in literature is especially apparent in such poetic forms as the seventeenth-century meditative image poem and the postromantic nature lyric. The work of the major philosopher most often cited as a harbinger of contemporary ecologism shows it: Martin Heidegger. Heidegger's achievement in "The Thing" (in *Poetry, Language, Thought),* for example, in some ways resembles that of Thoreau's *Journal* passage. As an antidote to the normal state of banal inattentiveness of modern life, he tries to reimagine an inconspicuous object so as to make it offer a true "nearing of the world" (p. 181). This synecdochic approach is meant to open up a vision of a world of magically luminous things: "Things, each thinging and each staying in its own way, are mirror and clasp, book and picture, crown and cross." But the dramatization of a protoecological sense of a "ring"/"ringing" of existence (p. 182) is constrained by the hyperfocus on *the* thing.

37. John Muir, *The Story of My Boyhood and Youth* (Boston: Houghton Mifflin, 1913), pp. 280–283.

38. Stephen A. Forbes, "The Lake as a Microcosm" (1887), reprinted in *Foundations of Ecology: Classic Papers with Commentaries,* ed. Leslie A. Real and James H. Brown (Chicago: University of Chicago Press, 1991), p. 14. On Thoreau as pioneer of limnology, see Donald G. Quick, "Thoreau as Limnologist," *Thoreau Journal Quarterly,* 4, no. 2 (1972): 13–20.

39. Susan Fenimore Cooper, *Rural Hours* (New York: Putnam, 1850), pp. 188, 194.

40. Wendell Berry, *Clearing* (New York: Harcourt, 1977), "The Clearing," p. 21. See also Berry's essay "The Making of a Marginal Farm," in *Recollected Essays, 1965–1980* (San Francisco: North Point, 1981), reprinted in *This Incomperable Lande: A Book of American Nature Writing,* ed. Thomas J. Lyon (Boston: Houghton Mifflin, 1989; rpt. New York: Penguin, 1991).

41. Robert E. Abrams, "Image, Object, and Perception in Thoreau's Landscapes: The Development of Anti-Geography," *Nineteenth Century Literature,* 46 (1991): 261. This discussion should, however, be set next to, for example, Don Scheese, "Thoreau's *Journal:* The Creation of a Sacred Place" (in *Mapping Ameri-*

can Culture, ed. Wayne Franklin and Michael Steiner [Iowa City: University of Iowa Press, 1992], pp. 139–151), which (like the present essay) stresses Thoreau's use of metaphors as a way of returning the reader to the landscape they recreate.

42. Paul Ricoeur, *The Rule of Metaphor,* trans. Robert Czerny et al. (Toronto: University of Toronto Press, 1977), especially pp. 216–277, "Metaphor and Reference." To be specific, Ricoeur argues that while metaphor "seeks the abolition of the reference by means of self-destruction of the meaning of metaphorical statements," ultimately it draws "a new semantic pertinence out of the ruins of literal meaning" and thereby "sustains a new referential design" (p. 230). Ricoeur's notion of reference has been attacked as stolid and monolithic, but the idea of metaphor's bidirectionality cannot thereby be disposed of.

43. Alexander Wilson, *The Culture of Nature: North American Landscape from Disney to the Exxon Valdez* (Oxford: Blackwell, 1992), p. 115. This book offers a sympathetic but critically circumspect view of restorationism, without minimizing for example the difficulty of how one determines what the target of a particular restorationist project should be. The journal *Restoration and Management Notes* is an excellent introduction to the discourse. Of special pertinence in the present context are two essays by William R. Jordan III, "Restoration at Walden Pond," *Restoration and Management Notes,* 7 (1989): 65–69; and "Renewal and Imagination: Thoreau's Thought and the Restoration of Walden Pond," in *Thoreau's World and Ours: A Natural Legacy,* ed. Edmund A. Schofield and Robert C. Baron (Golden, Colo.: North American Press, 1993), pp. 260–271. In the latter, Jordan calls Thoreau himself a restorationist.

44. Leopold offers the latter dictum as an ad hoc definition of a "conservationist." For the case on behalf of the biblical stewardship tradition yielding a positive ecological ethics rather than its opposite, as is often alleged, see Robin Attfield, *The Ethics of Environmental Concern,* rev. ed. (Athens: University of Georgia Press, 1991). Attfield tends to see Leopold as an adversary on account of his doctrine of biotic egalitarianism, but in general, and certainly in the passage at hand, Leopold's conservationism seems to me strongly grounded in the stewardship tradition. This is even truer of Berry; see his chapters "The Body and the Earth," in *The Unsettling of America* (San Francisco: Sierra Club, 1977), and "Two Economies," in *Home Economics* (San Francisco: North Point, 1987).

45. Berry, "Reverdure," in *Clearing,* p. 50.

46. It is customary to read "Solitude" as expressing the will to detachment, not the desire for embeddedness; and certainly the speaker does proclaim alienation from other people here ("What do we want most to dwell near to? Not to many men surely . . ." [p. 133]). But it would be truer to think of "Solitude" as part of a two-chapter sequence that unfolds a sense of emplacement such as will allow a person to replace factitious camaraderie with the sense of a "more normal and natural society" (p. 136). Thoreau's argument is not that we should seek

isolation for its own sake, though clearly he takes pleasure in solitude. Solitude is also important as a vantage point from which to recalibrate and renew one's relation with other people, as the following chapter, "Visitors," begins to show.

47. Stanley Cavell, *The Senses of Walden* (1972; rpt. San Francisco: North Point, 1981), p. 107n.

48. Robert David Sack, *Human Territoriality: Its Theory and History* (Cambridge, Eng.: Cambridge University Press, 1986), p. 30. Sack's "territoriality" and my "place-sense" differ in that for him the sense of rightful domain is primary, but the general point holds for both.

49. Tuan, *Topophilia*, pp. 30–44, among many other sources, very pertinently notes that ethnocentrism carries forward into such conventions of contemporary cartography as setting 0° longitude at Greenwich, England, and putting Europe at the center of the world map.

50. William Boelhower, "Saving Saukenuk: How Black Hawk Won the War and Opened the Way to Ethnic Semiotics," *Journal of American Studies,* 25 (1991): 345. See also Boelhower's "Nation-Building and Ethnogenesis: The Map as Witness and Maker," in *The Early Republic,* ed. Steve Ickringill (Amsterdam: Free University Press, 1988), pp.108–131.

51. John Stilgoe, in *Common Landscape of America, 1580–1845* (New Haven: Yale University Press, 1982), p. 103, gives a lucid, succinct historical account. "By the 1860s," he observes, "the grid objectified national, not regional order, and no one wondered at rural space marked by urban rectilinearity" (pp. 106–107). Philip Fisher, "Democratic Social Space: Whitman, Melville, and the Promise of American Transparency," *Representations,* 24 (1988): 60–101.

52. See for example Terry Cook, "A Reconstruction of the World: George R. Parkin's British Empire Map of 1893," *Cartographia,* 21, no. 4 (1984): 53–65; Graham Huggan, *Territorial Disputes: Maps and Mapping Strategies in Contemporary Canadian and Australian Fiction* (Toronto: University of Toronto Press, 1994), especially the conclusion, "Decolonizing the Map"; and William Boelhower, "Saving Saukenuk," and "Inventing America: A Model of Cartographic Semiosis," *Word and Image,* 4 (1988): 475–497. In the latter Boelhower observes that "the map both as a minimal and maximal cultural sign is the ideal text for studying the way Indian land was transformed into Euro-American territory and settlers from various nations into a homogeneous ethnos, as the ideological boast goes" (p. 478).

53. See for example the analysis, with accompanying cartographical illustrations, in Ward Churchill, "Struggle to Regain a Stolen Homeland: The Iroquois Land Claims in Upstate New York," in *Struggle for the Land: Indigenous Resistance to Genocide, Ecocide, and Expropriation in Contemporary North America* (Monroe, Me.: Common Courage Press, 1993), pp. 87–111.

54. For the basic concept of mental mapping, see Peter Gould and Rodney

White, *Mental Maps,* 2d ed. (Boston: Allen and Unwin, 1985), which, however, valorizes map over human perception in a one-sidedly positivistic way. ("Our images—the maps and models of the world we carry around with us—need larger and much more relevant information inputs. Only then can our visions of a larger world . . . grow to match the human-created problems we shall *all* face shortly" [p. 156].) For Gould and White, geographical science is an instrument for correcting the subjective bias that goes with place sense, not the instrument for deepening and enriching that subjectivity that I credit it with being in the cases discussed below.

55. Barry Lopez, *Arctic Dreams: Imagination and Desire in a Northern Landscape* (New York: Bantam, 1987), pp. 251, 238.

56. See Scott Slovic, *Seeking Awareness in American Nature Writing* (Salt Lake City: University of Utah Press, 1992), pp. 141–150, for a discussion of Lopez's attentiveness, over and beyond the customary procedures of the tradition of western travel writing to which *Arctic Dreams* broadly speaking belongs.

57. Lopez, *Arctic Dreams,* p. 180. In this regard, see also Lopez's essay "Renegotiating the Contracts," *Parabola* (Spring 1983), reprinted in *This Incomperable Lande: A Book of American Nature Writing,* ed. Thomas J. Lyon (Boston: Houghton Mifflin, 1989; rpt. New York: Penguin, 1991), pp. 381–388, as well as his book *Of Wolves and Men* (New York: Scribner's, 1978).

58. Lopez, *Arctic Dreams,* p. 258. Tuan, interestingly, uses the same example of near-correspondence between Eskimo and western maps to argue for the ethnocentricity of the former on the basis of the slight distortions of the home range (*Topophilia,* pp. 34–35).

59. Hugh Brody, *Maps and Dreams: Indians and the British Columbia Frontier* (Vancouver: Douglas and McIntyre, 1981), pp. 256–270. See pp. 146–177 for Brody's analysis of the accuracy of the Indians' conventional maps.

60. Lopez, *Arctic Dreams,* p. 261.

61. Ibid., p. 255.

62. Least Heat Moon, *PrairyErth,* pp. 363, 364.

63. Neither Lopez nor Least Heat Moon deals much with Native American modification of landscape in the manner of, say, William Cronon's environmental history of the Indian dispensation in New England, *Changes in the Land* (New York: Hill and Wang, 1983).

64. Least Heat Moon, *PrairyErth,* p. 598.

65. Ibid., pp. 93, 96.

66. Robert F. Stowell, in *A Thoreau Gazetteer,* ed. William L. Howarth (Princeton: Princeton University Press, 1970), prints several of Thoreau's maps, ventures a number of reflections on the relation of cartography to Thoreau's writing, and takes note of Thoreau's mixed feelings on the subject. Late in life Thoreau expressed the fear, for example, that having surveyed Walden Woods "so exten-

sively and minutely that I now see it mapped in my mind's eye . . . as so many men's wood lots," "it will not be easy to see so much wildness and native vigor there as formerly" (*J* 10: 233, noted by Stowell, p. ix).

67. Emerson, *Nature, Addresses, and Lectures*, p. 21.

68. Charles Anderson, *The Magic Circle of Walden* (New York: Holt, 1968), p. 274.

69. For sensitive discussion of this aspect of Thoreau's thought, see H. Daniel Peck, *Thoreau's Morning Work* (New Haven: Yale University Press, 1990), especially Chapter 4, "The Categorical Imagination" (pp. 79–114).

70. See in this regard Walter Benn Michaels, "*Walden*'s False Bottoms," *Glyph* 1 (1977): 132–149, which emphasizes the book's indeterminacy; and the reply by Joseph Allen Boone, "Delving and Diving for Truth: Breaking through to Bottom in Thoreau's *Walden*," *ESQ*, 27 (1981): 135–146, which redescribes the book's project as a confident, affirmative penetration of surface, both literal and figurative. Both essays are reprinted in *Critical Essays on Henry David Thoreau's Walden*, ed. Joel Myerson (Boston: Hall, 1988).

71. Wendell Berry, "Poetry and Place," in *Standing by Words* (San Francisco: North Point, 1983), p. 179.

72. Thomas Nagel, *The View from Nowhere* (New York: Oxford University Press, 1986), p. 63.

73. See note 9 above.

9. Environmental Apocalypticism

1. Most of these metaphors are noted and dealt with at least to a limited extent in Clarence J. Glacken's magisterial *Traces on the Rhodian Shore: Nature and Culture in Western Thought from Ancient Times to the End of the Eighteenth Century* (Berkeley: University of California Press, 1967). For a short study of the pervasiveness and influence of selected metaphors, see William J. Mills, "Metaphorical Vision: Changes in Western Attitudes to the Environment," *Annals of the Association of American Geographers*, 72 (1982): 237–253.

2. On this point, see Robert M. Young, *Darwin's Metaphor: Nature's Place in Victorian Culture* (Cambridge, Eng.: Cambridge University Press, 1985), especially "Darwin's Metaphor: Does Nature Select?" pp. 79–125. Young notes (p. 110) that "while Darwin grew increasingly unsympathetic to attempts to couple natural selection with a conception of design, it was Darwin's language which had given his interpreters a warrant for their views on designed evolution." For further reflections on Darwin's indecisiveness and its consequences for intellectual history, see David Kuhn, "Darwin's Ambiguity: The Secularization of Biological Meaning," *British Journal for the History of Science*, 22 (1989): 215–239.

3. For Thoreau on economy, see particularly Leonard Neufeldt's *The Econo-*

mist: *Henry Thoreau and Enterprise* (New York: Oxford University Press, 1989), an excellent study of *Walden* in relation to nineteenth-century economic discourse. Neufeldt emphasizes the instability of Thoreau's formulations but does not approach *Walden* as a text that alters its purpose and emphases in a major way as it unfolds.

4. Donald Worster, *Nature's Economy: The Roots of Ecology* (1977; rpt. Garden City, N.Y.: Doubleday, 1979), especially Parts I and V.

5. Thus, for example, "web" and "system" metaphors can easily be intermeshed in scientific writing; e.g. Lawrence E. Gilbert, "Food Web Organization and Conservation of Neotropical Diversity," in *Conservation Biology: An Evolutionary-Ecological Perspective*, ed. Michael E. Soulé and Bruce A. Wilcox (Sunderland, Mass.: Sinauer, 1980), pp. 11–33. What makes an example like this essay more interesting than many of the endless others that could have been cited is that it adopts conventional scientific "rhetoric of distance" (M. Jimmie Killingsworth and Jacqueline S. Palmer, *Ecospeak: Rhetoric and Environmental Politics in America* [Carbondale: Southern Illinois University Press, 1992], pp. 103ff.) notwithstanding the presentation of the volume as a whole in a context of ecological advocacy ("Foreword" by Thomas E. Lovejoy of the World Wildlife Fund, pp. ix–x). Conversely, the metaphor of "system" may be invoked in such a way as to subserve organicist holism, as in the declaration of the late Chico Mendes's Alliance of the Peoples of the [Amazonian] Forest, which "embraces all efforts to protect and preserve this immense, but fragile life-system that involves our forests, lakes, rivers and springs, the source of our wealth and the basis of our cultures and traditions" (*Fight for the Forest: Chico Mendes in His Own Words*, with Tony Gross [London: Latin American Bureau, 1989], p. 85).

6. See for example Raymond Williams, *Culture and Society* (New York: Oxford University Press, 1973), pp. 138, 258–259, 263–264.

7. Quoted in Worster, *Nature's Economy*, p. 50.

8. Darwin, *On the Origin of Species: A Facsimile of the First Edition*, intro. Ernst Mayr (Cambridge: Harvard University Press, 1964), p. 73. (Darwin retained this phraseology through the final [sixth] edition.) Commentators actually attach undue emphasis to "Darwin's 'web of life'" (cf. Glacken, *Traces on the Rhodian Shore*, p. 427) in light of his own preference for the image of the tree (*Origin*, p. 126).

9. Carson, *Silent Spring* (Boston: Houghton Mifflin, 1962), p. 56.

10. Wendell Berry, "The Body and the Earth," in *The Unsettling of America* (San Francisco: Sierra Club, 1977), p. 110. Cf. Gaston Bachelard, *The Poetics of Space*, trans. Maria Jolas (1958; rpt. Boston: Beacon, 1964), p. 103.

11. Carson, *Silent Spring*, p. 189.

12. See, in the first instance, Chapter 9 of Arthur O. Lovejoy, *The Great Chain of Being* (Cambridge: Harvard University Press, 1936).

13. Worster, *Nature's Economy,* pp. 292ff.; Wendell Berry, "Two Economies," in *Home Economics* (San Francisco: North Point, 1987), pp. 54–75.

14. Young, *Darwin's Metaphor,* p. 95.

15. On the continuum from Darwin to modern genetics, see for example Peter J. Bowler, *Evolution: The History of an Idea* (Berkeley: University of California Press, 1984), pp. 190–196. On the other side of the argument, Jeremy Rifkin's provocative *Algeny* (New York: Viking, 1983) emphasizes the sharp break between the Victorian dispensation of natural selection (which Rifkin sees as reflecting and legitimating laissez-faire economics and social Darwinism) and the modernist dispensation of genetic engineering ("algeny," derived from alchemy, is Rifkin's metaphor for the biotechnological vision); but even Rifkin stresses Darwin's fascination with artificial breeding (pp. 76–77).

16. Jonathan Schell, *The Fate of the Earth* (New York: Knopf, 1982), p. 109.

17. Bill McKibben, *The End of Nature* (New York: Random House, 1989), p. 160.

18. Albert Gore, *Earth in the Balance: Ecology and the Human Spirit* (Boston: Houghton Mifflin, 1992), p. 36. Hence Gore's title ("in the balance") itself gestures toward the possibility of apocalypse.

19. Herman E. Daly, "The Steady-State Economy: Postmodern Alternative to Growthmania" (1988), quoted in Andrew McLaughlin, *Regarding Nature: Industrialism and Deep Ecology* (Albany: State University of New York Press, 1993), p. 218.

20. Quotation from Worster, *Nature's Economy,* p. 23. On the landmark importance of Carson's book in galvanizing radical environmentalism in America, see for example George Sessions, "The Deep Ecology Movement: A Review," *Environmental Ethics,* 11 (1987): 105; Victor B. Scheffer, *The Shaping of Environmentalism in America* (Seattle: University of Washington Press, 1991), pp. ix, 119–121; and Philip Shabecoff, *A Fierce Green Fire: The American Environmental Movement* (New York: Hill and Wang, 1993), pp. 107–110. "There are very few books that can be said to have changed the course of history, but this was one of them," environmental historian Linda J. Lear declares of *Silent Spring* in "Rachel Carson's *Silent Spring,*" *Environmental History Review,* 17, no. 2 (1993): 28. By contrast, while stressing Carson's catalytic impact, Shirley A. Briggs, in "Silent Spring: The View from 1990," *Ecologist,* 20, no. 2 (March/April 1990): 54–60, points out how little long-term effect the book has had in controlling the pesticide industry.

21. Here and below, the text to which I refer is Leslie Marmon Silko, *Ceremony* (New York: Viking, 1977).

22. The court of first resort for precontemporary versions of Laguna mythography is Franz Boas, "Keresan Texts," *Publications of the American Ethnological Society,* 8, no. 1 (1928), but it is in need of supplementing by the other sources

it cites on pp. 227–228. In the process of trying to explain the Laguna myth of origins Boas includes an index of the many extant accounts. Not every account characterizes the creator as Spiderwoman, perhaps for the reason given by Anthony Purley in note 27 below. "Keresan Texts" includes versions of all the mythic stories used in *Ceremony*, such as the purification of the town by hummingbird, fly, buzzard, and caterpillar, and Sun Man's defeat of the gambler. For interpretation of how traditional Spiderwoman narratives figure in *Ceremony*, see especially the two articles by Edith Swan listed in note 24.

23. Silko to James Wright, 1 November 1978, in Silko and Wright, *The Delicacy and Strength of Lace*, ed. Anne Wright (St. Paul: Greywolf, 1986), p. 28. Silko was even more specific to Frederick Turner in an interview some years later, declaring that *Ceremony* "is as accurate as a map. . . Partly, this was because at the time I was writing it I was up in Alaska, and I was obsessive about the specifics of home" (Turner, "Leslie Marmon Silko's *Ceremony*," in *The Spirit of Place: The Making of an American Literary Landscape* [San Francisco: Sierra Club, 1989], p. 349). But see especially Silko, "Landscape, History, and the Pueblo Imagination," *Antaeus*, no. 57 (Autumn 1986): 83–94, for an extended essay on the symbiosis of detailed place sense and the narrative imagination among Laguna and other Pueblo peoples.

24. See particularly two articles by Edith Swan in *American Indian Quarterly*: "Laguna Symbolic Geography and Silko's *Ceremony*," 12 (1988): 229–249; and "Healing via the Sunwise Cycle in Silko's *Ceremony*," same volume, pp. 313–328. Claire R. Farrer takes exception to certain details, mainly ethnoastronomical, that do not in my opinion much affect the overall force of Swan's argument that Silko's environmental imagination reflects a highly sophisticated, indeed recondite, mythopoeic sense of place. For the Farrer-Swan exchange, see *American Indian Quarterly*, 14 (1990): 155–171.

25. In addition to Swan, "Laguna Symbolic Geography," Robert M. Nelson, "Place and Vision: The Function of Landscape in *Ceremony*," *Southwest Review*, 30 (1988): 281–316, is particularly helpful in identifying the place references in the novel and explaining the significance of why Silko has Tayo go where when.

26. E.g., Boas ("Keresan Texts," p. 7) records a story of the creation of whites by the Laguna I'tcts'ity'i (cf. *Ceremony*, p. 1), a substantiation of Betonie's astonishing claim, "we invented white people" (p. 132).

27. Quotation from Laguna scholar Anthony F. Purley, "Keres Pueblo Concepts of Deity," *American Indian Culture and Research*, 1, no. 1 (1974): 31. Purley, who stresses the creator's ability to transcend gender limits while remaining primarily female, comments further: "Some confusion is sometimes created concerning Tse che nako and Old Spider Woman, especially in secular discussions. Keres holy men hesitate to mention Tse che nako's name, especially for purely secular discussions; Thought Woman's name is reserved for use only in sacred ceremo-

nies. In secular discussions and teachings, Tse che nako is often symbolically referred to as Old Spider Woman or Spider Woman. As to the reason for the change, it is believed that only the holy men have the answer" (31).

28. Paula Gunn Allen, *The Sacred Hoop: Recovering the Feminine in American Indian Traditions* (Boston: Beacon, 1986), p. 11. See also Gunn's "The Feminine Landscape of Leslie Marmon Silko's *Ceremony,*" in ibid., pp. 118–126. It should be added that for Gunn, and undoubtedly for many other Native American writers also, the world-web metaphor is a less important master metaphor than the medicine wheel—on which subject see pp. 54–75 of Gunn's collection.

29. Boas ("Keresan Texts," p. 221) notes that the transmutation of I'tc'ts'ity'i from female to male was "a new development due to Catholic influence." Interestingly, the one early informant to preserve this figure's female identity was Silko's grandmother, as reported in Elsie Clews Parsons, "Notes on Ceremonialism at Laguna," *Anthropological Papers of the American Museum of Natural History,* 19, no. 4 (1920): 114. In her autobiographical work *Storyteller* (New York: Seaver, 1981), Silko disparages the "tone-deaf" Boas and praises the story collecting of Parsons, "his talented protégé" (254).

30. For the cultural prototype of Tayo's progress, see Katherine Spencer, "Navajo Chantway Myths," *Memoirs of the American Folklore Society,* 48 (1957): 18–40; for discussion of Tayo's case, see Swan, "Healing via the Sunwise Cycle," and "Laguna Prototypes of Manhood," *Melus,* 17, no. 1 (1992): 39–61.

31. On Ts'eh, see Gunn, "Feminine Landscape," pp. 119–123; Swan, "Laguna Symbolic Geography," pp. 244–247; and Nelson, "Place and Vision," pp. 300–308.

32. Following Swan, "Laguna Symbolic Geography," pp. 240–241, and Kenneth Lincoln, *Native American Renaissance* (Berkeley: University of California Press, 1983), p. 241, I put Betonie's Mexican grandmother in the company of Ts'eh and Night Swan.

33. Silko's letters to James Wright (see note 23) are studded with allusions to Plato, Vermeer, Spinoza, Hume, Camus, etc.

34. See Boas, "Keresan Texts," pp. 82–89, 256.

35. On the arcane symbolism of the color yellow, several of Silko's commentators are precise. E.g., Swan states that "it conveys the Laguna notion of personhood as well as the identity of the clan name" ("Laguna Symbolic Geography," p. 239). Lincoln (*Native American Renaissance,* pp. 234–235) further associates yellow with land and identifies Ts'eh with the mythic figure of Yellow Woman, suggesting as possible bases for this linkage "the Pueblo goddess complex of Yellow woman" as a "mountain spirit with yellow face" and "the generic term for mythic heroines of Laguna stories." Swan, in a later article, emphasizes to an even greater degree yellow's status as a way of feminizing the land by virtue of its association with the mythical Yellow Woman and with Ts'eh, whom Swan sees as her avatar ("Feminine Perspectives at Laguna Pueblo: Silko's *Ceremony,*"

Tulsa Studies in Women's Literature, 11 [1992]: 317–324). Yet Laguna critic Allen, who discusses Yellow Woman tales most fully and identifies yellow as "the color for women" (*Sacred Hoop,* p. 226), refrains from linking Yellow Woman to Ts'eh or developing the color symbolism in *Ceremony* notwithstanding her emphasis on the course of Tayo's feminization. Silko herself, when responding to an interviewer's questions about yellow imagery in a later work, was reluctant to be pinned down: "It's a color connected with the East, and corn, and corn pollen, and dawn, and Yellow Woman . . . So I don't think we can go too far in a traditional direction, with what yellow means" (Laura Coltelli, *Winged Words: American Indian Writers Speak* [Lincoln: University of Nebraska Press, 1990], p. 142). By the same token it seems clear that yellow in Laguna thinking is a symbolically multivalent color with astronomical, agricultural, and feminine ceremonial resonances.

36. Leslie Marmon Silko, *Almanac of the Dead* (New York: Simon and Schuster, 1991), pp. 760, 570, 569. These sentiments are expressed as individual characters' thoughts, but the characters seem at these moments more or less to be masks for the implied author.

37. Of the several biographical studies of Carson, I have found especially helpful the one by her editor, Paul Brooks, *The House of Life: Rachel Carson at Work* (Boston: Houghton Mifflin, 1972), which includes generous excerpts from her writing; and H. Patricia Hynes, *The Recurring Silent Spring* (New York: Pergamon, 1989), a feminist study that places Carson's life and legacy in the context of the history of women's achievement in science and victimage by patriarchally controlled technology. Lear, "Rachel Carson's *Silent Spring,*" gives a succinct, biographically focused account of the book's background, genesis, and influence.

38. From Carson's admission essay to the Pennsylvania College for Women, quoted in Hynes, *Recurring Silent Spring,* p. 65.

39. From "Undersea," *Atlantic Monthly,* September 1937, quoted in Brooks, *House of Life,* p. 26.

40. Rachel Carson, *The Sea around Us* (New York: Oxford University Press, 1951), p. 15. Carson claimed, however, in a 1948 letter to her friend the naturalist-writer William Beebe that "man's dependence upon the ocean" and "my belief that we will become even more dependent upon the ocean as we destroy the land, are really the theme of the book" (quoted in Brooks, *House of Life,* p. 110). This notion surfaces most explicitly in Chapter 13, "Wealth from the Salt Seas." Yet as Hynes notes, "the preponderant purpose and effect of this work, like that of *The Edge of the Sea* after it and *Under the Sea Wind* before it, was not a worldly call to stop polluting the sea" but a celebration of the sea's mystery and beauty (*Recurring Silent Spring,* p. 35). Carson does, however, directly confront human exploitation in her chapter on islands.

41. Quoted in Hynes, *Recurring Silent Spring*, p. 181.

42. Carson, *Silent Spring*, p. 93. Subsequent page references are noted in the text.

43. Mary Douglas, *Purity and Danger: An Analysis of the Concepts of Pollution and Taboo* (1966; rpt. London: Routledge, 1991), especially Chapter 2, "Secular Defilement."

44. Carson *The Sea around Us*, p. 93.

45. Brooks, *House of Life*, p. 214.

46. Ralph H. Lutts, in "Chemical Fallout: Rachel Carson's *Silent Spring*, Radioactive Fallout, and the Environmental Movement," *Environmental Review*, 9 (1985): 211–225, argues convincingly that Carson crafted *Silent Spring* with a view to refocusing fears about nuclear disaster already in the public consciousness and that *Silent Spring* ought thus to be considered "one of the first and most eloquent of books bridging the gap between the environmental movement and this new fearful vision of Armageddon" (p. 223).

47. These images were evidently implanted in her own mind as well. Sometimes Carson's military metaphors seem to spring out of control and infect the author herself, as when she assures us that "the chemical barrage" is unnecessary because there is "a whole battery" of other "armaments" available, such as the device of using one species to control another (pp. 197, 196).

48. The aggressive development of genetic engineering since Carson's death might have dampened her enthusiasm for microbial insecticides (pp. 289ff.), which she defends on the ground that "in contrast to chemicals, insect pathogens are harmless to all but their intended targets" (p. 291).

49. Ulf Hannerz, "Cosmopolitans and Locals in World Culture," *Theory, Culture, and Society*, 7, nos. 2–3 (1990): 239.

50. For a review of pertinent trends in Global Studies scholarship, see Frederick Buell, *National Culture and the New Global System* (Baltimore: Johns Hopkins University Press, 1994).

51. McKibben, *The End of Nature*, p. 143.

52. Killingsworth and Palmer, *Ecospeak*, pp. 23–48. For specific discussion of Carson, see pp. 64–78. The authors credit *Silent Spring* with being "perhaps the most widely read and most controversial of all books on environmental legislation" (p. 64)—a typical verdict. For the scientific and political debates instigated by Carson's book, see Frank Graham, Jr., *Since Silent Spring* (Boston: Houghton Mifflin, 1970); for more on Carson's legacy and its opponents, see Hynes, *Recurring Silent Spring*; for a "strict construction" view of Carson's influence, appraising the inertial weight of institutional forces as much greater in the long run than Carson's intervention, see Christopher J. Bosso, *Pesticides and Politics: The Life Cycle of a Public Issue* (Pittsburgh: University of Pittsburgh Press, 1987), pp. 125–127, 132, 179.

53. Schell, *The Fate of the Earth,* p. 5.

54. Sacvan Bercovitch, *The American Jeremiad* (Madison: University of Wisconsin Press, 1978). Rob Wilson calls attention to another way, especially pertinent in the present context, whereby the imagery of apocalypse can also be given an "optimistic" turn, i.e., the celebration of national or technological power; see "Towards the Nuclear Sublime: Representations of Technological Vastness in Postnuclear America," the provocative final chapter of his *The American Sublime: The Genealogy of a Poetic Genre* (Madison: University of Wisconsin Press, 1991), pp. 228–263.

55. See John R. May, *Toward a New Earth: Apocalypse in the American Novel* (Notre Dame: University of Notre Dame Press, 1972); Douglas Robinson, *American Apocalypses: The Image of the End of the World in American Literature* (Baltimore: Johns Hopkins University Press, 1985); Joseph Dewey, *In a Dark Time: The Apocalyptic Temper in the American Novel of the Nuclear Age* (West Lafayette, Ind.: Purdue University Press, 1990). *The End of the World,* ed. Eric S. Rabkin, Martin H. Greenberg, and Joseph D. Olander, (Carbondale: Southern Illinois University Press, 1983) is also useful for the contemporary period. Dewey's introduction to *In a Dark Time,* pp. 17–44, provides a panoramic chronological overview.

56. Perry Miller, "The End of the World," in *Errand into the Wilderness* (Cambridge: Harvard University Press, 1956), p. 232. It is no coincidence that "catastrophism" as an explanation of geological history and the origin of species (divinely ordained global cataclysms and rebirths of life) also fell into disrepute in the nineteenth century.

57. Theodore Dwight Bozeman, *To Live Ancient Lives* (Chapel Hill: University of North Carolina Press, 1988), pp. 311–343. It should be noted that Bozeman also argues persuasively that American Puritanism was not initially so millennial in its social vision as is commonly thought, although it became more so during and partially as a result of the British Civil War.

58. Ernest Tuveson, *Redeemer Nation: The Idea of America's Millennial Role* (Chicago: University of Chicago Press, 1968), p. 214. This monograph is especially useful for the early national and antebellum periods. On the politicization of millennial thought in pre-Revolutionary times, see for example Alan Heimert, *Religion and the American Mind* (Cambridge: Harvard University Press, 1966); Nathan O. Hatch, *The Sacred Cause of Liberty: Republican Thought and the Millennium in Revolutionary New England* (New Haven: Yale University Press, 1977); and Ruth Bloch, *Visionary Republic: Millennial Themes in American Thought, 1756–1800* (Cambridge, Eng.: Cambridge University Press, 1985).

59. James H. Moorhead, *American Apocalypse: Yankee Protestants and the Civil War, 1860–1869* (New Haven: Yale University Press, 1978), pp. 19, 38, the former

quotation taken from an anonymous 1859 article in the *American Theological Review*. Moorhead's is the fullest study of this subject.

60. Curtis Dahl, "The American School of Catastrophe," *American Quarterly*, 11 (1959): 380–390.

61. Paul Boyer, *When Time Shall Be No More: Prophecy Belief in Modern American Culture* (Cambridge: Harvard University Press, 1992), pp. 100–339. "In the early 1990s," Boyer asserts, "prophecy interest is surging to new heights," partly by virtue of the use evangelists have made of environmental degradation as a sign of the end times (pp. 325, 331–336). See also Michael Barkun, *Disaster and the Millennium* (New Haven: Yale University Press, 1974), and "Divided Apocalypse: Thinking about the End in Contemporary America," *Soundings*, 66 (1983): 257–280.

62. Mircea Eliade, *Cosmos and History*, trans. Willard R. Trask (New York: Harper and Row, 1959), p. 5.

63. Robinson, *American Apocalypses*, p. 250, n. 26.

64. On this point, see Eliade, *Cosmos and History*, pp. 112–127.

65. Robinson, *American Apocalypses*, p. 26. His fivefold taxonomy also includes these other apocalyptic modes: "biblical," "continuative" (no end at all, but "simple secular historical continuity"), "ethical" (apocalypse as a "figure for personal growth in ongoing history"), and "Romantic or visionary internalization of the fallen world by an act of imaginative incorporation, so that the world is revealed as the paradise it already is" (p. 26). For corroboration that in traditional mythical systems world cataclysm normally implies and leads to regeneration, see for example Bruce Lincoln, *Myth, Cosmos, and Society: Indo-European Themes of Creation and Destruction* (Cambridge: Harvard University Press, 1986), p. 138 and passim.

66. Sallie McFague, *Models of God: Theology for an Ecological, Nuclear Age* (Philadelphia: Fortress, 1987), p. 15.

67. Robinson, *American Apocalypses*, p. 229.

68. Here, however, I depart from Abbey scholarship, which while recognizing Abbey's humor tends to see it as less divided and more consistently the instrument of ecocritical satire (see Ann Ronald's discussion of *The Monkey Wrench Gang* in her *The New West of Edward Abbey* [Albuquerque: University of New Mexico Press, 1982], pp. 183ff).

69. Cecelia Tichi, *New World, New Earth: Environmental Reform in American Literature from the Puritans through Whitman* (New Haven: Yale University Press, 1979), traces, with special reference to literary sources, the force and decline of American visions of land transformation as they were energized by millennialist thinking in the Puritan and the Revolutionary eras and then called into question during the mid-nineteenth century as political disaffection with American insti-

tutions and aesthetic disaffection with industrialization took hold among intellectuals. (Tichi sees Walt Whitman as the last millennial transformationist.) Among the many histories of the rise of environmental protectionism that began to gather strength at about this same period, not the most scholarly but of special pertinence in this chapter's context for its emphasis on the apocalyptic urgency of the environmentalist cause is Shabecoff, *A Fierce Green Fire*.

70. See for example Roderick Nash, *Wilderness and the American Mind*, 3d ed. (New Haven: Yale University Press, 1982), pp. 105, 131, 194; and Shabecoff, *A Fierce Green Fire*, pp. 58–59.

71. Aldo Leopold, "Game and Wild Life Conservation," in *The River of the Mother of God and Other Essays*, ed. Susan L. Flader and J. Baird Callicott (Madison: University of Wisconsin Press, 1991), p. 166.

72. Aldo Leopold, "Adventures of a Conservation Commissioner," in *The River of the Mother of God*, pp. 334, 335.

73. Leopold, "The Ecological Conscience," in *The River of the Mother of God*, p. 345.

74. John Janovy, Jr., *Keith County Journal* (New York: St. Martin's, 1978), p. 13.

75. David Rains Wallace, *Idle Weeds: The Life of an Ohio Sandstone Ridge* (Columbus: Ohio State University Press, 1980), 164–169.

76. Ellery Channing, *Thoreau the Poet Naturalist*, rev. ed., ed. Franklin B. Sanborn (Boston: Goodspeed, 1902), p. 117–118.

77. Thoreau, *The Maine Woods*, ed. Joseph J. Moldenhauer (Princeton: Princeton University Press, 1972), pp. 153–155.

78. George Perkins Marsh, *Man and Nature; or, Physical Geography as Modified by Human Action*, ed. David Lowenthal (Cambridge: Harvard University Press, 1965), pp. 279, 280.

79. However, Tichi, *New World, New Earth*, pp. 218–220, does right to emphasize that Marsh belonged ultimately to the tranformationist tradition, that he was "at base . . . optimistic in his belief that man can engineer the New Earth after all" (p. 220).

80. Marsh told Harvard botanist Asa Gray that his early Vermont experience of "having been personally engaged to a considerable extent in clearing lands, and manufacturing and dealing in lumber" gave him "occasion both to observe and to feel the effects resulting from an injudicious system of managing woodlands and the products of the forest'" (quoted in Lowenthal's editorial introduction to *Man and Nature*, p. xviii).

81. Stephen D. O'Leary, *Arguing the Apocalypse: A Theory of Millennial Rhetoric* (New York: Oxford University Press, 1994), pp. 20–60.

82. Marsh, *Man and Nature*, p. 280.

83. Logan Reavis, quoted in William Cronon, *Nature's Metropolis: Chicago and the Great West* (New York: Norton, 1991), pp. 42–43. This study of the founding

of Chicago is the best single case history of premodern American attitudes toward environmental development in action.

84. Perhaps the third ingredient is most crucial, at least perceptually and rhetorically. Silko's climactic passage in *Ceremony* suggests this. Likewise, Michael Barkun concludes that "modern [envisionment of world] disaster is an artifact of interdependence. Where men are no longer able to encapsulate themselves in isolated communities, bad times, no less than good ones, soon become common property," especially when mass media make it possible for disaster to be "communicated almost instaneously to areas remote from the original source of stress" (*Disaster and the Millennium,* pp. 204, 205).

10. The Thoreauvian Pilgrimage

1. A striking case is reported by Chip Brown, "I Now Walk into the Wild," *New Yorker,* 8 February 1993, 36–47.

2. See Chapter 12 for further discussion of the promise of biographical imaging in reading Thoreau. Although I do not deal there with Thoreau's sexuality, I easily could have. The available biographical evidence strongly suggests that Thoreau responded more strongly to male than to female beauty, though apparently he was not active homosexually; see Walter Harding, "Thoreau's Sexuality," *Journal of Homosexuality,* 21, no. 3 (1991): 23–45. Gay criticism has begun to appraise how Thoreau's texts may have been shaped by the obliquities to which he would thereby have been led. Michael Warner, for example, sees *Walden*'s "organizing problematic" as "Thoreau's scene of reflective desire," manifested in such diverse ways as self-dissolution, narcissism, mirror imagery, and pond-bottom-sounding ("Thoreau's Bottom," *Raritan,* 11 [1992]: 67). Although I find some of Warner's inferences improbable, and although in general (am I showing my age?) sexual desire seems to me to have been a less central motive in Thoreau's life than Warner's essay suggests, I find it entirely plausible that Thoreau's environmental precocity was facilitated by the transfer of passion for a partner too close to oneself to the safer surrogate of the nonhuman otherworld. Some may consider this simply a polite way of saying that Thoreau was a misfit, or that *Walden* is a "perverse" book, or that there is something "queer" about ecocentrism. Such reductionisms are absurd. One ought to expect an extraordinary individual like Thoreau and an extraordinary book like *Walden* to comprise many strands and also to expect some of these to set both author and book at odds with "normality"; otherwise, nothing extraordinary would have been produced. On this point, see also Henry Abelove, "From Thoreau to Queer Politics," *Yale Journal of Criticism,* 6, no. 2 (1993): 17–28.

3. Lynn White, "Dynamo and Virgin Reconsidered," in *Machina ex Deo* (Cambridge: MIT Press, 1968), p. 57.

4. Jonathan Yardley, "Ten Books That Shaped the American Character," *American Heritage*, April/May 1985, 24.

5. Thomas D. Austin, "Thoreau, the First Hippie," *Ankh*, 1, no. 4 (Spring 1968): 12–21; Shirley Cochell, "Thoreau: A Man for Our Times," *Senior Scholastic*, 92 (15 February 1968): 9–10; *Thoreau Society Bulletin*, 110 (Winter 1970): 4; Stewart L. Udall, *The Quiet Crisis* (New York: Holt, 1963), p. 51; E. Merrill Root, "Henry Thoreau: Upon Finding a Fish in the Milk," *American Opinion*, 15 (February 1973): 19.

6. *Thoreau Society Bulletin*, 106 (Winter 1968): 5; 113 (Fall 1970): 6; 114 (Winter 1971): 5, 7; 119 (Spring 1972): 5; 122 (Winter 1972): 8; 126 (Winter 1974): 7. This is a tiny sampling of the Thoreauviana reported in the *Bulletin*, which makes it clear that by the 1960s, if not earlier, Thoreau and Walden were American household words, whatever the depth of knowledge underlying their use.

7. The proceedings have been published in part as *Thoreau's World and Ours: A Natural Legacy*, ed. Edmund A. Schofield and Robert C. Baron (Golden, Colo.: North American Press, 1993).

8. *Thoreau Society Bulletin*, 5 (September 1943).

9. A fascinating corroborating discussion, written however from an antiautobiographicalist view that opposes my underlying position here, is poet-critic Robert Pack's discussion of an incident when a woman who attended one of his readings told him that she felt betrayed when he afterward confessed that the narrative in a poem that especially moved her was invented, not lived. Pack then reports his students' consternation when he asked them whether they thought his story about the poetry reading was itself a fiction ("Lyric Narration: The Chameleon Poet," in *Affirming Limits* [Amherst: University of Massachusetts Press, 1985], pp. 23–40).

10. John Muir to Helen Muir, 9 June 1893, John Muir Papers, University of the Pacific, Stockton, Calif., hereafter abbreviated as JMP. This and other Muir manuscripts cited in this chapter I have examined in the Chadwyck-Healey comprehensive microfilm edition of Muir's papers. For an index, see *The Guide and Index to the Microform Editions of the John Muir Papers, 1858–1957*, ed. Ronald Limbaugh and Kirsten E. Lewis (Alexandria, Va.: Chadwyck-Healey, 1986).

11. John Muir to Louie Stanzel Muir, 12–13 June 1893, in *The Life and Letters of John Muir*, ed. William Fredric Badè (Boston: Houghton Mifflin, 1924), 2: 266–268.

12. John Muir to Wanda Muir, 14 June 1893 and 20 June 1893, John Muir Papers, quotation from the latter.

13. *Life and Letters of John Muir*, 2: 269.

14. *Life and Letters of John Muir*, 1: 259–260 (for Emerson's 5 February 1872 letter to Muir); *The Letters of Ralph Waldo Emerson*, ed. Ralph L. Rusk (New York: Columbia University Press, 1939), 6: 202 (for Muir's 18 March 1872 letter to

Emerson). For the most detailed accounts of the Muir-Emerson encounter from Emerson's perspective, see James Bradley Thayer, *A Western Journey with Mr. Emerson* (Boston: Little, Brown, 1884); and John McAleer, *Ralph Waldo Emerson: Days of Encounter* (Boston: Little, Brown, 1984), pp. 601–608. From Muir's perspective, see Muir, "The Forests of the Yosemite Park," *Our National Parks* (Boston: Houghton, Mifflin, 1901), pp. 131–136, and Linnie Marsh Wolfe, *Son of the Wilderness: The Life of John Muir* (New York: Knopf, 1945), pp. 145–151.

15. Muir to Robert U. Johnson, 3 June 1896, Robert U. Johnson Papers, Bancroft Library, University of California.

16. On the sacrality of the New England town as structure and as tradition, see for example John R. Stilgoe, *Common Landscape of America, 1580–1845* (New Haven: Yale University Press, 1982), pp. 56–58; Perry Westbrook, *The New England Town in Fact and Fiction* (Rutherford, N.J.: Fairleigh Dickinson University Press, 1982); Lawrence Buell, *New England Literary Culture: From Revolution through Renaissance* (Cambridge, Eng.: Cambridge University Press, 1986), pp. 283–318; and Belden C. Lane, *Landscapes of the Sacred: Geography and Narrative in American Spirituality* (New York: Paulist Press, 1988), pp. 103–124. On the rise of touristic pilgrimages, see John F. Sears, *Sacred Places: American Tourist Attractions in the Nineteenth Century* (New York: Oxford University Press, 1989).

17. John McWilliams's discussion of the memorialization of the events of 19 April 1775 during the century following, "Lexington, Concord, and the 'Hinge of the Future,'" *American Literary History*, 5 (1993): 1–29, gives an excellent sense of how the town of Concord became luminous in American public memory even before Thoreau's birth, as reflected in a series of important historical and literary works. See also the introduction to and final section of Edward Jarvis, *Traditions and Reminiscences of Concord, Massachusetts, 1779–1878*, ed. Sarah Chapin, intro. Robert A. Gross (Amherst: University of Massachusetts Press, 1993), pp. xv–xix, 222–232.

18. Victor Turner and Edith Turner, *Image and Pilgrimage in Christian Culture* (New York: Columbia University Press, 1978), pp. 9, 10, 11, 248. The title belies the fact that the Turners frequently discuss Christian pilgrimage with reference to diverse other regional and world religions. Sears, *Sacred Places*, pp. 5–6, 23, also invokes the Turners' model for explaining the allure of such tourist sites as Niagara Falls, Mammoth Cave, and Yosemite, understandably with more hesitation than I do with regard to the Walden pilgrimage given the emphasis Sears puts on the commercial entrepreneurialism and appeal to consumerism of the emerging tourist industry.

19. Kate Tryon, "A Day Afield," reprinted *New England Writers and the Press*, ed. Kenneth W. Cameron (Hartford: Transcendental Books, 1980), pp. 255–256; Philip Hubert, Jr., "At Thoreau's Pond," *Book Buyer*, 14 (1897): 550.

20. John Muir to Louie Stenzel Muir, 12–13 June 1893, in *Life and Letters of*

John Muir, 2: 268. For a contemporary urbanite's response to Walden, see Grant Allen, *Fortnightly Review*, 49 (1888): 675, which describes Walden as "a placid tarn embowered in drapery of shelving woods, and looking still as pure and untouched in every detail as when it came fresh from the hands of Nature." This was Allen's first glimpse, out the train window. On closer inspection, he noted "a gentleman's country house" overlooking the pond and was gratified by this echo of English taste; but the pond itself still impressed him as a "wild and beautiful prospect" (p. 684).

21. Henry Beers, "A Pilgrim in Concord," in *Four Americans* (New Haven: Yale University Press, 1919), p. 77; Lee Barber, "Walden—They Come in All Seasons, for All Reasons," *Concord Journal*, 1 December 1977, suppl. pp. 1, 5 (statistics for 1976 and 1977).

22. Edwin Way Teale, "Wildlife at Walden," in *The Lost Woods* (New York: Dodd, Mead, 1945), p. 273; H. D. Crawford, "Thoreau Country," *American Forests*, 75 (November 1969): 21; Caskie Stinnett, "It Wasn't as Easy as It Seemed," *Atlantic Monthly*, 243 (1979): 30.

23. See Brian Donahue, "Henry David Thoreau and the Environment of Concord," in *Thoreau's World and Ours*, pp. 181–182.

24. For the record of an early pilgrimage, in 1860, see William Dean Howells, "My First Visit to New England," *Harper's Monthly*, 89 (1894): 441–451.

25. Quotations from *Souvenir of Concord, Mass.* (Concord: Henry J. Walcott, Jr., 1895); *Concord in History and in Literature: A Tourist's Guide* (Concord: Albert Lane, [1903?]), pp. 40–45; Henry James, *The American Scene* (1907) ed. Leon Edel (Bloomington: Indiana University Press, 1968), pp. 264–265. Note, however, that the most popular late nineteenth-century Concord guidebook, George B. Bartlett's *The Concord Guide Book* (Boston: D. Lothrop, 1880), which went through at least eleven editions by 1885, put in a strong plug for Walden Pond, which was described under the heading "Thoreau's Home" (p. 63).

26. S. A. Jones to A. W. Hosmer, 18 December 1896, in *Toward the Making of Thoreau's Modern Reputation*, ed. Fritz Oehlschlaeger and George Hendrick, (Urbana: University of Illinois Press, 1979), p. 270; Franklin Benjamin Sanborn, "Thoreau and Emerson," *Forum*, 23 (April 1897): 218–227; Hubert, "At Thoreau's Pond," p. 522; Thomas Wentworth Higginson, "Henry David Thoreau," in *American Prose*, ed. George Rice Carpenter (New York: Macmillan, 1898), p. 340; Beers, "Pilgrim in Concord," p. 78. For the timber and the hatpins, see reprints in *Thoreau Society Bulletin*, 152 (Summer 1980): 7.

27. The best appraisal of the influences of Emerson and Thoreau on Burroughs is Perry Westbrook, *John Burroughs* (New York: Twayne, 1974), pp. 50–55, 57–63.

28. Muir's debts to Emerson and Thoreau have been variously appraised. Muir's admiration for Emerson is stressed by Frederick Turner, *Rediscovering*

America: John Muir in His Time and Ours (San Francisco: Sierra Club, 1985), pp. 213, 216–218. Stephen Fox, by contrast, stresses Muir's critical second thoughts about Emerson, quoting the negative comments in Muir's marginalia in his copies of Emerson, which Turner sees as confirming evidence of Muir's respect: *The American Conservation Movement: John Muir and His Legacy* (Madison: University of Wisconsin Press, 1985), pp. 6–7. In any case it is clear that the young Muir saw Emerson as a hero, whatever his second thoughts, before he saw Thoreau as one. Muir almost surely did not read *Walden* until the year after he met Emerson (Fox, *American Conservation Movement,* p. 83), although he had perused *The Maine Woods* as early as 1870 (*Life and Letters of John Muir* 1: 223). By the mid-1870s, Muir's style began at times to echo Thoreau's markedly. Noting Muir's absorption of the rhetoric of "Walking" in particular (cf. Muir's "Wild Wool," collected in *Steep Trails,* ed. William Frederick Badè [Boston: Houghton Mifflin, 1918]), Michael Cohen argues that "this was the tradition of rhetoric which Muir took as his model" (*The Pathless Way: John Muir and American Wilderness* [Madison: University of Wisconsin Press, 1984], p. 140). Muir was too eclectic and unbookish, however, to be classified as Thoreau's clone. The most sustained argument for Muir's discipleship, Richard Fleck's essay "Muir's Homage to Thoreau," demonstrates that Muir read Thoreau attentively and enthusiastically, but not that Thoreau was a fundamental formative influence: *Henry Thoreau and John Muir among the Indians* (Hamden, Conn.: Archon, 1985), pp. 22–27.

29. At the turn of the nineteenth century the indefatigable regional traveler Timothy Dwight, who never mentioned Walden Pond, declared that "from the plains of Concord will henceforth be dated a change in human affairs" (*Travels in New-England and New-York,* ed. Barbara Miller Solomon [Cambridge: Harvard University Press, 1969], 1: 280). This unshakable faith in the centrality of the Concord battle to the historical and spiritual landscape of Concord is reflected in Emerson's "Concord Hymn" and again in Thoreau's *A Week* but parodied in *Walden*'s dismissal of Fourth of July celebrations (*Wa* 160–161) and its mock-heroic account of the battle of the ants ("there is not the fight recorded in Concord history, at least, if in the history of America, that will bear a moment's comparison with this" [*Wa* 230]). Thoreau knew very well, as did Emerson when he saluted Concord's "embattled farmers" (with just a faint trace of condescension, however?) that "the fight in Concord history" was mythically the great exemplum of American military valor generally. Whereas *A Week* memorializes the Concord battle in a conventional way, *Walden* sets the tone for a counter-cultural definition of what counts as local sacred space.

30. With regard to nineteenth-century Concord's cosmopolitanization and its ambivalent relation to greater Boston, see Robert A. Gross, "Concord, Boston, and the Wider World: Transcendentalism and Urbanism," in *New Perspectives on Concord History,* ed. William M. Bailey et al. (Concord: Foundation for Humani-

ties and Public Policy, 1983), pp. 95–118, as well as Jarvis, *Traditions and Reminiscences of Concord*, pp. 141–142, 184–198, and Gross's introduction thereto. In the 1870s, according to Jarvis, trains stopped at Concord eighteen times daily in each direction.

31. Thomas Kean, "About a Visit to Boston and Concord," *Buffalo Courier*, 1869, in A. Bronson Alcott, "Autobiographical Collections," 1868–1871, p. 105 (Houghton Library, Harvard University, MS no. 59 M-307); "An Hour with a Philosopher," anon. 1868 newspaper clipping, in ibid., p. 47; "A Visit to Old Concord," 1870 unidentified newspaper article, reprinted in *Transcendental Log*, ed. Kenneth W. Cameron (Hartford: Transcendental Books, 1973), p. 232.

32. Kean, "About a Visit," p. 104; Thomas Lang, "Walden Pond," 1870 unidentified newspaper report, reprinted in *Transcendental Log*, p. 187; Edward King, "Rambles in Concord-I," 1869 *Springfield Republican* clipping, in Alcott "Autobiographical Collections," 1868–1871, p. 97; "A Visit to Old Concord," in *Transcendental Log*, p. 235; "Thoreau's Hermitage," clipping from *New York Evening Post*, 26 January 1877, reprinted in *Transcendental Log*, p. 296.

33. Wilson Flagg, *The Woods and By-Ways of New England* (Boston: Osgood, 1872), p. 392.

34. See for example Jeanne M. Zimmer, "A History of Thoreau's Hut and Hut Site," *ESQ*, 18 (1972): 134–140.

35. Hubert, "At Thoreau's Pond," p. 556.

36. Quotation from Winthrop Packard, *Literary Pilgrimages of a Naturalist* (Boston: Small, Maynard, 1911), p. 61. On contemporary attitudes I have revised my position a bit since receiving a number of letters both for and against swimming at Walden in the late twentieth century. The 1989 article version of this sentence read unequivocally: "Today the serious Thoreauvian considers swimming in Walden a form of pollution rather than a way of exorcising pollution." Several of my correspondents dispute this. But at the very least, Packard's attitude can no longer be taken as consensual. Thoreau himself, interestingly, acknowledged that "I myself have profaned Walden" (*Wa* 197).

37. "Clearly, the very substance and character of Walden are linked inextricably, in a cause-and-effect manner, to the characteristics of the Walden Ecosystem," declares ecologist Edmund A. Schofield, former president of the Thoreau Society; see "The Ecology of the Walden Woods," in *Thoreau's World and Ours*, p. 169. It is on this basis that the current campaign to save Walden Woods (by preventing projects by developers and purchasing tracts of land when possible) has been waged; see, for example, Don Henley's "Preface" to *Heaven Is under Our Feet*, ed. Henley and Dave Marsh (New York: Berkley, 1991), p. 13, which quotes Schofield approvingly. This remarkable volume, inspired by the founding by popular singer Don Henley of the preservationist Walden Woods Project in 1990, consists of thirty-three short testimonials from a mind-bogglingly diverse

group of politicians, Hollywood stars, singers, creative writers, professors, and environmental activists. A number of the contributors obviously know next to nothing about Thoreau, but academic Thoreauvians inclined to be disdainful of popular bandwagons are also in for some distinct surprises—e.g. Mike Farrell (pp. 121–123) and Gregory Peck (pp. 172–174).

38. Paul Tsongas, "Walden Our Living Heritage," in *Heaven Is under Our Feet,* p. 228.

39. Kenneth W. Cameron, "Thoreau's Disciple at Walden," *Emerson Society Quarterly,* 26 (1962): 34–45. See also Prentice Mulford, *The Swamp Angel* (Boston: Needham, 1888), which records a very similar, nearly contemporary experiment in hut building in the New Jersey Pine Barrens, in apparent innocence of Thoreau as a precedent.

40. Philip G. Hubert, Jr., *Liberty and a Living* (New York: Putnam's, 1889), pp. 171–190; Paul Elmer More, "A Hermit's Notes on Thoreau," *Atlantic Monthly,* 87 (1901): 857–864; Lewis Leary, "Walden Goes Wandering," *New England Quarterly,* 32 (1959): 3–30 (on Thoreau and van Eeden); Seymore L. Flaxman, "Thoreau and van Eeden," in *Thoreau Abroad,* ed. Eugene Timpe (Hamden, Conn.: Archon, 1971), pp. 61–69; Joseph Jones, "Thoreau in Australia," in *Thoreau Abroad,* pp. 186–192.

41. See for example *New England Quarterly,* 2 (1929): 694 (Van Wyck Brooks's review of Beston) and *San Francisco Chronicle,* 27 November 1949, p. 28 (review of Leopold by J. W. H., reprinted in *Book Review Digest, 1949,* p. 549). Two particular strategies often followed in Thoreauvian genealogy are tribute by imputation of sonship or daughtership and tribute by invidious comparison to the master. The first is illustrated by Curt Meine on Leopold: "By the late 1950s and early 1960s, Leopold was firmly established as a major figure in conservation history, philosophy, and practice, often mentioned in the same breath with Henry David Thoreau and John Muir" (*Aldo Leopold: His Life and Work* [Madison: University of Wisconsin Press, 1988], p. 525). The second can be seen in Edward B. Hinckley's comparative essay "Thoreau and Beston: Two Observers of Cape Cod," *New England Quarterly,* 4 (1931): 223: "Mr. Beston knew his Thoreau and has followed him in style, more or less, as he has followed him in subject; but in many respects he has surpassed his leader."

42. One of the striking features of *Heaven Is under Our Feet,* the volume of tributes assembled by Marsh and Henley, is how Thoreau's Walden experiment evokes a wide scattering of autobiographical reminiscences about places and episodes of pastoral retreat. See for example the contributions by James Earl Jones (pp. 40–41), Thomas McGuane (pp. 50–52), Jim Harrison (pp. 64–67), Paula Abdul (pp. 91–92), Bette Woody (pp. 124–125), Michael Dorris (pp. 154–156), Louise Erdrich (pp. 157–159), and Ed McMahon (p. 234: "In 1973, when I returned from military service, I visited my Walden Pond . . .").

43. Anne LaBastille reports, interestingly, that it was Beston, not Thoreau, who

inspired her first cabin-building experiment (cf. her *Woodswoman* [1976]); "I fell under the spell of *Walden* in my forties and it was Thoreau who inspired me to build a second tiny cabin." See her essay "Fishing in the Sky," in *New Essays on Walden*, ed. Robert F. Sayre (Cambridge, Eng.: Cambridge University Press, 1992), p. 58.

44. E. B. White, "Walden—1954," *Yale Review*, 44 (1954): 16–17.

45. Vena Angier and Bradford Angier, *At Home in the Woods: Living the Life of Thoreau Today* (New York: Sheridan House, 1951), p. 100.

46. Turner and Turner, *Image and Pilgrimage*, p. 18. The study of Thoreau that comes closest to a comprehensive discussion of Thoreau's Walden experience as a cultural archetype is Leo Marx's *The Machine in the Garden: Technology and the Pastoral Ideal in America* (New York: Oxford University Press, 1964), pp. 242–265.

47. Wallace Stegner, "Qualified Homage to Thoreau," in *Heaven Is under Our Feet*, p. 291. Stegner's contribution to this gathering is unique, however, in being astringent rather than encomiastic toward Thoreau.

48. Turner and Turner, *Image and Pilgrimage*, p. 6.

49. For a concise, suggestive treatment of ritual elements in *Walden*, see Reginald Cook, "Ancient Rites at *Walden*," *Emerson Society Quarterly*, 39 (1965): 52–56.

50. Thoreau, "Walking," in *Excursions and Poems*, ed. Bradford Torrey and Francis H. Allen (Boston: Houghton, Mifflin, 1906), pp. 205–206.

51. Emerson, *Journals and Miscellaneous Notebooks*, ed. William Gilman et al. (Cambridge: Harvard University Press, 1966–1982): 10, 344; Louisa May Alcott, "Thoreau's Flute," *Atlantic Monthly*, 12 (1863): 280–281; A. Bronson Alcott, sonnet 13 of *Sonnets and Canzonets* (Boston: Roberts, 1882); Edward C. Peple, Jr., "Thoreau and Donatello," *Thoreau Journal Quarterly*, 5 (1973): 22–25.

52. Bronson Alcott, *Concord Days* (Boston: Roberts, 1872), p. 14.

53. Frederick L. H. Willis, reported in *Alcott Memories* (1915), reprinted in *Thoreau: Man of Concord*, ed. Walter Harding (New York: Holt, 1960), p. 134.

54. Emerson, "Thoreau," in *The Complete Works of Ralph Waldo Emerson*, ed. Edward Waldo Emerson (Boston: Houghton, Mifflin, 1903–1904), 10: 472.

55. Ellery Channing, "Memorial Verses," in *Thoreau: The Poet-Naturalist* (Boston: Roberts, 1873), p. 329.

56. Emma Lazarus quoted in Frederick T. McGill, Jr., *Channing of Concord* (New Brunswick: Rutgers University Press, 1967), p. 169.

57. A. H. Japp, *Thoreau: His Life and Aims* (Boston: Osgood, 1877), pp. 1–14, 44–63; Moncure Conway, "Thoreau," *Fraser's Magazine*, 73 (1866): 462.

58. Joseph Wood Krutch, "Prologue" to *Great American Nature Writing*, ed. Krutch (New York: Sloane, 1950), pp. 5–6. Important concurrent essays by Krutch

are "Little Fishy Friend," *Nation*, 169 (8 October 1949): 350–351; and "A Kind of Pantheism," *Saturday Review*, 33 (10 June 1950): 7–8, 30–34. Krutch makes Thoreauvian respect and empathy for nature as humanity's equal the chief criterion for distinguishing the ethos of modern versus premodern nature writing.

59. In this respect, Krutch anticipates the influential albeit simplistic contemporary tradition of blaming Judeo-Christianity for technology's sins against the environment. The seminal indictment is Lynn White, "The Historical Roots of Our Ecologic Crisis," in *Machina ex Deo* (Cambridge: MIT Press, 1968), pp. 75–94. For a short discussion of the issue and the article, see Chapter 6, note 4 and related text.

60. Angier and Angier, *At Home in the Woods*, p. 251.

61. Jesse Jackson, "A Tribute to Henry David Thoreau," in *Heaven Is under Our Feet*, pp. 86, 87.

62. John Muir to David Muir (brother), 24 March 1870, in *Life and Letters of John Muir*, 1: 209.

63. For the pertinent evidence, see the correspondence during the years 1897–1899 between Muir and R. U. Johnson, W. H. Page, and C. S. Sargent, reels 9–10 of the microfilm edition of Muir's unpublished manuscripts. When Page relocated to Doubleday, Page, and Company, he unsuccessfully attempted to take Muir's business with him. Relations between the two remained cordial, but Page never succeeded in wheedling another major work from Muir.

64. *The Life and Letters of John Muir*, 2; 269.

65. James, *The American Scene*, p. 256.

66. Page to Muir, 1 September 1897, John Muir Papers.

67. See Warren S. Tryon, *Parnassus Corner: A Life of James T. Fields, Publisher to the Victorians* (Boston: Houghton Mifflin, 1963); Ellen B. Ballou, *The Building of the House: Houghton Mifflin's Formative Years* (Boston: Houghton Mifflin, 1970); Michael Winship, *American Literary Publishing in the Mid-Nineteenth Century: The Business of Ticknor and Fields* (Cambridge, Eng.: Cambridge University Press, 1995). Ellery Sedgwick, *A History of the Atlantic Monthly, 1857–1909* (Amherst: University of Massachusetts Press, 1994), pp. 245–273, provides an illuminating account of Page's success in recouping the fortunes of the *Atlantic* during his tenure as editor.

68. *Concord: A Few of the Things to Be Seen There* (Concord: Patriot Press, 1902), p. 3; *Concord: A Pilgrimage to the Historic and Literary Center of America* (Boston: Perry Walton, 1925), p. 11; Theodore F. Wolfe, *Literary Shrines: The Haunts of Some Famous American Authors* (Philadelphia: Lippincott, 1895), pp. 17–18; O. G. Seeley, *Views and Descriptive History of Lexington and Concord* (Lexington: Seeley, 1901), p. 50.

69. Albert Lane, *Concord Authors at Home* (Concord: Erudite Press, 1902),

p. 22; Charles Ferguson, *A Historical Sketch of the Town of Concord* (Concord: pvt., 1929), p. 21; *A Leaflet Guide to the Points of Interest in Historic Concord* (Concord: Concord Antiquarian Society, 1936).

70. See for example Frederick Turner's account of his visit in *Spirit of Place: The Making of an American Literary Landscape* (San Francisco: Sierra Club, 1989), pp. 45–52.

71. LaBastille, "Fishing in the Sky," pp. 55–56, 68–70.

72. William R. Jordan III, "The Ecology of Walden Woods," *Thoreau's World and Ours*, pp. 268, 270.

11. The Canonization and Recanonization of the Green Thoreau

1. George Orwell, "Reflections on Gandhi," in *A Collection of Essays* (Garden City, N.Y.: Doubleday: 1954), p. 177. On the contingent nature of literary reputation and evaluation, see Barbara Herrnstein Smith, *Contingencies of Value: Alternative Perspectives for Critical Theory* (Cambridge: Harvard University Press, 1988). Smith's intricate critique is itself critiqued with equal brilliance by John Guillory, *Cultural Capital: The Problem of Literary Canon Formation* (Chicago: University of Chicago Press, 1993), pp. 269–340, which historicizes her critique of canons as a phase within a modern discourse of autonomus aesthetic value that began to crystallize in Adam Smith's differential treatments of economics and aesthetics. Guillory's larger project is to deconstruct current critical debates over canonicity by calling attention to their characteristic neglect of the institutional forces that, as he sees it, shape the terms of those debates. From the standpoint of his argument, my treatment of Thoreauvian canonicity throughout this book and particularly in Chapters 10–12 seems exposed as a quixotic rearguard rescue attempt: to retrieve canonicity from a too narrow aestheticism by building most centrally around the case of a writer whom academia has long sanctioned as "great." For my own part, I take *Cultural Capital* as a metacritical superego, admonishing me of my inevitable duplicity as a maintainer of the pantheon I seek to redefine, though it treats canon debates more exclusively as instruments of pedagogical authority and focuses more on questions of aesthetic value than I do here. These restrictions of scope are valuable for the sake of dealing with the typical forms of self-interestedness manifested by literary academics as a body, but they do not enable one to reckon fully with the historical impact or potential cultural fertility of (some) actual canonical writers.

2. Gary Taylor, *Reinventing Shakespeare* (New York: Weidenfeld and Nicholson, 1989), p. 411. Two significant Americanist canonization studies that stress the politics of the process are Jane Tompkins, "Masterpiece Theater: The Politics of Hawthorne's Literary Reputation," in *Sensational Designs: The Cultural Work of American Fiction, 1790–1860* (New York: Oxford University Press, 1985); and

Lawrence H. Schwartz, *Creating Faulkner's Reputation: The Politics of Modern Literary Criticism* (Knoxville: University of Tennessee Press, 1988). The most comprehensive and circumspect study of an Anglo-American author is John Rodden, *The Politics of Literary Reputation: The Making and Claiming of "St. George" Orwell* (New York: Oxford University Press, 1989). A "political" reading that credits well-placed individuals and adept, well-timed interest groups with effecting canonization needs, however, to be pitted against broader examinations of the intersection of the text with pervasive cultural formations as well as against more concentrated textual readings that show how canonical texts give impetus to successor texts. An illuminating study of the former sort is Thomas F. Gossett, *Uncle Tom's Cabin and American Culture* (Dallas: Southern Methodist University Press, 1985); of the latter, Richard H. Brodhead, *The School of Hawthorne* (New York: Oxford University Press, 1986). My own view is that "politics," "culture," and "textual power" are interdependent forces that can neither be conflated under one head nor disentangled from each other. See note 7 below for previous studies of Thoreau's reputation.

3. On Thoreau's hostility to commodification, see Michael T. Gilmore, "*Walden* and the 'Curse of Trade,'" in *American Romanticism in the Marketplace* (Chicago: University of Chicago Press, 1985), pp. 35–51. For the history of Thoreau's ambivalent reactions to the marketplace, including the fullest available discussion of the Thoreau-Greeley and Thoreau-Fields relations, see Steven Fink, *Prophet in the Marketplace: Thoreau's Development as a Professional Writer* (Princeton: Princeton University Press, 1992). The services Greeley and Fields performed for Thoreau through their promotional networks are further dramatized by contemporary advertisements for and reviews of Thoreau's work. In this regard, see Bradley P. Dean and Gary Scharnhorst, "The Contemporary Reception of *Walden*," in *Studies in the American Renaissance, 1990,* ed. Joel Myerson (Charlottesville: University Press of Virginia, 1990), pp. 293–328, as well as Scharnhorst, *Henry David Thoreau: An Annotated Bibliography of Comment and Criticism before 1900* (New York: Garland, 1992).

4. An anonymous review in the *Chicago Evening Post* of Houghton, Mifflin's authoritative, twenty-volume 1906 edition of Thoreau's works (10 June 1907) concisely expressed the facts of the case: "Messrs. Houghton, Mifflin & Co. may be credited with something more than a commercial spirit in this enterprise, and the fine traditions of that house have never been better expressed than in this publication." My thanks to Michael Meyer for calling my attention to this review and to much else about the history of Thoreau's reputation.

5. Houghton, Osgood "Special Note to Postmasters," 1879, one-page printed circular, Houghton Mifflin Collection, Houghton Library, Harvard University, MS Am 2030 (236). Here and at a number of points below I have drawn on this valuable collection of printed and manuscript material.

6. George H. Mifflin to A. F. Houghton and O. R. Houghton, 8 April 1903, quoted in Ellen B. Ballou, *The Building of the House: Houghton Mifflin's Formative Years* (Boston: Houghton Mifflin, 1970), p. 489.

7. The following studies of Thoreau's reputation I have found especially helpful: Walter Harding and Michael Meyer, *The New Thoreau Handbook* (New York: New York University Press, 1980), pp. 202–224; *Toward the Making of Thoreau's Modern Reputation,* ed. Fritz Oehlschlaeger and George Hendrick (Urbana: University of Illinois Press, 1979), pp. 1–54; Michael Meyer, *Several More Lives to Live: Thoreau's Political Reputation in America* (Westport, Conn.: Greenwood, 1977); and *Thoreau Abroad,* ed. Eugene Timpe (Hamden, Conn.: Archon, 1971).

8. Bliss Perry, *And Gladly Teach* (Boston: Houghton Mifflin, 1935), p. 185. Late in life Perry reaffirmed that it was an uphill battle to persuade Houghton, Mifflin to publish both Thoreau's and Emerson's journals (Perry to Francis Allen, 7 June 1950, Concord Free Library).

9. George H. Mifflin to Albert F. Houghton, 6 April 1903, typescript copy, Houghton Library, Harvard University, MS Am 2030 (189).

10. Bliss Perry, *The American Spirit in Literature* (New Haven: Yale University Press, 1920), pp. 130–131, 130, 131–132, 137.

11. George H. Mifflin to A. F. Houghton and O. A. Houghton, 8 April 1903, typescript copy, Houghton Library, Harvard University, MS Am 2030 (189).

12. Bliss Perry to E. H. Russell, 9 April 1903 and 21 April 1903, Houghton Library, Harvard University, MS Am 2030 (217).

13. Houghton, Mifflin brochure for "Standard Library Series," 1895, Houghton Library, Harvard University, MS Am 2030 (242).

14. Houghton, Mifflin promotional brochure, c. 1888, Houghton Library, Harvard University, MS Am 2030 (238). The first titles in the series, issued five years earlier, had been Longfellow's *Evangeline* and *The Courtship of Miles Standish,* the dramatic rendition of *Courtship,* and Whittier's *Snowbound* and *Among the Hills.*

15. Emerson, "Thoreau," in *The Complete Works of Ralph Waldo Emerson,* ed. Edward Waldo Emerson (Boston: Houghton, Mifflin, 1903–1904), 10: 454. At the same time, it is clear that Thoreau's sponsors knew more than they were sometimes prepared to affirm. A good example was the literary naturalist Bradford Torrey, who relished the poet-naturalist side of Thoreau but also condescended to those who did not notice more than that. Torrey commended *Walden* in his 1897 edition (also by Houghton, Mifflin) as "a book for the individual soul against the world" (p. xxiv) and in his introduction to *The Journal of Henry David Thoreau* (Boston: Houghton, Mifflin, 1906) compared Thoreau to Jesus as a prophetic disrupter: "being a consistent idealist, he was of course an extremist, falling in that respect little behind the man out of Nazareth, whose hard sayings, by all accounts, were sometimes less acceptable than they might have been" (1:

xxxviii). Of course this apotheosis of Thoreau, while potentially scandalous, also guards itself through humor and by linking Thoreau with Christian truth. Another way Torrey halfway normalizes Thoreau in this introduction is by stressing that despite his crankiness Thoreau "was capable of a really human delight in familiar intercourse with his fellows" (xxviii).

16. Emerson, "Thoreau," in *Complete Works*, 10: 459.

17. The first four quotations are from book notices culled for Houghton, Mifflin scrapbooks or promotional brochures, Houghton Library, Harvard University, MS Am 2030 (236, 247, 242, 248); the last one is from an eight-page promotional piece advertising the 1906 edition of Thoreau's works, MS Am 2030 (246).

18. See Paul Brooks's account in *Two Park Street: A Publishing Memoir* (Boston: Houghton Mifflin, 1986), pp. 154–157. Tersely modest, it nevertheless indicates the major importance of his role. For a detailed glimpse of his professional relations with Carson, see Brooks's biography, *The House of Life: Rachel Carson at Work* (Boston: Houghton Mifflin, 1972). As for the commitment of individual editors to Thoreau's work, at least as impressive as any evidence as I have discussed above are the many minute revisions that Horace Scudder and Francis H. Allen made in the texts of the ten-volume Riverside Edition of Thoreau's works between 1894 and 1914, as revealed in Joseph J. Moldenhauer, "Textual Instability in the Riverside Edition of Thoreau," *Papers of the Bibliographical Society of America*, 85 (1991): 347–419. Moldenhauer is quite right in the claim he makes about the significance of this particular edition: "it is safe to say that vastly more readers have known Thoreau in the Riverside texts than in the texts of 1906" (p. 350).

19. I derive "official canon" from Alistair Fowler, "Genre and the Literary Canon," *New Literary History*, 11 (1979): 98–99, where it refers to the dominant institutionalized understanding of the canon of significant literature generally, rather than to the microlevel of an individual author's *oeuvre*. Fowler proposes "critical canon" to denote, as Wendell Harris usefully summarizes, "those works or parts of works that are repeatedly treated in critical articles and books" ("Canonicity," *PMLA*, 106 [1991]: 112); but this implies an academic sequestration of critical discussion not applicable to American literary studies until the 1920s.

20. William P. Trent, *A History of American Literature, 1607–1865* (New York: Appleton, 1903), p. 341.

21. Walter Harding, "The Early Printing Records of Thoreau's Books," *American Transcendental Quarterly*, 11 (1971): 44–59.

22. Charles F. Richardson, *American Literature, 1607–1885* (New York: Putnam's, 1886), 1: 288; Fred Lewis Pattee, *A History of American Literature* (New York: Silver, Burdett, 1899), p. 225; Barrett Wendell, *A Literary History of America* (New York: Scribner's, 1900), pp. 334–335.

23. John Nichol, *American Literature: An Historical Sketch, 1629–1880* (Edinburgh: Adam and Charles Black, 1882), p. 319; Julian Hawthorne and Leonard Lemmon, *American Literature: An Elementary Text-Book for Use in High Schools and Academies* (Boston: Heath, 1892), p. 150; John Beers, *An Outline Sketch of American Literature* (New York: Hunt and Eaton, 1893), p. 144; Pattee, *A History of American Literature*, p. 227; Katherine Lee Bates, *American Literature* (New York: Macmillan, 1898), p. 265.

24. For a social history of late nineteenth-century American naturism, the best survey, though excessively condescending in tone, is Peter J. Schmitt, *Back to Nature: The Arcadian Myth in Urban America* (New York: Oxford University Press, 1969). See also Chapters 7–10 of Roderick Nash, *Wilderness and the American Mind*, 3d ed. (New Haven: Yale University Press, 1982). For additional aesthetic ramifications, see John Stilgoe, *Borderland: Origins of the American Suburb, 1820–1939* (New Haven: Yale University Press, 1988). On turn-of-the-century antimodernism, see T. J. Jackson Lears, *No Place of Grace: Antimodernism and the Transformation of American Culture, 1880–1920* (New York: Pantheon, 1981).

25. Joseph Jackson, *Through Glade and Mead: A Contribution to Local Natural History* (Worcester, Mass.: Putnam Davis, 1894), pp. 18, 187.

26. F. O. Matthiessen, *American Renaissance* (New York: Oxford University Press, 1941), pp. 166–175.

27. James Russell Lowell, "Thoreau," *North American Review*, 101 (1865): 597–608.

28. Thomas Wentworth Higginson and Henry Walcott Boynton, *A Reader's History of American Literature* (Boston: Houghton, Mifflin, 1903), pp. 193–195. For an overview of Higginson's relationship with and advocacy of Thoreau, see Edgar McCormick, "Thoreau and Higginson," *Emerson Society Quarterly*, 31 (1963): 75–78.

29. John Macy, *The Spirit of American Literature* (Garden City, N.Y.: Doubleday, 1913), pp. 183, 172, 173, 183.

30. Cf. Emma Goldman, *Anarchism and Other Essays* (New York: Mother Earth, 1917), pp. 56–57. The essay seemingly dates from 1910. America's leading turn-of-the-century anarchist magazine, *Liberty*, called "Civil Disobedience" an "anarchist classic" as early as 1907 (vol. 16, no. 6, p. 1). Interestingly, however, *Liberty* took much more interest in Emerson and Whitman than it did in Thoreau—further evidence, perhaps, of the difference between early American and early Anglo-European readings of the overall importance of his social thought.

31. Nina Baym, "Early Histories of American Literature: A Chapter in the Institution of New England," *American Literary History*, 1 (1989): 470–471.

32. For discussion of Macy's career and the significance of *Spirit*, see Howard Mumford Jones, *Theory of American Literature*, rev. ed. (Ithaca: Cornell Univer-

sity Press, 1965), pp. 119–120; Richard Ruland, *The Rediscovery of American Literature* (Cambridge: Harvard University Press, 1967), p. 3; Jay B. Hubbell, *Who Are the Major American Writers?* (Durham: Duke University Press, 1972), pp. 110–111; and Kermit Vanderbilt, *American Literature and the Academy* (Philadelphia: University of Pennsylvania Press, 1986), pp. 201–205.

33. The rise of the conception of what I am calling an oppositional canon, starting with Macy, is discussed in Jones, *Theory of American Literature*, pp. 118–150. Gerald Graff connects this movement with the somewhat later rise of American literature as a scholarly profession, in *Professing Literature* (Chicago: University of Chicago Press, 1987), pp. 213–216. Thomas Bender's *New York Intellect* (Baltimore: Johns Hopkins University Press, 1987), pp. 206–252, is a valuable discussion of the turn from intellectual conservatism to radicalism. Chapter 1 of James Burkhart Gilbert, *Writers and Partisans: A History of Literary Radicalism in America* (New York: John Wiley, 1968), pp. 8–47; Edward Abrahams, *The Lyrical Left and the Origins of Cultural Radicalism in America* (Charlottesville: University Press of Virginia, 1986), pp. 1–20; and Casey Nelson Blake, *Beloved Community* (Chapel Hill: University of North Carolina Press, 1990) all shed light on the relationship between social and aesthetic radicalism during these prewar years.

34. Meyer, *Several More Lives to Live*, p. 20.

35. Van Wyck Brooks, *An Autobiography* (New York: Dutton, 1965), pp. 46, 328–329.

36. Waldo Frank, *Our America* (New York: Boni and Liveright, 1919), pp. 151–152.

37. Laurence Veysey, *The Communal Experience: Anarchist and Mystical Counter-Cultures in America* (New York: Harper and Row, 1973), pp. 18–33. Lloyd's two novels were *The Natural Man* (1902) and *The Dwellers in Vale Sunrise* (1904).

38. Odell Shepard, "Paradox of Thoreau," *Scribner's Magazine*, 68 (1920): 339, 340.

39. Vernon L. Parrington, *The Romantic Revolution in America* (New York: Harcourt, 1927), pp. 400, 413; Meyer, *Several More Lives to Live*, p. 20. On Parrington's significance as a literary historian generally, see Vanderbilt, *American Literature and the Academy*, pp. 301–354.

40. Harding and Meyer, *New Thoreau Handbook*, p. 208. This statement originally appeared in the first edition, authored solely by Harding, and was later quoted with approval by Meyer in his own *Several More Lives to Live*, p. 52. They do not restrict their point to the social Thoreau alone, but it is clear from their contexts that this is the avatar that played best in the 1930s.

41. Henry S. Canby "Thoreau in History; The Story of a Literary Reputation," *Saturday Review of Literature*, 20 (15 July 1939): 4, 14; Canby, *Thoreau* (Boston: Houghton Mifflin, 1939), p. 451. Canby's swipe at the image of Thoreau as a

writer for children recalls the Riverside Literature Series, the persistence of whose legacy can be seen in Melissa Stidham, "Thoreau's *Walden* for High School Study," *Education,* 48 (1928): 422–424. Canby had formerly authored such naturalist sketches as "Redwood Canyon," *Atlantic Monthly,* 113 (1914): 832–836, a staunchly preservationist essay, three excerpts from which supply the first three items of Aldo Leopold's manuscript commonplace book (Series 10-7, Box 1, Item 15, Leopold Papers, Wisconsin School of Agriculture).

42. Henry S. Canby, "Thoreau and Whitman on Democracy," *Saturday Review of Literature,* 24 (19 July 1941): 8.

43. Matthiessen, *American Renaissance,* pp. 171, 166, 173. The irony of Matthiessen's formalist legacy is discussed in Russell Reising, *The Unusable Past: Theory and the Study of American Literature* (New York: Methuen, 1986), pp. 170–183, and Meyer, *Several More Lives to Live,* pp. 95–103. Although Matthiessen's formalist innovations were especially influential, his overall achievement was much greater. For example, he also stands behind the "myth-symbol school" of American Studies scholarship, which has formalist elements but can hardly be reduced to them; both R. W. B. Lewis and Leo Marx pay tribute to his criticism and teaching: Lewis, *The American Adam* (Chicago: University of Chicago Press, 1955), p. iii; and Marx, "F. O. Matthiessen," in *The Pilot and the Passenger* (New York: Oxford University Press, 1988), pp. 179–227.

44. Stanley Edgar Hyman, "Thoreau in Our Time," *Atlantic Monthly,* 178, no. 5 (November 1946): 142.

45. Meyer, *Several More Lives to Live,* pp. 109–142. For a useful discussion of Cold War criticism and its notion of containment, see David Suchoff, "New Historicism and Containment: Toward a Post–Cold War Cultural Theory," *Arizona Quarterly,* 48 (1992): 137–161. The "solitary spiritual quester" reading of Thoreau deserves more extended treatment than I give it in this chapter. In the history of Thoreau interpretation, its most important proponent among early Thoreauvians is Thoreau's (first) disciple and literary executor, H. G. O. Blake; among modern Thoreauvians, the most influential critic in this vein has probably been Sherman Paul (note 47 below). My own *Literary Transcendentalism: Style and Vision in the American Renaissance* (Ithaca: Cornell University Press, 1973) tends to reaffirm a religiocentric approach to Thoreau as well as the symbiosis between it and formalist criticism in American scholarship between the 1940s and the 1970s. For this and other criticisms of its period-piece character, see Peter Carafiol, *The American Ideal: Literary History as a Worldly Activity* (New York: Oxford University Press, 1991), pp. 86–96.

46. George Hendrick, "The Influence of Thoreau's 'Civil Disobedience' on Gandhi's *Satyagraha,*" *New England Quarterly,* 29 (1956): 462–471. This kind of "exception," however, tends to prove the rule, insofar as the essay is documentary rather than polemical and mainstream America revered Gandhi. The most am-

bitious 1950s monograph on Thoreau's social thought, Leo Stoller's *After Walden* (Stanford: Stanford University Press, 1957), explains it in accommodationist terms, as an adaptation to the society Thoreau had sought to leave behind in his earlier work.

47. Joseph Wood Krutch, *Henry David Thoreau* (New York: Sloane, 1948), p. 239; Sherman Paul, *The Shores of America: Thoreau's Inward Exploration* (Urbana: University of Illinois Press, 1958), p. 246. Meyer, who discusses both biographies, quotes the latter passage (*Several More Lives to Live,* p. 120).

48. Meyer, *Several More Lives to Live,* p. 154.

49. Charles Anderson, *The Magic Circle of Walden* (New York: Holt, 1968).

50. J. Lyndon Shanley, *The Making of Walden* (Chicago: University of Chicago Press, 1957).

51. Not to cast stones elsewhere when my own prose is culpable, this passage from an article comparing Thoreau and V. S. Naipaul as postcolonial pastoralists exemplifies the trend: for both "the game of animating the provincial quotidian with imagery from the repertoire of metropolitan culture is of course class-specific (the elegant recreation of the cultivated person for whom Euroculture is the touchstone for local knowledge)" ("American Literary Emergence as a Postcolonial Phenomenon," *American Literary History,* 4 [1992]: 434). What nonacademic is going to want to read this? And this rhetoric is actually a rather lucid example of scholarship produced in accordance with a self-conscious interpretative methodology (colonial discourse analysis, in this case).

52. Meyer's statement that "the formalistic approach was limited to academic treatments of Thoreau" (*Several More Lives to Live,* p. 157) is borne out by the reports of Thoreau Society meetings and the membership correspondence printed in the *Thoreau Society Bulletin* (1941–), although the *Bulletin* has also included short professorial exegeses. Of special interest in this regard are its annotated bibliographies maintained for more than half a century by the society's secretary and prime mover, Professor Walter Harding. Although consistently receptive to innovative, challenging interpretations written in nontechnical language—e.g., Stanley Cavell's *The Senses of Walden* (1972)—Harding has also repeatedly chided what he takes to be in-group exercises in literary criticism and theory. See also Jim Aton, "Stalking Henry Thoreau: An Interview with Walter Harding," *South Dakota Review,* 22, no. 4 (1984): 47–60.

53. For the resurgence of the radical Thoreau in the 1960s, see Meyer, *Several More Lives to Live,* pp. 151–152. That Meyer, writing in the mid-1970s, does not deal with green radicalism is a sign of its belated emergence as a subject of major concern to humanist scholars.

54. Paul, *The Shores of America,* p. 305. For Paul's literary naturist interests, see especially his *For Love of the World: Essays on Nature Writers* (Iowa City: University of Iowa Press, 1992), which begins with three essays on Thoreau, one

of which notes that for Thoreau "empirical Law [was] a warrant of redemption superior to, because more secure than, epiphany" (p. 32)—a measure of Paul's shift of emphasis during the several decades he has meditated on Thoreau. Paul's scholarly career is reviewed and honored in *The Green American Tradition*, ed. H. Daniel Peck (Baton Rouge: Louisiana State University Press, 1989).

55. Krutch, *Thoreau*, pp. 33, 147.

56. Joseph Wood Krutch, "Little Fishy Friend," *Nation*, 169 (8 October 1949): 350–351; "A Kind of Pantheism," *Saturday Review*, 33 (10 June 1950): 7–8, 30–34; "The Wilderness at Our Doorstep," *New York Times Book Review*, 21 June 1953, pp. 1, 15. See also the "Prologue" to *Great American Nature Writing*, ed. Krutch (New York: Sloane, 1950).

57. Important early discussions are E. S. Deevey, Jr., "Re-Examination of Thoreau's *Walden*," *Quarterly Review of Biology*, 17 (March 1942): 1–11; Raymond Adams, "Thoreau's Science," *Scientific Monthly*, 60 (1945): 379–382; Kathryn Whitford, "Thoreau and the Woodlots of Concord," *New England Quarterly*, 23 (1950): 291–306; Philip Whitford and Kathryn Whitford, "Thoreau: Pioneer Ecologist and Conservationist," *Scientific Monthly*, 73 (November 1951): 291–306. An excellent synopsis of claims made up to 1980 for Thoreau's scientific accomplishments is Walter Harding, "*Walden*'s Man of Science," *Virginia Quarterly Review*, 57 (1981): 45–61.

58. Robin McDowell, "Thoreau in the Current Scientific Literature," *Thoreau Society Bulletin*, 143 (Spring 1982): 2, and 172 (Summer 1985): 3–4; P. A. Keddy and A. A. Reznicek, "Great Lakes Vegetation Dynamics," *Journal of Great Lakes Research*, 12, no. 1 (1986): 25–36; L. Kilham, "Reproductive Behavior of White-Breasted Nuthatches," *Auk*, 89 (1972): 115–129; Gordon G. Whitney and William C. Davis, "Thoreau and the Forest History of Concord, Massachusetts," *Journal of Forest History*, 30 (April 1986): 69–81; Frederick L. Paillet, "Character and Distribution of American Chestnut Sprouts in Southern New England Woodlots," *Bulletin of the Torrey Botanical Club*, 115 (1988): 32–44.

59. William Howarth, *The Book of Concord: Thoreau's Life as a Writer* (New York: Penguin, 1983), p. 219; Robert Richardson, Jr., *Henry David Thoreau: A Life of the Mind* (Berkeley: University of California Press, 1986), p. 363. We can measure the shift in Thoreau Studies respecting Thoreau's scientific pursuits by comparing Richardson's article "Thoreau and Science," in *American Literature and Science*, ed. Robert J. Scholnick (Lexington: University Press of Kentucky, 1992), pp. 110–127, with the classic statement of Thoreau's ambivalence: Nina Baym, "Thoreau's View of Science," *Journal of the History of Ideas*, 26 (1965): 221–234. Both stress, rightly, that Thoreau's criticisms of the narrowness of scientific method increased as he became more committed to the pursuit of natural history; but Richardson emphasizes to a much greater degree the growth of Thoreau's scientific activities, notwithstanding his antimodernism. A different

tack is taken by William Rossi, "Roots, Leaves, and Method: Henry Thoreau and Nineteenth-Century Natural Science," *Journal of the American Studies Association of Texas,* 19 (October 1988): 1–19, which relates Thoreau's ambivalences to the transitional stage of professional scientific emergence in his era. Still another body of commentary by both literary scholars and historians of science rigorously evaluates Thoreau's natural history as serious, respectable work albeit somewhat modest in accomplishment: e.g., Ray Angelo, "Thoreau as Botanist: An Appreciation and a Critique," *Arnoldia,* 45 (1985): 13–23.

60. Thoreau, *Faith in a Seed: The Dispersion of Seeds and Other Late Natural History Writings,* ed. Bradley P. Dean (Washington: Island Press, 1993).

61. Joel Porte, *Emerson and Thoreau: Transcendentalists in Conflict* (Middletown, Conn.: Wesleyan University Press, 1966); Victor Friesen, *The Spirit of the Huckleberry: Sensuousness in Henry Thoreau* (Edmonton: University of Alberta Press, 1984); James McIntosh, *Thoreau as Romantic Naturalist: His Shifting Stance toward Nature* (Ithaca: Cornell University Press, 1974); Stanley Cavell, *The Senses of Walden* (1972; rpt. San Francisco: North Point Press, 1981), pp. 95, 107; Sharon Cameron, *Writing Nature: Henry Thoreau's Journal* (New York: Oxford University Press, 1985), p. 6; H. Daniel Peck, *Thoreau's Morning Work* (New Haven: Yale University Press, 1990); John Hildebidle, *Thoreau: A Naturalist's Liberty* (Cambridge: Harvard University Press, 1983); Joan Burbick, *Thoreau's Alternative History* (Philadelphia: University of Pennsylvania Press, 1987).

62. Emerson, "Thoreau," in *Complete Works,* 10: 468.

63. Donald Culross Peattie, *An Almanac for Moderns* (1935; rpt. Boston: Godine, 1980), p. 123.

64. Thomas Merton, "The Wild Places," in *The Ecological Conscience: Values for Survival,* ed. Robert Disch (Englewood Cliffs, N.J.: Prentice-Hall, 1970), p. 40; Douglas H. Strong, *Dreamers and Defenders: American Conservationists* (1971; rpt. Lincoln: University of Nebraska Press, 1988), p. 12; Michael Frome, *Battle for the Wilderness* (New York: Praeger, 1974), p. 43; Joseph Wood Krutch, "In Dubious, Desperate Battle," in *What We Save Now . . .: An Audubon Primer of Defense,* ed. Les Line (Boston: Houghton Mifflin, 1973), p. 4. Roderick Nash, *The Rights of Nature: A History of Environmental Ethics* (Madison: University of Wisconsin Press, 1989), is a good bibliographical guide to recent environmentalist writing of a scholarly nature as well as to a number of popular discussions; a considerable number of the items listed refer at least in passing to Thoreau. The strong (although not unanimous) perception of Thoreau as a patron of radical environmental activism has continued; cf. Jonathon Porritt, *Seeing Green: The Politics of Ecology Explained* (Oxford: Blackwell, 1984), p. 4; Tim Palmer, *Endangered Rivers and the Conservation Movement* (Berkeley: University of California Press, 1986), pp. 230–231; Christopher Manes, *Green Rage: Radical Environmentalism and the Unmaking of Civilization* (Boston: Little, Brown, 1990), pp. 245–246;

Philip Shabecoff, *A Fierce Green Fire: The American Environmental Movement* (New York: Hill and Wang, 1993), pp. 51–55.

65. The Sierra Club had a great deal to do with propagating both mottoes. For the first, see for example Kenneth Brower, "Wilderness," in *The Environmental Handbook* (New York: Ballantine, 1970), p. 147; Stuart L. Udall, "Total Environment: A New Political Reality," in *Agenda for Survival: The Environmental Crisis—2*, ed. Harold W. Helfrich, Jr. (New Haven: Yale University Press, 1970), p. 1; and John McPhee, *Encounters with the Archdruid* (New York: Farrar, Straus, 1971), p. 84. The second, from "Walking" (*Excursions and Poems*, ed. Bradford Torrey and Francis H. Allen [Boston: Houghton, Mifflin, 1906], p. 224), was one of John Muir's favorite Thoreau sayings (as per annotations in his copies of *Excursions*, Muir Papers, University of the Pacific); Aldo Leopold reprinted it in *SCA* 133; the Eliot Porter book (San Francisco: Sierra Club, 1962) was excerpted the same year in *American Heritage*, 14 (December 1962): 112–120, with an introduction by Krutch.

66. Leo Marx, *The Machine in the Garden: Technology and the Pastoral Ideal in America* (New York: Oxford University Press, 1964); Nash, *Wilderness and the American Mind*, p. 102 (wording unchanged from the first edition); Worster's *Nature's Economy: The Roots of Ecology*, (1977; rpt. Garden City, N.Y.: Doubleday, 1979). All have long sections on Thoreau. As I have noted in earlier chapters, however, Marx is much less interested in Thoreau's interest in literal nature than are Nash and Worster. The major English-language history of European ecologism, Anna Bramwell's *Ecology in the Twentieth Century: A History* (New Haven: Yale University Press, 1989), gives Thoreau frequent honorable mention as precursor.

67. Emerson, "Thoreau," in *Complete Works*, 10: 485.

68. Edward Abbey, "Down the River with Henry Thoreau," in *Slumgullion Stew: An Edward Abbey Reader* (New York: Dutton, 1984), pp. 307, 289; Wendell, *Literary History of America*, p. 335.

69. William Blake, "The Everlasting Gospel," in *The Poetry and Prose of William Blake*, ed. David V. Erdman (Garden City, N.Y.: Doubleday, 1970), p. 516.

70. Against Worster, see for example Frank N. Egerton, "The History of Ecology: Achievements and Opportunities, Part One," *Journal of the History of Biology*, 16 (1983): 259–260.

71. Marx, *Machine in the Garden*, pp. 242–265; Max Oelschlaeger, *The Idea of Wilderness* (New Haven: Yale University Press, 1991), pp. 133–171. The difficulty of pinning down Thoreau's green politics is scrupulously discussed in an influential work of nearly contemporary ecotheological ethics, H. Paul Santmire, *Brother Earth: Nature, God, and Ecology in a Time of Crisis* (New York: Nelson, 1970), pp. 17–22. Thoreau's readers, writes Santmire, have understood him to "express

an *ethic of adoration* toward nature," which entails withdrawal from "the practical social-political arena" rather than direct confrontation. Thoreau's "obligation to withdraw," as Santmire interprets it, is an unresolved mixture "of hostility toward social injustice" and "a continually and passionately expressed morality of withdrawal from institutions in the name of nature." Santmire considers this mix "an unstable compound that tended to disintegrate in the hands of less sensitive and gifted followers"—and, in particular, to encourage retreat rather than engagement. Certainly that is what tended to happen in late Victorian America: among Thoreauvians, for one John Muir there were probably ten William Hamilton Gibsons. In any case, the chief interest of a discussion like Santmire's is its judicious understanding that nature meant various things to Thoreau. Nor is this awareness confined to scholarly analyses. Joyce Carol Oates shows an equally shrewd sense of it in "Looking for Thoreau," in *(Woman) Writer: Occasions and Opportunities* (New York: Dutton, 1988), pp. 155–157: "Surely it is doubtful that Nature is a single entity."

72. *Thoreau's World and Ours: A Natural Legacy,* ed. Edmund A. Schofield and Robert C. Baron (Golden, Colo.: North American Press, 1993). It is of course significant that Schofield, then the president of the Thoreau Society and the prime mover behind the jubilee, happens himself to be an ecologist; but that the society chose an ecologist as its president during that historic year is even more telling.

73. "Deep ecology" was coined by Norwegian ecophilosopher Arne Naess, in "The Shallow and the Deep, Long-Range Ecology Movement: A Summary," *Inquiry*, 16 (1973): 95–100, and popularized in America most influentially in the wake of Bill Devall and George Sessions, *Deep Ecology* (Salt Lake City: Gibbs Smith, 1985). Devall and Sessions argue that environmentalism cannot affect the "assumptions of the dominant worldview in our culture" without a transformation of "ecological consciousness" beginning with the individual consciousness (pp. 8–9). Their prescriptions include study of "the lives and works of great naturalists, such as St. Francis of Assisi, Henry David Thoreau, and John Muir" (p. 34). For a clear, succinct analytical overview of its premises, see Andrew McLaughlin, *Regarding Nature: Industrialism and Deep Ecology* (Albany: State University of New York Press, 1993), especially Chapter 9. Clearly this is a "transcendentalist" approach to social reform in which degradation of the natural environment is seen as the central problem in need of remediation.

74. Shabecoff, *A Fierce Green Fire*, p. 52.

75. "Positions: Ecology, Feminism, and Thoreau," *Interdisciplinary Studies in Literature and Environment*, 1, no. 1 (Spring 1993): 121–150. See my Introduction, note 20, for a brief definition of ecocriticism; for further details, see Glen A. Love, "*Et in Arcadia Ego:* Pastoral Theory meets Ecocriticism," *Western American*

Literature, 27 (1992): 197–207. The term was apparently introduced by William Rueckert, in "Into and out of the Void: Two Essays," *Iowa Review*, 9, no. 1 (Winter 1978): 62–86.

76. Wendell Glick, autobiographical statement, *Thoreau Society Bulletin*, 144 (Summer 1978): 5.

12. Text as Testament

1. T. S. Eliot, "Tradition and the Individual Talent," in *Selected Essays*, new ed. (New York: Harcourt, 1950), pp. 6–8.

2. Roland Barthes, "The Death of the Author," in *Image, Music, Text*, ed. and trans. Stephen Heath (1968; rpt. New York: Hill and Wang, 1977), pp. 142–148: "To give a text an Author is to impose a limit on that text, to furnish it with a final signified, to close the writing" (p. 147). It should be emphasized that Barthes's essay does not fully disclose his thinking about the subject, which seems to have evolved over time. The essay suggests that Barthes is mainly interested in ensuring the flexibility of the text for the sake of reading pleasure and ingenuity. But at least as important to him was to retain a Thoreauvian liberty, as an author, not to be bound by his own utterances but to change his shape at will, as it were. This emerges quite explicitly in his autobiography *Roland Barthes* (1975), trans. Richard Howard (New York: Hill and Wang, 1977).

3. See for example Jacques Derrida, "Signature Event Context," *Glyph*, 1 (1977): 172–197. Although Derrida grants that a "general *maintenance* is in some way inscribed" by the signature, his larger claim is that "by definition, a written signature implies the actual or empirical non-presence of the signer" and thus the disjunction of text from source (p. 194). Thus Derrida would undoubtedly also put biographicalist myth under the sign of text and hold that the contrast I draw in this section is a false opposition.

4. See Michel Foucault, "What Is an Author?" (1969), in *Language, Counter-Memory, Practice*, trans. Donald F. Bouchard and Sherry Simon, ed. Bouchard (Ithaca: Cornell University Press, 1977), pp. 114–138, though Foucault is more explicit in *The Archaeology of Knowledge*, trans. A. M. Sheridan Smith (New York: Pantheon, 1972), in which he insists that "the rule of materiality that statements necessarily obey is therefore of the order of the institution rather than of the spatio-temporal localization; it defines *possibilities of reinscription and transcription . . .* rather than limited and perishable individualities" (p. 103).

5. Henry Louis Gates, Jr., "The Master's Pieces: On Canon-Formation and the Afro-American Experience," in *Reconstructing American Literary and Historical Studies*, ed. Günter H. Lenz, Hartmut Keil, and Sabine Bröck-Sallah (Frankfurt am Main: Campus Verlag; New York: St. Martin's, 1990), pp. 184–185. Gates most specifically criticizes deconstructionism here, but his final thrust ("far from

constraining its agency") also disassociates him from the Foucaultian/new historicist premises that seem to have propelled his critique.

6. For the contrast between the two "orders," see Harry Berger, Jr., "Bodies and Texts," *Representations*, 17 (1987): 147. (The distinction basically derives from Derrida on voice versus text; cf. *Of Grammatology*, trans. Gayatri Chakravorty Spivak [Baltimore: Johns Hopkins University Press, 1976], p. 9.) Berger himself is clearly a "text" person rather than a "body" person. The best direct critiques of antiauthorism that I have seen are William Gass, *Habitations of the Word* (New York: Simon and Schuster, 1985), "The Death of the Author," pp. 265–288 (responding to Barthes' essay); Paul Smith, *Discerning the Subject* (Minneapolis: University of Minnesota Press, 1988), especially "Autobiography," pp. 100–116, which also focuses on Barthes; Paul John Eakin, *Touching the Word: Reference in Autobiography* (Princeton: Princeton University Press, 1992), whose "Introduction" focuses especially on Barthes's autobiography; and Sean Burke, *The Death and Return of the Author: Criticism and Subjectivity in Barthes, Foucault, and Derrida* (Edinburgh: Edinburgh University Press, 1992), the most extensive study to date. As I see it, four main arguments are presented in these critiques: (1) the position of putative antiauthorists is not so extreme or stable as has been alleged (e.g., Eakin on Barthes, Burke on Derrida); (2) antiauthorists refute themselves by assuming the position of author in their turn (Burke on all three of his primary subjects); (3) the antiauthor position is more objectionable than the biographicalism it displaces (e.g., Gass's charge that depersonalization potentially abets arrogance both in author [who is thereby given a space to deny his human fallibility] and in critic [who is freed to deny author's authority]); (4) the careers of the great antiauthorists themselves show that the author as historical person cannot be bracketed if one is to understand the meaning or significance of the work (e.g., Burke on Paul de Man). The third and fourth arguments seem to me the most promising. That they are taken very seriously indeed even by scholars uninterested in discussing antiauthorism as an abstract issue is clear from recent discussions of de Man's early fascism and the homosexuality of Foucault and Barthes. From the standpoint, for example, of D. A. Miller's appraisal of Barthes's *Incidents,* the order of the authorial body is not so easily dispensed with: "even when not spoken about in this writing, homosexuality does not fail to be spoken any the less" (*Bringing Out Roland Barthes* [Berkeley: University of California Press, 1992], p. 25). Indeed Jerrold Siegel, in "Avoiding the Subject: A Foucaultian Itinerary," *Journal of the History of Ideas*, 51 (1990): 273–299, envisages a direct connection between the desire to occlude the author figure and the state of the homosexual authorial body. In feminist literary theory there has of course been a more long-standing controversy over the question of whether to ascribe the differences of women's writing (in themselves a subject of debate) to discourse or to the existential condition of women in history. As the reader of this chapter

will quickly infer, it seems to me self-evident that the question is not whether either of these alternatives is correct (the order of the body *or* the order of the text) but how to formulate a position in which due regard will be paid to the claims of both.

7. Stanley Edgar Hyman, "Thoreau in Our Time," *Atlantic Monthly,* 178 (1946): 137ff.

8. Edward Abbey, "Down the River with Henry Thoreau," in *Slumgullion Stew: An Edward Abbey Reader* (New York: Dutton, 1984), p. 195.

9. Stanley Cavell, *The Senses of Walden* (1972; rpt. San Francisco: North Point, 1981), pp. 51–52.

10. Emerson, "Thoreau," in *The Complete Works of Ralph Waldo Emerson,* ed. Edward Waldo Emerson (Boston: Houghton, Mifflin, 1903–1904), 10: 454.

11. Of the many appraisals of their relationship from Emerson's perspective, two especially good sources are Robert D. Richardson, Jr., *Emerson* (Berkeley: University of California Press, forthcoming), sections 47 and 78; and David M. Robinson, *Emerson's Pragmatic Turn* (Cambridge, Eng.: Cambridge University Press, 1993), pp. 139–145, on Emerson's *Conduct of Life* as a critique of Thoreau's ideas of economy. The minds of Emerson and Thoreau were so intertwined, however, notwithstanding their estrangement around 1850, that as Richardson writes, "it is sometimes impossible to say who took what from whom."

12. Julie Ellison, "Aggressive Allegory," *Raritan,* 3 (1984): 100–115.

13. Emerson, "Experience," in *Essays, Second Series,* ed. Alfred R. Ferguson and Jean Ferguson Carr (Cambridge: Harvard University Press, 1983), p. 33.

14. On this point, see Michael Fischer, "Speech and Writing in *The Senses of Walden,*" *Soundings,* 68 (1985): 394–401, as well as Robert Milder, *Reimagining Thoreau* (Cambridge, Eng.: Cambridge University Press, forthcoming 1994), pp. 78–79.

15. In other words, Thoreau anticipates what we now consider the postmodern fracturing of the subject, although within limits. Paul Smith, in *Discerning the Subject,* usefully posits a "third 'I'" in autobiography, that is, the superintending principle that mediates between autobiographical actor and autobiographical narrator, *discourse* and *récit.* Within Augustine's sentence "I am not what I was," for example, Smith discerns in addition to the past actor and present speaker "the 'I' that would be prefigured or desired by the moral and ideological operation of trying to maintain the coherence (the wholeness) and the propriety (the wholesomeness) of the ideological subject" (p. 105). By this means, traditional autobiographies like Augustine's enforce a coherence that contemporary anti-authorism tries to undermine. Although Smith does not identify such a case, Thoreau seems to occupy an intermediate position between Augustine and Roland Barthes (Smith's key example of both the antiauthorist type and the latter-day autobiographer who seeks to jettison the coherent "third 'I'"). Thoreau

certainly has a keen sense of the non-identity of *discourse* and *récit* and, like Barthes (see notes 2 and 23), he has a horror of being pinned down to any one avatar; but he will not on that account refuse to see the "I" as a (potentially) coherent figure, an actual person, a responsible agent.

16. See especially Michael West, "Scatology and Eschatology: The Heroic Dimensions of Thoreau's Wordplay," *PMLA*, 89 (1974): 1043–1064.

17. See David Leverenz, *Manhood and the American Renaissance* (Ithaca: Cornell University Press, 1989), as well as the works listed in note 21 below.

18. Frederick Garber, *Thoreau's Fable of Inscribing* (Princeton: Princeton University Press, 1991), pp. 68, 16, 102, 149. Garber's Heideggerian model is "Building Dwelling Thinking," in *Poetry, Language, Thought,* trans. and ed. Albert Hofstadter (New York: Harper and Row, 1971), pp. 143–161. A more recent, also important study of Thoreau's conception of art as work, a study that stresses, however, the difficulty of reconciling intellectual and manual spheres, is Nicholas Bromell, *By the Sweat of the Brow: Literature and Labor in Antebellum America* (Chicago: University of Chicago Press, 1993). Chapters 4 and 11 deal, respectively, with *A Week* and *Walden,* Chapter 11 being the culmination of the book.

19. My chief reservation about Garber's account is the emphasis he places on "self-locating" (*Thoreau's Fable,* pp. 76, 110, etc.)—on Thoreau's drive to make himself at home in the world. Such is also the main theme of Garber's Thoreau chapter in the *Columbia Literary History of the United States,* ed. Emory Elliott (New York: Columbia University Press, 1988), pp. 399–412. This emphasis seems to me one-sided and more applicable to early than to late Thoreau. I read Thoreau as becoming steadily less interested in self, more in environment. Certainly by the mid-1850s his own mind and body were no longer of the first importance to him as objects of contemplation.

20. Bromell, *By the Sweat of the Brow,* p. 238.

21. One of the striking paradoxes of the antebellum period is that American literary emergence, both as a marketplace phenomenon and as an enduring aesthetic achievement, took place in a climate of considerable suspicion toward creativity disjunct from practicality. The suspiciousness reflected a combination of post-Puritan moralism, Yankee practicality, and stereotypical associations of art with European "decadence" and the sphere of the feminine. For discussions of public suspicion of the arts on one or more of these grounds, see for example William Charvat, *Origins of American Critical Thought, 1810–1835* (Philadelphia: University of Pennsylvania Press, 1936); Neil Harris, *The Artist in American Society: The Formative Years, 1790–1860* (New York: Braziller, 1966); Ann Douglas, *The Feminization of American Culture* (New York: Knopf, 1977); Nina Baym, *Novels, Readers, and Reviewers: Responses to Fiction in Antebellum America* (Ithaca: Cornell University Press, 1984); Lawrence Buell, *New England Literary Culture: From Revolution through Renaissance* (Cambridge, Eng.: Cambridge Univer-

sity Press, 1986); and Susan Coultrap-McQuin, *Doing Literary Business: American Women Writers in the Nineteenth Century* (Chapel Hill: University of North Carolina Press, 1990). As I, McQuin, and others have shown, such prejudice as Victorian America held against art loomed larger for men (whose ideas of secular vocation were generally more exalted and rarefied) than for women (whose entrepreneurial literary undertakings were more matter-of-fact and, unlike most professional aspirations, considered legitimate—at least when certain decorums were observed—in cases of financial need). On the tendency of the period to associate "work" with physical rather than mental labor, see Bromell, *By the Sweat of the Brow,* pp. 1–12; on the crisis of masculinity caused by this (among other) factors, see David Leverenz, *Manhood and the American Renaissance* (Ithaca: Cornell University Press, 1989).

22. Allen Ginsberg, "A Supermarket in California," in *Howl and Other Poems* (San Francisco: City Lights, 1956), p. 23.

23. Barthes, *Roland Barthes,* p. 56. Foucault's theoretical humiliation of authorial authority was argued on different grounds from Barthes', as we saw earlier, yet he too desired to free the author from the yoke of authority. In the "Introduction" to his *Archaeology of Knowledge* he imagines replying to a hostile interlocutor: "Do not ask who I am and do not ask me to remain the same: leave it to our bureaucrats and our police to see that our papers are in order. At least spare us their morality when we write" (p. 17).

24. Carole Anne Taylor, "Authorship without Authority: *Walden,* Kierkegaard, and the Experiment in Points of View," in *Kierkegaard and Literature,* ed. Ronald Schleifer and Robert Markley (Norman: University of Oklahoma Press, 1984), p. 175.

25. Elaine Scarry, *The Body in Pain: The Making and Unmaking of the World* (New York: Oxford University Press, 1985), provides a powerful demonstration of the hazards of deleting bodies from acts of representation and overlooking the plenitude of the vision of text as incarnation. I have been influenced by her work at a number of points in this chapter.

26. This is essentially Gass's judgment on Barthes's theory: "It may at first seem that the effacement of the author was an act of modesty . . . but the opposite is clearly the case." Whereas Trollope, manipulative storyteller as he was, fits comfortably within "the well-known world of his readers," "Flaubert is not telling a tale, he is constructing a world" (*Habitations of the Word,* p. 273).

27. The relationship between the romantic aesthetic and the theory of individual creativity that forms the basis of modern copyright law is traced in Martha Woodmansee, *The Author, Art, and the Market: Rereading the History of Aesthetics* (New York: Columbia University Press, 1994), especially pp. 35–55; and in *The Construction of Authorship: Textual Appropriation in Law and Literature,* ed.

Woodmansee and Peter Jaszi (Durham: Duke University Press, 1994), particularly in the introductory essays by the two editors.

28. Scott Slovic, *Seeking Awareness in American Nature Writing* (Salt Lake City: University of Utah Press, 1992), p. 45.

29. Though the author does not claim so, this seems a corollary of Robert C. Elliott's account of the nature, background, and emergence of "persona" as a literary category: *The Literary Persona* (Chicago: University of Chicago Press, 1982).

30. Edward O. Wilson, *Biophilia* (Cambridge: Harvard University Press, 1984).

31. Robert Sayre, "Aldo Leopold's Sentimentalism: 'A Refined Taste in Natural Objects,'" *North Dakota Quarterly*, 59, no. 2 (1991): 112–125. Sayre calls attention to Smith as both economic and moral theorist.

32. This position has been advanced by Thomas L. Haskell in "Capitalism and the Origins of the Humanitarian Sensibility," *American Historical Review*, 90 (1985): 339–361, 547–566; and in "Convention and Hegemonic Interest in the Debate over Antislavery," *American Historical Review*, 92 (1987): 829–878. I believe that Haskell overstates the case for the moral originality and productivity of capitalism, but I am persuaded that there is, historically, a correlation between the globalization of the western entrepreneurial impulse and the extension of moral consideration beyond the parochial bounds of family, clan, tribe, and even church.

33. Kai Nielson, "Why Should I Be Moral?" quoted in A. S. Cua, *Dimensions of Moral Creativity: Paradigms, Principles, and Ideals* (University Park: Pennsylvania State University Press, 1978), p. 37.

34. Robert Sayre, "Autobiography and Images of Utopia" *Salmagundi*, 19 (Spring 1972): 20.

35. Charles Taylor, *Sources of the Self: The Making of the Modern Identity* (Cambridge: Harvard University Press, 1989), p. 510.

36. Cua, *Dimensions of Moral Creativity*, p. 35.

37. Gabriel Josipovici, *Writing and the Body* (Princeton: Princeton University Press, 1981), p. 96.

38. Among the endless number of quotable put-downs, let one suffice: "What I miss in him," writes Wallace Stegner, "as I missed it in the more extreme rebels of the 1960s, is the acknowledgement that their society shaped them, that without it every individual of them would be a sort of Sasquatch, a solitary animal without language, thought, tradition, obligation, or commitment" ("Qualified Homage to Thoreau," in *Heaven Is under Our Feet*, ed. Don Henley and Dave Marsh [New York: Berkley, 1991], p. 281).

39. I could refine this point by pointing out how Thoreau's seeming misanthropy belied his actual loyalty to the town of Concord, despite his lover's quarrel

with it. (See my *New England Literary Culture*, pp. 319–334, and the studies by Robert Gross cited therein, 484n). In the present context, however, I want to stick with the basic myth of Thoreau's character in the public memory, the level to which Stegner's remark above speaks, which has enshrined him as abrasively individualistic rather than as community-oriented despite generations of attempts to make the case for him as a devoted son of Concord.

40. George Kateb, "Democratic Individuality and the Claims of Politics," in *The Inner Ocean: Individualism and Democratic Culture* (Ithaca: Cornell University Press, 1992), pp. 77–105, quotation from p. 95. See also Robert D. Richardson, Jr., "The Social Ethics of *Walden*," in *Critical Essays on Henry David Thoreau's Walden*, ed. Joel Myerson (Boston: Hall, 1988), pp. 235–248.

41. On the rise of tourism in America during Thoreau's lifetime, see Hans Huth, *Nature and the American: Three Centuries of Changing Attitudes* (1957; rpt. Lincoln: University of Nebraska Press, 1990), pp. 50–86; John F. Sears, *Sacred Places: American Tourist Attractions in the Nineteenth Century* (New York: Oxford University Press, 1989); and Anne Farrar Hyde, *An American Vision: Far Western Landscape and National Culture, 1820–1920* (New York: New York University Press, 1990).

42. Tu Wei-ming, "The Continuity of Being," in *Nature in Asian Traditions of Thought*, ed. J. Baird Callicott and Roger T. Ames (Albany: State University of New York Press, 1989), p. 78.

43. Roderick Nash, *Wilderness and the American Mind*, 3d ed. (New Haven: Yale University Press, 1982), p. 384. Others have painted similar portraits of environmental faddism for earlier periods. For the early twentieth century, see Peter J. Schmitt, "The Search for Scenery," in *Back to Nature: The Arcadian Myth in Urban America* (New York: Oxford University Press, 1969), pp. 167–176.

44. David Shi, in "Thoreau for Commuters," *North American Review*, 272 (June 1987), comments wryly on the release of *Walden* on audiocassette targeted for the California car commuter (p. 65). Shi tries to put an engaging face on this development ("Thoreau was not an anchorite but a commuter of sorts himself" [p. 67]) and to emphasize the transferability of Thoreau's gospel of simplicity to "cities and suburbs, town-houses and condominiums" (p. 69). Shi is a first-rate historian of voluntary simplicity in America and of Thoreau's place in that tradition (see his *The Simple Life* [New York: Oxford University Press, 1985]), but in this particular article I think he exposes to a greater degree than he intends the ease with which *Walden* can become a placebo and the complicity of Thoreau in that process of tranquilization, when it occurs.

45. Henri Lefebvre, *The Production of Space*, trans. Donald Nicholson-Smith (1974; rpt. Oxford: Blackwell, 1984), p. 383.

46. Herbert Marcuse, *One-Dimensional Man* (Boston: Beacon, 1964), pp. 74, 75.

47. Culled from Joel Myerson's selection of early journalistic reviews in *Critical*

Essays on Henry David Thoreau's Walden, pp. 18, 19, 21. See also Bradley P. Dean and Gary Scharnhorst, "The Contemporary Reception of *Walden,*" in *Studies in the American Renaissance, 1990,* ed. Joel Myerson (Charlottesville: University Press of Virginia, 1990), pp. 293–328.

48. Cavell, *The Senses of Walden,* p. 4.

49. Bromell, *By the Sweat of the Brow,* p. 229.

50. See David M. Robinson, "'Unchronicled Nations': Agrarian Purpose and Thoreau's Ecological Knowing," *Nineteenth-Century Literature,* 49 (1993): 326–340.

51. For documentation of the compositional process, see J. Lyndon Shanley, *The Making of Walden* (Chicago: University of Chicago Press, 1957), pp. 190–191, and Ronald Earl Clapper, "The Development of *Walden:* A Genetic Text" (Ph.D. diss., UCLA, 1967), pp. 564–598.

52. I certainly do not wish to deny the traces of the more conflicted and somber aspects of Thoreauvian sublimation that have been pointed out by such scholars as Richard Bridgman, *Dark Thoreau* (Lincoln: University of Nebraska Press, 1982), and Robert Milder, *Reimagining Thoreau.* Milder, for example, sees "Higher Laws" as the culmination of a "purity triptych," starting with "The Ponds" and intertextually linked to the "Shipwreck" chapter in *Cape Cod,* in which Thoreau struggles to rationalize the savagery and uncleanness in nature as well as in himself (p. 132 and pp. 123–138 passim). To my thinking, however, the doubts and struggles that surface especially in "Higher Laws" do not seriously undermine Thoreau's overriding ideal of personal and natural purity but, on the contrary, mainly testify in its favor: as evidence of his awareness of the difficulty of attaining the ethic of relinquishment to which he was committed. Thoreau's occasional revulsions against nature's own unchastity (for example, his well-known horror at phallic fungi) strike me mainly as epiphenomenal projections of fears about the "beast" within. As one *Journal* passage has it, "perhaps man's impurity begets a monster somewhere, so proclaim his sin" (*PJ* 4: 309).

53. Obviously one would look at Thoreau's theory of "chastity" in "Higher Laws" quite differently if one's reference point were the old construction of him as a repressed heterosexual or the more recent (and more sophisticated) construction of him as a closeted homosexual, and if one imagined that repression of sexuality as tragic. To me, what is more striking is the positive personal and cultural result eventuating from that repression. I would by no means generalize from this observation, as Freud does, that sexual repression is the key to culture's survival. I suggest only that in this case Thoreau's "queerness" helped make him a prophet of modern ecologism.

54. Michael Oriard, *Sporting with the Gods: The Rhetoric of Play and Game in American Culture* (Cambridge, Eng.: Cambridge University Press, 1991), p. 374.

55. Oriard claims that the postromantic writers of the American literary

emergence period developed the "first American theology of play," which was, however, manifested rather fitfully and hesitantly by the transcendentalists (as "an ideal of holy play competed with a contradictory insistence on purposeful striving"); see *Sporting with the Gods*, p. 368 and pp. 368–406 passim.

56. By the same token, the position was also precarious; as William Gleason remarks, Thoreau sought "to dissolve the distinctions between work and play at precisely the moment in American history when these activities were becoming more, not less, rigidly demarcated" ("Thoreau's Economy of Work and Play," *American Literature*, 65 (1993): 687). Gleason is right in thinking that this caused Thoreau some anxiety, as seen, for example, in the pains he took to distinguish his own position from such apparently similar ones on the margins of Concord's emerging agrarian-capitalist economy as that of the slackard laborer John Field.

57. Sayre, "Aldo Leopold's Sentimentalism," p. 124.

Appendix

1. See Linck C. Johnson, "Revolution and Renewal: The Genres of *Walden*," in *Critical Essays on Henry David Thoreau's Walden*, ed. Joel Myerson (Boston: Hall, 1988), pp. 215–235, in which Johnson argues that "Thoreau used genre to free himself from generic restrictions" (p. 216).

2. Two previous discussions of "Brute Neighbors" that comment sensitively on the issue of aesthetic control, although they stop short of my notion that Thoreau sought to engineer a planned aesthetic decontrol, are Gerry Brenner, "Thoreau's 'Brute Neighbors': Four Levels of Nature," *Emerson Society Quarterly*, 39 (1965): 37–40; and H. Daniel Peck, *Thoreau's Morning Work* (New Haven: Yale University Press, 1990), pp. 117–125.

3. These are M. M. Bakhtin's terms for designating the interplay of different voices and different linguistic strata in novelistic discourse. For succinct definitions, see Katerina Clark and Michael Holquist, *Mikhail Bakhtin* (Cambridge: Harvard University Press, 1984), pp. 241ff., 292–293. Thoreauvian multigenericism seems to me to combine a greater array of genres and mimetic modes (e.g., "fictional" and "nonfictional" mimesis) and to create larger fissures within a text than the discursive universe of the novel as mapped by Bakhtin.

4. These and all other early American writers mentioned in this paragraph are listed in the annotated bibliography of Robert Sattelmeyer's *Thoreau's Reading: A Study in Intellectual History with Bibliographical Catalogue* (Princeton: Princeton University Press, 1988). All works of environmental prose mentioned subsequently in this chapter that are listed in Sattelmeyer are designated by number (e.g., *TR* #791 for Josselyn).

5. For critical history and extensive discussion of early American environmental prose, see Wayne Franklin, *Discoverers, Explorers, Settlers: The Diligent*

Writers of Early America (Chicago: University of Chicago Press, 1979); David Schofield Wilson, *In the Presence of Nature* (Amherst: University of Massachusetts Press, 1978); and Pamela Regis, *Describing Early America: Bartram, Jefferson, Crèvecoeur, and the Rhetoric of Natural History* (DeKalb: Northern Illinois University Press, 1992). For a more popular account of natural history writing, see Joseph Kastner, *A Species of Eternity* (New York: Knopf, 1977). For a helpful short historical-critical overview of pre-Thoreauvian environmental prose, see the introduction to *This Incomperable Lande: A Book of American Nature Writing,* ed. Thomas J. Lyon (Boston: Houghton Mifflin, 1989; rpt. New York: Penguin, 1991), pp. 24–48 ("Beginnings"). For reflections on the relation between landscape representation and issues of cultural nationalism in the late eighteenth century, see Larzer Ziff's chapter "Realizing the Landscape," in *Writing in the New Nation* (New Haven: Yale University Press, 1991), pp. 34–53.

6. See *This Incomperable Lande* for a good representation of early American ornithological writing (Wilson, Audubon, Nuttall).

7. For example, an anonymous writer in *The Outlook* (1903) identifies a "little group of men, among whom Emerson and Thoreau were the most conspicuous," as those "who early gave direction and impulse" to the literature of observation ("Back to Nature," 74: 305). Hamilton Wright Mabie (1897) credits "the modern writers about nature"—meaning Thoreau, Burroughs, and Richard Jefferies— with creating "a new kind of literature," approaching "their subjects as artists rather than as scientists" ("John Burroughs," *Century,* 32: 562). This tradition continues, even among those fully aware of the pre-thoreauvian history. Lyon declares, for example, that "the possibilities of the nature essay as a modern literary form were first outlined in Thoreau's first essay, published in July, 1842" (*This Incomperable Lande,* p. 52). Lyon especially has in mind Thoreau's achievement of "a pure and direct experience, that is, a nondual experience, which would transcend the usual distance between subject and object" (p. 53), yet his anthology shows that some of Thoreau's precursors were also capable of this. The major critical discussions bearing on the emergence of nature writing in America are Philip Marshall Hicks's *The Development of the Natural History Essay in American Literature* (Philadelphia: University of Pennsylvania Press, 1924); Joseph Wood Krutch's editoral introduction to *Great American Nature Writing* (New York: Sloane, 1950), pp. 5–73; and Peter Fritzell's *Nature Writing and America: Essays upon a Cultural Type* (Ames: Iowa State University Press, 1990).

8. John Godman, *Rambles of a Naturalist* (Philadelphia: Ash, 1833). The series of twelve essays is prefaced with a copious memoir, pp. 13–36, praising Godman's polymathy. During a one-year stint as professor of surgery at the Medical College of Ohio, for instance, Godman practiced medicine, wrote most of the local medical journal, "created an apparatus for sulphurous fumigation," "translated and published a French pamphlet" on the subject, studied German and French,

and "labeled the ancient coins and medals of the Western Museum" (p. 27). *This Incomperable Lande,* pp. 127–131, prints Godman's essay on pine trees.

9. Anon., "A Few Memoirs of William Henry Herbert," in *Frank Forester's Field Sports of the United States and British Provinces of North America,* new ed. (New York: Woodward, 1848), 1: xii. See this and the *Dictionary of American Biography* for details on Forester's life.

10. See David E. Allen, *The Naturalist in Britain* (London: Allen Lane, 1976); Lynn Barber, *The Heyday of Natural History* (Garden City, N.Y.: Doubleday, 1980); and Lynn Merrill, *The Romance of Victorian Natural History* (New York: Oxford University Press, 1989), the last of which includes a helpful secondary bibliography. "A generation ahead" is a crude approximation. In America, the nineteenth-century apogee of literary naturism did come later than in mid-Victorian Britain, but serious amateur collecting started earlier, although according to Allen, as early as 1746 a British correspondent wrote Linnaeus, "we are very fond of all branches of Natural history; they sell the best of any books in England" (*Naturalist in Britain,* p. 36). However, by the "literary classics" test, it could be argued that natural history "came of age" about the same time on both sides of the Atlantic, with Gilbert White's *The Natural History of Selbourne* (1789) and William Bartram's *Travels* (1791).

11. Thoreau, *Early Essays and Miscellanies,* ed. Joseph Moldenhauer and Edwin Moser (Princeton: Princeton University Press, 1975), specifically, "The Book of the Seasons," pp. 26–36.

12. William Howitt, *The Book of the Seasons* (Philadelphia: Carey and Lea, 1831), pp. xxi, 97.

13. Thoreau, "Book of the Seasons," p. 26.

14. *The Complete Works of Ralph Waldo Emerson,* ed. Edward Waldo Emerson (Boston: Houghton, Mifflin, 1903–1904), 9: 41–42; cf. Howitt, *Book of the Seasons,* pp. 26–27. Emerson's 1835 journal refers slightingly to Howitt as "not so much the model as the parody" for a very Thoreauvian-sounding work Emerson projects that "should contain the Natural history of the woods around my shifting camp for every month in the year"; see *Journals and Miscellaneous Notebooks of Ralph Waldo Emerson,* ed. William H. Gilman et al. (Cambridge: Harvard University Press, 1960–1982), 5: 25. This Emerson wrote a few months after composing "The Snow-Storm"—interesting collateral testimony to the potency of the literary almanac idea and Howitt's attempt particularly.

15. Ralph Waldo Emerson, *Nature, Addresses, and Lectures,* ed. Robert E. Spiller and Alfred R. Ferguson (Cambridge: Harvard University Press, 1971), p. 76. V. Michael Colacurcio, in the most complex discussion of Emerson's address to date: "If historical imagination is any guide in such matters, it probably took the original audience . . . a moment or two to get over a certain electric thrill at the lavishly sensual, even voluptuary mood of its opening sentences" ("'Pleasing

God': The Lucid Strife of Emerson's 'Address,'" *ESQ*, 37 [1991]: 145). To amend Colacurcio here, however, is simply to bring Emerson's exordium into line with what Colacurcio says later about "the relative mildness" of Emerson's "strategy of revision" in the address: "it seeks not at all to triumph over or to supplant but merely to equalize the authority of Jesus" (p. 177).

16. Thoreau "The Seasons," in *Early Essays and Miscellanies*, p. 3.

17. In 1851, *Harper's* serialized an elegantly illustrated printing of the first two parts of *The Seasons*, 2: 433–448 ("Spring"); 3: 1–24 ("Summer"). This suggests that the taste for this poem was still very much alive in Thoreau's America. Using the seasons as a topic of American school assignments dates back at least as early as the mid-eighteenth century; cf. John Lovell, *The Seasons* (Boston: Fleet, 1765), a poem that identifies itself as "an interlocutory exercise at the South Grammar School, June 26, 1765."

18. Robert Richardson, Jr., *Henry David Thoreau: A Life of the Mind* (Berkeley: University of California Press, 1986), p. 87; see pp. 307–308 for Thoreau's interest in the other Roman agriculturists.

19. Howitt, *Book of the Seasons*, p. 224.

20. Virginia Woolf, "Thoreau," *Times Literary Supplement*, 12 July 1917, p. 325.

21. *Through the Year with the Poets*, ed. Oscar Fay Adams, 12 vols. (Boston: Lothrop, 1885–1886); Thoreau's *Journal* was excerpted by his literary executor Harrison Gray Otis Blake and published by Houghton, Mifflin as *Early Spring in Massachusetts* (1881), *Summer* (1884), *Winter* (1887), and *Autumn* (1892).

22. William Howitt, *The Year-Book of the Country* (London: Colburn, 1850), p. iii. This work expresses great concern for the plight of the rural poor, indignation at the speculators and absentee landlords that have exploited them, satisfaction at the failures of agricultural speculators after the repeal of the Corn Laws, along with optimism at what Howitt takes to be the progress of humanitarian reform legislation.

23. Cyrus Bartol, *Discourses on the Christian Spirit and Life*, 2d ed. (Boston: Crosby and Nichols, 1850), pp. 357–367; N. L. Frothingham, *Sermons, in the Order of a Twelvemonth* (Boston: Crosby and Nichols, 1852), pp. 341–351; Henry Ward Beecher, *Star Papers; or, Experiences of Art and Nature* (New York: Derby, 1855). The *Star Papers* stands on the borderline between homily and the picturesque, being a collection of essays written by a vacationer for an audience of potential well-to-do vacationers.

24. *Sacred Philosophy of the Seasons: Illustrating the Perfections of God in the Phenomena of the Year*, by Henry Duncan, ed. F. W. P. Greenwood, 4 vols. (Boston: Marsh, Capen, Lyon, and Webb, 1839). Greenwood had given the Boston Natural History Society's ceremonial "Address . . . at the Opening of Their New Hall in Tremont Street," *Boston Journal of Natural History*, 1 (1834–1837): 7–13. In it he issued a Thoreauvian call "to attend particularly to the formation or completion

of such collections as may give a good idea of the natural features of our own country, and of our own section of our country" (p. 11).

25. Edward Hitchcock, *Religious Lectures on Peculiar Phenomena in the Four Seasons* (Amherst: Adams, 1849), pp. 9–52. Quotation from Herbert Hovenkamp, *Science and Religion in America, 1800–1860* (Philadelphia: University of Pennsylvania Press, 1978), p. 132.

26. Hitchcock, *Religious Lectures,* pp. 72–78.

27. The rainbow imagery in "Baker Farm" is discussed in Charles Anderson, *The Magic Circle of Walden* (New York: Holt, 1968), pp. 135–141.

28. As I myself have to some extent done in "Democratic Ideology and Autobiographical Personae in American Renaissance Writing," *Amerikastudien,* 35 (1990): 270–271.

29. Sandra A. Zagarell, "Narrative of Community: The Identification of a Genre," *Signs,* 13 (1988): 498–527. For more background on the genres of regionalism in New England and their bearing on Thoreau, see Chapters 12–14 of my *New England Literary Culture: From Revolution through Renaissance* (Cambridge, Eng.: Cambridge University Press, 1986), pp. 283–334.

30. On this point, see Vera Norwood's discussion of Susan Cooper's historical significance, in *Made from This Earth: American Women and Nature* (Chapel Hill: University of North Carolina Press, 1993), pp. 25–53. Norwood's chapter provides the best discussion to date of Cooper's ecological vision.

31. Susan Fenimore Cooper, *Rural Hours* (New York: Putnam, 1850), pp. 145–146.

32. Ibid., pp. 254–266.

33. Quotation from Cooper's introduction to her American edition of John Leonard Knapp's *Journal of a Naturalist* (which she retitled *Country Rambles in England* [Buffalo: Phinney, 1853], p. 16). For her historical essay (considerably indebted to Humboldt), see the introduction to her anthology, *The Rhyme and Reason of Country Life* (New York: Putnam, 1855), pp. 13–34. Cooper's patriotic belief is that "the union of Christianity with this general diffusion of a high degree of civilization" that in her opinion marks American against European culture "has led us to a more deeply felt appreciation of the works of the creation" (p. 27), although she warns that "probably there never has been a social condition in which the present is more absolutely absorbing, more encroaching . . . than in our American towns" (p. 32).

34. Cooper, *Rural Hours,* p. 215.

35. Thoreau, *Excursions and Poems,* ed. Bradford Torrey and Francis H. Allen (Boston: Houghton, Mifflin, 1906), p. 247.

36. Cooper, *Rural Hours,* pp. 333, 335.

37. *The Home Book of the Picturesque; or American Scenery, Art, and Literature* (1852; rpt. Gainesville, Fla.: Scholars' Facsimiles and Reprints, 1967). Perhaps the

first important manifesto by a participating artist was Thomas Cole's "Essay on American Scenery," *American Monthly Magazine*, 1 (1836): 1–12.

38. For Thoreau's reading in Gilpin and Ruskin, see Richardson, *HDT: A Life of the Mind*, pp. 260–262, 357–362; and Sattelmeyer, *Thoreau's Reading*, pp. 70–71.

39. E. L. Magoon, "Scenery and Mind," in *Home Book*, p. 39.

40. Cooper, *Rural Hours*, p. 113.

41. William Gilpin, *Remarks on Forest Scenery*, 3d ed. (London: Cadell and Davies, 1808), 1: 46–47. This is the edition Thoreau apparently consulted.

42. In this regard, see H. Daniel Peck's chapter "Picturing the World," in *Thoreau's Morning Work* (New Haven: Yale University Press, 1990), pp. 49–66.

43. *Letters of Ralph Waldo Emerson*, ed. Ralph Leslie Rusk (New York: Columbia University Press, 1939), 3: 383.

44. Susan Cooper, "A Dissolving View," in *Home Book*, pp. 92–93.

45. Bayard Taylor, "The Erie Railroad," in *Home Book*, p. 149.

46. On this point, see Ronald J. Zboray, *A Fictive People: Antebellum Economic Development and the American Reading Public* (New York: Oxford University Press, 1993), especially Chapter 5, "The Railroad, the Community, and the Book" (pp. 69–82).

47. Leo Marx, *The Machine in the Garden: Technology and the Pastoral Ideal in America* (New York: Oxford University Press, 1964), pp. 242–265 and passim.

48. Alfred B. Street, "The Adirondack Mountains," in *Home Book*, p. 161.

49. James Russell Lowell, "A Week on the Concord and Merrimack Rivers," in *Pertaining to Thoreau*, ed. Samuel A. Jones (1901), reprinted in *Emerson Society Quarterly*, no. 62, suppl. (1971); 16.

50. James Russell Lowell, "A Moosehead Journal" (1853), in *Fireside Travels* (Boston: Houghton, Mifflin, 1885), p. 135.

51. Steven Fink carefully traces Thoreau's many accommodations to the picturesque in his early environmental prose. Fink characterizes "A Winter Walk," for instance, as "a veritable catalog of conventional images of picturesque New England—from the barnyard at dawn, to the smoke ascending from the rustic cabin, to skating on the river, to the solitary fisherman, to the snug farmer's hearth" (*Prophet in the Marketplace: Thoreau's Development as a Professional Writer* [Princeton: Princeton University Press, 1992], p. 120). The "walk" itself was a long-established picturesque subgenre; see Jeffrey C. Robinson, *The Walk: Notes on a Romantic Image* (Norman: University of Oklahoma Press, 1989).

52. Thoreau, "Natural History of Massachusetts," in *Excursions*, p. 39.

53. Wilson Flagg's nature essays, begun in the early 1840s and resumed more intensively in the 1850s with the advent of the *Atlantic Monthly* (1857), were collected in *Studies in the Field and Forest* (Boston: Little, Brown, 1855), *The Woods and By-Ways of New England* (Boston: Osgood, 1872), and *The Birds and Seasons of New England* (Boston: Osgood, 1875). Thomas Wentworth Higginson's nature

essays of the early 1860s were collected in *Out-Door Papers* (Boston: Ticknor and Fields, 1868).

54. Quotations from C. T. Jackson, "Henry D. Thoreau," *Proceedings of the Boston Society of Natural History,* 7 (1862–1863): 71; Higginson, *Out-Door Papers,* pp. 312, 257. For Flagg's reactions to Thoreau, whose response to him had been conveyed by their mutual friend Daniel Ricketson, see *Woods and By-Ways,* pp. iv, 392–396. For Burroughs' reactions to Thoreau, see Perry Westbrook, *John Burroughs* (New York: Twayne, 1974), pp. 57–63, and the last of Burroughs' own many pronouncements, "Another Word on Thoreau," in *The Last Harvest,* ed. Clara Barrus (Boston: Houghton Mifflin, 1922), pp. 103–171. For a short survey of Flagg, Higginson, and other Thoreauvian contemporaries, see Hicks, *Development of the Natural History Essay,* pp. 100–158. For a nearly contemporary appraisal of literary naturalists, see W. G. Barton, "Thoreau, Flagg, and Burroughs," *Essex Institute Historical Collections,* 22 (1895): 53–79, which gives Thoreau *qua* writer the palm while preferring the more genial personae of the other two—a standard judgment for the period. Although it did not imply the highest echelon of authorship, the category of literary natural history writer was at all events the one most often assigned to Thoreau during his lifetime, e.g., by Emerson when heralding Thoreau as an American Isaac Walton or Gilbert White (see Fink, *Prophet in the Marketplace,* pp. 51, 136, 143).

55. Anon., "The Night-Birds of North America," *Putnam's,* 2 (1853): 617, 618. This owlish contributor had previously published "A Few Words on the Day Owls of North America," in ibid., vol. 2, pp. 277–288. Such articles were standard mid-century magazine fare. The first volume of *Harper's* (1850) included several naturalist pieces from Howitt's *Year-Book of the Country,* including "Singular Proceedings of the Sand Wasp" and a substantial article on astronomy, "Shooting Stars and Meteoric Showers" (pp. 439–448). The *Atlantic* of the late 1850s and 1860s, in which Thoreau's "Chesuncook," "Wild Apples," and other essays appeared, ran several articles by Flagg on birds and by Higginson on flowers, birds, and snow. Thoreau read all these journals, and his library included a copy of the *Putnam's* issue in which "Night-Birds" appeared (*TR* #1131)—along with the second half of Melville's "Bartleby the Scrivener."

56. "Night-Birds," p. 616n; Flagg, *Woods and By-Ways,* p. 70. Such prejudice also existed in Britain. When young Charles Darwin first proposed accepting the position of naturalist for the voyage of the *Beagle* in 1831, his physician father treated the proposition disdainfully, as if he thought that "beetle hunting was not far removed from rat-catching" (Gertrude Himmelfarb, *Darwin and the Darwinian Revolution* [London: Chatto and Windos, 1959], p. 46).

57. "Night-Birds," p. 618.

58. William O. Ayres, "Enumeration," *Boston Journal of Natural History,* 4 (1843–1844): 255–264; communication from Henry Bryant regarding birds ob-

served in East Florida, in *Proceedings of the Boston Society of Natural History*, 7 (19 January 1859): 15. Elected a corresponding member of the Boston Society, Thoreau "read widely" in its *Proceedings* (Sattelmeyer, *Thoreau's Reading*, p. 137), and he was probably familiar with its more formal organ, the *Boston Journal.*

59. John James Audubon and John Bachman, *Vivaparous Quadrupeds* (New York: Audubon, 1846), pp. 302–305.

60. Higginson, "April Days," in *Out-Door Papers*, p. 231.

61. On Thoreau's late efforts to capitalize on the appeal of his natural history writing while maintaining his intellectual integrity, see especially Fink, *Prophet in the Marketplace*, pp. 268–285. Thoreau seems to have been quite aware, and by no means wholly contemptuous of, the typicality of this 1857 appraisal of his work in a British journal: "The natural sights and sounds of the woods, as described by Mr. Thoreau, form much pleasanter reading than his vague and scarcely comprehensible social theories" ("An American Diogenes," *Chambers's Journal*, 8 [21 November 1857], reprinted in *Thoreau: A Century of Criticism*, ed. Walter Harding [Dallas: Southern Methodist University Press, 1954], pp. 12–21.

62. Among the various contemporary discussions of the late-century rise of natural history writing, see for example Francis Halsey, "The Rise of the Nature Writers," *American Monthly Review of Reviews*, 26 (1902): 567–571. Peter Schmidt provides a short overview of the vogue in *Back to Nature: The Arcadian Myth in Urban America* (New York: Oxford University Press, 1969), pp. 33–44. Hicks, *Development of the Natural History Essay*, pp. 100–123, sheds light on the emergence of home and garden writing.

63. John Christie, *Thoreau as World Traveler* (New York: Columbia University Press, 1965), pp. 44–47. Christie notes that half of the bibliography of Thoreau's reading in this genre consisted of travel books published 1830 and after (p. 47).

64. Ibid., p. 80.

65. Josiah Gregg, *The Commerce of the Prairies* (1844), ed. Max L. Moorhead (Norman: University of Oklahoma Press, 1954), pp. 369, 379–381.

66. Charles Darwin, *The Voyage of the Beagle* (New York: Collier, 1909), p. 9.

67. Ibid., p. 224. On the imperialistic ideology of natural historians' travelogues, see Mary Louise Pratt, *Imperial Eyes: Travel Writing and Transculturation* (London: Routledge, 1992), Chapters 2–4, 6. For further complexities inherent in nineteenth-century travel narrative as a Eurocentric ideological form, see James Buzard, *The Beaten Track: European Tourism, Literature, and the Ways to "Culture," 1800–1918* (Oxford: Clarendon Press, 1993).

68. As Joan Burbick points out, another way in which Thoreau dissented from Darwin was in his desire to keep natural history from becoming completely secularized; he opposed "both the providential and materialistic histories" (*Thoreau's Alternative History: Changing Perspectives on Nature, Culture, and Language* (Philadelphia: University of Pennsylvania Press, 1987), p. 125.

69. Darwin, *Voyage of the Beagle,* p. 459.

70. See Alfred W. Crosby, *Ecological Imperialism: The Biological Expansion of Europe, 900–1900* (Cambridge, Eng.: Cambridge University Press, 1986), and "Ecological Imperialism: The Overseas Migration of Western Europeans as a Biological Phenomenon," in *The Ends of the Earth,* ed. Donald Worster (Cambridge, Eng.: Cambridge University Press, 1988), pp. 103–117. Crosby's findings bear out the ecological truth of Susan Cooper's botanical nationalism: "many—often a majority—of the most aggressive plants in the temperate humid regions of North America, South America, Australia, and New Zealand are of European origin" ("Ecological Imperialism," p. 115).

71. Darwin, *Voyage of the Beagle,* pp. 256–257.

72. James Krasner, *The Entangled Eye: Visual Perception and the Representation of Nature in Post-Darwinian Narrative* (New York: Oxford University Press, 1992), pp. 36, 57. For the quotation, see Darwin, *On the Origin of Species* (1859; rpt. Cambridge: Harvard University Press, 1964), p. 12. Krasner's "entangled bank" allusion is to the final paragraph of *Origin* (p. 489), where Darwin asks us to reflect that "these elaborately constructed forms" of life inhabiting "an entangled bank," "so different from each other, and dependent upon each other in so complex a manner, have all been produced by laws acting around us."

73. For Thoreau's reading of Darwin, see Christie, *Thoreau as World Traveler,* pp. 74–80, and Richardson, *HDT: A Life of the Mind,* pp. 242–245.

74. On the intellectual genealogy of this passage, see Philip Gura, *The Wisdom of Words: Language, Theology, and Literature in the New England Renaissance* (Middletown: Wesleyan University Press, 1981), pp. 132–137.

75. Cooper, *Rural Hours,* p. 107; *Home Book,* pp. 91–94.

76. Emerson, *Nature, Addresses, and Lectures,* p. 286.

77. The first draft is more straightforward: "The beauty of the dropping and sheaf-like head of the rush all men have admired in all ages—and it must have some such near and unaccountable relation to human life, as astronomy has to those laws and figures which first existed in the mind of man" (J. Lyndon Shanley, *The Making of Walden* [Chicago: University of Chicago Press, 1957], p. 204).

Acknowledgments

This book would not have been completed without much generous assistance. My research and writing were supported by a Guggenheim Fellowship and by research and sabbatical leaves from Oberlin College and Harvard University. Along the way I benefited greatly from my colleagues in the Environmental Studies Program at Oberlin College; Harvard University's Committee on the Environment; the Harvard Seminar on Environmental Values; the MIT Science, Technology, and Society Program's Seminar on Humanistic Perspectives on the Environment; and the DeCordova Museum's workshop on the natural and cultural history of the Sudbury River Valley. For reading and criticism of portions of this work, I have been grateful to: Nina Baym, Sacvan Bercovitch, Denise Buell, Philip Fisher, Philip Gura, Myra Jehlen, Leo Marx, Michael Meyer, Joel Myerson, Leonard Neufeldt, Elaine Scarry, and Sam Bass Warner. John Elder and H. Daniel Peck critically evaluated the entire manuscript with admirable care and judiciousness. Many of the improvements made in revising I owe to these fellow scholars; many of the faults that remain result from not attending to them sufficiently. A number of other scholars as well have given me valuable advice, among them Thomas Blanding, John Cooper, James Engell, Donna Gerstenberger, Cheryl Burgess Glotfelty, Alan Heimert, Eric Higgs, Abiola Irele, Clayton Koppes, Glen Love, Derek Pearsall, Robert Richardson, Jr., David Robinson, Donald Ross, Robert Sayre, Scott Slovic, Taylor Stoehr, Edith Swan, Donald Swearer, John Tallmadge, Lynn Wardley, Joseph Wiesenfarth, Elizabeth Witherell, Sandra Zagarell, and Grover Zinn. A series of research assistants have performed heroic labors for me, including in some cases the critical reading of parts or all of the manuscript: Stephanie Foote, Steven Holmes, Masanobu Horiyama, Nathaniel Lewis, Timothy McCarthy, John Nielson, William Pannapacker, and Suzanne Schneider.

The remote origin of this project was a small pedagogical grant from the National Endowment for the Humanities to support the development of an undergraduate course in American literature and the American environment, as part of the humanities' contribution to Oberlin College's recently established Environmental Studies Program. I have since taught versions of that course eight times, at Oberlin, Bread Loaf, and Harvard; and I have learned much from my students and teaching assistants, among whom I should especially mention my former students Greg Harris, Abram Kaplan, Adam Rogoff, Damion Searls, Robin Sherman, Daniel Smith, Carol Stumbo, Brian Trelstad, and Jennifer Wheat; and my teaching fellows Susan Ferguson, Rebecca Gould, Mary Lou Kete, and Suzanne Klingenstein.

Portions of four chapters were first delivered as lectures at the Bread Loaf School of English, Cornell University, Harvard University, the University of North Carolina at Chapel Hill, the University of Pennsylvania, Purdue University, and the University of Wisconsin at Madison, as well as the annual meetings of the Modern Language Association, the American Literature Association, and the Thoreau Society. I am grateful for the feedback I received on all those occasions. Versions of three of these same chapters, and one other, have been published previously in *American Literary History* (Oxford University Press, 1989) (Chapter 1), *The Cambridge Companion to Thoreau,* ed. Joel Myerson (Cambridge University Press, 1995) (Chapter 4), *American Literature* (Duke University Press, 1989) (Chapter 10), and *New Essays on Thoreau's Walden,* ed. Robert F. Sayre (Cambridge University Press, 1992) (Chapter 11). I thank the university presses of Oxford, Cambridge, and Duke for permission to reprint.

For their kind assistance, I am grateful to the staff of the Bancroft Library, Berkeley; the Concord Free Library; the Holt-Atherton Pacific Center for Western Studies, University of the Pacific; the Houghton Library, Harvard University; the Steenbock Archives of the University of Wisconsin; and the Special Collections Division of the Vassar College Libraries. Quotations from the Houghton Mifflin archival papers donated to the Houghton Library at Harvard are used by permission of the Houghton Mifflin Company and Houghton Library. Quotations from the John Muir Papers at the University of the Pacific are by permission of the Holt-Atherton Pacific Center for Western Studies, University of the Pacific, Copyright 1984 Muir-Hanna Trust. Quotations from the Robert U. Johnson collection at the University of California, Berkeley, are by permission of the Bancroft Library. For permission to quote from the journals of John Burroughs, I am indebted to the Special Collections

Division of the Vassar Libraries and to Elizabeth Burroughs Kelley. My quotation from George Perkins Marsh's letter in the Norton Papers at Harvard is by permission of the Houghton Library.

The editorial team of Harvard University Press has been unfailingly supportive: William Sisler, Aïda Donald, Lindsay Waters, Alison Kent, and Elizabeth Hurwit. Their ministrations have been equaled only by those of the members of my family, particularly Kim Buell, without whose encouragement and resilience during my seven years of work on this project it might well have foundered. The book is dedicated to the one who first awakened me, by her instruction and by her example, to the complexity and beauty of the natural environment.

Index

ronmental writing, 14–22; African American, 17–19, 42–44, 56, 435; Anglo-Canadian, 58–62; Australian, 58–62; in cartography, 269–276; Euro-American, 16–17, 58–62, 68–82; hybridization in, 20, 436; Jewish American, 15–16, 18–19; Native American, 19–20, 63–64, 76, 435–436; Pan-African, 62–68; South African, 58–62. *See also* Environmental racism; Silko

Ettin, Andrew, 36

Evernden, Neil, 157, 243 and n, 279, 426, 465, 482 497, 509; quoted 156

Excursion. *See* Genre; Travel/excursion narrative

Fairbanks, Carol, 434, 437

Falkenstein, Linda Anne, 458

Farnham, Eliza, 25

Faulkner, William, 15, 64, 260, 296, 300; "The Bear," 10, 16, 85, 144, 156

Feminist revisionism. *See* Gender

Fetterley, Judith, 504

Fiedler, Leslie, 33–34, 39, 434, 440; quoted, 53

Fields, James T., 233, 340

Fink, Steven, 432, 468, 478, 479, 484, 535, 559, 561

Fischer, Michael, 548

Fisher, Philip, 269, 461

Fitzgerald, F. Scott, 34, 50

Flader, Susan L., 471

Flagg, Wilson, 246 and n, 406, 413 and n, 414, 507; quoted, 246, 324

Fleck, Richard, 479, 529

Foerster, Norman, 11

Forbes, Stephen A.: quoted, 265

Foucault, Michel: on concept of author, 372 and n, 384, 547–548; on representation, 86, 114, 186; mentioned, 449; quoted, 83

Fowler, Alistair, 537

Fox, Warwick, 497

Francis of Assisi, 183, 331, 363, 545

Frank, Waldo, 358

Franklin, Wayne, 554–555

Fried, Michael, 87

Fritzell, Peter, 75, 179, 429, 458, 473, 510, 555

Frost, Robert, 19, 36, 85, 108, 128, 199, 210, 259

Frye, Northrop, 60, 451–452

Fuller, Margaret, 314, 339, 393

Fussell, Edwin, 434, 440

Gaia theory, 200–201, 204, 215, 304. *See also* Ecocentrism; Ecofeminism; Goddess; Personification

Gallagher, Winifred, 509

Gandhi, Mohandas, 9, 336, 340, 360

Garber, Frederick, 379–380, 438, 510–511, 549

Gass, William, 547, 550

Gates, Henry Louis, Jr., 372 and n

Gender, and environmental attitudes/writing, 16–17, 25–27, 34–36; botany as "female" pursuit, 44, 47–48; intertextuality within women's environmental writing, 25, 80, 177; men's writing and "female" traditions, 25–27, 177–178, 247; women's writing and "male" traditions, 16–17, 25, 44–49, 175–177, 234–235, 487

Genette, Gérard, 2

Genre, of/and environmental nonfiction: almanac tradition in, 223–224, 399–402; animal story, 195–199, 204–207; bioregionalist tradition in, 405–408; literary theory's privileging of fictive genres at expense of (environmental) nonfiction, 8–10, 84–86; multi-generic character of, 397; natural history tradition in, 402–405; picturesque mode in, 408–412; travel/excursion narrative tradition in,

Library of Congress Cataloguing-in-Publication Data

Buell, Lawrence.
The environmental imagination: Thoreau, nature writing, and the
formation of American culture / Lawrence Buell.
p.   cm.
Includes bibliographical references and index.
ISBN 0-674-25861-4
1. Thoreau, Henry David, 1817–1862—Knowledge—Natural history.
2. National characteristics, American, in literature.
3. Environmental protection—United States—History.
4. Environmental protection in literature.   5. Natural history—
United States—History.   6. Nature in literature.   I. Title.
PS3057.N3B84   1995
818'.309—dc20

94-31321
CIP